THE CONCISE
THESAURUS

A dictionary of synonyms
and antonyms

First published in this edition 1977

This edition 1986, reprinted 1991

© Wm Collins Sons & Co Ltd 1964, 1967

ISBN 0 85501 135 2
Printed in Great Britain by
Wm Collins Sons & Co Ltd

CONTENTS

ABBREVIATIONS

a. adjective
Abbrev. Abbreviation
adv. adverb
Agric. Agriculture
Arab. Arabic
Arch. Archaic
Archit. Architecture

Bib. Biblical
Biol. Biology
Bot. Botany

cf. compare
Ch. Chapter
Chem. Chemistry
Colloq. Colloquial
Comm. Commerce
conj. conjunction

Eccl. Ecclesiastical
e.g. for example
esp. especially
etc. et cetera

fem. feminine
Fig. Figurative
Fr. French

Geog. Geography
Ger. German
Gk. Greek
Gram. Grammar

Heb. Hebrew
Her. Heraldry
Hist. History

i.e. that is
interj. interjection
Ital. Italian

Lat. Latin
lit. literally
Lit. Literature

med. medieval
Med. Medicine
Mil. Military
Mus. Music

n. noun
Naut. Nautical
N.B. Nota Bene
(note well)

Obs. Obsolete
O.Fr. Old French
orig. originally

pa.p. past participle
pl. plural
Poet. Poetic
Pol. Polish
Polit. Political
Pop. Popular
pref. prefix
prep. preposition
Print. Printing

R. River
Russ. Russian

Scot. Scottish
Sl. Slang
Sp. Spanish

Theat. Theatre
Turk. Turkish

Univ. University
U.S.A. United States
of America

v. verb

5

SYNONYMS
& ANTONYMS

A

abaft (*Naut.*) aft, astern, behind.

abalienate alienate, estrange; (*Law*) bequeath, convey, demise, transfer.

abandon (1) *v.* abdicate, cede, desert, evacuate, forsake, leave, relinquish, renounce, resign, surrender, vacate, waive, withdraw from, yield; (2) *n.* dash, careless freedom, wild impulse.
  Ant. cherish, defend, hold, keep, maintain, uphold.

abandoned (1) cast aside, cast away, cast out, deserted, discarded, dropped, forsaken, left, rejected; (2) (*Morally, of a person*) corrupt, depraved, dissolute, profligate, sinful, wicked.
  Ant. of (2) good, honest, righteous, upright, virtuous.

abase debase, degrade, depress, disgrace, dishonour, humble, humiliate, lower.
  Ant. elevate, exalt, honour, raise.

abash affront, confound, confuse, discomfit, discompose, disconcert, embarrass, humiliate, mortify, shame.
  Ant. assure, encourage, sustain.

abate decline, decrease, diminish, ebb, lessen, mitigate, moderate, reduce, sink, slacken, subside, wane.
  Ant. increase, intensify.

abatement alleviation, allowance, cessation, decline, decrease, diminution, discount, extenuation, mitigation, remission, slackening.
  Ant. increase, intensification.

abbey monastery, priory.

abbreviate abridge, compress, condense, contract, cut, epitomise, reduce, shorten.
  Ant. amplify, enlarge, expand, extend, lengthen, prolong.

abdicate abandon, quit, relinquish, renounce, resign, retire, surrender, vacate.
  Ant. maintain, retain.

abdomen *n.* belly, paunch, stomach; (*Colloq.*) corporation; (*Sl.*) guts.

abduct carry off, kidnap, run away with, run off with.

abduction carrying off, kidnapping.

aberration abnormality, delusion, deviation, divergence, eccentricity, hallucination, illusion, irregularity, peculiarity, rambling, wandering; (*Mental*) disorder, instability, moral lapse.

abet aid, assist, condone, encourage, help, incite, succour, support, sustain, uphold.
  Ant. hinder, impede, obstruct, oppose.

abettor accomplice, assistant, confederate, co-operator, helper, instigator.

abeyance inactivity, intermission, reservation, suspense,

suspension; (*Law*) anticipation, calculation, expectancy, expectation.

Ant. action, renewal, revival.

abhor abominate, detest, execrate, hate, loathe, regard with repugnance, shrink from.

Ant. admire, love.

abide (1) dwell, lodge, remain, reside, rest, stay, tarry, wait; (2) bear, brook, endure, stand, suffer, tolerate.

Ant. of (1) move, proceed.

ability aptitude, capability, capacity, competency, dexterity, endowment, energy, expertness, faculty, force, gift, power, proficiency, qualification, skill, talent.

Ant. inability, incapability.

abject base, cringing, degraded, despicable, dishonourable, fawning, grovelling, mean, outcast, slavish, sordid, vile, worthless.

Ant. dignified, esteemed, exalted, worthy.

able accomplished, clever, competent, effective, efficient, expert, gifted, highly endowed, masterly, powerful, practised, skilled, strong.

Ant. incapable, incompetent, inefficient, inept, unskilled, weak.

ablution bathing, cleansing, lavation, purification, washing.

abnegation abjuration, denial and renunciation, disallowance.

abnormal anomalous, eccentric, erratic, exceptional, irregular, monstrous, peculiar, singular, strange, unnatural, unusual, weird.

Ant. customary, natural, normal, regular, usual.

abode domicile, dwelling, habitation, home, house, lodging, quarters, residence.

abolish abrogate, annihilate, annul, cancel, destroy, eliminate, extinguish, nullify, obliterate, overturn, repeal, revoke, subvert, suppress.

Ant. establish, promote, reinstate.

abominable abhorrent, accursed, contemptible, detestable, disgusting, execrable, foul, hateful, horrid, loathsome, nauseous, obnoxious, odious, repugnant, revolting, vile.

Ant. admirable, delightful, desirable, lovable.

abominate abhor, detest, execrate, hate, loathe, recoil from, regard with repugnance.

Ant. admire, enjoy, like, love.

aboriginal indigenous, native, original, primary, primeval, primordial, pristine.

abortion (*Med.*) miscarriage; (*Law*) deliberate miscarriage, disappointment, failure, misadventure, vain effort.

abortive (1) *a.* fruitless, futile, idle, ineffectual, unavailing, unsuccessful, vain; (2) *n.* (*Med.*) abortifacient (*i.e.* a drug producing abortion).

abound flourish, increase, luxuriate, overflow, superabound, swarm, swell, teem.

about almost, approximately, around, concerning, connected with, near, over, relative to, round, surrounding.

above (1) *prep.* beyond, exceeding, higher than, on top of, over; (2) *adv.* in heaven, on high, overhead; (3) *a.* foregoing, preceding.

aboveboard candidly, frankly, honourably, openly, without guile.

Ant. treacherously, underhandedly.

abrade erase, erode, rub off,

scrape out, wear away, wear off.

abrasion (1) (*Med.*) scrape, scratch, surface injury; (2) abrading, erosion, friction, rubbing.

abridge compress, condense, contract, curtail, digest, diminish, epitomise, lessen, reduce, shorten.

Ant. amplify, expand, extend.

abridgment abstract, compendium, condensation, curtailment, epitome, précis, reduction, restriction, shortening, summary, synopsis.

abroad (1) beyond the sea, in foreign lands, overseas; (2) away, extensively, far, forth, out-of-doors, outside, widely, without.

abrogate abolish, annul, cancel, nullify, repeal, rescind, revoke, set aside.

Ant. enforce, maintain, ratify.

abrupt (1) blunt, brusque, curt, discourteous, rude, unceremonious; (2) precipitous, steep, sudden.

Ant. of (1) courteous; of (2) gradual.

abscond bolt, decamp, disappear, escape, flee, run off, sneak away.

absence (1) non-appearance, non-attendance; (2) defect, deficiency, lack, need, privation, want; (3) abstraction, distraction, inattention, preoccupation, reverie.

Ant. of (1) presence; of (2) sufficiency; of (3) attention.

absent (1) *a.* away, elsewhere, gone, lacking, missing, not present; (2) *v.* depart, keep away, stay away, withdraw (*oneself*).

absent-minded absorbed,

abstracted, dreaming, engrossed, forgetful, inattentive, musing, preoccupied.

Ant. attentive.

absolute actual, arbitrary, autocratic, categorical, certain, complete, despotic, dictatorial, infallible, peremptory, perfect, positive, supreme, unbounded, unconditional, unlimited, unquestionable.

absolve acquit, clear, discharge, excuse, exempt, exonerate, forgive, pardon, release.

Ant. blame, censure.

absorb (1) assimilate, consume, devour, drink in, exhaust, imbibe; (2) engross, monopolise.

abstain avoid, cease, desist, forbear, keep from, refrain, refuse, stop, withhold.

Ant. indulge.

abstemious abstinent, frugal, moderate, self-denying, sober, temperate.

Ant. greedy, intemperate.

abstinence abstemiousness, avoidance, forbearance, moderation, self-restraint, soberness, teetotalism, temperance.

Ant. indulgence.

abstract (1) *v.* abbreviate, abridge, condense, digest, epitomise, outline, summarise; (2) *n.* abridgment, compendium, condensation, digest, epitome, essence, summary, synopsis; (3) *a.* abstruse, complex, non-concrete, occult, recondite, separate, subtle, unpractical, unrealistic.

abstruse dark, enigmatical, hidden, latent, mysterious, mystical, occult, recondite, vague.

Ant. clear, concrete.

absurd foolish, irrational, nonsensical, preposterous, ridiculous, senseless, silly, stupid, unreasonable.

Ant. sensible, wise.

absurdity folly, foolishness, idiocy, irrationality, nonsense, preposterousness, unreasonableness.

abundance affluence, ampleness, copiousness, exuberance, fulness, plenteousness, plenty, profusion, riches, wealth.

Ant. lack, need.

abundant ample, copious, exuberant, overflowing, plenteous, plentiful, profuse, rich, teeming.

Ant. poor, scarce.

abuse (1) *v.* damage, deceive, harm, hurt, injure, maltreat, misapply, misuse, revile, scold, spoil, upbraid, vilify; (2) *n.* blame, censure, contumely, defamation, derision, insult, maltreatment, misuse, opprobrium, reproach.

abut adjoin, border, impinge, project.

abyss abysm, bottomless depth, chasm, gorge, gulf, pit.

academic lettered, literary, scholastic, theoretical, university, unscientific.

accede acquiesce, agree, assent, comply, consent, succeed to (*as heir*).

accelerate expedite, forward, further, hasten, hurry, quicken, speed.

accent (1) *n.* beat, cadence, emphasis, force, intonation, modulation, rhythm, stress, tone; (2) *v.* accentuate, stress.

accept acknowledge, acquiesce in, admit, allow, approve, assent to, believe, consent, receive, take.

Ant. reject.

acceptable agreeable, delight-ful, grateful, gratifying, pleasant, pleasing, welcome.

access adit, admission, admittance, approach, avenue, entrance, entry, passage; (*Med.*) attack, fit, onset, paroxysm.

accession addition, augmentation, enlargement, extension, increase, succession (*to a throne, dignity, or office*).

accessory (1) *n.* abettor, accomplice, associate (*in crime*), confederate, helper; (2) *a.* abetting, additional, aiding, auxiliary, subordinate, supplementary.

accident calamity, casualty, chance, disaster, misadventure, misfortune, mishap.

accidental casual, chance, contingent, fortuitous, incidental, uncertain, unessential, unintended.

Ant. designed, planned.

acclamation approbation, cheer, loud homage, outcry, plaudit, salutation, shouting.

acclivity ascent, hill, rising ground, steep upward slope.

accommodate adapt, adjust, afford, assist, compose, fit, harmonise, oblige, reconcile, settle, supply.

accommodating considerate, kind, obliging, polite, unselfish.

Ant. disobliging.

accompany attend, convoy, escort, go with.

accomplice abettor, accessory, assistant, associate, coadjutor, confederate, partner.

accomplish achieve, attain, complete, consummate, do, execute, finish, fulfil, perform, realise.

accord agree, allow, assent, concede, conform, correspond, fit, grant, harmonise, suit, vouchsafe.

accost address, greet, hail, salute, solicit (*as a prostitute*).

account (1) description, detail, explanation, narration, narrative, recital, reckoning, relation, report, story, value; (2) (*Comm.*) balance, bill, book, books, charge, computation, inventory, ledger, register, score, statement; (3) *v.* assess, calculate, compute, consider, count, deem, estimate, explain, judge, rate, reckon, regard.

accountable amenable, answerable, liable, responsible.

accoutre array, decorate, equip, fit out, furnish.

accredit authorise, commission, depute, empower, entrust.

accrue accumulate, arise, be added, enlarge, ensue, flow, follow, increase, issue, spring up.

accumulate accrue, amass, collect, gather, grow, hoard, increase, store.
Ant. decrease, diminish.

accumulation augmentation, collection, heap, mass, pile, store.

accuracy carefulness, correctness, exactitude, exactness, fidelity, niceness, nicety, precision, strictness, truth.
Ant. carelessness, inaccuracy.

accurate careful, correct, exact, just, nice, precise, regular, right, strict, true.
Ant. inaccurate.

accusation arraignment, charge, crimination, impeachment, indictment.

accuse arraign, blame, censure, impeach, incriminate, indict, tax.

accustom discipline, exercise, familiarise, habituate, inure, train, use.

ace (1) (*Cards, dice, etc.*) single point; (2) best, highest, iota, item, jot, particle, point, tittle, unit, whit; (3) (*Sl.*) expert.

acerbity acrimony, astringency, bitterness, churlishness, harshness, rancour, sharpness, sternness, tartness.

achieve accomplish, attain, complete, consummate, effect, execute, finish, fulfil, gain, perform, procure, realise.

achievement attainment, completion, deed, execution, exploit, feat, performance, realisation.

acid biting, pungent, sharp, sour, stinging, tart, vinegary.
Ant. mild, sweet.

acknowledge admit, allow, concede, confess, declare, grant, own, profess, recognise.

acme apex, climax, culmination, height, peak, pinnacle, summit, top, vertex, zenith.
Ant. base, foot, nadir.

acquaint announce, appraise, disclose, enlighten, inform, notify, tell.

acquaintance (1) associate, companion, comrade, friend; (2) companionship, experience, familiarity, fellowship, intimacy, knowledge.

acquiesce accede, agree in, approve of, assent, comply, concur, consent, submit, yield.
Ant. dissent, object.

acquire attain, earn, gain, get, obtain, procure, realise, secure, win.

acquirement accomplishment, acquisition, attainment, gathering, learning, mastery, mental gains.

acquit absolve, clear, discharge, exonerate, fulfil, liberate, pay, release, settle.

acquittal absolution, clearance, deliverance, discharge, exoneration, liberation, release.

acquittance discharge, receipt, release.

acrimonious biting, bitter, caustic, censorious, crabbed, petulant, pungent, rancorous, severe, sharp, spiteful, testy.

Ant. good-tempered.

acrimony asperity, bitterness, churlishness, harshness, rancour, tartness, virulence.

act (1) v. do, enact, exert, function, imitate, make, operate, perform, play the part of, pretend, represent, sham, simulate; (2) n. (*Law*) bill, decree, enactment, law, ordinance.

active agile, alert, assiduous, brisk, diligent, efficient, energetic, enterprising, hard-working, indefatigable, nimble, prompt, sprightly, quick, vigorous.

Ant. inactive, slow.

actual absolute, categorical, certain, existent, genuine, living, positive, present, substantial, tangible, true.

Ant. unreal, untrue.

actuate animate, dispose, impel, incite, induce, influence, instigate, prompt, urge.

acumen acuteness, astuteness, keenness, penetration, perspicacity, perspicuity, sagacity, sharpness, shrewdness.

acute clever, distressing, high-toned, ingenious, intense, keen, penetrating, piercing, poignant, pointed, severe, sharp, shrill, smart, subtle, violent.

Ant. blunt, dull, stupid.

adage aphorism, apothegm, axiom, maxim, proverb, saw, saying.

adapt accommodate, adjust,

apply, conform, fashion, fit, harmonise, make, match, prepare, qualify, suit.

add adjoin, affix, amplify, annex, append, attach, augment, count up, sum up, supplement.

Ant. deduct, subtract.

addicted accustomed, disposed, habituated, inclined, prone.

Ant. unaddicted.

addition accession, addendum, adjunct, appendage, appendix, augmentation, enlargement, extension, increase, increment, supplement.

address (1) n. adroitness, appeal, application, art, dexterity, discourse, expertness, harangue, manners, oration, petition, skill, solicitation, speech, superscription (*on a letter*), tact; (2) v. accost, hail, invoke, salute.

adduce advance, allege, cite, mention, name, quote.

adept (1) a. accomplished, expert, practised, proficient, skilful, versed; (2) n. expert, genius, master.

adequate capable, commensurate, competent, enough, requisite, satisfactory, sufficient.

Ant. inadequate, insufficient.

adhere abide by, attach, be faithful, cleave to, cling, cohere, follow, hold fast, unite.

adherent (1) n. disciple, follower, partisan, supporter, upholder, votary; (2) a. adhering, clinging, sticking.

adhesion adherence, attachment, coherence, union.

adhesive clinging, glutinous, sticky, tenacious.

adieu farewell, goodbye, leave-taking, valediction.

adipose fat, fatty, greasy, obese, oily, oleaginous, sebaceous.

Ant. skinny, thin.

adit access, approach, entrance, opening, passage.

adjacent abutting, adjoining, bordering, contiguous, near, neighbouring, touching.

Ant. distant.

adjoin abut, add, annex, append, approximate, attach, border, combine, couple, link, neighbour, touch, unite, verge.

adjourn defer, delay, interrupt, postpone, prorogue.

adjudge adjudicate, allot, apportion, assign, award, decide, decree, determine, distribute.

adjunct addendum, addition, appendage, appurtenance, auxiliary, supplement.

adjure beg, beseech, entreat, implore, invoke, pray, supplicate.

adjust accommodate, adapt, arrange, compose, dispose, fit, harmonise, make, conform, measure, reconcile, rectify, redress, regulate, removel, set, settle, suit.

Ant. disarrange, disturb.

administer conduct, contribute, control, direct, dispense, execute, give, govern, manage, oversee, superintend, supervise.

admirable astonishing, choice, excellent, exquisite, fine, praiseworthy, rare, surprising, valuable, wonderful.

Ant. commonplace, displeasing, mediocre.

admiration affection, appreciation, approbation, approval, astonishment, delight, esteem, pleasure, regard, surprise, wonder.

Ant. abhorrence, displeasure, hatred.

admission (1) access, admittance, entrance, initiation, introduction; (2) acknowledgement, allowance, concession, confession.

Ant. refusal, rejection.

admit (1) allow, give (access to), receive; (2) acknowledge, allow, concede, confess, grant, permit.

Ant. deny, reject.

admonish advise, caution, censure, chide, counsel, forewarn, rebuke, reprove, warn.

admonition advice, caution, rebuke, remonstrance, reproof, warning.

adolescent (1) a. growing, juvenile, young, youthful; (2) n. minor, teenager, youth.

adopt (1) appropriate, approve, assume, choose, maintain, select, support; (2) foster.

adore admire, bow to, esteem, honour, idolise, love, reverence, venerate, worship.

Ant. abhor, despise, execrate, hate.

adorn beautify, bedeck, deck, decorate, embellish, enhance, enrich, garnish, grace, ornament.

Ant. deface, disfigure.

adroit able, adept, apt, clever, dexterous, expert, ingenious, skilful.

Ant. clumsy, inept, maladroit.

adulation blandishment, extravagant flattery, fulsome praise, servile flattery, sycophancy.

Ant. defamation, detraction, obloquy.

adult (1) a. full grown, grown-up, mature, of age, ripe; (2) n. grown-up person (man or *woman*), person of mature age.

Ant. adolescent, immature.

adulterate contaminate, corrupt, debase, deteriorate, make impure, mix with, vitiate.

advance (1) *v.* accelerate, adduce, allege, benefit, bring forward, elevate, exalt, grow, hasten, improve, progress, prosper, thrive; (2) *n.* advancement, forward movement, growth, improvement, march, preferment, progress, progression, promotion; (3) *v.* (*Comm.*) increase (*price*), lend, pay beforehand, raise (*price*), supply on credit; (4) *n.* (*Comm.*) appreciation, credit, loan, rise.

Ant. decrease, retreat.

advantage ascendency, assistance, benefit, convenience, gain, good, interest, profit, service, superiority, upperhand, utility.

advent approach, arrival, coming, coming (*of Christ*), visitation.

adventitious accidental, casual, extraneous, foreign, incidental, non-essential.

adventure (1) *n.* chance, contingency, enterprise, hazard, incident, occurrence, risk, speculation, undertaking, venture; (2) *v.* dare, hazard, imperil, risk, venture.

adventurous daring, enterprising, foolhardy, hazardous, headstrong, rash, reckless, venturesome.

Ant. cautious, timid, unenterprising.

adversary antagonist, competitor, contestant, enemy, foe, opponent, opposer.

Ant. ally, friend, partner.

adverse antagonistic, conflicting, contrary, hostile, inimical,

opposing, reluctant, repugnant, unfavourable, unfortunate, unfriendly, unlucky, unwilling.

Ant. favourable, friendly, lucky.

adversity affliction, calamity, catastrophe, distress, ill-luck, misery, misfortune, sorrow, trouble, wretchedness.

Ant. good luck, happiness.

advert allude, attend, notice, observe, refer, regard.

advertise advise, announce, apprise, declare, inform, make known, notify, proclaim, promulgate, publish.

Ant. conceal, hush.

advice admonition, caution, counsel, guidance, information, instruction, intelligence, notice, notification, opinion, recommendation, warning.

advisable desirable, expedient, fit, judicious, profitable, proper, prudent.

advise acquaint, admonish, apprise, caution, confer, consult, inform, notify, recommend, suggest, warn.

advocate (1) *v.* argue for, countenance, defend, favour, justify, plead for, recommend, support, urge, vindicate; (2)*n.* counsellor, defender, pleader, promoter, supporter; (3) *n.* (*Law*) attorney, barrister, counsel, lawyer, solicitor.

Ant. of (1) oppose; of (2) opponent.

affable amiable, approachable, civil, cordial, courteous, gracious, obliging, sociable, urbane.

affair (1) *n.* business, circumstance, concern, event, incident, matter, occurrence, question, subject, transaction;

n. (*Mil.*) battle, combat, conflict, encounter, engagement, skirmish.

affect (1) *v.* accomplish, act on, alter, change, impress, influence, interest, modify, move, overcome, regard, sway, transform; (2) *v.* adopt, aspire to, assume, feign, imitate, pretend.

affectation affectedness, artificiality, assumed manners, mannerism, pose, pretension, simulation, unnatural imitation.
Ant. artlessness, unaffectedness.

affection (1) *n.* amity, attachment, desire, feeling, fondness, friendliness, good-will, inclination, kindness, love, passion, propensity, tenderness; (2) *n.* (*Med.*) ailment, complaint, disease, disorder, illness.

affectionate attached, devoted, fond, kind, loving, tender, warm-hearted.

affiliate annex, associate, connect, incorporate, unite.

affinity alliance, attraction, connection, likeness, resemblance, similarity, sympathy.

affirm assert, asseverate, aver, avouch, confirm, declare, depone, maintain, ratify, swear, testify.
Ant. deny.

affix annex, append, attach, bind, fasten, subjoin, tack.

afflict distress, grieve, harass, hurt, pain, plague, torment, trouble, try, wound.

affliction adversity, calamity, depression, distress, hardship, misfortune, scourge, sorrow, torment, trial, trouble, woe, wretchedness.
Ant. relief.

affluence abundance, exuber-ance, opulence, plenty, riches, wealth.

afford bestow, furnish, give, grant, impart, offer, produce, spare, supply, yield.

affray brawl, contest, disturbance, encounter, feud, fight, outbreak, scuffle, tumult.

affright alarm, appal, confound, daunt, dismay, frighten, intimidate, overawe, shock, startle.

affront (1) *v.* abuse, anger, annoy, displease, insult, offend, outrage, provoke, vex; (2) *n.* abuse, indignity, injury, insult, offence, outrage, vexation, wrong.
Ant. of (2) compliment, courtesy.

afraid alarmed, anxious, apprehensive, fainthearted, fearful, frightened, suspicious, timid, timorous.
Ant. fearless, inapprehensive, unafraid.

afresh again, anew, newly, over again.

after afterwards, behind, following, later, succeeding.

again (1) afresh, anew, another time, once more; (2) besides, furthermore, in addition, moreover, on the contrary.

against abutting, close up to, counter, facing, fronting, in opposition to, in preparation for, opposing, opposite to, resisting.

age (1) *n.* date, duration, epoch, era, generation, period, time; (2) *n.* decline (*of life*), majority, maturity, old age, senility, seniority; (3) *v.* decline, grow old, mature.

agency (1) action, efficiency, force, influence, instrumentality, intervention, operation; (2) charge, direction, management, supervision.

agent (1) actor, doer, operator, performer; (2) attorney, commissioner, deputy, procurator, promoter, representative, substitute.

agglomeration accumulation, clump, cluster, heap, lump, mass, pile.

agglutinate cement, fasten, glue, solder, unite.

aggrandise advance, augment, dignify, elevate, ennoble, enrich, exalt, promote.

aggravate (1) heighten, increase, intensify, magnify, make worse, overstate; (2) exasperate, irritate, provoke, tease.

Ant. of (1) diminish, lessen; of (2) soothe.

aggregate (1) v. accumulate, amass, heap, pile; (2) n. amount, body, bulk, heap, lump, mass, sum, total, whole; (3) a. added, collected, combined, total.

aggression assault, attack, encroachment, injury, invasion, offence.

aggressor assailant, assaulter, attacker, invader.

aghast affrighted, amazed, appalled, astonished, astounded, awe-struck, startled, thunderstruck.

agile active, alert, brisk, lively, nimble, prompt, quick, sprightly, spry, supple.

agitate (1) rock, rouse, shake, stir, toss; (2) confuse, disconcert, distract, disturb, excite, ferment, rouse, ruffle; (3) debate, discuss, dispute, examine, ventilate.

Ant. of (2) allay, calm, pacify.

agitation (1) shake, shaking, stir; (2) commotion, discomposure, distraction, disturb-

ance, excitement, flurry, fluster; (3) controversy, debate, discussion, ventilation.

agony anguish, distress, pangs, throes, torment, suffering.

Ant. comfort, peace.

agree (1) accede, acquiesce, allow, assent, comply, concur, consent, engage, grant, permit; (2) accord, answer, conform, correspond, harmonise, match, suit, tally.

agreement (1) accordance, compliance, concord, concurrence, harmony, suitableness, union; (2) bargain, compact, contract, covenant, pact, treaty, understanding.

agriculture cultivation, culture, farming, husbandry, tillage.

aid (1) v. abet, assist, befriend, encourage, favour, help, relieve, second, subsidise, succour; (2) n. assistance, assistant, favour, help, helper, relief, succour, support.

aim (1) v. design, direct, intend, level, mean, point, purpose, seek; (2) n. course, design, direction, end, goal, intent, intention, mark, object, purpose, target.

airy animated, buoyant, ethereal, fairy-like, light, sprightly, subtile, trifling, unsubstantial.

Ant. substantial.

akin allied, analogous, cognate, congenial, consanguineous, related, similar.

Ant. dissimilar, unrelated.

alacrity alertness, briskness, cheerfulness, eagerness, gaiety, hilarity, joyousness, liveliness, readiness, sprightliness.

alarm (1) v. daunt, dismay, frighten, scare, startle, terrify; (2) (n) apprehension, consternation, dismay, fear, fright, scare.

terror; (3) alarm-bell, distress signal, tocsin.

Ant. of (1) calm.

alert active, agile, brisk, circumspect, heedful, lively, nimble, quick, spirited, vigilant, wary, watchful.

Ant. listless, slow.

alertness agility, briskness, nimbleness, promptitude, vigilance, watchfulness.

alien (1) *a.* adverse, estranged, foreign, inappropriate, not native, not naturalised, remote, repugnant; (2) *n.* foreigner, stranger.

Ant. native.

alienate (1) disaffect, estrange, make unfriendly; (2) (*Law*) abalienate, convey, transfer.

alienation (1) disaffection, estrangement, rupture; (2) (*Law*) abalienation, conveyance, transfer; (3) (*Med.*) aberration, hallucination, insanity, lunacy, mental derangement.

alike akin, analogous, equal, equivalent, identical, resembling, similar.

Ant. dissimilar, unlike.

aliment fare, food, meat, nourishment, nutriment, provender, sustenance.

alive active, animated, brisk, cheerful, existing, functioning, having life, lively, living, quick, sensitive, sprightly, susceptible, swarming, vivacious.

Ant. dead, dull, inanimate.

allay alleviate, appease, assuage, calm, check, compose, ease, mitigate, pacify, relieve, soothe.

Ant. aggravate.

allege adduce, advance, affirm, assert, asseverate, aver, cite, declare, depose, maintain, plead, quote.

Ant. deny.

allegiance duty, fealty, fidelity, homage, loyalty, obedience, obligation.

Ant. disloyalty, treason.

allegory apologue, fable, myth, parable, story, tale.

alleviate abate, allay, assuage, diminish, ease, lessen, lighten, mitigate, mollify, quiet, relieve, soften, soothe.

Ant. aggravate, increase.

alleviation diminution, mitigation, palliation, relief.

alliance affiliation, affinity, association, coalition, combination, compact, confederacy, confederation, connection, league, marriage, partnership, treaty, union.

Ant. discord, disunion, separation.

allow (1) acknowledge, admit, concede, confess, own; (2) approve, authorise, bear, endure, let, permit, sanction, suffer, tolerate; (3) abate, deduct, give, grant, remit, spare.

Ant. of (2) forbid, prohibit.

allude advert, glance, hint, imply, intimate, refer, remark, suggest.

allure attract, cajole, coax, decoy, entice, inveigle, persuade, seduce, tempt, win over.

allusion casual remark, hint, indirect reference, innuendo, mention, suggestion.

ally (1) *n.* abettor, accessory, accomplice, associate, coadjutor, colleague, confederate, friend, helper; (2) *v.* associate, combine, connect, join, marry, unify, unite.

Ant. of (1) enemy, foe, opponent.

alms benefaction, bounty, charity, donation, gift.

alone apart, desolate, isolated, separate, single, solitary, uncombined, unconnected.

Ant. accompanied, together.

aloud audibly, clamorously, loudly, noisily, vociferously.

Ant. inaudibly, silently.

alter change, convert, diversify, metamorphose, modify, remodel, shift, transform, turn, vary.

Ant. keep, retain.

altercation bickering, contention, controversy, dispute, dissension, quarrel, wrangle.

alternative choice, option, other (of two), preference, selection.

although albeit, even if, even supposing, notwithstanding, though.

altitude elevation, height, loftiness, summit.

always continually, constantly, eternally, ever, everlastingly, evermore, forever, perpetually, unceasingly.

Ant. never.

amalgamate blend, combine, commix, compound, fuse, incorporate, mingle.

amass accumulate, aggregate, collect, gather, heap up, hoard, pile up, rake up, scrape together.

Ant. disperse, divide, scatter.

amaze alarm, astonish, astound, bewilder, daze, dumbfound, electrify, startle, stupefy, surprise.

amazement admiration, astonishment, bewilderment, confusion, marvel, perplexity, wonder.

ambassador deputy, legate, minister, plenipotentiary.

ambiguous dubious, enigmatical, equivocal, indefinite, indeterminate, obscure, puzzling, vague.

Ant. clear, obvious, unequivocal.

ambition aspiration, avidity, eagerness, emulation, enterprise, hankering, longing, yearning.

ambush ambuscade, cover, hiding-place, retreat, shelter.

ameliorate alleviate, amend, assuage, benefit, better, elevate, improve, lessen, mend, promote, raise, relieve.

Ant. aggravate, deteriorate.

amenable (1) accountable, answerable, liable, responsible; (2) able to be influenced by, open to.

amend ameliorate, better, change, improve, mend, rectify, reform, repair.

Ant. impair, mar.

amends apology, atonement, compensation, indemnity, redress, reparation, satisfaction.

amenity affability, agreeableness, amiability, complaisance, courtesy, mildness, pleasantness (of situation), politeness, refinement, suavity.

Ant. churlishness, disagreeableness.

amiable agreeable, attractive, benign, charming, cheerful, delightful, engaging, good-humoured, kind, lovable, pleasant, pleasing, sweet-tempered, winsome.

Ant. ill-natured, unfriendly.

amicable amiable, brotherly, cordial, fraternal, friendly, good-humoured, harmonious, kindly, neighbourly.

Ant. inimical, unfriendly.

amiss defective, faulty, inaccurate, inappropriate, incorrect, wrong.

Ant. right.

amity cordiality, friendliness, friendship, goodwill, harmony, kindliness, peacefulness.
Ant. hatred.

amnesty absolution, condonation, dispensation, general pardon, oblivion, remission (*of penalty*).
Ant. penalty, retribution.

amorous affectionate, amatory, ardent, attached, erotic, fond, loving, lustful, passionate, tender.
Ant. cold.

amorphous formless, irregular, shapeless, unformed, unshaped.

ample abounding, abundant, broad, capacious, extensive, full, large, lavish, liberal, plenteous, plentiful, rich, roomy, spacious, unrestricted, wide.
Ant. insufficient, restricted.

amplify augment, develop, dilate, enlarge, expand, extend, go into detail, magnify, stretch, widen.
Ant. abbreviate, curtail.

amputate curtail, lop, remove, separate, sever, truncate.

amuse charm, cheer, delight, divert, enliven, entertain, gratify, recreate.
Ant. bore, sadden.

analogy correspondence, likeness, relation, resemblance, similarity, similitude.
Ant. dissimilarity, incongruity.

analysis dissection, dissolution, segregation, separation.
Ant. synthesis.

anarchy chaos, confusion, disorder, lawlessness, misgovernment, misrule, rebellion, riot.
Ant. control, law, order.

anathema ban, curse, excommunication, execration, imprecation, malediction, proscription.
Ant. blessing.

anatomy analysis, dissection, dismemberment, division.

ancestry descent, family, genealogy, house, line, lineage, pedigree, stock.
Ant. posterity.

ancient aged, antiquated, antique, archaic, obsolete, old, old-fashioned, out-of-date, primeval, primordial.
Ant. modern.

angelic adorable, celestial, cherubic, entrancing, ethereal, heavenly, lovely, pure, seraphic.

anger (1) *n.* choler, displeasure, exasperation, fury, indignation, ire, passion, rage, resentment, spleen, wrath; **(2)** *v.* affront, displease, exasperate, excite, fret, incense, irritate, madden, nettle, offend, provoke, vex.
Ant. of **(1)** patience, peace; of **(2)** appease, calm.

angle (1) *n.* bend, corner, crook, crotch, cusp, elbow, knee, nook, point; **(2)** *v.* fish.

angry furious, hot, indignant, infuriated, irate, irritated, nettled, passionate, piqued, provoked, raging, resentful, tumultuous, wrathful.
Ant. calm, peaceful.

anguish distress, grief, pain, pang, throe, torment, torture.
Ant. comfort.

animadversion blame, censure, comment, criticism, rebuke, reprehension, reproof, strictures.
Ant. approbation, commendation.

animate embolden, encourage, enliven, gladden, incite, inspire, inspirit, instigate, kindle.

quicken, revive, rouse, stimulate, urge, vitalise, vivify.

Ant. discourage, dishearten.

animosity acrimony, antipathy, bitterness, enmity, hatred, ill-will, malevolence, malice, malignity, rancour, virulence.

Ant. kindliness, sympathy.

annals (*Hist.*), accounts, archives, chronicles, memorials, records, registers.

annex add, adjoin, affix, append, attach, fasten, subjoin, tack, unite.

Ant. detach, separate.

annihilate abolish, destroy, eradicate, exterminate, extinguish, extirpate, nullify, obliterate.

Ant. keep, preserve.

annotation comment, commentary, elucidation, explanation, gloss, illustration, note, observation.

announce advertise, declare, disclose, divulge, intimate, proclaim, promulgate, propound, publish, report, reveal.

Ant. conceal, suppress.

annoy bore, bother, disturb, incommode, irritate, molest, pester, plague, provoke, tease, trouble, vex.

Ant. appease, soothe.

annul abolish, abrogate, cancel, countermand, nullify, repeal, rescind, reverse, revoke.

anoint consecrate, hallow, sanctify.

anomaly abnormality, eccentricity, exception, irregularity, peculiarity, rarity.

Ant. conformity, regularity.

anonymous nameless, unacknowledged, unattested, unauthenticated, unidentified, unknown, unsigned.

Ant. signed.

answer (**1**) *n.* defence, plea, refutation, rejoinder, reply, report, solution, vindication; (**2**) *v.* fulfil, refute, reply, respond, satisfy, serve.

Ant. of (**1**) question; of (**2**) differ.

answerable accountable, agreeing, amenable, correspondent, liable, responsible, solvable, suited.

Ant. unanswerable.

antagonist adversary, competitor, enemy, foe, opponent, rival.

Ant. ally, friend.

antecedent anterior, earlier, foregoing, former, preceding, precursory, preliminary, previous.

Ant. posterior, later.

anterior antecedent, foregoing, former, introductory, preceding, previous.

anticipate apprehend, await, count upon, expect, forecast, foresee, forestall, hope for, prepare for, prevent.

anticipation apprehension, awaiting, expectation, foresight, foretaste, forethought, hope, preconception, presentiment, prospect.

Ant. non-expectation.

antidote corrective, counteragent (*of poison*), preventive, remedy, specific.

antipathy abhorrence, aversion, contrariety, disgust, dislike, distaste, hatred, loathing, opposition, repugnance.

Ant. sympathy.

anxiety apprehension, care, concern, disquietude, distress, foreboding, misgiving, restlessness, solicitude, uneasiness, watchfulness, worry.

Ant. contentment, security.

anxious apprehensive, careful,

concerned, distressed, disturbed, restless, solicitous, troubled, uneasy, watchful.

Ant. certain, confident.

apart alone, aloof, aside, asunder, away, separately.

Ant. together.

apathy coldness, impassibility, indifference, insensibility, phlegm, stoicism, torpor, unconcern, unfeelingness.

Ant. anxiety, concern.

ape affect, copy, counterfeit, imitate, mimic.

aperture cleft, eye, eyelet, gap, hole, opening, orifice, passage, perforation.

aphorism adage, apothegm, axiom, dictum, proverb, saw, saying.

apish affected, foolish, foppish, imitative, mimicking, silly, trifling.

apocryphal doubtful, equivocal, fictitious, legendary, spurious, uncanonical, unauthenticated.

apologue allegory, fable, parable, story, tale.

apology confession, defence, excuse, explanation, extenuation, justification, makeshift, plea, reparation, vindication.

apostate (1) n. backslider, deserter, renegade, turncoat; (2) a. backsliding, disloyal, faithless, false, recreant, traitorous, treacherous, untrue.

Ant. of (2) faithful, loyal.

apostle angel, herald, messenger, missionary, preacher.

apothegm adage, aphorism, dictum, maxim, proverb, saw, saying.

appal alarm, astound, daunt, dismay, frighten, intimidate, scare, shock, terrify.

Ant. assure.

apparel attire, clothes, clothing, costume, dress, garb, garments, habiliments, habit, outfit, raiment, robes, trappings, vestments.

apparent clear, conspicuous, discernible, distinct, evident, indubitable, manifest, obvious, ostensible, plain, seeming, specious, unmistakable.

Ant. dubious, uncertain.

apparition chimera, ghost, phantom, shade, spectre, spirit, vision.

appeal (1) n. application, entreaty, invocation, petition, prayer, request, supplication; (2) v. apply, ask, call, entreat, petition, refer, request, (Law) transfer.

appearance advent, air, apparition, arrival, aspect, coming, demeanour, expression, face, figure, look, manifestation, manner, mien, presence.

appease allay, assuage, calm, compose, conciliate, ease, lessen, pacify, placate, quell, quiet, soothe, subdue, tranquillise.

Ant. aggravate, perturb.

appellation address, description, designation, epithet, style, term, title.

append add, affix, annex, attach, fasten, hang, join, subjoin.

appendix addendum, addition, adjunct, appendage, supplement.

appetite craving, demand, desire, hankering, hunger, longing, proclivity, propensity, zeal.

Ant. aversion.

applaud approve cheer, clap, commend, compliment, encourage, extol, magnify, praise.

applause acclaim, acclamation, approbation, approval,

cheers, commendation, hand-clapping, plaudit.

Ant. disapproval, hissing.

applicable apposite, appropriate, apt, fitting, germane, pertinent, relevant, suitable, suited, useful.

Ant. inapplicable, irrelevant.

application (1) assiduity, attention, effort, industry, perseverance, study; (2) appeal, petition, request, solicitation; (3) exercise, practice, use.

Ant. of (1) inattention, laziness, sloth.

apply (1) address, appeal, entreat, petition, solicit; (2) appropriate, employ, exercise, use, utilise; (3) dedicate, devote, direct, engage.

appoint (1) allot, assign, designate, fix, settle; (2) command, decree, direct, enjoin, ordain; (3) elect, name, nominate, select.

apportion allocate, allot, assign, deal, dispense, distribute, divide, share.

apposite appropriate, apropos, apt, befitting, germane, pertinent, relevant, suitable.

Ant. inappropriate, unsuitable.

appraise appreciate, estimate, price, rate, survey, value.

appreciate acknowledge, esteem, estimate, prize, raise the value of, realise, recognise, value.

Ant. depreciate, disparage.

apprehend (1) arrest, capture, catch, seize, take; (2) believe, comprehend, conceive, imagine, think; (3) fear, dread.

Ant. of (1) release.

apprehension (1) arrest, capture, seizure; (2) belief, conception, opinion, sentiment,

view; (3) anxiety, dread, fear, uneasiness.

Ant. of (1) release; of (3) serenity.

apprise acquaint, advise, communicate, inform, make known, notify, tell.

approach (1) v. advance, approximate, come near, make overtures to, push forward, resemble; (2) n. access, advance, advent, approximation, arrival, avenue, coming, drawing near, entrance, nearing, passage.

approbation approval, assent, commendation, encouragement, endorsement, praise, ratification, support.

Ant. disapproval, disavowal.

appropriate (1) a. adapted, apposite, apt, becoming, felicitous, fit, opportune, pertinent, proper, suitable, well-timed; (2) v. allocate, allot, apportion, assign, devote, set apart.

Ant. of (1) inappropriate, inopportune, untimely.

approximate approach, come near, reach, touch.

Ant. differ, diverge.

apt (1) applicable, apposite, appropriate, apropos, befitting, fit, fitting, relevant, suitable, to the point; (2) disposed, inclined, liable, prone; (3) bright, clever, expert, handy, intelligent, prompt, quick, skilful, teachable.

Ant. inapt.

aptitude (1) bent, disposition, inclination, proclivity, proneness, tendency; (2) aptness, capacity, cleverness, faculty, fitness, gift, intelligence, suitability, talent.

arbitrary (1) absolute, despotic, dictatorial, domineering, imperious, irresponsible, over-bearing, uncontrolled, unlimited; (2) capricious, discretionary, fanciful, optional, voluntary.

Ant. of (1) limited.

arch chief, consummate, cunning, first class, principal, roguish, shrewd, sly, waggish, wily.

archaic ancient, antiquated, antique, bygone, obsolete, old, old-fashioned, out-moded, primitive.

Ant. modern, up-to-date.

archives annals, chronicles, muniments, record office, records, registers, registry, rolls.

ardent eager, earnest, enthusiastic, fervent, fervid, fierce, fiery, intense, keen, passionate, vehement, warm, zealous.

Ant. apathetic, cool, lukewarm.

ardour eagerness, enthusiasm, fervour, heat, passion, spirit, warmth, zeal.

Ant. indifference.

arduous burdensome, difficult, exhausting, hard, laborious, painful, severe, toilsome.

Ant. easy, simple.

area (1) district, domain, realm, region, sphere, territory; (2) sunken space, yard.

argue contend in argument, controvert, convince, debate, discuss, dispute, expostulate, question, reason.

Ant. assent.

arid barren, dried up, dry, moistureless, parched, sterile.

Ant. damp, moist.

aright correctly, in due order, justly, rightly, truly, without error.

Ant. incorrectly, wrongly.

arise (1) ascend, get up, go up, mount, rise, soar, stand up,

tower; (2) ensue, follow, issue, originate, proceed, result; (3) rebel, revolt, rise.

aristocracy body of nobles, gentry, nobility, noblesse, peerage, upper classes, (*Colloq.*) upper ten.

army (1) armed force, host, legions, military force, troops; (2) (*Fig.*) multitude, throng, vast number.

aromatic balmy, fragrant, odoriferous, perfumed, redolent, spicy, sweet-scented.

Ant. fetid, ill-smelling.

around about, encircling, encompassing, environing, on every side of, surrounding.

arouse animate, awaken, call forth, incite, instigate, provoke, rouse, stimulate, stir up, warm, whet.

Ant. allay, calm, pacify.

arraign accuse, call to account, charge, denounce, impeach, indict, prosecute.

arrange (1) array, class, classify, dispose, group, marshal, put in order, range, rank; (2) adjust, contrive, construct, determine, devise, plan, prepare, project, settle.

arrant atrocious, downright, gross, infamous, monstrous, notorious, rank, utter, vile.

array (1) *v.* arrange, dispose, draw up, marshal, place in order, (*Mil.*) set in line; (2) accoutre, adorn, clothe, deck, decorate, dress, equip, invest; (3) *n.* arrangement, disposition, marshalling, order; (4) apparel, attire, clothes, dress, garments.

Ant. of (1) disarray.

arrest (1) *v.* apprehend, capture, catch, check, delay, detain, fix, hinder, lay hold of, obstruct, seize, stop; (2) *n.*

apprehension, capture, delay, detention, hindrance, obstruction, seizure.

Ant. of (1) release.

arrive attain, come, get to, reach.

Ant. depart.

arrogant assuming, blustering, contemptuous, disdainful, haughty, imperious, insolent, over-bearing, presumptuous, proud, scornful, supercilious.

Ant. bashful, humble, servile.

arrogate assume, claim unduly, demand, presume, usurp.

art (1) adroitness, aptitude, dexterity, ingenuity, knack, profession, skill, trade; (2) artfulness, astuteness, cunning, deceit, duplicity, guile, wiliness.

artful adroit, crafty, cunning, deceitful, designing, dexterous, intriguing, sly, wily.

Ant. artless, open.

article (1) branch, clause, division, head, heading, item, paragraph, part, particular, point, portion; (2) commodity, substance, thing; (3) discourse, essay, treatise.

artifice artfulness, chicanery, craft, cunning, deception, device, finesse, machination, ruse, stratagem, subterfuge, trickery.

artificial affected, assumed, counterfeit, false, feigned, fictitious, forced, sham, simulated, spurious, unnatural.

Ant. genuine, natural.

artless candid, fair, frank, honest, ingenuous, naïve, natural, open, simple, straightforward, trustful, undesigning.

Ant. artful, cunning, designing.

ascend climb, mount, rise, scale, soar, tower.

Ant. descend.

ascendency authority, command, domination, influence, mastery, power, predominance, prevalence, sovereignty, superiority, supremacy, sway, upperhand.

Ant. inferiority, weakness.

ascertain determine, discover, establish, find out, fix, learn, make certain, settle, verify.

Ant. guess, presume.

ascribe assign, attribute, charge, impute, refer, set down.

ask appeal, beg, beseech, claim, crave, demand, entreat, implore, inquire, interrogate, petition, pray, question, request, seek, solicit, sue, supplicate.

Ant. answer.

aspect (1) air, appearance, attitude, condition, countenance, expression, feature, look, mien; (2) bearing, direction, outlook, point of view, position, prospect, situation, view.

asperity acrimony, bitterness, churlishness, crabbedness, harshness, moroseness, roughness, ruggedness, severity, sourness, sullenness.

Ant. cheerfulness.

aspersion abuse, calumny, censure, defamation, detraction, obloquy, reproach, slander, vituperation.

Ant. eulogy.

aspiration aim, ambition, craving, desire, eagerness, endeavour, hankering, hope, longing, yearning.

aspire aim, desire, hope, long, seek, yearn.

assail assault, attack, charge, encounter, fall upon, impugn, invade, malign, maltreat.

assassinate kill, murder, slay.

assault (1) n. aggression, attack, charge, incursion, invasion, onslaught, storm; (2) v. assail, attack, charge.

assay (1) v. analyse, examine, prove, test, try; (2) n. analysis, examination, test, trial.

assemble call together, collect, congregate, convene, convoke, gather, muster, put together, set up.
Ant. disperse.

assembly assemblage, collection, company, conclave, conference, convocation, council, crowd, diet, group, meeting, multitude, synod, throng.

assent (1) v. accede, acquiesce, admit, agree, approve, concur, consent; (2) n. accord, acquiescence, agreement, approval, concurrence, consent.
Ant. of (1) disagree, dissent; of (2) denial, refusal.

assert (1) affirm, allege, asseverate, aver, avouch, avow, declare, maintain, pronounce; (2) claim, defend, press, uphold, vindicate.
Ant. of (1) deny.

assertion (1) affirmation, allegation, asseveration, avowal, declaration, predication, statement; (2) defence, maintenance, vindication.

assess appraise, compute, estimate, fix, impose, rate, tax, value.

asseverate affirm, assert, aver, declare, maintain, protest.
Ant. contradict.

assiduous attentive, constant, diligent, hard-working, indefatigable, industrious, laborious, persevering, sedulous, studious, untiring, unwearied.
Ant. inattentive, lazy.

assign advance, allocate, allot, apportion, appropriate, ascribe, attribute, convey, designate, determine, distribute,

fix, make over, offer, specify.

associate (1) v. accompany, affiliate, combine, conjoin, connect, couple, fraternise, link, unite; (2) n. ally, companion, compeer, comrade, confederate, consort, follower, friend, mate, partner.
Ant. of (1) dissociate; of (2) opponent.

assort arrange, classify, distribute, group, rank, sort.

assuage allay, alleviate, appease, calm, ease, lessen, mitigate, pacify, relieve, soothe, tranquillise.
Ant. aggravate, increase.

assume adopt, affect, appropriate, arrogate, infer, pretend to, put on, suppose, take for granted, undertake, usurp.

assurance arrogance, assuredness, boldness, certainty, confidence, conviction, courage, declaration, effrontery, engagement, firmness, impudence, persuasion, pledge, presumption, promise, protestation, self-reliance, word of honour.
Ant. diffidence, self-effacement, timidity.

assure certify, confirm, declare confidently, embolden, encourage, hearten, insure, secure against loss, vouch for.

astonish alarm, amaze, astound, daze, dum(b)found, scare, startle, stun, stupefy, surprise.

astronaut cosmonaut, spaceman, space-pilot.

astute crafty, cunning, discerning, keen, penetrating, sagacious, sharp, shrewd, sly, subtle, wily.
Ant. ingenuous, naïve, straightforward.

asylum haven, hospital, institution, refuge, retreat, sanctuary, shelter.

atheist agnostic, freethinker, heathen, infidel, non-believer, pagan, sceptic, unbeliever.

Ant. believer, Christian, theist.

athletic (1) brawny, herculean, lusty, muscular, powerful, robust, sinewy, strapping, strong, sturdy; (2) *n. pl.* games of strength, gymnastics, contests, exercises, races, sports.

Ant. of (1) puny, weak.

atom bit, dot, grain, jot, mite, molecule, mote, scrap, whit.

atone answer for, compensate, do penance for, make amends for, expiate, satisfy.

atonement amends, compensation, propitiation, satisfaction.

atrocious diabolical, enormous, flagrant, grievous, horrible, infamous, infernal, monstrous, nefarious, villainous.

Ant. kind, humane.

attach add, adhere, affix, annex, append, bind, connect, fasten, join, subjoin, tie, unite, win.

Ant. detach, loosen, untie.

attack (1) *n.* aggression, assault, blame, censure, charge, inroad, invasion, onslaught; (2) *v.* assail, assault, blame, censure, criticise, impugn, invade, storm, threaten.

Ant. of (1) defence; of (2) defend.

attain accomplish, achieve, acquire, effect, gain, get, grasp, obtain, procure, reach, secure.

Ant. lose, miss.

attempt (1) *n.* effort, endeavour, essay, experiment, trial, undertaking; (2) *v.* endeavour, essay, experiment, seek, strive, try, undertake.

attend (1) accompany, escort, follow, frequent, guard, minister, regard, serve, wait on, watch; (2) hear, hearken, heed, listen, pay attention.

attention alertness, application, care, civility, consideration, contemplation, courtesy, deference, heed, notice, regard, respect.

Ant. inattention, disrespect.

attentive careful, civil, considerate, courteous, heedful, intent, mindful, observant, polite, regardful, respectful, studious, watchful.

Ant. distracted, inattentive, remiss.

attenuate contract, dilute, diminish, draw out, elongate, lengthen, lessen, make slender, rarefy, reduce, thin, weaken.

Ant. increase, thicken.

attest adjure, affirm, authenticate, aver, certify, confirm, corroborate, exhibit, invoke, manifest, prove, ratify, seal, show, testify, witness.

Ant. deny, refute.

attic chaste, classical, correct, graceful, elegant, polished, pure, refined.

attire (1) *n.* accoutrements, apparel, array, clothes, clothing, costume, dress, garments, habit, raiment, robes, uniform, vestment; (2) *v.* accoutre, apparel, array, clothe, dress, equip.

Ant. of (1) bareness, undress.

attitude aspect, bearing, condition, manner, mien, phase, pose, posture, standing, state.

attract allure, captivate, charm, decoy, endear, engage, entice, fascinate, incline, induce, invite, tempt.

Ant. repel, repulse.

attractive agreeable, alluring,

beautiful, charming, enticing, fascinating, interesting, inviting, tempting, winning.

Ant. deterrent, disagreeable, repulsive.

attribute (1) *v.* apply, ascribe, assign, charge, impute, refer; (2) *n.* character, characteristic, indication, mark, note, peculiarity, property, quality, sign, symbol.

attune accord, adapt, adjust, harmonise, modulate, tune.

audacious adventurous, bold, courageous, daring, enterprising, fearless, impudent, insolent, intrepid, presumptuous, rash, reckless, valiant.

Ant. cowardly, timid, unenterprising.

audience assemblage, congregation, hearing, interview, reception.

augment add to, amplify, dilate, enhance, enlarge, extend, grow, magnify, multiply, swell.

Ant. abate, decrease, reduce.

augmentation accession, addition, amplification, enlargement, extension, increase.

Ant. deduction, diminution.

augury auspice, divination, forerunner, harbinger, portent, prediction, presage, prophecy, prognostication, omen, sign, soothsaying.

august dignified, exalted, grand, imposing, kingly, magnificent, majestic, noble, regal, solemn, stately, superb.

Ant. commonplace, undignified.

auspicious encouraging, favourable, fortunate, happy, lucky, opportune, promising, propitious, prosperous.

Ant. unfavourable, unpromising.

austere ascetic, exacting, formal, hard, harsh, inflexible, rigorous, stern, stiff, straitlaced, strict, unrelenting.

Ant. affable, genial, indulgent, sweet.

authentic accurate, authoritative, certain, faithful, genuine, legitimate, pure, real, reliable, trustworthy, veritable.

Ant. fictitious, spurious.

uthor composer, creator, doer, fabricator, maker, mover, originator, parent, producer, writer.

authority ascendency, authorisation, control, dignity, dominion, empire, government, ground, influence, interest, jurisdiction, order, permission, permit, rule, sanction, supremacy, sway, testimony, warrant, weight of evidence.

auxiliary (1) *a.* aiding, ancillary, assisting, helping, subsidiary; (2) *n.* ally, assistant, confederate, helper.

Ant. chief.

avail (1) *n.* advantage, benefit, help, profit, service, use, utility; (2) *v.* be of use, benefit, profit, serve.

available accessible, advantageous, applicable, attainable, beneficial, handy, helpful, profitable, ready, useful.

Ant. unavailable, useless.

avarice acquisitiveness, covetousness, cupidity, greediness, miserliness, niggardliness, penuriousness, rapacity.

Ant. bountifulness, liberality.

avenge punish, requite, retaliate, revenge, take satisfaction for.

Ant. forgive, pardon.

avenue access, alley, approach, channel, entrance, entry, pass, passage, path, road, route, way.

aver affirm, allege, assert, asseverate, avouch, declare, pronounce, protest, say.

averse backward, disinclined, loath, reluctant, unwilling.

Ant. disposed, willing.

aversion abhorrence, antipathy, detestation, disgust, disinclination, dislike, distaste, hate, hatred, loathing, reluctance, repugnance, unwillingness.

Ant. desire, liking.

avidity avarice, cupidity, desire, eagerness, greediness, hankering, longing, ravenousness, voracity.

Ant. aversion.

avocation business, calling, employment, job, occupation, profession, trade, vocation.

avoid dodge, elude, escape, eschew, evade, forbear, refrain from, shirk, shun.

Ant. approach, confront.

avouch affirm, allege, assert, asseverate, aver, declare, maintain.

avow acknowledge, admit, affirm, aver, confess, declare, own, profess, recognise.

Ant. refute, renounce.

awaken arouse, awake, call forth, excite, kindle, provoke, stimulate, stir up.

award (1) v. accord, adjudge, allot, apportion, assign, bestow, decree, distribute, grant; (2) n. adjudication, allotment, bestowal, decree, decision, gift, order.

Ant. of (1) withhold.

awe (1) n. dread, fear, horror, terror, veneration, wonder; (2) v. cow, daunt, frighten, intimidate, terrify.

Ant. of (1) boldness, fearlessness.

awful alarming, appalling, dreadful, frightful, horrible, horrific, majestic, portentous, solemn, tremendous, ugly, unsightly, venerable.

Ant. ordinary, unimposing.

awkward bungling, clownish, clumsy, coarse, crude, gauche, gawky, embarrassing, ill-bred, inconvenient, inexpert, maladroit, rude, rustic, stiff, uncouth, ungraceful, unhandy, unmanageable, unpolished, unrefined, unwieldy.

Ant. adroit, handy, skilful.

axiom adage, aphorism, apothegm, maxim, postulate, truism.

azure blue, cerulean, sky-blue, sky-coloured.

B

babble blab, cackle, chatter, gabble, gibber, jabber, prate, prattle.

babe baby, (Scot.) bairn, brat, infant, nursling, suckling.

babel clamour, confusion, din, disorder, hubbub, hurly-burly, jargon, tumult.

Ant. distinctness.

bacchanal carouser, debauchee, drunkard, reveller, roysterer, wine-bibber.

Ant. abstainer, teetotaler.

back (1) v. abet, assist, countenance, endorse, favour, second, side with, support, sustain; (2) v. go back, move back, retire, retreat, withdraw; (3) n. end, hind part, posterior, rear.

Ant. of (2) advance; of (3) face, front.

backbite abuse, calumniate, defame, detract, libel, malign, revile, slander, traduce, vilify.

backbone (1) n. (Med.) spine,

vertebral column; (2) *n.* (*Fig.*) courage, essence, firmness, hardihood, marrow, nerve, pith, pluck, resolution, stamina, steadfastness.

Ant. of (2) weakness.

backslider apostate, deserter recreant, renegade, turncoat.

Ant. adherent, loyalist.

backward (1) *a.* behind, behindhand, dull, hesitating, late, reluctant, shy, slow, sluggish, tardy, undeveloped, unwilling, wavering; (2) *adv.* aback, behind, rearward.

bad abandoned, abominable, baneful, criminal, decayed, dishonest, evil, harmful, hurtful, ill, immoral, inferior, injurious, poor, rotten, scurvy, serious, severe, shabby, sick, sorry, unfair, unwholesome, vile, wicked.

Ant. good, moral.

badge brand, device, emblem, mark, sign, stamp, token.

baffle balk, bewilder, check, checkmate, confound, confuse, defeat, disconcert, elude, foil, frustrate, perplex, thwart, upset.

Ant. aid, assist.

bait allurement, decoy, enticement, inducement, lure, refreshment, snare, temptation.

Ant. deterrent.

balance (1) *v.* adjust, assay, compare, compensate, counteract, counterpoise, equalise, estimate, make up for, settle, square, weigh; (2) *n.* equilibrium, equipoise, residue, self-control, self-possession, surplus.

baleful calamitous, deadly, hurtful, injurious, mournful, noxious, pernicious, ruinous, sad, woeful.

Ant. beneficial, good, healthy.

balk baffle, bar, counteract, defeat, disconcert, foil, frustrate, hinder, prevent, thwart.

Ant. encourage, help.

balmy ambrosial, aromatic, easing, fragrant, healing, odoriferous, odorous, perfumed, redolent, refreshing, soothing, spicy, sweet-scented, sweet-smelling.

Ant. malodorous, noisome, noxious.

band (1) bandage, belt, binding, bond, chain, cord, fetter, fillet, ligature, manacle, shackle, strap, strip, tie; (2) assembly, association, body, clique, club, company, coterie, crew, gang, horde, party, society, troop.

bandit brigand, footpad, freebooter, highwayman, marauder, outlaw.

baneful baleful, deadly, deleterious, destructive, harmful, hurtful, injurious, noxious, pestilential, venomous.

Ant. beneficial, good, salutary.

banish drive away, eject, exclude, exile, expatriate, expel, ostracise, outlaw, shut out, transport.

Ant. accept, admit.

banner colours, ensign, fanion, fanon, flag, pennant, pennon, standard, streamer.

banter (1) *v.* (*Colloq.*) chaff, deride, jeer, jest, joke, make fun of, ridicule, tease, twit; (2) *n.* badinage, (*Colloq.*) chaff, derision, jeering, jesting, joking, mockery, pleasantry, ridicule.

bar (1) *n.* barricade, barrier, deterrent, hindrance, impediment, obstacle, obstruction, rail, railing, stop; (2) *v.* exclude, hinder, obstruct, prevent, prohibit, restrain; **(3)** (*Law*) barristers, body of lawyers, counsel, court, judgment, tribunal.

Ant. of (2) admit, allow.

barbarian boor, brute, philistine, ruffian, savage.

barbarous barbarian, barbaric, brutal, coarse, crude, cruel, ferocious, ignorant, inhuman, primitive, rough, rude, ruthless, savage, truculent, uncivilised, uncouth, uncultured, unlettered, vulgar.

Ant. cultured, refined.

bare denuded, empty, exposed, mean, naked, nude, open, plain, poor, scanty, scarce, simple, unadorned, unclothed, uncovered, undressed, unfurnished.

Ant. clothed, dressed.

bargain **(1)** *n.* agreement, business, compact, contract, convention, engagement, negotiation, pact, (*cheap*) purchase, stipulation, transaction, treaty; **(2)** *v.* agree, contract, covenant, sell, stipulate, trade, traffic, transact.

barren bare, desert, desolate, empty, infecund, infertile, poor, scanty, sterile, unfruitful, unproductive, unprolific.

Ant. fertile, fruitful.

barricade barrier, obstruction, palisade, stockade.

barrier bar, barricade, boundary, fence, hindrance, impediment, obstacle, obstruction, railing, stop.

barter bargain, exchange, sell, trade, traffic.

base abject, contemptible, counterfeit, debased, dishonourable, disreputable, grovelling, ignoble, infamous, inferior, low, mean, menial, paltry, pitiful, scandalous,

servile, shameful, slavish, sordid, sorry, spurious, vile, villainous, vulgar, worthless.

Ant. good, lofty, noble.

bashful coy, diffident, overmodest, reserved, retiring, self-effacing, shamefaced, sheepish, shrinking, shy, timid.

Ant. immodest.

basis base, bottom, chief ingredient, foundation, ground, groundwork, principal element.

bastard **(1)** *n.* illegitimate (*child*), love-child, natural child; **(2)** *a.* adulterated, base-born, counterfeit, false, illegitimate, sham, spurious.

Ant. of (1) legitimate (*child*).

bathe cover, flood, go into the sea or water, immerse, lave, steep, swim, wash.

batter beat, break, bruise, dash against, deface, demolish, destroy, disfigure, mar, pelt, ruin, shatter, shiver, smash, smite.

battle **(1)** *n.* action, combat, conflict, contest, encounter, engagement, fight, skirmish, war; **(2)** *v.* combat, contend, contest, fight, strive, struggle, war.

bauble gewgaw, gimcrack, knick-knack, plaything, toy, trinket.

bawl bellow, clamour, cry, halloo, roar, shout, squall, vociferate, yell.

Ant. murmur, whisper.

bay **(1)** (*Geog.*) bight, gulf, inlet; **(2)** (*Archit.*) compartment, opening, recess; **(3)** chaplet, garland, glory, laurel-crown, praise, prize, renown, trophy; **(4)** (*Dogs*) bark, barking, baying, yelp.

beach bank, littoral, margin, sands, shore, strand.

beacon lighthouse, pharos, sign, signal-fire, watch-tower.

beak (1) bill, mandible, (*Colloq.*) neb, (*Colloq.*) nose; (2) (*Naut.*) bow, prow, stem.

beaming beautiful, bright, brilliant, flashing, gleaming, glistening, glittering, radiant, scintillating, shining, sparkling.
Ant. dull, lustreless.

bear (1) carry, cherish, convey, entertain, exhibit, harbour, have, hold, maintain, possess, support, sustain, transport, uphold, weigh upon; (2) abide, admit, allow, brook, endure, permit, tolerate; (3) beget, generate, give birth to, produce, yield.

bearable endurable, supportable, sustainable, tolerable.
Ant. insufferable, unbearable.

bearing (1) aim, aspect, behaviour, carriage, demeanour, dependency, deportment, effect, endurance, gesture, import, mien, posture, relation, suffering; (2) (*Naut.*) course, direction, point of compass.

beat bang, batter, break, bruise, buffet, cane, checkmate, cudgel, defeat, drub, excel, flog, hammer, hit, knock, lash, maul, outdo, overcome, pelt, pound, pulsate, punch, strike, surpass, thrash, throb, thump, thwack, vanquish, whip.

beatitude beatification, blessedness, bliss, ecstasy, felicity, happiness, holy joy.

beau coxcomb, dandy, fop, gallant, ladies' man, lover, popinjay, suitor, sweetheart.

beautify adorn, array, bedeck, deck, decorate, embellish, garnish, gild, grace, ornament.
Ant. deface, disfigure.

beauty attraction, attractiveness, charm, comeliness, elegance, exquisiteness, grace, loveliness, seemliness, symmetry.
Ant. ugliness.

becoming (1) comely, graceful, neat, pretty; (2) befitting, congruous, decent, decorous, fit, proper, seeming, suitable.
Ant. of (1) ugly; of (2) unbecoming, unsuitable.

bedim becloud, bedarken, cloud, darken, dim, obscure.
Ant. brighten.

befall bechance, betide, come to pass, happen, occur, supervene, take place.

befitting appropriate, becoming, fit, fitting, meet, right, seemly.
Ant. inappropriate, unbecoming.

befool bamboozle, beguile, cheat, delude, dupe, fool, hoax, hoodwink, impose on, trick.

befriend aid, assist, back, benefit, encourage, favour, help, patronise, succour, support, sustain.

beg beseech, crave, desire, entreat, implore, importune, petition, pray, request, supplicate.
Ant. demand.

beggarly abject, base, contemptible, despicable, destitute, indigent, low, mean, miserly, needy, niggardly, pitiful, poor, stingy, vile, wretched.
Ant. liberal, profuse.

begin commence, inaugurate, initiate, institute, originate, prepare, set about, set on foot, start.
Ant. end, finish.

beginning birth, commencement, inauguration, initiation, opening, origin, outset, preface, prelude, rise, rudiments, source, start.

Ant. completion, conclusion, end.

beguile (1) befool, cheat, deceive, delude, hoodwink, impose on, mislead, trick; (2) amuse, charm, cheer, divert, entertain, solace.

behaviour actions, bearing, carriage, conduct, demeanour, deportment, manners.

behest bidding, charge, command, commandment, direction, expressed desire, injunction, precept, wish.

behindhand backward, behind time, dilatory, late, slow, tardy.

Ant. early, up to time.

behold (1) v. consider, contemplate, discern, eye, look at, observe, perceive, regard, survey, view, witness; (2) *interj.* lo, look, mark, observe, see.

behoove become, befit, beseem.

being animal, body, creature, life, living spirit, nature, reality, substance, thing.

beleaguer beset, besiege, blockade, encompass, environ, hem in, invest, surround.

Ant. relieve.

belief (1) admission, assent, confidence, conviction, credit, opinion, persuasion, reliance, trust, view; (2) credence, creed, doctrine, dogma, faith, tenet.

Ant. unbelief.

bellow bawl, clamour, cry, howl, roar, shout, vociferate.

Ant. whisper.

belt (1) band, cincture, girdle, girth; (2) (*Geog.*) region, stretch, strip, zone.

bemoan bewail, deplore, express sorrow, grieve for, lament, moan over, mourn.

bemused bewildered, confused, fuddled, half-drunk, muddled, stupefied, tipsy.

Ant. sober.

bend bow, crack, curve, deflect, direct, diverge, incline, incurvate, lean, persuade, stoop, subdue, submit, sway, swerve, tend, yield.

Ant. resist, stiffen.

benediction beatitude, benison, blessing, favour, grace, gratitude, invocation, prayer, thankfulness, thanksgiving.

Ant. curse, malediction.

benefaction alms, bequest, boon, charity, contribution, donation, endowment, gift, grant, gratuity, offering, present.

beneficent benevolent, bounteous, bountiful, charitable, generous, kind, liberal, munificent, princely.

Ant. mean, stingy, ungenerous.

beneficial advantageous, favourable, gainful, helpful, profitable, salutary, serviceable, useful, wholesome.

Ant. disadvantageous.

benefit advantage, avail, blessing, boon, favour, good turn, interest, kindness, profit, use.

Ant. disadvantage, injury.

benevolent altruistic, beneficent, benign, bountiful, charitable, generous, humane, kind-hearted, liberal, philanthropic, tender-hearted, well-disposed.

Ant. egoistic, selfish.

benign amiable, complaisant, favourable, friendly, generous, gracious, kind, liberal, obliging.

Ant. disobliging.

bequeath bestow, give, grant, hand down, impart, leave to by will, transmit, will.

bereave afflict, deprive of

kindred, despoil, dispossess, divest, make destitute, rob, spoil, strip, take away from.
Ant. compensate.

beseech adjure, ask, beg, crave, entreat, implore, importune, petition, pray, solicit, supplicate.

beset (1) assail, besiege, encircle, enclose, encompass, environ, hem in; (2) (*Fig.*) embarrass, entangle, harass, perplex.

besides also, further, furthermore, in addition, moreover, otherwise, too.

besiege beleaguer, beset, blockade, encircle, encompass, environ, hem in, invest, lay siege, surround.
Ant. relieve.

bespatter bedaub, befoul, besmirch, besprinkle, smear, spatter.

bespeak accost, address, declare, forestall, imply, indicate, order beforehand, prearrange, predict, proclaim, show, solicit.

best chief, first, foremost, highest, leading, most excellent, most good, pre-eminent, principal.
Ant. worst.

bestial animal, beastlike, beastly, brutal, brutish, carnal, degraded, depraved, gross, low, sensual, vile.

bestir animate, awaken, exert, incite, rouse, stimulate, stir up, trouble.
Ant. appease.

bestow accord, allot, confer, donate, give, grant, impart, present, store, stow.

bet hazard, pledge, risk, stake, wager.

bethink cogitate, consider, ponder, recall, recollect, reflect, remember, take thought.

betide bechance, befall, come to pass, happen, occur, overtake, supervene, take place.

betimes beforehand, early, forward, in good time, seasonably, soon.
Ant. behindhand, late.

betoken augur, declare, denote, evidence, indicate, manifest, mark, portend, presage, prognosticate, represent, signify, typify.

betray beguile, corrupt, deceive, delude, disclose, divulge, dupe, ensnare, entrap, lead astray, mislead, reduce, reveal, show, undo.
Ant. protect.

betroth affiance, engage to marry, pledge in marriage, plight.

better (1) *a.* bigger, fitter, greater, higher grade, larger, less ill, more (appropriate, expert, fitting, suitable, useful, valuable), superior; (2) *v.* advance, ameliorate, amend, correct, exceed, improve, meliorate, mend, promote, rectify, reform.
Ant. of (1) worse; of (2) worsen.

between amidst, among, betwixt.

bewail bemoan, deplore, express sorrow, grieve for, lament, moan, mourn, rue.

beware avoid, be (careful, cautious, wary), heed, look out, mind, refrain from.
Ant. brave, dare.

bewitch captivate, charm, enchant, enrapture, entrance, fascinate, hypnotise.
Ant. disenchant.

beyond above, at a distance, before, farther, out of reach, over, past, remote, superior to, yonder.

bias bent, inclination, leaning, partiality, penchant, predisposition, prejudice, propensity, tendency, turn.

Ant. impartiality.

bid (1) ask, call, charge, command, desire, direct, enjoin, require, solicit, summon, tell; (2) greet, say, wish; (3) offer, proffer, propose, tender.

Ant. of (1) forbid.

big (1) bulky, burly, enormous, extensive, gigantic, great, huge, immense, inflated, large, massive, ponderous, pregnant, swollen; (2) arrogant, conceited, haughty, pompous, proud.

Ant. of (1) small; of (2) humble, unaffected.

bigoted dogmatic, intolerant, narrow-minded, obstinate, opinionative, prejudiced, zealous.

bill (1) account, invoice, note of charge, reckoning, score, statement; (2) advertisement, bulletin, circular, handbill, notice, placard, poster; (3) beak, mandible, (*Colloq.*) neb; (4) measure, projected law.

billow breaker, roller, surge, swell, wave.

bind compel, confine, detain, engage, fasten, oblige, restrict, secure, tie, wrap.

Ant. loosen, untie.

birth ancestry, beginning, descent, extraction, line, lineage, nativity, noble extraction, nobility, parentage, parturition, race, rise, source.

Ant. death, end.

bit atom, chip, crumb, fragment, grain, iota, jot, mite, morsel, mouthful, part, speck, tittle, whit.

bite (1) *v.* blast, burn, champ, chew, corrode, crush, cut, gnaw, nip, pierce, pinch, rend, seize, smart, sting, tear, tingle, wound; (2) *n.* burn, cut, nip, pinch, sting; (3) food, morsel, mouthful, snack.

biting blighting, cold, cutting, freezing, nipping, piercing, pungent, (*Fig.*) severe, sharp, stinging.

bitter acrid, calamitous, cruel, dire, distressing, fierce, grievous, harsh, merciless, painful, poignant, ruthless, savage, severe, sore, sour, stern, tart.

Ant. mellow, sweet.

black (1) dark, dingy, dirty, dusky, ebon, murky, (*Poet.*) sable, soiled, stained, swarthy; (2) (*Fig.*) atrocious, depressing, dismal, distressing, doleful, foreboding, funereal, gloomy, horrible, infamous, infernal, lugubrious, mournful, ominous, sad, sombre, villainous, wicked.

Ant. of (1) white; of (2) bright, good.

blacken befoul, calumniate, cloud, darken, decry, defame, grow black, make black, malign, slander, soil, sully, traduce, vilify.

Ant. clear.

blamable blameworthy, culpable, deserving of censure, faulty, reprehensible, reproachable, reprovable.

Ant. praiseworthy.

blame accuse, censure, charge, chide, condemn, criticise, disapprove, express disapprobation, find fault with, reprehend, reproach, reprove, tax, upbraid.

Ant. credit, praise.

blameless faultless, guiltless, immaculate, impeccable, innocent, irreproachable, perfect, stainless, unblemished, unimpeachable, unspotted, unsullied.

Ant. guilty.

blanch become (or grow) white, bleach, fade, pale, whiten.

Ant. blacken.

bland affable, affectionate, amiable, congenial, courteous, friendly, gentle, gracious, kind, mild, (Med.) non-irritating, soft, soothing, tender.

Ant. harsh, rough, uncongenial.

blandishment cajolery, coaxing, compliment, fawning, flattery, soft words, wheedling, winning caresses.

blank (1) bare, empty, unfilled, unmarked, void; (2) amazed, astonished, confounded, confused, disconcerted, non-plussed, dum(b)founded.

blasphemy impiety, impiousness, indignity (to God), irreverence, profaneness, profanity, sacrilege, swearing.

Ant. piety, reverence.

blast (1) n. and v. blare, blow, clang, peal; (2) n. burst, discharge, explosion, outburst; (3) n. gale, gust, squall, storm, strong breeze, tempest; (4) v. blight, destroy, kill, ruin, shrivel, wither.

blaze burn, fire, flame, flare, glare, gleam, glow.

bleach blanch, etiolate, grow pale (or wan), whiten.

Ant. blacken, darken.

bleak bare, cheerless, chilly, cold, desolate, drear, dreary, exposed, open, unsheltered.

Ant. sheltered.

blemish blot, blur, defect, disfigurement, disgrace, dishonour, fault, flaw, imperfection, speck, spot, stain, taint.

Ant. purity.

blend (1) v. amalgamate, coalesce, combine, compound, confuse, harmonise, mingle, mix, unite; (2) n. amalgamation, combination, mixture.

Ant. of (1) separate.

bless consecrate, delight, enrich, extol, give thanks to, gladden, glorify, invoke happiness on, magnify, praise, sanctify, thank.

Ant. curse, deprive.

blessedness beatitude, bliss, blissfulness, content, felicity, happiness, heavenly joy, pleasure.

blight (1) blast, destroy, injure, nip in the bud, ruin, shrivel, taint with mildew, wither; (2) (Fig.) annihilate, crush, disappoint, frustrate, nullify.

blind (1) destitute of vision, eyeless, sightless, stone-blind; (2) (Fig.) careless, heedless, ignorant, inconsiderate, indiscriminate, injudicious, morally darkened, prejudiced, thoughtless, unaware of, uncritical, undiscerning, unreasoning; (3) closed, concealed, dark, dim, hidden, leading nowhere, without exit.

blink (1) flicker, gleam, glimmer, twinkle, wink; (2) (Fig.) connive at, disregard, overlook, pass by.

Ant. of (2) mark, notice.

bliss beatitude, blessedness, blissfulness, ecstasy, felicity, gladness, happiness, joy, rapture.

Ant. misery, wretchedness.

blithe animated, cheerful, gay, gladsome, happy, lighthearted, merry, mirthful, sprightly, vivacious.

Ant. dejected, unhappy.

block (1) v. arrest, check, close, deter, hinder, impede, obstruct, stop; (2) n. hindrance, impediment, jam, obstacle, obstruction, stoppage; (3) lump, mass; (4) blockhead, dunce, fool, idiot.

Ant. of (1) clear; of (4) genius.

blood (1) *n.* children, consanguinity, descendants, family, kindred, noble extraction, offspring, relation; (2) (*Fig.*) anger, disposition, feeling, passion, temper.

bloom (1) *n.* blossom, efflorescence, flower, opening (*of flowers*); (2) *v.* blossom, blow, bud, open; (3) (*Fig.*) beauty, flush, freshness, vigour.

Ant. of (2) die.

blossom (1) *n.* bloom, bud, flower; (2) (*Fig.*) flourish, prosper.

blot (1) bespatter, disfigure, disgrace, spoil, spot, sully, tarnish; (2) cancel, destroy, efface, erase, expunge, obliterate; (3) blemish, blur, disgrace, spot, stain.

Ant. of (1) cleanse.

blow (1) *n. and v.* bang, buffet, knock, rap, stroke, thump, whack; (2) (*Fig.*) affliction, calamity, disappointment, disaster, misfortune, reverse; (3) *v.* bloom, blossom, flower; (4) *v.* breathe, pant, puff, sound; (5) *n.* blast, gale, gust, strong breeze, wind.

blue (1) azure, cerulean, sapphire, sky-coloured; (2) (*Fig.*) dejected, depressed, dismal, downcast, down-hearted, gloomy, glum, melancholy, sad.

Ant. of (2) cheerful, mirthful.

bluff (1) *v.* deceive, defraud, lie, mislead; (2) *n.* deceit, feint, fraud, lie; (3) *a.* abrupt, blunt, blustering, coarse, frank, good-natured, open.

blunder (1) *n.* error, fault, inaccuracy, mistake, oversight; (2) *v.* err, flounder, mistake, stumble.

Ant. of (1) accuracy, correctness.

blunt (1) edgeless, pointless, rounded; (2) (*Fig.*) bluff, brusque, discourteous, impolite, outspoken, rude, uncivil, unpolished; (3) dull, obtuse, slow, stolid, stupid.

Ant. of (1) sharp; of (2) courteous.

blur (1) *v.* blemish, blot, disfigure, injure, spot, stain, sully, tarnish; (2) *n.* blemish, blot, disfigurement, spot, stain; (3) *v.* dim, obscure.

blush colour, flush, redden.

bluster (1) *v.* boast, brag, bully, domineer, roar, swagger, swell, vaunt; (2) *n.* boasting, bragging, swaggering.

board (1) piece of timber, plank, table; (2) diet, fare, food, meals, provisions, victuals; (3) committee, conclave, council, directors.

boast bluster, bounce, brag, crow, exaggerate, (*Sl.*) talk big, vaunt.

Ant. depreciate.

bode augur, betoken, forbode, foreshadow, foretell, portend, predict, presage.

bodily altogether, completely, entirely, fully, wholly.

Ant. partly.

body (1) carcass, corpse, dead body, trunk; (2) being, creature, individual, mortal, person; (3) association, band, collection, company, corporation, coterie; (4) bulk, mass, matter, substance.

boggle demur, doubt, falter, hesitate, shrink from, waver.

bogle apparition, bugbear,

hobgoblin, imp, scarecrow, spectre.

boil (1) *v.* agitate, bubble, ebulliate, effervesce, foam, froth, rage, seethe; (2) *n.* (*Med.*) gathering, pustule, tumour, ulcer.

Ant. of (1) cool.

boisterous clamorous, furious, impetuous, loud, noisy, obstreperous, stormy, tempestuous, turbulent, unrestrained, uproarious, vociferous.

Ant. calm, quiet.

bold (1) adventurous, audacious, brave, courageous, daring, dauntless, fearless, gallant, heroic, intrepid, valiant, valorous; (2) confident, forward, impudent, insolent.

Ant. of (1) timorous; of (2) modest.

bolster aid, assist, defend, help, maintain, prop, stay, support.

bolt (1) *n.* arrow, dart, missile, shaft, thunderbolt; (2) *v.* abscond, flee, fly.

Ant. of (2) remain.

bombast bluster, brag, braggadocio, extravagant boasting, fustian, gasconade, grandiloquence, rant, rodomontade, pomposity.

Ant. humility.

bond (1) band, chain, cord, fetter, ligature, link, manacle, shackle, tie; (2) (*Fig.*) binding, compact, contract, obligation.

bondage captivity, confinement, enslavement, enthralment, serfdom, servitude, slavery, subjection, thraldom, vassalage.

Ant. freedom.

bondsman bond-servant, captive, serf, slave, vassal.

Ant. freeman.

bonny (1) beautiful, comely, fair, handsome, pretty; (2) buxom, chubby, plump, shapely, round; (3) blithe, cheerful, gay, joyful, merry, winsome.

Ant. of (1) ugly; of (3) dull.

bonus benefit, bounty, dividend, gift, honorarium, premium, reward, subsidy.

booby blockhead, dunce, fool, idiot, simpleton.

Ant. sage.

book manual, roll, scroll, textbook, tome, tract, volume, work.

bookish erudite, learned, literary, scholarly, studious.

Ant. unlearned.

boon (1) *n.* advantage, blessing, donation, favour, gift, grant, gratuity, present; (2) *a.* benign, bountiful, generous, kind; (3) *a.* convivial, gay, jolly, jovial, merry.

Ant. of (2) unkind; of (3) sad.

boor bumpkin, clodhopper, clodpole, clown, countryman, lout, peasant, rustic, swain.

boorish awkward, bearish, clownish, gruff, ill-bred, loutish, lubberly, rude, rustic, uncivilised, uneducated.

Ant. refined.

booty loot, pillage, plunder, prey, spoil.

border bound, boundary, brim, brink, confine, edge, hem, limit, lip, margin, rim, skirt, verge.

Ant. centre.

bore (1) *v.* drill, penetrate, perforate, pierce; (2) *n.* calibre, hole; (3) *v.* annoy, bother, fatigue, tire, trouble, worry, vex; (4) *n.* wearisome talker.

borrow adopt, appropriate, imitate, obtain, simulate, take, use.

Ant. lend.

boss (1) knob, point, protuberance, stud, tip; (2) employer, foreman, master, overseer, superintendent.

Ant. of (2) employee.

botch (1) *v.* blunder, bungle, clout, cobble, mar, mend, mess, patch, spoil; (2) *n.* bungling, failure, miscarriage.

Ant. of (2) success.

bother (1) *n.* annoyance, bustle, flurry, fuss, irritation, molestation, perplexity, trouble, vexation, worry; (2) *v.* annoy, harass, irritate, molest, pester, plague, vex.

Ant. calm, comfort.

bottom (1) base, basis, foot, foundation, groundwork, support; (2) buttocks, fundament, seat; (3) endurance, stamina, strength; (4) dregs, grounds, lees, sediment.

Ant. of (1) top.

bounce (1) bound, jump, leap, rebound, recoil, spring; (2) boast, brag, lie.

bound (1) *n.* border, boundary, confine, edge, limit, march, termination, verge; (2) *v.* circumscribe, confine, enclose, limit, restrain, terminate; (3) *v.* frisk, jump, leap, skip, spring.

boundary barrier, bounds, confines, march, precinct, termination, verge.

boundless illimitable, immeasurable, infinite, unconfined, unlimited.

Ant. finite, restricted.

bountiful beneficent, bounteous, generous, liberal, munificent.

Ant. mean, stingy.

bounty beneficence, benevolence, charity, donation, generosity, gift, kindness, liberality, premium, present, reward.

bourn (1) border, boundary, confine, goal, limit; (2) brook,

burn, rill, rivulet, stream, torrent; (3) (*Fig.*) death.

bow (1) bend, buckle, crook, curve, droop, inflect, yield; (2) cast down, crush, depress, subdue, submit, weigh down; (3) (*Naut.*) beak, prow, stem.

bowels (1) entrails, guts, insides, intestines, viscera; (2) (*Fig.*) compassion, mercifulness, mercy, pity, sympathy, tenderness.

Ant. (2) hardness.

bower alcove, arbour, grotto, shady recess, summer-house.

box (1) case, chest, portmanteau, receptacle, trunk; (2) blow, buffet, cuff, stroke; (3) *v.* fight, spar.

boyish childish, juvenile, puerile, young, youthful.

brace bandage, bind, fasten, fortify, prop, strap, strengthen, support, tie, tighten.

Ant. loose.

brag bluster, boast, bully, swagger, (*Sl.*) talk big, vaunt.

Ant. deprecate, whimper.

brains capacity, intellect, mind, reason, sense, understanding.

branch (1) arm, bough, limb, offshoot, ramification, shoot; (2) department, part, section, subdivision, subsection.

Ant. of (1) root, stem.

brand (1) kind, grade, make, quality, stamp; (2) blot, disgrace, infamy, mark, reproach, stain, stigma; (3) (*Poet.*) sword.

bravado bluster, boast, bombast, brag, swaggering, vaunting.

Ant. modesty.

brave bold, courageous, daring, dauntless, fearless, gallant, heroic, intrepid, plucky, valiant, valorous.

Ant. cowardly, craven.

bravo assassin, bandit, brigand, murderer, villain.

brawl altercation, argument, disorder, dispute, fray, quarrel, rumpus, squabble, tumult, uproar, wrangle.

brawny athletic, bulky, fleshy, hardy, herculean, lusty, muscular, powerful, robust, stalwart, strong, sturdy, vigorous.

Ant. flabby, weak.

bray (1) v. beat, break, bruise, grind, pound, pulverise, triturate; (2) n. blare, crash, harsh sound, roar.

brazen bold, forward, immodest, insolent, pert, saucy, shameless.

Ant. modest.

breach (1) aperture, break, chasm, cleft, crack, gap, opening, rent, rift; (2) difference, disagreement, dissension, falling-out, quarrel, schism, variance.

Ant. of (2) reconciliation.

bread aliment, diet, fare, food, nourishment, nutriment, provisions, sustenance, viands, victuals.

break (1) batter, crash, demolish, destroy, fracture, rend, sever, shatter, shiver, tear; (2) contravene, disobey, infringe, transgress, violate; (3) dispirit, enervate, enfeeble, impair, subdue, tame, weaken; (4) interrupt, pause, stop, suspend; (5) degrade, discharge, dismiss, make bankrupt.

Ant. of (1) repair; of (2) obey.

breast (1) bosom, chest, teat, thorax, udder; (2) (*Fig.*) conscience, heart, seat of the affections.

breath (1) air, animation, breathing, exhalation, existence, inhalation, life, respiration; (2) aroma, odour; (3)

breathing-space, instant, moment, pause, respite, rest; (4) faint breeze, slight movement.

breed (1) v. bear, beget, engender, generate, hatch, originate, produce; (2) v. bring up, discipline, educate, instruct, nourish, nurture, raise, rear; (3) n. extraction, family, line, lineage, pedigree, progeny, race, stock, strain.

brevity briefness, conciseness, condensation, curtness, pithiness, shortness, succinctness, terseness.

Ant. prolixity.

brew (1) ferment, infuse (*tea*), make (*beer*), prepare by fermentation; (2) (*Fig.*) concoct, contrive, devise, excite, foment, hatch, plot, project, stir up.

bribe (1) n. allurement, corrupting gift, enticement, reward for treachery; (2) v. influence by gifts, lure, reward, suborn.

bridal conjugal, connubial, hymeneal, matrimonial, nuptial.

bridle (1) v. check, control, curb, govern, master, moderate, repress, restrain, subdue; (2) n. check, control, curb, restraint.

Ant. of (1) decontrol, free.

brief (1) compendious, concise, curt, laconic, limited, pithy, short, terse; (2) ephemeral, fleeting, short-lived, temporary, transitory.

Ant. of (1) lengthy; of (2) long.

brigand bandit, footpad, freebooter, highwayman, marauder, outlaw, robber.

bright (1) beaming, brilliant, dazzling, effulgent, flashing, glistening, glittering, glowing, luminous, lustrous, radiant, resplendent, scintillating, shining, sparkling, twinkling; (2) clear, cloudless, limpid, lucid, pellucid, transparent, unclouded; (3) acute, clever, ingenious, intelligent, sharp, smart; (4) auspicious, distinguished, famous, glorious, illustrious, promising, propitious; (5) cheerful, gay, genial, happy, light-hearted, lively, vivacious.

Ant. of (1) dull; of (3) stupid.

brilliant (1) bright, glittering, luminous, lustrous, radiant, refulgent, shining; (2) famous, glorious, illustrious.

Ant. of (1) dull.

brim border, brink, circumference, edge, lip, margin, rim, skirt, verge.

Ant. centre.

bring (1) accompany, bear, carry, convey, fetch, import, lead, transfer, transport; (2) draw, induce, obtain, occasion, prevail on, procure.

Ant. of (1) remove, withdraw.

brisk active, agile, alert, animated, gay, nimble, quick, sprightly, spry, vivacious.

Ant. slow.

brittle brash, breakable, crumbling, fragile, frail, frangible, shivery.

broach (1) open, pierce, start, tap; (2) approach, hint, suggest; (3) announce, give out, proclaim, publish, utter.

Ant. of (1) close.

broad (1) ample, capacious, comprehensive, expansive, extensive, large, roomy, spacious, vast, wide; (2) liberal, open, tolerant; (3) coarse, gross, indecent, indelicate, unrefined, vulgar.

Ant. of (1) narrow; of (2) bigoted.

broadcast disseminate, publish, spread, transmit, utter.

broil affray, altercation, brawl, feud, fray, quarrel, strife.

broken (1) demolished, destroyed, fractured, rent, separated, severed, shattered, shivered; (2) defective, exhausted, feeble, imperfect, spent, weak; (3) halting, hesitating, stammering.

Ant. of (2) strong.

broker agent, dealer, factor, middleman, negotiator.

brood (1) v. meditate, muse, ponder, ruminate, think upon; (2) v. incubate, sit upon; (3) n. breed, family, issue, kind, line, lineage, litter, offspring, progeny, strain, young.

brook (1) v. abide, bear, endure, put up with, stand, suffer, tolerate; (2) n. beck, burn, rill, rivulet, stream.

Ant. of (1) repel.

brotherhood association, brotherliness, clan, clique, coterie, fraternity, friendliness, society.

brotherly affectionate, amicable, cordial, friendly, kind, neighbourly.

Ant. unfriendly.

browbeat bully, intimidate, overawe, overbear.

bruise bray, contuse, crush, deface, pound, pulverise.

brush (1) besom, broom; (2) brushwood, bushes, copse, shrubs, thicket, underwood; (3) action, affair, conflict, encounter, fight, scrap, skirmish, slight engagement.

brutal (1) barbarous, bloodthirsty, cruel, ferocious, inhuman, ruthless, savage, uncivilised; (2) beastly, bestial, carnal, coarse, sensual; (3) bearish, gruff, harsh, impolite, rough, rude, uncivil, unmannerly.

Ant. of (1) humane; of (3) polite.

bubble (1) blister, blob, vesicle; (2) bagatelle, toy, trifle.

buccaneer corsair, freebooter, pirate, sea-rover.

buck beau, blade, blood, dandy, fop, gallant, spark.

bud (1) n. embryo, germ, shoot; (2) v. bourgeon, burst forth, shoot, sprout.

budget assortment, batch, collection, financial statement, fiscal estimate, pack, package, stock, store.

buffet (1) n. and v. box, cuff, knock, slap, rap; (2) n. counter, cupboard, refreshment-counter, sideboard.

buffoon clown, droll, fool, harlequin, jester, merry andrew, mountebank, wag.

build construct, erect, establish, fabricate, form, make, raise.

building architecture, construction, domicile, dwelling, edifice, erection, fabric, house, pile, structure.

bulk (1) amplitude, bigness, largeness, magnitude, size, volume; (2) body, main part, majority, mass, most.

Ant. of (2) minority.

bully bluster, browbeat, hector, intimidate, overbear, swagger.

bulwark bastion, defence, fortification, guard, outwork, partition, rampart, redoubt, security.

bumpkin boor, clodhopper, clown, hind, lout, lubber, peasant, rustic.

bunch (1) assortment, batch, bundle, cluster, collection, lot, parcel, tuft; (2) knob, lump, protuberance.

bundle bunch, package, packet, parcel, roll.

bungler botcher, fumbler, lubber, novice.

Ant. expert.

burden (1) clog, grievance, load, obstruction, sorrow, trial, weight; (2) (*Naut.*) cargo, freight, lading, tonnage; (3) chorus, refrain.

Ant. of (1) release.

bureau chest, coffer, department, desk, office.

burial entombment, inhumation, interment, sepulture.

Ant. exhumation.

burial-ground cemetery, churchyard, God's acre, graveyard, necropolis.

burlesque caricature, humour, mock-comedy, parody, satire, travesty.

burn blaze, brand, calcine, char, flame, flare, flash, incinerate, parch, reduce to ashes, scorch, shrivel, singe, toast, wither.

burning (1) fiery, flaming, glowing, hot, scorching; (2) (*Fig.*) ardent, earnest, fervent, fervid, impassioned, intense, vehement.

Ant. of (1) cool; of (2) calm.

burnish brighten, furbish, glaze, polish.

Ant. dull.

burst (1) v. blow up, break, crack, explode, fly open, rend asunder, shatter, shiver, split; (2) n. blast, blasting, crack, explosion, split.

Ant. join together.

bury (1) entomb, inearth, inhume, inter; (2) conceal, cover, enshroud, hide, secrete, shroud.

Ant. of (1) exhume; of (2) uncover.

business (1) calling, craft, employment, function, job,

occupation, profession, pursuit, trade, vocation; (2) commerce, company, concern, corporation, dealing, enterprise.

bustle activity, ado, agitation, commotion, excitement, flurry, fuss, haste, stir.

Ant. calm.

busy (1) active, assiduous, brisk, bustling, diligent, employed, engaged, engrossed, industrious, occupied, restless, working; (2) fussy, meddling, officious, prying, stirring, troublesome.

Ant. indolent, lazy.

but (1) further, however, moreover, nevertheless, still, yet; (2) barring, except, excepting, excluding, notwithstanding, save.

butchery bloodshed, carnage, massacre, murder, slaughter.

butt (1) mark, object, point, target; (2) barrel, cask, pipe.

buttonhole v. (*Fig.*) bore, catch, detain in talk, importune. persuade importunately.

buttress n. and v. brace, prop, shore, stay, support.

buxom (*Poet.*) blithe, brisk, comely, debonair, fresh-looking, frolicsome, gay, healthy, hearty, jocund, jolly, lively, merry, plump, sprightly, winsome.

Ant. slim.

byword adage, aphorism, apothegm, dictum, epithet, maxim, precept, proverb, saw, saying.

C

cabal clique, coalition, combination, conspiracy, coterie, faction, intrigue, junta, league, machination, party, plot, set.

cabalistic dark, fanciful, mysterious, mystic, occult, secret.

Ant. open.

cabin berth, bunk, cot, cottage, crib, hovel, shack, shanty, shed.

cabinet (1) apartment, boudoir, chamber, closet; (2) case, davenport, escritoire; (3) council, ministry.

cackle babble, chatter, giggle, prattle, snigger, titter.

cacophonous discordant, grating, harsh, inharmonious, jarring.

Ant. harmonious.

cadaverous bloodless, deathlike, exsanguineous, ghastly, pale, pallid, wan.

Ant. ruddy.

cage v. confine, immure, imprison, incarcerate, shut up.

Ant. free.

caitiff coward, knave, miscreant, rascal, rogue, scoundrel, traitor, vagabond, villain, wretch.

cajole beguile, coax, decoy, dupe, entice, entrap, flatter, inveigle, lure, mislead, tempt, wheedle.

Ant. repel.

calamity adversity, affliction, cataclysm, catastrophe, disaster, distress, downfall, hardship, mischance, misfortune, mishap.

Ant. boon.

calculate adjust, compute, consider, count, determine, estimate, figure, rate, value, weigh.

Ant. guess.

calibre (1) bore, diameter, gauge, measure; (2) (*Fig.*) ability, endowment, faculty, force, gifts, parts, scope, strength, talent.

call (1) announce, arouse, awaken, cry out, proclaim, rouse, shout, waken; (2) assemble, bid, convene, convoke, invite, muster, summon, telephone; (3) christen, denominate, dub, entitle, name, style; (4) appoint, elect, ordain, set apart.

callous apathetic, hardened, indifferent, indurated, insensible, inured, obdurate, torpid, unfeeling, unsusceptible.

Ant. considerate.

calm (1) a. collected, composed, mild, peaceful, placid, quiet, sedate, serene, smooth, still, tranquil, unruffled; (2) v. allay, alleviate, appease, assuage, becalm, compose, lull, moderate, pacify, smooth, soften, tranquillise.

Ant. of (1) disturbed; of (2) stir.

calumniate asperse, backbite, blacken, defame, detract, lampoon, libel, slander, traduce, vilify.

Ant. praise.

calumny abuse, aspersion, backbiting, defamation, detraction, evil-speaking, insult, libel, lying, obloquy, slander, vilification, vituperation.

Ant. commendation.

canaille mob, populace, proletariat, rabble, rag-tag, riff-raff, scum, vulgar herd.

Ant. aristocracy.

cancel abolish, abrogate, annul, blot out, countermand, delete, do away, efface, erase, expunge, quash, repeal, rescind, revoke.

Ant. ratify.

candid artless, fair, frank, free, impartial, ingenuous, just, naïve, outspoken, plain, sincere, straightforward, unbiased, unprejudiced.

Ant. biased.

candidate applicant, aspirant, claimant, competitor, solicitant.

candour artlessness, fairness, frankness, guilelessness, honesty, impartiality, ingenuousness, sincerity, straightforwardness, truthfulness.

Ant. cunning.

canker (1) v. blight, consume, corrupt, embitter, envenom, inflict, poison, rot, rust, waste away; (2) n. bane, blight, corrosion, corruption, infection, rot.

canon catalogue, criterion, formula, regulation, roll, rule, standard, statute.

cant (1) v. slant, tilt; (2) n. affected piety, humbug, hypocrisy, pretence, sham holiness; (3) argot, jargon, lingo, slang, thieves' vocabulary.

canvass (1) examine, inspect, investigate, scrutinise, sift, solicit, study, ventilate; (2) agitate, debate, discuss, dispute.

cap v. complete, cover, crown, exceed, finish, overtop, surpass, transcend.

capable able, accomplished, adapted, clever, competent, efficient, fitted, gifted, intelligent, qualified, skilful, suited, susceptible.

Ant. incapable, incompetent.

capacious ample, broad, comprehensive, extended, extensive, liberal, roomy, spacious, vast, wide.

Ant. narrow.

capacity (1) amplitude, dimensions, extent, magnitude, size, volume; (2) ability, aptitude, aptness, brains, capability, cleverness, competency, efficiency, faculty, forte, genius, gift, intelligence, readiness; (3) appointment, function, office, province, service, sphere.

caper (1) v. bound, dance, frisk, gambol, hop, jump, leap, skip, spring; (2) n. gambol, hop, jump, leap, prank.

capital (1) excellent, first, first-rate, prime, splendid; (2) cardinal, chief, controlling, essential, important, leading, main, major, pre-eminent, prominent, vital.

Ant. of (1) poor; of (2) minor.

caprice changeableness, crotchet, fancy, fickleness, fitfulness, freak, inconstancy, vagary, whim, whimsy.

Ant. constancy.

capricious changeful, crotchety, fanciful, fickle, fitful, freakish, inconstant, odd, queer, variable, wayward, whimsical.

Ant. constant.

capsize overturn, upset.

Ant. right.

capsule (1) case, covering, envelope, sheath, shell, wrapper; (2) (Bot.) pericarp, pod, seed-vessel.

captain chief, chieftain, commander, leader, officer, soldier, warrior.

captious (1) carping, cavilling, censorious, critical, fault-finding; (2) acrimonious, cantankerous, crabbed, cross, peevish, testy, touchy.

Ant. affable.

captivate allure, attract, bewitch, enamour, enchant, enslave, enthral, fascinate, gain, hypnotise, win.

Ant. repel.

captivity bondage, confinement, durance, duress, enthralment, imprisonment, servitude, slavery, thraldom, vassalage.

Ant. freedom.

capture (1) v. apprehend, arrest, catch, make prisoner, seize; (2) n. apprehension, arrest, catch, imprisonment, seizure, taking captive.

Ant. release.

carcass corpse, corse, dead body, framework, remains.

cardinal capital, central, chief, essential, first, important, main, pre-eminent, primary.

Ant. subordinate.

care (1) anxiety, concern, perplexity, solicitude, trouble, worry; (2) attention, carefulness, caution, circumspection, direction, management, prudence, regard, vigilance, watchfulness.

Ant. of (1) lightheartedness; of (2) carelessness, neglect.

career advance, conduct, course, passage, procedure, profession, progress, race, walk of life.

careful (1) attentive, cautious, chary, circumspect, discreet, heedful, thoughtful, thrifty, vigilant, watchful; (2) anxious, concerned, perplexed, solicitous, troubled, uneasy, worried.

Ant. of (1) careless; (2) untroubled.

careless forgetful, heedless, incautious, inconsiderate, listless, neglectful, negligent, regardless, remiss, unguarded, unmindful.

Ant. careful, cautious, attentive.

caress (1) v. coddle, cuddle, embrace, fondle, hug, kiss, pet; (2) n. cuddle, embrace, fondling, hug, kiss.

caricature burlesque, cartoon, farce, mimicry, parody, satire, take-off, travesty.

carnage bloodshed, butchery, havoc, massacre, murder, slaughter.

carnal (1) animal, fleshly, lascivious, lecherous, lewd, libidinous, licentious, lustful, salacious, sensual, voluptuous, wanton; (2) earthly, human, mundane, natural, secular, unregenerate, unspiritual.
Ant. of (1) chaste, pure; of (2) spiritual.

carol canticle, canzonet, chorus, ditty, hymn, lay, song, strain.

carp cavil, censure, criticise, find fault, hypercriticise.
Ant. approve.

carriage (1) brougham, cab, conveyance, transport, vehicle; (2) (*Fig.*) bearing, behaviour, conduct, demeanour, deportment, manner, mien.

carry (1) bear, bring, convey, transfer, transmit, transport; (2) accomplish, capture, effect, gain, secure, win; (3) drive, impel, urge; (4) bear, stand, suffer, support.

carve chisel, cut, divide, engrave, fashion, form, grave, hack, hew, indent, mould, sculpture, slice.

case (1) box, capsule, chest, container, covering, envelope, receptacle, sheath, shell; (2) circumstance, condition, contingency, event, occurrence, plight, predicament, situation, state; (3) (*Law*) action, cause, lawsuit, process, suit, trial.

cash bank-notes, bullion, coin, currency, money, payment, ready money, specie.

cashier (1) *n.* cash-keeper; (2)

v. break, cast off, discard, discharge, dismiss.

cast (1) *v.* drive, drop, fling, hurl, impel, pitch, project, shed, shy, sling, throw, thrust, toss; (2) *n.* fling, throw, thrust, toss; (3) (*Comm.*) calculate, compute, forecast, reckon; (4) *v.* form, found, mould; (5) air, appearance, demeanour, look, manner, mien, style, tone, turn.

caste class, grade, lineage, order, race, rank, social order, species, status.

castigate beat, cane, chasten, chastise, correct, discipline, flog, lash, scourge, whip.
Ant. caress.

casual accidental, contingent, fortuitous, irregular, occasional, random, uncertain, unforeseen, unintentional, unpremeditated.
Ant. systematic.

casualty accident, calamity, catastrophe, chance, contingency, disaster, misadventure, misfortune, mishap.

catacomb crypt, tomb, vault.

catalogue inventory, list, record, register, roll, roster, schedule.

cataract (1) cascade, fall, waterfall; (2) (*Med.*) opacity (*of the eye*).

catastrophe (1) adversity, blow, calamity, cataclysm, disaster, ill, mischance, misfortune, mishap, trial, trouble; (2) conclusion, dénouement, end, finale, termination, upshot, winding-up.
Ant. of (1) blessing; of (2) beginning.

catch (1) apprehend, arrest, capture, clutch, ensnare, entangle, entrap, grasp, grip, lay hold of, seize, take; (2) bewitch, captivate, charm, enchant, fascinate.

Ant. of (1) release; of (2) repel.

catching (1) attractive, captivating, charming, enchanting, fascinating, taking, winning; (2) (*Med.*) contagious, infectious.

Ant. of (1) repulsive.

catechise examine, interrogate, question.

catechumen convert, disciple, learner, neophyte, novice, tyro.

categorical absolute, direct, downright, emphatic, explicit, express, unconditional, unqualified, unreserved.

category class, division, head, heading, list, order, rank, sort.

catholic charitable, general, liberal, tolerant, unbigoted, universal, unsectarian, whole, wide, world-wide.

Ant. bigoted, illiberal.

cause (1) agent, creator, origin, producer, source, spring; (2) account, agency, aim, consideration, end, incentive, inducement, motive, object, purpose, reason; (3) attempt, enterprise, undertaking; (4) (*Law*) action, case, suit, trial.

caustic acrid, biting, burning, corroding, corrosive, cutting, keen, mordant, pungent, sarcastic, severe, stinging, trenchant, virulent.

Ant. kindly, mild.

caution (1) care, carefulness, circumspection, discretion, forethought, heed, heedfulness, prudence, vigilance, watchfulness; (2) admonition, advice, counsel, injunction, warning; (3) (*Scots Law*) security, surety, pledge.

Ant. carelessness, rashness.

cautious alert, careful, chary,

circumspect, discreet, heedful, prudent, vigilant, **wary.**

Ant. heedless.

cavalier (1) chevalier, equestrian, horseman, knight, royalist; (2) arrogant, curt, disdainful, haughty, insolent, scornful, supercilious; (3) debonair, gallant, gay.

Ant. of (2) humble.

cave cavern, cavity, den, grotto.

cavil carp, censure, hypercriticise, object.

Ant. approve.

cavilling carping, censorious, critical, hypercritical.

cease culminate, desist, discontinue, end, fail, finish, stay, stop.

Ant. begin, continue.

cede abandon, abdicate, convey, grant, relinquish, resign, surrender, transfer, yield.

Ant. hold, maintain.

celebrate bless, commemorate, commend, eulogise, extol, glorify, honour, laud, observe, praise, solemnise.

celebrated distinguished, eminent, famed, famous, glorious, illustrious, notable, renowned.

Ant. obscure, undistinguished.

celebrity (1) distinction, eminence, fame, glory, honour, notability, renown, reputation; (2) (*Colloq.*) lion, star.

Ant. of (1) obscurity; (2) nobody.

celerity fleetness, haste, quickness, rapidity, speed, velocity.

Ant. slowness.

celestial angelic, divine, elysian, eternal, godlike, heavenly, immortal, seraphic, supernatural.

Ant. earthly.

cement attach, bind, cohere, combine, join, solder, stick together, unite, weld.
Ant. disjoin, separate.

cemetery burial - ground, churchyard, God's acre, graveyard, necropolis.

censorious captious, carping, cavilling, condemnatory, faultfinding, hypercritical, severe.
Ant. appreciative.

censurable blamable, blameworthy, culpable, faulty, reprehensible.
Ant. commendable.

censure (1) v. abuse, blame, chide, condemn, rebuke, reprehend, reprimand, reproach, reprove, scold, upbraid; (2) n. blame, condemnation, criticism, disapproval, rebuke, remonstrance, reprehension, reprimand, reproach, stricture.
Ant. of (1) praise; of (2) commendation.

ceremonious civil, courteous, courtly, deferential, exact, formal, precise, punctilious, solemn, stately, stiff.
Ant. informal.

ceremony ceremonial, etiquette, form, formal courtesy, formality, observance, parade, pomp, rite, show.

certain actual, ascertained, assured, constant, convinced, dependable, determinate, established, fixed, incontrovertible, indubitable, irrefutable, plain, positive, real, regular, reliable, settled, true, trustworthy, trusty, undoubted, unfailing, unmistakable, unquestionable.
Ant. doubtful, uncertain.

certainty assurance, certitude, conviction, indubitableness, inevitability, positiveness, reality, surety, truth.
Ant. doubt, uncertainty.

certify ascertain, assure, attest, aver, avow, declare, notify, show, verify, vouch, witness.
Ant. disavow.

cessation abeyance, ceasing, discontinuance, ending, halt, intermission, interruption, interval, pause, respite, rest, stay, stoppage, suspension.
Ant. beginning.

cession abandonment, capitulation, concession, conveyance, grant, renunciation, surrender, yielding.
Ant. resistance.

chafe anger, annoy, exasperate, fret, fume, gall, incense, inflame, irritate, offend, provoke, rage, rub, ruffle, vex, worry.
Ant. soothe.

chaff (1) n. glumes, hulls, husks, refuse, trash, waste; (2) v. banter, deride, jeer, mock, ridicule, scoff.

chaffer bargain, haggle, higgle, negotiate.

chagrin annoyance, displeasure, disquiet, dissatisfaction, fretfulness, ill-humour, irritation, mortification, peevishness, spleen.
Ant. pleasure.

chain (1) v. bind, confine, enslave, fetter, manacle, restrain, shackle, trammel, unite to; (2) n. bond, fetter, manacle, shackle, union.

challenge (1) v. brave, call out, claim, dare, defy, demand, dispute, investigate, object to, provoke, question, require, summon; (2) n. defiance, interrogation, question, summons to contest.
Ant. of (1) accept, agree.

chamber (1) apartment, cavity, hall, hollow; (2) legislative body.

champion (1) *n.* challenger, defender, hero, protector, victor, vindicator, warrior, winner; (2) *v.* advocate, defend, fight for, support, uphold.

Ant. of (1) loser; of (2) oppose.

chance (1) *n.* accident, casualty, contingency, fortuity, fortune, hap, hazard, jeopardy, luck, misfortune, peril, possibility, risk, uncertainty; (2) *v.* befall, betide, happen, occur, risk.

Ant. of (1) certainty.

change (1) *v.* alter, displace, diversify, exchange, fluctuate, modify, remove, shift, substitute, transmit, turn, vary, veer; (2) *n.* alteration, alternation, exchange, innovation, mutation, novelty, revolution, substitution, transition, transmutation, variety, vicissitude.

Ant. of (1) remain.

changeable capricious, changeful, fickle, fitful, inconstant, mutable, shifting, unsettled, unstable, unsteady, vacillating, versatile, volatile, wavering.

Ant. constant, reliable, steady.

changeless abiding, consistent, constant, fixed, immutable, permanent, regular, reliable, resolute, settled, stationary, unalterable, unchanging.

Ant. variable.

channel (1) canal, chamber, conduit, fluting, furrow, groove, gutter, passage, route, strait; (2) (*Fig.*) avenue, means, medium, way.

chant *v.* carol, intone, sing, warble.

chaos anarchy, confusion, disorder.

Ant. order.

chapfallen crestfallen, dejected, despondent, discouraged, dispirited, downcast, downhearted, low-spirited, melancholy, sad.

Ant. cheerful.

chaplet bouquet, coronal, garland, wreath.

character (1) emblem, figure, letter, mark, sign, symbol, type; (2) bent, cast, constitution, disposition, individuality, marked traits, nature, personality, quality, reputation, temperament; (3) eccentric, oddity.

characteristic (1) *a.* distinctive, peculiar, singular, special, specific, typical; (2) *n.* attribute, feature, idiosyncrasy, mark, peculiarity, quality, trait.

charge (1) *v.* bid, command, enjoin, exhort, order, require; (2) *n.* command, direction, exhortation, injunction, instruction, mandate, precept; (3) *v.* accuse, arraign, blame, impeach, incriminate, indict, involve; (4) *n.* accusation, allegation, imputation, indictment; (5) *v.* assail, assault, attack; (6) *n.* assault, attack, onset, onslaught; (7) *v.* burden, commit, entrust, load; (8) *n.* burden, care, custody, duty, office, responsibility, trust, ward; (9) cost, expenditure, expense, outlay, price.

charitable (1) beneficent, benevolent, bountiful, generous, kind, lavish, liberal; (2) broadminded, considerate, favourable, indulgent, kindly, lenient.

Ant. of (1) mean, stingy; of (2) inconsiderate.

charity (1) affection, benevolence, benignity, bountifulness bounty, fellow-feeling, generosity, goodness, indulgence, philanthropy, tenderheartedness; (2) alms-giving, benefaction, gift.

Ant. of (1) miserliness, selfishness.

charlatan cheat, impostor, mountebank, pretender, quack.

charm (1) v. allure, attract, bewitch, captivate, delight, enamour, enchant, enrapture, entrance, fascinate, mesmerise, please, win; (2) n. allurement, attraction, enchantment, fascination, magic, sorcery, spell.

Ant. of (1) repel; of (2) revulsion.

charter bond, deed, indenture, instrument, prerogative, privilege, right.

chary careful, cautious, circumspect, heedful, reluctant, scrupulous, shy, slow, thrifty, wary.

Ant. reckless.

chase (1) v. drive, follow, hound, hunt, pursue, track; (2) n. hunt, hunting, pursuit, race.

chasm breach, cavity, cleft, fissure, gap, hiatus, hollow, opening, void.

chaste decent, elegant, immaculate, incorrupt, modest, neat, pure, quiet, refined, simple, unaffected, uncontaminated, undefiled, virtuous.

Ant. impure.

chasten afflict, castigate, chastise, humble, repress, subdue.

Ant. indulge.

chastise beat, castigate, chasten, correct, discipline, flog, lash, punish, scourge, whip.

Ant. caress.

chatter babble, chat, gossip, jabber, prate, prattle, tattle, twaddle.

cheap (1) inexpensive, low-priced, uncostly; (2) base, common, inferior, low, mean, paltry, poor, worthless.

Ant. of (1) dear; of (2) honourable, superior.

cheat (1) v. beguile, deceive, defraud, delude, dupe, fool, hoax, hoodwink, mislead, swindle, trick, victimise; (2) n. artifice, deceit, deception, fraud, imposture, swindle, trickery, wile; (3) n. charlatan, cheater, deceiver, dodger, impostor, knave, rogue, sharper, trickster.

Ant. of (1) disabuse.

check (1) bridle, control, curb, delay, halt, hinder, impede, obstruct, repress, restrain, stop; (2) blame, chide, rebuke, reprimand, reprove; (3) (*Comm.*) compare, examine, investigate, note, test, tick, verify.

Ant. of (1) advance; of (2) encourage.

cheer (1) v. acclaim, animate, applaud, clap, comfort, console, elate, elevate, encourage, enliven, exhilarate, gladden, incite, inspirit, solace; (2) n. acclamation, applause, cheerfulness, comfort, gaiety, gladness, glee, joy, merriment, mirth, solace.

Ant. of (2) dejection, depression.

cheerful animated, blithe, bright, cheery, contented, enlivening, gay, glad, gladsome, happy, jolly, joyful, lightsome, merry, pleasant, sprightly.

Ant. melancholy.

cheerless dark, dejected, depressed, despondent, disconsolate, dismal, dreary, dull, forlorn, gloomy, joyless, melancholy, mournful, sombre, sullen, unhappy.

Ant. cheerful.

cherish care for, comfort, encourage, entertain, foster, harbour, hold dear, nourish, nurse, nurture, support, sustain, treasure.

Ant. abandon, neglect.

chew (1) bite, champ, gnaw, masticate, munch; (2) (*Fig.*) meditate, muse on, reflect upon, ruminate.

chicanery artifice, chicane, deception, duplicity, intrigue, sophistry, stratagems, trickery, underhandedness, wiles, wire-pulling.

Ant. straightforwardness.

chide admonish, blame, censure, check, criticise, reprehend, reprimand, reprove, scold, upbraid.

Ant. praise.

chief (1) *a.* capital, cardinal, especial, essential, grand, highest, leading, main, most important, paramount, pre-eminent, prime, principal, superior, supreme, vital; (2) *n.* captain, chieftain, commander, head, leader, master, principal, ruler.

Ant. of (1) minor.

child babe, baby, (*Scot.*) bairn, brat, chit, infant, issue, nursling, offspring, progeny, suckling.

Ant. adult.

childbirth child-bearing, delivery, labour, parturition, travail.

childish boyish, foolish, frivolous, infantile, ingenuous, juvenile, puerile, silly, simple, trifling, weak, young.

Ant. adult, sensible.

chill (1) *a.* bleak, chilly, cold, frigid; (2) (*Fig.*) cool, depres-sing, unfriendly, ungenial; (3) *v.* (*Fig.*) deject, depress, discourage, dishearten; (4) *n.* cold, coldness, frigidity.

Ant. of (1) warm; of (4) warmth.

chimerical delusive, fanciful, fantastic, illusory, imaginary, quixotic, unfounded, vain, visionary, wild.

Ant. real.

chink aperture, cleft, crack, cranny, crevice, fissure, gap, opening, rift.

chivalrous adventurous, bold, brave, courageous, courteous, enterprising, gallant, heroic, high-minded, intrepid, knightly, magnanimous, valiant.

Ant. cowardly, uncourtly.

chivalry courage, courtesy, gallantry, knight-errantry, knighthood, politeness.

choice (1) *n.* alternative, discrimination, election, option, preference, selection; (2) *a.* dainty, excellent, exquisite, nice, precious, rare, select, superior, uncommon, unusual, valuable.

Ant. of (2) cheap, common.

choke bar, block, close, obstruct, overpower, smother, stifle, stop, strangle, suffocate, suppress, throttle.

choleric angry, fiery, hasty, hot, irascible, irritable, passionate, petulant, testy.

Ant. good-tempered.

choose adopt, cull, designate, elect, pick, predestine, prefer.

Ant. exclude.

christen baptise, call, designate, dub, name, style, term, title.

chronicle account, annals, diary, history, journal, narrative, record, register.

chuckle crow, exult, giggle, laugh, snigger, titter.
Ant. sob.

chum companion, comrade, crony, friend, (*Colloq.*) mate, pal.

churl (1) boor, bumpkin, clodhopper, clown, lout, peasant, rustic; (2) curmudgeon, miser, niggard, skinflint.
Ant. of (1) gentleman.

churlish (1) brusque, crabbed, harsh, ill-tempered, impolite, morose, rude, sullen, surly, uncivil; (2) close-fisted, illiberal, inhospitable, mean, miserly, niggard, stingy, unneighbourly, unsociable.
Ant. of (1) good-tempered; of (2) generous.

cicatrice cicatrix, mark, scar, seam.

cincture band, belt, cestus, girdle.

cipher (1) nothing, nought, zero; (2) nobody, nonentity; (3) character, code, device, monogram.

circle (1) circumference, cycle, globe, orb, perimeter, periphery, ring, round, sphere; (2) area, bounds, circuit, compass, enclosure, field, province, range, region; (3) assembly, class, clique, club, company, coterie, fellowship, fraternity, set, society.

circuit (1) area, journey, perambulation, revolution, round, tour; (2) boundary, bounding line, compass, district, range, region, tract.

circuitous ambagious, devious, indirect, roundabout, tortuous, winding.
Ant. direct.

circulate diffuse, disseminate, make known, promulgate, propagate, publish, spread.

Ant. suppress.

circumference boundary, circuit, outline, perimeter, periphery.
Ant. diameter.

circumscribe bound, confine, define, encircle, enclose, encompass, environ, limit, restrict, surround.

circumspect attentive, careful, cautious, discreet, heedful, observant, prudent, vigilant, wary, watchful.
Ant. imprudent, rash.

circumstance accident, condition, detail, event, fact, happening, incident, occurrence, particular, position, situation.

circumstantial detailed, founded on circumstances, indirect, inferential, particular, presumptive, specific.
Ant. substantial.

circumvent beguile, deceive, dupe, ensnare, entrap, hoodwink, mislead, outgeneral, outwit, overreach, thwart, trick.
Ant. guide, lead.

circumvention chicanery, deceit, deception, duplicity, fraud, guile, imposition, imposture, trickery, wiles.
Ant. honesty.

cistern basin, pond, reservoir, tank.

cite (1) adduce, enumerate, extract, mention, name, quote; (2) (*Law*) call, summon.

citizen burgess, burgher, denizen, dweller, freeman, inhabitant, resident, subject, townsman.
Ant. alien.

civil (1) civic, domestic, home, interior, municipal, political; (2) accommodating, affable, civilised, complaisant, courteous, courtly, obliging,

polished, polite, refined, urbane, well-bred, well-mannered.
Ant. ill-mannered, rude.

civilise christianise, educate, enlighten, humanise, improve, polish, refine.

civility affability, amiability, breeding, complaisance, courtesy, politeness, urbanity.
Ant. rudeness.

claim (1) v. ask, assert, call for, challenge, demand, exact, insist, require, uphold; (2) n. call, demand, privilege, request, requirement, right.
Ant. of (1) renounce.

clamour blare, din, exclamation, hubbub, hullabaloo, noise, outcry, shout, shouting, uproar, vociferation.
Ant. quiet.

clan band, brotherhood, clique, coterie, family, fraternity, group, race, sect, set, society, sodality, tribe.

clandestine concealed, fraudulent, hidden, private, secret, sly, stealthy, underhand.
Ant. above-board.

clap (1) pat, slap, strike gently, thrust; (2) applaud, cheer.

clarify cleanse, defecate, infiltrate, purify, refine.
Ant. defile.

clash clang, clank, clatter, collide, contend, differ, disagree, interfere, jar.
Ant. agree.

clasp (1) v. attack, clutch, concatenate, connect, embrace, fasten, grapple, grasp, grip, hug; (2) n. brooch, buckle, catch, clip, hasp, hook, pin.
Ant. of (1) loose.

class category, collection, denomination, division, genus, grade, group, kind, order, set, sort, species, value.

classical (1) chaste, elegant,

first-rate, master, model, pure, refined, standard; (2) Attic, Augustan, Grecian, Greek, Latin, Roman.
Ant. of (1) unrefined; of (2) Romantic.

classify arrange, assort, dispose, distribute, rank, systematise, tabulate.
Ant. disarrange.

clause article, chapter, condition, paragraph, part, passage, proviso, section, stipulation.

clean (1) faultless, flawless, immaculate, pure, unblemished, unsoiled, unspotted, unstained, unsullied; (2) clarified, purified, unadulterated, uncontaminated; (3) chaste, honourable, innocent moral, pure, undefiled; (4) delicate, graceful, neat, tidy, trim; (5) complete, entire, perfect, unimpaired, whole.
Ant. of (1) dirty; of (2) impure; of (3) immoral; of (4) clumsy; of (5) imperfect.

cleanse clean, clear, purge, purify, rinse, scour, scrub, wash, wipe.
Ant. soil.

clear (A) a. (1) bright, cloudless, crystalline, light, limpid, luminous, shining, sunny, transparent, undimmed; (2) apparent, comprehensible, distinct, evident, intelligible, manifest, obvious, patent, plain, unmistakable, unquestionable; (3) empty, free, open, unhampered, unhindered, unlimited, unobstructed; (4) clean, guiltless, immaculate, innocent, moral, pure, sinless, stainless, unblemished, undefiled, virtuous.
Ant. of (1) dark; of (2) doubtful; of (3) obstructed; of (4) impure.

clear (B) *v.* (1) clean, cleanse, purify, refine; (2) absolve, acquit, excuse, exonerate, justify, vindicate; (3) emancipate, free, liberate; (4) disengage, extricate, loosen, rid; (5) jump, leap, vault.

Ant. of (1) pollute; of (2) condemn; of (3) enslave; of (4) block; of (5) stumble, trip.

cleave (A) adhere, agree, cling, cohere, hold, remain devoted to, stick.

Ant. abandon.

cleave (B) crack, divide, open, part, rend, rive, sever, split, sunder.

Ant. unite.

cleft breach, break, chasm, chink, crack, cranny, crevice, fissure, fracture, gap, opening, rent.

clemency compassion, forgiveness, indulgence, kindness, leniency, mercifulness, mercy, mildness, tenderness.

Ant. intolerance, severity.

clement compassionate, forgiving, gentle, humane, indulgent, kind, kind-hearted, lenient, merciful, tender.

Ant. harsh, severe.

clever able, adroit, apt, dexterous, discerning, expert, gifted, ingenious, knowing, quick, skilful, smart, talented.

Ant. stupid.

click (1) *v.* beat, clack, clink, tick; (2) *n.* catch, pawl, ratchet.

climate clime, country, region, temperature, weather.

climax culmination, head, height, summit, top, zenith.

cling adhere, attach to, clasp, cleave to, embrace, fasten, stick, twine round.

Ant. abandon.

clip (1) *v.* curtail, cut, cut short, pare, prune, shear; (2) *n.*

(*Colloq.*) blow, knock, thump, whack.

cloak (1) *v.* conceal, cover, disguise, hide, mask, screen, veil; (2) *n.* blind, coat, cover, mantle, mask, pretext.

Ant. of (1) expose.

clog (1) *n.* burden, dead weight, drag, encumbrance, hindrance, impediment, obstruction; (2) *v.* burden, encounter, hamper, hinder, impede, obstruct, shackle.

Ant. of (2) free.

close (A) *v.* (1) bar, block, choke, clog, obstruct, shut, shut up; (2) cease, complete, conclude, end, finish, terminate; (3) come together, join, unite.

Ant. of (1) open; of (2) begin; of (3) part.

close (B) *a.* (1) hidden, private, reticent, retired, secluded, secret, secretive, taciturn, uncommunicative; (2) close-fisted, illiberal, mean, miserly, niggardly, parsimonious, penurious, stingy, ungenerous; (3) adjacent, adjoining, near, nearby, neighbouring; (4) assiduous, earnest, fixed, intense, intent; (5) accurate, exact, faithful, nice, strict; (6) compressed, confined, heavy, stifling, stuffy, thick, unventilated; (7) attached, confidential, dear, devoted; (8) *n.* cessation, conclusion, end, termination.

Ant. of (1) open; of (2) liberal; of (3) distant; of (4) indifferent; of (5) inexact; of (6) airy; of (7) faithless; of (8) beginning.

clothe apparel, array, attire, cover, deck, drape, dress, enwrap, rig, swathe.

Ant. strip.

clothes apparel, attire, clothing, costume, dress, garb, garments, habits, raiment, vestments, vesture.

Ant. nakedness.

cloud (1) darkness, fog, gloom, haze, mist, nebulosity, obscurity, vapour; (2) crowd, dense mass, horde, host, multitude, swarm; (3) v. becloud, darken, dim, obscure, shade, shadow.

Ant. of (3) brighten, clarify.

cloudy blurred, confused, dark, dim, dismal, dusky, gloomy, indistinct, sullen.

Ant. clear, distinct.

clown (1) buffoon, dolt, droll, fool, jester, mountebank; (2) boor, clodhopper, countryman, hind, peasant, swain, yokel.

clownish awkward, boorish, churlish, clumsy, ill-bred, rough, rude, rustic, uncivil, ungainly, vulgar.

Ant. adroit.

club (1) bat, bludgeon, cosh, cudgel, stick, truncheon; (2) association, circle, clique, company, fraternity, group, set, society, sodality.

clumsy awkward, heavy, inept, inexpert, ill-shaped, lumbering, maladroit, ponderous, uncouth, ungainly, unhandy, unskilful, unwieldy.

Ant. expert, handy.

cluster assemblage, bunch, clump, collection, gathering, group.

clutch catch, clasp, fasten, grapple, grasp, grip, seize, snatch.

Ant. release.

coadjutor abettor, accomplice, aider, ally, assistant, associate, auxiliary, collaborator, colleague, co-operator, fellow-helper, helpmate, partner.

Ant. opponent.

coagulate clot, congeal, curdle, thicken.

coalesce amalgamate, blend, cohere, combine, commix, concur, fraternise, incorporate, mix.

Ant. separate.

coalition alliance, association, combination, compact, confederacy, confederation, conjunction, conspiracy, league, union.

Ant. separation.

coarse boorish, brutish, clownish, gross, gruff, immodest, impolite, impure, indelicate, inelegant, mean, rough, rude, uncivil, unpolished, unpurified, unrefined, vile, vulgar.

Ant. refined.

coast beach, border, littoral, seaboard, seaside, shore, strand.

coax allure, beguile, cajole, decoy, entice, flatter, persuade, soothe, wheedle.

Ant. force.

cobble botch, bungle, clout, mend, patch, tinker.

coddle caress, fondle, humour, indulge, nurse, pamper, pet.

Ant. treat roughly.

codify condense, digest, summarise, systematise, tabulate.

coerce check, compel, constrain, curb, drive, force, repress, subdue, urge.

Ant. persuade.

coeval coetaneous, coexistent, contemporaneous, contemporary, synchronous.

Ant. anterior, posterior.

cogent compelling, conclusive, convincing, effective, forcible, influential, irresistible, potent, powerful, strong, urgent.

Ant. feeble.

cogitate consider, contemplate, deliberate, meditate,

muse, ponder, reflect, ruminate, think.

cognate affiliated, akin, alike, allied, analogous, connected, related, similar.
Ant. unrelated.

coherence agreement, coalition, cohesion, congruity, connection, correspondence, intelligibility, union, unity.
Ant. incongruity.

coin (1) *v.* counterfeit, create, fabricate, forge, invent, mint, mould, originate; (2) *n.* cash, money, specie; (3) *n.* coign, corner, key, plug, prop, quoin, wedge.

coincide acquiesce, agree, concur, correspond, harmonise, quadrate, square, tally.

cold (1) bleak, chill, chilly, cool, freezing, frigid, frosty, frozen, gelid, icy, raw, wintry; (2) apathetic, cold-blooded, dead, distant, indifferent, lukewarm, passionless, phlegmatic, reserved, spiritless, unfeeling, unresponsive.
Ant. warm.

collapse (1) *v.* break down, come to nothing, fail, faint, fall, subside; (2) *n.* breakdown, exhaustion, failure, faint, prostration, subsidence.
Ant. of (1) recover, rise; of (2) recovery.

collate adduce, collect, compare, compose.

collateral concurrent, confirmatory, corroborative, indirect, not lineal, related, subordinate.
Ant. direct.

colleague aider, ally, assistant, associate, auxiliary, coadjutor, collaborator, companion, confederate, helper, partner.
Ant. competitor, opponent.

collect accumulate, aggregate, amass, assemble, gather, heap.
Ant. spread, strew.

collected *a.* calm, composed, cool, not disconcerted, placid, self-possessed, serene, unperturbed.
Ant. agitated, perturbed.

collection (1) assemblage, assembly, cluster, crowd, gathering, group, heap, hoard, mass, pile, set, store; (2) alms, contribution, offering, offertory.
Ant. of (1) dispersion.

collision clash, clashing, concussion, conflict, encounter, interference, opposition, shock.

colloquy confabulation, conference, conversation, dialogue, discourse, talk, tête-à-tête.
Ant. soliloquy.

collusion connivance, conspiracy, craft, deceit, fraudulent artifice, secret understanding.

colossal enormous, gigantic, herculean, huge, immense, monstrous, prodigious, vast.
Ant. diminutive.

colour (1) *n.* complexion, dye, hue, paint, pigment, shade, tinge, tint; (2) (*Fig.*) appearance, disguise, excuse, false show, plea, pretence, pretext; (3) *v.* dye, paint, redden, stain, tinge, tint; (4) (*Fig.*) disguise, distort, garble, gloss over, misrepresent, pervert.
Ant. of (2) sincerity.

colours banner, ensign, flag, standard.

column file, line, pilaster, pillar, row.

coma drowsiness, lethargy, somnolence, stupor, torpor.
Ant. activity.

comatose drowsy, lethargic,

sleepy, somnolent, stupefied.
Ant. alert.

combat (1) *v.* battle, contend, contest, cope, engage, fight, oppose, resist, strive, struggle, withstand; (2) *n.* action, battle, conflict, contest, encounter, engagement, fight, skirmish.
Ant. of (2) peace.

combination alliance, amalgamation, association, cabal, cartel (*Comm.*), coalescence, coalition, combine, compound, confederacy, confederation, connection, conspiracy, federation, mixture.
Ant. separation.

combine amalgamate, associate, blend, compound, co-operate, incorporate, mix, unite.
Ant. separate.

combustible consumable, inflammable.

comely beautiful, becoming, decent, fair, fit, good-looking, graceful, handsome, pleasing, pretty, proper, seemly.
Ant. ugly.

comfort (1) *v.* alleviate, animate, cheer, console, encourage, enliven, gladden, inspirit, invigorate, refresh, relieve, soothe, strengthen; (2) *n.* aid, alleviation, consolation, ease, enjoyment, help, satisfaction, succour, support.
Ant. of (1) agitate; of (2) irritation.

comfortable agreeable, commodious, convenient, cosy, delightful, enjoyable, happy, pleasant, prosperous, snug.
Ant. cheerless, uncomfortable.

comfortless cheerless, desolate, disconsolate, dreary, forlorn, miserable, woe-begone, wretched.

Ant. cheerful.

comical amusing, comic, diverting, droll, farcical, funny, humorous, laughable, ludicrous, whimsical.
Ant. serious, tragic.

command (1) *v.* bid, charge, compel, control, demand, direct, dominate, enjoin, govern, lead, require, rule, sway; (2) *n.* authority, behest, bidding, charge, control, direction, dominion, government, injunction, mandate, precept, requirement, rule, sway.
Ant. of (1) beseech; of (2) entreaty.

commemorate celebrate, keep, observe, solemnise.

commence begin, inaugurate, initiate, open, originate, start.
Ant. end, finish.

commend (1) applaud, approve, eulogise, extol, praise, recommend; (2) commit, entrust, hand over, yield.
Ant. of (1) disapprove.

commendation approbation, approval, encomium, encouragement, good opinion, panegyric, praise, recommendation.
Ant. blame, censure.

commensurate adequate, appropriate, co-extensive, due, proportionate, sufficient.
Ant. insufficient.

comment (1) *v.* annotate, criticise, explain, interpret, remark; (2) *n.* annotation, commentary, criticism, elucidation, explanation, exposition, illustration, note, observation, remark.

commentator annotator, commenter, critic, expositor, interpreter, scholiast.

commerce business, communication, dealing, exchange, intercourse, trade, traffic.

commingle amalgamate, blend, combine, commix, intermingle, join, mingle, unite.
Ant. separate.

commiserate compassionate, condole, feel for, pity, sympathise.

commiseration compassion, condolence, fellow-feeling, pity, sympathy.
Ant. antipathy.

commission (1) *n.* appointment, authority, charge, duty, employment, errand, function, mandate, trust, warrant; (2) allowance, brokerage, compensation, fee; (3) body of commissioners, committee, delegation, deputation; (4) *v.* appoint, authorise, delegate, depute, send on a commission.

commit (1) do, enact, execute, perform, perpetrate; (2) commend, confide, consign, deliver, deposit, engage, entrust, give; (3) compromise, endanger, pledge; (4) imprison.

commodious ample, comfortable, convenient, fit, proper, roomy, spacious, suitable, useful.
Ant. cramped.

commodity *pl.* goods, merchandise, produce, wares.

common (1) customary, familiar, frequent, general, habitual, ordinary, usual; (2) general, popular, public, universal; (3) commonplace, hackneyed, inferior, low, stale, trite, undistinguished, vulgar.
Ant. of (1) unusual; of (3) refined.

commonplace common, ordinary, stale, threadbare, trite, worn out.
Ant. novel.

commotion ado, agitation, bustle, disorder, disturbance, excitement, perturbation, tumult, turmoil, uproar.
Ant. quietness.

communicate acquaint, announce, correspond, declare, disclose, divulge, give, impart, inform, make known, publish, report, reveal, unfold.
Ant. conceal.

communication announcement, commerce, conference, conversation, correspondence, disclosure, information, intelligence, intercourse, message, news.

communion (1) agreement, concord, converse, fellowship, intercourse, participation, unity; (2) (*Church*) Eucharist, Lord's Supper, Mass, Sacrament.

community (1) association, body politic, brotherhood, commonwealth, company, people, public, society; (2) identity, likeness, sameness, similarity.

compact (1) *a.* close, compressed, dense, firm, pressed together, solid; (2) *a.* brief, compendious, concise, laconic, pithy, pointed, succinct, terse; (3) *n.* agreement, arrangement, bargain, contract, covenant, pact, stipulation, treaty.
Ant. of (1) loose; of (2) lengthy.

companion accomplice, ally, associate, comrade, confederate, consort, crony, friend, partner.
Ant. enemy.

companionable affable, conversable, familiar, friendly, genial, neighbourly, sociable.
Ant. unfriendly.

company (1) assemblage, assembly, band, circle, collection, community, concourse, corporation, coterie, crew, gathering, group, partnership, set, syndicate, troop; (2) companionship, fellowship, guests, party, society, visitors.

Ant. solitude.

compare assimilate, collate, compete, liken, parallel, resemble.

Ant. contrast.

compass (1) *n.* area, bound, boundary, circle, circuit, circumference, enclosure, extent, limit, range, reach, round, stretch; (2) *v.* beset, besiege, blockade, circumscribe, enclose, encompass, environ, invest, surround; (3) *v.* accomplish, achieve, effect, execute, fulfil, perform, procure, realise.

Ant. of (2) exclude; of (3) fail.

compassion clemency, commiseration, condolence, fellow-feeling, humanity, kindness, mercy, sorrow, sympathy, tender-heartedness, tenderness.

Ant. mercilessness.

compatible accordant, agreeable to, congruous, consistent, consonant, reconcilable, suitable.

Ant. incompatible.

compel coerce, constrain, drive, enforce, force, impel, necessitate, oblige, restrain, urge.

Ant. persuade.

compend abbreviation, abridgment, abstract, compendium, conspectus, digest, epitome, summary, syllabus, synopsis.

Ant. enlargement.

compendious abbreviated, abridged, brief, comprehensive, concise, short, succinct, summary.

Ant. diffuse.

compensate atone, counterbalance, indemnify, make amends, recompense, reimburse, remunerate, repay, requite, reward, satisfy.

compensation amends, atonement, damages, indemnification, indemnity, payment, recompense, remuneration, reparation, reward, salary, satisfaction.

Ant. deprivation.

compete contend, contest, cope, emulate, strive, struggle, vie.

Ant. support.

competent able, adapted, adequate, capable, clever, endowed, equal, pertinent, qualified.

Ant. incompetent, unqualified.

competitor adversary, antagonist, contestant, emulator, opponent, rival candidate.

Ant. ally, friend.

complacency affability, civility, complaisance, contentment, courtesy, gratification, pleasure, politeness, satisfaction.

Ant. rudeness.

complacent (1) affable, civil, complaisant, courteous, gracious, grateful, polite; (2) contented, pleased, satisfied.

Ant. of (1) rude; of (2) dissatisfied.

complain bemoan, bewail, deplore, find fault, grieve, groan, growl, grumble, lament, moan, whine.

Ant. be uncomplaining.

complaint (1) accusation, annoyance, charge, grievance, grumble, plaint, remonstrance, wail; (2) ailment, disease, disorder, illness, sickness.

Ant. of (1) approbation; of (2) health.

complete (1) *v.* accomplish, achieve, conclude, do, end, execute, finish, fulfil, perfect, perform, realise, terminate; (2) *a.* accomplished, achieved, adequate, all, consummate, ended, entire, faultless, full, intact, integral, thorough, unbroken, undivided, unimpaired, whole.
Ant. of (1) begin; of (2) incomplete.

complex complicated, composite, compound, compounded, intricate, involved, mingled, mixed, tangled.
Ant. simple.

compliance acquiescence, agreement, assent, concession, concurrence, consent, obedience, submission, yielding.
Ant. refusal.

complicate confuse, entangle, interweave, involve, make intricate.
Ant. simplify.

complication combination, complexity, confusion, entanglement, intricacy, mixture.
Ant. simplification.

compliment (1) *n.* admiration, commendation, courtesy, eulogy, favour, flattery, gift, honour, praise, tribute; (2) *v.* commend, congratulate, extol, flatter, laud, praise.
Ant. insult.

complimentary commendatory, congratulatory, eulogistic, flattering, laudatory, panegyrical.
Ant. disparaging.

comply accede, accord, acquiesce, adhere to, agree to, conform to, consent to, discharge, obey, observe, perform, satisfy, yield.
Ant. refuse.

component (1) *n.* constituent, element, ingredient, part; (2) *a.* composing, constituent.

comport (1) accord, agree, coincide, correspond, fit, harmonise, suit, tally; (2) act, behave, conduct, demean.

compose (1) compound, constitute, make, put together; (2) build, contrive, create, imagine, indite, invent; (3) adjust, arrange, regulate, settle; (4) appease, assuage, calm, pacify, quell, quiet, soothe, still, tranquillise.
Ant. of (3) unsettle; of (4) excite.

composition (1) adjustment, compound, compromise, conjunction, constitution, formation, making, mixture, settlement, union; (2) (*Arts*) invention, literary work, writing.

composure calmness, coolness, equanimity, placidity, sedateness, self-possession, serenity, tranquillity.
Ant. agitation.

compound (1) *v.* amalgamate, blend, combine, intermingle, mingle, mix, unite; (2) *v.* adjust, arrange, compose, settle; (3) *n.* combination, composition, medley, mixture; (4) *a.* complex, intricate.
Ant. of (1) separate.

comprehend (1) conceive, discern, grasp, know, perceive, see, understand; (2) apprehend, comprise, contain, embody, embrace, enclose, include.
Ant. of (1) misunderstand.

comprehension (1) conception, discernment, intelligence, judgment, knowledge, perception, understanding; (2) compass, domain, field, limits, province, range, reach, scope.

comprehensive ample, broad, capacious, extensive, full, inclusive, large, wide.
Ant. limited.

compress abbreviate, condense, constrict, contract, crowd, press, shorten, squeeze, summarise.
Ant. expand.

compromise (1) v. adjust, agree, arbitrate, commit, compose, compound, engage, pledge, settle; (2) n. adjustment, concession, settlement.

compulsion coercion, constraint, force, pressure, urgency.
Ant. freedom.

compunction contrition, penitence qualm, regret, reluctance, remorse, repentance, sorrow, sting of conscience.
Ant. impenitence.

compute calculate, cast up, count, enumerate, estimate, figure measure, rate, reckon, sum.

comrade accomplice ally, associate, companion, compatriot, compeer, confederate, (Colloq.) mate, pal.
Ant. foe.

concatenation chain, connection linking, sequence, series, succession.

concave depressed, excavated, hollow, hollowed, scooped.
Ant. convex.

conceal bury, cover, disguise, dissemble, hide, mask, screen secrete, shelter.
Ant. reveal.

concede acknowledge, allow, confess, give up, grant, surrender, yield.
Ant. deny.

conceit (1) amour-propre, complacency, egotism, priggishness, self-sufficiency,

vanity; (2) belief, fancy, idea, image imagination, judgment, notion, opinion, quip, thought, vagary, whim.
Ant. of (1) humility.

conceive (1) apprehend, believe, fancy, imagine, suppose, understand; (2) contrive, create, design, devise, form, project, purpose; (3) bear, become pregnant.

concern (1) v. affect, interest, involve, regard, touch; (2) n. affair, business, interest, matter, transaction; (3) v. disquiet, disturb, make uneasy, trouble; (4) n. anxiety, burden, care, responsibility, solicitude, worry; (5) (Comm.) business, company, corporation, establishment, firm.

concert (1) n. agreement, concord, concordance harmony, union, unison; (2) v. combine, concoct, contrive design, devise, invent, plot, project; (3) musical entertainment.
Ant. of (1) opposition.

concession acknowledgment, admission, allowance, boon, confession, grant, privilege, surrender.
Ant. denial

conciliate appease, engage, gain, pacify, placate, propitiate, reconcile, win over.
Ant. antagonise.

concise brief, compact, compendious, comprehensive, compressed, condensed, laconic, pithy, short, succinct, summary, terse.
Ant. prolix.

conclave assembly, cabinet, council meeting.

conclude (1) close, complete, end, finish, terminate; (2) decide, deduce, determine, gather, infer, resolve, sum up.

Ant. of (1) begin.

conclusion (1) close, completion, end, finale, finish, result, termination; (2) decision, deduction, inference, judgment, settlement.

Ant. of (1) beginning.

conclusive convincing, decisive, definite, final, irrefutable, ultimate, unanswerable.

Ant. inconclusive.

concoct brew, contrive, design, devise, hatch, invent, mature, plot, prepare, project.

concord accord, agreement, amity, concert, consonance, friendship, good understanding, harmony, unanimity, unison.

Ant. discord.

concourse assemblage, assembly, collection, confluence, convergence, crowd, gathering, meeting, multitude, throng.

Ant. solitude.

concrete (1) *a.* compact, condensed, consolidated, firm, incorporated, not abstract, solid; (2) *n.* cement, concretion, mixture.

concupiscent lascivious, lecherous, lewd, libidinous, lustful, morbidly passionate, prurient, salacious, sensual.

Ant. ascetic.

concur accede, acquiesce, agree, approve, assent, combine, consent, co-operate, harmonise, join.

Ant. disagree.

concussion agitation, clash, collision, crash, shaking, shock.

condemn (1) blame, censure, damn, disapprove, reproach, reprove, upbraid; (2) convict, doom, sentence.

Ant. of (1) approve; of (2), acquit.

condemnation (1) blame,

censure, disapproval, reproach, reprobation, reproof; (2) conviction, doom, judgment, sentence.

Ant. of (1) praise; of (2) acquittal.

condense abbreviate, abridge, compact, compress, concentrate, contract, curtail, epitomise, summarise.

Ant. expand.

condescend bend, deign, stoop, submit, vouchsafe.

condescension affability, civility, courtesy, deference, favour, graciousness, humiliation, obeisance.

Ant. arrogance.

condign adequate, deserved, just, meet, merited, suitable.

Ant. inadequate.

condition (1) case, circumstances, plight, predicament, situation; (2) arrangement, article, provision, proviso, requirement, requisite, rule, stipulation, terms; (3) class, estate, grade, order, rank.

condole commiserate, compassionate, console, sympathise.

condone excuse, forgive, overlook, pardon.

Ant. punish.

conduce advance, aid, avail, contribute, lead, promote, tend.

conduct (1) *n.* bearing, behaviour, carriage, demeanour, deportment, manners, mien; (2) *v.* act, behave, deport; (3) *n.* administration, control, direction, guidance, leadership; (4) *v.* administer, control, convey, direct, escort, govern, guard, lead, manage, preside over, regulate, supervise.

conduit canal, channel, duct, passage, pipe, tube.

confederacy alliance, coalition, compact, confederation, conspiracy, covenant, federation, league, union.

Ant. opposition.

confer (1) consult, converse, deliberate, discourse, parley, talk; (2) award, bestow, give, grant.

Ant. of (2) refuse.

confess (1) acknowledge, admit, allow, concede, grant, own, recognise; (2) attest, aver, confirm, declare, prove.

Ant. deny.

confidence (1) belief, dependence, faith, reliance, trust; (2) assurance, boldness, courage, firmness, self-reliance; (3) secrecy.

Ant. of (1) distrust; of (2) fear.

confidential (1) intimate, private, secret; (2) faithful, trustworthy.

Ant. of (1) public; of (2) unreliable.

configuration conformation, contour, figure, form, outline, shape.

confine (1) v. bind, bound, circumscribe, enclose, immure, imprison, limit, restrain, restrict, shut up; (2) n. border, boundary, frontier, limit, march, precinct.

confirm (1) assure, establish, fix, settle, strengthen; (2) approve, corroborate, sanction, substantiate, verify.

Ant. of (1) refute; of (2) disprove.

conflict (1) n. battle, collision, combat, contention, contest, encounter, engagement, fight, strife; (2) n. antagonism, disagreement, discord, interference, opposition; (3) v. clash, combat, contend, contest, disagree, fight, interfere, strive, struggle.

Ant. of (2) agreement; of (3) agree.

confluence assemblage, assembly, concourse, concurrence, conflux, convergence, crowd, host, meeting, multitude, union.

conform accord, adapt, adjust, agree, assimilate, comply, harmonise, suit, yield.

Ant. disagree.

confound (1) amaze, astonish, astound, baffle, confuse, perplex, startle, surprise; (2) abash, disconcert, dismay, mortify, shame, trouble; (3) annihilate, demolish, destroy, overthrow, overwhelm, ruin.

Ant. of (1) compose; of (2) encourage; of (3) maintain.

confuse (1) blend, confound, disorder, intermingle, involve, mingle, mix; (2) bewilder, darken, mystify, obscure, perplex.

Ant. of (1) order; of (2) clarify.

confute disprove, oppugn, overthrow, prove false, refute, set aside.

Ant. prove right.

congeal benumb, condense, curdle, freeze, stiffen, thicken.

Ant. thaw.

congenial adapted, agreeable, complaisant, favourable, fit, friendly, genial, kindly, pleasant, pleasing, suitable, sympathetic.

Ant. disagreeable.

congratulate compliment, felicitate, greet, hail, salute.

Ant. condole.

congregate assemble, collect, convene, convoke, meet, muster.

Ant. disperse.

congress assembly, conclave, conference, convention, convocation, council, diet, legislature, meeting.

congruous appropriate, becoming, compatible, concordant, consistent, consonant, correspondent, meet, seemly, suitable.

Ant. unfit, unseemly.

conjecture (1) v. assume, guess, imagine, suppose, surmise, suspect; (2) n. assumption, guess, hypothesis, notion, supposition, surmise, theory.

Ant. of (2) certainty.

conjugal bridal, connubial, hymeneal, marital, matrimonial, nuptial, spousal.

conjuncture combination, concurrence, connection, crisis, emergency, exigency.

conjure (1) adjure, beseech, crave, entreat, implore, importune, pray, supplicate; (2) bewitch, charm, enchant, fascinate; (3) juggle, play tricks.

Ant. of (1) order; of (2) repel.

connect associate, cohere, combine, couple, join, link, unite.

Ant. separate.

connection (1) alliance, association, junction, link, union; (2) affinity, commerce, communication, correspondence, intercourse, relationship; (3) kin, kindred, kinsman, kith, relation, relative.

Ant. of (1) disjunction.

connive disregard, overlook, pass by, wink at.

Ant. obstruct.

conquer checkmate, crush, defeat, discomfit, humble, master, overcome, overpower, overthrow, prevail, rout, subdue, subjugate, surmount, triumph, vanquish.

Ant. lose, yield.

conquest defeat, discomfiture, mastery, overthrow, rout, subjection, subjugation, triumph.

consanguinity affinity, blood-relationship, kin, kindred.

conscientious careful, exact, faithful, high-principled, honest, honourable, incorruptible, scrupulous, straightforward, strict, upright.

Ant. unprincipled, unscrupulous.

conscious (1) awake, aware, cognisant, percipient, sentient; (2) deliberate, intentional, knowing, rational, reasoning, reflective, self-conscious.

Ant. unconscious.

consecrate dedicate, devote, hallow, ordain, sanctify, set apart, venerate.

Ant. desecrate.

consent (1) v. accede, acquiesce, agree, allow, assent, comply, concede, concur, permit, yield; (2) n. acquiescence, agreement, assent, compliance, concession, permission.

Ant. of (1) refuse; of (2) refusal.

consequence (1) effect, end, event, issue, outcome, result; (2) concern, importance, interest, moment, value, weight.

Ant. of (1) cause; of (2) unimportance.

consequential arrogant, conceited, inflated, pompous, pretentious, self-sufficient, vainglorious.

Ant. modest.

conservation guardianship, maintenance, preservation, protection.

consider (1) cogitate, consult, contemplate, examine, meditate, muse, ponder, reflect, revolve, ruminate, study; (2) care for, regard, respect.

Ant. of (2) despise.

considerate attentive, charitable, circumspect, discreet, forbearing, kind, patient, prudent, thoughtful, unselfish.

Ant. selfish.

consign commit, deliver, deposit with, entrust, ship (*cargo*), transfer, transmit.

Ant. withhold.

consistency (1) compactness, density, thickness; (2) agreement, compatibility, congruity, correspondence, harmony.

consistent accordant, agreeing, compatible, congruous, consonant, harmonious, logical.

Ant. inconsistent.

consolation alleviation, comfort, encouragement, relief, solace, support.

console assuage, calm, cheer, comfort, encourage, relieve, solace.

consolidate cement, combine, compact, conduce, conjoin, fuse, harden, solidify, stabilise, thicken, unite.

Ant. break up.

consonance accord, agreement, concord, conformity, congruity, harmony, suitableness.

Ant. discord.

consonant accordant, according, compatible, congruous, consistent, harmonious.

Ant. discordant, inconsistent.

consort (1) *n.* associate, companion, fellow, husband, partner, spouse, wife (*of a king*); (2) *v.* associate, fraternise.

conspectus abstract, compendium, digest, epitome, outline, précis, summary, syllabus, synopsis.

Ant. extension.

conspicuous apparent, celebrated, clear, discernible, distinguished, eminent, famous, illustrious, manifest, noticeable, obvious, outstanding, perceptible, remarkable.

Ant. insignificant, obscure.

conspiracy cabal, confederacy, intrigue, league, machination, plot, scheme.

conspire combine, concur, conduce, confederate, co-operate, devise, hatch treason, intrigue, plot, scheme.

constancy decision, determination, firmness, fixedness, permanence, regularity, resolution, stability, steadfastness, tenacity, uniformity.

Ant. inconstancy, instability.

constant (1) continual, firm, fixed, immutable, permanent, perpetual, stable, steadfast, steady, unalterable, unbroken, uniform; (2) determined, resolute, unshaken, unwavering; (3) devoted, faithful, loyal, true.

Ant. of (3) fickle.

consternation alarm, amazement, awe, bewilderment, dread, fear, fright, panic, terror.

Ant. equanimity.

constituent (1) component part, element, ingredient, principle; (2) elector, voter.

constitute (1) compose, enact, establish, fix, form, make; (2) appoint, delegate, depute, empower.

Ant. dissolve.

constitution (1) establishment, formation, organisation; (2) character, disposition, form, habit, peculiarity, physique, temper, temperament.

constrain (1) coerce, drive,

force, impel, oblige, urge; (2) chain, confine, constrict, curb, restrain.

Ant. of (1) entice; of (2) release.

construct build, erect, establish, fabricate, form, found, frame, make, organise, raise.

Ant. demolish, raze.

construction (1) building, composition, edifice, erection, fabric, fabrication, figure, form, formation, shape, structure; (2) explanation, interpretation, rendering.

Ant. of (1) demolition, destruction.

construe analyse, explain, expound, interpret, parse, render, translate.

consult ask, confer, consider, deliberate, interrogate, question, take counsel.

Ant. dictate.

consume absorb, decay, destroy, dissipate, eat up, exhaust, expend, lavish, lessen, spend, squander, vanish, waste.

Ant. save.

consummate (1) v. accomplish, achieve, compass, complete, conclude, effectuate, end, finish, perfect, perform; (2) a. complete, done, effected, finished, fulfilled, supreme.

Ant. of (1) attempt; of (2) unfinished.

consumption (1) decay, decrease, destruction, diminution, expenditure, loss, use, waste; (2) (*Med.*) atrophy, emaciation, phthisis, tuberculosis.

contact approximation, contiguity, juxtaposition, touch, union.

Ant. detachment, separation.

contagious catching, deadly,

epidemic, infectious, pestiferous, pestilential, poisonous.

contain accommodate, comprehend, comprise, embody, embrace, enclose, hold, include.

Ant. exclude.

contaminate corrupt, defile, deprave, infect, pollute, soil, stain, sully, tarnish, vitiate.

Ant. purify.

contemn despise, disdain, disregard, neglect, scorn, slight, spurn.

Ant. respect.

contemplate (1) behold, consider, meditate on, observe, ponder, reflect (*upon*), revolve in the mind, study; (2) design, intend, mean, plan.

Ant. of (2) forego.

contemporary coetaneous, coeval, co-existing, contemporaneous.

Ant. antecedent, succeeding.

contempt derision, disdain, disgrace, disregard, disrespect, mockery, neglect, slight.

Ant. honour, respect.

contemptible abject, base, despicable, low, mean, paltry, pitiful, vile, worthless.

Ant. honourable.

contemptuous arrogant, disdainful, haughty, insolent, insulting, supercilious.

Ant. humble.

contend (1) compete, contest, cope, emulate, litigate, strive, struggle, vie; (2) argue, assert, debate, dispute, maintain.

Ant. of (1) yield.

content (1) v. appease, delight, gladden, gratify, humour, indulge, please, satisfy, suffice; (2) n. contentment, ease, peace, satisfaction; (3) a. agreeable, contented, satisfied.

Ant. of (1) displease; of (2) discontent, displeasure.

contentious captious, cavilling, cross, disputatious, litigious, peevish, perverse, pugnacious, quarrelsome, wrangling.
Ant. genial.

contest (1) *n.* affray, altercation, battle, combat, conflict, controversy, debate, discord, dispute, encounter, fight, shock, struggle; (2) *v.* argue, debate, dispute, doubt, litigate, oppose, question.

contiguous abutting, adjacent, adjoining, beside, bordering, conterminous, near, neighbouring, touching.
Ant. distant.

contingency accident, casualty, chance, event, fortuity, happening, incident, possibility, uncertainty.

contingent accidental, casual, conditional, dependent, fortuitous, uncertain.
Ant. calculated.

continual constant, continuous, endless, eternal, everlasting, incessant, perpetual, recurrent, repeated, unceasing, uninterrupted, unremitting.
Ant. sporadic.

continue abide, endure, extend, keep on, last, persist, prolong, remain, rest, stay.
Ant. cease, stop.

continuous connected, continued, extended, prolonged, unbroken, uninterrupted.
Ant. severed.

contraband banned, forbidden, illegal, illicit, interdicted, prohibited, smuggled, unlawful.
Ant. lawful.

contract (1) *v.* abbreviate, abridge, condense, confine, curtail, epitomise, lessen, reduce, shrink, shrivel, wrinkle; (2) *v.* agree, bargain, stipulate;

(3) *n.* agreement, arrangement, bargain, bond, compact, convention, covenant, engagement, stipulation, treaty.
Ant. of (1) expand.

contradict assail, challenge, contravene, controvert, counteract, deny, dispute, gainsay, impugn, oppose.
Ant. agree, defend.

contradictory antagonistic, contrary, incompatible, inconsistent, opposed, opposite, repugnant.
Ant. affirmative.

contrary adverse, antagonistic, counter, discordant, hostile, inconsistent, inimical, obstinate, perverse, wayward.
Ant. agreeable.

contrast (1) *n.* comparison, contrariety, difference, differentiation, distinction, opposition; (2) *v.* compare, differentiate, distinguish, oppose.
Ant. of (1) similarity.

contravene abrogate, annul, contradict, counteract, cross, go against, hinder, interfere, nullify, oppose, set aside, thwart.
Ant. assist.

contribute afford, aid, bestow, conduce, donate, furnish, give, subscribe, supply, tend.
Ant. withhold.

contribution bestowal, donation, gift, grant, offering, subscription.

contrite humble, penitent, repentant, sorrowful.
Ant. unrepentant.

contrition compunction, humiliation, penitence, remorse, repentance, self-reproach, sorrow.
Ant. remorselessness.

contrivance fabrication, formation, design, device,

gadget, invention, machine, plan, plot, project, scheme.

contrive arrange, concoct, design, devise, effect, frame, invent, manage, plan, plot, scheme, succeed.

control (1) *n.* command, direction, government, guidance, management, mastery, oversight, rule, superintendence, supremacy; (2) *v.* bridle, check, command, counteract, curb, direct, dominate, govern, manage, oversee, regulate, restrain, rule, superintend.

Ant. of (2) free.

controversy altercation, argument, contention, debate, discussion, dispute, quarrel, strife, wrangle.

Ant. agreement.

contumacious haughty, headstrong, intractable, obdurate, obstinate, perverse, rebellious, refractory, stubborn.

Ant. yielding.

contumacy contempt, disobedience, haughtiness, obstinacy, perverseness, rebelliousness, stubbornness.

Ant. obedience.

contumely abuse, affront, arrogance, disdain, indignity, insolence, insult, opprobrium, rudeness, scorn.

Ant. reverence.

contusion bruise, injury, knock, wound.

convene assemble, call, congregate, convoke, gather, meet, summon.

Ant. disperse.

convenient adapted, appropriate, beneficial, commodious, fit, fitted, handy, helpful, opportune, seasonable, suitable, suited, timely, useful.

Ant. inconvenient.

convention (1) assembly, congress, convocation, meeting; (2) agreement, bargain, compact, contract, pact, stipulation, treaty.

conventional accepted, common, customary, formal, habitual, ordinary, regular, usual.

Ant. unusual.

conversation chat, colloquy, communion, confabulation, conference, dialogue, discourse, intercourse, talk.

converse (1) *v.* associate, chat, commune, confer, discourse; (2) *n.* chat, conference, conversation, dialogue, talk; (3) opposite, reverse.

convert (A) *v.* (1) alter, change, interchange, transform, transmute, transpose, turn; (2) apply, appropriate, convince.

convert (B) *n.* catechumen, disciple, neophyte, proselyte.

Ant. recreant.

convey (1) bear, bring, carry, communicate, conduct, grant, impart, support, transport; (2) (*Law*) cede, demise, devolve, transfer.

convict (1) *v.* condemn, confute, convince, imprison, sentence; (2) *n.* criminal, culprit, felon, malefactor, prisoner.

Ant. of (1) acquit.

convivial festive, gay, jolly, jovial, merry, mirthful, social.

Ant. sad.

convocation assembly, congregation, congress, convention, council, diet, meeting, synod.

convoke assemble, collect, convene, gather, summon.

Ant. disband.

convoy (1) *n.* attendance, attendant, escort, guard, protection; (2) *v.* accompany, attend, escort, guard, protect.

Ant. of (2) desert.

convulse agitate, derange, disorder, disturb, shake, shatter.

Ant. soothe.

convulsion (1) agitation, commotion, disturbance, shaking, tumult; (2) (*Med.*) cramp, fit, spasm.

cool (1) apathetic, calm, chilling, coldish, collected, composed, dispassionate, frigid, placid, quiet, self-possessed, unexcited; (2) (*Colloq.*) bold, impertinent, impudent, shameless; (3) *v.* abate, allay, assuage, calm, moderate, quiet.

Ant. of (1) warm; of (2) respectful.

coop (1) *v.* cage, confine, immure, imprison, shut up; (2) *n.* barrel, box, cage, pen.

Ant. of (1) free.

co-operate abet, aid, assist, combine, concur, conduce, conspire, contribute, help.

Ant. oppose.

co-ordinate co-equal, equal, equivalent, tantamount.

cope combat, compete, contend, encounter, engage, struggle, vie.

copious abundant, ample, exuberant, full, overflowing, plenteous, plentiful, profuse, rich.

Ant. scarce.

copiousness abundance, amplitude, exuberance, fulness, plenty, richness.

Ant. scarcity.

copy (1) *v.* counterfeit, duplicate, follow, imitate, reproduce, transcribe; (2) *n.* archetype, duplicate, facsimile, image, imitation, likeness, model, pattern, transcription.

Ant. of (1) originate.

cord line, rope, string.

cordial affectionate, agreeable, cheerful, earnest, friendly, heartfelt, hearty, invigorating, warm, warm-hearted.

Ant. cold, formal, frigid.

core centre, heart, kernel.

corner (1) angle, bend, joint; (2) cavity, hole, nook, recess, retreat; (3) *v.* confound, confuse, perplex, puzzle.

corollary conclusion, consequence, induction, inference.

corporal bodily, corporeal, material, physical.

Ant. spiritual.

corporeal bodily, corporal, fleshy, material, physical, substantial.

Ant. spiritual.

corps band, body, company, contingent, division, regiment, squad, squadron, troop.

corpse ashes, body, carcass, dust, remains.

corpulent burly, fat, fleshy, large, lusty, obese, stout, portly, robust.

Ant. lean.

correct (1) *a.* accurate, equitable, exact, faultless, just, regular, right, strict, true, upright; (2) *v.* adjust, amend, chasten, chastise, cure, discipline, improve, punish, rectify, reform, regulate, remedy.

Ant. of (1) inaccurate.

correctness accuracy, exactness, faultlessness, precision, propriety, regularity, truth.

correspond (1) accord, agree, coincide, conform, fit, harmonise, match, tally; (2) communicate, write.

Ant. of (1) differ.

correspondence (1) agreement, coincidence, concurrence, congruity, fitness, harmony, match; (2) communication, writing.

corroborate confirm, establish, ratify, substantiate, support, sustain.

Ant. disprove.

corrode canker, consume, corrupt, deteriorate, erode, gnaw, impair, rust, waste, wear away.

corrosive acrid, biting, caustic, consuming, corroding, erosive, virulent, wasting, wearing.

Ant. harmless.

corrugate crease, furrow, groove, pucker, rumple, wrinkle.

Ant. smooth.

corrupt (1) v. contaminate, debase, defile, infect, putrefy, spoil, taint, vitiate; (2) a. contaminated, decayed, defiled, infected, polluted, putrescent, putrid, rotten, tainted; (3) v. bribe, demoralise, deprave, entice, lure, pervert; (4) a. abandoned, debased, defiled, demoralised, depraved, profligate, venal.

Ant. of (1) purify; of (2) undefiled; of (3) correct; of (4) honest.

corruption (1) adulteration, decay, defilement, infection, pollution, putrefaction, putrescence, rot; (2) bribery, bribing, demoralisation, depravity, immorality, impurity, perversion, profligacy, sinfulness, wickedness.

Ant. of (1) purity; of (2) honesty.

corsair buccaneer, picaroon, pirate, rover, sea-rover.

corset bodice, (Pop.) girdle, stays.

cosmonaut astronaut, spaceman, space-pilot.

cost (1) n. amount, charge, damage, detriment, expenditure, expense, figure, loss, outlay, penalty, sacrifice, worth; (2) v. absorb, consume, require.

costly dear, expensive, high-priced, luxurious, precious, splendid, sumptuous, valuable.

Ant. cheap.

costume apparel, attire, dress, robes, uniform.

cottage cabin, cot, hut, lodge, shack, shanty.

couch (1) bend down, crouch, lie, recline, squat, stoop; (2) conceal, cover up, deposit, hide; (3) express, set forth, utter; (4) n. bed, chesterfield, divan, seat, sofa.

council assembly, cabinet, chamber, conclave, conference, congress, convention, convocation, diet, ministry, parliament.

counsel (1) admonition, advice, caution, consideration, consultation, deliberation, forethought, information, recommendation, suggestion, warning; (2) advocate, attorney, barrister, lawyer, solicitor; (3) v. advise, caution, recommend, warn.

Ant. of (2) client.

count (1) calculate, compute, enumerate, estimate, number, reckon; (2) consider, deem, esteem, impute, rate, regard.

countenance (1) appearance, aspect, expression, features, look, mien, physiognomy, visage; (2) aid, approval, assistance, favour, sanction, support; (3) v. abet, aid, approve, help.

Ant. of (3) condemn, disapprove.

counter adverse, against, contrary, opposed, opposite.

counteract annul, contravene, counterbalance, countervail, cross, defeat, foil, frustrate, hinder, neutralise, offset, oppose, resist, thwart.
Ant. aid.

counterbalance balance, compensate, counterpoise, countervail, make up for, set off.

counterfeit (1) v. copy, fake, feign, forge, imitate, impersonate, pretend, sham, simulate; (2) a. copied, faked, false, feigned, forged, fraudulent, sham, spurious, supposititious; (3) n. copy, fake, forgery, fraud, imitation, sham.
Ant. of (2) genuine.

countermand annul, cancel, repeal, rescind, revoke.

counterpart complement, copy, correlative, duplicate, fellow, match, mate, tally, twin, supplement.
Ant. antithesis.

country (1) n. kingdom, people, region, rural parts, state, territory; (2) a. landed, rural, rustic.
Ant. of (2) urban.

countryman (1) boor, clown, farmer, hind, husbandman, peasant, rustic, swain, yokel; (2) compatriot, fellow-citizen.
Ant. of (1) townsman; of (2) foreigner.

couple (1) n. brace, pair, twain; (2) v. buckle, clasp, conjoin, connect, join, link, marry, pair, unite, wed, yoke.
Ant. of (2) separate.

courage boldness, bravery, daring, dauntlessness, fearlessness, firmness, fortitude, gallantry, hardihood, heroism, intrepidity, pluck, resolution, valour.
Ant. cowardice.

courageous audacious, brave' bold, daring, dauntless, fearless, gallant, hardy, heroic, intrepid, plucky, resolute, valiant, valorous.
Ant. timid.

course (1) continuity, direction, line, order, path, race, road, route, sequence, succession, way; (2) behaviour, conduct, manner, method, mode, plan; (3) v. chase, follow, hunt, pursue, run, race.

court (1) v. fawn upon, flatter, make love to, seek, solicit, woo; (2) n. attention, homage, respects; (3) n. courtyard, lawcourt, palace, quadrangle, retinue, tribunal.
Ant. of (1) shun.

courteous affable, attentive, ceremonious, civil, complaisant, elegant, gracious, polished, polite, refined, respectful, wellbred, well-mannered.
Ant. discourteous.

courtesy affability, civility, complaisance, courteousness, elegance, good breeding, graciousness, polish, politeness, urbanity.
Ant. discourtesy.

courtly affable, ceremonious, civil, elegant, flattering, highbred, lordly, obliging, polished, refined, urbane.
Ant. impolite.

covenant (1) arrangement, bargain, compact, concordat, contract, convention, pact, stipulation, treaty; (2) bond, deed; (3) v. agree, bargain, contract, stipulate.
Ant. of (1) disagreement.

cover (1) v. cloak, conceal, disguise, enshroud, hide, mask, screen, secrete, shroud, veil; (2) n. cloak, disguise, mask, screen, veil; (3) v. defend, guard, protect, shelter, shield; (4) *n.* defence, guard, protection, refuge, shelter, shield; (5) *v.* clothe, dress, envelop, invest, wrap; (6) *n.* case, clothing, covering, dress, envelope, lid, top; (7) *v.* comprise, embody, embrace, include; (8) balance, compensate, make up for.

Ant. of (1) uncover.

covert (1) *a.* clandestine, concealed, disguised, hidden, private, secret, stealthy, underhand; (2) *n.* coppice, shrubbery, thicket, underwood.

Ant. of (1) open, overt.

covet aspire to, desire, envy, hanker after, long for, lust after, yearn for.

Ant. relinquish.

covetous acquisitive, avaricious, close-fisted, grasping, greedy, miserly, niggardly, parsimonious, penurious, rapacious.

Ant. generous.

cow awe, daunt, dishearten, frighten, intimidate, overawe, subdue.

Ant. hearten.

coward (1) *n.* craven, dastard, poltroon, renegade, skulker, sneak; (2) *a.* timid, cowardly.

Ant. of (1) hero.

cowardly base, chicken-hearted, craven, dastardly, faint-hearted, fearful, mean, pusillanimous, timorous, white-livered, (*Colloq.*) yellow.

Ant. brave, valiant.

cower bend, cringe, crouch, fawn, shrink, stoop, squat.

Ant. face.

coxcomb beau, dandy, dude, fop, prig, puppy.

coy backward, bashful, demure, modest, reserved, retiring, self-effacing, shrinking, shy, timid.

Ant. bold, forward.

coyness backwardness, bashfulness, diffidence, modesty, reserve, shrinking, shyness, timidity.

Ant. boldness, effrontery.

cozen cheat, chouse, circumvent, deceive, diddle, dupe, gull, impose on, swindle, victimise.

crabbed acrid, acrimonious, captious, churlish, cross, cynical, difficult, fretful, harsh, ill-tempered, irritable, morose, perplexing, petulant, sour, splenetic, tart, testy, tough, trying.

Ant. cordial, genial.

crack (1) *v.* burst, chop, cleave, crackle, fracture, snap, splinter; (2) *n.* breach, break, chink, cleft, cranny, crevice, fissure, interstice; (3) *n.* burst, clap, explosion, pop, report, snap.

craft (1) ability, aptitude, art, cleverness, dexterity, expertness; (2) artfulness, artifice, deceit, duplicity, guile, shrewdness, stratagem, subtlety, trickery; (3) business, calling, employment, occupation, trade, vocation; (4) barque, boat, ship, vessel.

crafty artful, astute, cunning, deceitful, designing, fraudulent, guileful, insidious, scheming, shrewd, sly, subtle, wily.

Ant. ingenuous, naïve.

craggy broken, cragged, jagged, rocky, rough, uneven.

cram compress, crowd, glut, gorge, over-crowd, over-eat, pack, press, satiate, squeeze, stuff.

Ant. disgorge.

cramp check, clog, confine, hamper, hinder, impede, obstruct, restrict.

Ant. loose, relax.

cranny breach, chink, cleft, crack, crevice, fissure, gap, hole, nook.

crash (1) n. clang, clash, collision, concussion, jar; (2) v. break, shatter, shiver, smash, splinter.

crass coarse, confused, dense, gross, muddled, obtuse, stupid, thick, unrefined.

crave (1) ask, beg, beseech, entreat, implore, petition, seek, solicit, supplicate; (2) desire, hanker after, long for, need, require, want, yearn for.

craven coward, dastard, poltroon, recreant, renegade.

Ant. hero.

craw crop, gullet, stomach, throat.

craze (1) v. bewilder, confuse, dement, derange, madden, make insane; (2) n. fashion, mania, mode, novelty, passion.

crazy a. (1) broken, full of cracks, rickety, shattered, tottering; (2) delirious, demented, deranged, idiotic, insane, lunatic, mad, silly.

Ant. of (1) unbroken; of (2) sane, sensible.

create appoint, cause, constitute, invent, make, occasion, originate, produce.

Ant. destroy.

creator framer, God, inventor, maker, originator.

creature (1) animal, beast, being, body, brute, man, person; (2) dependant, hanger-on, minion, retainer, wretch.

credence belief, confidence, credit, faith, reliance, trust.

Ant. distrust.

credential certificate, diploma, missive, recommendation, testament, testimonial, title, voucher, warrant.

credit (1) belief, confidence,

credence, faith, trust; (2) esteem, estimation, reputation, repute, standing; (3) commendation, honour, merit, praise; (4) v. accept, believe, have faith in, trust, rely on.

creditable commendable, estimable, honourable, meritorious, praiseworthy, reputable, respectable.

Ant. dishonourable.

credulity credulousness, gullibility, silliness, simplicity, stupidity.

Ant. scepticism.

creed belief, confession, doctrine, dogma, profession (of faith), tenet.

creek bay, bight, cove, inlet, rivulet, streamlet.

creep crawl, cringe, fawn, glide, grovel, insinuate, kowtow, steal upon.

crepitate crack, crackle, snap.

crest (1) apex, crown, head, ridge, summit, top; (2) comb, plume, tuft; (3) (Her.) arms, badge, bearings.

crevice chink, cleft, crack, cranny, fissure, fracture, gap, hole, interstice, opening, rent, rift.

crew band, (ship's) company, crowd, gang, herd, horde, mob, party, set, swarm.

crib (1) n. bed, bin, box, bunker, cot, manger, rack; (2) v. cage, confine, coop, enclose, imprison, limit, restrict; (3) v. cheat, pilfer, purloin, steal.

crick convulsion, cramp, spasm.

crime delinquency, fault, felony, guilt, iniquity, misdeed, misdemeanour, offence, sin, transgression, violation, wickedness, wrong.

Ant. guiltlessness.

criminal (1) n. convict,

culprit, delinquent, felon, malefactor, offender, sinner, transgressor; (2) *a.* culpable, felonious, illegal, immoral, iniquitous, nefarious, unlawful, vicious, wicked, wrong.

Ant. of (2) lawful.

criminate accuse, arraign, charge, convict, impeach, indict.

Ant. acquit.

cringe bend, bow, cower, crouch, fawn, grovel, kowtow, kneel, sneak, stoop, truckle.

Ant. dare.

cripple cramp, destroy, disable, enfeeble, impair, lame, maim, ruin, weaken.

Ant. strengthen.

crisis acme, climax, conjecture, exigency, height, strait, turning-point, urgency.

criterion canon, gauge, measure, principle, proof, rule, standard, test, touchstone.

critic arbiter, carper, caviller, censor, censurer, connoisseur, fault-finder, judge, reviewer.

critical (1) captious, carping, cavilling, censorious; (2) accurate, discriminating, fastidious, precise; (3) crucial, dangerous, momentous, perilous, precarious, psychological, risky.

Ant. of (1) appreciative; of (3) unimportant.

criticism analysis, animadversion, comment, critical remarks, critique, judgment, notice, review, stricture.

croak complain, groan, grumble, moan, murmur, repine.

Ant. rejoice.

crony ally, associate, chum, companion, comrade, friend, (*Colloq.*) mate, pal.

Ant. foe.

crooked (1) askew, awry, bent, bowed, crippled, curved, de-

formed, disfigured, distorted, misshapen, twisted; (2) (*Fig.*) crafty, deceitful, dishonest, dishonourable, fraudulent, knavish, treacherous, underhand, unscrupulous.

Ant. of (1) straight; of (2) honest, upright.

crop (1) *v.* browse, gather, mow, nibble, pick, pluck, reap; (2) *v.* clip, curtail, lop, reduce, shorten; (3) *n.* harvest, produce, yield.

cross (1) *a.* cantankerous, captious, churlish, crusty, fractious, fretful, ill-humoured, ill-tempered, irascible, irritable, peevish, pettish, petulant, querulous, splenetic, sullen, surly, testy, waspish; (2) *v.* pass over, traverse; (3) *v.* hinder, obstruct, thwart; (4) *v.* cross-breed, hybridise, interbreed; (5) *n.* (*Fig.*) affliction, burden, misery, misfortune, trouble, woe, worry.

Ant. of (1) agreeable, good-tempered.

cross-grained cantankerous, disobliging, ill-natured, morose, peevish, perverse, stubborn, wayward.

Ant. genial, obliging.

crotchet caprice, fad, fancy, vagary, whim.

crouch bend, bow, cower, cringe, fawn, kneel, squat, stoop, truckle.

crow bluster, boast, brag, exult, flourish, swagger, triumph over, vaunt.

Ant. bewail, whimper.

crowd (1) *n.* assembly, company, concourse, flock, herd, horde, host, mass, mob, pack, rabble, swarm, throng; (2) *v.* congregate, cram, flock, gather, press, push, squeeze, throng.

crown (1) chaplet, coronal, coronet, diadem, (*Fig.*) distinction, garland, honour, laurel wreath; (2) monarchy, royalty, sovereignty; (3) apex, crest, head, summit, top; (4) *v.* adorn, dignify, honour, reward; (5) *v.* cap, complete, consummate, finish, perfect.
 Ant. of (3) bottom; of (4) dishonour.

crucial critical, decisive, psychological, searching, severe, testing, trying.
 Ant. indecisive.

crude (1) raw, uncooked, undigested, undressed, unprepared, unripe; (2) (*Fig.*) coarse, immature, unfinished, unrefined.
 Ant. of (1) cooked, ripe; of (2) refined.

cruel barbarous, bitter, brutal, ferocious, fierce, hard, hard-hearted, harsh, inexorable, inhuman, merciless, pitiless, ruthless, severe, truculent, unrelenting.
 Ant. gentle, kind, merciful.

crumble bruise, crush, decay, disintegrate, perish, pound, pulverise, triturate.

crush (1) bray, break, bruise, comminute, compress, contuse, crumble, pound, pulverise, rumple, smash, squeeze; (2) (*Fig.*) conquer, overcome, overwhelm, quash, quell, subdue.

crust coat, coating, concretion, incrustation, outside, shell, surface.
 Ant. inside.

crusty (1) brittle, friable, hard, short; (2) captious, cross, fractious, fretful, ill-humoured, irritable, peevish, snappish, snarling, surly, testy, touchy.
 Ant. of (2) genial.

cry (1) *v.* bawl, bellow, call, ejaculate, exclaim, howl, roar, scream, screech, shriek, yell; (2) *n.* bawl, bellow, ejaculation, exclamation, howl, outcry, roar, scream, screech, shriek, yell; (3) *v.* lament, shed tears, sob, weep; (4) *n.* crying, lament, lamentation, plaint, sobbing, weeping; (5) *v.* announce, proclaim, publish; (6) *n.* announcement, proclamation, publication.
 Ant. of (1) laugh.

crypt catacomb, tomb, vault.

cuddle cosset, embrace, fondle, hug, nestle, pet, snuggle.

cudgel (1) *n.* baton, bludgeon, club, stick, truncheon; (2) *v.* bang, baste, batter, beat, cane, drub, maul, pound, thrash, thump, thwack.
 Ant. of (2) caress.

cue catchword, hint, nod, prompting, sign, signal, suggestion.

cuff *v.* beat, box, buffet, knock, pommel, punch, slap, smack, thump.

cull choose, collect, gather, glean, pick, pluck, select.

culmination acme, apex, completion, consummation, crown, summit, top, zenith.
 Ant. base, bottom.

culpable blamable, blameworthy, censurable, faulty, guilty, sinful, wrong.
 Ant. blameless, innocent.

culprit criminal, delinquent, evil-doer, felon, malefactor, offender.

cultivate (1) farm, fertilise, till, work; (2) cherish, civilise, develop, elevate, foster, improve, promote, train; (3) investigate, prosecute, search, study.

culture (1) agriculture, cultivation, farming, husbandry;

(2) civilisation, elevation, improvement, refinement.

Ant. of (1) neglect; of (2) ignorance.

cumber (1) burden, clog, encumber, hamper, impede, oppress, trouble; (2) annoy, embarrass, harass, perplex.

cumbersome burdensome, clumsy, cumbrous, embarrassing, heavy, inconvenient, oppressive, unmanageable, unwieldy.

Ant. light.

cunning (1) a. artful, astute, crafty, foxy, guileful, sharp, shrewd, subtle, tricky, wily; (2) n. artfulness, astuteness, craftiness, deceitfulness, guile, shrewdness, slyness, trickery, wiliness; (3) a. adroit, dexterous, ingenious, skilful; (4) n. ability, adroitness, art, skill.

Ant. of (1) artless; of (3) dull, maladroit.

cup beaker, bowl, chalice, cupful, draught, goblet, potion.

cupidity acquisitiveness, avarice, covetousness, greediness, longing, stinginess.

Ant. liberality.

curb (1) v. bridle, check, control, hinder, moderate, repress, restrain, restrict; (2) n. bridle, check, control, rein, restraint.

Ant. of (1) encourage.

cure (1) alleviation, antidote, corrective, healing, recovery, remedy, restorative, specific; (2) (Eccl.) charge of souls; (3) v. alleviate, correct, heal, help, mend, remedy, restore.

curiosity (1) inquisitiveness, interest; (2) celebrity, marvel, novelty, oddity, rarity, sight, spectacle, wonder.

curious (1) inquiring, inquisitive, meddling, peeping, peering, prying; (2) extraordinary,

marvellous, novel, queer, rare, singular, strange, unique, unusual, wonderful.

Ant. of (1) uninquisitive; of (2) common, ordinary.

curl v. bend, coil, crisp, ripple, turn, twist, wind, writhe.

currency (1) bills, coins, money, notes; (2) acceptance, circulation, publicity, transmission.

current (1) a. circulating, common, customary, general, popular, present, prevailing, rife, widespread; (2) n. course, progression, river, stream, tide.

Ant. of (1) uncommon.

curse (1) n. anathema, ban, denunciation, excommunication, execration, imprecation, malediction, malison; (2) n. (Fig.) affliction, calamity, disaster, evil, misfortune, plague, scourge, trouble, vexation; (3) v. accurse, anathematise, blaspheme, damn, execrate, fulminate, swear; (4) v. (Fig.) afflict, blight, destroy, doom, plague, scourge, torment.

Ant. of (1) bless; of (2) blessing.

cursed abominable, accursed, confounded, damnable, detestable, execrable, unholy, unsanctified, villainous.

Ant. blessed.

cursory brief, careless, desultory, hasty, rapid, slight, summary, superficial, transient, transitory.

Ant. constant, thorough.

curtail abbreviate, abridge, contract, cut, decrease, dock, lessen, lop, reduce, retrench, shorten.

Ant. extend.

curvature bend, curve, curvity, flexure, incurvation.

curve v. bend, inflect, turn, twist, wind.

Ant. straighten.

custody care, charge, confinement, custodianship, durance, duress, guardianship, imprisonment, keeping, observation, preservation, protection, safe-keeping, ward, watch.

Ant. freedom, release.

custom (1) convention, fashion, form, formality, habit, manner, mode, observation, patronage, practice, rule, usage, use, way; (2) duty, import, tax, toll, tribute.

customary accustomed, common, conventional, familiar, fashionable, general, habitual, regular, usual, wonted.

Ant. rare, unusual.

cut (1) v. carve, chop, cleave, divide, sever, slash, slice, slit, wound; (2) v. carve, chisel, sculpture; (3) v. abbreviate, abridge, curtail, shorten; (4) v. (Fig.) avoid, hurt, ignore, insult, slight, wound; (5) n. gash, incision, slash, slice, slit, wound; (6) n. fashion, mode, shape, style.

cutting acid, biting, bitter, caustic, piercing, sarcastic, sardonic, severe, trenchant, wounding.

Ant. kind.

cycle age, circle, era, period, revolution, round (of years).

cynical cantankerous, captious, censorious, cross, crusty, cutting, fretful, ill-natured, misanthropical, morose, pessimistic, petulant, sarcastic, sardonic, scornful, snarling, sour, surly, testy, touchy.

Ant. cheery, good-natured.

cynosure attraction, centre, point (of attraction).

D

dabble (1) dip, moisten, spatter, splash, sprinkle, wet; (2) meddle, tamper, trifle.

daft absurd, foolish, giddy, idiotic, insane, silly, simple, stupid, witless.

Ant. sane, sensible.

dagger bayonet, dirk, poniard, stiletto.

dainty (1) charming, delicate, elegant, exquisite, fine, neat, nice, refined; (2) delicious, palatable, savoury, tasty, tender; (3) fastidious, finical, particular, scrupulous; (4) n. delicacy, nicety, tidbit.

Ant. of (1) coarse; of (2) unpalatable.

dale bottom, dell, dingle, glen, vale, valley.

Ant. hill.

dally (1) dawdle, delay, linger, loiter; (2) caress, fondle, play, tamper, trifle.

Ant. of (1) hasten.

damage (1) n. detriment, harm, hurt, impairment, injury, loss, mischief; (2) (pl.) compensation, fine, indemnity, reparation, satisfaction; (3) v. harm, hurt, impair, injure, spoil.

Ant. of (1) gain; of (3) improve.

damp (1) n. dampness, fog, humidity, mist, moisture; (2) a. humid, moist, wet; (3) v. dampen, moisten; (4) v. (Fig.) allay, check, chill, cool, deaden, deject, depress, discourage, dispirit, moderate, restrain.

Ant. of (1) aridity, dryness; of (4) encourage.

dandle amuse, caress, dance, fondle, pet, toss, toy (with).

danger hazard, insecurity, jeopardy, peril, risk, venture.
Ant. safety.

dangerous hazardous, insecure, perilous, risky, unsafe.
Ant. safe.

dapper active, brisk, chic, dainty, neat, nice, nimble, pretty, smart, spruce, spry, trim.
Ant. inactive, inelegant.

dare challenge, defy, endanger, hazard, presume, provoke, risk.

dark (1) black, dusky, ebon, sable, swarthy; (2) cloudy, darksome, dim, murky, overcast, pitchy, shadowy, shady, sunless; (3) abstruse, enigmatic, mysterious, mystic, obscure, occult, puzzling, recondite; (4) cheerless, dismal, gloomy, morbid, morose, mournful, sombre; (5) benighted, ignorant, unenlightened, unlettered, untaught; (6) atrocious, damnable, foul, hellish, horrible, infamous, infernal, nefarious, satanic, sinful, vile; (7) *n*. darkness, dimness, obscurity; (8) *n*. (*Fig.*) concealment, ignorance, secrecy.
Ant. of (1) light; of (2) clear; of (3) plain, obvious; of (4) cheerful; of (5) well-informed; of (6) clean, good.

darkness (1) blackness, dimness, gloom, obscurity; (2) (*Fig.*) blindness, concealment, ignorance, privacy, secrecy.

dart cast, fling, fly, launch, propel, run, rush, send, shoot, sling, throw.

dash (1) break, destroy, smash, shatter; (2) bolt, dart, fly, haste, run, rush, speed; (3) cast, hurl, throw; (4) abash, confound, disappoint, frustrate, thwart; (5) *n*. haste, onset, rush; (6) *n*. élan,

flourish, spirit, vigour; (7) *n*. bit, hint, smack, tinge, flavour.

dastard (1) *n*. coward, craven, poltroon, recreant, renegade, traitor; (2) *a*. base, cowardly, craven, faint-hearted, recreant, spiritless.
Ant. brave.

date age, epoch, era, time.

daub bedaub, begrime, besmear, blur, cover, deface, grime, plaster, smear, smirch, smudge, stain.
Ant. clean.

daunt alarm, appal, cow, discourage, dismay, frighten, intimidate, scare, subdue, terrify.
Ant. encourage.

dauntless bold, brave, courageous, doughty, fearless, gallant, heroic, indomitable, intrepid, valiant, valorous.
Ant. cowardly.

dawdle dally, delay, fiddle, idle, lag, loiter, trifle.
Ant. hurry.

dawn (1) *n*. dawning, daybreak, sunrise; (2) *v*. appear, begin, gleam, glimmer, open, rise.
Ant. of (1) sunset.

daze amaze, befog, bewilder, blind, confuse, dazzle, perplex, stagger, stun.

dead (1) breathless, deceased, defunct, departed, extinct, gone, inanimate, lifeless; (2) apathetic, callous, cold, dull, frigid, indifferent, inert, lukewarm, numb, spiritless, torpid; (3) barren, inactive, sterile, still, unemployed, unprofitable, useless; (4) flat, tasteless, vapid; (5) (*Fig.*) absolute, complete, entire, total.
Ant. of (1) alive; of (2) animated.

deaden abate, benumb, blunt,

damp, dampen, dull, impair, lessen, paralyse, weaken.
Ant. enliven.

deadly baleful, baneful, destructive, fatal, lethal, malignant, mortal, noxious, pernicious, poisonous, rancorous, venomous.
Ant. innocuous, wholesome.

deal (1) allot, apportion, assign, bestow, dispense, distribute, divide, dole out, give, mete out, reward, share; (2) bargain, trade, traffic, treat (*with*); (3) act, behave; (4) *n.* amount, degree, distribution, extent, portion, quantity, share, transaction.
Ant. of (1) collect.

dear (1) beloved, cherished, darling, esteemed, precious, treasured; (2) costly, expensive, high-priced.
Ant. of (1) disliked; of (2) cheap.

dearth deficiency, famine, insufficiency, lack, need, scarcity, shortage, want.
Ant. plenty.

death cessation, decease, demise, departure, destruction, dissolution, end, extinction, mortality, passing.
Ant. birth.

deathless eternal, everlasting, immortal, imperishable, incorruptible, undying.
Ant. mortal.

debar blackball, deny, exclude, hinder, obstruct, prevent, prohibit, restrain, shut out, stop.
Ant. admit.

debase (1) abase, degrade, disgrace, dishonour, humble, humiliate, lower, reduce, shame; (2) adulterate, contaminate, corrupt, defile, impair, pollute, taint.
Ant. of (1) exalt; of (2) purify.

debate (1) *v.* argue, contend, contest, deliberate, discuss, dispute, question, wrangle; (2) *n.* altercation, argument, contention, controversy, dispute.
Ant. of (1) agree.

debauch corrupt, deflower, deprave, pollute, ravish, seduce, violate, vitiate.
Ant. purify.

debauchery carousal, dissipation, dissoluteness, excess, gluttony, indulgence, intemperance, lewdness, licentiousness, lust, orgy, revel.
Ant. purity, temperance.

debilitate enervate, enfeeble, exhaust, prostrate, relax, weaken.
Ant. strengthen.

debility enervation, faintness, feebleness, frailty, infirmity, languor, weakness.
Ant. strength.

débris bits, fragments, pieces, remains, rubbish, rubble, ruins, wreck.

debt (1) arrears, claim, debit, due, duty, liability, obligation, score; (2) (*Bib.*) offence, sin, transgression, trespass.
Ant. of (1) credit.

decadence decay, decline, degeneration, deterioration, fall, retrogression.
Ant. progress, rise.

decamp abscond, bolt, break up camp, escape, flee, fly, march off, run away, steal away.

decay (1) *v.* decline, decompose, degenerate, deteriorate, dwindle, perish, putrefy, rot, sink, spoil, wane, wither; (2) *n.* decadence, decline, decomposition, degeneracy, degeneration, deterioration, dying, fading, failing, perishing, putrefaction, rot, wasting, withering.

Ant. of (1) grow; of (2) growth.

decease death, demise, departure, dissolution, dying, release.

Ant. birth.

deceit artifice, cheat, craftiness, cunning, deception, double-dealing, duplicity, fraud, guile, hypocrisy, imposition, pretence, sham, shift, slyness, treachery, trick, trickery, wile.

Ant. honesty.

deceitful counterfeit, crafty, deceiving, deceptive, designing, fallacious, false, fraudulent, guileful, illusory, insincere, knavish, tricky, two-faced.

Ant. sincere.

deceive beguile, betray, cheat, delude, disappoint, double-cross, dupe, ensnare, entrap, fool, gull, hoodwink, impose upon, mislead, outwit.

deceiver betrayer, charlatan, cheat, hypocrite, impostor, pretender, sharper.

decent appropriate, becoming, befitting, chaste, comely, decorous, delicate, fit, modest, passable, pure, respectable, seemly, suitable, tolerable.

Ant. improper, indecent.

deception artifice, cheat, deceit, duplicity, fraud, guile, hoax, imposition, imposture, ruse, sham, snare, stratagem, treachery, trickery, wile.

Ant. honesty.

decide adjudge, adjudicate, award, conclude, decree, determine, end, purpose, resolve, settle.

Ant. begin.

decided absolute, categorical, certain, definite, determined, distinct, express, firm, indis-

putable, positive, resolute, undeniable, undisputed, unquestionable.

Ant. hesitant, irresolute.

decipher explain, interpret, make out, read, reveal, solve, unfold, unravel.

Ant. cipher.

decision conclusion, determination, firmness, judgment, resolution, settlement.

Ant. indecision.

decisive conclusive, decided, determined, final, firm, positive, resolute.

Ant. indecisive.

deck adorn, apparel, array, attire, beautify, bedeck, clothe, decorate, dress, embellish, grace, ornament.

Ant. undress.

declamatory bombastic, discursive, incoherent, inflated, grandiloquent, pompous, rhetorical, turgid.

Ant. quiet, simple.

declaration affirmation, announcement, assertion, averment, avowal, proclamation, protestation, statement.

declaratory affirmative, declarative, definite, enunciatory, explanatory, expressive.

declension (1) decadence, decay, decline, degeneracy, deterioration, diminution, fall; (2) inflection, variation.

Ant. of (1) rise.

declination decay, decline, declivity, descent, deterioration, deviation, divergence, inclination, obliquity, slope.

decline (1) v. decay, decrease, degenerate, deteriorate, diminish, droop, languish, lean, lessen, pine, wane, weaken; (2) v. avoid, deny, refuse, reject; (3) n. abatement, decay, deficiency, deterioration, diminution, enfeeblement, failing, lessening, weakening; (4) n. declivity, hill, incline, slope; (5) n. (*Med.*) consumption, phthisis.

Ant. of (1) increase; of (2) agree.

declivity descent, incline, slope.

Ant. ascent.

decompose (1) decay, putrefy, rot; (2) analyse, decompound, disintegrate, dissolve, distil, separate.

decorate adorn, beautify, bedeck, deck, embellish, enrich, grace, ornament.

Ant. spoil.

decorous appropriate, becoming, befitting, comely, decent, proper, sedate, seemly, staid.

Ant. unseemly.

decorum behaviour, courtliness, decency, deportment, dignity, good grace, gravity, politeness, good manners, propriety.

Ant. impropriety.

decoy allure, deceive, ensnare, entice, entrap, inveigle, lure, seduce, tempt.

decrease (1) v. abate, contract, curtail, decline, diminish, dwindle, lessen, lower, reduce, shrink, subside, wane; (2) n. abatement, contraction, decline, diminution, dwindling, lessening, reduction, shrinkage, subsidence.

Ant. enlarge, increase.

decree (1) n. act, command, edict, enactment, law, mandate, order, ordinance, precept, regulation, statute; (2) v. command, decide, determine, enact, ordain, order.

decrepit aged, broken down, crippled, effete, feeble, infirm, wasted, weak, worn out.

Ant. strong, virile.

decry abuse, belittle, blame, condemn, denounce, depreciate, detract, discredit, disparage, rail against, traduce, underrate, undervalue.

Ant. commend, praise.

dedicate address, assign, consecrate, devote, hallow, inscribe, offer, sanctify, set apart.

Ant. desecrate.

deduce conclude, derive, draw, gather, infer.

deduct abate, detract, remove, subtract, withdraw.

Ant. add.

deduction (1) conclusion, consequence, inference; (2) abatement, allowance, diminution, discount, reduction, withdrawal.

Ant. of (2) addition.

deed (1) achievement, act, action, exploit, fact, feat, performance, reality, truth; (2) (*Law*) contract, document, indenture, instrument, transaction.

deem believe, conceive, consider, estimate, hold, imagine, judge, regard, suppose, think.

Ant. doubt.

deep (1) dark, hard, intense, profound, unfathomable; (2) abstract, abstruse, hidden, mysterious, obscure, recondite, secret; (3) astute, cunning, designing, discerning, insidious, penetrating, sagacious, shrewd; (4) absorbing, grave, great, serious; (5) n. main, ocean, sea, water.

Ant. of (1) shallow; of (3) simple.

deeply (1) completely, gravely, profoundly, thoroughly; (2) affectingly, distressingly, feelingly, mournfully, sadly.

deface deform, destroy, disfigure, injure, mar, obliterate, spoil, sully, tarnish.

Ant. improve, preserve.

defalcation (1) abatement, diminution, reduction; (2) default, deficiency, deficit, embezzlement, fraud, shortage.

Ant. of (1) addition.

defamation aspersion, calumny, disparagement, libel, obloquy, opprobrium, slander.

Ant. praise.

defame asperse, blacken, belie, calumniate, detract, disgrace, dishonour, libel, slander, traduce, vilify.

Ant. praise.

default defect, delinquency, destitution, failure, fault, lack, lapse, neglect, offence, omission, want.

Ant. supply.

defaulter delinquent, embezzler, offender, peculator.

defeat (1) v. beat, conquer, disappoint, discomfit, foil, frustrate, overpower, overthrow, repulse, rout, ruin, vanquish; (2) n. conquest, discomfiture, frustration, overthrow, repulse, rout, vanquishment.

Ant. of (1) submit; of (2) victory.

defect (1) n. blemish, blotch, deficiency, error, failing, fault, flaw, foible, imperfection, mistake, shortcoming, spot, taint, want; (2) v. abandon, desert, rebel, revolt.

Ant. of (1) perfection.

defection abandonment, backsliding, dereliction, desertion, rebellion, revolt.

Ant. loyalty.

defective deficient, faulty, imperfect, inadequate, incomplete, insufficient, scant, short.

Ant. adequate.

defence (1) buckler, bulwark, fortification, guard, protection, rampart, resistance, shield; (2) apology, excuse, justification, plea, vindication.

Ant. of (2) attack.

defend (1) cover, fortify, guard, preserve, protect, safeguard, screen, secure, shelter, shield; (2) assert, espouse, justify, maintain, plead, uphold, vindicate.

Ant. of (1) attack; of (2) accuse.

defer adjourn, delay, postpone, procrastinate, prorogue, protract, put off.

Ant. expedite.

deference attention, complaisance, condescension, consideration, esteem, homage, honour, regard, respect, reverence, veneration.

Ant. disrespect.

defiance challenge, contempt, disobedience, disregard, opposition, spite.

Ant. reverence.

defiant (1) disobedient, insolent, insubordinate, rebellious, recalcitrant; (2) bold, brave, courageous, daring, fearless.

Ant. of (1) respectful; of (2) cowardly.

deficient defective, faulty, inadequate, incomplete, insufficient, lacking, scanty, scarce, short, wanting.

Ant. adequate.

defile (1) contaminate, corrupt, debase, dirty, soil, stain, sully, taint, tarnish, vitiate; (2) deflower, ravish, seduce, violate.

Ant. of (1) purify.

define bound, circumscribe, designate, determine, explain, expound, limit, specify.

Ant. confuse.

definite assured, certain, clear, determined, exact,

explicit, fixed, positive, precise, restricted, specific.

Ant. inconclusive, uncertain.

deflect bend, deviate, diverge, swerve, turn, twist, wind.

Ant. straighten.

deform deface, disfigure, distort, injure, mar, misshape, ruin, spoil.

Ant. beautify.

deformity abnormality, defect, disfigurement, distortion, irregularity, malformation, misproportion, misshapenness, ugliness.

Ant. beauty, perfection.

defraud beguile, cheat, chouse, cozen, delude, diddle, dupe, embezzle, gull, outwit, pilfer, rob, swindle, trick.

defray discharge, liquidate, meet, pay, settle.

Ant. dishonour.

deft adroit, clever, dexterous, expert, handy, skilful.

Ant. clumsy.

defunct dead, deceased, departed, gone.

Ant. living.

defy brave, challenge, contemn, dare, despise, disregard, face, flout, provoke, result, scorn, slight, spurn.

Ant. encourage, help.

degeneracy corruption, debasement, decadence, decay, decline, decrease, degradation, deterioration, inferiority, meanness, poorness.

Ant. betterment.

degenerate (1) a. base, corrupt, degenerated, deteriorated, fallen, low, mean, perverted; (2) v. decay, decline, decrease, deteriorate.

Ant. of (2) improve.

degeneration debasement, decline, degeneracy, deterioration.

Ant. improvement.

degradation (1) abasement, debasement, decadence, decline, degeneracy, degeneration, deterioration, perversion; (2) discredit, disgrace, dishonour, humiliation.

Ant. honour.

degrade (1) corrupt, debase, demean, deteriorate, discredit, disgrace, dishonour, humble, humiliate, impair, injure, pervert, vitiate; (2) break, cashier, depose, demote, downgrade, lower, reduce to inferior rank.

Ant. exalt, promote.

degree (1) class, grade, order, rank, standing, station; (2) division, extent, interval, limit, measure, stage, step.

deify apotheosise, elevate, ennoble, exalt, glorify, idolise.

Ant. degrade.

deign accord, condescend, grant, vouchsafe.

dejected cast down, crestfallen, depressed, despondent, disheartened, doleful, downcast, downhearted, lowspirited, miserable, sad, wretched.

Ant. cheerful, lighthearted.

delay (1) v. defer, postpone, procrastinate, prolong, protract, put off; (2) n. deferment, postponement, procrastination; (3) v. arrest, detain, hinder, obstruct, retard, slow up, stop; (4) n. detention, hindrance, impediment, obstruction; (5) v. dawdle, lag, linger, loiter, tarry; (6) n. dawdling, loitering, tarrying.

Ant. of (1) hurry.

delectable agreeable, charming, delightful, enjoyable, gratifying, pleasant.

Ant. disagreeable.

delegate (1) *n.* ambassador, commissioner, deputy, envoy, legate, representative, vicar; (2) *v.* appoint, authorise, commission, depute, entrust, transfer.

delete blot out, cancel, efface, erase, expunge, obliterate.
Ant. insert.

deliberate (1) *v.* cogitate, consider, consult, meditate, ponder, reflect, think, weigh; (2) *a.* considered, intentional, premeditated, purposeful, studied, thoughtful; (3) *a.* careful, cautious, heedful, methodical, unhurried, wary.
Ant. of (2) haphazard; of (3) heedless.

deliberation (1) caution, circumspection, consideration, coolness, meditation, prudence, purpose, wariness; (2) consultation, discussion.

delicacy (1) agreeableness, daintiness, deliciousness, elegance, fineness, nicety, pleasantness; (2) frailty, slenderness, tenderness, weakness; (3) discrimination, fastidiousness, purity, refinement, sensibility, sensitiveness, tact; (4) dainty, relish, savoury, tidbit, titbit.
Ant. of (2) strength; of (3) coarseness.

delicate (1) fragile, frail, slender, slight, tender, weak; (2) dainty, delicious, elegant, exquisite, fine, graceful, savoury; (3) careful, critical, discriminating, fastidious, pure, refined, scrupulous.
Ant. of (1) strong; of (2) coarse.

delicious charming, choice, dainty, delicate, luscious, palatable, pleasant, pleasing, savoury.

Ant. unpleasant.

delight (1) *n.* ecstasy, enjoyment, gladness, happiness, joy, pleasure, rapture, transport; (2) *v.* charm, enchant, gratify, please, ravish, rejoice, satisfy.
Ant. of (1) disgust; of (2) displease.

delightful agreeable, captivating, charming, delectable, enchanting, enjoyable, rapturous, ravishing.
Ant. unpleasant.

delineate depict, describe, design, draw, figure, paint, picture, portray, sketch.

delineation account, description, design, drawing, outline, picture, portrayal.

delinquency crime, fault, misdemeanour, offence, wrongdoing.
Ant. innocence.

delinquent criminal, culprit, defaulter, evil-doer, malefactor, offender, miscreant.

delirious crazy, demented, deranged, frantic, frenzied, mad, insane, raving.
Ant. sane.

delirium aberration, derangement, frenzy, hallucination, insanity, lunacy, madness, raving.

deliver (1) cede, commit, grant, relinquish, resign, surrender, transfer, yield; (2) acquit, discharge, emancipate, free, liberate, loose, redeem, rescue, save; (3) announce, declare, give forth, proclaim, pronounce, publish, utter.

delivery (1) conveyance, distribution, surrender, transmission; (2) elocution, enunciation, speech, utterance; (3) (*Med.*) childbirth, confinement, labour, parturition.

delude beguile, cheat, chouse,

cozen, deceive, dupe, gull, misguide, mislead, impose on, trick.

Ant. enlighten.

deluge cataclysm, downpour, flood, inundation, overflowing, rush.

Ant. drought.

delusion (1) deception, error, fallacy, fancy, hallucination, illusion, mistake, phantasm; (2) artifice, cheat, deceit, fraud, imposition, imposture, ruse, snare, trap, wile.

Ant. of (1) reality.

demand (1) v. ask, challenge, claim, exact, inquire, interrogate, question, request, require; (2) n. call, claim, inquiry, interrogation, question, request, requisition, want.

Ant. of (1) relinquish.

demarcation bound, boundary, confine, distinction, division, enclosure, limit, separation.

demeanour air, bearing, behaviour, carriage, conduct, deportment, mien.

demented crazy, (Scot.) daft, deranged, (Colloq.) dotty, foolish, idiotic, insane, lunatic.

Ant. sane.

demise (1) death, decease, departure; (2) (Law) alienation, conveyance, transfer, transmission; (3) v. (Law) bequeath, convey, grant, leave, will, transfer.

Ant. of (1) birth.

demolish annihilate, destroy, dismantle, level, overthrow, overturn, raze, ruin.

Ant. construct.

demon devil, evil spirit, fiend, goblin.

Ant. angel.

demoniacal devilish, diabolical, fiendish, hellish.

Ant. angelic.

demonstrate establish, exhibit, illustrate, indicate, manifest, prove, show.

Ant. disprove.

demoralise (1) corrupt, debase, debauch, deprave, vitiate; (2) depress, discourage, dishearten, weaken.

Ant. of (2) encourage.

demulcent emollient, lenitive, mild, mollifying, sedative, soothing.

Ant. harsh, irritating.

demur doubt, halt, hesitate, object, pause, refuse, stop, waver.

Ant. consent.

demure coy, decorous, grave, modest, priggish, prudish, sedate, sober, staid.

Ant. forward, immodest.

den cave, cavern, haunt, lair, resort, retreat.

denial adjuration, contradiction, disclaimer, negation, refusal, renunciation.

denizen citizen, dweller, inhabitant, resident.

denominate call, christen, designate, dub, entitle, name, phrase, style, term.

denomination (1) appellation, designation, name, style, term, title; (2) body, class, group, school, sect.

denote betoken, designate, imply, indicate, mark, show, signify, typify.

denounce accuse, arraign, attack, brand, censure, condemn, decry, denunciate, proscribe, stigmatise, threaten.

Ant. commend.

dense (1) close, compact, compressed, condensed, heavy, opaque, solid, substantial, thick; (2) dull, slow, stupid.

Ant. of (1) thin; of (2) clever.

denude bare, divest, strip.
Ant. dress.

deny (1) contradict, gainsay, oppose, refute; (2) abjure, disavow, disclaim, disown, renounce; (3) refuse, reject, withhold.
Ant. of (1) agree; of (2) accept; of (3) receive.

depart (1) absent, go, decamp, deviate, disappear, diverge, leave, migrate, quit, remove, vanish, vary, withdraw; (2) decease, die.
Ant. of (1) arrive.

department (1) district, division, function, part, portion, province; (2) branch, bureau, office, section, station.
Ant. of (1) whole.

departure (1) exit, removal, retirement, withdrawal; (2) abandonment, deviation, variation; (3) death, decease, demise.
Ant. of (1) arrival.

depend build upon, confide in, count upon, hang, lean on, rely upon, trust in, turn to.

dependant (also —ent) n. client, hanger-on, henchman, minion, retainer, subordinate, vassal.
Ant. freeman, patron.

dependence (1) buttress, prop, staff, stay, support; (2) concatenation, confidence, reliance, trust.
Ant. of (2) independence.

dependent (also —ant) a. contingent, depending, relative, relying, subject, subordinate.
Ant. independent.

depict delineate, describe, draw, outline, paint, picture, portray, reproduce, sketch.

deplete drain, empty, evacuate, exhaust, reduce.

Ant. fill.

deplorable calamitous, disastrous, distressing, grievous, lamentable, melancholy, miserable, pitiable, regrettable, sad, wretched.
Ant. fortunate.

deplore bemoan, bewail, grieve for, lament, mourn, regret, sorrow over.
Ant. rejoice.

deportment air, bearing, behaviour, breeding, carriage, comportment, conduct, demeanour, manner, mien.

depose (1) break, cashier, degrade, dethrone, dismiss, displace, oust; (2) (*Law*) avouch, declare, dispone, testify.

deposit (1) v. drop, lay, place, precipitate, put; (2) v. bank, hoard, lodge, save, store; (3) n. dregs, lees, precipitate, sediment; (4) n. money (*in bank*), pledge, security, stake.

deposition (1) dethronement, dismissal, displacement, removal; (2) (*Law*) affidavit, declaration, evidence, testimony.

depot (1) depository, storehouse, warehouse; (2) (*Mil.*) headquarters, (*U.S.A.*) station.

depraved corrupt, debased, debauched, degenerate, dissolute, evil, immoral, lascivious, lewd, licentious, profligate, sinful, vicious, wicked.
Ant. pure, upright.

depravity baseness, contamination, corruption, criminality, degeneracy, depravation, immorality, iniquity, profligacy, vice, viciousness, vitiation, wickedness.
Ant. virtue.

depreciate belittle, decry, detract, disparage, traduce, underestimate, underrate, undervalue.

Ant. appreciate.

depredation despoiling, devastation, pillage, plunder, rapine, robbery, spoliation, theft.

Ant. reparation.

depress (1) abase, debase, degrade, disgrace, drop, humble, humiliate, lower, reduce; (2) chill, damp, deject, discourage, dishearten, dispirit, oppress, sadden.

Ant. of (1) raise; of (2) hearten.

depression (1) abasement, debasement, degradation, humiliation, reduction; (2) dejection, despondency, dolefulness, (*Colloq.*) dumps, gloominess, melancholy; (3) (*Comm.*) dullness, inactivity, lowness, stagnation; (4) cavity, dent, dimple, dip, excavation, hollow, indentation, pit, valley.

Ant. of (1) elevation; of (2) joy; of (3) boom; of (4) hill, mound.

deprive bereave, despoil, dispossess, divest, rob, strip.

Ant. furnish.

depth (1) abyss, deepness, extent, measure; (2) (*Fig.*) astuteness, discernment, penetration, profoundness, sagacity, wisdom.

deputation commission, delegates, delegation, deputies, envoys.

depute *v.* accredit, appoint, authorise, charge, commission, delegate, empower, entrust.

Ant. withhold.

deputy agent, ambassador, commissioner, delegate, legate, lieutenant, nuncio, proxy, substitute, vice-regent.

derange confound, confuse, disarrange, discompose, disconcert, disorder, displace, disturb, madden, ruffle, unsettle, upset.

Ant. arrange, settle.

derangement (1) confusion, disarrangement, disorder, disturbance, irregularity; (2) aberration, alienation, delirium, hallucination, insanity, lunacy, madness, mania.

Ant. of (1) order; of (2) sanity.

dereliction abandonment, delinquency, desertion, failure, faithlessness, fault, neglect, negligence, relinquishment, renunciation.

Ant. attention, observance.

deride chaff, flout, gibe, insult, jeer, mock, ridicule, scoff, scorn, sneer, taunt.

Ant. respect.

derision contempt, disrespect, insult, laughter, mockery, ridicule, scorn.

Ant. respect.

derivation beginning, descent, etymology, extraction, foundation, genealogy, origin, root, source.

derive deduce, draw, follow, get, infer, obtain, receive, trace.

derogate compromise, depreciate, detract, diminish, disparage, lessen.

Ant. appreciate.

derogatory depreciative, detracting, disparaging, injurious.

Ant. appreciative.

descant (1) *v.* amplify, animadvert, dilate, discuss, enlarge, expatiate; (2) *n.* animadversion, commentary, discourse, discussion; (3) *n.* melody, song, tune.

descend (1) alight, dismount, drop, fall, plunge, sink,

swoop; (2) derive, originate, proceed.

Ant. of (1) ascend.

descent (1) declivity, drop, fall, incline, slope; (2) extraction, genealogy, lineage, parentage, transmission; (3) assault, attack, foray, incursion, invasion, raid.

Ant. of (1) ascent.

describe characterise, define, delineate, depict, express, illustrate, mark out, narrate, portray, recount, relate, specify, trace.

description (1) account, delineation, detail, explanation, narration, narrative, report, representation; (2) class, kind, sort, species.

descry behold, detect, discern, discover, distinguish, espy, mark, observe, recognise, see, spy out.

desecrate abuse, pervert, pollute, profane.

Ant. consecrate, purify.

desert (A) v. abandon, abscond, forsake, give up, leave, relinquish, renounce, resign, quit, vacate.

Ant. stand fast.

desert (B) (1) n. solitude, waste, wilderness; (2) a. barren, desolate, lonely, solitary, uncultivated, uninhabited, unproductive, untilled.

Ant. of (2) fertile.

desert (C) n. due, excellence, merit (or demerit), worth.

deserter apostate, fugitive, (Colloq.) rat, recreant, renegade, runaway, traitor.

Ant. loyalist.

deserve earn, gain, justify, merit, procure, win.

desiderate desire, lack, long for, miss, need, want.

design (1) v. delineate, describe, draw, outline, plan, sketch, trace; (2) n. delineation, draught, drawing, outline, plan, scheme, sketch; (3) v. contrive, devise, intend, mean, plan, project, propose, purpose, scheme; (4) n. aim, intent, intention, meaning, object, purpose, purport.

designate (1) call, christen, entitle, name, nominate, style, term; (2) allot, appoint, assign; (3) characterise, define, denote, describe, indicate, show, specify.

designing artful, astute, crafty, crooked, cunning, deceitful, intriguing, scheming, sly, treacherous, unscrupulous, wily.

Ant. artless, frank.

desirable agreeable, beneficial, covetable, eligible, enviable, good, pleasing, preferable.

Ant. undesirable.

desire ask, covet, crave, entreat, fancy, hanker after, request, solicit, want, yearn for.

Ant. refuse.

desist break off, cease, discontinue, end, give over, leave off, pause, stop.

Ant. continue.

desolate (1) v. depopulate, despoil, destroy, devastate, lay waste, pillage, plunder, ravage; (2) a. bare, barren, desert, dreary, ruined, solitary, unfrequented, uninhabited, waste, wild; (3) a. cheerless, comfortless, companionless, disconsolate, forlorn, forsaken, miserable, wretched.

Ant. of (2) populous; of (3) cheerful.

desolation (1) destruction,

devastation, havoc, ravage, ruin; (2) barrenness, bleakness, desolateness, loneliness, solitude, wildness; (3) (*Fig.*) gloom, gloominess, melancholy, misery, sadness, unhappiness.

Ant. of (3) happiness.

despair (1) *v.* despond, lose hope; (2) *n.* dejection, desperation, despondency, disheartenment, hopelessness.

Ant. of (2) confidence, hope.

despatch (1) *v.* accelerate, conclude, dismiss, expedite, finish, forward, hasten, hurry, quicken; (2) *v.* assassinate, butcher, kill, murder, slaughter, slay; (3) *n.* diligence, expedition, haste, rapidity, speed; (4) *n.* communication, document, instruction, letter, message, report.

Ant. of (1) retard; of (3) delay.

desperate (1) despairing, forlorn, hopeless, irrecoverable, irremediable, irretrievable, serious; (2) audacious, daring, determined, foolhardy, frantic, furious, headstrong, rash, reckless, violent, wild.

Ant. of (1) hopeful; of (2) careful.

despicable abject, base, contemptible, degrading, low, mean, pitiful, shameful, sordid, vile, worthless.

Ant. commendable, laudable.

despise contemn, disdain, disregard, neglect, scorn, slight, spurn, undervalue.

Ant. admire.

despoil bereave, denude, deprive, dispossess, divest, fleece, plunder, rifle, rob, strip.

Ant. enrich, furnish.

despond despair, lose hope, mourn, sorrow.

Ant. hope.

despondency dejection, depression, discouragement, gloom, hopelessness, melancholy, sadness.

Ant. elation, hopefulness.

despot autocrat, dictator, oppressor, tyrant.

Ant. slave.

despotic absolute, arbitrary, arrogant, autocratic, dictatorial, domineering, imperious, oppressive, tyrannical, unconstitutional.

Ant. mild.

despotism absolutism, autocracy, dictatorship, oppression, tyranny.

Ant. constitutionalism.

destination (1) end, goal, harbour, haven, journey's end, landing-place, resting-place; (2) aim, design, intention, object, purpose; (3) appointment, decree, design, doom, fate, lot, ordination.

Ant. of (1) beginning.

destine allot, appoint, assign, consecrate, decree, design, devote, doom, intend, mark out, purpose.

destiny destination, divine decree, doom, fate, fortune, lot.

destitute deficient in, distressed, indigent, moneyless, necessitous, needy, penniless, penurious, poor, wanting.

Ant. rich.

destroy annihilate, demolish, desolate, devastate, dismantle, eradicate, extinguish, extirpate, kill, raze, ruin, slay, waste.

Ant. create.

destruction annihilation, demolition, devastation, downfall, eradication, extermination, extinction, havoc, massacre, ruin, slaughter.

Ant. construction, creation.

destructive baleful, baneful, deadly, deleterious, detrimental, fatal, hurtful, injurious, lethal, noxious, pernicious, ruinous.
Ant. salutary, wholesome.

desultory capricious, cursory, discursive, erratic, fitful, inconstant, inexact, irregular, loose, rambling, roving, spasmodic, unsettled, unsystematic, vague.
Ant. steady.

detach disconnect, disengage, disjoin, disunite, divide, separate, sever.
Ant. attach.

detail (1) n. account, description, enumeration, narrative, recital, relation; (2) n. pl. minutiae, particulars, parts; (3) v. delineate, depict, describe, enumerate, individualise, portray, recount, specify; (4) v. appoint, detach, send.
Ant. of (3) generalise.

detain arrest, check, confine, delay, hinder, hold, keep, restrain, retain, stay, stop.
Ant. release.

detect ascertain, catch, descry, disclose, discover, expose, reveal, unmask.
Ant. conceal.

detention confinement, delay, hindrance, restraint, withholding.
Ant. freedom.

deter debar, discourage, frighten, hinder, prevent, prohibit, restrain, stop.
Ant. encourage.

deteriorate corrupt, debase, degenerate, degrade, deprave, depreciate, impair, injure, lower, spoil, worsen.
Ant. improve.

determinate absolute, certain, conclusive, decided, decisive, definite, definitive, determined, established, explicit, express, fixed, limited, positive, settled.
Ant. uncertain.

determination (1) constancy, firmness, persistence, resoluteness, steadfastness; (2) conclusion, decision, judgment, purpose, resolve, result.
Ant. of (1) indecision.

determine (1) conclude, decide, end, finish, regulate, settle, terminate; (2) ascertain, certify, check, find out, verify; (3) decide, establish, fix, resolve; (4) impel, incline, induce, influence, lead.

detest abhor, abominate, despise, execrate, hate, loathe.
Ant. love.

detestable abhorred, abominable, accursed, disgusting, execrable, hateful, loathsome, odious, offensive, shocking, vile.
Ant. lovable.

dethrone depose, uncrown.
Ant. enthrone.

detract asperse, belittle, calumniate, debase, decry, defame, depreciate, disparage, slander, traduce, vilify.
Ant. praise.

detriment damage, disadvantage, harm, hurt, injury, loss, mischief, prejudice.
Ant. advantage.

detrimental baleful, deleterious, destructive, harmful, injurious, mischievous, pernicious, prejudicial.
Ant. advantageous.

devastate desolate, destroy, lay waste, pillage, plunder, ravage, sack, spoil, waste.
Ant. reconstruct.

devastation desolation, destruction, havoc, pillage, plunder, ruin, spoliation.
Ant. reconstruction.

develop cultivate, disclose, expand, expose, grow, mature, open out, progress, uncover, unfold, unravel.
Ant. hide, neglect.

development disclosure, disentanglement, evolution, exhibition, expansion, exposure, growth, increase, maturity, progress, unfolding, unravelling.
Ant. degeneration.

deviate avert, deflect, depart, differ, digress, diverge, err, stray, swerve, turn aside, vary, wander.
Ant. continue.

device (1) contraption, contrivance, gadget, gimmick, invention; (2) artifice, expedient, manoeuvre, plan, project, purpose, ruse, scheme, shift, stratagem, trick; (3) badge, crest, design, emblem, motto, symbol.

devil Apollyon, (*Scot.*) Auld Nick, Belial, demon, (*Colloq.*) deuce, fiend, Lucifer, Satan.
Ant. angel.

devilish atrocious, damnable, detestable, diabolical, execrable, fiendish, hellish, infernal, satanic, wicked.
Ant. godly.

devious circumlocutory, confusing, crooked, deviating, erratic, excursive, misleading, roundabout, tortuous, wandering.
Ant. straightforward.

devise arrange, conceive, concoct, contrive, design, discover, imagine, invent, plan, prepare, project, scheme.

devoid destitute, empty, lacking, unprovided with, vacant, void, wanting.
Ant. full.

devolve alienate, authorise, be handed down, be transferred, commission, consign, convey, deliver, depute, fall upon, transfer.

devote (1) consecrate, dedicate, enshrine; (2) apply, appropriate, destine, doom.
Ant. of (1) withhold.

devotion (1) consecration, dedication; (2) adoration, devoutness, holiness, piety, prayer, religiousness, sanctity, worship; (3) affection, ardour, attachment, earnestness, love, zeal.
Ant. of (2) irreverence.

devour (1) bolt, consume, eat, gobble, gorge, swallow; (2) annihilate, destroy, ravage, spend, waste.
Ant. of (1) disgorge; of (2) spare.

devout devoted, earnest, fervent, holy, pious, prayerful, pure, religious, reverent, saintly, serious, sincere, zealous.
Ant. irreverent.

dexterity ability, address, adroitness, aptitude, aptness, art, cleverness, expertness, facility, skilfulness, tact.
Ant. clumsiness.

dexterous able, active, adroit, apt, clever, handy, ingenious, nimble, prompt, quick, skilful, versed.
Ant. clumsy.

diabolical atrocious, damnable, demoniac, devilish, fiendish, hellish, impious, malevolent, nefarious, satanic, wicked.
Ant. angelic, heavenly.

dialect accent, idiom, jargon, language, patois, pronunciation, provincialism, speech, tongue.

dialectic argumentative, idiomatical, logical, rhetorical.

dialogue colloquy, conversation, discourse.

diaphanous clear, pellucid, translucent, transparent.
Ant. opaque.

diatribe abuse, disputation, dissertation, invective, philippic, reviling, tirade.

dictate (1) *v.* command, direct, enjoin, ordain, order, prescribe, pronounce, speak, urge, utter; (2) *n.* command, decree, direction, order, precept, rule.

dictator autocrat, despot, oppressor, tyrant.
Ant. slave.

dictatorial absolute, arbitrary, dogmatical, domineering, imperious, overbearing, tyrannical.
Ant. servile.

diction enunciation, expression, language, phraseology, speech, style, usage.

dictionary encyclopedia, glossary, lexicon, vocabulary, word-book.

didactic instructive, moral, preceptive.

die (1) decease, demise, depart, expire, finish; (2) decay, decline, disappear, fade, sink, vanish, wane, wilt, wither.
Ant. of (1) live; of (2) grow.

diet (A) aliment, fare, food, nourishment, nutriment, regimen, provisions, subsistence, sustenance, viands, victuals.

diet (B) chamber, congress, convention, council, meeting, parliament, sitting.

differ (1) diverge, vary; (2) altercate, argue, contend, de-

bate, disagree, dispute, oppose, quarrel, wrangle.
Ant. of (1) correspond; of (2) agree.

difference (1) dissimilarity, distinction, diversity, variation, variety; (2) argument, contention, contrariety, controversy, debate, disagreement, discordance, dispute, quarrel, strife, wrangle.
Ant. of (1) similarity; of (2) agreement.

difficult (1) arduous, hard, laborious, painful; (2) austere, fastidious, forbidding, intractable, rigid, unaccommodating, unamenable; (3) enigmatical, intricate, involved, obscure, perplexing.
Ant. of (1) easy; of (2) accommodating; of (3) plain, obvious.

difficulty (1) arduousness, hardship, impediment, objection, obstacle, obstinacy, opposition, stubbornness, unwillingness; (2) dilemma, distress, embarrassment, perplexity, predicament, quandary, trial, trouble.
Ant. of (1) ease, willingness.

diffidence bashfulness, doubt, fear, hesitation, humility, modesty, self-consciousness, shyness, timidity.
Ant. boldness, self-confidence.

diffident bashful, distrustful, doubtful, modest, reserved, self-conscious, self-effacing, shy, suspicious, timid.
Ant. bold, forward.

diffuse (1) *a.* copious, diffusive, discursive, long-winded, loose, prolix, vague, verbose, wordy; (2) *v.* circulate, disperse, disseminate, distribute, propagate, scatter, spread.
Ant. of (1) terse; of (2) collect.

diffusion circulation, dispersion, dissemination, distribution, expansion, propaganda, spread.

dig (1) break up, delve, excavate, hoe, hollow out, penetrate, pierce into, scoop, tunnel; (2) poke, punch, thrust.

Ant. of (1) fill in.

digest (1) *v.* assimilate, concoct, incorporate, macerate; (2) arrange, classify, codify, dispose, methodise, reduce, systematise, tabulate; (3) assimulate, con, consider, contemplate, master, meditate, ponder, study, (4) *n.* abridgment, abstract, epitome, précis, summary, synopsis.

Ant. of (2) expand.

dignify adorn, advance, aggrandise, elevate, ennoble, exalt, grace, honour, promote.

Ant. degrade.

dignity (1) elevation, eminence, excellence, glory, grandeur, greatness, honour, majesty, nobleness, nobility, rank, respectability, standing, stateliness, station; (2) dignitary, magistrate.

Ant. of (1) lowliness.

digress depart, deviate, diverge, expatiate, wander.

Ant. continue.

digression departure, deviation, divergence.

dilapidate demolish, destroy, disintegrate, pull down, ruin, waste.

Ant. preserve, reconstruct.

dilapidation decay, demolition, destruction, disintegration, dissolution, downfall, ruin, waste.

Ant. preservation, reconstruction.

dilate (1) distend, expand, extend, stretch, swell, widen; (2) amplify, be profuse, be

prolix, dwell on, enlarge, expatiate, spin out.

Ant. of (1) shrink.

dilatory backward, behindhand, delaying, laggard, lingering, loitering, off-putting, procrastinating, slack, slow, sluggish.

Ant. expeditious.

dilemma difficulty, (*Sl.*) fix, plight, predicament, problem, quandary, strait.

diligence activity, application, assiduity, assiduousness, attention, care, constancy, earnestness, heedfulness, industry, laboriousness, perseverance.

Ant. laziness.

diligent active, assiduous, attentive, busy, careful, constant, earnest, hard-working, indefatigable, industrious, laborious, painstaking, persevering, persistent, tireless.

Ant. lazy.

dim (1) *a.* cloudy, dark, darkish, dusky, hazy, obscure; (2) blurred, dull, faint, imperfect, indefinite, indistinct, obtuse, sullied, tarnished; (3) *v.* blur, cloud, darken, dull, obscure, tarnish.

Ant. of (1) clear.

dimension amplitude, bigness, bulk, capacity, extent, greatness, largeness, magnitude, measure.

diminish abate, contract, curtail, cut, decrease, lessen, lower, reduce, retrench, shrink, weaken.

Ant. increase.

diminution abatement, contraction, curtailment, cut, decay, decrease, deduction, lessening, reduction, retrenchment, weakening.

Ant. increase.

din clamour, clash, clatter, crash, hullabaloo, noise, outcry, racket, row, shout, uproar.
Ant. peace, quiet.

dingle dale, dell, glen, vale, valley.

dingy bedimmed, colourless, dark, dim, dirty, dull, dusky, faded, obscure, soiled, sombre.
Ant. bright.

dint (1) blow, dent, indentation, stroke; (2) force, power.

dip (1) v. bathe, dive, douse, duck, immerse, plunge, souse; (2) n. bend, incline.

dire alarming, awful, calamitous, cruel, dismal, dreadful, fearful, gloomy, horrible, horrid, terrible, terrific, woeful.
Ant. harmless.

direct (1) a. straight, not crooked, undeviating; (2) a. absolute, categorical, downright, earnest, express, frank, obvious, outspoken, plain, sincere, straightforward, unambiguous, unequivocal; (3) v. aim, cast, point, turn; (4) v. advise, conduct, control, dispose, govern, guide, lead, manage, regulate, rule; (5) v. command, enjoin, instruct, order; (6) v. address, superscribe.
Ant. of (1) crooked; of (2) devious.

direction (1) administration, command, control, government, guidance, management, order, oversight, superintendence; (2) aim, bearing, course, tendency; (3) address, superscription.

directly at once, expressly, forthwith, immediately, instantaneously, instantly, promptly, quickly, soon, speedily, straightaway.
Ant. by-and-by.

direful awful, calamitous, dire, dreadful, fearful, gloomy, horrible, horrid, shocking, terrible, tremendous.

dirge coronach, elegy, lament, requiem, threnody.

dirty (1) a. begrimed, filthy, foul, mucky, nasty, unclean, soiled, sullied; (2) a. clouded, dark, dull, miry, muddy; (3) a. base, beggarly, contemptible, low, mean, shabby, sordid, squalid; (4) v. begrime, defile, foul, soil, sully.
Ant. of (1) and (4) clean.

disability disqualification, impotency, inability, incapacity, incompetency, unfitness, weakness.
Ant. aptitude, fitness.

disable cripple, disqualify, enfeeble, impair, incapacitate, paralyse, unfit, unman, weaken.
Ant. strengthen.

disabuse correct, set right, undeceive.

disadvantage damage, detriment, disservice, drawback, harm, hurt, inconvenience, injury, loss, prejudice.
Ant. advantage, benefit.

disadvantageous deleterious, detrimental, harmful, hurtful, inconvenient, injurious, prejudicial, unfavourable.
Ant. advantageous, favourable.

disaffect alienate, disdain, dislike, disorder, estrange.

disaffection alienation, breach, disagreement, dislike, disloyalty, dissatisfaction, estrangement, repugnance, ill-will, unfriendliness.
Ant. loyalty.

disagree (1) deviate, differ, vary; (2) argue, debate, differ (*in opinion*), dispute, quarrel, wrangle.

Ant. agree.

disagreeable contrary, displeasing, distasteful, nasty, offensive, unpleasant, unsuitable.

Ant. agreeable, pleasant.

disagreement (1) difference, discrepancy, dissimilitude, diversity, unlikeness, variance; **(2)** argument, debate, discord, dispute, dissent, division, misunderstanding, strife, wrangle.

Ant. of (1) similarity; of (2) accord, agreement.

disallow disclaim, dismiss, disown, prohibit, refuse, reject, repudiate.

Ant. accept.

disappear cease, depart, fade, vanish.

Ant. appear.

disappoint baffle, balk, deceive, defeat, delude, disconcert, frustrate, mortify, tantalise, vex.

Ant. please, satisfy.

disappointment balk, failure, frustration, ill-success, miscarriage, mortification, unfulfilment.

Ant. fulfilment.

disapprobation blame, censure, condemnation, disapproval, dislike, displeasure, reproof.

Ant. approval.

disapprove blame, censure, condemn, disallow, dislike, reject.

Ant. approve.

disarrange confuse, derange, disorder, disturb, unsettle.

Ant. order.

disaster accident, adversity, blow, calamity, catastrophe, misadventure, mischance, misfortune, mishap, reverse, stroke.

Ant. good luck.

disastrous adverse, calamitous, catastrophic, detrimental, ill-starred, ruinous, unfortunate, unlucky, unpropitious, untoward.

Ant. fortunate, lucky.

disburden alleviate, diminish, discharge, disencumber, ease, free, relieve.

Ant. load.

discard banish, cashier, discharge, dismiss, displace, reject, remove, repudiate.

discern (1) behold, descry, discover, espy, notice, observe, perceive, recognise, see; **(2)** differentiate, discriminate, distinguish, judge, make distinction.

Ant. of (2) confuse.

discerning acute, astute, clear-sighted, discriminating, ingenious, intelligent, judicious, knowing, sagacious, sharp, shrewd.

Ant. stupid.

discernment acuteness, astuteness, clear-sightedness, cleverness, discrimination, ingenuity, insight, intelligence, judgment, perception, sagacity, sharpness, shrewdness.

Ant. stupidity.

discharge (1) *v.* disburden, unburden, unload; **(2)** cashier, discard, dismiss, eject, emit, excrete, expel, remove; **(3)** do, execute, fulfil, observe, perform; **(4)** absolve, acquit, clear, free, liberate, release, relieve, settle; **(5)** *n.* unburdening, unloading; **(6)** dismissal, ejection, emission, vent, voiding; **(7)** execution, fulfilment, observance, payment, performance; **(8)** acquittal, clearance, exoneration, liberation, release, settlement.

disciple adherent, catechumen, follower, learner, partisan, pupil, student, supporter, tyro.

Ant. master.

discipline (1) *n.* chastisement, control, correction, culture, drill, education, exercise, government, instruction, regulation, strictness, subjection, training; (2) *v.* bring up, chasten, chastise, control, correct, drill, educate, exercise, form, govern, instruct, punish, regulate, train.

Ant. of (1) unruliness; of (2) pamper.

disclaim abandon, deny, disallow, disavow, disown, reject, renounce, repudiate.

disclose communicate, discover, divulge, exhibit, expose, impart, make known, uncover, unveil, utter, reveal, tell.

Ant. conceal.

discolour stain, tarnish, tinge.

discomfit baffle, beat, checkmate, conquer, defeat, foil, frustrate, overpower, overthrow, subdue, vanquish, worst.

Ant. encourage.

discomfiture confusion, defeat, frustration, overthrow, rout, ruin.

Ant. encouragement.

discomfort annoyance, disquiet, inquietude, trouble, uneasiness, unpleasantness, vexation.

Ant. comfort, ease.

discommode annoy, disquiet, disturb, harass, incommode, inconvenience, molest, trouble.

Ant. assist.

discompose (1) agitate, annoy, bewilder, disconcert,

displease, embarrass, fret, irritate, perplex, provoke, ruffle, vex, worry; (2) confuse, derange, disorder, disturb, unsettle, upset.

Ant. of (1) calm, help; of (2) settle.

disconcert (1) abash, agitate, bewilder, disturb, perplex, perturb, unbalance, worry; (2) baffle, balk, confuse, defeat, disarrange, frustrate, thwart, undo.

Ant. of (1) calm; of (2) arrange, assist.

disconsolate cheerless, dejected, desolate, forlorn, gloomy, heart-broken, melancholy, miserable, sad, unhappy, woeful, wretched.

Ant. cheerful.

discontent discontentment, displeasure, dissatisfaction, restlessness, uneasiness.

Ant. contentment, satisfaction.

discontinuance cessation, discontinuation, disjunction, intermission, interruption, separation, stop, stopping, suspension.

Ant. continuation.

discord contention, difference, disagreement, discordance, dissension, dissonance, harshness, jarring, opposition, rupture, strife, variance, wrangling.

Ant. harmony.

discordant contradictory, contrary, disagreeing, dissonant, harsh, incongruous, inharmonious, jarring, opposite, repugnant.

Ant. harmonious.

discount allowance, deduction, drawback, rebate, reduction.

Ant. addition.

discourage (1) abash, awe, damp, daunt, deject, depress, dishearten, dismay, dispirit, frighten, intimidate; (2) deter, discountenance, disfavour, dissuade, hinder.

Ant. of (1) encourage; of (2) countenance.

discourse (1) n. conversation, dissertation, essay, homily, sermon, speech, talk, treatise; (2) v. advise, confer, converse, expatiate, parley, speak, talk.

discourteous abrupt, brusque, curt, disrespectful, ill-bred, ill-mannered, impolite, rude, uncivil, ungentlemanly, unmannerly.

Ant. courteous.

discover (1) ascertain, detect, determine, discern, disclose, espy, find out, notice, reveal, see, uncover; (2) contrive, invent, originate.

Ant. of (1) conceal.

discredit (1) v. disbelieve, doubt, question; (2) n. doubt, question; (3) v. disgrace, dishonour, reproach; (4) n. disgrace, dishonour, disrepute, ignominy, odium, reproach.

Ant. of (1) believe; of (3) and (4) honour.

discreet careful, cautious, circumspect, considerate, discerning, judicious, prudent, sagacious, wary.

Ant. imprudent, indiscreet.

discrepancy difference, disagreement, discordance, dissonance, inconsistency, variance, variation.

Ant. agreement.

discretion (1) care, carefulness, caution, circumspection, consideration, heedfulness, wariness; (2) choice, option, pleasure, will.

discrimination (1) acuteness, clearness, discernment, insight, judgment, penetration, sagacity; (2) differentiation, distinction.

discursive argumentative, casual, desultory, digressive, erratic, loose, rambling, roving, vague.

Ant. coherent.

discuss agitate, argue, consider, debate, deliberate, examine, reason about, sift, ventilate.

disdain (1) v. contemn, deride, despise, disregard, reject, scorn, slight, spurn, undervalue; (2) n. arrogance, contempt, scorn, sneer, superciliousness.

Ant. of (1) admire; of (2) admiration.

disdainful contemptuous, haughty, scornful, supercilious.

Ant. amiable.

disease affection, affliction, ailment, complaint, disorder, illness, indisposition, infirmity, malady, sickness.

Ant. good health.

disembodied bodiless, immaterial, incorporeal, spiritual, unbodied.

Ant. corporeal.

disengage (1) deliver, discharge, disentangle, ease, extricate, free, liberate, release, set free, unloose; (2) detach, disjoin, disunite, divide, separate, withdraw.

Ant. entangle, involve.

disentangle clear, detach, disconnect, disengage, evolve, extricate, free, loose, separate, sever, unfold, unravel, untwist.

Ant. entangle.

disfigurement blemish, defacement, defect, deformity, injury, spot, stain.

disgorge (1) belch, discharge, spew, throw up, vomit; **(2)** relinquish, resign, surrender, yield.

disgrace (1) *n.* baseness, contempt, degradation, discredit, disesteem, disfavour, dishonour, disrepute, ignominy, infamy, odium, opprobrium, reproach, scandal; **(2)** *v.* abase, defame, degrade, discredit, disfavour, dishonour, disparage, reproach, shame, taint.
Ant. of **(1)** credit, repute.

disgraceful discreditable, dishonourable, disreputable, ignominious, infamous, opprobrious, scandalous, shameful.
Ant. honourable.

disguise (1) *v.* cloak, conceal, cover, dissemble, hide, mask, screen, secrete, shroud, veil; **(2)** *n.* cloak, cover, mask, screen, veil.
Ant. of **(1)** disclose, reveal.

disgust (1) *n.* abhorrence, abomination, antipathy, aversion, detestation, dislike, distaste, hatefulness, hatred, loathing, nausea, repugnance; **(2)** *v.* abhor, abominate, detest, displease, nauseate, repel, revolt, sicken.
Ant. delight.

dishearten cast down, damp, daunt, deject, depress, deter, discourage, dispirit.
Ant. encourage, hearten.

dishevelled disarranged, disordered, hanging loose, untidy, untrimmed.
Ant. tidy.

dishonest cheating, corrupt, crafty, deceiving, deceptive, designing, fraudulent, guileful, knavish, perfidious, treacherous, unfair.
Ant. honest.

dishonour (1) *v.* corrupt, de-

base, debauch, degrade, discredit, disgrace, pollute, ravish; **(2)** *n.* abasement, degradation, discredit, disrepute, ignominy, infamy, odium, opprobrium, scandal, shame.
Ant. honour.

dishonourable base, discreditable, disgraceful, disreputable, ignominious, infamous, scandalous, shameful.
Ant. honourable.

disinclination alienation, antipathy, aversion, dislike, reluctance, repugnance, unwillingness.
Ant. willingness.

disinfect cleanse, deodorise, fumigate, purify.
Ant. infect.

disingenuous artful, deceitful, dishonest, insidious, insincere, uncandid, unfair, wily.
Ant. candid, frank.

disintegrate crumble, disunite, reduce to fragments, separate.

disinterested (1) impartial, indifferent, unbiased, uninterested, unprejudiced; **(2)** generous, liberal, magnanimous, unselfish.
Ant. of **(1)** biased; of **(2)** selfish.

disjoin detach, disconnect, disintegrate, dissociate, divide, separate, sever, sunder.
Ant. join, unite.

dislike (1) *n.* antagonism, aversion, disapprobation, disapproval, disgust, disinclination, displeasure, distaste, loathing; **(2)** *v.* abominate, detest, disapprove, hate, loathe.
Ant. of **(1)** delight, liking; of **(2)** like.

disloyal disaffected, faithless, false, perfidious, traitorous, treacherous, treasonable, unfaithful, unpatriotic.

Ant. faithful, loyal.

dismal black, calamitous, cheerless, dark, dolorous, dreary, funereal, gloomy, lonesome, lugubrious, melancholy, sad, sorrowful.

Ant. cheerful.

dismantle dispossess, divest, strip, unrig.

Ant. build, rig.

dismay (1) v. affright, alarm, appal, daunt, discourage, dishearten, frighten, horrify, paralyse, scare, terrify; (2) n. alarm, consternation, fear, fright, horror, terror.

Ant. of (1) hearten; of (2) security.

dismember disjoint, dislimb, dislocate, divide, mutilate, rend, sever.

dismiss banish, cashier, discard, discharge, disperse, reject, release, remove.

Ant. keep.

dismount alight, descend, dismantle, unhorse.

Ant. mount.

disorder (1) confusion, derangement, disarray, irregularity, jumble, mess; (2) brawl, clamour, commotion, fight, hubbub, quarrel, riot, unrest, uproar; (3) (Med.) ailment, complaint, disease, indisposition, malady, sickness; (4) v. confound, confuse, derange, disarrange, discompose, disorganise, disturb, unsettle, upset.

Ant. of (1), (2) and (4) order.

disorderly confused, immethodical, inordinate, intemperate, irregular, lawless, rebellious, refractory, riotous, tumultuous, turbulent, ungovernable, unruly, unsystematic.

Ant. orderly.

disorganise break up, confuse, derange, destroy, disarrange, discompose, disorder, unsettle, upset.

Ant. organise.

disown abnegate, deny, disallow, disavow, disclaim, reject, renounce, repudiate.

Ant. acknowledge.

disparage belittle, decry, defame, degrade, depreciate, derogate, detract from, reproach, traduce, underestimate, underrate, undervalue, vilify.

Ant. praise.

disparagement belittlement, debasement, degradation, depreciation, derogation, detraction, disgrace, dishonour, impairment, lessening, prejudice, reproach, underestimation.

disparity difference, dissimilarity, dissimilitude, disproportion, distinction, inequality, unlikeness.

Ant. parity, similarity.

dispassionate (1) calm, collected, composed, cool, imperturbable, moderate, quiet, serene, sober, temperate, unexcitable, unexcited, unruffled; (2) candid, disinterested, fair, impartial, indifferent, neutral, unbiased.

Ant. of (1) excited; of (2) biased, partial.

dispel banish, disperse, dissipate, scatter.

Ant. collect.

dispensation (1) allotment, appointment, apportionment, distribution; (2) administration, stewardship; (3) economy, plan, scheme, system; (4) exemption, immunity, indulgence, licence, privilege.

dispense (1) allot, apportion,

assign, deal out, distribute, mix; (2) administer, apply, carry out, execute; (3) excuse, exempt, exonerate, release, relieve.

disperse diffuse, disappear, disseminate, dissipate, distribute, separate, spread, vanish.

Ant. assemble.

dispirit damp, depress, discourage, dishearten.

Ant. encourage.

displace (1) derange, disarrange, dislodge, misplace, move; (2) cashier, depose, discard, discharge, dismiss, oust, remove, replace.

Ant. of (1) arrange; of (2) retain.

display (1) *n.* exhibition, manifestation, ostentation, pageant, parade, pomp, show; (2) *v.* evince, exhibit, expand, expose, extend, flaunt, manifest, open, present, show.

Ant. of (2) conceal.

displease aggravate, anger, annoy, disgust, dissatisfy, irritate, nettle, offend, pique, provoke, vex.

Ant. please.

displeasure anger, annoyance, disapproval, dislike, dissatisfaction, distaste, indignation, irritation, offence, pique, resentment, vexation.

Ant. pleasure, satisfaction.

disport amuse, beguile, caper, cheer, divert, entertain, frisk, frolic, gambol, make merry.

Ant. work.

disposal (1) conduct, control, direction, government, management, ordering, regulation; (2) arrangement, dispensation, disposition, distribution.

dispose (1) adjust, arrange, determine, fix, group, order,

place, rank, regulate, set, settle; (2) bias, incline, induce, lead, move; (3) (*Law*) alienate, convey, demise, sell, transfer.

disposition (A) (1) adjustment, arrangement, classification, control, direction, disposal, grouping, management, ordering, regulation.

disposition (B) bent, bias, character, inclination, nature, predisposition, proneness, propensity, temper, temperament, tendency.

dispossess deprive, dislodge, divest, eject, evict, oust, strip.

dispraise blame, censure, depreciation, discredit, disgrace, dishonour, disparagement, opprobrium, reproach, shame.

Ant. praise.

disproportion disparity, inequality, insufficiency, unsuitableness.

Ant. equality.

disprove confute, rebut, refute.

Ant. confirm.

disputatious argumentative, captious, cavilling, contentious, litigious, polemical, pugnacious, quarrelsome.

Ant. conciliatory.

dispute (1) *v.* argue, brawl, contest, controvert, debate, deny, discuss, doubt, impugn, quarrel, question, wrangle; (2) *n.* altercation, argument, brawl, contention, controversy, debate, disagreement, discussion, quarrel, wrangle.

Ant. of (1) agree; of (2) agreement.

disqualify disable, incapacitate, prohibit, unfit.

Ant. qualify.

disquiet (1) *v.* agitate, annoy.

bother, discompose, disturb, harass, incommode, pester, plague, trouble, worry, vex; (2) *n.* anxiety, disquietude, disturbance, restlessness, solicitude, trouble, uneasiness, unrest, worry.

Ant. of (2) peace.

disquisition discourse, dissertation, essay, paper, thesis, treatise.

disregard (1) *v.* contemn, despise, disdain, disobey, disparage, ignore, neglect, overlook, slight; (2) *n.* disrespect, ignoring, inattention, indifference, neglect, oversight, slight.

Ant. respect.

disrelish (1) *v.* dislike, loathe; (2) *n.* antipathy, aversion, disgust, dislike, repugnance.

Ant. of (1) like; of (2) liking.

disreputable base, contemptible, derogatory, discreditable, disgraceful, dishonourable, ignominious, infamous, low, mean, opprobrious, shameful, vicious, vile.

Ant. reputable, respectable.

dissect analyse, anatomise, explore, investigate, open, scrutinise.

dissemble affect, cloak, conceal, counterfeit, cover, disguise, feign, mask, simulate.

Ant. reveal.

dissembler dissimulator, feigner, hypocrite, pretender.

disseminate circulate, diffuse, disperse, proclaim, promulgate, propagate, publish, scatter, spread.

Ant. conceal.

dissension contention, difference, disagreement, discord, quarrel, strife, variance.

Ant. agreement.

dissent (1) *v.* decline, differ, disagree, refuse; (2) *n.* differ-ence, disagreement, opposition, refusal.

Ant. of (1) agree; of (2) agreement.

dissertation discourse, disquisition, essay, thesis, treatise.

dissimilar different, divergent, diverse, heterogeneous, unlike, various.

Ant. alike, similar.

dissimilitude difference, disparity, dissimilarity, diversity, heterogeneity, unlikeness.

Ant. similarity.

dissimulation concealment, deceit, double-dealing, duplicity, feigning, hypocrisy, pretence.

Ant. sincerity.

dissipate (1) consume, expend, lavish, spend, squander, waste; (2) dispel, disperse, scatter, vanish.

Ant. of (1) save; of (2) unite.

dissipation (1) debauchery, dissoluteness, drunkenness, excess, profligacy, squandering, waste; (2) disappearance, dispersion, dissemination, scattering, vanishing.

dissolute abandoned, corrupt, debauched, depraved, disorderly, dissipated, lax, lewd, licentious, loose, rakish, vicious, wanton, wild.

Ant. chaste, temperate.

dissolution (1) breaking up, death, destruction, end, extinction, overthrow, ruin, termination; (2) corruption, putrefaction; (3) decomposition, liquefaction, melting, solution.

Ant. of (1) revival.

dissolve (1) break, disorganise, disunite, loose, separate, sever; (2) destroy, end, overthrow, ruin, terminate; (3) crumble, disappear, fade, perish, vanish; (4) liquefy, melt.

dissonance disagreement, discord, discordance, discrepancy, harshness, incongruity, inconsistency, jarring, want of harmony.

Ant. harmony.

distance (1) absence, interval, remoteness, separation, space; (2) (*Fig.*) coldness, frigidity, reserve, stiffness.

Ant. of (1) nearness; of (2) friendliness.

distant (1) far, remote, removed; (2) (*Fig.*) aloof, ceremonious, cold, haughty, reserved; (3) faint, indirect, indistinct, slight.

Ant. of (1) near; of (2) friendly; of (3) clear.

distaste antipathy, aversion, disgust, disinclination, dislike, displeasure, disrelish, dissatisfaction, repugnance.

Ant. liking.

distasteful disagreeable, displeasing, loathsome, nauseous, offensive, repulsive, unpalatable, unpleasant, unsavoury.

Ant. agreeable, tasteful.

distemper ailment, complaint, disease, disorder, illness, indisposition, malady, sickness.

Ant. good health.

distend bloat, dilate, enlarge, expand, increase, inflate, puff, stretch, swell, widen.

Ant. contract, shrink.

distinct (1) clear, manifest, obvious, plain, unmistakable, well-defined; (2) definite, detached, different, individual, separate, unconnected.

Ant. of (1) indistinct, vague.

distinction (1) difference, division, separation; (2) account, celebrity, credit, discrimination, eminence, fame, honour, name, rank, renown, superiority.

Ant. of (1) similarity; of (2) disrepute.

distinguish (1) discern, know, perceive, recognise, see, tell; (2) characterise, classify, differentiate, discriminate, divide, mark; (3) celebrate, honour, signalise.

Ant. of (1) confuse.

distinguished (1) celebrated, conspicuous, eminent, famous, illustrious, noted; (2) conspicuous, extraordinary, marked.

Ant. of (1) common; of (2) ordinary.

distort contort, deform, falsify, misrepresent, twist, wrest.

Ant. straighten.

distortion contortion, deformity, falsification, misrepresentation, twist.

distract bewilder, confound, confuse, derange, discompose, disconcert, disturb, divert, harass, madden, mystify, perplex, puzzle.

Ant. compose.

distracted crazy, deranged, frantic, insane, mad, raving, wild.

Ant. sane.

distraction (1) abstraction, agitation, bewilderment, commotion, confusion, discord, disorder, disturbance; (2) aberration, alienation, delirium, derangement, frenzy, hallucination, incoherence, insanity, mania.

Ant. of (1) equanimity; of (2) sanity.

distress (1) *n.* adversity, affliction, agony, anguish, anxiety, calamity, destitution, grief, hardship, indigence, misery, misfortune, need, poverty, privation, sorrow, straits, suffering, trial; (2) *v.* afflict, grieve, harass, pain, perplex, trouble, worry.

Ant. comfort, delight.

distribute administer, allocate, allot, apportion, arrange, assign, classify, deal, dispense, dispose, divide, give, mete, spare.

Ant. collect.

distribution allocation, allotment, apportionment, arrangement, assortment, classification, dispensation, disposition, division, dole, grouping, partition, sharing.

Ant. collection.

distrust (1) *v.* disbelieve, discredit, doubt, misbelieve, mistrust, question, suspect; (2) *n.* doubt, misgiving, mistrust, question, suspicion.

Ant. of (1) believe; of (2) belief.

disturb (1) confuse, derange, disarrange, disorder, unsettle, upset; (2) agitate, annoy, discompose, distract, excite, harass, hinder, impede, incommode, interrupt, molest.

Ant. of (1) arrange; of (2) pacify, soothe.

disturbance (1) agitation, annoyance, confusion, derangement, disorder, hindrance, molestation, perturbation; (2) brawl, commotion, disorder, riot, tumult, turmoil, uproar.

Ant. of (1) order; of (2) calm.

disunion (1) disconnection, disjunction, separation, severance; (2) breach, rupture, schism.

Ant. union.

disunite detach, disconnect, disjoin, divide, estrange, part,

segregate, separate, sever, sunder.

Ant. join.

divaricate bifurcate, branch, diverge, fork, part, separate.

Ant. converge.

diverge bifurcate, branch, depart, deviate, divaricate, divide, fork, radiate, separate, wander.

Ant. unite.

divers different, manifold, many, numerous, several, sundry, various.

Ant. few.

diverse differing, dissimilar, divergent, multiform, separate, unlike, various, varying.

Ant. similar.

diversify alter, change, variegate, vary.

diversion (1) amusement, delight, distraction, enjoyment, entertainment, game, gratification, pastime, play, pleasure, recreation, sport; (2) detour, digression.

Ant. of (1) work.

divert (1) deflect, distract, turn aside; (2) amuse, delight, entertain, gratify, recreate.

Ant. of (1) straighten; of (2) bore.

divest denude, deprive, dispossess, disrobe, strip, unclothe, undress.

Ant. clothe, dress.

divide (1) bisect, cleave, cut, segregate, sever, shear, sunder; (2) allocate, allot, apportion, deal out, dispense, distribute, portion, share; (3) alienate, disunite, estrange.

Ant. of (1) join; of (2) retain; of (3) unite.

divination augury, divining, foretelling, magic, prediction, presage, prophecy, soothsaying, sorcery.

divine (1) angelic, celestial, godlike, heavenly, holy, sacred, spiritual, superhuman, supernatural; (2) exalted, rapturous, supreme, transcendent; (3) v. conjecture, foretell, prognosticate, suppose, surmise, suspect; (4) n. clergyman, ecclesiastic, minister, pastor, priest.

Ant. of (1) devilish; of (2) low; of (3) assert; of (4) layman.

division (1) category, class, demarcation, group, head, section; (2) bisection, partition, portion, separation; (3) breach, disagreement, discord, disunion, estrangement, feud, rupture, variance.

Ant. of (1) collection; of (3) unison.

divorce disconnect, dissolve (marriage), disunite, part, separate, sever, sunder.

Ant. join.

divulge communicate, declare, disclose, exhibit, expose, impart, proclaim, promulgate, publish, reveal, tell, uncover.

Ant. conceal.

do (1) accomplish, achieve, act, complete, conclude, effect, end, execute, produce, serve, suffice, transact, work; (2) (Sl.) cheat, hoax, swindle.

docile amenable, obedient, pliant, teachable, tractable.

Ant. disobedient.

dock clip, curtail, cut short, diminish, lessen, shorten.

Ant. lengthen.

doctrine article, belief, creed, dogma, opinion, precept, principle, teaching, tenet.

dogged (1) cantankerous, headstrong, intractable, obstinate, perverse, resolute, stubborn, unyielding, wilful; (2)

churlish, morose, sour, sullen, surly.

Ant. of (1) docile; of (2) friendly.

dogma article, belief, creed, doctrine, opinion, precept, principle, tenet.

dogmatic (1) arrogant, dictatorial, imperious, magisterial, opinionated, overbearing, peremptory; (2) authoritative, categorical, oracular, positive.

Ant. of (1) diffident, moderate.

dole (1) v. allocate, allot, apportion, assign, deal, distribute, divide, share; (2) n. allocation, allotment, apportionment, distribution, division, part, share; (3) alms, benefit, donation, gift, grant, gratuity, pittance; (4) n. affliction, distress, grief, sorrow, woe.

Ant. of (3) payment; of (4) joy.

doleful cheerless, dismal, distressing, dolorous, gloomy, lugubrious, melancholy, painful, pitiful, rueful, sad, sombre, woebegone, woeful.

Ant. cheerful.

dolt ass, blockhead, booby, dullard, dunce, fool, ignoramus, (Sl.) nitwit, simpleton.

Ant. genius.

domain (1) empire, estate, lands, province, realm, region, territory; (2) authority, dominion, jurisdiction, power, sway.

domestic (1) a. domiciliary, family, home, household, private; (2) domesticated, tame; (3) internal; (4) n. charwoman, (Colloq.) help, maid, servant.

Ant. of (1) public; of (2) wild; of (3) foreign; of (4) mistress.

domicile abode, dwelling,

habitation, home, house, mansion, residence, settlement.

dominant ascendant, controlling, governing, influential, outstanding, paramount, predominant, pre-eminent, presiding, prevailing, prevalent, ruling.

Ant. subordinate.

domineer bluster, bully, hector, lord, menace, overbear, swagger, threaten, tyrannise.

Ant. encourage.

dominion (1) ascendancy, authority, command, control, domination, government, jurisdiction, supremacy; (2) country, kingdom, realm, region, territory.

Ant. of (1) servitude, submission.

donation alms, benefaction, boon, contribution, gift, grant, gratuity, largess, offering, present, subscription.

doom (1) destiny, destruction, fate, fortune, lot, ruin; (2) condemnation, decree, judgment, sentence, verdict; (3) v. condemn, decree, destine, foreordain, judge, sentence.

Ant. of (2) acquittal.

dormant asleep, inactive, inert, latent, lazy, quiescent, sleeping, sluggish, slumbering, suspended, torpid.

Ant. active.

dose draught, drench, potion, quantity.

dotage imbecility, second childhood, senility, weakness.

Ant. infancy.

double (1) a. coupled, paired, twice, twofold; (2) a. deceitful, dishonest, false, insincere, knavish, perfidious, treacherous, vacillating; (3) v. duplicate, fold, plait, repeat; (4) n. (*Fig.*) artifice, ruse, trick,

shift, stratagem; (5) n. copy, counterpart, twin.

doublet jacket, jerkin, vest, waistcoat.

doubt (1) v. distrust, mistrust, question, suspect; (2) n. distrust, mistrust, suspicion; (3) v. demur, fluctuate, hesitate, scruple, vacillate, waver; (4) n. dubiety, hesitancy, hesitation, indecision, irresolution, suspense, uncertainty, vacillation.

Ant. of (1) trust; of (3) decide; of (4) resolution.

doubtful (1) ambiguous, dubious, equivocal, hazardous, obscure, precarious, problematic, questionable, uncertain, undecided, unsure; (2) distrustful, hesitating, irresolute, sceptical, suspicious.

Ant. of (1) certain; of (2) resolute.

doubtless certainly, clearly, indisputably, precisely, unquestionably.

doughty bold, brave, courageous, daring, dauntless, fearless, gallant, heroic, intrepid, redoubtable, valiant, valorous.

Ant. cowardly, timid.

dowdy dingy, ill-dressed, old-fashioned, scrubby, shabby, slovenly, unfashionable.

Ant. fashionable, smart.

dower dowry, endowment, gift, portion, share.

downfall descent, destruction, fall, ruin.

Ant. rise.

downhearted chapfallen, crestfallen, dejected, depressed, despondent, discouraged, dispirited, downcast, low-spirited, sad, unhappy.

Ant. happy, optimistic.

downright (1) categorical, clear, explicit, plain, positive, simple, unequivocal, undisguised; (2) artless, blunt, frank, honest, sincere, straightforward.

Ant. of (1) equivocal; of (2) insincere.

doze drowse, nap, sleep, slumber.

draft (1) v. delineate, draw, outline, select, sketch; (2) n. abstract, delineation, outline, sketch; (3) n. bill (of exchange), cheque, order.

drag (1) draw, haul, pull, tow, trail, tug; (2) linger, loiter.

Ant. of (1) push; of (2) hasten.

draggle befoul, bemire, besmirch, daggle, drabble, trail.

drain (1) v. draw off, dry, empty, evacuate, exhaust; (2) n. channel, ditch, sewer, sink, trench, watercourse; (3) exhaustion, withdrawal.

Ant. of (1) fill.

draught (1) cup, dose, drench, drink, potion, quantity; (2) delineation, design, draft, outline, sketch; (3) current (of air), drawing, pulling, traction.

draw (1) drag, haul, pull, tow; (2) delineate, depict, design, sketch, trace; (3) deduce, derive, infer; (4) allure, attract, engage, induce, influence, persuade; (5) extort, extract, pull out; (6) extend, lengthen, stretch; (7) drain, inhale, inspire, suck; (8) compose, formulate, frame, prepare, write; (9) (Med.) blister, vesicate.

Ant. of (1) push.

drawback (1) defect, deficiency, detriment, disadvantage, fault, flaw, imperfection, injury; (2) allowance, deduction, discount, rebate.

Ant. of (1) advantage.

dread (1) v. fear; (2) n. affright, alarm, apprehension, awe, dismay, fear, horror, terror; (3) a. awful, dire, dreadful, frightful, horrible, terrible.

Ant. of (2) bravery; of (3) pleasant.

dreadful alarming, appalling, awful, dire, formidable, frightful, horrible, monstrous, shocking, terrible, tremendous.

Ant. pleasing.

dream (1) v. fancy, imagine, think; (2) n. delusion, fantasy, hallucination, illusion, imagination, reverie, speculation, trance, vagary, vision.

Ant. of (2) reality.

dreamy absent, abstracted, fanciful, ideal, misty, shadowy, speculative, unreal, visionary.

Ant. practical.

dreary (1) cheerless, comfortless, depressing, dismal, drear, gloomy, lonely, lonesome, sad, solitary, sorrowful; (2) boring, dull, monotonous, tedious, uninteresting, wearisome.

Ant. of (1) cheerful; of (2) interesting.

dregs draff, dross, grounds, lees, residuum, scourings, scum, sediment, trash, waste.

drench (1) drown, duck, imbrue, saturate, soak, steep, wet; (2) (Med.) physic, purge.

Ant. of (1) dry.

dress (1) v. adorn, apparel, array, attire, bedeck, deck, decorate, drape, embellish, rig, robe, trim; (2) n. apparel, attire, clothes, clothing, costume, frock, garb, garment, gown, guise, habiliment, habit, suit, vestment; (3) v. adjust, align, arrange, dispose, fit, prepare, straighten.

Ant. of (1) undress; of (3) disarrange.

driblet bit, drop, fragment, morsel, piece, scrap.

drift (1) *v.* accumulate, drive, float, go (*aimlessly*), wander; (2) *n.* accumulation, diluvium, heap, mass, pile; (3) current, impulse, rush, sweep; (4) (*Fig.*) aim, design, direction, meaning, object, purport, scope, tendency, tenor.

Ant. of (4) aimlessness.

drill (1) *v.* discipline, exercise, instruct, teach, train; (2) *n.* discipline, exercise, instruction, training; (3) *v.* bore, perforate, pierce; (4) *n.* borer, boring-tool.

drink (1) absorb, drain, imbibe, quaff, sip, suck, swallow, swig, swill; (2) carouse, indulge, revel, tipple, tope; (3) *n.* beverage, cup, draught, liquid, potion, refreshment.

Ant. of (1) pour.

drive (1) *v.* coerce, compel, constrain, force, harass, impel, oblige, overburden, overwork, press, rush; (2) *v.* hurl, propel, push, send; (3) *n.* effort, energy, pressure; (4) *v.* go, guide, ride, travel.

Ant. of (1) restrain.

drivel (1) *v.* babble, blether, dote, drool, slaver, slobber; (2) *n.* balderdash, fatuity, nonsense, prating, rubbish, stuff, twaddle.

Ant. of (2) coherence.

droll (1) *a.* amusing, comical, diverting, farcical, funny, humorous, jocular, laughable, ludicrous, odd, quaint, waggish, whimsical; (2) *n.* buffoon, clown, comedian, harlequin, jester, mountebank, wag.

Ant. of (1) dull, serious.

drollery archness, buffoonery, comicality, fun, humour, jocu-

larity, pleasantry, waggishness, whimsicality.

Ant. seriousness.

drone (1) *n.* idler, loafer, lounger, sluggard; (2) *v.* dawdle, drawl, idle, loaf, lounge, read monotonously.

Ant. of (1) worker.

droop bend, decline, drop, fade, faint, fall down, flag, hang, languish, wilt, wither.

Ant. rise.

drop (1) decline, depress, descend, droop, lower, sink; (2) abandon, cease, desert, discontinue, forsake, leave, quit, relinquish, remit; (3) *n.* globule, sip, spot, taste.

Ant. of (2) hold.

dross crust, dregs, lees, recrement, refuse, scoria, scum, waste.

drought aridity, drouth, dryness, thirstiness.

Ant. deluge.

drove collection, company, crowd, flock, herd.

drown (1) deluge, engulf, flood, immerse, inundate, sink, submerge, swamp; (2) (*Fig.*) overcome, overpower, overwhelm.

Ant. of (1) float, rise.

drowse doze, nap, sleep, slumber.

drowsy comatose, dozy, heavy, lethargic, lulling, sleepy, somnolent, soporific.

Ant. alert, awake.

drub bang, beat, cane, cudgel, flog, hit, knock, pommel, pound, strike, thrash, thump, whack.

drudge (1) *v.* plod, slave, toil, work; (2) *n.* hack, menial, plodder, scullion, slave, toiler, worker.

drug medicine, physic, poison, remedy.

drunk drunken, fuddled,

inebriated, intoxicated, maudlin, muddled, soaked, tipsy.
Ant. sober.

drunkard alcoholic, carouser, dipsomaniac, drinker, sot, tippler, toper.

dry (1) arid, barren, juiceless, parched, sapless, thirsty; (2) (*Fig.*) boring, dreary, dull, plain, tedious, tiresome, uninteresting; (3) (*Fig.*) cutting, keen, sarcastic, sharp; (4) *v.* desiccate, drain, make dry, parch.
Ant. of (1) wet; of (2) interesting; of (4) moisten.

dub call, denominate, designate, entitle, name, style, term.

dubious (1) doubtful, hesitant, uncertain, undecided, wavering; (2) ambiguous, doubtful, equivocal, obscure, problematical, questionable.
Ant. of (1) certain; of (2) obvious.

duck (1) dip, dive, immerse, plunge, submerge, souse; (2) bend, bow, dodge, stoop.

duct canal, blood-vessel, channel, conduit, pipe, tube.

ductile compliant, docile, extensible, flexible, malleable, tractable, yielding.
Ant. obstinate, unyielding.

dudgeon indignation, ire, resentment, umbrage, wrath.
Ant. content, mildness.

due (1) *a.* appropriate, becoming, bounden, fit, just, obligatory, owed, owing, proper, suitable, right; (2) *n.* debt.
Ant. of (1) unfit, unjust.

dug nipple, pap, teat.

dulcet charming, delightful, euphonious, harmonious, honeyed, luscious, melodious, pleasant, pleasing, soothing, sweet.
Ant. harsh

dull (1) *a.* doltish, solid, stupid, unintelligent; (2) apathetic, callous, dead, heavy, insensible, lifeless, listless, passionless, slow, sluggish; (3) cheerless, dismal, gloomy, sad; (4) boring, commonplace, dreary, dry, plain, tedious, tiresome, uninteresting; (5) blunt, dulled, obtuse; (6) cloudy, dim, opaque, turbid; (7) *v.* deject, depress, discourage, dishearten, dispirit, sadden; (8) allay, alleviate, assuage, mitigate, moderate, paralyse, soften, stupefy; (9) dim, stain, sully, tarnish.

dumb inarticulate, mute, silent, (*Colloq.*) stupid, soundless, speechless, voiceless.
Ant. talkative.

dum(b)found(er) amaze, astonish, astound, bewilder, confound, confuse, nonplus.

dumps blues, dejection, depression, despondency, gloom, gloominess, hypochondria, melancholy, sadness.
Ant. cheerfulness.

dun beset, importune, press, urge.

dunce ass, blockhead, dolt, donkey, dullard, dunderhead, goose, halfwit, ignoramus, loon, nincompoop, numskull, simpleton.
Ant. genius.

dupe (1) *v.* beguile, cheat, cozen, deceive, delude, gull, hoodwink, outwit, overreach, swindle, trick; (2) *n.* gull, simpleton.

duplicity artifice, deceit, deception, dishonesty, dissimulation, double-dealing, fraud, hypocrisy, perfidy.
Ant. honesty.

durable abiding, constant, enduring, firm, lasting,

permanent, persistent, stable.
Ant. temporary, unstable.

duration continuance, continuation, period, permanency, perpetuation, prolongation, time.

duress (1) captivity, confinement, constraint, hardship, imprisonment, restraint; (2) (*Law*) compulsion (*by threat of personal violence*).
Ant. of (1) liberty.

dusky (1) dark, swarthy, tawny; (2) cloudy, darkish, dim, murky, obscure, overcast, shadowy.
Ant. light.

dutiful deferential, docile, respectful, reverential, submissive.
Ant. disrespectful.

duty (1) allegiance, business, engagement, function, obedience, obligation, office, responsibility, reverence, service, work; (2) custom, excise, tariff, tax, toll.

dwarf (1) *n.* homunculus, manikin, midget, pygmy; (2) lower, stunt.
Ant. of (1) giant.

dwarfish diminutive, dwarfed, low, pygmean, small, stunted, tiny, undersized.
Ant. huge.

dwell abide, inhabit, live, remain, reside, rest, sojourn, stay, stop.
Ant. travel.

dwelling abode, domicile, habitation, home, house, lodging, quarters, residence.

dwindle decay, decline, decrease, diminish, grow less, lessen, pine, shrink, waste away.
Ant. increase.

dynasty dominion, empire, government, rule, sovereignty.

E

eager anxious, ardent, earnest, fervent, fervid, greedy, glowing, hot, impatient, longing, vehement, yearning, zealous.
Ant. apathetic.

eagerness ardour, avidity, earnestness, fervour, greediness, heartiness, impatience, impetuosity, vehemence.
Ant. apathy.

ear (*Fig.*) attention, hearing, heed, musical perception, regard, taste.

early (1) *a.* forward, opportune, premature, seasonable, timely; (2) *adv.* anon, beforehand, betimes, ere, seasonably, shortly, soon.
Ant. late.

earn acquire, deserve, gain, get, merit, obtain, procure, realise, reap, win.
Ant. lose, spend.

earnest (1) ardent, eager, enthusiastic, fervent, fervid, keen, purposeful, warm, zealous; (2) close, determined, firm, fixed, grave, intent, resolved, sincere, solemn, stable, steady; (3) *n.* determination, reality, seriousness, sincerity, truth; (4) foretaste, pledge, promise; (5) (*Law*) arles, earnest-money, handsel, token.
Ant. of (1) slack; of (2) insincere; of (3) indifference.

earnings allowance, emolument, income, pay, profits, remuneration, reward, salary, stipend, wages.
Ant. expenditure.

earth (1) globe, orb, planet, world; (2) clay, clod, (*Scot.*) divot, ground, land, loam, sod, soil, turf.

earthly (1) mundane, terrestrial, worldly; (2) (*Fig.*) base, carnal, gross, grovelling, low, sensual, sordid, vile; (3) (*Sl.*) conceivable, imaginable, possible.

Ant. of (1) heavenly; of (2) spiritual.

ease (1) calmness, comfort, contentment, enjoyment, happiness, peace, quiet, quietude, relaxation, repose, rest, serenity, tranquillity; (2) easiness, facility, readiness; (3) flexibility, freedom, informality, naturalness, unaffectedness; (4) *v.* abate, allay, alleviate, appease, assuage, disburden, mitigate, moderate, quiet, relieve, soothe, still, tranquillise.

Ant. of (1) discomfort; of (3) formality; of (4) aggravate.

easy (1) facile, light, not difficult; (2) comfortable, contented, quiet, satisfied, undisturbed, untroubled; (3) accommodating, compliant, manageable, submissive, tractable, yielding; (4) affable, gentle, graceful, informal, smooth, unconstrained.

Ant. of (1) difficult; of (2) uncomfortable; of (3) exacting; of (4) unnatural.

eat (1) chew, consume, devour, ingest, swallow; (2) corrode, erode, wear away.

eatable edible, esculent, harmless, wholesome.

Ant. inedible, uneatable.

ebb (1) *v.* abate, fall away, fall back, recede, retire, sink, subside, wane; (2) *n.* reflux, regression, retrocession, subsidence, wane; (3) *v.* decay, decline, degenerate, deteriorate; (4) *n.* decay, decline, degeneration, deterioration.

Ant. of (1) flow, wax.

ebullition (1) boiling, bubbling, effervescence, fermentation, outburst, overflow; (2) fit, outbreak, paroxysm.

eccentric aberrant, abnormal, anomalous, erratic, irregular, odd, peculiar, singular, strange, uncommon, whimsical.

Ant. natural, normal.

eccentricity aberration, abnormality, anomaly, irregularity, oddity, oddness, peculiarity, singularity, strangeness, waywardness.

Ant. normality.

echo (1) *v.* repeat, resound, reverberate; (2) *n.* answer, repetition, reverberation.

éclat acclamation, applause, brilliancy, effect, lustre, pomp, renown, show, splendour.

Ant. disapproval.

eclipse (1) *v.* blot out, cloud, darken, dim, extinguish, obscure, overshadow, shroud, surpass, veil; (2) *n.* darkening, diminution, extinction, failure, obscuration, occultation, shading.

Ant. of (1) illumine.

economise husband, retrench, save, utilise.

Ant. squander.

economy (1) frugality, husbandry, parsimony, retrenchment, saving, stinginess, thrift; (2) administration, arrangement, management, method, order, regulation, system.

Ant. of (1) prodigality; of (2) mismanagement.

ecstasy delight, enthusiasm, fervour, frenzy, joy, rapture, ravishment, trance, transport.

Ant. misery.

ecumenical catholic, general, universal.

eddy counter-current, swirl, vortex, whirlpool.

Ant. flow.

edge (1) border, brim, brink, lip, margin, rim, verge; **(2)** animation, interest, keenness, point, sharpness, sting, zest; **(3)** v. sharpen.

Ant. of (1) centre; of (2) bluntness; of (3) blunt.

edible eatable, esculent, harmless, wholesome.

Ant. harmful, noxious.

edict act, command, decree, law, mandate, manifesto, order, ordinance, proclamation, regulation, statute.

edifice building, fabric, habitation, house, structure.

edify educate, elevate, enlighten, improve, inform, instruct, nurture, teach.

educate cultivate, develop, discipline, drill, edify, exercise, indoctrinate, inform, instruct, mature, rear, train.

Ant. neglect.

education breeding, cultivation, development, discipline, drilling, indoctrination, instruction, nurture, schooling, training, tuition.

Ant. illiteracy.

educe bring out, draw out, elicit, extract.

Ant. insert.

eerie awesome, fearful, frightening, strange, uncanny, weird.

efface blot out, cancel, delete, destroy, erase, expunge, obliterate.

Ant. restore.

effect (1) n. consequence, event, fruit, issue, outcome; **(2)** efficiency, fact, force, power, reality, validity, weight; **(3)** import, impression, meaning, purport, significance, tenor; **(4)** v. accomplish, achieve,

cause, complete, consummate, create, effectuate, execute, fulfil, perform.

Ant. of (1) cause.

effective able, active, adequate, cogent, competent, convincing, efficacious, efficient, energetic, forcible, operative, potent, powerful.

Ant. incompetent, ineffective.

effects chattels, furniture, goods, property.

effectuate accomplish, achieve, complete, do, effect, execute, fulfil, perform.

Ant. neglect.

effeminate delicate, feminine, soft, tender, unmanly, womanish, womanlike, womanly.

Ant. manly.

effervesce v. bubble, ferment, foam, froth.

effete barren, decayed, decrepit, exhausted, spent, sterile, unfruitful, unproductive, unprolific, worn out.

Ant. fertile, vigorous.

efficacious active, adequate, competent, effective, effectual, energetic, operative, powerful.

Ant. ineffective, weak.

efficacy ability, competence, efficiency, energy, force, power, strength, vigour, virtue.

Ant. inefficiency.

efficient able, capable, competent, effective, effectual, energetic, powerful, ready, skilful.

Ant. inefficient, weak.

effigy figure, image, likeness, picture, portrait, statue.

effluence discharge, effluvium, efflux, emanation, emission, flow, outpouring.

Ant. influx.

effort application, attempt, endeavour, essay, exertion, strain, stretch, struggle.

Ant. ease.

effrontery assurance, audacity, boldness, (*Colloq.*) brass, disrespect, impudence, incivility, insolence, presumption, rudeness, shamelessness.
Ant. respectfulness.

effulgent blazing, bright, brilliant, dazzling, flaming, glowing, lustrous, radiant, resplendent, shining, splendid.
Ant. dull.

effusion (1) discharge, effluence, emission, gush, outpouring; (2) address, speech, talk, utterance.

egotism egoism, self-conceit, selfishness, self-importance, self-praise, vanity.
Ant. altruism, modesty.

egotistic(al) conceited, egotistic(al), opinionated, self-important, vain.
Ant. altruistic, modest.

egregious conspicuous, enormous, extraordinary, huge, monstrous, outrageous, prodigious, remarkable.
Ant. commonplace.

egress departure, emergence, exit, outlet, passage out.
Ant. entrance.

eject banish, discard, discharge, dismiss, dispossess, emit, evacuate, expel, oust, reject, throw out, vomit.
Ant. retain.

elaborate (1) v. develop, improve, mature, produce, refine; (2) a. complicated, decorated, laboured, ornate, perfected, studied.
Ant. of (1) simplify; of (2) plain, simple.

elapse go, lapse, pass.
Ant. remain.

elated animated, cheered, elevated, excited, exhilarated, puffed up, roused.
Ant. depressed.

elbow (1) n. angle, bend, corner, turn; (2) v. crowd, hustle, jostle, push.

elder (1) a. ancient, earlier born, older, senior; (2) n. presbyter, prior, senator, senior, (*Eccl.*) office-bearer.
Ant. of (1) younger.

elect (1) v. appoint, choose, designate, pick, prefer, select; (2) a. choice, chosen, picked, selected.
Ant. of (1) reject; of (2) rejected.

election appointment, choice, preference, selection.
Ant. rejection.

elector chooser, constituent, selector, voter.
Ant. candidate.

electrify (*Fig.*) astonish, enchant, excite, rouse, startle, stir, thrill.
Ant. tranquillise.

elegance beauty, gentility, grace, gracefulness, polish, politeness, propriety, refinement, symmetry, taste.
Ant. awkwardness, inferiority.

elegant accomplished, beautiful, chaste, choice, comely, cultivated, delicate, fashionable, genteel, graceful, nice, polished, refined, tasteful.
Ant. inelegant, unrefined.

elegy dirge, lament, threnody.

element (1) basis, component, constituent, essential factor, ingredient, part, principle, rudiment, unit; (2) environment, milieu, sphere.
Ant. of (1) compound.

elementary basic, fundamental, initial, introductory, primary, rudimentary, simple, uncombined, uncompounded.
Ant. advanced, secondary.

elevate (1) advance, augment,

evict, exalt, heighten, lift, promote, raise, set up, swell; (2) animate, cheer, elate, excite, exhilarate, rouse.

Ant. of (1) lower; of (2) depress.

elicit acquire, deduce, draw out, educe, eliminate, evoke, evolve, extort, obtain.

eligible desirable, preferable, qualified, suitable, worthy.

Ant. ineligible.

eliminate disengage, eradicate, exclude, expel, ignore, omit, reject, remove, separate.

Ant. include.

elliptical (1) oval; (2) defective, incomplete.

elocution declamation, delivery, oratory, rhetoric, speech, utterance.

elongate draw, extend, lengthen, protract, stretch.

Ant. shorten.

elope abscond, bolt, decamp, disappear, leave.

eloquence fluency, oratory, rhetoric.

elucidate clarify, explain, expound, illustrate, interpret, unfold.

Ant. obscure.

elucidation annotation, clarification, comment, commentary, explanation, exposition, illustration, interpretation.

elude (1) avoid, dodge, evade, escape, shun; (2) baffle, disappoint, disconcert, foil, frustrate, thwart.

Ant. of (1) confront; of (2) aid.

elusive deceitful, deceptive, elusory, equivocal, evasive, fallacious, fraudulent, illusory, misleading, slippery.

Elysian blissful, celestial, charming, delightful, enchanting, happy, heavenly, ravishing, seraphic.

Ant. hellish.

emaciation attenuation, leanness, meagreness, tabes, thinness, wasting away.

Ant. fatness.

emanate arise, emerge, flow, issue, originate, proceed, spring.

emancipate deliver, discharge, disenthrall, enfranchise, free, liberate, release, unchain, unfetter.

Ant. enslave.

emancipation deliverance, enfranchisement, freedom, liberation, manumission, release.

Ant. enslavement.

embalm consecrate, conserve, enshrine, perfume, preserve, scent, store, treasure.

Ant. abandon.

embargo ban, bar, hindrance, prohibition, restraint, restriction.

Ant. permit.

embarrass abash, annoy, complicate, confound, confuse, disconcert, distress, hamper, harass, impede, involve, mystify, plague, puzzle, trouble, vex.

Ant. comfort, simplify.

embellish adorn, beautify, bedeck, deck, decorate, enhance, enrich, garnish, grace, ornament.

Ant. deface.

embellishment adornment, decoration, enrichment, ornament, ornamentation.

embezzle appropriate, filch, misappropriate, peculate, pilfer, purloin, steal.

emblem badge, device, figure, image, mark, representation, sign, symbol, token, type.

embody (1) collect, combine, comprehend, comprise,

concentrate, contain, incarnate, include, incorporate, integrate; (2) codify, methodise, systematise.

Ant. of (1) exclude.

embolden animate, cheer, elate, encourage, gladden, incite, inspirit, reassure.

Ant. dishearten.

embrace (1) v. clasp, encircle, grasp, hug, seize; (2) comprehend, comprise, contain, cover, enclose, encompass, include; (3) n. clasp, hug.

Ant. of (1) release; of (2) except.

embroil confound, disorder, disturb, encumber, entangle, implicate, involve, perplex, trouble.

Ant. disentangle.

embryo beginning, germ, nucleus, root, rudiment.

emendation amendment, correction, improvement, rectification.

Ant. error.

emerge appear, become visible, emanate, issue, rise, spring up.

Ant. enter.

emergency conjecture, crisis, difficulty, dilemma, exigency, necessity, pass, pinch, quandary, strait.

emigration departure, exodus, migration, removal.

Ant. immigration.

eminence (1) celebrity, dignity, distinction, fame, note, prominence, rank, renown, reputation, repute; (2) elevation, height, hill.

eminent celebrated, conspicuous, distinguished, elevated, exalted, famous, high, illustrious, notable, prominent, renowned.

Ant. commonplace, ordinary.

emissary messenger, scout, secret agent, spy.

emit breathe forth, discharge, eject, exhale, exude, give out, vent.

Ant. inhale.

emollient assuaging, balsamic, laxative, mollifying, softening, soothing.

Ant. irritating.

emolument advantage, benefit, compensation, fee, gain, hire, profits, remuneration, salary, stipend, wages.

emotion agitation, excitement, feeling, passion, perturbation, sympathy, trepidation.

Ant. apathy.

emphasis force, importance, impressiveness, moment, significance, stress, weight.

Ant. insignificance.

emphatic earnest, energetic, decided, definite, distinct, forcible, impressive, momentous, positive, powerful, pronounced, significant, striking, strong.

Ant. undecided, weak.

empire authority, command, control, dominion, government, power, rule, supremacy, sway.

empiric experimental, hypothetical, provisional, tentative.

Ant. theoretical.

employ (1) v. apply, commission, engage, enlist, hire, occupy, retain; (2) n. employment, service.

Ant. of (1) dismiss.

employment agency, avocation, business, calling, craft, employ, engagement, profession, pursuit, trade, vocation, work.

emporium market, mart, store.

empower authorise, commission, enable, permit, qualify, sanction, warrant.
Ant. forbid.

empty (1) *v.* deplete, discharge, drain, evacuate, exhaust, pour out, unload; (2) *a.* bare, blank, desolate, destitute, unfurnished, unoccupied, unsupplied, vacant, void, waste; (3) *a.* hollow, ineffective, unreal, unsatisfactory, unsubstantial; (4) (*Fig.*) frivolous, senseless, silly, vain, weak.
Ant. of (1) fill; of (2) occupied; of (3) satisfactory; of (4) serious.

empyreal aerial, airy, ethereal, heavenly, refined, sublime.

emulation competition, contention, contest, envy, jealousy, rivalry, strife.
Ant. association.

enable authorise, capacitate, commission, empower, fit, permit, prepare, qualify, sanction, warrant.
Ant. forbid.

enact (1) authorise, command, decree, establish, ordain, order, sanction; (2) act, perform, personate, play, represent.
Ant. of (1) annul.

enamour bewitch, captivate, charm, enchant, endear, fascinate.
Ant. repel.

enchain bind, enslave, fetter, hold, manacle, shackle.
Ant. free.

enchant bewitch, captivate, charm, delight, enamour, enrapture, fascinate.
Ant. repel.

enchantment (1) bliss, delight, fascination, rapture, ravishment, transport; (2) charm, incantation, magic, necromancy, sorcery, spell, witchcraft, wizardry.
Ant. of (1) disenchantment.

encircle circumscribe, enclose, encompass, enfold, environ, gird in, surround.
Ant. exclude.

enclose circumscribe, cover, encircle, encompass, environ, wrap.

encomium applause, compliment, eulogy, laudation, panegyric, praise.
Ant. blame, censure, invective.

encompass beset, besiege, circumscribe, encircle, enclose, environ, hem in, include, invest.

encounter (1) *v.* confront, face, meet; (2) *v.* attack, combat, contend, cope with, engage, strive, struggle, withstand; (3) *n.* clash, collision, meeting; (4) *n.* action, battle, combat, conflict, contest, dispute, engagement, fight, skirmish.
Ant. of (1) avoid.

encourage (1) animate, cheer, comfort, console, embolden, hearten, incite, rouse, stimulate; (2) abet, advance, aid, foster, help, promote, strengthen, support, urge.
Ant. of (1) discourage; of (2) dispirit.

encroach infringe, intrude, invade, trench, trespass.

encumber burden, clog, embarrass, hamper, hinder, impede, obstruct, oppress, overload, retard.
Ant. unburden.

encumbrance burden, clog, drag, embarrassment, hindrance, impediment, liability, load, obstruction.
Ant. ease.

end (1) bound, boundary, extreme, extremity, limit, terminus; (2) attainment, close, conclusion, consequence, finish, issue, outcome, termination; (3) aim, design, drift, intention, object, objective, purpose; (4) bit, fragment, remnant, scrap; (5) v. cease, complete, conclude, finish, terminate; (6) destroy, kill, put to death.
Ant. of (5) begin.

endanger compromise, hazard, imperil, jeopardise, risk.
Ant. protect, secure.

endear attach, bind, captivate, charm, win.
Ant. estrange.

endeavour (1) n. aim, attempt, effort, essay, trial; (2) v. aim, attempt, essay, labour, strive, struggle, try.

endless boundless, continual, eternal, everlasting, incessant, infinite, interminable, unending, uninterrupted, unlimited, perpetual.
Ant. limited.

endorse back, confirm, indorse, ratify, sanction, superscribe, support, vouch for.
Ant. oppose.

endow bequeath, bestow, confer, dower, endue, enrich, furnish, give, grant, invest, supply.
Ant. deprive.

endowment (1) benefaction, bequest, boon, fund, gift, grant, largess, property, provision, revenue; (2) ability, aptitude, capability, capacity, faculty, genius, power, qualification, quality, talent.
Ant. of (2) inability.

endurance bearing, fortitude, patience, resignation, submission, sufferance, toleration.
Ant. cessation, impatience.

endure abide, bear, brook, continue, experience, last, persist, remain, suffer, support, sustain, tolerate, undergo.
Ant. cease, fail.

enemy adversary, antagonist, foe, opponent, rival.
Ant. ally, friend.

energetic active, forcible, effective, effectual, efficacious, potent, powerful, strong, vigorous.
Ant. lazy, weak.

energy activity, animation, efficacy, efficiency, force, intensity, life, manliness, pluck, power, spirit, strength, strenuousness, vigour, zeal.
Ant. inactivity.

enervate debilitate, emasculate, enfeeble, exhaust, paralyse, relax, unhinge, unnerve, unstring, weaken.
Ant. strengthen.

enfeeble debilitate, exhaust, relax, render feeble, weaken, unhinge, unnerve.
Ant. strengthen.

enforce compel, constrain, exact, execute, oblige, put in force, require, urge.
Ant. persuade.

enfranchise emancipate, free, give the vote to, liberate, release, set free.
Ant. disenfranchise, enslave.

engage (1) agree, betroth, bind, commit, pledge, promise, stipulate, undertake, vouch; (2) employ, enlist, hire; (3) busy, engross, occupy; (4) allure, arrest, attach, attract, draw, fix, gain, win; (5) attack, encounter, fight with.

engagement (1) assurance, betrothal, bond, compact, contract, obligation, pact, pledge, promise, stipulation, troth, undertaking, word; (2) avocation, business, calling, employment, occupation, work; (3) action, battle, combat, conflict, contest, encounter, fight.

engender beget, breed, cause, create, excite, generate, incite, occasion, procreate, produce.
Ant. kill.

engine agency, agent, implement, instrument, machine, means, tool, weapon.

engorge bolt, devour, eat, gobble, gorge, gulp.
Ant. digest.

engrave carve, chisel, cut, grave, impress, imprint, infix, sculpture.
Ant. efface.

engross absorb, engage, engulf, forestall, monopolise, occupy.

enhance aggravate, augment, elevate, exalt, heighten, improve, increase, swell.
Ant. diminish, spoil.

enigma mystery, problem, puzzle, riddle.

enigmatical ambiguous, doubtful, equivocal, mystic, mystical, obscure, occult, perplexing, puzzling, recondite, uncertain, unintelligible.
Ant. lucid.

enjoin (1) advise, bid, command, direct, order, prescribe, require, urge; (2) (*Law*) prohibit, restrain.
Ant. of (1) submit.

enjoy like, possess, relish.
Ant. dislike.

enjoyment comfort, delectation, delight, fruition, gladness, gratification, happiness, indulgence, pleasure, possession, satisfaction.
Ant. displeasure.

enlarge (1) amplify, augment, diffuse, expand, grow, increase, magnify, multiply, stretch, swell, widen; (2) descant, dilate, expatiate.
Ant. decrease, lessen.

enlighten counsel, edify, educate, illuminate, illumine, inform, instruct, teach.
Ant. confuse.

enlist engage, enrol, list, record, register.
Ant. decline.

enliven animate, excite, exhilarate, gladden, inspire, invigorate, quicken, rouse.
Ant. depress.

enmity animosity, animus, aversion, bitterness, hate, hostility, ill-will, malevolence, malignity, rancour.
Ant. friendliness.

ennoble aggrandise, dignify, elevate, exalt, raise.
Ant. degrade.

enormity atrociousness, atrocity, depravity, disgrace, heinousness, nefariousness, outrage, outrageousness, villainy.

enormous (1) colossal, excessive, gigantic, gross, huge, immense, mammoth, monstrous; (2) atrocious, depraved, disgraceful, heinous, nefarious, outrageous, villainous, wicked.
Ant. of (1) diminutive; of (2) honourable.

enough (1) *a.* abundant, adequate, ample, plenty, sufficient; (2) *n.* abundance, plenty, sufficiency.
Ant. of (1) inadequate; of (2) scarcity.

enrage aggravate, anger, incense, exasperate, incite, inflame, infuriate, irritate, madden, provoke.
Ant. calm, soothe.

enrapture bewitch, captivate, charm, delight, enchant, entrance.
Ant. repel.

enrich adorn, aggrandise, decorate, embellish, endow, grace, ornament.
Ant. deplete.

enrol (1) engage, enlist, register; (2) chronicle, record.

ensconce conceal, cover, hide, protect, screen, shelter, shield.
Ant. uncover.

enshrine cherish, consecrate, dedicate, embalm, preserve, treasure.
Ant. desecrate.

ensign badge, banner, colours, flag, pennant, pennon, standard, streamer.

ensue accrue, arise, befall, flow, follow, issue, proceed, result, supervene.
Ant. precede.

entangle bewilder, complicate, confuse, ensnare, entrap, implicate, involve, knot, mat, perplex, puzzle, ravel.
Ant. disentangle, unravel.

enterprise (1) adventure, effort, endeavour, essay, plan, project, undertaking, venture; (2) activity, boldness, daring, dash, energy, readiness, spirit.
Ant. of (2) caution.

enterprising active, adventurous, alert, audacious, bold, daring, dashing, eager, energetic, ready, resourceful, spirited, stirring, venturesome, zealous.
Ant. cautious.

entertain (1) amuse, cheer, divert, please, recreate; (2) cherish, consider, harbour, hold, foster, lodge, maintain, support, treat.
Ant. of (1) tire; of (2) reject.

entertainment amusement, banquet, cheer, diversion, feast, festival, pastime, recreation, sport, treat.
Ant. mirthlessness.

enthusiasm ardour, devotion, earnestness, fanaticism, frenzy, passion, vehemence, warmth, zeal.
Ant. coolness.

enthusiast bigot, devotee, dreamer, (Sl.) fan, fanatic, visionary, zealot.

entice allure, attract, cajole, coax, decoy, inveigle, lure, persuade, prevail on, seduce, tempt, wheedle.
Ant. deter, repel.

enticement allurement, attraction, bait, blandishment, inducement, inveiglement, lure, persuasion, seduction.
Ant. repulsion.

entire complete, continuous, full, mere, intact, perfect, pure, thorough, unbroken, undiminished, unmitigated, unmixed, unrestricted.
Ant. partial.

entitle (1) call, characterise, christen, denominate, designate, name, style; (2) empower, fit for, qualify for.
Ant. of (2) disqualify.

entomb bury, inhume, inter.
Ant. exhume.

entrails bowels, guts, intestines, inwards, offal, viscera.

entrance (A) n. (1) access, avenue, door, doorway, entry, gate, ingress, inlet, passage, portal; (2) beginning, commencement, initiation, introduction.
Ant. of (1) egress, exit, outlet.

entrance (B) v. bewitch, captivate, charm, delight, enchant, enrapture, fascinate, ravish, transport.
Ant. repel.

entrap (1) allure, beguile, decoy, ensnare, entice, inveigle, seduce, tempt; (2) entangle.

hamper, hinder, impede, involve, obstruct, perplex.
Ant. of (2) liberate.

entreat ask, beg, beseech, crave, implore, importune, petition, pray, supplicate.
Ant. demand.

entreaty appeal, importunity, petition, prayer, request, solicitation, suit, supplication.
Ant. command.

entwine embrace, encircle, entwist, interlace, surround, twine, weave.
Ant. disentangle.

enumerate calculate, compute, count, detail, mention, number, recapitulate, reckon, relate, specify, tell.

enunciate articulate, declare, proclaim, promulgate, pronounce, propound, publish, say, speak, utter.
Ant. suppress.

envelop conceal, cover, encase, encircle, enclose, encompass, enfold, enwrap, hide, surround, wrap.
Ant. expose.

envenom aggravate, enrage, exasperate, incense, inflame, irritate, madden, poison, provoke, taint.
Ant. soothe.

environ beset, besiege, encircle, enclose, encompass, engird, envelop, gird, hem, invest, surround.

envoy ambassador, courier, legate, messenger, minister, plenipotentiary.

envy (1) n. enviousness, grudge, hatred, jealousy, ill-will, invidiousness, malice, malignity; (2) v. begrudge, covet, grudge.
Ant. disdain.

ephemeral brief, evanescent, fleeting, flitting, fugitive, momentary, short, short-lived, transient, transitory.
Ant. abiding, permanent.

epicure epicurean, gastronome, glutton, gourmand, gourmet, sensualist, sybarite, voluptuary.
Ant. ascetic.

epidemic a. general, prevailing, prevalent.

epigrammatic concise, laconic, piquant, pointed, sharp, short, terse.
Ant. diffuse, pointless.

epistle letter, missive, note.

epithet appellation, description, designation, name, title.

epitome abbreviation, abridgment, abstract, compendium, condensation, conspectus, contraction, digest, summary, syllabus, synopsis.
Ant. expansion.

epitomise abbreviate, abridge, condense, contract, curtail, cut, reduce, shorten, summarise.
Ant. expand.

epoch age, date, era, period, time.

equable even, regular, serene, smooth, steady, temperate, tranquil, uniform.
Ant. uneven, variable.

equal (1) even, regular, uniform, unvarying; (2) alike, balanced, commensurate, equivalent, like, proportionate, tantamount; (3) adequate, equable, fair, fit, just, suitable; (4) n. compeer, fellow, match, mate, peer; (5) v. equalise, even, match.
Ant. of (1) uneven; of (3) inadequate.

equanimity calmness, composure, coolness, peace, sangfroid, self-possession, serenity, steadiness.

Ant. excitability.

equestrian cavalier, horseman, knight, rider.

equip accoutre, arm, array, dress, furnish, provide, rig, supply.
Ant. divest.

equipage (1) accoutrements, apparatus, baggage, carriage, effects, turn-out, vehicle; (2) attendants, retinue, suite, train.

equipment accoutrements, apparatus, baggage, equipage, furniture, gear, outfit, paraphernalia.

equipoise balance, equilibrium.

equitable adequate, candid, fair, honest, impartial, just, proper, proportionate, reasonable, right.
Ant. unfair, unreasonable.

equity fairness, honesty, impartiality, justice, rectitude, righteousness, uprightness.
Ant. injustice, unfairness.

equivalent commensurate, equal, interchangeable, synonymous, tantamount.
Ant. unequal.

equivocal ambiguous, doubtful, dubious, indeterminate, questionable, uncertain.
Ant. certain, clear.

equivocate dodge, evade, fence, prevaricate, quibble, shuffle.
Ant. admit, confess.

equivocation evasion, prevarication, quibbling, shuffling.
Ant. admission, confession.

era age, date, epoch, period, time.

eradicate abolish, annihilate, destroy, exterminate, extirpate, uproot.
Ant. plant.

erase blot, cancel, delete, efface, expunge, obliterate.
Ant. restore.

erect (1) v. build, construct, elevate, establish, found, institute, lift, raise; (2) a. elevated, firm, standing, upright.
Ant. of (1) destroy.

erelong early, quickly, shortly, soon, speedily.

eremite anchoret, anchorite, hermit, recluse.

erode canker, consume, corrode, destroy, eat away.

err (1) blunder, deviate, go astray, misapprehend, misjudge, mistake, ramble, rove, wander; (2) fall, lapse, offend, sin, trespass, trip.
Ant. correct.

errand charge, commission, message.

erratic aberrant, abnormal, capricious, changeable, desultory, eccentric, irregular, unreliable, wandering.
Ant. steady, undeviating.

erroneous false, inaccurate, incorrect, inexact, mistaken, untrue, wrong.
Ant. correct, right.

error (1) blunder, fallacy, inaccuracy, misapprehension, oversight; (2) delinquency, fault, misdeed, offence, sin, transgression, trespass, wrong.
Ant. correction.

erudition knowledge, learning, lore, scholarship.
Ant. illiteracy.

eruption (1) discharge, explosion, outbreak, outburst, sally; (2) (*Med.*) rash.

escape (1) v. abscond, avoid, bolt, decamp, elude, evade, flee, fly, shun, slip; (2) n. avoidance, evasion, flight, passage, release.
Ant. of (1) confront.

eschew abstain, avoid, elude, shun.

escort (1) *v.* accompany, conduct, convoy, guard, guide, protect; (2) *n.* convoy, guard, guidance, guide, protection, protector, safeguard.

esculent eatable, edible, wholesome.

Ant. uneatable.

esoteric hidden, inner, mysterious, private, secret.

Ant. open.

especial chief, distinguished, marked, particular, principal, special, specific, unusual.

Ant. ordinary.

espousal (1) affiancing, betrothing, espousing, plighting; (2) (*Fig.*) adoption, defence, maintenance, support.

espouse (1) betroth, marry, wed; (2) (*Fig.*) adopt, champion, defend, maintain, support.

Ant. of (2) oppose.

espy descry, detect, discern, discover, observe, perceive, spy, watch.

essay (A) (1) *n.* aim, attempt, effort, endeavour, exertion, struggle; (2) *v.* attempt, endeavour, try.

essay (B) article, composition, dissertation, paper.

essence (1) being, entity, life, nature, quintessence; (2) extract, odour, perfume, scent.

essential (1) basic, fundamental, important, indispensable, inherent, innate, necessary, requisite, vital; (2) rectified, refined, volatile.

Ant. of (1) non-essential, superfluous.

establish (1) constitute, decree, enact, fix, found, inaugurate, install, institute, organise, plant, settle; (2)

confirm, demonstrate, prove, ratify, substantiate, verify.

Ant. of (1) destroy; of (2) disprove.

estate (1) position, quality, rank, standing, state; (2) demesne, domain, effects, fortune, lands, possessions, property.

esteem (1) *v.* admire, honour, like, love, prize, respect, revere; (2) appreciate, estimate, rate, reckon, value; (3) account, believe, consider, deem, fancy, hold, imagine, suppose, think; (4) *n.* admiration, credit, honour, regard, respect, reverence, veneration.

Ant. of (1) dislike; of (4) disregard.

estimable admirable, excellent, good, honourable, meritorious, reputable, respectable, valuable, worthy.

Ant. inferior.

estimate (1) *v.* appraise, appreciate, assess, calculate, count, evaluate, judge, number, reckon, value; (2) *n.* appraisement, calculation, estimation, judgment, valuation.

estimation appreciation, esteem, judgment, opinion, regard, respect, reverence.

Ant. disregard.

estrange alienate, destroy, disaffect, divert, withdraw, withhold.

Ant. propitiate.

estuary creek, fiord, firth, inlet, mouth.

eternal abiding, ceaseless, deathless, endless, everlasting, immortal, immutable, imperishable, indestructible, infinite, interminable, perennial, perpetual, unceasing, undying.

Ant. temporal.

ethereal aerial, airy, celestial,

delicate, empyreal, fairy, heavenly, light, refined, spiritual, tenuous, volatile.

Ant. material.

eulogise applaud, commend, extol, laud, magnify, praise.

Ant. condemn.

eulogy applause, commendation, encomium, laudation, panegyric, praise.

Ant. condemnation, disapproval.

euphonious clear, harmonious, mellifluous, mellow, melodious, musical, silvery, sweet-toned.

Ant. discordant.

evacuate (1) discharge, eject, empty, excrete, void; (2) abandon, depart, desert, forsake, leave, quit, relinquish, vacate.

Ant. of (1) fill; of (2) hold.

evade (1) avoid, decline, dodge, elude, escape, shun; (2) equivocate, hedge, prevaricate, quibble.

evanescent brief, ephemeral, fleeting, fugitive, passing, short-lived, transient, transitory.

Ant. permanent.

evaporate (1) dehydrate, dry, vaporise; (2) (*Fig.*) disappear, disperse, dissolve, fade, vanish.

Ant. of (1) condense.

evaporation (1) dehydration, drying, vaporisation; (2) disappearance, dispersal, dissolution.

Ant. of (1) condensation.

evasion artifice, avoidance, dodge, equivocation, escape, excuse, pretext, prevarication, shift, shuffling, subterfuge.

Ant. straightforwardness.

evasive elusive, elusory, equivocating, prevaricating, shuffling, slippery, sophistical.

Ant. straightforward.

even (1) flat, horizontal, level, plane, regular, smooth, steady, uniform; (2) calm, composed, equable, peaceful, placid, tranquil, undisturbed, unruffled, well-balanced; (3) equitable, fair, impartial, just; (4) *adv.* actually, exactly, just.

Ant. of (1) uneven; of (2) agitated; of (3) biased.

event (1) adventure, affair, circumstance, episode, fact, happening, incident, occurrence; (2) conclusion, consequence, effect, end, issue, outcome, result, termination.

Ant. of (1) antecedent; of (2) origin.

eventful critical, important, memorable, momentous, notable, remarkable.

Ant. ordinary, uneventful.

ever always, constantly, continually, eternally, evermore, forever, incessantly, perpetually, unceasingly.

Ant. never.

everlasting continual, deathless, endless, eternal, immortal, imperishable, incessant, indestructible, interminable, unceasing, undying, uninterrupted.

Ant. ephemeral, passing.

everyday accustomed, common, customary, habitual, usual, wonted.

evidence (1) *n.* affirmation, attestation, averment, confirmation, corroboration, declaration, deposition, grounds, indication, manifestation, proof, sign, testimony, witness; (2) *v.* manifest, prove, show, witness.

Ant. of (1) disproof; of (2) disprove.

evident apparent, clear, conspicuous, incontestable, indisputable, manifest, obvious, patent, plain, unmistakable.

Ant. doubtful, obscure.

evil (1) *a.* bad, base, corrupt, depraved, malevolent, malignant, nefarious, vile; (2) *n.* badness, baseness, corruption, curse, depravity, guilt, iniquity, malignity, sinfulness, wickedness, wrong; (3) *a.* calamitous, destructive, disastrous, harmful, inauspicious, injurious, mischievous, noxious, painful, sorrowful, woeful; (4) *n.* calamity, disaster, harm, mischief, misery, misfortune, pain, sorrow, suffering, woe.

Ant. good.

evince demonstrate, display, establish, evidence, exhibit, manifest, show.

Ant. conceal.

evolve develop, disclose, expand, open, unfold, unroll.

exacerbate aggravate, embitter, enrage, exasperate, excite, inflame, infuriate, irritate, provoke, vex.

Ant. propitiate, soothe.

exact (A) *v.* claim, compel, demand, extort, extract, force, require.

exact (B) (1) accurate, careful, correct, faithful, literal, methodical, orderly, precise, punctilious; (2) rigorous, scrupulous, severe, strict.

Ant. of (1) inaccurate; of (2) loose.

exaction contribution, extortion, oppression, rapacity, tribute.

exactness accuracy, carefulness, exactitude, faultlessness, nicety, precision, regularity, scrupulousness, strictness, truth.

Ant. carelessness, inaccuracy.

exaggerate amplify, enlarge, magnify, overestimate, overstate, strain.

Ant. minimise.

exalt (1) dignify, elevate, ennoble, promote, raise; (2) bless, extol, glorify, praise.

Ant. of (1) humiliate.

examination inquiry, inquisition, inspection, investigation, observation, research, scrutiny, search, test, trial.

examine catechise, consider, explore, inquire, inspect, interrogate, investigate, question, scrutinise, study.

example case, copy, illustration, instance, model, pattern, precedent, prototype, sample, specimen, warning.

exasperate anger, annoy, embitter, enrage, exacerbate, excite, incense, inflame, infuriate, irritate, nettle, provoke, rouse.

Ant. assuage, calm.

exasperation anger, annoyance, exacerbation, fury, ire, irritation, passion, provocation, rage, wrath.

Ant. appeasement.

excavate cut, delve, dig, hollow, scoop, trench.

exceed cap, excel, outdo, outstrip, surpass, transcend.

excel beat, eclipse, exceed, outdo, outrival, outvie, surpass.

Ant. equal.

excellence distinction, eminence, goodness, merit, perfection, purity, superiority, worth.

Ant. inferiority.

excellent admirable, choice, distinguished, estimable, exquisite, fine, first-rate, good, meritorious, noted, outstanding, prime, select, worthy.

Ant. inferior.

except (1) *v.* exclude, object,

omit, reject; **(2)** *prep.* bar, but, excepting, excluding, save.

exceptional abnormal, anomalous, irregular, peculiar, uncommon, unusual, rare, strange.
Ant. normal, usual.

excerpt (1) *v.* cite, cull, extract, quote, take; **(2)** *n.* citation, extract, quotation, selection.

excess (1) remainder, superabundance, superfluity, surplus; **(2)** debauchery, dissipation, dissoluteness, extravagance, immoderation, intemperance, over-indulgence.
Ant. of **(1)** lack; of **(2)** sobriety.

excessive (1) disproportionate, enormous, exorbitant, inordinate, superfluous, undue, unreasonable; **(2)** extreme, immoderate, intemperate.
Ant. of **(1)** reasonable; of **(2)** sober.

exchange (1) *v.* barter, change, commute, interchange, swap, trade, truck; **(2)** *n.* barter, dealing, interchange, reciprocity, trade, traffic; **(3)** bourse, market.

excision destruction, eradication, extermination, extirpation.

excitable emotional, hasty, hot-tempered, irascible, irritable, passionate, sensitive, susceptible, violent.
Ant. impassive.

excite (1) animate, arouse, awaken, incite, inflame, kindle, raise, rouse, stimulate, stir; **(2)** agitate, discompose, disturb, irritate, provoke.
Ant. calm, soothe.

excitement (1) agitation, commotion, discomposure, heat, irritation, passion, perturbation, warmth; **(2)** in-

citement, motive, stimulus.
Ant. of **(1)** calmness.

exclaim call, cry, declare, shout, utter, vociferate.

exclude (1) ban, bar, debar, except, eliminate, interdict, omit, prohibit, proscribe, veto, withhold; **(2)** eject, expel, extrude.
Ant. of **(1)** include; of **(2)** admit.

exclusive (1) debarring, excepting, excluding, restricting; **(2)** aristocratic, choice, cliquish, fashionable, limited, narrow, narrow-minded, select, selfish, snobbish.
Ant. of **(1)** inclusive; of **(2)** sociable.

excommunicate anathematise, ban, denounce, eject, exclude, expel, proscribe.
Ant. absolve.

excoriate abrade, flay, gall, scarify, skin.

excrescence (1) (*Med.*) swelling, tumour, wart; **(2)** knob, lump, prominence.

excruciate agonise, rack, torment, torture.
Ant. alleviate, comfort.

exculpate absolve, acquit, clear, discharge, exonerate, free, justify, release, vindicate.
Ant. accuse, blame.

excursion (1) expedition, jaunt, journey, outing, pilgrimage, ramble, tour, trip; **(2)** digression, episode.

excursive devious, diffusive, digressive, discursive, rambling, roaming, roving, wandering.
Ant. straightforward.

excusable forgivable, justifiable, pardonable, venial, warrantable.
Ant. inexcusable.

excuse (1) *v.* absolve, acquit,

exculpate, exonerate, extenuate, forgive, overlook, pardon; (2) v. exempt, free, liberate, release; (3) n. absolution, apology, justification, plea; (4) disguise, evasion, makeshift, pretence, pretext, semblance, subterfuge.

Ant. of (1) condemn; of (2) oblige.

execrable abominable, accursed, damnable, detestable, disgusting, hateful, loathsome, nauseous, odious, offensive, repulsive, revolting, sickening, vile.

Ant. agreeable, blessed.

execrate abhor, abominate, curse, damn, detest, hate, imprecate, loathe.

Ant. bless.

execute (1) accomplish, achieve, administer, complete, consummate, effect, finish, fulfil, perform; (2) (*Law*) seal, sign; (3) behead, electrocute, guillotine, hang.

Ant. of (1) attempt.

execution (1) accomplishment, achievement, completion, consummation, effect, operation, performance, workmanship; (2) (*Law*) warrant, writ.

exemplary commendable, correct, estimable, excellent, good, honourable, laudable, meritorious, praiseworthy, punctilious.

Ant. blameworthy, objectionable.

exemplify evidence, exhibit, illustrate, manifest, show.

exempt (1) v. absolve, except, excuse, exonerate, free, release, relieve; (2) a. absolved, excepted, excused, free, immune, liberated, privileged, released, unamenable.

Ant. of (1) oblige.

exemption absolution, dispensation, exception, freedom, immunity, privilege.

Ant. obligation.

exercise (1) n. appliance, application, enjoyment, exertion, practice, use; (2) action, activity, effort, labour, toil, work; (3) discipline, drill, drilling, lesson, schooling, task, training; (4) v. apply, employ, enjoy, exert, practise, use; (5) effect, produce, test, try; (6) afflict, annoy, burden, pain, trouble, try; (7) discipline, drill, habituate, inure, train.

Ant. of (1) disuse; of (2) laziness.

exert employ, endeavour, exercise, labour, strain, strive, struggle, toil, work.

exertion action, attempt, effort, endeavour, labour, strain, stretch, struggle, toil, trial.

Ant. inertness.

exhalation damp, effluvium, evaporation, fog, fume, mist, smoke.

exhale breathe, discharge, eject, emit, evaporate.

Ant. inhale.

exhaust (1) drain, dry, empty, strain, void; (2) cripple, debilitate, disable, enfeeble, enervate, fatigue, tire, weaken; (3) consume, dissipate, spend, squander, waste.

Ant. of (1) replenish; of (2) strengthen; of (3) economise.

exhaustion debilitation, enervation, fatigue, lassitude, weariness.

Ant. energy.

exhibit demonstrate, disclose, display, expose, express, indicate, manifest, offer, present, reveal, show.

Ant. conceal.

exhibition (1) demonstration, display, exposition, manifestation, representation, spectacle; **(2)** (*Univ.*) allowance, benefaction, scholarship.

exhilarate animate, cheer, elate, enliven, gladden, inspirit, rejoice, stimulate.

Ant. depress.

exhilaration animation, cheerfulness, gaiety, gladness, gleefulness, hilarity, joyfulness, liveliness, mirth, sprightliness.

Ant. depression.

exhort advise, caution, counsel, encourage, persuade, stimulate, urge, warn.

exhume disinter, disentomb, unbury, unearth.

Ant. inter.

exigency (1) demand, distress, necessity, need, requirement, urgency, want; **(2)** crisis, difficulty, emergency, juncture, pass, pinch, plight, quandary, strait.

exile (1) *v.* banish, expatriate, expel, ostracise, proscribe; **(2)** *n.* banishment, expatriation, expulsion, ostracism, proscription, separation.

Ant. of **(1)** repatriate.

exist abide, be, breathe, continue, endure, last, live, occur.

Ant. cease, die.

existence animation, being, breath, continuation, duration, life.

Ant. cessation, death.

exit (1) departure, egress, outlet, withdrawal; **(2)** death, decease, demise.

Ant. of **(1)** entrance.

exonerate absolve, acquit, clear, discharge, except, exculpate, exempt, free, justify, pardon, release.

Ant. condemn.

exorbitant enormous, excessive, extravagant, inordinate, unreasonable.

Ant. moderate, reasonable.

exorcise cast out, deliver, expel, purify.

exordium introduction, opening, preamble, preface, prelude, prologue.

Ant. epilogue.

exotic extraneous, foreign.

Ant. native.

expand develop, diffuse, dilate, distend, enlarge, extend, increase, inflate, stretch, unfold, widen.

Ant. contract.

expansion development, diffusion, dilatation, distension, enlargement, expanse, increase, inflation, swelling, unfolding.

Ant. contraction.

expatiate amplify, dilate, enlarge, range, rove.

Ant. abridge.

expatriate banish, exile, expel, ostracise, proscribe.

Ant. repatriate.

expect anticipate, await, calculate, forecast, foresee, hope, reckon, rely.

expectation anticipation, confidence, expectancy, foresight, hope, prospect, reliance, trust.

Ant. realisation.

expedient (1) *a.* advantageous, advisable, appropriate, convenient, desirable, fit, profitable, proper, suitable, useful; **(2)** *n.* contrivance, device, means, method, resort, resource, scheme, shift, substitute.

Ant. of **(1)** inadvisable.

expedite accelerate, advance, despatch, forward, hasten, hurry, precipitate, press, quicken, urge.

Ant. delay.

expedition (1) celerity, despatch, haste, hurry, quickness, speed; (2) enterprise, excursion, safari, trip, undertaking, voyage.

Ant. of (1) slowness.

expeditious active, alert, diligent, hasty, nimble, prompt, quick, ready, speedy, swift.

Ant. slow.

expel banish, discharge, dislodge, dismiss, eject, exclude, exile, expatriate, oust, remove.

Ant. accept.

expend consume, disburse, dissipate, employ, exhaust, spend, use, waste.

Ant. save.

expenditure charge, cost, disbursement, expense, outlay.

Ant. income.

expensive costly, dear, extravagant, high-priced, lavish, wasteful.

Ant. cheap, inexpensive.

experience (1) v. encounter, endure, feel, suffer, try, undergo; (2) n. endurance, evidence, knowledge, practice, proof, test, testimony, trial.

Ant of (2) inexperience.

experiment (1) n. assay, examination, investigation, procedure, proof, research, test, trial; (2) v. examine, investigate, test, try.

expert (1) a. adroit, apt, clever, dexterous, handy, facile, prompt, quick, ready, skilful; (2) n. authority, master, specialist.

Ant. of (1) maladroit.

expertness adroitness, aptness, dexterity, facility, promptness, skilfulness, skill.

expiate atone, satisfy.

expiration (1) cessation, close, conclusion, end, termination; (2) death, decease, demise, departure.

Ant. of (1) beginning.

expire (1) cease, close, conclude, end, stop, terminate; (2) emit, exhale; (3) depart, die, perish.

Ant. of (1) begin.

explain clarify, define, disclose, elucidate, expound, illustrate, interpret, justify, solve, teach, unfold.

Ant. confirm.

explanation (1) clarification, definition, description, elucidation, exposition, illustration, interpretation; (2) account, answer, detail, justification, meaning, recital, sense.

explicit absolute, categorical, clear, definite, exact, express, plain, positive, precise, unambiguous, unequivocal, unreserved.

Ant. ambiguous, vague.

explode (1) burst, detonate, discharge, displode, shatter, shiver; (2) contemn, discard, repudiate, scorn.

exploit (1) n. accomplishment, achievement, adventure, deed, feat; (2) v. befool, use, utilise.

explore examine, inquire, inspect, investigate, prospect, scrutinise, seek.

explosion blast, burst, clap, crack, detonation, discharge, displosion.

exponent (1) example, illustration, indication, specimen, type; (2) commentator, demonstrator, elucidator, expounder, illustrator, interpreter.

expose (1) bare, display, exhibit, reveal, show, uncover; (2) betray, denounce, detect, disclose, unmask; (3) endanger, imperil, jeopardise, risk.

Ant. of (1) and (2) conceal.

exposition (1) demonstration, display, exhibition, show; (2) commentary, critique, elucidation, explanation, illustration, interpretation.

expound elucidate, explain, illustrate, interpret, unfold.

Ant. obscure.

express (1) v. assert, asseverate, declare, say, speak, utter; (2) denote, designate, exhibit, indicate, intimate, represent, show, signify, testify; (3) a. accurate, clear, definite, distinct, exact, explicit, plain, precise, unambiguous; (4) special, particular; (5) fast, nonstop, quick, rapid, speedy, swift.

Ant. of (1) conceal; of (3) vague; of (5) slow.

expression (1) assertion, asseveration, declaration, statement, utterance; (2) language, phrase, remark, speech, term, word; (3) air, aspect, countenance, look, mien.

expressive (1) emphatic, energetic, forcible, lively, striking, strong, telling, vivid; (2) indicative, significant, suggestive; (3) appropriate, modulated, sympathetic.

Ant. of (1) dull, expressionless.

expulsion banishment, discharge, dismissal, dismission, ejection, exclusion, extrusion.

expunge annihilate, annul, cancel, delete, destroy, efface, erase, obliterate.

Ant. insert, restore.

expurgate clean, cleanse, purge, purify.

exquisite admirable, beauti-

ful, charming, choice, consummate, delicate, elegant, excellent, fine, matchless, perfect, polished, rare, refined, select.

Ant. common, unrefined.

extant existent, existing, surviving, undestroyed.

Ant. extinct.

extempore extemporaneous, extemporary, impromptu, improvised, off-hand, unpremeditated, unprepared.

Ant. prepared.

extend (1) augment, continue, dilate, enlarge, expand, increase, lengthen, prolong, protract, stretch, widen; (2) give, grant, offer, yield.

Ant. of (1) shorten.

extension augmentation, continuation, delay, dilatation, distension, enlargement, expansion, increase, prolongation, protraction.

extensive broad, capacious, comprehensive, expanded, extended, large, wide.

Ant. confined.

extent amount, amplitude, area, bulk, compass, expanse, expansion, length, magnitude, measure, reach, size, stretch, width, volume.

extenuate diminish, excuse, lessen, mitigate, palliate, qualify, reduce, underrate, soften, weaken.

Ant. increase.

exterior (1) a. external, outer, outside, superficial; (2) n. outside, surface.

Ant. interior.

exterminate abolish, annihilate, destroy, eliminate, eradicate, extirpate.

Ant. originate.

external (1) exterior, outer, outside, outward, superficial;

(2) extrinsic, foreign; (3) apparent, visible.

Ant. of (1) and (2) internal.

extinction abolition, annihilation, destruction, eradication, excision, extermination, extirpation.

extinguish abolish, annihilate, destroy, eradicate, exterminate, extirpate, kill, obscure, put out, quench, suppress.

Ant. kindle, light, secure.

extirpate abolish, annihilate, destroy, eradicate, exterminate, uproot.

Ant. establish.

extol applaud, celebrate, commend, eulogise, exalt, glorify, laud, magnify.

Ant. condemn, damn.

extort exact, extract, squeeze, wrench, wrest, wring.

extortion compulsion, demand, exaction, exorbitance, oppression, rapacity.

extortionate exacting, exorbitant, hard, harsh, oppressive, rapacious, rigorous, severe.

Ant. moderate, reasonable.

extract (1) v. draw, extort, pull, take; (2) derive, distil, draw, express, squeeze; (3) cite, determine, quote, select; (4) n. decoction, distillation, essence; (5) citation, excerpt, passage, quotation, selection.

Ant. of (1) insert.

extraction (1) drawing, pulling; (2) derivation, distillation; (3) birth, descent, lineage, origin, parentage.

extraneous additional, adventitious, external, extrinsic, foreign, superfluous, supplementary, unessential.

Ant. essential, intrinsic.

extraordinary exceptional, marvellous, particular, peculiar, rare, remarkable, singular, strange, uncommon, unprecedented, unusual, unwonted, wonderful.

Ant. ordinary, usual.

extravagance (1) dissipation, excess, lavishness, prodigality, profusion, recklessness, waste, wastefulness; (2) absurdity, folly, preposterousness, unreasonableness, wildness.

Ant. of (1) economy; of (2) reasonableness.

extravagant (1) excessive, exorbitant, immoderate, inordinate, prodigal, wasteful; (2) absurd, foolish, preposterous, unreasonable, wild.

Ant. of (1) economical; of (2) reasonable.

extreme (1) farthest, final, greatest, last, ultimate, utmost, uttermost; (2) excessive, immoderate, unreasonable; (3) n. climax, edge, end, extremity, termination, top.

Ant. of (1) initial; of (2) reasonable; of (3) beginning.

extremity border, boundary, end, extreme, terminal, termination, verge.

Ant. beginning.

extricate clear, deliver, disengage, disentangle, free, liberate, release, relieve.

Ant. entangle.

extrinsic external, extraneous, foreign, outside, superficial.

exuberance abundance, copiousness, excess, lavishness, luxuriance, profusion, superabundance, superfluity.

Ant. scarcity.

exuberant abundant, copious, excessive, lavish, luxuriant, plenteous, profuse, rich, superabundant.

Ant. scarce.

exult rejoice, triumph, taunt, vaunt.
Ant. grieve.

exultation delight, elation, joy, jubilation, transport, triumph.
Ant. depression, grief.

F

fable (1) allegory, apologue, legend, myth, parable story, tale; (2) fabrication, falsehood, fiction, figment, invention, lie, untruth.
Ant. of (2) truth.

fabric (1) building, edifice, pile, structure; (2) cloth, texture.

fabricate (1) build, construct, erect, frame, make, manufacture; (2) coin, fake, feign, forge, form, invent.
Ant. of (1) destroy.

fabrication (1) building, construction, erection, manufacture; (2) fable, fake, falsehood, fiction, figment, forgery, invention, lie.

fabulous amazing, fabricated, false, fictitious, forged, imaginary, incredible, invented, legendary, mythical, unbelievable, unreal.
Ant. real.

face (1) appearance, aspect, countenance, expression, look, prestige, reputation, visage; (2) assurance, audacity, boldness, confidence, effrontery, impudence; (3) cover, exterior, front, surface; (4) v. confront, encounter, meet, oppose; (5) coat, cover, level, veneer.
Ant. of (2) shyness.

facetious amusing, comical, droll, funny, humorous, jocose, jocular, merry, pleasant, waggish, witty.

Ant. dull, sad.

facile (1) affable, complaisant, courteous, docile, easy, flexible, manageable, mild, tractable, yielding; (2) dexterous, easy, fluent, ready, skilful.
Ant. of (1) difficult, intractable; of (2) clumsy.

facilitate ease, expedite, help.
Ant. hinder.

facility (1) ability adroitness, dexterity, ease, expertness, knack, quickness, readiness; (2) advantage, convenience, means, opportunity, resource; (3) affability, civility, complaisance, politness.
Ant. of (1) clumsiness.

fact (1) act, deed, event, incident, occurrence, performance; (2) certainty, truth, reality.
Ant. of (2) fiction.

faction (1) cabal, clique, coalition, combination, confederacy, group, junta, party, set; (2) disagreement, discord, dissension, rebellion, recalcitration, sedition, tumult, turbulence.
Ant. of (2) agreement.

factious litigious, malcontent, rebellious, refractory, seditious, tumultous, turbulent.
Ant. harmonious.

factitious artful, artificial, conventional, unnatural, unreal.
Ant. natural.

faculty (1) ability, adroitness, aptitude, capacity, cleverness, dexterity, facility, knack, readiness, skill, talent, turn; (2) body, craft, department, profession; (3) (*Law*) licence, prerogative, privilege, right.

fade blanch, blench, change, decline, disappear, disperse, droop dwindle, fail, fall, languish, pale, perish, vanish, wither.

Ant. flourish, last.

fail (1) cease, decline, disappear, dwindle, fade, sink, wane, weaken; (2) desert, disappoint, forget, forsake; (3) fall, miscarry, miss.

Ant. of (3) succeed.

failing defect, deficiency, error, failure, fault, foible, frailty, lapse, miscarriage, misfortune, shortcoming, weakness.

Ant. success.

failure (1) breakdown, decay, decline, default, deficiency, loss, miscarriage, neglect, non-observance, non-success, omission, shortcoming; (2) bankruptcy, downfall, insolvency, ruin.

Ant. of (1) success.

fain (1) a. anxious, eager, glad, well-pleased; (2) adv. cheerfully, eagerly, gladly, willingly.

Ant. of (2) unwillingly.

faint (1) v. fade, fail, languish, swoon, weaken; (2) a. drooping, exhausted, fatigued, feeble, languid, weak; (3) dim, dull, ill-defined, indistinct, slight.

Ant. of (2) strong; of (3) clear.

fair (1) blond, clean, clear, light, unblemished, unspotted, untarnished, white; (2) candid, equitable, frank, honest, impartial, unbiased, upright; (3) mediocre, middling, passable, promising, tolerable; (4) attractive, beautiful, comely, handsome, pretty; (5) bright, clear, cloudless, dry, unclouded; (6) distinct, open, plain, unobstructed.

Ant. of (1) dark; of (2) biased, unfair; of (3) good (or poor); of (5) cloudy.

faith (1) assurance, confidence, credence, credit, reliance, trust;

(2) belief, creed, doctrine, dogma, persuasion, religion, tenet; (3) constancy, faithfulness, fidelity, loyalty, truth, truthfulness.

Ant. of (1) distrust.

faithful (1) attached, constant, dependable, devoted, loyal, reliable, staunch, steadfast, truthful; (2) accurate, exact, strict, true.

Ant. of (1) unfaithful.

faithless disloyal, doubting, false, perfidious, treacherous, unbelieving, unreliable, untrustworthy, untrue.

Ant. faithful, loyal.

fall (1) v. abate, decline, decrease, descend, drop, ebb, sink, subside, tumble; (2) err, lapse, offend, sin, transgress, trespass; (3) die, perish; (4) become, befall, chance, happen, occur, pass; (5) n. descent, drop, tumble; (6) collapse, death, destruction, downfall, ruin, surrender; (7) degradation, failure, lapse, sin, slip, transgression; (8) cascade, cataract, waterfall; (9) declivity, slope.

Ant. of (1) and (3) ascend, rise.

fallacious deceptive, delusive, erroneous, false, fictitious, illusory, incorrect, misleading, untrue.

Ant. true.

fallacy deceit, deception, delusion, error, falsehood, illusion, misconception, mistake, sophistry, untruth.

Ant. truth.

fallible erring, frail, ignorant, imperfect, uncertain, weak.

Ant. infallible.

fallow dormant, idle, inactive, inert, neglected, uncultivated, untilled.

false (1) lying, mendacious, truthless, unreliable, untrue, untrustworthy, untruthful; (2) dishonest, dishonourable, disloyal, faithless, perfidious, treacherous; (3) erroneous, improper, incorrect, unfounded, wrong; (4) deceitful, deceiving, deceptive, delusive, hypocritical, misleading; (5) counterfeit, feigned, forged, sham, spurious.

Ant. genuine, true.

falsehood deception, fabrication, (*Colloq.*) fib, fiction, lie, mendacity, untruth.

Ant. truth.

falsify alter, belie, (*Sl.*) cook, counterfeit, fake, garble, misrepresent, misstate.

falter fail, hesitate, stammer, stumble, stutter, totter, tremble, vacillate, waver.

fame celebrity, credit, eminence, glory, honour, notoriety, renown, reputation, repute.

Ant. dishonour, disrepute.

familiar (1) accustomed, affable, amicable, close, cordial, easy, free, friendly, informal, intimate, near, over-free, presuming, unceremonious, unconstrained, well-known; (2) common, domestic, domiciliary, household; (3) conversant; (4) *n.* acquaintance, associate, intimate.

Ant. of (1) unfriendly.

familiarise accustom, habituate, inure, train, use.

familiarity acquaintance, closeness, disrespect, fellowship, friendliness, friendship, informality, intercourse, intimacy, liberty, over-freedom, presumption, sociability, understanding.

Ant. unfamiliarity.

family (1) ancestors, clan, descent, genealogy, house, household, kindred, lineage, race, tribe; (2) class, genus, group, kind, sub-division.

Ant. of (2) individual.

famine dearth, destitution, hunger, scarcity, starvation.

Ant. plenty.

famous celebrated, conspicuous, distinguished, eminent, excellent, glorious, honoured, illustrious, notable, noted, notorious, remarkable, renowned, signal.

Ant. undistinguished.

fan *v.* (1) agitate, blow, excite, increase, rouse, stimulate; (2) cool, refresh, ventilate.

Ant. of (1) calm.

fanatic *n.* bigot, devotee, enthusiast, visionary, zealot.

fanatical bigoted, enthusiastic, frenzied, mad, rabid, visionary, wild, zealous.

Ant. apathetic.

fanciful capricious, chimerical, fantastic, ideal, imaginary, imaginative, unreal, visionary, whimsical, wild.

Ant. practical.

fancy (1) *v.* believe, conceive, desire, imagine, like, think, wish; (2) *n.* conception, idea, image, imagination, impression, notion, thought; (3) fondness, inclination, liking, preference; (4) caprice, crotchet, fantasy, humour, whim; (5) *a.* decorated, elegant, extravagant, fanciful, ornamental, whimsical.

fang claw, nail, talon, tooth, tusk.

fantastic capricious, chimerical, fanciful, grotesque, imaginative, odd, queer, unreal, visionary, whimsical, wild.

Ant. realistic.

farcical absurd, amusing,

comic, diverting, droll, funny, laughable, ludicrous, ridiculous.

Ant. sad, tragic.

fare (1) *v.* feed, live, manage, subsist; (2) go, travel; (3) *n.* eatables, food, provisions, rations, victuals; (4) passenger, traveller; (5) charge, passage-money, price, ticket-money.

farewell adieu, departure, good-bye, leave-taking, valediction.

Ant. welcome.

farrago hodge-podge, hotch-potch, jumble, medley, miscellany, mixture.

fascinate allure, bewitch, captivate, charm, delight, enamour, entrance, infatuate.

Ant. repel.

fascination attraction, charm, enchantment, incantation, magic, sorcery, spell.

Ant. disenchantment.

fashion (1) appearance, cut, figure, form, make, model, mould, pattern; (2) convention, craze, custom, mode, style, usage, vogue; (3) manner, method, way; (4) (*Arch.*) gentry, quality; (5) *v.* construct, form, make, mould, shape; (6) accommodate, adapt, adjust, suit.

fashionable current, customary, genteel, modern, prevailing, stylish, up-to-date, usual, well-bred.

Ant. dowdy.

fast (1) *a.* fleet, quick, rapid, speedy, swift; (2) *adv.* quickly, rapidly, swiftly; (3) *a.* constant, firm, fixed, fortified, immovable, impregnable, secure, sound; (4) *adv.* firmly, securely; (5) *a.* dissipated, dissolute, extravagant, gay, reckless,

wild; (6) *adv.* extravagantly, recklessly, wildly.

Ant. of (1) slow; of (3) loose; of (5) sober.

fasten (1) attach, bind, bolt, chain, connect, fix, join, link, secure, tie, unite; (2) (*Naut.*) belay, bend.

Ant. of (1) unfix.

fastidious critical, dainty, difficult, finical, hypercritical, meticulous, over-nice, particular, punctilious, squeamish.

Ant. indifferent.

fat (1) corpulent, fleshy, obese, plump, portly, stout; (2) fatty, greasy, oily; (3) fertile, fruitful, lucrative, productive, rich.

Ant. of (1) lean, thin; of (3) poor.

fatal (1) baleful, baneful, calamitous, catastrophic, deadly, destructive, lethal, mortal; (2) destined, doomed, foreordained, inevitable, predestined.

Ant. of (1) harmless; of (2) unordained.

fate chance, death, destiny, destruction, doom, end, fortune, lot.

fatherly (*Fig.*) benign, kind, paternal, protecting, protective, tender.

Ant. harsh.

fathom comprehend, divine, estimate, gauge, measure, penetrate, plumb, probe, sound.

fathomless abysmal, bottomless, deep, profound, unfathomable.

Ant. shallow.

fatigue (1) *v.* exhaust, (*Colloq.*) fag, jade, tire, weaken, weary; (2) *n.* exhaustion, hardship, labour, lassitude, toil, weakness, weariness.

Ant. rest.

fatuity absurdity, folly, foolishness, idiocy, imbecility, infatuation, madness, stupidity.

Ant. sense.

fatuous absurd, dense, dull, foolish, idiotic, infatuated, mad, silly, stupid, weak, witless.

Ant. sensible.

fault (1) blemish, defect, failing, flaw, imperfection, weakness; (2) blunder, error, mistake, omission, slip; (3) delinquency, lapse, misdemeanour, misdeed, offence, sin, transgression, trespass, wrong.

Ant. of (1) merit; of (2) correctness; of (3) goodness.

faultless (1) accurate, correct, perfect, unblemished; (2) blameless, guiltless, immaculate, innocent, pure, sinless, spotless, stainless, unsullied.

Ant. of (1) imperfect; of (2) sinful.

faulty bad, blamable, culpable, defective, erroneous, imperfect, incorrect, wrong.

Ant. correct.

favour (1) aid, approve, assist, befriend, countenance, encourage, facilitate, help, patronise, support; (2) ease, extenuate, indulge, spare; (3) n. benefit, boon, friendliness, goodwill, grace, kindness, patronage, support; (4) communication, epistle, letter; (5) gift, love-token, present; (6) leave, pardon, permission; (7) decoration, knot, ribbons, rosette.

Ant. of (1) disapprove.

favourable (1) advantageous, auspicious, beneficial, convenient, fit, suitable; (2) fond, friendly, kind, well-disposed.

Ant. of (1) useless; of (2) unfriendly.

favourite (1) n. beloved, darling, dear, pet; (2) esteemed, preferred.

fealty allegiance, devotion, faithfulness, fidelity, homage, loyalty, obeisance, submission.

Ant. treachery.

fear (1) n. alarm, apprehension, awe, consternation, dismay, dread, fright, horror, panic; (2) anxiety, concern, solicitude; (3) awe, reverence, veneration; (4) v. apprehend, dread; (5) revere, reverence, venerate.

Ant. of (1) courage; of (2) unconcern; of (3) irreverence.

fearful (1) afraid, alarmed, apprehensive, diffident, faint-hearted, nervous, pusillanimous, shrinking, timid, timorous; (2) awful, distressing, dreadful, frightful, ghastly, horrible, shocking, terrible.

Ant. of (1) courageous.

fearless bold, brave, courageous, daring, dauntless, doughty, gallant, heroic, intrepid, valiant, valorous.

Ant. timid.

feasible achievable, attainable, possible, practicable.

Ant. impracticable.

feast (1) banquet, carousal, entertainment, repast, revels, treat; (2) celebration, festival, fête, holiday; (3) delight, enjoyment, pleasure; (4) v. delight, gladden, gratify, rejoice.

Ant. of (1) fast; of (4) disappoint.

feat accomplishment, achievement, act, deed, exploit, performance.

Ant. failure.

feature appearance, aspect, characteristic, conformation, lineament, mark, outline, peculiarity, property, trait.

fecundity fertility, fruitfulness, productiveness.
Ant. barrenness.

federation alliance, coalition, combination, co-partnership, confederacy, entente, federacy, league, union.
Ant. separation.

fee account, bill, charge, compensation, hire, pay, recompense, remuneration, reward.

feeble debilitated, enervated, exhausted, faint, frail, infirm, languid, powerless, sickly, weak.
Ant. strong.

feed (1) v. cherish, eat, nourish, subsist, supply, sustain; (2) n. fodder, food, forage, provender.
Ant. of (1) starve.

feel (1) handle, touch; (2) prove, sound, test, try; (3) enjoy, experience, suffer.

feeling (1) perception, sensation, sense, touch; (2) affection, emotion, passion, sensibility, sentiment, sentimentality, sympathy; (3) consciousness, impression, notion, sense.

feign affect, assume, counterfeit, devise, dissemble, fabricate, forge, imagine, imitate, pretend, sham, simulate.

felicitate compliment, congratulate.
Ant. condole.

felicity (1) blessedness, bliss, blissfulness, happiness, joy; (2) appropriateness, aptness, propriety, suitableness.
Ant. of (1) misfortune.

fell (A) v. cut, demolish, hew, level, prostrate.

fell (B) a. barbarous, bloody, cruel, ferocious, fierce, implacable, inhuman, malicious, malignant, merciless, pitiless, relentless, ruthless, sanguinary, savage.

Ant. gentle, mild.

fellow associate, companion, compeer, comrade, counterpart, equal, friend, mate, member, partner, peer.
Ant. stranger.

fellowship affability, association, brotherhood, communion, companionship, familiarity, intercourse, intimacy, kindliness, sociability.
Ant. animosity.

felon convict, criminal, culprit, delinquent, malefactor, outlaw.
Ant. well-doer.

felonious atrocious, cruel, heinous, infamous, malicious, malignant, nefarious, perfidious, vicious, villainous.
Ant. kind.

feminine (1) affectionate, delicate, gentle, graceful, modest, soft, tender, womanish, womanly; (2) effeminate, unmanly, weak.
Ant. of (2) manly.

fen bog, marsh, moor, morass, quagmire, slough, swamp.

fence (1) n. barrier, defence, guard, hedge, paling, palisade, rampart, security, shield, wall; (2) v. circumscribe, defend, enclose, fortify, guard, protect, surround.
Ant. of (2) uncover.

ferment (1) v. boil, brew, bubble, concoct, heat, seethe; (2) n. barm, leaven, yeast; (3) v. (Fig.) agitate, excite, heat; (4) (Fig.) agitation, commotion, excitement, fever, glow, heat.
Ant. of (3) calm, soothe.

ferocious (1) fierce, rapacious, savage, untamed, violent, wild; (2) barbarous, brutal, cruel, inhuman, merciless, pitiless, relentless, ruthless.
Ant. of (1) tame; of (2) gentle.

ferocity barbarity, cruelty, ferociousness, fierceness, inhumanity, rapacity, savageness, wildness.

Ant. gentleness.

fertile abundant, fruitful, luxuriant, plenteous, plentiful, productive, prolific, rich.

Ant. barren, sterile.

fervent animated, ardent, eager, earnest, enthusiastic, excited, impassioned, vehement, warm, zealous.

Ant. cool.

fervour animation, ardour, eagerness, earnestness, excitement, intensity, vehemence, warmth, zeal.

Ant. coolness.

fester corrupt, decay, suppurate, ulcerate.

festival (1) anniversary, feast, fête, holiday; (2) banquet, carousal, celebration, entertainment, treat.

festive convivial, festal, gay, gleeful, happy, jolly, jovial, joyous, merry, mirthful.

Ant. sad.

festivity conviviality, festival, gaiety, joviality, joyfulness, merrymaking, mirth.

Ant. sadness.

fetch bring, carry, convey, get, perform, reach.

fetid corrupt, foul, malodorous, noisome, noxious, offensive, rancid, stinking.

Ant. pure.

fetter (1) *n.* bond, chain, clog, shackle; (2) *v.* bind, chain, confine, encumber, hamper, restrain, shackle, tie, trammel.

Ant. of (2) untie.

feud argument, broil, contention, discord, dissension, enmity, grudge, hostility, quarrel, strife, vendetta.

Ant. accord.

fever (*Fig.*) agitation, excitement, ferment, fervour, flush, heat, passion.

Ant. calmness.

fibre (1) filament, pile, staple, texture, thread; (2) (*Fig.*) stamina, strength, toughness.

Ant. of (2) weakness.

fickle capricious, changeable, fitful, inconstant, irresolute, mercurial, unstable, unsteady, vacillating, variable, volatile.

Ant. steadfast.

fiction (1) fable, legend, myth, novel, romance, story, tale; (2) fabrication, falsehood, fancy, fantasy, imagination, invention.

Ant. fact.

fictitious artificial, counterfeit, false, fanciful, feigned, imagined, invented, spurious, unreal, untrue.

Ant. genuine.

fidelity (1) allegiance, devotion, faithfulness, fealty, integrity, loyalty, trustworthiness; (2) accuracy, closeness, exactness, preciseness.

Ant. of (1) disloyalty; of (2) inaccuracy.

fidget chafe, fret, twitch, worry.

fidgety impatient, restless, uneasy.

Ant. patient.

fiendish atrocious, cruel, demoniac, devilish, diabolical, hellish, implacable, infernal, malevolent, malicious, malignant.

Ant. angelic.

fierce barbarous, brutal, cruel, ferocious, fiery, furious, passionate, savage, truculent, untamed, violent.

Ant. tame.

fiery ardent, burning, fervent, fervid, fierce, flaming, glowing,

fig 136 **fin**

heated, impetuous, irritable, passionate.

Ant. cool.

fight (1) v. battle, combat, conflict, contend, engage, strive, struggle, war; (2) n. action, affray, battle, brawl, combat, conflict, contest, dispute, duel, encounter, engagement, fray, mêlée, riot, skirmish, struggle, war.

figment fable, fabrication, falsehood, fiction, invention.

Ant. fact.

figurative (1) emblematical, metaphorical, representative, symbolical, typical; (2) florid, flowery, ornate, poetical.

Ant. of (1) straightforward; of (2) plain.

filament fibre, pile, staple, strand, string, thread.

filch abstract, (*Colloq.*) crib, pilfer, purloin, rob, steal, thieve.

file (A) v. burnish, furbish, polish, rasp, refine, smooth.

Ant. dull.

file (B) n. column, line, list, row.

filibuster (1) adventurer, buccaneer, freebooter, pirate, sea-robber, sea-rover; (2) (*U.S.A.*) obstructionist.

fill (1) furnish, glut, gorge, pervade, replenish, satiate, satisfy, stock, store, stuff, supply, swell; (2) engage, fulfil, hold, occupy, officiate, perform.

Ant. of (1) empty.

film coating, layer, membrane, pellicle, skin, thread.

filter clarify, exude, filtrate, leak, ooze, percolate, purify, strain.

filth corruption, defilement, dirt, foulness, grossness, impurity, nastiness, obscurity,

pollution, pornography, uncleanness.

Ant. cleanliness.

filthy (1) dirty, foul, impure, licentious, nasty, obscene, pornographic, unclean, vile; (2) miry, muddy.

Ant. clean.

final conclusive, decisive, definitive, eventual, last, latest, terminal, ultimate.

Ant. primary.

find (1) attain, get, obtain, procure; (2) discover, experience, notice, observe, perceive, remark; (3) contribute, furnish, provide, supply.

Ant. lose.

fine (A) (1) admirable, beautiful, choice, elegant, excellent, exquisite, nice, select, showy, splendid, superior; (2) little, minute, slender, small, tenuous, thin; (3) clear, pure, refined, unadulterated; (4) acute, critical, keen, sharp.

Ant. of (1) inferior; of (2) thick; of (3) unrefined; of (4) blunt.

fine (B) (1) v. amerce, mulct, penalise, punish; (2) n. amercement, forfeit, penalty, punishment.

finery decorations, gewgaws, ornaments, splendour, showiness, trappings, trinkets.

finesse artifice, craft, cunning, manoeuvre, ruses, stratagems, tricks, wiles.

finger handle, manipulate, play, touch.

finical critical, dainty, fastidious, over-particular, scrupulous, squeamish.

Ant. careless, indifferent.

finish (1) v. accomplish, achieve, close, complete, conclude, do, end, execute, terminate; (2) n. close, completion, conclusion, end, termination; (3) v. elaborate, perfect, polish; (4) n. elaboration, perfection, polish.

Ant. of (1) begin; of (2) beginning.

finite bounded, circumscribed, conditioned, restricted.

Ant. unbounded.

fire (1) v. ignite, kindle, light; (2) discharge, eject, hurl; (3) (*Fig.*) animate, excite, inflame, irritate, rouse; (4) n. blaze, combustion, conflagration; (5) (*Fig.*) animation, ardour, enthusiasm, excitement, fervour, heat, impetuosity, intensity, light, lustre, passion, radiance, spirit, splendour, vigour, vivacity.

Ant. of (5) coldness, coolness.

firm (1) compact, compressed, dense, hard; (2) constant, fast, fixed, resolute, robust, secure, settled, steadfast, steady, strong, sturdy; (3) n. (*Comm.*) association, business, company, concern, corporation, house.

Ant. of (1) soft; of (2) unstable.

firmament heavens, sky, vault, welkin.

firmness (1) compactness, fixedness, hardness, solidity; (2) constancy, soundness, stability, steadfastness, steadiness, strength.

Ant. of (1) softness; of (2) instability.

first (1) chief, foremost, highest, leading, principal; (2) earliest, elementary, original, primeval, primitive, primordial, pristine, rudimentary.

Ant. of (1) least; of (2) secondary.

fissure breach, break, chasm, chink, crack, cranny, crevice,

gap, hole, interstice, opening, rent, rift.

fit (1) a. adequate, appropriate, apt, becoming, competent, convenient, expedient, fitted, fitting, meet, qualified, seemly; (2) v. adapt, adjust, conform, suit; (3) accommodate, equip, prepare, provide; (4) n. (*Med.*) convulsion, paroxysm, spasm; (5) n. fancy, humour, whim.

fitful capricious, changeable, desultory, fanciful, fickle, impulsive, irregular, spasmodic, unstable, variable, whimsical.

Ant. constant, steady.

fitness adaptation, appropriateness, aptness, pertinence, preparedness, propriety, qualification, seemliness, suitability.

Ant. unfitness.

fix (1) establish, locate, place, plant, root, set, settle; (2) attach, bind, connect, fasten, secure, tie; (3) appoint, define, determine, limit; (4) correct, mend, repair; (5) congeal, solidify, stiffen; (6) n. difficulty, dilemma, plight, predicament.

Ant. of (2) detach.

flabbergasted abashed, amazed, astonished, astounded, confounded, disconcerted, dumbfounded, nonplussed.

flaccid drooping, flabby, lax, limp, loose, soft, weak.

Ant. firm, tight.

flag (A) v. decline, droop, fall, fail, faint, languish, pine, sink, succumb, weaken, weary.

Ant. strengthen.

flag (B) n. banner, colours, ensign, pennant, pennon, standard, streamer.

flagellate beat, castigate, chastise, flog, scourge, thrash, whip.

flagitious abandoned, atrocious, corrupt, flagrant, heinous, infamous, monstrous, nefarious, profligate, scandalous, vile, villainous, wicked.
Ant. decent.

flagrant atrocious, awful, dreadful, enormous, flagitious, glaring, heinous, notorious, scandalous.
Ant. mild.

flake lamina, layer, scale.

flame (1) v. blaze, burn, flash, glow, shine; (2) n. blaze, brightness, fire; (3) (Fig.) affection, ardour, enthusiasm, fervour, fire, keenness, warmth; (4) (Sl.) sweetheart.
Ant. of (3) coolness.

flap (1) v. beat, flutter, shake, vibrate, wave; (2) n. beating, shaking, swinging, waving.

flare (1) v. blaze, dazzle, flicker, flutter, glare, waver; (2) n. blaze, dazzle, flame, glare.

flash (1) v. blaze, glare, gleam, glisten, light, sparkle; (2) n. (Colloq.) instant, moment, twinkling.

flashy gaudy, gay, ostentatious, showy, tawdry.
Ant. quiet.

flat (1) even, horizontal, level, low, plane, prostrate, smooth; (2) dead, dull, insipid, lifeless, prosaic, spiritless, stale, uninteresting, vapid; (3) absolute, direct, downright, peremptory, positive; (4) n. lowland, plain, shallow, shoal, strand; (5) apartment, floor, lodging, storey; (6) (Arch.) fool, ninny, simpleton.
Ant. of (1) uneven, upright.

flatter blandish, cajole, compliment, court, entice, fawn, humour, inveigle, praise, wheedle.
Ant. offend.

flattery adulation, (Colloq.) blarney, blandishment, cajolery, fawning, obsequiousness, servility, sycophancy, toadyism.
Ant. sincerity.

flaunt boast, display, disport, flourish, parade, sport, vaunt.

flavour aroma, odour, relish, savour, seasoning, smack, taste, zest.
Ant. tastelessness.

flaw (1) blemish, defect, fault, imperfection, speck, spot; (2) breach, break, cleft, crack, crevice, fissure, fracture, rent, rift.
Ant. of (1) merit.

flay excoriate, skin.

fleck (1) v. dapple, speckle, spot, streak, variegate; (2) n. speckle, spot, streak.

flee abscond, avoid, decamp, depart, escape, fly, leave, shun.
Ant. pursue.

fleece (1) clip, shear; (2) (Fig.) despoil, plunder, rifle, rob, steal.

fleet (A) a. nimble, quick, rapid, speedy, swift.
Ant. slow.

fleet (B) n. armada, flotilla, navy, squadron.

fleeting brief, ephemeral, evanescent, flitting, fugitive, temporary, transient, transitory.
Ant. long-lived.

fleetness celerity, nimbleness, quickness, rapidity, speed, swiftness, velocity.
Ant. slowness.

flesh (1) body, food, meat; (2) carnality, sensuality; (3) kindred, man, mankind, race, stock, world.

fleshly animal, bodily, carnal, lascivious, lustful, sensual.
Ant. pure, spiritual.

fleshy corpulent, fat, obese, plump, stout.

Ant. thin.

flexible (1) elastic, lithe, pliable, pliant, supple, yielding; (2) complaisant, compliant, docile, gentle, tractable.

Ant. of (1) stiff; of (2) intractable.

flight (1) flying, mounting, soaring; (2) departure, exodus, fleeing, retreat.

flighty capricious, fickle, frivolous, giddy, light-headed, unbalanced, volatile, wild.

Ant. steady.

flimsy feeble, frail, frivolous, light, shallow, slight, superficial, thin, trivial, unsubstantial.

Ant. serious.

flinch blench, flee, recoil, retreat, shirk, shrink, swerve, wince, withdraw.

Ant. sustain.

fling (1) cast, hurl, pitch, shy, throw, toss; (2) n. cast, throw, toss.

Ant. catch.

flippant bold, forward, glib, impertinent, irreverent, pert, saucy, talkative, voluble.

Ant. serious.

flirt (1) n. coquette, philanderer; (2) v. coquet, philander; (3) fling, flutter, gibe, hurl, pitch, shy, throw, toss, twirl, wave.

flit dart, fleet, flutter, fly, pass.

flitting brief, ephemeral, evanescent, fleeting, fugitive, passing, short, transient, transitory.

Ant. constant, permanent.

flock (1) v. collect, congregate, gather, herd, group, throng; (2) n. bevy, collection, company, congregation, convoy, crowd, drove, flight, gaggle, group, herd, multitude, skein, throng.

Ant. of (1) scatter.

flog beat, castigate, chastise, flagellate, lash, scourge, thrash, whip.

flood (1) v. deluge, inundate, overflow, submerge, swamp; (2) n. deluge, downpour, freshet, inundation, overflow, spate, tide; (3) (*Fig.*) abundance, multitude, rush.

Ant. of (1) subside.

floor (*Fig.*) v. beat, confound, conquer, disconcert, nonplus, overthrow, prevail, puzzle.

florid (1) embellished, figurative, flowery, ornate; (2) bright-coloured, flushed, rubicund.

Ant. of (1) plain; of (2) pale.

flounce fling, jerk, spring, throw, toss, wince.

flounder v. flounce, struggle, stumble, toss, tumble, wallow.

flourish (1) grow, prosper, succeed, thrive; (2) brandish, shake, wave; (3) bluster, boast, brag, vaunt; (4) n. bombast, dash, display, parade, show.

Ant. of (1) fade, fail.

flout deride, gibe, insult, jeer, mock, ridicule, scoff, sneer, taunt.

Ant. respect.

flow (1) v. glide, gush, move, pour, roll, run, spurt, stream; (2) deluge, flood, inundate, overflow, teem; (3) arise, emanate, emerge, issue, result, spring; (4) n. current, flood, flux, stream; (5) (*Fig.*) abundance, plenty.

Ant. of (1) stop; of (5) scarcity.

flower (1) n. and v. bloom, blossom; (2) n. (*Fig.*) best, cream, élite, freshness, pick, vigour.

flowery embellished, figurative, florid, ornate, overwrought.

Ant. plain.

fluctuate change, oscillate, undulate, vacillate, vary, waver.

fluency ease, facility, glibness, readiness, smoothness, volubility.

Ant. hesitation.

fluent easy, facile, flowing, glib, ready, smooth, voluble.

Ant. hesitating, terse.

flummery (1) porridge, (*Scot.*) sowens; (2) (*Fig.*) adulation, blarney, chaff, emptiness, flattery, froth, nonsense.

flunkey (1) footman, lackey, man-servant, valet; (2) toady, (*Colloq.*) yes-man.

flurry (1) *n.* flaw, gust, squall; (2) (*Fig.*) agitation, bustle, commotion, disturbance, excitement, fluster, flutter, hurry, tumult; (3) *v.* agitate, bustle, confuse, disconcert, disturb, fluster, flutter, hurry, ruffle.

Ant. of (2) steadiness.

flush (1) *v.* blush, colour, glow, redden; (2) animate, elate, elevate, excite; (3) cleanse, drench, flood; (4) *a.* bright, fresh, glowing, vigorous; (5) affluent, generous, lavish, liberal, prodigal, rich, wealthy; (6) even, flat, level, plane; (7) *n.* bloom, blush, glow, redness, rosiness.

Ant. of (5) miserly.

fluster (1) *v.* agitate, bustle, confound, confuse, disturb, excite, flurry, heat, hurry, perturb, ruffle; (2) *n.* agitation, bustle, commotion, disturbance, flurry, flutter, perturbation, ruffle.

Ant. of (2) calmness

fluted channelled, corrugated, grooved.

flutter (1) *v.* agitate, beat, flap, flip, fluctuate, hover, palpitate, quiver, ruffle, vibrate, waver; (2) *n.* agitation, commotion, confusion, excitement flurry, fluster, perturbation, quivering, tumult.

Ant. of (1) calm; of (2) calmness.

flux (1) change, flow, motion, mutation, transition; (2) (*Med.*) diarrhoea, dysentery.

Ant. of (1) inactivity.

fly (1) *v.* flap, flit, flutter, hover, mount, soar, wing; (2) elapse, glide, pass; (3) abscond, avoid, decamp, escape, flee, hasten, hurry, shun.

Ant. of (2) and (3) remain.

foam bubbles, froth, spray, spume.

fodder feed, food, forage, provender, rations.

foe adversary, antagonist, enemy, foeman, opponent.

Ant. friend.

foggy (1) blurred, cloudy, dim, hazy, indistinct, misty, obscure; (2) (*Fig.*) befuddled, bewildered, confused, dazed, muddled, stupid.

Ant. of (1) clear.

foible defect, failing, fault, imperfection, infirmity, penchant, weakness.

Ant. strength.

foil *v.* baffle, balk, check, checkmate, circumvent, defeat, elude, frustrate.

Ant. aid.

foist impose, insert, interpolate, introduce, palm.

follow (1) ensue, succeed; (2) chase, hunt, pursue, track, trail; (3) comply, conform, heed, obey, observe; (4) accompany, attend; (5) copy, imitate; (6) cherish, cultivate, seek; (7) arise, flow, issue, proceed, result, spring.

Ant. of (1) lead; of (3) disobey.

folly absurdity, dullness, fatuity, foolishness, imbecility, imprudence, indiscretion, madness, nonsense, silliness, stupidity.

Ant. sense, wisdom.

foment abet, brew, encourage, excite, instigate, promote, stimulate.

Ant. allay.

fond (1) affectionate, doting, loving, tender; (2) absurd, empty, foolish, indiscreet, vain, weak.

Ant. of (2) sensible.

fondle caress, coddle, dandle, pet.

food (1) aliment, board, bread, commons, fare, meat, nutriment, nutrition, provisions, rations, subsistence, sustenance, viands, victuals; (2) (*Cattle, etc.*) feed, fodder, forage, provender.

fool (1) *n.* blockhead, dolt, dunce, idiot, imbecile, nincompoop, simpleton; (2) buffoon, clown, harlequin, jester, mountebank; (3) *v.* beguile, cheat, deceive, delude, dupe, gull, hoax, hoodwink, trick; (4) jest, play, toy, trifle.

Ant. of (1) sage.

foolhardy adventurous, bold, incautious, precipitate, rash, reckless, venturesome, venturous.

Ant. cautious.

foolish (1) brainless, crazy, daft, fatuous, idiotic, insensate, mad, senseless, silly, simple, stupid, weak, witless; (2) absurd, ill-judged, imprudent, indiscreet, nonsensical, unreasonable, unwise.

Ant. sensible.

footing (1) basis, establishment, foothold, foundation, groundwork, installation, settlement; (2) condition, grade, position, rank, standing, state, status.

footpad bandit, brigand, freebooter, highwayman, robber.

footstep (1) footfall, step, tread; (2) footmark, footprint, trace, track.

fop beau, coxcomb, dandy, prig, swell.

foppish coxcombical, dandified, dandyish, dressy, finical, spruce, vain.

Ant. slovenly.

forage *n.* (*Cattle, etc.*) feed, fodder, food, provender.

foray incursion, inroad, invasion, irruption, raid.

forbear (1) abstain, avoid, cease, decline, desist, omit, pause, refrain, stop, withhold; (2) endure, indulge, spare, tolerate.

Ant. of (1) continue; of (2) resist.

forbearance abstinence, avoidance, indulgence, lenity, long-suffering, mildness, moderation, patience, refraining.

Ant. harshness, impatience.

forbid ban, debar, disallow, hinder, inhibit, interdict, prohibit, proscribe, veto.

Ant. allow.

forbidding abhorrent, disagreeable, displeasing, odious, offensive, repellent, repulsive, threatening.

Ant. attractive.

force (1) *v.* coerce, compel, constrain, drive, impel, necessitate, oblige, overcome, press, urge; (2) *n.* coercion, compulsion, constraint, enforcement, vehemence, violence; (3) cogency, efficacy, emphasis, energy, impulse, intensity, might, momentum, potency, power, strength, stress, vigour; (4) army, battalion, host, legion, regiment, squadron, troop.

Ant. of (1) induce; of (3) weakness.

forcible (1) active, cogent, effective, efficient, energetic, impressive, mighty, potent, powerful, strong, valid, weighty; (2) compulsory impetuous, violent.

Ant. weak.

forebode augur, betoken, foreshadow, foretell, indicate, portend, predict, presage, prognosticate, promise.

foreboding augury, omen, prediction, premonition, presage, presentiment, prognostication.

forecast (1) v. anticipate, calculate, contrive, estimate, foresee, plan, predict, prophesy; (2) n. anticipation, foresight, forethought, planning, prediction, prophecy.

forefend avert, forbid, hinder, prevent.

forego abandon, abjure, cede, relinquish, renounce, resign, surrender, waive, yield.

Ant. retain.

foregoing antecedent, anterior, former, preceding, previous, prior.

Ant. retain.

foreign (1) alien, distant, exotic, external, outlandish, remote, strange; (2) extraneous, extrinsic, irrelevant.

Ant. of (1) native; of (2) pertinent.

foreknowledge foresight, prescience.

foremost first, front, highest, leading, principal.

Ant. hindmost.

foreordain foredoom, predestine, predetermine.

forerunner (1) foregoer, harbinger, herald, precursor, predecessor; (2) omen, premonition, prognostic, sign.

foresee anticipate, forebode, forecast, foretell, prophesy.

foreshadow forebode, predict, presage, prophesy.

foresight anticipation, care, caution, forethought, precaution, prescience, prevision, prudence.

Ant. imprudence.

forestall anticipate, balk, frustrate, hinder, intercept, preclude, prevent, thwart.

Ant. assist.

foretell augur, bode, forebode, forecast, foreshadow, portend, predict, presage, prognosticate, prophesy.

forethought anticipation, foresight, precaution, prudence.

forewarn admonish, advise, caution, dissuade.

forfeit (1) n. amercement, damages, fine, forfeiture, loss, mulct, penalty; (2) v. lose, renounce.

Ant. gain.

forge (A) v. construct, contrive, fabricate, frame, invent, make.

orge (B) v. coin, counterfeit, falsify, feign, imitate.

forgery counterfeit, fake, falsification, imitation.

forgetful careless, heedless, inattentive, neglectful, negligent, oblivious, unmindful.

Ant. careful, mindful.

forgive absolve, acquit,

condone, excuse, exonerate, pardon, remit.

Ant. blame, censure.

forgiveness absolution, acquittal, condonation, exoneration, overlooking, pardon, remission.

Ant. punishment.

forlorn abandoned, desolate, destitute, disconsolate, forsaken, friendless, helpless, hopeless, lost, miserable, pitiable, pitiful, unhappy, woebegone, wretched.

Ant. cheerful.

form (A) v. (1) construct, contrive, create, devise, fashion, invent, make, model, mould, produce, shape; (2) arrange, combine, compose, constitute, organise; (3) discipline, educate, teach, train.

form (B) n. (1) appearance, cast, cut, fashion, figure, model, mould, pattern, shape; (2) arrangement, kind, manner, method, order, practice, sort, style, system, type; (3) ceremony, convention, etiquette, formality, ritual, rule; (4) application, document, paper; (5) bench, class, rank, seat.

formal (1) affected, ceremonious, conventional, correct, exact, precise, prim, punctilious, stiff; (2) explicit, express, fixed, methodical, regular, rigid, set, strict.

Ant. informal, unceremonious.

formality ceremony, conventionality, custom, etiquette, procedure, ritual.

former ancient, antecedent, anterior, bygone, earlier, foregoing, past, previous, prior.

Ant. latter.

formidable appalling, dangerous, dreadful, fearful, fright-ful, horrible, menacing, shocking, terrific, threatening, tremendous.

Ant. harmless, pleasant.

forsake abandon, desert, forego, forswear, leave, quit, relinquish, renounce, yield.

Ant. retain.

forsooth certainly, indeed, really, surely, truly.

forswear abandon, abjure, deny, disown, drop, forsake, recant, reject, repudiate, retract.

Ant. affirm.

forthwith directly, instantly, quickly, straightway.

Ant. later.

fortification bulwark, castle, citadel, fastness, fort, fortress, keep, stronghold.

fortify brace, confirm, corroborate, encourage, garrison, protect, reinforce, stiffen, strengthen.

Ant. discourage, weaken.

fortitude braveness, courage, determination, endurance, firmness, hardihood, patience, pluck, resolution, strength, valour.

Ant. weakness.

fortuitous accidental, casual, chance, contingent, incidental.

Ant. calculated.

fortunate auspicious, favourable, favoured, felicitous, happy, lucky, propitious, prosperous, successful.

Ant. unfortunate.

fortune (1) accident, chance, contingency, destiny, fate, fortuity, hap, lot, luck; (2) affluence, estate, opulence, possessions, property, riches, wealth; (3) event, issue, result, success.

Ant. of (2) poverty.

forward (1) a. advanced

advancing, early, onward, premature, progressive; (2) assuming, bold, brazen, brazenfaced, confident, impertinent, impudent, pert, presuming, presumptuous; (3) eager, earnest, hasty, impulsive, quick, ready, zealous; (4) fore, front, head; (5) *adv.* ahead, onward; (6) *v.* advance, aid, encourage, expedite, favour, foster, further, hasten, hurry, speed; (7) (*Comm.*) despatch, post, send, ship, transmit.

Ant. of (2) modest; of (6) retard.

foul (1) dirty, disgusting, filthy, impure, loathsome, nasty, noisome, offensive, polluted, putrid, squalid, stinking, sullied, unclean; (2) abusive, blasphemous, coarse, foulmouthed, indecent, low, obscene, profane, scurrilous, vulgar; (3) abominable, base, detestable, disgraceful, dishonourable, shameful, vile, wicked; (4) *v.* besmirch, defile, dirty, pollute, soil, stain, sully; (5) catch, clog, collide, entangle, jam.

Ant. of (1) pure; of (2) clean; of (3) attractive; of (4) cleanse; of (5) clear.

found (1) base, build, constitute, construct, endow, erect, establish, fix, ground, institute, originate, plant, raise, settle; (2) cast, mould.

Ant. of (1) destroy.

foundation (1) base, basis, bottom, footing, groundwork; (2) endowment, establishment, institution, settlement.

Ant. of (1) superstructure.

founder (A) *n.* (1) author, beginner, builder, constructor, establisher, originator, planter; (2) caster, moulder.

Ant. of (1) follower.

founder (B) *v.* (1) sink, submerge; (2) collapse, fall, stumble, trip; (3) (*Fig.*) fail, miscarry.

fountain (1) font, reservoir, jet, spring, well; (2) (*Fig.*) beginning, cause, commencement, origin, rise, source.

foxy artful, crafty, cunning, sly, wily.

Ant. artless.

fracas affray, brawl, disturbance, quarrel, riot, row, uproar.

fractious captious, cross, fretful, irritable, peevish, pettish, petulant, querulous, refractory, testy.

Ant. good-tempered, tractable.

fracture (1) *n.* breach, break, cleft, crack, fissure, gap, opening, rent, rift, rupture, split; (2) *v.* break, crack, split.

fragile breakable, brittle, delicate, feeble, frail, frangible, infirm, weak.

Ant. strong.

fragility brittleness, feebleness, frailty, frangibility, infirmity, weakness.

Ant. strength.

fragment bit, chip, fraction, morsel, part, piece, remnant, scrap.

Ant. whole.

fragrant ambrosial, aromatic, balmy, odoriferous, odorous, perfumed, redolent, sweetscented, sweet-smelling.

Ant. malodorous.

frail breakable, brittle, delicate, feeble, frangible, infirm, weak.

Ant. strong.

frailty (1) feebleness, frailness, infirmity, weakness; (2) blemish, defect, failing, fault, foible, peccability, short-coming.

Ant. strength.

frame (1) v. build, compose, constitute, construct, contrive, devise, fabricate, fashion, forge, form, invent, make, mould, plan, shape; (2) n. body, carcass, fabric, form, framework, scheme, shell, skeleton, system; (3) condition, humour, mood, state, temper.

franchise exemption, immunity, privilege, right, suffrage, vote.

frank artless, candid, direct, downright, honest, ingenuous, open, outright, outspoken, plain, sincere, straightforward, truthful, unreserved, unrestricted.

Ant. artful, secretive.

frankness candour, ingenuousness, openness, truth.

Ant. cunning.

frantic distracted, frenzied, furious, mad, outrageous, raging, raving, wild.

Ant. calm.

fraternise associate, coalesce, concur, consort, co-operate, harmonise, sympathise, unite.

Ant. disagree.

fraternity association, brotherhood, circle, clan, company, league, set, sodality.

fraud artifice, cheat, craft, deceit, duplicity, guile, imposture, stratagem, treachery, trickery, wile.

Ant. honesty.

fraudulent crafty, deceitful, deceptive, dishonest, false, knavish, treacherous, wily.

Ant. honest.

fraught abounding, charged, filled, freighted, full, laden, pregnant.

Ant. empty.

fray (A) n. affray, battle, broil, combat, conflict, fight, quarrel, riot.

Ant. peace.

fray (B) v. chafe, fret, rub, wear.

freak caprice, crotchet, fancy, folly, humour, vagary, whim, whimsy.

Ant. steadfastness.

freakish capricious, erratic, fanciful, humorous, odd, whimsical.

Ant. sober, steady.

free (1) v. deliver, disenthrall, emancipate, liberate, loose, release, unchain, unfetter; (2) clear, disengage, extricate, relieve, rid; (3) a. gratis, gratuitous; (4) delivered, emancipated, independent, liberated, loose, unrestrained; (5) allowed, clear, exempt, immune, open, permitted, unobstructed, unregulated; (6) easy, familiar, frank, informal, lax, loose, open, unconstrained; (7) bountiful, charitable, eager, hospitable, lavish, liberal, munificent, open-handed, prodigal, willing.

freebooter bandit, brigand, buccaneer, highwayman, marauder, pillager, pirate, plunderer, robber, rover.

freedom (1) emancipation, independence, liberty; (2) ingenuousness, frankness, openness; (3) ease, facility, familiarity, informality, laxity, licence; (4) opportunity, range, scope.

Ant. of (1) slavery.

freethinker agnostic, deist, doubter, infidel, sceptic, unbeliever.

Ant. believer.

freeze benumb, chill, congeal, harden, stiffen.

Ant. melt.

frenzy aberration, delirium, derangement, distraction, fury, insanity, lunacy, madness, mania, paroxysm, rage.

Ant. sanity.

frequent (A) *a.* common, customary, everyday, habitual, numerous, repeated, usual.

Ant. rare.

frequent (B) *v.* attend, haunt, resort, visit.

fresh (1) new, novel, recent; (2) blooming, fair, florid, good, hardy, healthy, keen, lively, rosy, ruddy, unfaded, unwearied, unwithered, vigorous, young; (3) cool, pure, refreshing, sweet; (4) artless, inexperienced, raw, uncultivated, untrained; (5) uncured, undried, unsalted.

Ant. of (1) old; of (2) stale; of (3) warm; of (4) experienced.

fret (A) affront, annoy, chagrin, goad, harass, irritate, provoke, ruffle, torment, worry.

Ant. appease.

fret (B) abrade, chafe, erode, gall, fray, rub, wear.

fretful captious, cross, fractious, irritable, peevish, petulant, querulous, short-tempered, splenetic, testy, touchy, uneasy.

Ant. contented.

friable brittle, crisp, powdery, pulverisable.

friction (1) abrasion, attrition, grating, rubbing; (2) (*Fig.*) bickering, disagreement, dispute, dissension, wrangling.

Ant. of (2) agreement.

friend adherent, advocate, ally, associate, benefactor, chum, companion, comrade, confidant, crony, intimate, pal, patron, supporter, well-wisher.

Ant. enemy.

friendly affectionate, amiable, amicable, auspicious, benevolent, conciliatory, cordial, favourable, fraternal, good, intimate, kind, neighbourly, peaceable, propitious, sociable, well-disposed.

Ant. unfriendly, unsociable.

friendship affection, amity, attachment, benevolence, familiarity, fondness, friendliness, good-fellowship, goodness, harmony, intimacy, love, regard.

Ant. enmity.

fright alarm, consternation, dismay, dread, fear, panic, terror.

frighten affright, alarm, appal, daunt, dismay, intimidate, scare, shock, terrify.

Ant. hearten, reassure.

frightful alarming, awful, dire, dread, dreadful, fearful, ghastly, grim, gruesome, hideous, horrible, horrid, shocking, terrible.

Ant. attractive.

frigid chill, cold, cool, dull, forbidding, formal, gelid, icy, lifeless, passionless, repellent, rigid, stiff, unfeeling.

Ant. warm.

fringe border, edging, tassel, trimming.

frisk caper, dance, frolic, gambol, hop, jump, play, romp, skip, sport, wanton.

frivolous childish, flimsy, flippant, foolish, idle, light, paltry, petty, puerile, silly, trivial, unimportant, vain.

Ant. serious.

frolic (1) caper, frisk, gambol, lark, play, romp, sport; (2) *n.*

drollery, escapade, fun, gambol, lark, prank.

frolicsome frisky, gay, lively, merry, playful, sportive, wanton.

front (1) brow, face, forehead; (2) anterior, façade, forepart, head, obverse, van; (3) (*Fig.*) assurance, boldness, effrontery, face; (4) *v.* confront, encounter, face, oppose.

Ant. of (3) bashfulness.

frosty chilly, cold, frigid, icy, wintry.

frothy (1) foamy, spumous, spumy; (2) (*Fig.*) empty, frivolous, light, trivial, unsubstantial, vain.

Ant. of (2) serious.

froward captious, contrary, cross, defiant, difficult, fractious, impudent, intractable, obstinate, perverse, refractory, stubborn, ungovernable, wayward, wilful.

Ant. tractable.

frown glower, scowl.

frugal careful, cheese-paring, economical, miserly, niggard, parsimonious, provident, saving, sparing, stingy, temperate, thrifty.

Ant. wasteful.

fruit (1) crop, harvest, produce, product; (2) (*Fig.*) advantage, consequence, effect, outcome, profit, result; (3) issue, offspring, young.

fruitful abundant, copious, fecund, fertile, plenteous, plentiful, productive, prolific, rich.

Ant. barren.

fruition completion, enjoyment, fulfilment, perfection.

Ant. failure.

fruitless abortive, barren, bootless, futile, ineffectual, profitless, unavailing, unfruit-

ful, unproductive, unprofitable, unprolific, useless, vain.

Ant. fruitful.

frustrate baffle, balk, check, confront, defeat, disappoint, foil, nullify, thwart.

Ant. stimulate.

fuddled drunk, inebriated, intoxicated, muddled, tipsy.

Ant. sober.

fugitive (1) *n.* deserter, runaway; (2) *a.* brief, ephemeral, evanescent, flitting, momentary, passing, short, short-lived, temporary, transient, transitory, unstable.

Ant. of (2) permanent.

fulfil accomplish, achieve, answer, complete, comply, conclude, discharge, execute, effect, fill, finish, keep, meet, obey, observe, perfect, perform, realise.

Ant. fail.

full (1) complete, filled, replete, satiated, satisfied, stocked, sufficient; (2) abundant, adequate, ample, copious, plenteous, plentiful; (3) clear, deep, distinct, loud; (4) broad, capacious, extensive, large, loose.

Ant. of (1) empty.

ful(l)ness (1) abundance, adequateness, copiousness, glut, plenty, profusion, repletion, satiety; (2) clearness, loudness, strength; (3) dilation, distension, enlargement, extensiveness, swelling.

Ant. of (1) emptiness.

fully abundantly, completely, entirely, full, largely.

fulminate (1) burst, detonate, explode, thunder; (2) (*Fig.*) curse, denounce, menace, rage, threaten.

Ant. of (2) praise.

fulsome disgusting, excessive,

extravagant, fawning, loathsome, nauseous, offensive, repulsive, sickening.

Ant. moderate.

fume (1) v. reek, smoke, vaporise; (2) (*Fig.*) chafe, rage, rave, storm; (3) n. reek, smoke, vapour; (4) (*Fig.*) agitation, fury, passion, rage.

fun amusement, diversion, frolic, gaiety, jesting, jocularity, joy, merriment, mirth, play, playfulness, sport.

Ant. melancholy.

function (1) v. act, operate, work; (2) n. discharge, execution, exercise, operation, performance; (3) business, ceremony, duty, employment, occupation, office, part, province.

Ant. of (2) neglect.

fund capital, foundation, stock, store, supply.

fundamental (1) a. basic, constitutional, elementary, essential, important, indispensable, necessary, organic, primary, principal, underlying; (2) n. essential, principle, rule.

Ant. of (1) incidental.

funeral burial, cremation, interment, obsequies.

funereal dark, death-like, dismal, gloomy, lugubrious, mournful, sad, sepulchral, sombre, woeful.

Ant. cheerful.

funny amusing, comic, comical, diverting, droll, facetious, farcical, humorous, jocose, jocular, laughable, ludicrous, witty.

Ant. serious.

furbish burnish, brighten, polish, rub, shine.

Ant. tarnish.

furious angry, boisterous, fierce, frantic, frenzied, impetuous, mad, raging, stormy, tempestuous, tumultuous, turbulent, vehement, violent, wild.

Ant. calm.

furnish (1) decorate, equip, fit, provide, rig, stock, store, supply; (2) afford, bestow, give, offer, present.

Ant. of (1) dismantle.

furniture (1) appliances, chattels, effects, fittings, furnishings, goods, movables; (2) decorations, embellishments, ornaments.

furore commotion, craze, enthusiasm, excitement, fury, rage.

furrow chamfer, channel, crease, fluting, groove, hollow, seam, trench, wrinkle.

further (1) a. additional; (2) adv. also, besides, furthermore, moreover; (3) v. advance, aid, assist, encourage, help, promote, succour.

Ant. of (3) hinder.

furtive clandestine, hidden, secret, sly, stealthy, surreptitious, underhand.

Ant. open.

fury (1) anger, fierceness, frenzy, impetuosity, ire, madness, passion, rage, vehemence, violence, wrath; (2) bacchante, hag, shrew, termagant, virago, vixen.

Ant. of (1) calm.

fuse amalgamate, blend, coalesce, combine, commingle, dissolve, intermingle, intermix, melt, merge, smelt.

Ant. solidify.

fusion amalgamation, blending, commingling, commixture, liquefaction, mixture, smelting.

fuss (1) n. ado, agitation, bustle, commotion, excitement, fidget, flurry, hurry, stir, to-do, worry; (2) v. bustle, fidget, fret, fume, worry.

Ant. of (1) peace.

fusty ill-smelling, malodorous, mildewed, mouldy, musty, rank.

Ant. sweet-smelling.

futile bootless, fruitless, ineffectual, profitless, trivial, unavailing, unimportant, unprofitable, unsuccessful, useless, vain, valueless, worthless.

Ant. profitable, valuable.

futility bootlessness, fruitlessness, triviality, uselessness, vanity.

Ant. advantage.

future a. coming, forthcoming, hereafter, subsequent.

Ant. bygone, past.

G

gabble (1) v. babble, chatter, gibber, gossip, jabber, prate; (2) n. chatter, gossip, jargon, prating, twaddle.

gaffer foreman, overseer.

gag muffle, muzzle, silence, stifle, throttle.

gage (1) v. pawn, pledge; (2) n. pawn, pledge, security; (3) challenge, gauntlet, glove.

gaiety animation, blithesomeness, cheerfulness, glee, good-humour, hilarity, jollity, joviality, joyousness, light-heartedness, merriment, mirth, vivacity.

Ant. sadness.

gain (1) v. achieve, acquire, attain, get, obtain, reach, realise, secure, win; (2) conciliate, enlist, persuade, prevail; (3) n. acquisition, advantage, benefit, earnings, emolument, lucre, winnings.

Ant. of (1) lose.

gainful advantageous, beneficial, lucrative, paying, productive, profitable, remunerative.

Ant. unprofitable.

galaxy assemblage, assembly, cluster, collection, constellation, group.

gale blast, hurricane, squall, storm, tempest, tornado, typhoon.

Ant. zephyr.

gall (1) v. chafe, excoriate, fret, rub; (2) (*Fig.*) annoy, exasperate, harass, incense, irritate, plague, provoke, vex; (3) n. (*Fig.*) bitterness, malice, malignity, rancour, spite.

Ant. of (3) kindliness.

gallant (1) bold, brave, courageous, daring, dauntless, doughty, fearless, heroic, intrepid, valiant, valorous; (2) chivalrous, courteous, courtly, dignified, magnanimous, noble, polite; (3) n. lover, suitor, wooer.

Ant. of (1) cowardly; of (2) impolite.

gallantry (1) boldness, bravery, courage, courageousness, fearlessness, heroism, intrepidity, prowess, valour; (2) chivalry, courteousness, courtesy, elegance, politeness.

Ant. of (1) cowardice; of (2) discourtesy.

gallop fly, hurry, run, rush, speed.

Ant. trot, walk.

gambol v. caper, frisk, frolic, hop, jump, skip.

game (A) (1) n. amusement, diversion, frolic, pastime, play, recreation, sport; (2) adventure, enterprise, plan, scheme undertaking.

Ant. of (1) work.

game (B) brave, courageous, dauntless, fearless, gallant, heroic, intrepid, resolute, valiant, valorous.

Ant. cowardly.

gamesome frisky, frolicsome, gay, lively, merry, playful, sportive, vivacious.

Ant. sedate.

gammon (1) *v.* beguile, cheat, dupe, gull, hoax, hoodwink, humbug, trick; (2) *n.* hoax, imposition, trick.

gang band, clique, company, coterie, crew, crowd, horde, party, set.

gaol bridewell, dungeon, jail, lock-up, penitentiary, prison.

gap breach, break, chink, cleft, crack, cranny, crevice, hole, interstice, opening, rift, vacuity.

gape open, stare, yawn.

garb apparel, attire, clothes, costume, garment, habit, habiliment, raiment, robes, uniform, vestments.

Ant. nakedness.

garbage filth, offal, offscourings, refuse, remains, rubbish, trash, waste.

garble corrupt, distort, falsify, misquote, misrepresent, misstate, mutilate, pervert.

Ant. quote.

gargantuan big, colossal, enormous, gigantic, huge, prodigious, tremendous.

Ant. small.

garish flaring, flashy, gaudy, glaring, glittering, loud, showy, tawdry.

Ant. elegant.

garland chaplet, coronal, crown, wreath.

garner accumulate, collect, deposit, gather, hoard, husband, reserve, save, store, treasure.

Ant. dissipate.

garnish adorn, beautify, bedeck, decorate, embellish, enhance, grace, ornament.

Ant. spoil.

garniture adornments, appendages, decorations, furniture, ornaments.

garrulous babbling, chattering, loquacious, prating, prolix, prosy, talkative, verbose, wordy.

Ant. succinct.

gasp blow, pant, puff.

gather (1) assemble, collect, congregate, marshal, melt, muster; (2) accumulate, amass, collect, garner, hoard; (3) crop, cull, glean, harvest, pluck, reap, select; (4) assume, conclude, deduce, infer, learn; (5) fold, plait, pucker, tuck; (6) condense, grow, increase, thicken.

Ant. of (1) scatter, separate.

gathering (1) assemblage, assembly, company, congregation, concourse, crowd, throng; (2) accumulation, acquisition, collecting, collection, gain, heap, pile, procuring; (3) (*Med.*) abscess, boil, pimple, pustule, sore, tumour.

Ant. of (1) dispersal.

gaudy brilliant, flashy, garish, glaring, loud, showy, tawdry.

Ant. quiet.

gaunt angular, attenuated, emaciated, haggard, lank, meagre, skinny, slender, slim, spare, thin.

Ant. stout.

gawky awkward, clownish, clumsy, loutish, uncouth, ungainly.

Ant. graceful.

gay (1) animated, blithe, cheerful, glad, gleeful, happy, hilarious, jolly, jovial, joyful, joyous, lively, merry, vivacious;

(2) bright, brilliant, flashy, garish, gaudy, showy.

Ant. of (1) sad.

gaze gape, look, regard, stare, view, wonder.

gear (1) accessories, accoutrements, apparatus, armour, array, dress, equipment, harness, rigging, rig-out, tackle, trappings; (2) cogs, gearing, machinery, mechanism.

gelid chilly, cold, freezing, frigid, icy.

Ant. warm.

genealogy ancestry, descent, lineage, pedigree, progeniture, stock.

general (1) common, customary, extensive, ordinary, prevalent, usual, regular; (2) imprecise, inaccurate, indefinite, inexact, loose, vague; (3) catholic, total, universal.

Ant. of (1) rare; of (2) precise.

generally commonly, ordinarily, usually.

generate beget, breed, create, engender, form, make, procreate, produce.

Ant. destroy.

generation (1) creation, formation, procreation, production; (2) breed, children, family, offspring, progeny, race, stock; (3) age, epoch, era, period, time.

generosity (1) benevolence, bounteousness, bounty, charity, liberality, open-handedness; (2) disinterestedness, magnanimity, nobleness.

Ant. of (1) stinginess; of (2) meanness.

generous (1) benevolent, bounteous, bountiful, charitable, hospitable, liberal, munificent, open-handed; (2) highminded, magnanimous, noble;

(3) abundant, ample, copious, plentiful.

Ant. of (1) close-fisted; of (2) mean; of (3) scanty.

genial agreeable, cheerful, cordial, enlivening, friendly, hearty, inspiring, jovial, joyous, merry, warm, warm-hearted.

Ant. frigid.

genius (1) ability, aptitude, capacity, endowment, faculty, gift, talent, turn; (2) adept, master, master-hand, master-mind; (3) deity, demon, spirit.

genteel aristocratic, civil, courteous, courtly, elegant, fashionable, refined, stylish, well-bred.

Ant. ill-bred, rude.

gentility civility, courtesy, courtliness, good-breeding, refinement, urbanity.

Ant. incivility.

gentle (1) amiable, bland, clement, compassionate, docile, dove-like, kind, meek, merciful, mild, pacific, peaceful, placid, quiet, soft, tame, tender, tractable; (2) aristocratic, courteous, genteel, noble, polished, polite, refined, well-born, well-bred; (3) gradual, light, moderate, slight.

Ant. of (1) unkind; of (2) impolite; of (3) harsh.

gentlemanly civil, complaisant, courteous, cultivated, genteel, honourable, obliging, polite, refined, urbane, well-bred.

Ant. impolite.

genuine authentic, frank, natural, pure, real, sincere, sound, true, unadulterated, unaffected, unalloyed, veritable.

Ant. spurious.

genus class, group, kind, race, sort.

Ant. species.

germ (1) embryo, nucleus, ovary, seed; (2) (*Fig.*) beginning, cause, origin, source.

Ant. maturity.

germane allied, appropriate, cognate, fitting, kindred, pertinent, relevant, suitable.

Ant. irrelevant.

germinate bud, develop, grow, shoot, sprout, swell, vegetate.

Ant. die.

gesture action, attitude, posture, sign, signal.

gewgaw bauble, gimcrack, kickshaw, plaything, toy, trifle, trinket.

ghastly deathlike, frightful, grim, grisly, hideous, horrible, pale, pallid, shocking, spectral, wan.

Ant. pleasing.

ghost apparition, phantom, shade, soul, spectre, spirit, sprite, wraith.

giant (1) *n.* colossus, Hercules, monster; (2) *a.* colossal, enormous, huge, large, monstrous, prodigious, vast.

Ant. of (1) dwarf.

gibberish babble, balderdash, drivel, jabber, jargon, nonsense, twaddle.

Ant. sense.

gibbous convex, humped, hunched, protuberant, rounded, swelling.

Ant. concave.

gibe deride, flout, ridicule, scoff, sneer, taunt.

Ant. praise.

giddiness dizziness, vertigo.

giddy (1) dizzy, vertiginous; (2) careless, changeable, fickle, flighty, heedless, inconstant,

irresolute, thoughtless, unstable, unsteady, vacillating, wild.

Ant. of (2) constant.

gift (1) benefaction, bequest, boon, bounty, contribution, donation, grant, gratuity, largesse, legacy, offering, present, subscription; (2) ability, capability, capacity, endowment, faculty, power, talent, turn.

gifted able, capable, clever, ingenious, intelligent, inventive, sagacious, talented.

Ant. incapable.

gigantic colossal, cyclopean, enormous, giant, herculean, huge, immense, prodigious, titanic, tremendous.

Ant. diminutive, puny.

giggle cackle, grin, snigger, titter.

gild adorn, beautify, bedeck, brighten, deck, embellish, garnish, grace, ornament.

Ant. mar.

gimcrack bauble, gewgaw, kickshaw, plaything, toy, trinket.

gingerly carefully, cautiously, daintily, fastidiously, warily.

Ant. boldly.

gird (A) (1) bind, encircle, enclose, encompass, enfold, engird, environ, girdle; (2) clothe, equip, furnish, invest.

gird (B) gibe, ridicule, scoff, sneer.

girdle (1) *v.* bind, gird, enclose, encompass, environ, surround; (2) *n.* band, belt, cincture, fillet, girth, sash, waistband.

gist core, essence, force, marrow, meaning, pith, point, substance.

give (1) accord, allow, confer, contribute, donate, furnish, grant, permit, present, provide, supply, vouchsafe; (2) communicate, emit, impart, issue, pronounce, publish, render, utter; (3) cede, fall, recede, retire, sink, surrender, yield; (4) cause, occasion, produce.

glad (1) blithesome, contented, delightful, gleeful, gratified, happy, joyful, pleased; (2) animated, cheerful, cheering, cheery, joyous, merry.
Ant. of (1) miserable; of (2) sad.

gladden cheer, delight, elate, enliven, exhilarate, gratify, rejoice.
Ant. dishearten.

gladness animation, cheerfulness, delight, gaiety, happiness, hilarity, jollity, joy, joyousness, pleasure.
Ant. sadness.

gladsome blithesome, cheerful, delighted, gleeful, happy, jocund, jovial, joyful, joyous, light-hearted, merry, sprightly, vivacious.
Ant. dismal.

glamour bewitchment, charm, enchantment, fascination, ravishment, spell, witchery.

glance (1) v. flash, gleam, glisten, glitter, shine; (2) gaze, glimpse, look, view; (3) dart, flit; (4) n. gleam, glimpse, look, view.

glare (1) dazzle, flame, flare, gleam, glisten, sparkle; (2) frown, gaze, glower.
Ant. of (1) glimmer.

glaring (1) dazzling, gleaming, glistening, glittering, sparkling; (2) (*Fig.*) conspicuous, manifest, obvious, open, visible.
Ant. of (2) obscure.

glaze burnish, calendar, coat,

enamel, furbish, gloss, lacquer, polish, varnish.
Ant. dull.

gleam (1) n. brightness, coruscation, flash, lustre, ray, splendour; (2) beam, glimmer, ray; (3) v. coruscate, flash, glimmer, glitter, shine, sparkle.

glean collect, cull, gather, harvest, pick, select.
Ant. reject.

glee exhilaration, fun, gaiety, gladness, hilarity, jollity, joviality, joyousness, liveliness, merriment, verve.
Ant. melancholy.

glib artful, flippant, fluent, garrulous, ready, slippery, smooth, talkative, voluble.
Ant. stammering.

glide flow, roll, run, skim, slide, slip.
Ant. rest.

glimmer (1) v. flicker, gleam, glitter, shine; (2) beam, gleam, ray.

glimpse glance, gleam, look.

glisten glare, gleam, glimmer, glitter, scintillate, shine, sparkle, twinkle.

glitter (1) v. flare, flash, glare, gleam, glisten, shine, sparkle; (2) n. beam, brilliance, brightness, gleam, radiance, scintillation, splendour.
Ant. of (2) dullness.

gloaming dusk, eventide, nightfall, twilight.

gloat exult, gaze, stare, triumph.

globe ball, earth, orb, sphere.

globular globate, globose, globulous, round, spherical.

globule bead, drop, particle.

gloom (1) cloud, cloudiness, darkness, dimness, dullness, gloominess, obscurity, shade, shadow; (2) dejection, depression, despondency, downheartedness, melancholy, sadness.

Ant. of (1) brightness; of (2) happiness.

gloomy (1) dark, dim, dusky, obscure, shadowy; (2) cheerless, dejected, despondent, dismal, dispirited, downcast, downhearted, glum, moody, morose, pessimistic, sad, sullen.

Ant. of (1) light; of (2) cheerful.

glorify adore, bless, celebrate, exalt, extol, laud, magnify, worship.

Ant. humiliate.

glorious (1) celebrated, distinguished, eminent, excellent, famed, famous, illustrious, noted, renowned; (2) bright, brilliant, grand, magnificent, radiant, splendid.

Ant. of (1) ordinary; of (2) dull.

glory (1) n. celebrity, dignity, distinction, eminence, fame, honour, praise, renown; (2) brilliance, lustre, magnificence, pomp, radiance, splendour; (3) v. boast, exult, triumph.

Ant. of (1) disrepute.

glossy bright, brilliant, glazed, lustrous, sheeny, shiny, smooth.

glow (1) v. brighten, burn, gleam, redden, shine; (2) n. brightness, burning, incandescence, luminosity, reddening; (3) (Fig.) ardour, enthusiasm, excitement, fervour, impetuosity, vehemence, warmth.

Ant. of (3) coolness.

glower frown, glare, scowl.

Ant. smile.

glum churlish, crabbed, crestfallen, crusty, gloomy, gruff, moody, morose, sour, sulky, sullen.

Ant. jovial.

glutinous adhesive, cohesive, gluey, gummy, sticky, viscid, viscous.

glutton gobbler, gormandiser, gourmand.

Ant. ascetic.

gnarled a. contorted, knotted, knotty, twisted.

Ant. smooth.

go (1) advance, depart, fare, journey, pass, proceed, travel; (2) extend, lead, reach, run; (3) avail, concur, contribute, tend; (4) accept, approve, bear, endure.

goad annoy, arouse, excite, harass, impel, incite, irritate, instigate, prod, spur, stimulate, sting, urge, worry.

Ant. pacify.

goal aim, ambition, design, end, limit, object, purpose.

Ant. start.

gobble bolt, devour, gorge, gulp, swallow.

Ant. disgorge.

goblin apparition, elf, gnome, hobgoblin, phantom, sprite.

godless atheistic, impious, irreligious, profane, ungodly, wicked.

Ant. godly, righteous.

godly devout, holy, pious, religious, righteous, saintly.

Ant. ungodly.

golden (1) bright, brilliant, precious, resplendent, shining, valuable, yellow; (2) (Fig.) auspicious, excellent, favourable, opportune, propitious.

good (A) (1) benevolent, friendly, gracious, humane, kind, merciful, obliging, well-disposed; (2) honourable, pious, religious, righteous, unsullied, upright, virtuous, worthy; (3) advantageous, auspicious, convenient, favourable, fit, profitable, satisfactory, serviceable, suitable, useful; **(4)** admirable, capital, commendable, excellent, precious, valuable; **(5)** able, dexterous, expert, qualified, reliable, skilful, trustworthy; **(6)** agreeable, gratifying, pleasant.

Ant. bad.

good (B) *n.* **(1)** excellence, merit, morality, righteousness, virtue; **(2)** advantage, benefit, blessing, gain, profit, prosperity, usefulness, welfare.

goodbye adieu, farewell.

goodly (1) agreeable, comely, desirable, elegant, good-looking, graceful, pleasant; **(2)** considerable, large.

Ant. of **(1)** unpleasing.

goodness (1) honesty, integrity, morality, probity, rectitude, righteousness, uprightness, virtue; **(2)** benevolence, generosity, goodwill, kindliness, kindness; **(3)** excellence, quality, value, worth.

Ant. of **(1)** badness, evil.

goods belongings, chattels, effects, furnishings, furniture, movables, property, wares.

gore *v.* pierce, stab, wound.

gorge (A) *v.* bolt, cram, devour, feed, fill, glut, gobble, gormandise, sate, satiate, stuff, surfeit, swallow.

Ant. starve.

gorge (B) *n.* cleft, defile, fissure, pass, ravine.

gorgeous brilliant, dazzling, luxuriant, magnificent, resplendent, showy, splendid, sumptuous, superb.

Ant. shabby, ugly.

gory bloody, ensanguined.

gospel creed, doctrine, message, news, revelation, tidings.

gossip (1) *n.* chit-chat, hear-

say, newsmongering, prattle, scandal; **(2)** babbler, chatterer, newsmonger, prattler, tattler, tell-tale; **(3)** *v.* cackle, chat, gabble, prate, prattle, tattle.

govern administer, check, command, conduct, control, curb, direct, guide, manage, order, pilot, reign, rule, steer, superintend, supervise.

Ant. misgovern, obey.

government (1) command, control, direction, guidance, management, regulation, restraint, sway; **(2)** administration, cabinet, commonwealth; dominion, execution, polity, rule, sovereignty, state.

Ant. of **(1)** disorder; of **(2)** anarchy.

governor (1) commander, comptroller, controller, director, manager, overseer, ruler, superintendent, supervisor; **(2)** director, executive, guardian, instructor, magistrate, tutor.

grace (1) *n.* attractiveness, beauty, charm, comeliness, elegance, polish, refinement; **(2)** beneficence, favour, generosity, goodwill, kindliness, kindness; **(3)** clemency, devotion, devoutness, forgiveness, holiness, mercy, pardon, piety, salvation; **(4)** blessing, prayer, thanks; **(5)** *v.* adorn, beautify, bedeck, deck, decorate, embellish, honour, ornament.

Ant. of **(1)** ungainliness; of **(2)** disfavour; of **(3)** condemnation; of **(5)** spoil.

graceful beautiful, becoming, comely, easy, elegant, flowing, natural, symmetrical.

Ant. ungainly.

graceless abandoned, base, corrupt, degenerate, depraved, dissolute, hardened, incorrigible, profligate, reprobate.

shameless, vicious, wicked, worthless.

Ant. righteous.

gracious affable, beneficent, benevolent, benign, benignant, civil, courteous, courtly, friendly, kind, lenient, loving, mild, pleasing, polite, tender.

Ant. ungracious.

grade (1) brand, degree, quality, rank, stage, step; (2) gradient, incline, slope.

gradual approximate, continuous, gentle, progressive, regular, slow, successive, unintermittent.

Ant. broken, sudden.

graduate (A) *n.* alumnus, laureate.

graduate (B) *v.* adapt, adjust, proportion, regulate.

graft (1) *n.* bud, scion, shoot, sprout; (2) *v.* ingraft, insert, transplant; (3) *n.* (*U.S.A.*) corruption, favouritism, influence, nepotism.

grain (1) cereals, corn, kernel, seed; (2) atom, bit, iota, jot, particle, piece, scrap, trace, whit; (3) disposition, humour, temper; (4) fibre, shade, texture.

grand (1) august, eminent, exalted, fine, glorious, great, illustrious, imposing, lordly, magnificent, majestic, noble, pompous, princely, regal, splendid, stately, sublime; (2) chief, main, principal.

Ant. insignificant, small.

grandeur augustness, dignity, greatness, loftiness, magnificence, majesty, splendour, state, stateliness, sublimity.

Ant. lowliness.

grant (1) allot, allow, award, bestow, confer, give, impart, vouchsafe, yield; (2) (*Law*)

convey, transfer, transmit; (3) *n.* admission, benefaction, boon, bounty, concession, donation, endowment, gift, present.

Ant. of (1) receive.

graphic descriptive, forcible, lively, picturesque, striking, telling, vivid.

Ant. dull.

grapple catch, clasp, clutch, grasp, grip, hold, hug, seize, wrestle.

Ant. loose.

grasp (1) *v.* catch, clasp, clinch, clutch, grapple, hold, seize; (2) comprehend, understand; (3) *n.* clasp, grip, hold, possession; (4) comprehension, power, reach, scope, understanding.

Ant. of (1) release.

grasping acquisitive, avaricious, close-fisted, covetous, greedy, miserly, niggardly, rapacious.

Ant. generous.

grate (1) *v.* abrade, comminute, grind, rasp, rub, scrape, scratch, triturate; (2) creak, fret, irritate, jar, vex.

grateful (1) appreciative, beholden, indebted, obliged, thankful; (2) acceptable, agreeable, gratifying, nice, pleasing, refreshing, satisfactory, satisfying, welcome.

Ant. of (1) ungrateful; of (2) unsatisfactory.

gratification delight, enjoyment, fruition, pleasure, recompense, reward, satisfaction.

Ant. disappointment, dissatisfaction.

gratify delight, fulfil, humour, indulge, please, recompense, requite, satisfy.

Ant. dissatisfy.

grating *a.* disagreeable,

displeasing, harsh, irritating, offensive.

Ant. pleasant.

gratis freely, gratuitously.

gratitude gratefulness, indebtedness, thankfulness.

Ant. ingratitude.

gratuitous (1) free, spontaneous, unrewarded, voluntary; (2) assumed, baseless, groundless, unfounded, unwarranted.

Ant. of (1) compulsory; of (2) justifiable.

gratuity benefaction, bonus, boon, bounty, charity, donation, endowment, gift, grant, largess, present, (*Colloq.*) tip.

grave (1) *n.* mausoleum, pit, sepulchre, vault; (2) *a.* critical, important, momentous, serious, weighty; (3) *a.* demure, earnest, sage, sedate, serious, sober, solemn, staid, thoughtful; (4) *v.* carve, chisel, cut, imprint, sculpture.

Ant. of (2) unimportant; of (3) flippant.

graveyard burial-ground, cemetery, churchyard, God's acre, necropolis.

gravity (1) importance, moment, momentousness, seriousness, weightiness; (2) demureness, sedateness, seriousness, sobriety, solemnity, thoughtfulness.

Ant. of (1) triviality; of (2) frivolity.

graze (1) brush, rub, scrape, shave, skim, touch; (2) browse, crop, feed, pasture.

great (1) big, bulky, enormous, gigantic, immense, vast; (2) considerable, excessive, grievous, high, important, much, numerous, weighty; (3) celebrated, distinguished, eminent, exalted, excellent, famed,

famous, illustrious, notable, renowned; (4) august, chivalrous, dignified, magnanimous, noble, sublime; (5) chief, grand, main, leading, principal.

Ant. of (1) small; of (2) insignificant; of (3) undistinguished.

greatness (1) bulk, enormity, largeness, magnitude, size, vastness; (2) distinction, eminence, fame, grandeur, renown; (3) chivalry, dignity, disinterestedness, generosity, majesty, nobility, nobleness, sublimity.

Ant. smallness.

greediness (1) gluttony, greed, hunger, ravenousness, voracity; (2) (*Fig.*) avidity, desire, eagerness, longing, rapacity, selfishness.

Ant. of (1) self-restraint; of (2) unselfishness.

greedy (1) gluttonous, insatiable, ravenous, voracious; (2) (*Fig.*) avaricious, covetous, desirous, eager, grasping, rapacious, selfish.

Ant. of (1) self-restrained; of (2) unselfish.

green (1) blooming, emerald, flourishing, fresh, new, undecayed, verdant; (2) (*Fig.*) ignorant, immature, inexperienced, inexpert, raw, unripe, unskilful; (3) *n.* grassplot, lawn, sward, turf.

Ant. of (1) faded; of (2) expert.

greet accost, address, compliment, hail, salute, welcome.

grief affliction, agony, anguish, dejection, distress, grievance, misery, mournfulness, mourning, regret, sadness, sorrow, suffering, trial, tribulation, trouble, woe.

Ant. joy.

grievance affliction, burden, complaint, distress, grief, hardship, injury, injustice, sorrow, trial, tribulation, trouble, wrong.

Ant. justice.

grieve (1) afflict, annoy, hurt, injure, pain, trouble, vex, wound; (2) bemoan, bewail, complain, deplore, lament, sorrow, suffer.

Ant. of (1) comfort; of (2) rejoice.

grievous (1) afflicting, calamitous, distressing, harmful, heavy, hurtful, injurious, offensive, oppressive, provoking; (2) atrocious, dreadful, flagrant, intolerable, lamentable, outrageous.

Ant. of (1) happy; of (2) pleasant.

grim cruel, ferocious, fierce, forbidding, frightful, grisly, hideous, horrid, ruthless, stern, sullen, surly, terrible, unrelenting.

Ant. gentle.

grimy begrimed, dirty, filthy, foul, unclean.

Ant. clean.

grind (1) bruise, comminute, crush, grate, pound, powder, pulverise, rub, sharpen, triturate; (2) (*Fig.*) afflict, harass, oppress, persecute, plague, trouble.

Ant. of (2) relieve.

grip v. clasp, clutch, grasp, hold, seize.

gripe (1) v. clasp, clutch, grasp, grip, seize, snatch; (2) compress, pinch, press, squeeze; (3) n. clutch, grasp, hold, seizure; (4) affliction, distress, griping, pinching.

grisly appalling, awful, dreadful, ghastly, grim, hideous, terrible.

Ant. agreeable,

grit (1) bran, gravel, pebbles,

sand; (2) (*Fig.*) courage, determination, perseverance, pluck, resolution, spirit.

Ant. of (2) cowardice.

groan complain, lament, moan, whine.

groom hostler, manservant, stableman, valet, waiter.

groove channel, cutting, furrow, rut.

grope feel, fumble, grabble.

gross (1) big, bulky, dense, great, large, massive, thick; (2) coarse, common, impure, indecent, indelicate, lewd, low, rude, sensual, vulgar; (3) apparent, flagrant, glaring, grievous, manifest, obvious, serious, shameful; (4) aggregate, entire, total, whole.

Ant. of (1) small; of (2) decent, pure.

grossness (1) bigness, bulkiness, greatness, thickness; (2) bestiality, coarseness, impurity, indecency, indelicacy, licentiousness, rudeness, sensuality, vulgarity.

Ant. of (1) smallness; of (2) decency.

grotesque bizarre, extravagant, fanciful, ludicrous, odd, ridiculous, unnatural, whimsical.

Ant. natural.

ground (1) clod, earth, field, loam, mould, sod, soil, turf; (2) country, domain, estate, land, property, territory; (3) base, basis, cause, factor, foundation, motive, reason; (4) deposit, dregs, lees, sediment; (5) v. base, establish, fix, found, set; (6) instruct, train.

groundless baseless, false, idle, unauthorised, unfounded, unjustified, unwarranted.

Ant. true.

group (1) bunch, clump,

cluster, collection; (2) v. arrange, assemble, dispose, order.
Ant. of (1) individual; of (2) disarrange.

grove copse, thicket, wood, woodland.

grovel cower, crawl, creep, cringe, crouch, fawn, flatter, sneak.
Ant. face.

grow (1) develop, enlarge, expand, extend, increase, spread, swell; (2) germinate, shoot, sprout, vegetate; (3) advance, become, improve, progress, wax; (4) cultivate, produce, raise.
Ant. of (1) decrease.

growl complain, groan, grumble, lament, murmur, snarl.
Ant. purr.

growth (1) augmentation, development, expansion, extension, growing, increase; (2) cultivation, germination, produce, shooting, sprouting, vegetation; (3) advance, advancement, improvement, progress; (4) (Med.) tumour.
Ant. decline.

grudge (1) v. begrudge, complain, covet, envy, repine; (2) n. aversion, dislike, enmity, grievance, hate, ill-will, malevolence, malice, pique, rancour, spite, venom.
Ant. goodwill.

gruff bearish, blunt, brusque, churlish, grumpy, harsh, impolite, rough, rugged, surly, uncivil, ungracious.
Ant. polite.

grumble complain, croak, murmur, repine, roar, rumble, snarl.

guarantee (1) v. assure, insure, pledge, warrant; (2) n. assurance, pledge, security, surety, warranty.

guard (1) v. defend, keep, protect, safeguard, save, secure, shield, watch; (2) n. protector, sentinel, sentry, watch, watchman; (3) convoy, escort, patrol; (4) bulwark, defence, protection, rampart, safeguard, security, shield; (5) attention, care, caution, heed, watchfulness.
Ant. of (1) attack.

guarded careful, cautious, circumspect, reserved, reticent, wary.
Ant. rash.

guardian custodian, defender, guard, keeper, preserver, protector, trustee, warden.
Ant. ward.

guerdon recompense, remuneration, reward.
Ant. loss.

guess (1) v. believe, conjecture, divine, fancy, hazard, imagine, judge, reckon, suppose, surmise, suspect; (2) estimate, fathom, penetrate, solve; (3) n. conjecture, notion, supposition.
Ant. of (1) know.

guest caller, company, visitant, visitor.
Ant. host.

guidance conduct, control, direction, government, leadership.

guide (1) v. conduct, control, direct, escort, govern, lead, manage, pilot, regulate, rule, steer, superintend, supervise, train; (2) n. adviser, cicerone, conductor, controller, counsellor, director, mentor, monitor, pilot, steersman; (3) clue, guide-book, key, mark, sign, signal, signpost.
Ant. of (1) follow; of (2) follower.

guild association, brotherhood,

company, corporation, fellowship, fraternity, union.

guile art, artfulness, artifice, craft, cunning, deceit, deception, duplicity, knavery, ruse, treachery, trickery, wiliness.
Ant. honesty.

guileless artless, candid, frank, honest, ingenuous, open, simple-minded, sincere, truthful, undesigning.
Ant. cunning.

guilt (1) culpability, guiltiness, iniquity, sinfulness, wickedness, wrong; (2) crime, offence, sin, wrong.
Ant. of (1) innocence.

guiltless blameless, immaculate, innocent, pure, sinless, spotless, unsullied.
Ant. culpable, guilty.

guilty criminal, culpable, evil, sinful, wicked, wrong.
Ant. innocent.

guise (1) appearance, aspect, dress, fashion, form, semblance, shape; (2) custom, habit, manner, mode, practice; (3) air, behaviour, demeanour.

gulf (1) bay, sea-inlet; (2) abyss, chasm, opening, whirlpool.

gull v. beguile, cheat, deceive, defraud, dupe, hoax, swindle, trick.

gullibility credulity, simplicity.
Ant. astuteness.

gumption ability, astuteness, cleverness, commonsense, discernment, nous, sagacity, shrewdness.
Ant. simplicity, stupidity.

gun blunderbuss, cannon, carbine, fowling-piece, musket, pistol, revolver, rifle.

gurgle babble, murmur, purl, ripple.

gush burst, flood, flow, pour, rush, spout, stream.
Ant. stop.

gust (1) blow, breeze, gale, squall; (2) (*Fig.*) fit, outburst, paroxysm, passion.
Ant. calm, lull.

gusto enjoyment, liking, pleasure, relish, savour, zest.
Ant. distaste.

gusty blustering, blustery, squally, stormy, tempestuous, windy.
Ant. calm.

gut (1) v. disembowel, eviscerate; (2) n. pl. bowels, entrails, intestines, inwards, viscera.

gutter channel, conduit, pipe, tube.

guttural deep, gruff, hoarse, thick, throaty.
Ant. clear, mellow.

guzzle carouse, drink, gorge, gormandise, quaff, swill, tope.

gyration revolution, rotation, spinning, whirling.

gyves bonds, chains, fetters, handcuffs, manacles, shackles.

H

habiliment apparel, array, clothes, costume, dress, garb, garment, habit, raiment, robes, uniform, vestments.
Ant. undress.

habit (1) n. bent, constitution, custom, disposition, manner, mode, practice, tendency, usage, way, wont; (2) apparel, dress, garb, garment, habiliment, riding-coat; (3) v. array, attire, clothe, dress, equip.
Ant. of (3) undress.

habitation abode, domicile, dwelling, home, house, lodging, quarters, residence.

habitual accustomed, com-

mon, confirmed, customary, inveterate, ordinary, regular, usual.
Ant. unusual.

habituate accustom, familiarise, harden, inure, train, use.

hack (1) v. chop, cut, haggle, hew, mangle, notch; (2) a. hackney, hired, hireling, mercenary; (3) n. drudge, plodder, slave.

hackneyed common, commonplace, over-worked, stale, threadbare, trite, worn-out, unoriginal.
Ant. original.

hag beldam, fury, Jezebel, shrew, termagant, virago, vixen.

haggard (1) care-worn, emaciated, gaunt, ghastly, lank, lean, meagre, spare, thin, wasted, wrinkled; (2) intractable, refractory, unruly, wayward, wild.
Ant. of (1) robust.

haggle (1) bargain, boggle, chaffer, higgle, stickle; (2) chop, cut, hack, hackle, hew; (3) annoy, badger, bait, harass, tease, worry.

hail accost, address, call, greet, salute, speak, welcome.
Ant. avoid.

halcyon (1) calm, peaceful, placid, quiet, serene, still, tranquil, undisturbed, unruffled; (2) (Fig.) golden, happy, palmy.
Ant. of (1) stormy; of (2) unhappy.

hale healthy, hearty, robust, strong, sound, vigorous, well.
Ant. feeble.

half-witted doltish, dull, dull-witted, feeble-minded, foolish, silly, simple, stupid.
Ant. intelligent.

hall (1) chamber, corridor, entrance-hall, entry, lobby, vestibule; (2) college, (Univ.) diningroom manor, mansion.

halloo call, cry, holla, shout.

hallow consecrate, dedicate, devote, enshrine, respect, reverence, sanctify, venerate.
Ant. desecrate.

hallowed blessed, holy, honoured, revered, sacred.
Ant. desecrated.

hallucination (1) aberration, delusion, dream, illusion, phantasy, vision; (2) blunder, error, fallacy, mistake.
Ant. reality.

halt (1) v. cease, desist, hold, rest, stop; (2) hesitate, pause, stammer, waver; (3) falter, hobble, limp; (4) a. crippled, lame, limping; (5) n. stop, stand, standstill; (6) limp, limping, stammer.
Ant. of (1) continue.

hammer v. forge, form, make, shape.

hamper v. bind, curb, encumber, entangle, fetter, hinder, impede, obstruct, prevent, restrain.
Ant. encourage.

hand (1) v. conduct, convey, give, guide, lead, present, transmit; (2) n. fist, palm; (3) artificer, artisan, craftsman, employee, labourer, operative, worker, workman; (4) agency, direction, part, participation, share.

handcuff fetter, manacle, shackle.

handle (1) v. feel, manage, manipulate, operate, touch, use, wield; (2) discourse, discuss, treat; (3) n. haft, helve, hilt, stock.

handsome (1) admirable, becoming, comely, elegant,

fine, good-looking, graceful; (2) ample, considerable, generous, large, liberal, magnanimous, plentiful.

Ant. of (1) ugly; of (2) stingy.

handy (1) adroit, clever, dexterous, expert, ready, skilful, skilled, useful; (2) close, convenient, near.

Ant. of (1) awkward; of (2) inconvenient.

hang (1) bend, dangle, depend, droop, incline, suspend; (2) execute; (3) adhere, cling, hold, rest, stick; (4) attach, cover, decorate, drape, furnish; (5) float, hover, loiter, swing.

hanker covet, crave, desire, hunger, long, lust, want, yearn.

hap accident, chance, fate, fortune, lot.

hapless ill-fated, ill-starred, miserable, unfortunate, unhappy, unlucky, wretched.

Ant. lucky.

happen befall, betide, chance, come, occur, supervene.

happiness beatitude, blessedness, contentment, delight, enjoyment, felicity, gaiety, joy, merriment, prosperity, well-being.

Ant. sadness.

happy (1) blessed, blest, blissful, contented, delighted, glad, gratified, joyous, merry, pleased; (2) fortunate, lucky, successful; (3) able, adroit, apt, dexterous, expert, ready; (4) appropriate, auspicious, befitting, favourable, felicitous, opportune, propitious, seasonable, well-timed.

Ant. of (1) unhappy; of (2) unlucky; of (3) inapt.

harangue (1) n. address, bombast, declamation, oration, screed, speech, tirade; (2) v. address, declaim, spout.

harass annoy, badger, disturb, exhaust, fatigue, harry, jade, perplex, pester, plague, tease, tire, torment, trouble, vex, weary, worry.

Ant. soothe.

harbour (1) n. anchorage, destination, haven, port; (2) asylum, covert, refuge, retreat, sanctuary, security; (3) v. cherish, conceal, entertain, foster, hide, lodge, protect, relieve, secrete, shelter.

Ant. of (3) banish.

hard (1) compact, dense, firm, impenetrable, rigid, solid, stiff, unyielding; (2) arduous, exacting, fatiguing, laborious, toilsome, wearying; (3) complicated, difficult, intricate, perplexing, puzzling; (4) callous, cruel, hard-hearted, harsh, obdurate, severe, stern, stubborn, unfeeling, unjust, unkind, unsympathetic; (5) calamitous, disagreeable, distressing, grievous, painful, unpleasant; (6) coarse, harsh, rough, sour, tough, uneatable.

Ant. of (1) soft; of (2) light; of (3) easy; of (4) kind; of (5) agreeable.

hard-headed astute, cool, intelligent, sagacious, shrewd, well-balanced, wise.

Ant. simple.

harden (1) accustom, habituate, inure, season, train; (2) brace, fortify, indurate, nerve, steel, strengthen, toughen.

Ant. of (2) soften.

hardihood (1) boldness, bravery, courage, daring, determination, firmness, intrepidity, mettle, pluck, resolution, strength; (2) assurance, audacity, effrontery, impertinence.

Ant. of (1) timidity; of (2) politeness.

hardship adversity, affliction, austerity, burden, calamity, fatigue, grievance, labour, misfortune, need, oppression, persecution, privation, suffering, toil, trial, trouble.

Ant. prosperity.

hardy (1) bold, brave, courageous, heroic, intrepid, manly, resolute, stout-hearted, valiant, valorous; (2) firm, hale, healthy, hearty, robust, stout, sound, vigorous.

Ant. of (1) faint-hearted; of (2) weak.

hare-brained careless, flighty, giddy, harum-scarum, heedless, rash, reckless, unstable, unsteady, wild.

Ant. reliable.

hark attend, hear, hearken, listen.

harm (1) v. abuse, damage, hurt, ill-treat, ill-use, injure, maltreat, molest; (2) n. damage, detriment, evil, hurt, injury, loss, mischief, misfortune, wickedness, wrong.

Ant. of (1) benefit; of (2) good.

harmful baleful, baneful, deleterious, disadvantageous, hurtful, injurious, noxious.

Ant. harmless, innocuous.

harmless gentle, innocent, innocuous, inoffensive, innoxious, safe.

Ant. harmful.

harmonious (1) concordant, congruous, consonant, correspondent, dulcet, euphonious, harmonic, mellifluous, melodious, musical, tuneful; (2) agreeable, amicable, congenial, cordial, fraternal, friendly, sympathetic.

Ant. of (1) discordant; of (2) unfriendly.

harmonise accord, adapt, agree, arrange, cohere, correspond, reconcile, tally.

Ant. differ.

harmony (1) euphony, melodiousness, melody; (2) accord, agreement, amity, concord, friendship, peace, understanding, unity; (3) congruity, consonance, correspondence, fitness, suitability.

Ant. of (1) cacophony; of (2) disagreement; of (3) unsuitability.

harness equipment, gear, tackle.

harp v. reiterate, renew, repeat.

harping n. reiteration, repetition.

harrow v. (Fig.) harass, lacerate, rend, tear, torment, torture, wound.

Ant. soothe.

harry (1) devastate, pillage, plunder, raid, ravage, rob; (2) (Fig.) annoy, disturb, fret, harass, molest, pester, plague, tease, trouble, vex, worry.

Ant. of (2) comfort.

harsh (1) abusive, austere, bitter, brutal, cruel, hard, severe, sharp, stern, unfeeling, unkind, unpleasant; (2) discordant, dissonant, grating, jarring, rough, unmelodious.

Ant. of (1) gentle; of (2) harmonious.

harshness acerbity, acrimony, asperity, austerity, churlishness, hardness, ill-temper, rigour, roughness, severity, sourness, sternness, tartness.

Ant. mildness.

harvest (1) crop, harvest-time, ingathering, produce, yield; (2) (Fig.) consequence, effect, result.

haste alacrity, bustle, celerity,

despatch, expedition, hurry, nimbleness, promptitude, quickness, rapidity, rapidness, speed, swiftness, velocity.
Ant. slowness.

hasten accelerate, expedite, hurry, precipitate, press, push, quicken, speed, urge.
Ant. retard.

hasty (1) eager, expeditious, fast, hurried, rapid, speedy; (2) excited, irascible, irritable, passionate, quick-tempered; (3) foolhardy, indiscreet, precipitate, rash, reckless, thoughtless.
Ant. of (1) deliberate; of (2) dispassionate; of (3) cautious.

hatch (1) breed, incubate; (2) (*Fig.*) concoct, contrive, design, devise, plot, project, scheme.

hate (1) *v.* abhor, abominate, detest, dislike, execrate, loathe; (2) *n.* abomination, animosity, antipathy, detestation, dislike, enmity, execration, hatred, loathing.
Ant. love.

hateful abhorrent, abominable, detestable, disgusting, execrable, forbidding, foul, horrible, obnoxious, odious, offensive, repugnant, repulsive, revolting, vile.
Ant. attractive.

hatred abomination, animosity, antipathy, aversion, detestation, dislike, hate, odium, repugnance, revulsion.
Ant. love.

haughtiness arrogance, contempt, contemptuousness, disdain, insolence, loftiness, pride, snobbishness, superciliousness.
Ant. humility.

haughty arrogant, assuming, contemptuous, disdainful, high, imperious, lofty, over-

weening, proud, scornful, snobbish, supercilious.
Ant. humble.

haul drag, draw, lug, pull, tow, trail, tug.
Ant. push.

haunt (1) frequent, repair, resort, visit; (2) follow, importune.
Ant. of (1) desert.

hauteur arrogance, contempt, dignity, disdain, haughtiness, loftiness, pride, stateliness, superciliousness.
Ant. condescension.

have (1) accept, acquire, gain, get, obtain, receive, take; (2) hold, obtain, occupy, own, possess.
Ant. lose.

haven (1) anchorage, harbour, port; (2) (*Fig.*) asylum, refuge, retreat, shelter.

havoc carnage, damage, desolation, destruction, devastation, ravage, ruin, slaughter, waste, wreck.
Ant. restoration.

hazard (1) *v.* endanger, imperil, jeopardise, risk, venture; (2) *n.* accident, chance, danger, hap, jeopardy, luck, peril, risk.
Ant. of (2) safety.

hazardous dangerous, insecure, perilous, precarious, risky, uncertain, unsafe.
Ant. secure.

haze cloud, dimness, fog, mist, obscurity, smog, vapour.
Ant. clearness.

hazy (1) cloudy, dim, foggy, misty, nebulous, obscure; (2) (*Fig.*) indefinite, indistinct, loose, uncertain, vague.
Ant. clear.

head (1) apex, height, pitch, summit, top; (2) chief, chieftain, commander, director, leader, manager, master, principal, superintendent, supervisor; (3) beginning, commencement, origin, rise, source; (4) brain, crown, headpiece, mind, (*Colloq.*) noddle, intellect, thought, understanding; (5) branch, category, class, department, division, section, subject, topic; (6) conclusion, crisis, culmination; (7) (*Geog.*) cape, headland, point, promontory; (8) *v.* beat, command, control, direct, excel, govern, guide, lead, outdo, precede, rule, surpass; (9) *a.* chief, first, foremost, front, leading, main, principal, topmost.

headlong (1) *a.* dangerous, hasty, impulsive, inconsiderate, precipitate, reckless, thoughtless; (2) perpendicular, precipitous, sheer, steep; (3) *adv.* hastily, helter-skelter, hurriedly, precipitately, rashly, thoughtlessly.
Ant. of (3) cautiously.

headstrong cantankerous, froward, intractable, obstinate, pig-headed, self-willed, stubborn, ungovernable, unruly.
Ant. tractable.

heady (1) hasty, impetuous, impulsive, inconsiderate, precipitate, rash, reckless, stubborn, thoughtless, violent; (2) exciting, inebriating, intoxicating, spirituous, strong.
Ant. of (1) cautious; of (2) sobering, weak.

heal (1) cure, remedy, restore; (2) harmonise, reconcile, settle, soothe.
Ant. of (1) injure.

healing (1) curative, palliative, remedial, restorative, restoring; (2) assuaging, comforting, gentle, mild, soothing.
Ant. of (1) injurious.

health robustness, salubrity, soundness, strength, vigour.
Ant. sickness, weakness.

healthy (1) active, hale, hearty, vigorous, sound, well; (2) bracing, healthful, health-giving, hygienic, invigorating, nourishing, salubrious, wholesome.
Ant. of (1) unwell; of (2) unwholesome.

heap (1) *n.* accumulation, collection, lot, mass, pile, stack, store; (2) *v.* accumulate, amass, augment, collect, increase, pile, store.

heart (1) centre, core, essence, kernel, marrow, nucleus, pith; (2) affection, benevolence, character, disposition, feeling, inclination, love, mind, purpose, will; (3) boldness, courage, fortitude, resolution, spirit.
Ant. of (1) exterior; of (3) timidity.

heartache affliction, anguish, bitterness, distress, grief, heartbreak, sorrow.
Ant. joy.

hearten animate, assure, cheer, comfort, console, encourage, incite, reassure, stimulate.
Ant. depress.

heartfelt cordial, deep, hearty, profound, sincere, warm.
Ant. insincere.

heartily (1) cordially, profoundly, sincerely, warmly; (2) ardently, eagerly, earnestly, resolutely, zealously.

heartless (1) brutal, cruel, hard, harsh, merciless, pitiless, unfeeling; (2) fearful, spiritless, timid.
Ant. of (1) kind; of (2) brave.

hearty (1) ardent, cordial, eager, earnest, genuine, honest, real, true, unfeigned, warm, zealous; (2) active, energetic, hale, healthy, robust, sound, strong, vigorous, well.

Ant. of (1) cold, insincere; of (2) weak.

heat (*Fig.*) (1) *n.* ardour, earnestness, excitement, fervour, fever, impetuosity, intensity, passion, vehemence, violence, warmth, zeal; (2) *v.* animate, excite, rouse, stimulate, stir, warm.

Ant. of (1) coolness; of (2) cool.

heathen idolater, idolatress, infidel, pagan, unbeliever.

Ant. Christian.

heathenish barbarous, cruel, heathen, inhuman, irreligious, pagan, savage.

Ant. humane.

heave (1) elevate, hoist, lift, raise; (2) cast, fling, hurl, send, strive, struggle, throw, toss; (3) breathe, dilate, exhale, expand, pant, rise, swell.

Ant. of (1) drop.

heaven (1) firmament, sky, welkin; (2) (*Fig.*) bliss, ecstasy, Elysium, felicity, happiness, paradise, rapture, transport.

Ant. of (2) hell.

heavenly angelic, beatific, blest, celestial, cherubic, delightful, divine, glorious, godlike, holy, immortal, rapturous, ravishing, seraphic, superhuman, supernatural.

Ant. earthly.

heaviness (1) gravity, ponderousness, weight; (2) grievousness, oppressiveness, severity; (3) dullness, languor, lassitude, sluggishness; (4) dejection, depression, despondency, gloom, melancholy, sadness, seriousness.

Ant. of (1) lightness; of (4) gaiety.

heavy (1) bulky, massive, ponderous, weighty; (2) burdensome, difficult, grievous, hard, laborious, oppressive, severe, tedious, wearisome; (3) drowsy, dull, inactive, indolent, inert, slow, sluggish, stupid; (4) crestfallen, dejected, depressed, despondent, disconsolate, downcast, gloomy, melancholy, sad, serious; (5) abundant, burdened, copious, encumbered, loaded; (6) boisterous, rough, stormy, tempestuous, violent.

Ant. of (1) light; of (2) easy; of (3) alert; of (6) calm.

hebetate (1) *v.* blunt, stupefy; (2) *a.* dull, obtuse, sluggish, stupid, stupefied.

Ant. of (2) sharp.

hectic animated, excited, fevered, feverish, flushed, heated, hot, wild.

Ant. calm.

hector (1) *v.* bluster, boast, browbeat, bully, harass, menace, provoke, threaten, worry; (2) *n.* boaster, browbeater, bully, swaggerer.

Ant. of (1) encourage, persuade.

hedge (1) *n.* hedge-fence, hedgerow; (2) *v.* block, enclose, fence, hinder, obstruct, surround; (3) fortify, guard, protect, shield; (4) disappear, dodge, hide, skulk.

Ant. of (2) admit.

heed (1) *v.* attend, consider, mark, mind, note, obey, observe, regard; (2) *n.* attention, care, caution, consideration heedfulness, watchfulness.

Ant. of (1) disregard; of (2) neglect.

heedful attentive, careful, cautious, circumspect, mindful, observant, wary, watchful.
Ant. careless.

heedless careless, inattentive, neglectful, negligent, precipitate, rash, reckless, thoughtless, unmindful, unobservant.
Ant. careful.

height (1) acme, altitude, apex, elevation, hill, mountain, peak, summit, top, zenith; (2) dignity, eminence, exaltation, grandeur, loftiness.
Ant. of (1) bottom; of (2) baseness.

heighten (1) aggravate, amplify, augment, greaten, improve, increase, intensify; (2) elevate, enhance, ennoble, exalt, magnify, raise.
Ant. of (1) lower; of (2) abase.

heinous abominable, atrocious, awful, execrable, flagrant, grave, hateful, infamous, nefarious, odious, outrageous, villainous.
Ant. praiseworthy.

hellish (1) damnable, damned, demoniacal, devilish, diabolical, fiendish, infernal; (2) abominable, accursed, atrocious, detestable, execrable, monstrous, nefarious.
Ant. of (1) angelic.

helm (1) (*Naut.*) rudder, steering-gear, tiller, wheel; (2) (*Fig.*) command, control, direction, rule; (3) (*Poet.*) casque, head-piece, helmet, morion.

help (1) *v.* abet, aid, assist, back, co-operate, promote, relieve, save, second, succour, support; (2) alleviate, ameliorate, cure, heal, improve, remedy, restore; (3) avoid, control, forbear, hinder, prevent, resist, withstand; (4) *n.* aid, assistance, assistant,

helper, remedy, relief, succour, support.
Ant. of (1) obstruct; of (2) aggravate.

helper abettor, aider, ally, assistant, auxiliary, coadjutor, colleague, helpmate, partner, supporter.
Ant. adversary.

helpful (1) advantageous, beneficial, useful; (2) beneficent, benevolent, kind.
Ant. of (1) disadvantageous.

helpless abandoned, defenceless, disabled, exposed, feeble, impotent, infirm, irreparable, irretrievable, powerless, unprotected.
Ant. strong.

helpmate assistant, associate, companion, consort, helper, partner, wife.
Ant. adversary.

hem (1) *v.* beset, border, confine, edge, enclose, environ, skirt, surround; (2) *n.* edge, border, fringe, margin.

herald (1) *n.* crier, forerunner, harbinger, messenger, precursor, publisher; (2) *v.* announce, proclaim, publish.

herbage grass, herbs, pasture, vegetation.

herculean (1) athletic, brawny, massive, mighty, muscular, powerful, sinewy, stalwart, sturdy; (2) colossal, huge, gigantic, great, large; (3) (*Fig.*) arduous, dangerous, difficult, hard, laborious, toilsome.
Ant. of (1) puny; of (2) slight; of (3) easy.

herd (1) assemblage, collection, crowd, drove, flock, multitude; (2) (*Fig.*) populace, rabble; (3) drover, herdsman, shepherd; (4) *v.* assemble, associate, flock.

hereditary ancestral, inheritable, inherited, patrimonial, transmitted.

heresy error, heterodoxy, impiety, unorthodoxy.
Ant. orthodoxy.

heretic dissenter, nonconformist, sectarian, schismatic, separatist.

heretical heterodox, impious, schismatic, unorthodox.
Ant. orthodox.

heritage estate, inheritance, legacy, patrimony, portion.

hermetic(al) (1) air-tight; (2) cabalistic, emblematic, mysterious, mystic, mystical, occult, symbolical.
Ant. open.

hermit anchoret, anchorite, monk, recluse, solitary.

heroic bold, brave, courageous, daring, dauntless, fearless.
Ant. cowardly.

heroism fearlessness, fortitude, gallantry, intrepidity, spirit, valour.
Ant. cowardice.

hesitate deliberate, demur, doubt, falter, stammer, stutter, vacillate, wait, waver.
Ant. resolve.

hesitation delay, doubt, dubiety, hesitancy, indecision, irresolution, reluctance, stammering, stuttering, suspense, vacillation.
Ant. certainty.

heterodox heretical, schismatic, unorthodox, unsound.
Ant. orthodox.

heterogeneous contrary, contrasted, different, dissimilar, diverse, incongruous, miscellaneous, mixed, opposed, unlike.
Ant. alike, homogeneous.

hew (1) chop, cut, hack; (2) fashion, form, shape, smoothe.

hiatus aperture, breach, break,

chasm, interval, gap, lacuna opening, rift.

hidden abstruse, clandestine, close, concealed, covered, covert, dark, hermetic, hermetical, mysterious, mystic, mystical, obscure, occult, recondite, secret, shrouded, unrevealed, veiled.
Ant. revealed.

hide bury, cloak, conceal, cover, disguise, mask, screen, secrete, shelter, shroud, suppress, veil, withhold.
Ant. reveal.

hideous abominable, appalling, awful, detestable, dreadful, ghastly, grim, grisly, horrible, horrid, repulsive, shocking, terrible, terrifying, ugly.
Ant. pleasing.

hie fly, hasten, speed.
Ant. stroll.

hieroglyph picture-word, picture-writing, sign, symbol.

hieroglyphic(al) enigmatical, figurative, obscure, symbolical.

higgle bargain, chaffer, haggle, hawk, peddle.

higgledy-piggledy confusedly, disorderly, helter-skelter, pell-mell, topsy-turvy.
Ant. orderly.

high (1) elevated, lofty, tall, towering; (2) extreme, great, strong; (3) chief, distinguished, eminent, exalted, prominent, superior; (4) arrogant, boastful, bragging, despotic, domineering, haughty, lordly, overbearing, ostentatious, proud, tyrannical vainglorious; (5) capital, extreme, grave, important, serious; (6) boisterous, strong, tumultuous, turbulent; (7) costly, dear, expensive; (8) acute, high-pitched, sharp,

shrill, strident; (9) strong-flavoured, tainted.
Ant. low.

high-handed arbitrary, despotic, dictatorial, domineering, imperious, oppressive, overbearing, self-willed, wilful.
Ant. retiring.

high-minded (1) arrogant, haughty, lofty, proud, snobbish; (2) elevated, honourable, magnanimous, noble.
Ant. of (1) modest.

high-strung ardent, excitable, high-spirited, irascible, quick, sensitive.
Ant. imperturbable.

hilarious convivial, exhilarated, gay, happy, jolly, jovial, joyful, joyous, merry, mirthful, noisy.
Ant. downcast.

hilarity cheerfulness, conviviality, exhilaration, gaiety, glee, jollity, joviality, joyousness, merriment.
Ant. sadness.

hill ben, elevation, eminence, height, hillock, knoll, mound, mount, mountain, prominence, tor.
Ant. valley.

hind boor, bumpkin, clodhopper, countryman, herd, peasant, ploughman, rustic, swain.

hinder arrest, check, debar, delay, embarrass, encumber, impede, interrupt, obstruct, oppose, retard, stop, thwart, trammel.
Ant. assist.

hindrance check, deterrent, difficulty, encumbrance, hitch, impediment, interruption, obstacle, obstruction, restraint, stoppage.
Ant. support.

hinge depend, hang, rest, turn.

hint (1) v. allude, imply, insinuate, intimate, mention, suggest; (2) n. allusion, implication, innuendo, insinuation, intimation, mention, reminder, suggestion.

hire (1) n. allowance, pay, recompense, remuneration, rent, reward, salary, stipend, wages; (2) v. bribe, buy, charter, employ, engage, lease, let, rent.

hirsute (1) bearded, bristly, hairy, hispid, shaggy; (2) boorish, coarse, loutish, rough, rude, rustic, uncouth.
Ant. of (1) beardless, hairless; of (2) refined.

hiss (1) shrill, sibilate, whirr, whistle, whiz; (2) condemn, damn, decry, hoot, ridicule.
Ant. of (2) applaud, cheer.

historian annalist, autobiographer, biographer, chronicler, narrator, recorder, storyteller.

history account, autobiography, biography, annals, chronicle, memoirs, narration, narrative, recital, record, relation, story.

hit (1) beat, clash, collide, smite, strike; (2) accomplish, achieve, attain, reach, secure; (3) gain, succeed, win; (4) n. blow, clash, collision, stroke; (5) chance, fortune, gain, success, venture.
Ant. miss.

hitch (1) v. attach, connect, fasten, harness, join, tether, tie, unite, yoke; (2) n. catch, check, hindrance, impediment.
Ant. of (1) loose, untie.

hoard accumulate, amass, collect, deposit, garner, gather, hive, save, store, treasure.
Ant. squander.

hoarse discordant, grating,

gruff, harsh, husky, raucous, rough.

Ant. melodious.

hoary gray, grey, frosty, hoar, silvery, white.

Ant. dark.

hoax (1) *n.* cheat, deception, fraud, imposture, joke, swindle, trick; (2) *v.* befool, deceive, dupe, fool, gammon, gull, hoodwink, swindle, trick.

hobble (1) falter, halt, limp; (2) fasten, fetter, shackle, tie; (3) *n.* difficulty, embarrassment, perplexity, strait.

Ant. of (1) run; of (2) unfasten.

hobgoblin apparition, bogey, goblin, imp, spectre, spirit, sprite.

hocus-pocus (1) cheater, juggler, impostor, sharper, swindler; (2) artifice, cheat, deceit, deception, delusion, hoax, imposture, swindle.

Ant. of (2) honesty.

hodge-podge farrago, gallimaufry, hash, hotch-potch, jumble, miscellany, mixture, olla-podrida, olio, ragout.

hoggish brutish, filthy, gluttonous, greedy, mean, piggish, sordid, swinish.

Ant. decent, refined.

hoiden hoyden, romp, tomboy.

hoidenish boisterous, bold, hoydenish, inelegant, uncouth, ungenteel, unladylike, unruly.

Ant. ladylike.

hoist (1) *v.* elevate, heave, lift, raise; (2) *n.* elevator, lift.

Ant. of (1) lower.

hold (1) *v.* have, keep, occupy, own, possess, retain; (2) adhere, cleave, clinch, cling, clutch, grasp, grip, stick; (3) arrest, bind, check, confine, detain, imprison, restrain, stay, stop, suspend; (4) believe, consider,

deem, entertain, esteem, judge, maintain, reckon, regard; (5) continue, endure, last, persist, remain; (6) assemble, call, convene; (7) celebrate, preside, solemnise; (8) *n.* clutch, control, grasp, grip, influence; (9) footing, prop, stay, support, vantage; (10) fort, fortification, fortress, keep, stronghold, tower.

hole (1) aperture, breach, break, opening, perforation; (2) cave, cavern, cavity, excavation, hollow, pit; (3) burrow, cover, den, hovel, lair, retreat.

holiday anniversary, celebration, feast, festival, festivity, fête, gala, recess, vacation.

Ant. work-day.

holiness blessedness, devoutness, godliness, piety, purity, religiousness, righteousness, sacredness, saintliness, sanctity.

Ant. sinfulness.

hollow (1) cavernous, concave, empty, sunken, vacant, void; (2) artificial, deceitful, faithless, false, flimsy, hollowhearted, insincere, treacherous, unsound, weak; (3) deep, low, rumbling; (4) *n.* cave, cavern, cavity, concavity, cup, den, dent, depression, dimple, excavation, hole, pit; (5) basin, canal, channel, groove; (6) *v.* dig, excavate, groove, scoop.

Ant. of (1) full; of (2) genuine.

holy (1) devout, divine, godly, hallowed, pious, pure, religious, righteous, saintly; (2) blessed, consecrated, dedicated, hallowed, sacred.

Ant. of (1) sinful; of (2) desecrated.

homage (1) allegiance, devotion, faithfulness, fealty, fidelity, loyalty, obeisance, service, tribute; (2) adoration, deference, duty, honour, respect, reverence, worship.

Ant. of (1) disloyalty; of (2) disrespect.

homely coarse, commonplace, domestic, familiar, homelike, homespun, inelegant, plain, simple, unattractive, uncomely, unpolished, unpretentious.

Ant. elaborate.

homespun coarse, homely, home-made, inelegant, plain, rough, rude, unpolished.

Ant. fine.

homicide manslaughter, murder.

homily address, discourse, lecture, sermon.

homogeneous akin, cognate, kindred, similar, uniform.

Ant. heterogeneous.

honest candid, conscientious, creditable, decent, equitable, fair, frank, honourable, genuine, ingenuous, just, proper, reliable, reputable, sincere, straightforward, suitable, true, trustworthy, trusty, upright, virtuous.

Ant. dishonest.

honesty candour, equity, fairness, faithfulness, fidelity, genuineness, honour, probity, rectitude, sincerity, trustworthiness, truthfulness, uprightness, veracity, virtue.

Ant. dishonesty.

honorary formal, nominal, titular, unofficial, unpaid.

honour (1) credit, dignity, distinction, elevation, esteem, fame, glory, rank, renown, reputation; (2) deference, homage, respect, reverence, veneration; (3) honesty, integrity, probity, rectitude, uprightness; (4) chastity, purity, virginity, virtue; (5) v. celebrate, commemorate, dignify, respect; (6) adore, exalt, glorify, hallow, revere, reverence, venerate, worship.

Ant. dishonour.

honourable (1) fair, just, honest, true, trustworthy, trusty, upright, virtuous; (2) distinguished, great, illustrious, noble, renowned; (3) creditable, estimable, proper, reputable, respected, right.

Ant. of (1) untrustworthy; of (2) low; of (3) disreputable.

honours adornments, decorations, dignities, distinctions, titles.

hoodwink (1) blind, blindfold, conceal, cloak, cover, hide; (2) befool, cheat, delude, dupe, gull, hoax, fool, impose, swindle, trick.

Ant. of (1) disclose.

hook (1) v. catch, clasp, hasp; (2) catch, ensnare, entrap, snare, trap; (3) n. catch, clasp, fastener, hasp, holder; (4) cutter, grass-hook, sickle.

hooked aquiline, bent, curved, hamate.

Ant. straight.

hoop (1) band, circlet, girdle, ring; (2) crinoline, farthingale, hoop-skirt.

hoot (1) cry, shout, toot, yell; (2) (Fig.) condemn, decry, denounce, execrate, hiss.

Ant. of (2) applaud.

hop (1) v. bound, caper, dance, jump, leap, skip, spring; (2) halt, limp.

hope (1) n. anticipation, belief, confidence, desire, faith, longing, prospect, reliance, trust; (2) v. anticipate, await, believe, desire, expect, long, rely, trust.

Ant. of (1) despair.

hopeful (1) confident, expec-

tant, optimistic, sanguine; (2) cheerful, encouraging, promising.
Ant. of (1) hopeless; of (2) cheerless.

hopeless (1) despairing, desperate, despondent, disconsolate, forlorn, woebegone; (2) helpless, incurable, irremediable, remediless; (3) impossible, impracticable, unachievable, unattainable.
Ant. of (1) hopeful.

horde band, crew, crowd, gang, host, multitude, pack, troop.

horrible abominable, appalling, awful, dreadful, fearful, frightful, ghastly, grim, grisly, hideous, horrid, repulsive, revolting, shocking, terrible, terrifying, unpleasant.
Ant. agreeable.

horrid abominable, alarming, appalling, awful, formidable, hair-raising, harrowing, hideous, horrible, horrific, odious, repulsive, revolting, shocking, terrible, terrific, terrifying, terrorising.
Ant. delightful.

horrify affright, alarm, frighten, shock, terrify, terrorise.
Ant. hearten.

horror (1) alarm, awe, consternation, dismay, dread, fear, fright; (2) abhorrence, abomination, detestation, disgust, hatred, loathing.
Ant. of (1) courage; of (2) approval.

horse (1) charger, cob, colt, filly, gelding, mare, nag, palfrey, pony, stallion, steed; (2) cavalry, horseman.

horseman cavalier, cavalryman, dragoon, equestrian, horse-soldier, rider.

hospitable attentive, bountiful, charitable, generous, kind,

liberal, receptive, sociable.
Ant. parsimonious.

host (1) entertainer, innkeeper, landlord, proprietor; (2) army, assemblage, horde, legion, multitude, throng.

hostile adverse, antagonistic, contrary, inimical, opposed, opposite, unfriendly.
Ant. friendly.

hostilities conflict, fighting, war, warfare.
Ant. peace.

hostility animosity, antagonism, antipathy, aversion, enmity, hatred, ill-will, opposition, unfriendliness.
Ant. friendliness.

hot (1) boiling, burning, fiery, flaming, heated, roasting, warm; (2) acrid, biting, peppery, piquant, pungent, spicy; (3) (*Fig.*) animated, ardent, excited, fervent, fervid, impetuous, irascible, passionate, touchy, vehement, violent.
Ant. cold.

hotel guest-house, hostel, hostelry, inn, motel, pension, public-house, road-house, tavern.

hound (1) chase, drive, hunt, pursue; (2) goad, harass, harry, incite, spur, stimulate, urge.

house (1) abode, building, domicile, dwelling, edifice, home, mansion, residence; (2) family, household, kindred, lineage, race, tribe; (3) business, company, concern, establishment, firm, partnership; (4) hotel, inn, public house, tavern; (5) *v.* lodge, protect, shelter.

household (1) *n.* family, home, house; (2) *a.* domestic, domiciliary, family.

hovel cabin, den, hole, hut, shed.

Ant. mansion.

hover flutter, fly, hang, waver.
Ant. rest.

however but, nevertheless, notwithstanding, still, though, yet.

howl cry, lament, roar, wail, weep, yell.

hoyden hoiden, romp, tomboy.

hoydenish boisterous, bold, hoidenish, ill-mannered, inelegant, uncouth, ungenteel, unladylike, unruly.

hubbub clamour, confusion, din, disorder, disturbance, noise, racket, riot, uproar.
Ant. calm.

huckster hawker, peddler, retailer.

huddle confusion, crowd, disorder, disturbance, tumult.

hue colour, complexion, dye, shade, tinge, tint, tone.

huff anger, passion, pet, rage, temper.

hug (1) clasp, cling, grasp, grip; (2) cherish, embrace, nurse, retain.

huge bulky, colossal, enormous, gigantic, immense, large, mammoth, prodigious, stupendous, tremendous, vast.
Ant. tiny.

hull covering, husk, peel, shell.

hullabaloo clamour, confusion, din, disturbance, hubbub, noise, outcry, racket, uproar.
Ant. calm.

hum buzz, drone, mumble, murmur.

humane benevolent, benign, charitable, clement, compassionate, gentle, kind, kind-hearted, merciful, mild, sympathetic, tender.
Ant. cruel, inhumane.

humanise civilise, cultivate, educate, enlighten, improve, polish, reclaim, refine, soften.

Ant. brutalise.

humanity (1) mankind, men; (2) benevolence, benignity, charity, compassion, fellow-feeling, kind-heartedness, philanthropy, sympathy, tenderness.
Ant. of (2) cruelty.

humble (1) a. common, low, lowly, mean, meek, modest, obscure, poor, submissive, unassuming, unpretentious; (2) courteous, polite, respectful; (3) v. abase, abash, break, crush, debase, degrade, depress, disgrace, humiliate, lower, mortify, reduce, sink, subdue.
Ant. of (1) conceited; of (3) raise.

humbug (1) cheat, deception, dodge, feint, fraud, hoax, imposition, imposture, swindle, trick; (2) cant, charlatanry, hypocrisy, quackery; (3) charlatan, cheat, impostor, quack; (4) v. befool, deceive, delude, dupe, fool, hoax, impose, mislead, swindle, trick.

humdrum boring, dreary, dull, monotonous, tedious, tiresome, uninteresting, unvaried, wearisome.
Ant. interesting.

humid damp, dank, moist, watery, wet.
Ant. arid.

humiliate abase, abash, debase, degrade, depress, disgrace, humble, mortify, shame.
Ant. exalt.

humiliation abasement, affront, condescension, degradation, disgrace, humbling, indignity, mortification, self-abasement, shame, submission, submissiveness, resignation.
Ant. elevation.

humility diffidence, humbleness, lowliness, meekness, modesty, submissiveness.

humorist droll, eccentric, jester, wag, wit.

humorous capricious, comical, funny, jocose, jocular, laughable, merry, playful, pleasant, whimsical, witty.
Ant. serious.

humour (1) bent, bias, fancy, freak, mood, propensity, vagary, whim; (2) amusement, facetiousness, fun, jocularity, wit; (3) v. favour, gratify, indulge.
Ant. of (2) seriousness.

hunch (1) n. bunch, hunk, knob, lump; (2) v. punch, push, shove.

hunger v. crave, desire, hanker, long, pine, wish.

hungry covetous, craving, desirous, famishing, greedy, starved, starving.
Ant. satisfied.

hunt (1) v. chase, hound, pursue; (2) look, search, seek; (3) n. chase, hunting, pursuit, search.
Ant. of (1) flee.

hurl cast, fling, project, send, sling, throw, toss.

hurricane cyclone, gale, storm, tempest, tornado, typhoon.
Ant. zephyr.

hurry (1) v. accelerate, expedite, haste, hasten, quicken, speed, urge; (2) n. bustle, celerity, commotion, despatch, expedition, haste, precipitation, promptitude, quickness, speed, urgency.
Ant. of (1) retard; of (2) slowness.

hurt (1) bruise, damage, harm, impair, injure, wound; (2) (*Fig.*) afflict, annoy, grieve, pain; (3) n. bruise, detriment,

disadvantage, injury, loss, mischief, wound, wrong.
Ant. repair.

hurtful baleful, baneful, destructive, detrimental, disadvantageous, harmful, injurious, mischievous, noxious, pernicious, unwholesome.
Ant. beneficial.

husband v. economise, hoard, save, store.
Ant. squander.

husbandry (1) agriculture, cultivation, farming, tillage; (2) economy, frugality, thrift.

hush allay, appease, calm, conceal, quiet, repress, silence, suppress.

husk bark, chaff, covering, glume, hull, rind.

huskiness harshness, hoarseness, roughness.

husky (1) dry, shrivelled; (2) harsh, hoarse, raucous, rough.
Ant. of (2) mellifluous.

hussy jade, quean, wench.

hustle bustle, crowd, elbow, haste, hasten, hurry, jog, push, shove, thrust.
Ant. loiter.

hut cabin, cot, den, hovel, shed.

hutch bin, box, chest, coffer, cupboard.

hybrid n. cross-breed, half-breed, mongrel, mule.
Ant. thoroughbred.

hymeneal bridal, conjugal, connubial, matrimonial, nuptial.

hypercritical captious, cavilling, fault-finding, over-critical.
Ant. tolerant.

hypnotic mesmeric, narcotic, opiate, somniferous, soporific.

hypochondria dejection, despondency, depression, melancholy, spleen.
Ant. elation.

hypochondriac(al) dejected,

depressed, despondent, dispirited, melancholic.
Ant. elated.

hypocrisy cant, deceit, deception, imposture, insincerity, pretence, sanctimoniousness.
Ant. sincerity.

hypocrite deceiver, dissembler, impostor, pharisee, pretender.

hypocritical canting, deceitful, deceptive, dissembling, false, hollow, insincere, pharisaical, sanctimonious.
Ant. honest, sincere.

hypothesis supposition, theory.

I

icy (1) chilling, cold, freezing, frosty, glacial; (2) (*Fig.*) cold, frigid, indifferent.
Ant. warm.

idea (1) belief, concept, conception, fancy, impression, judgment, notion, thought; (2) archetype, essence, form, pattern; (3) aim, intention, object, plan.

ideal (1) intellectual, mental; (2) fanciful, imaginary, impractical, unreal, visionary; (3) complete, consummate, perfect; (4) *n.* criterion, example, model, standard.
Ant. of (2) actual.

identity existence, individuality, oneness, personality, sameness.
Ant. difference.

idiocy fatuity, foolishness, imbecility, insanity.
Ant. sanity.

idiosyncrasy caprice, crotchet, fad, peculiarity, singularity.

idiot booby, fool, imbecile, natural, simpleton.

idiotic fatuous, foolish, imbecile, insane, senseless, stupid.
Ant. sensible.

idle (1) inactive, indolent, lazy, slothful, sluggish, unemployed; (2) fruitless, futile, groundless, ineffective, unavailing, useless, vain, worthless.
Ant. of (1) industrious; of (2) profitable.

idler dawdler, drone, laggard, loafer, lounger, sluggard.
Ant. worker.

idol (1) deity, god, icon, image, pagan symbol; (2) (*Fig.*) beloved, darling, favourite, pet.

idolater (1) heathen, pagan; (2) admirer, adorer, worshipper.

idolise admire, adore, deify, love, reverence, worship.
Ant. hate.

if admitting, allowing, granting, provided, providing, supposing, though, whether.

ignite burn, fire, kindle, light.
Ant. extinguish.

ignoble (1) low-born, mean, plebeian, vulgar; (2) base, contemptible, degenerate, degraded, dishonourable, humble, infamous, insignificant, shameless, unworthy.
Ant. of (1) noble; of (2) haughty.

ignominious despicable, disgraceful, dishonourable, disreputable, humiliating, scandalous, shameful.
Ant. reputable.

ignominy contempt, discredit, disgrace, dishonour, disrepute, infamy, odium, opprobrium, reproach, shame.
Ant. honour.

ignoramus ass, blockhead, donkey, dullard, dunce, fool, simpleton.
Ant. intellectual.

ignorant illiterate, unenlightened, unlearned, unlettered, untaught, untutored.
Ant. wise.

ignore disregard, neglect, overlook, reject.
Ant. heed.

ill (1) *a.* ailing, diseased, indisposed, sick, unwell; (2) bad, evil, iniquitous, unfortunate, unlucky, wicked, wrong; (3) cross, harsh, hateful, hostile, malevolent, surly, unkind; (4) unhealthy, unwholesome; (5) ill-favoured, ugly, unprepossessing; (6) *n.* ailment, disease, illness, indisposition; (7) badness, depravity, evil, wickedness; (8) affliction, harm, hurt, injury, misfortune, pain, trouble; (9) *adv.* badly, poorly, unfortunately.
Ant. of (1) well; of (2) good.

ill-bred discourteous, ill-mannered, impolite, rude, uncivil, uncouth, unrefined.
Ant. polite.

illegal forbidden, illicit, unauthorised, unconstitutional, unlawful, unlicensed.
Ant. legal.

illegible indecipherable, obscure, undecipherable, unreadable.
Ant. legible.

illegitimate (1) illegal, illicit, improper, unauthorised; (2) bastard, spurious.
Ant. legitimate.

ill-fated ill-starred, unfortunate, unlucky.
Ant. lucky.

illiberal (1) close-fisted, mean, miserly, niggardly, parsimonious, selfish, sordid, stingy, ungenerous; (2) narrow-minded, uncharitable.
Ant. of (1) generous; of (2) broad-minded.

illicit (1) illegal, illegitimate, unauthorised, unlawful, unlicensed; (2) forbidden, guilty, improper, wrong.
Ant. of (1) legal; of (2) proper.

illimitable boundless, immense, infinite, unbounded, unlimited, vast.
Ant. limited.

illiterate ignorant, uneducated, unlettered, untaught, untutored.
Ant. literate.

ill-natured churlish, crabbed, cross, cross-grained, disobliging, malevolent, perverse, petulant, sulky, sullen, surly, unkind.
Ant. kind.

illness (1) ailment, complaint, disease, disorder, indisposition, malady, sickness; (2) badness, wickedness.
Ant. of (1) health; of (2) goodness.

illogical fallacious, faulty, inconclusive, inconsistent, incorrect, invalid, sophistical.
Ant. logical.

illude cheat, deceive, delude, disappoint, mock, swindle, trick.

illuminate (1) adorn, brighten, decorate, depict, illumine, light; (2) edify, enlighten, inform, inspire, instruct.
Ant. of (1) darken.

illumination (1) brightening, brightness, lighting, splendour; (2) edification, enlightenment, inspiration, instruction.

illusion chimera, deception, delusion, error, fallacy, fantasy, hallucination, mockery.
Ant. reality.

illusive beguiling, deceitful, deceptive, delusive, fallacious.

illustrate (1) demonstrate,

elucidate, exemplify, explain, interpret; (2) adorn, depict, draw.

illustration (1) demonstration, elucidation, exemplification, explanation, interpretation; (2) adornment, decoration, picture.

illustrious brilliant, celebrated, distinguished, eminent, exalted, famous, glorious, noble, noted, remarkable, renowned, signal.
Ant. undistinguished.

ill-will antipathy, aversion, dislike, enmity, envy, grudge, hatred, malevolence, malice.
Ant. goodwill.

image (1) effigy, figure, likeness, picture, portrait, representation, similitude; (2) idol, statue.

imaginary assumed, chimerical, fanciful, hypothetical, ideal, illusive, illusory, imagined, shadowy, supposed, unreal.
Ant. real.

imagination chimera, conception, device, fancy, idea, ideality, illusion, image, invention, notion, supposition, unreality, vision.
Ant. reality.

imaginative creative, dreamy, fanciful, inventive, poetical, visionary.
Ant. unpoetical.

imagine (1) apprehend, assume, believe, conceive, deem, picture, realise, suppose, think; (2) create, devise, frame, invent, plan, project, scheme.

imbecile (1) *n.* dotard, fool, idiot, silly; (2) *a.* fatuous, foolish, idiotic, silly, witless; (3) decrepit, feeble, helpless, infirm.
Ant. of (2) sane.

imbecility (1) childishness, fatuity, foolishness, idiocy; (2) debility, helplessness, infirmity, weakness.
Ant. of (1) sanity.

imbibe absorb, acquire, drink, gain, gather, receive, suck, swallow.
Ant. eject.

imbroglio complexity, complication, embarrassment, entanglement, misunderstanding.
Ant. composure.

imbue (1) colour, dye, stain, tinge, tint; (2) (*Fig.*) bathe, impregnate, inculcate, infuse, instil, permeate, pervade, steep.
Ant. of (1) bleach.

imitate ape, burlesque, copy, counterfeit, duplicate, follow, mimic, mock, parody, personate, repeat, simulate, travesty.
Ant. distort.

imitation copy, counterfeit, likeness, mimicry, mockery, parody, resemblance, travesty.

immaculate clean, faultless, guiltless, innocent, perfect, pure, sinless, spotless, stainless, unblemished, uncontaminated, undefiled, unpolluted, unsullied.
Ant. contaminated.

immanent congenital, inborn, inherent, innate, internal, intrinsic, natural, subjective.
Ant. external.

immaterial (1) inconsiderable, insignificant, trifling, trivial, unessential, unimportant; (2) disembodied, incorporeal, spiritual, unembodied, unsubstantial.
Ant. of (1) important; of (2) substantial.

immature crude, green, imperfect, premature, raw, undeveloped, unfinished, unformed, unripe, unseasonable, untimely.

Ant. ripe.

immaturity crudeness, crudity, greenness, imperfection, rawness, unpreparedness, unripeness,

Ant. ripeness.

immeasurable bottomless, boundless, illimitable, immense, infinite, limitless, measureless, unbounded, unfathomable, vast.

Ant. finite.

immediate (1) close, contiguous, direct, near, next, proximate; (2) instant, instantaneous, present.

Ant. of (1) remote; of (2) later.

immense enormous, extensive, gigantic, great, huge, illimitable, immeasurable, infinite, interminable, large, prodigious, stupendous, vast.

Ant. small, tiny.

immerse (1) dip, douse, duck, plunge, sink, submerge; (2) absorb, engage, involve.

immethodical confused, desultory, disorderly, irregular, unmethodical, unsystematic.

Ant. orderly.

imminent close, dangerous, impending, near, perilous, threatening.

Ant. remote.

immobile (1) fixed, immovable, motionless, stable, stationary; (2) dull, rigid, steadfast, stiff, stolid.

Ant. of (1) mobile; of (2) pliant.

immoderate enormous, excessive, exorbitant, extravagant, extreme, inordinate, intemperate, unreasonable.

Ant. moderate, reasonable.

immodest (1) coarse, gross, impure, indecent, indecorous, indelicate, obscene, unchaste; (2) bold, brazen, forward, impudent, shameless.

Ant. of (1) pure; of (2) modest.

immolate kill, sacrifice.

immoral abandoned, amoral, bad, corrupt, debauched, depraved, dishonest, dissolute, evil, licentious, profligate, sinful, unchaste, unprincipled, vicious, wicked, wrong.

Ant. good, moral.

immorality badness, corruption, depravity, evil, licentiousness, profligacy, sin, vice, wickedness, wrong.

Ant. goodness, virtue.

immortal deathless, endless, eternal, everlasting, imperishable, incorruptible, indestructible, lasting, undying, unfading.

Ant. perishable.

immortality deathlessness, endlessness, incorruptibility, indestructibility, perpetuity.

Ant. death, mortality.

immovable firm, fixed, immutable, stable, stationary, steadfast, unchangeable, unshaken.

Ant. mobile.

immunity charter, exoneration, franchise, freedom, liberty, licence, prerogative, privilege, release, right.

Ant. liability.

immure confine, imprison, incarcerate.

Ant. free, release.

immutability constancy, invariability, permanence, stability, unalterableness, unchangeableness.

immutable constant, fixed,

invariable, permanent, stable, unalterable, unchangeable.
Ant. changeable.

imp (1) brat, demon, devil, scamp, sprite; (2) graft, shoot, scion.
Ant. of (1) angel.

impact collision, contact, impression, shock, stroke.

impair damage, decrease, deteriorate, diminish, enervate, enfeeble, harm, injure, lessen, spoil, weaken, worsen.
Ant. strengthen.

impalpable delicate, fine, imperceptible, indistinct, intangible, shadowy, thin, unsubstantial.
Ant. tangible.

impart afford, bestow, communicate, confer, disclose, discover, divulge, grant, relate, reveal.
Ant. conceal.

impartial disinterested, equitable, fair, just, unbiased, unprejudiced.
Ant. partial.

impassable impenetrable, impermeable, impervious, pathless.

impassioned animated, ardent, excited, fervent, fervid, glowing, intense, passionate, vehement, vivid, warm.
Ant. cool.

impassive apathetic, callous, calm, impassible, indifferent, insensible, insusceptible, unfeeling, unimpressible.
Ant. feeling.

impatience disquietude, fretfulness, haste, heat, impetuosity, irritableness, uneasiness, vehemence, violence.
Ant. quietness.

impatient abrupt, brusque, curt, eager, fretful, hasty, hot-tempered, impetuous, intoler-

ant, rebellious, restless, sudden, testy, vehement, violent.
Ant. patient.

impeach accuse, arraign, censure, challenge, criminate, denounce, disparage, indict.
Ant. uphold, vindicate.

impeachment accusation, arraignment, blame, censure, crimination, imputation, indictment, reproach.
Ant. vindication.

impeccable faultless, immaculate, incorrupt, innocent, perfect, pure, sinless, stainless.
Ant. sinful.

impede bar, block, check, curb, delay, hamper, hinder, obstruct, restrain, slow, stop, thwart.
Ant. help.

impediment bar, block, check, curb, difficulty, encumbrance, hindrance, obstacle, obstruction, stumbling-block.
Ant. help.

impel actuate, compel, constrain, drive, force, incite, induce, influence, instigate, move, push, stimulate, urge.
Ant. restrain.

impend approach, menace, near, threaten.

impending approaching, imminent, menacing, near, threatening.
Ant. remote.

impenetrable dark, dense, impassable, impermeable, impervious, obscure, undiscernible.
Ant. penetrable.

impenitence impenitency, hard-heartedness, obduracy, stubbornness.

impenitent hard-hearted, hardened, obdurate, relentless, uncontrite, unrepentant.
Ant. repentant.

imperative authoritative, binding, commanding, compulsory, obligatory, peremptory, urgent.

Ant. discretional, optional.

imperceptible faint, fine, impalpable, inaudible, invisible, minute, shadowy, small, undiscernible.

Ant. perceptible.

imperfect defective, faulty, immature, impaired, incomplete, undeveloped, unfinished.

Ant. complete, perfect.

imperfection blemish, defect, deficiency, failing, fault, flaw, incompleteness, insufficiency, stain, taint, weakness.

imperial (1) kingly, majestic, queenly, regal, royal, sovereign; (2) exalted, grand, great, magnificent, noble, supreme.

imperil endanger, expose, hazard, jeopardise, risk.

Ant. secure.

imperious arrogant, authoritative, despotic, dictatorial, domineering, exacting, haughty, imperative, overbearing, tyrannical.

Ant. docile.

imperishable eternal, everlasting, immortal, indestructible, perpetual, unfading.

Ant. perishable.

impermeable impassable, impenetrable, impervious.

impermissible deniable, insufferable, objectionable, unallowable, unallowed, unlawful.

Ant. allowable, permissible.

impersonate act, ape, enact, imitate, mimic, personate, personify, represent.

impertinence assurance, boldness, (*Colloq.*) cheek, effrontery, forwardness, impudence, incivility, insolence, pertness, presumption, rudeness.

Ant. politeness.

impertinent (1) bold, brazen, (*Colloq.*) cheeky, forward, impudent, insolent, interfering, pert, presumptuous, rude, uncivil, unmannerly; (2) inapplicable, inappropriate, incongruous, irrelevant.

Ant. of (1) polite; of (2) appropriate.

imperturbable calm, collected, composed, cool, sedate, tranquil, undisturbed, unmoved, unruffled.

Ant. excitable, fussy.

impervious impassable, impenetrable, imperviable.

impetuosity force, fury, haste, precipitancy, vehemence, violence.

impetuous ardent, eager, fierce, furious, hasty, impassioned, impulsive, passionate, rash, vehement, violent.

Ant. cautious.

impiety atheism, iniquity, irreligion, irreverence, profaneness, profanity, sinfulness, ungodliness, unholiness, unrighteousness, wickedness.

Ant. piety.

impinge clash, collide, dash, infringe, strike, touch.

impious blasphemous, iniquitous, irreligious, irreverent, profane, sinful, ungodly, unholy, unrighteous, wicked.

Ant. pious, righteous.

implacable cruel, inexorable, merciless, pitiless, rancorous, relentless, remorseless, unappeasable, unbending, unyielding.

Ant. merciful.

implant (1) fix, ingraft, insert, place, plant, sow; (2) (*Fig.*) inculcate, infuse, instil.

Ant. of (1) uproot.

implement (1) *n.* appliance, instrument, tool, utensil; (2) *v.* effect, execute, fulfil.

Ant. of (2) ignore, neglect.

implicate concern, enfold, entangle, imply, include, involve.

Ant. disentangle.

implication conclusion, entanglement, inference, meaning, signification.

implicit (1) implied, inferred, tacit, understood; (2) absolute, constant, entire, firm, full, steadfast, unhesitating, unreserved, unshaken.

Ant. of (2) doubtful.

implore beg, beseech, crave, entreat, pray, solicit, supplicate.

Ant. order.

imply betoken, denote, import, include, infer, involve, mean, signify.

Ant. declare.

impolite boorish, discourteous, disrespectful, ill-mannered, insolent, rough, rude, uncivil, ungentlemanly, unmannerly, unrefined.

Ant. polite.

impoliteness boorishness, disrespect, incivility, insolence, rudeness, unmannerliness.

Ant. politeness.

impolitic ill-advised, imprudent, indiscreet, inexpedient, injudicious, unwise.

Ant. prudent.

import (1) *v.* bring, introduce, transport; (2) denote, imply, mean, purport, signify; (3) *n.* goods, importation, merchandise; (4) bearing, drift, gist, intention, meaning, purport; (5) consequence, importance, significance, weight.

Ant. of (1) export; of (3)

exportation; of (5) insignificance.

importance concern, consequence, import, moment, momentousness, significance, value, weight.

Ant. insignificance.

important grave, influential, material, momentous, prominent, serious, significant, urgent, weighty.

Ant. insignificant.

importunate busy, clamorous, earnest, pertinacious, pressing, solicitous, urgent.

Ant. hesitant.

importune beset, dun, entreat, press, solicit.

impose (1) fix, lay, place, put, set; (2) appoint, change, dictate, enjoin, prescribe; (3) deceive, dupe, trick.

imposing august, commanding, dignified, effective, grand, impressive, majestic, stately, striking.

Ant. unimpressive.

imposition (1) artifice, cheating, deception, dupery, fraud, imposture, trickery; (2) burden, charge, constraint, duty, levy, tax.

impossibility impracticability, inability, inconceivability, unfeasibility.

impossible impracticable, inconceivable, unachievable, unattainable, unfeasible.

Ant. possible.

impost custom, duty, exercise, tax, toll, tribute.

impostor charlatan, cheat, deceiver, hypocrite, knave, pretender, quack, rogue, trickster.

Ant. gentleman.

imposture artifice, cheat, deception, fraud, imposition, quackery, trick, wile.

impotence disability, feebleness, frailty, helplessness, inability, incapacity, incompetence, inefficiency, infirmity, powerlessness, weakness.

Ant. strength.

impotent disabled, feeble, frail, incapable, incapacitated, incompetent, infirm, powerless, unable, weak.

Ant. strong.

impoverish beggar, deplete, exhaust, pauperise, reduce.

Ant. enrich.

impracticable (1) impossible, unachievable, unattainable, unfeasible; **(2)** impassable, unsurmountable.

Ant. of **(1)** practicable; of **(2)** surmountable.

imprecate anathematise, curse, execrate.

Ant. bless.

imprecation anathema, curse, denunciation, execration, malediction.

Ant. blessing.

impregnable invincible, invulnerable, unassailable.

Ant. vulnerable.

impregnate fecundate, fill, imbue, infuse, saturate, steep.

impress (1) engrave, imprint, print, stamp; **(2)** (*Fig.*) affect, fix, inculcate, move, strike.

impressible excitable, impressionable, sensitive, susceptible.

Ant. insensitive.

impression (1) brand, dent, impress, imprinting, indentation, mark, printing, stamp, stamping; **(2)** (*Fig.*) effect, fancy, idea, influence, notion, opinion, recollection.

impressive affecting, exciting, forcible, moving, powerful, stirring, touching.

Ant. weak.

imprint engrave, fix, impress, print, stamp.

imprison confine, immure, incarcerate, jail.

Ant. release.

imprisonment confinement, custody, durance, duress, incarceration, restraint.

Ant. liberty.

improbability doubt, uncertainty, unlikelihood.

Ant. probability.

improbable doubtful, uncertain, unlikely.

Ant. probable.

improbity dishonesty, faithlessness, fraud, knavery, unfairness.

Ant. honesty.

impromptu extempore, improvised, off-hand, ready, spontaneous, unpremeditated, unprepared, unrehearsed, unstudied.

Ant. prepared.

improper (1) erroneous, false, inaccurate, incorrect, wrong; **(2)** indecent, indecorous, unbecoming, unfitting, unseemly; **(3)** inapplicable, inapposite, inappropriate, unfit, unsuitable, unsuited.

Ant. of **(1)** correct; of **(2)** proper; of **(3)** suitable.

improve (1) amend, ameliorate, better, correct, mend, rectify; **(2)** enhance, increase, progress, reform, rise, use.

Ant. worsen.

improvement (1) advancement, amelioration, amendment, betterment, correction, rectification; **(2)** enhancement, increase, proficiency, progress, reformation, rise.

improvident careless, heedless, imprudent, inconsiderate, negligent, prodigal, reckless, shiftless, short-sighted.

thoughtless, thriftless, unthrifty, wasteful.
Ant. saving, thrifty.

improvise extemporise, fabricate, imagine, invent.
Ant. prepare, rehearse.

imprudence carelessness, heedlessness, improvidence, incautiousness, inconsideration, indiscretion, rashness.
Ant. caution, prudence.

imprudent careless, heedless, ill-advised, improvident, incautious, inconsiderate, indiscreet, injudicious, rash, unwise.
Ant. cautious, prudent.

impudence assurance, audacity, boldness, (Colloq.) cheek, effrontery, impertinence, insolence, (Sl.) lip, pertness, presumption, rudeness, sauciness.
Ant. courtesy, modesty.

impudent audacious, bold, bold-faced, brazen, (Colloq.) cheeky, forward, immodest, impertinent, insolent, pert, presumptuous, rude, saucy, shameless.
Ant. courteous, modest.

impugn assail, attack, challenge, dispute, gainsay, oppose, question, resist.
Ant. defend.

impulse (1) force, impetus, momentum, push, thrust; (2) (Fig.) feeling, incitement, inclination, influence, instinct, motive, passion, resolve.
Ant. of (1) pull.

impulsive emotional, forcible, hasty, impelling, impetuous, moving, passionate, quick, rash, vehement, violent.
Ant. cool, restrained.

impunity exemption, immunity, liberty, licence, permission, security.
Ant. liability.

impure (1) admixed, adulterated, mixed; (2) defiled, dirty, filthy, foul, polluted, tainted, unclean, vitiated; (3) coarse, corrupt, immodest, immoral, indecent, lewd, licentious, obscene, ribald, unchaste.

impurity (1) admixture, adulteration, mixture; (2) defilement, filth, foulness, pollution, uncleanness; (3) coarseness, corruption, grossness, immodesty, immorality, indecency, lewdness, licentiousness, obscenity, unchastity, vulgarity.
Ant. purity.

imputable ascribable, attributable, chargeable, referable, referrible, traceable.

imputation accusation, attribution, blame, censure, change, insinuation, reproach.
Ant. denial.

impute ascribe, assign, attribute, charge, insinuate, reproach.
Ant. deny.

inability disability, disqualification, impotence, incapability, incapacity, incompetence, inefficiency.
Ant. ability.

inaccessible unapproachable, unattainable.

inaccuracy blunder, defect, erroneousness, error, fault, incorrectness, inexactness, mistake.
Ant. accuracy.

inaccurate defective, erroneous, faulty, incorrect, inexact, mistaken, wrong.
Ant. accurate.

inactive dormant, dull, idle, immobile, indolent, inert, inoperative, lazy, passive, slothful, sluggish.
Ant. active.

inactivity dilatoriness, inaction, indolence, inertness, laziness, sloth, sluggishness, torpor.

Ant. activity.

inadequacy defectiveness, inadequateness, inaptness, incapacity, incompetence, incompetency, insufficiency, unfitness, unsuitableness.

Ant. fitness.

inadequate defective, faulty, inapt, incapable, incommensurate, incompetent, incomplete, insufficient, unequal.

Ant. adequate.

inadmissible improper, incompetent, unacceptable, unallowable, unqualified, unreasonable.

Ant. admissible.

inadvertency blunder, carelessness, error, heedlessness, inadvertence, inattention, inconsideration, inobservance, mistake, negligence, oversight, thoughtlessness.

Ant. attention, care.

inadvertently accidentally, carelessly, heedlessly, negligently, thoughtlessly, unintentionally.

Ant. carefully, heedfully.

inalienable (*Law*) entailed, untransferable.

inane empty, fatuous, frivolous, futile, idiotic, puerile, senseless, stupid, trifling, vacuous, vain, void, worthless.

Ant. sensible.

inanimate dead, defunct, extinct, inactive, inert, lifeless, soulless, spiritless.

Ant. alive, animate.

inanition exhaustion, hunger, malnutrition, starvation, want.

Ant. plenty.

inanity emptiness, fatuity, folly, frivolity, puerility, sense-

lessness, vacuity, vanity, worthlessness.

Ant. sense.

inapplicable inapposite, inappropriate, inapt, irrelevant, unsuitable, unsuited.

Ant. relevant.

inapposite inapplicable, irrelevant, unfit, unsuitable.

inappropriate improper, unbecoming, unfit, unfitting, unsuitable.

Ant. appropriate.

inapt (1) inapposite, inappropriate, unsuitable, unsuited; (2) awkward, clumsy, dull, slow, stupid.

Ant. of (1) apt; of (2) efficient.

inaptitude awkwardness, unfitness, unreadiness, unsuitableness.

inarticulate (1) indistinct; (2) unjointed.

inartificial artless, natural, simple, unaffected.

Ant. artificial, unnatural.

inattention carelessness, disregard, heedlessness, inadvertence, indifference, neglect, thoughtlessness.

Ant. attention.

inattentive absent-minded, careless, heedless, inadvertent, neglectful, negligent, regardless, remiss, thoughtless, unmindful, unobservant.

Ant. attentive.

inaudible indistinct, low, mumbling, mute, noiseless, silent, stifled.

Ant. audible.

inaugurate begin, celebrate, commence, induct, initiate, install, invest, originate.

Ant. terminate.

inauspicious bad, discouraging, ill-omened, unfavourable, unfortunate, unlucky,

unpromising, unpropitious, untoward.
Ant. auspicious, favourable.

inborn inbred, ingrained, inherent, inherited, innate, native, natural.
Ant. acquired.

incalculable countless, enormous, incomputable, innumerable, numberless, uncountable.
Ant. few, small.

incapable feeble, impotent, incompetent, insufficient, unable, unfit, unfitted, unqualified, weak.
Ant. capable.

incapacitate cripple, disable, disqualify, unfit.
Ant. fit, rehabilitate.

incapacity disqualification, inability, incapability, incompetency, unfitness.
Ant. fitness.

incarcerate commit, confine, immure, imprison, jail, restrain, restrict.
Ant. release.

incarnation embodiment, exemplification, impersonation, manifestation, personification.

incautious careless, heedless, improvident, imprudent, inconsiderate, indiscreet, injudicious, negligent, rash, reckless, thoughtless, unwary.
Ant. careful, cautious.

incendiary (1) a. dissentious, inflammatory, seditious; (2) n. agitator, firebrand, fire-raiser.

incense (A) v. anger, enrage, exasperate, excite, inflame, infuriate, irritate, madden, provoke.
Ant. pacify.

incense (B) n. aroma, fragrance, perfume, scent.

incentive encouragement, enticement, impulse, incitement,

inducement, motive, spur, stimulus.
Ant. discouragement.

inception beginning, commencement, inauguration, origin, rise, start.
Ant. finish.

incessant ceaseless, constant, continual, continuous, eternal, everlasting, never-ending, perpetual, unceasing, unending, unremitting.
Ant. periodic.

incident circumstance, episode, event, fact, happening, occurrence.

incidental accidental, casual, chance, concomitant, contingent, fortuitious, non-essential, occasional, subordinate.
Ant. essential.

incipient beginning, commencing, inceptive, originating, starting.
Ant. ending.

incision cut, gash, notch, opening.

incisive acid, acute, biting, keen, sarcastic, sardonic, satirical, severe, sharp, trenchant.
Ant. mild.

incite animate, encourage, excite, goad, impel, instigate, prompt, provoke, rouse, spur, stimulate, urge.
Ant. calm.

incitement encouragement, goad, impulse, inducement, motive, provocation, spur, stimulus.
Ant. hindrance.

incivility discourtesy, disrespect, ill-breeding, impoliteness, rudeness, unmannerliness.
Ant. politeness.

inclemency (1) cruelty, harshness, mercilessness, severity, tyranny; (2) boisterousness, rigour, roughness, storminess.

Ant. of (1) clemency; of (2) mildness.

inclement (1) cruel, harsh, merciless, severe, tyrannical, unmerciful; (2) boisterous, rigorous, rough, stormy.

Ant. of (1) merciful; of (2) mild.

inclination (1) bend, bending, leaning, slant, slope; (2) aptitude, bent, bias, disposition, partiality, predilection, predisposition, prejudice, proclivity, proneness, propensity, tendency; (3) affection, desire, fondness, liking, wish.

Ant. of (3) dislike.

incline (1) *v.* bend, bow, diverge, slant, slope, stoop, tend; (2) bias, predispose, tend, turn; (3) *n.* ascent, descent, grade, gradient, rise, slope.

inclose circumscribe, cover, encircle, enclose, encompass, envelop, surround, wrap.

include comprehend, comprise, contain, embody, embrace.

Ant. exclude.

inclusive comprehending, embracing, including.

Ant. exclusive.

incognito disguised, unknown.

incoherent confused, detached, disconnected, incongruous, inconsistent, loose, rambling, unconnected, unintelligible, wandering.

Ant. coherent, connected.

income earnings, gains, interest, pay, proceeds, profits, receipts, rents, revenue, salary, wages.

Ant. expenditure, outlay.

incommensurate disproportionate, inadequate, insufficient, unequal.

incommode annoy, disturb, embarrass, hinder, impede, inconvenience, trouble, upset, vex.

Ant. aid.

incommodious (1) annoying, disadvantageous, harassing, irritating, vexatious; (2) awkward, cumbersome, inconvenient, unhandy, unmanageable, unwieldy.

Ant. of (1) helpful; of (2) handy.

incomparable inimitable, matchless, paramount, peerless, unequalled, unparalleled, unrivalled.

Ant. comparable.

incompatible contradictory, incongruous, inconsistent, irreconcilable, unsuitable.

Ant. consistent.

incompetence disqualification, inability, incapability, incapacity, inadequacy, insufficiency, unfitness.

Ant. capability.

incompetent disqualified, incapable, incapacitated, improper, insufficient, unable, unconstitutional, unfit.

Ant. competent, fit.

incomplete defective, deficient, imperfect, unaccomplished, undone, unexecuted, unfinished.

Ant. complete.

incomprehensible inconceivable, perplexing, puzzling, unimaginable, unintelligible, unthinkable, ununderstandable.

Ant. understandable.

incongruous absurd, contradictory, contrary, discordant, improper, inappropriate, incoherent, incompatible, inconsistent, unbecoming, unsuitable, unsuited.

Ant. consistent.

inconsiderable insignificant, minor, petty, slight, trivial, unimportant.
   Ant. important.
inconsiderate (1) impatient, intolerant, selfish, thoughtless, uncharitable, unkind; (2) careless, hasty, heedless, impetuous, imprudent, inattentive, indiscreet, rash.
   Ant. of (1) unselfish; of (2) careful.
inconsistent (1) contradictory, contrary, incoherent, incompatible, incongruous, irreconcilable; (2) changeable, unstable, unsteady, variable.
   Ant. of (2) steady.
inconstant capricious, changeable, fickle, fluctuating, inconsistent, uncertain, unreliable, unsettled, unstable, unsteady, vacillating, variable, volatile, wavering.
   Ant. constant, steady.
incontestable certain, incontrovertible, indisputable, indubitable, sure, undeniable, unquestionable.
   Ant. doubtful.
incontinent debauched, lascivious, lewd, lustful, unchaste.
   Ant. pure.
incontrovertible certain, incontestable, indisputable, indubitable, irrefutable, sure, undeniable, unquestionable.
   Ant. questionable.
inconvenience (1) annoyance, disadvantage, disturbance, uneasiness, trouble, vexation; (2) awkwardness, incommodiousness, unfitness, unhandiness, unsuitableness, unwieldiness.
   Ant. of (1) advantage; of (2) fitness.
inconvenient (1) annoying, disadvantageous, disturbing,

inopportune, troublesome, unseasonable, unsuitable, vexatious; (2) awkward, cumbersome, incommodious, unhandy, unmanageable, unwieldy.
   Ant. of (1) advantageous; of (2) commodious.
incorporate blend, combine, consolidate, embody, merge, mix, unite.
   Ant. exclude.
incorporeal bodiless, disembodied, immaterial, spiritual, supernatural, unsubstantial.
   Ant. material.
incorrect erroneous, false, faulty, improper, inaccurate, inexact, untrue, wrong.
   Ant. correct.
increase (1) advance, augment, dilate, enhance, enlarge, extend, grow, heighten, magnify, multiply, prolong, spread; (2) addition, augmentation, enlargement, expansion, extension, growth, increment.
   Ant. decrease.
incredulity disbelief, distrust, doubt, scepticism, unbelief.
   Ant. belief.
incredulous distrustful, doubtful, dubious, sceptical, unbelieving.
   Ant. credulous.
increment addition, augmentation, enlargement, increase.
   Ant. decrease.
inculcate enforce, implant, impress, infuse, ingraft, instill.
inculpate accuse, blame, censure, charge, impeach, incriminate.
   Ant. exonerate.
incumbent binding, compulsory, obligatory.
incur acquire, bring, contract.
incurable helpless, hopeless,

irrecoverable, irremediable, remediless.

Ant. curable.

incursion foray, inroad, invasion, raid.

indebted beholden, obliged, owing, unpaid.

Ant. paid.

indecency coarseness, foulness, grossness, immodesty, impropriety, impurity, indecorum, indelicacy, lewdness, licentiousness, obscenity, pornography, outrageousness, unseemliness, vileness.

Ant. purity.

indecent coarse, dirty, filthy, foul, gross, immodest, improper, impure, indecorous, indelicate, lewd, licentious, outrageous, pornographic, unbecoming, unseemly, vile.

Ant. decent, pure.

indecipherable illegible, unintelligible, unreadable.

Ant. readable.

indecision hesitation, inconstancy, irresolution, shilly-shallying, vacillation, wavering.

Ant. resolution.

indecisive doubtful, hesitating, inconclusive, irresolute, uncertain, undecided, undetermined, unsettled, vacillating, wavering.

Ant. firm.

indecorous coarse, impolite, improper, indecent, rude, uncivil, unseemly.

Ant. polite.

indeed actually, certainly, positively, really, strictly, truly, verily, veritably.

indefatigable assiduous, persevering, tireless, unflagging, unremitting, untiring, unwearied.

Ant. idle, weary.

indefeasible irreversible, irrevocable, unalterable.

Ant. changeable.

indefensible faulty, inexcusable, unjustifiable, untenable, unwarrantable, wrong.

Ant. justifiable.

indefinite confused, doubtful, equivocal, indistinct, loose, obscure, uncertain, undefined, undetermined, unsettled, vague.

Ant. definite.

indelible indestructible, ineffaceable, ingrained, lasting, permanent.

Ant. temporary.

indelicate coarse, gross, immodest, improper, indecent, indecorous, low, obscene, rude, unbecoming, unchaste, unseemly, vulgar.

Ant. modest.

indemnify compensate, reimburse, remunerate, repair, requite, satisfy.

Ant. injure.

indemnity compensation, reimbursement, remuneration, requital, satisfaction, security.

Ant. injury.

indentation dent, depression, dimple, dip, hollow, jag, notch.

Ant. elevation.

independence (1) ease, freedom, liberty; (2) autonomy, self-government, separation.

Ant. of (1) dependence; of (2) subjection.

independent (1) absolute, free, unconnected, uncontrolled, unrelated; (2) autonomous, decontrolled, self-governing, separated; (3) bold, self-reliant, unconventional.

indescribable ineffable, inexpressible, unutterable.

indestructible abiding, enduring, everlasting, imperishable, incorruptible, lasting, permanent.

Ant. destructible, fragile.

indeterminate indefinite, uncertain, undetermined, unfixed, vague.

Ant. definite.

index director, forefinger, hand, indication, pointer, table.

indicate betoken, denote, designate, manifest, mark, show, signify, specify.

indication evidence, explanation, hint, index, manifestation, mark, note, sign, suggestion, symptom.

indict (*Law*) accuse, arraign, charge, impeach, prosecute, summon.

Ant. acquit, defend.

indictment accusation, allegation, charge, impeachment, prosecution.

Ant. defence.

indifference (1) apathy, callousness, carelessness, coldness, coolness, disregard, heedlessness, inattention, negligence, unconcern; (2) disinterestedness, impartiality, neutrality; (3) insignificance, triviality.

Ant. of (1) concern, regard.

indifferent (1) apathetic, callous, careless, cold, cool, heedless, inattentive, regardless, unconcerned, uninterested, unmoved; (2) disinterested, impartial, neutral, unbiased; (3) mediocre, ordinary, passable.

Ant. of (1) concerned; of (2) partial; of (3) excellent.

indigence destitution, distress, necessity, need, poverty, privation, want.

Ant. plenty.

indigenous home-grown, native.

Ant. foreign.

indigent destitute, necessitous, needy, penniless, poor, poverty-stricken, straitened.

Ant. rich.

indigestion dyspepsia, dyspepsy.

indignant angry, annoyed, exasperated, furious, incensed, irate, provoked, wrathful.

Ant. peaceful.

indignation anger, exasperation, fury, ire, rage, resentment.

Ant. composure.

indignity abuse, affront, contumely, dishonour, disrespect, humiliation, injury, insult, obloquy, opprobrium, outrage, reproach, slight.

Ant. dignity, honour.

indirect circuitous, crooked, oblique, roundabout, tortuous.

Ant. direct, straight.

indiscernible imperceptible, indistinguishable, invisible, undiscernible.

indiscreet foolish, hasty, heedless, imprudent, incautious, inconsiderate, injudicious, rash, reckless, unwise.

Ant. wise.

indiscretion error, folly, foolishness, imprudence, inconsiderateness, mistake, rashness, recklessness, slip.

Ant. caution, prudence.

indiscriminate confused, mingled, miscellaneous, mixed, promiscuous, undistinguishable.

Ant. classified.

indispensable essential, necessary, needed, needful, requisite.

Ant. unnecessary.

indisposed (1) ailing, ill, sick, unwell; (2) averse, disinclined, loath, reluctant, unwilling.

Ant. of (1) well; of (2) willing.

indisposition (1) ailment, illness, sickness; (2) aversion, disinclination, reluctance, unwillingness.

Ant. of (1) health; of (2) willingness.

indisputable certain, evident, incontestable, incontrovertible, indubitable, sure, undeniable, unquestionable.

Ant. dubious, uncertain.

indissoluble abiding, enduring, imperishable, incorruptible, indestructible, inseparable, lasting, permanent.

Ant. separable.

indistinct ambiguous, confused, dim, doubtful, faint, ill-defined, indefinite, obscure, undefined, undistinguishable, vague.

Ant. clear.

indite compose, dictate, pen, write.

individual (1) a. characteristic, distinctive, identical, particular, personal, separate, single, singular, special, specific, unique; (2) n. body, character, person, personage, unit.

Ant. of (1) general.

indoctrinate ground, imbue, initiate, instruct, teach, train.

indolence idleness, inactivity, inertness, laziness, sloth, sluggishness.

Ant. industry.

indolent idle, inactive, inert, lazy, listless, slothful, sluggish.

Ant. industrious.

indomitable invincible, unconquerable, untameable, unyielding.

Ant. weak, yielding.

indorse approve, back, confirm, ratify, sanction.

Ant. disapprove.

indubitable certain, evident, incontestable, incontrovertible, indisputable, sure, unarguable, undeniable.

Ant. doubtful.

induce (1) actuate, encourage, impel, incite, influence, instigate, move, persuade, press, prevail; (2) cause, effect, produce.

Ant. of (1) discourage.

inducement cause, consideration, encouragement, impulse, incentive, incitement, influence, motive, spur, stimulus, urge.

Ant. discouragement.

induct inaugurate, initiate, install, introduce, invest.

induction (1) inauguration, initiation, installation, institution, introduction, investiture; (2) conclusion, generalisation, inference.

indulge allow, cherish, concede, favour, foster, gratify, harbour, humour, pamper, spoil, suffer.

Ant. deny.

indulgent clement, compliant, favourable, favouring, forbearing, gentle, gratifying, kind, lenient, liberal, mild, tender, tolerant.

Ant. harsh.

industrious active, assiduous, busy, diligent, hard-working, laborious, persevering, persistent, sedulous, steady.

Ant. indolent.

industry activity, assiduity, diligence, effort, labour, perseverance, persistence, toil.

Ant. indolence.

inebriate (1) v. intoxicate; (2) n. drunkard.

inebriation drunkenness, insobriety, intemperance, intoxication.

Ant. temperance.

ineffable indescribable, inexpressible, unspeakable, unutterable.
Ant. ordinary.

ineffective feeble, fruitless, futile, idle, ineffectual, inefficacious, unavailing, useless, vain, weak.
Ant. effective.

ineffectual (1) abortive, bootless, fruitless, futile, idle, ineffective, inefficacious, inefficient, unavailing, useless, vain; (2) feeble, impotent, powerless, weak.
Ant. of (1) effective.

inefficient feeble, incapable, incompetent, ineffectual, inefficacious, weak.
Ant. capable.

ineligible disqualified, objectionable, undesirable, unfitted, unqualified.
Ant. eligible, qualified.

inept (1) absurd, foolish, inane, nonsensical, ridiculous, silly, stupid; (2) improper, inappropriate, unfit, unsuitable.
Ant. of (1) sensible; of (2) suitable.

inequality difference, disparity, diversity, irregularity, unevenness.
Ant. equality.

inert dead, dull, idle, inactive, indolent, lazy, lifeless, slothful, sluggish, torpid.
Ant. active, alert.

inestimable incalculable, invaluable, precious, priceless.
Ant. worthless.

inevitable certain, necessary, sure, unavoidable, unpreventable.
Ant. avoidable.

inexcusable inadmissible, indefensible, unjustifiable, unpardonable.
Ant. pardonable.

inexhaustible endless, illimitable, indefatigable, never-ending, unwearied.
Ant. restricted.

inexorable cruel, hard, harsh, implacable, inflexible, merciless, pitiless, severe, unbending, unrelenting, unyielding.
Ant. merciful.

inexpedient disadvantageous, improper, indiscreet, imprudent, unadvisable, undesirable, unfit, unwise.
Ant. advisable.

inexperienced fresh, green, raw, unfamiliar, unpractised, unschooled, unskilled, untrained, unversed.
Ant. skilled.

inexpert awkward, clumsy, inept, maladroit, unhandy, unskilled.
Ant. dexterous.

inexplicable incomprehensible, inscrutable, mysterious, strange, unintelligible.
Ant. evident.

infallible certain, dependable, reliable, sure, unerring, unfailing.
Ant. unreliable.

infamous atrocious, base, detestable, disgraceful, dishonourable, disreputable, heinous, ignominious, ill-famed, odious, scandalous, shameful, villainous, vile, wicked.
Ant. honourable.

infamy atrocity, discredit, disgrace, dishonour, disrepute, ignominy, obloquy, odium, opprobrium, scandal, villainy.
Ant. honour.

infantile babyish, childish, immature, puerile, tender, weak, young.
Ant. adult.

infatuate befool, besot, delude, mislead, stupefy.

infatuation fatuity, folly, foolishness, hallucination, madness, self-deception.

Ant. sanity.

infect affect, contaminate, corrupt, defile, poison, pollute, taint, vitiate.

Ant. cleanse.

infection contagion, contamination, corruption, defilement, poison, pollution, virus.

infectious catching, communicable, contagious, contaminating, corrupting, defiling pestilential, poisoning, polluting, vitiating.

Ant. harmless.

infer conclude, conjecture, deduce, gather, presume. surmise.

Ant. know.

inference conclusion, conjecture. consequence, corollary, deduction, presumption, surmise.

Ant. statement.

inferior bad, imperfect, indifferent, lower, mean, mediocre, poor, poorer, secondary, subordinate, subsidiary, underneath.

Ant. superior.

infernal accursed, damnable, devilish, diabolical, fiendish, hellish, malicious, satanic.

Ant. heavenly.

infertile barren, sterile, unfruitful, unproductive.

Ant. fertile.

infest (1) overrun, swarm, throng; (2) annoy, disturb, harass, irritate, molest, plague, torment, trouble, vex, worry.

Ant. of (2) please.

infidel atheist, freethinker, heretic, sceptic, unbeliever.

Ant. Christian, Muslim.

infidelity (1) adultery, disloyalty, faithlessness, unfaith-fulness; (2) disbelief, scepticism, treachery, unbelief.

Ant. of (1) fidelity.

infinite boundless, enormous, eternal, illimitable, immeasurable, immense, interminable, limitless, stupendous, unbounded, vast, wide.

Ant. finite, limited.

infinitesimal inappreciable, microscopic, minute, tiny.

Ant. huge.

infirm debilitated, decrepit, enfeebled, failing, faltering, feeble, frail, insecure, irresolute, lame, unsound, wavering, weak.

Ant. healthy, strong.

infirmity debility, decrepitude, defect, failing, fault, feebleness, frailty, weakness.

Ant. health, strength.

infix implant, infuse, ingraft, insert, instil, introduce, place, set.

Ant. uproot.

inflame anger, arouse, embitter, enrage, exasperate, excite, heat, ignite, incense, infuriate, kindle, madden, rouse, stimulate.

Ant. discourage, soothe.

inflammatory (1) exciting, fiery, inflaming; (2) incendiary, seditious.

Ant. of (1) appeasing.

inflate blow, dilate, distend, enlarge, expand, increase, puff, swell.

Ant. deflate.

inflation (1) blowing, distension, enlargement, expansion, extension, increase, swelling; (2) (*Fig.*) conceit, self-complacency self-importance, vainglory, vanity.

inflect (1) bend, bow, curve, (2) (*Gram.*) conjugate, decline.

inflection (1) bend, bow,

crook, curvature; (2) (*Gram.*) conjugation, declension.

inflexible adamant, firm, headstrong, implacable, intractable, obdurate, obstinate, relentless, resolute, rigid, rigorous, stiff, stubborn, unbending, unchangeable, unyielding.
Ant. complaisant, pliable.

inflict apply, impose, punish.

influence (1) *n.* agency, authority, control, credit, direction, power, rule, sway, weight; (2) *v.* arouse, bias, control, direct, impel, impress, incite, induce, instigate, modify, move, persuade, rouse, sway.
Ant. of (1) weakness; of (2) dissuade.

influential controlling, efficacious, forcible, guiding, leading, persuasive, potent, powerful.
Ant. ineffective, weak.

inform acquaint, advise, apprise, communicate, enlighten, instruct, notify, teach, tell.
Ant. conceal.

information (1) advice, counsel, instruction, intelligence, knowledge, news, notice; (2) (*Law*) accusation, complaint, denunciation.
Ant. of (1) concealment.

informer (*Law*) accuser, complainant, complainer, informant.

infraction breach, breaking, infringement, non-fulfilment, transgression, violation.
Ant. compliance.

infrequent rare, seldom, uncommon, unusual.
Ant. frequent.

infringe break, disobey, encroach, transgress, violate.
Ant. obey.

infuriate anger, enrage,

exasperate, incense, irritate, madden, provoke.
Ant. calm.

infuse (1) implant, inculcate, ingraft, inspire, introduce; (2) macerate, soak, steep.

ingenious able, adept, adroit, apt, bright, clever, dexterous, gifted, inventive, ready, resourceful, skilful.
Ant. unskilful.

ingenuity ability, adroitness, aptitude, aptness, capacity, cleverness, faculty, genius, gift, ingeniousness, knack, skill, turn.
Ant. clumsiness.

ingenuous artless, candid, frank, guileless, honest, innocent, naïve, open, plain, simple, sincere, unreserved.
Ant. insincere, sly.

ingraft graft, implant, inculcate, infix, infuse, instil.
Ant. uproot.

ingratitude thanklessness, ungratefulness.

ingredient component, constituent, element, part.
Ant. whole.

ingress access, entrance, entry.
Ant. egress, exit.

inhabit abide, dwell, live, occupy, possess, reside.

inhabitant citizen, denizen, dweller, native, occupier, resident, residenter, tenant.

inharmonious discordant, dissonant, harsh, jarring, unharmonious, unmelodious, unmusical.
Ant. melodious.

inherent congenital, essential, inborn, ingrained, inherited, innate, intrinsic, native, natural.
Ant. acquired.

inheritance bequest, heritage, legacy, patrimony.

inhibit arrest, bar, check, debar, discourage, forbid, hinder, obstruct, prohibit, restrain, stop.
Ant. support.

inhibition bar, check, disallowance, drawback, embargo, hindrance, interdict, obstacle, prohibition, restraint.

inhospitable mean, unfriendly, ungenerous, unkind, unreceptive.
Ant. hospitable, kind.

inhuman barbarous, brutal, cruel, heartless, merciless, pitiless, remorseless, ruthless, savage, unfeeling.
Ant. human.

inhume bury, entomb, inter.
Ant. exhume.

inimical adverse, antagonistic, harmful, hostile, hurtful, ill-disposed, noxious, opposed, pernicious, repugnant, unfavourable, unfriendly.
Ant. friendly.

inimitable consummate, incomparable, matchless, peerless, supreme, unequalled, unexampled, unmatched, unparalleled, unrivalled, unsurpassable.
Ant. comparable.

iniquitous criminal, heinous, immoral, nefarious, sinful, unjust, unrighteous, vicious, wicked.
Ant. righteous.

iniquity crime, injustice, misdeed, offence, sin, sinfulness, unrighteousness, wickedness, wrong.
Ant. righteousness.

initial a. beginning, commencing, early, first, incipient, opening.
Ant. final.

initiate (1) v. begin, commence, inaugurate, indoctrinate, instruct, introduce, invest, open, originate, start, teach, train; (2) n. beginner, learner, tyro.
Ant. of (1) end.

initiative advantage, beginning, commencement, example, leadership, start.

injudicious foolish, hasty, ill-advised, ill-judged, ill-timed, imprudent, incautious, inconsiderate, indiscreet, inexpedient, rash, unwise.
Ant. wise.

injunction command, exhortation, mandate, order, precept.
Ant. disobedience.

injure abuse, break, damage, harm, hurt, impair, maltreat, mar, ruin, spoil, wrong.
Ant. benefit, right.

injurious baneful, damaging, deleterious, destructive, detrimental, disadvantageous, harmful, hurtful, iniquitous, mischievous, pernicious, ruinous, slanderous, unjust, wrongful.
Ant. profitable.

injury damage, detriment, evil, harm, hurt, ill, injustice, mischief, ruin, wrong.
Ant. benefit.

injustice grievance, iniquity, unfairness, unlawfulness, wrong.
Ant. fairness.

inkling conception, hint, idea, intimation, notion, suggestion, whisper.

inlet bay, bight, cove, creek, entrance, ingress, passage.
Ant. outlet.

innate congenital, inborn, inbred, ingrained, inherent, inherited, natural.
Ant. acquired.

innocence artlessness, guiltlessness, harmlessness, ingenuousness, innocuousness, innoxiousness, purity, righteousness, simplicity, stainlessness, uprightness.

Ant. impurity.

innocent artless, blameless, faultless, guileless, guiltless, harmless, honest, immaculate, impeccable, ingenuous, innocuous, inoffensive, pure, righteous, simple, sinless, stainless, upright.

Ant. culpable.

innocuous harmless, innocent, inoffensive, innoxious, safe, uninjurious.

Ant. harmful.

innovation alteration, change, novelty.

innoxious harmless, innocent, innocuous, inoffensive, safe, uninjurious, wholesome.

Ant. harmful.

innuendo hint, insinuation, intimation, suggestion.

innumerable countless, infinite, many, numberless, numerous.

Ant. few.

inoffensive harmless, innocent, innocuous, innoxious, unoffending.

inordinate excessive, extravagant, immoderate, intemperate, unreasonable.

Ant. moderate.

inquest inquiry, inquisition, investigation.

inquire ask, examine, interrogate, investigate, query, question, seek.

Ant. answer.

inquiry examination, interrogation, query, question, research, scrutiny, search, study.

Ant. reply.

inquisition examination, inquest, inquiry, investigation.

inquisitive curious, inquiring,

peering, prying, questioning, scrutinising, snooping.

inroad foray, incursion, invasion, irruption, raid.

Ant. retreat.

insalubrious injurious, noxious, unhealthy, unwholesome.

Ant. salubrious.

insane (1) crazed, crazy, demented, deranged, lunatic, mad; (2) foolish, senseless, stupid.

Ant. of (1) sane; of (2) sensible.

insanity aberration, alienation, craziness, delirium, dementia, frenzy, lunacy, madness.

Ant. sanity.

insatiable gluttonous, greedy, insatiate, intemperate, rapacious, ravenous, unappeasable, unquenchable.

Ant. temperate.

inscribe (1) carve, cut, engrave, impress, imprint, write; (2) address, dedicate.

Ant. of (1) obliterate.

inscrutable hidden, incomprehensible, inexplicable, mysterious, undiscoverable, unexplainable, unfathomable.

Ant. understandable.

insecure dangerous, exposed, hazardous, ill-protected, perilous, shaky, uncertain, unguarded, unprotected, unsafe, unstable, weak.

Ant. safe.

insecurity danger, hazard, instability, peril, risk, uncertainty, weakness.

Ant. safety.

insensate apathetic, dull, foolish, indifferent, insensible, stolid, stupid, torpid, unfeeling, unperceiving.

Ant. sensitive.

insensibility apathy, dullness, indifference, lethargy, numbness, stupidity, torpor.

insensible (1) apathetic, callous, hard-hearted, indifferent, unfeeling, unsusceptible; (2) dull, insensate, stupid, torpid; (3) imperceivable, imperceptible.

inseparable indissoluble, indivisible, intimate.

Ant. separate.

insert infix, introduce, place, put, set.

insidious artful, crafty, crooked, cunning, deceitful, deceptive, designing, guileful, intriguing, sly, subtle, treacherous, tricky, wily.

Ant. honest, upright.

insight discernment, judgment, observation, penetration, perception, understanding, vision.

insignificant inconsiderable, immaterial, paltry, petty, trifling, trivial, unimportant, unsubstantial.

Ant. important.

insincere deceitful, deceptive, dishonest, disingenuous, dissembling, dissimulating, faithless, false, hypocritical, pretended, unfaithful, untrue.

Ant. sincere.

insincerity deceitfulness, dishonesty, disingenuousness, dissimulation, duplicity, faithlessness, hypocrisy.

Ant. honesty, sincerity.

insinuate (1) allude, hint, intimate, suggest; (2) inculcate, infuse, ingratiate, inject, instil, introduce.

Ant. of (2) withdraw.

insinuation (1) allusion, hint, innuendo, suggestion; (2) inculcation, infusion, ingratiating, injection, instillation, introduction.

Ant. of (2) withdrawal.

insipid characterless, dull, flat, flavourless, lifeless, prosy, spiritless, stale, tasteless, uninteresting, vapid.

Ant. interesting, tasteful.

insist contend, demand, persist, press, urge.

Ant. yield.

insobriety drunkenness, intemperance, intoxication.

Ant. sobriety.

insolence abuse, arrogance, boldness, contemptuousness, contumely, disrespect, effrontery, impertinence, impudence, insubordination, offensiveness, pertness, rudeness.

Ant. courtesy.

insolent abusive, arrogant, bold, contemptuous, domineering, impertinent, impudent, insubordinate, insulting, overbearing, pert.

Ant. courteous.

insolvent bankrupt, failed, ruined.

Ant. solvent.

insomnia (*Med.*) sleeplessness, wakefulness.

inspect examine, investigate, oversee, scrutinise, search, superintend, supervise.

inspection examination, investigation, scrutiny, search, superintendence, supervision.

inspector censor, critic, examiner, investigator, overseer, scrutiniser, superintendent, supervisor, visitor.

inspiration (1) breathing, inhalation; (2) (*Fig.*) afflatus, elevation, enthusiasm, exaltation, genius, insight.

inspire (1) breathe, inhale; (2) (*Fig.*) animate, encourage, enliven, imbue, infuse, inspirit, instil.

Ant. of (1) exhale; of (2) discourage.

inspirit animate, cheer, embolden, encourage, enliven, exhilarate, fire, hearten, incite, inspire, invigorate, rouse, stimulate.

Ant. dishearten.

instability changeableness, fickleness, inconstancy, insecurity, mutability, variability, wavering.

Ant. constancy, steadfastness.

instal(1) inaugurate, induct, institute, introduce, invest.

instance (1) *n.* case, example, illustration; (2) application, entreaty, importunity, impulse, incitement, instigation, pressure, prompting, request, solicitation; (3) *v.* cite, mention, specify.

instant (A) flash, jiffy, moment, second, trice, twinkling.

instant (B) (1) earnest, importunate, pressing, solicitous, urgent; (2) immediate, prompt, quick; (3) (*Comm.*) current, present.

Ant. of (1) half-hearted; of (2) slow.

instantly forthwith, immediately, instantaneously, instanter, now.

Ant. later.

instauration reconditioning, reconstitution, reconstruction, redintegration, re-establishment, rehabilitation, renewal, renovation, repair.

Ant. demolition.

instigate actuate, encourage, impel, incite, influence, move, persuade, prompt, provoke, rouse, spur, stimulate, urge.

Ant. discourage.

instil implant, inculcate, infuse, ingraft, insinuate, introduce.

Ant. remove.

instinct impulse, intuition, proclivity, prompting, tendency.

Ant. reason.

instinctive automatic, intuitional, involuntary, natural, spontaneous.

Ant. reasoned.

institute (A) appoint, begin, commence, enact, establish, fix, found, invest, ordain, originate, settle, start.

institute (B) (1) academy, college, institution, school, seminary, society; (2) doctrine, dogma, maxim, precept, principle, tenet.

institution (1) custom, enactment, establishment, foundation, investiture, investment, practice; (2) academy, college, hospital, school, seminary, society, university.

instruct (1) coach, discipline, educate, enlighten, guide, inform, school, teach, train, tutor; (2) command, direct, enjoin, order.

Ant. learn.

instruction (1) coaching, discipline, education, enlightenment, guidance, information, schooling, teaching, training, tuition; (2) advice, command, counsel, direction, injunction, mandate, order.

instructor coach, master, pedagogue, preceptor, schoolmaster, teacher, tutor.

Ant. pupil.

instrument (1) agent, apparatus, appliance, implement, means, medium, tool, utensil; (2) (*Law*) charter, deed, document, indenture, writing.

instrumental assisting,

auxiliary, conducive, helpful, helping, subsidiary, useful.

instrumentality agency, intervention, mediation, medium.

insubordinate disobedient, disorderly, mutinous, rebellious, riotous, seditious, turbulent, ungovernable, unruly.

Ant. obedient.

insubordination disobedience, indiscipline, insurrection, mutiny, rebellion, revolt, riotousness, sedition.

Ant. obedience.

insufferable (1) insupportable, intolerable, unbearable, unendurable; (2) (*Fig.*) detestable, disgusting, outrageous.

Ant. bearable.

insufficiency (1) dearth, defect, deficiency, lack; (2) inadequateness, incompetence.

Ant. plenty.

insufficient (1) deficient, lacking; (2) inadequate, incapable, incompetent, unfitted, unqualified.

Ant. of (1) plenty; of (2) capable.

insular (*Fig.*) contracted, limited, narrow, narrow-minded, petty, prejudiced.

Ant. broad-minded.

insulate detach, disconnect, disengage, disunite, isolate, separate.

Ant. unite.

insult (1) *n.* abuse, affront, contumely, indignity, insolence, offence, outrage, slander; (2) *v.* abuse, affront, injure, offend, outrage, slander.

Ant. of (1) compliment; of (2) respect.

insuperable impassable, insurmountable, invincible, unconquerable.

insupportable insufferable,

intolerable, unbearable, unendurable.

Ant. bearable.

insuppressible irrepressible, unconquerable, uncontrollable.

Ant. suppressible.

insure assure, guarantee, indemnify, underwrite, warrant.

insurgent (1) *n.* rebel, revolter, rioter; (2) *a.* disobedient, insubordinate, rebellious, riotous, seditious.

Ant. of (1) loyalist; of (2) loyal.

insurmountable impassable, impossible, insuperable, invincible.

insurrection mutiny, rebellion, revolt, rising, sedition, uprising.

insusceptible indifferent, insensible, insensitive, unimpressible.

intact (1) complete, scatheless, sound, undamaged, unharmed, unimpaired, uninjured, unscathed, untouched, whole; (2) undefiled, unviolated, virgin.

Ant. of (1) harmed.

intangible dim, impalpable, imperceptible, indefinite, unreal, unsubstantial, vague.

Ant. solid, tangible.

integral complete, entire, whole.

Ant. fractional.

integrity candour, goodness, honesty, probity, purity, rectitude, righteousness, uprightness, virtue.

Ant. disrepute.

intellect brains, intelligence, judgment, mind, reason, sense, understanding.

intellectual intelligent, mental, rational, thoughtful.

intelligence (1) alertness, aptitude, brightness, capacity, cleverness, discernment, mind, penetration, quickness, reason, understanding; (2) advice, information, knowledge, news, notice, notification, report, rumour, tidings.

Ant. of (2) ignorance.

intelligent acute, alert, apt, bright, clever, discerning, enlightened, instructed, knowing, sharp, smart, well-informed.

Ant. stupid.

intelligible clear, comprehensible, distinct, evident, obvious, plain.

Ant. incomprehensible.

intemperance excess, extravagance, immoderation, inebriation, intoxication.

Ant. moderation.

intemperate excessive, extravagant, extreme, immoderate, inordinate, intoxicated, passionate, uncontrollable, ungovernable.

Ant. moderate.

intend aim, contemplate, contrive, design, determine, meditate, plan, propose, purpose, scheme.

intense (1) close, severe, strained, stretched, strict; (2) acute, deep, excessive, extreme, great, profound; (3) ardent, eager, earnest, energetic, forcible, keen.

Ant. of (1) slight.

intensify aggravate, concentrate, deepen, strengthen.

Ant. weaken.

intensity ardour, concentration, earnestness, energy, excess, extremity, force, intenseness, severity, strain, strength, tension, vehemence, vigour.

Ant. weakness.

intent (1) a. bent, eager, earnest, fixed, resolute, set, stead-

fast; (2) n. aim, design, end, intention, object, plan, purpose.

Ant. of (1) irresolute.

intention aim, design, end, intent, meaning, object, purpose, scope, view.

intentional contemplated, deliberate, designed, intended, planned, preconcerted, premeditated, purposed, studied, wilful.

Ant. unintentional.

inter bury, entomb, inhume.

Ant. exhume.

intercede advocate, arbitrate, interpose, intervene, mediate, plead.

Ant. accuse.

intercept arrest, interrupt, obstruct, seize.

Ant. release.

intercession advocacy, entreaty, intervention, mediation, plea, pleading, prayer, solicitation, supplication.

Ant. non-intervention.

intercessor advocate, interceder, mediator, pleader.

interchange alternate, bandy, exchange, reciprocate.

intercourse commerce, communication, communion, connection, converse, correspondence, dealings, inter-communication, intimacy.

Ant. separation, silence.

interdict (1) v. ban, bar, debar, disallow, forbid, prevent, prohibit, proscribe, veto; (2) n. ban, disallowance, interdiction, prohibition, veto.

Ant. of (1) allow.

interest (1) v. affect, attract, concern, engage, move, touch; (2) n. affection, attraction, attention, concern, curiosity, regard, sympathy; (3) advantage, authority, benefit, good, influence, portion, premium, profit, share.

Ant. of (3) loss.

interested (1) affected, attracted, concerned, excited, moved; (2) biased, partial, predisposed, prejudiced.

Ant. of (2) impartial.

interesting absorbing, attractive, engaging, entertaining.

Ant. dull.

interfere clash, collide, conflict, intermeddle, intervene, intrude, meddle.

Ant. support.

interference clashing, collision, conflict, intermeddling, intervention, intrusion, opposition.

interior (1) inner, inside, internal, inward; (2) (*Geog.*) inland, remote; (3) (*Polit.*) domestic, home.

Ant. exterior.

interlace cross, intertwine, interweave, intwine, reticulate, twine.

Ant. untwist.

interloper intermeddler, intruder, meddler.

intermeddle interfere, interlope, meddle.

intermediate interposed, intervening, middle.

interment burial, inhumation, sepulture.

Ant. exhumation.

interminable boundless, endless, immeasurable, infinite, limitless, long, long-drawn, never-ending, protracted, unbounded, unlimited.

Ant. limited.

intermingle blend, commingle, commix, intermix, mix.

Ant. separate.

intermission cessation, interruption, interval, pause,

respite, rest, stop, stoppage, suspense, suspension.

Ant. continuance.

intermit cease, discontinue, interrupt, stop, suspend.

Ant. continue.

internecine deadly, destructive, exterminating, exterminatory, fatal, mortal.

interpolate add, insert, introduce.

Ant. delete.

interpose (1) interfere, intermeddle, intrude, intervene; (2) insert, introduce; (3) arbitrate, intercede, mediate.

Ant. of (1) withdraw.

interpret clarify, construe, decipher, decode, define, elucidate, explain, expound, render, solve, translate, understand.

Ant. obscure.

interpretation clarification, construction, elucidation, explanation, exposition, meaning, sense, signification, translation, understanding, version.

interrogate ask, catechise, enquire, examine, inquire, investigate, question.

Ant. answer, reply.

interrogation examination, enquiry, inquiry, query, question, questioning.

Ant. answer.

interrupt break, cut, delay, disconnect, discontinue, disjoin, disturb, disunite, divide, hinder, interfere, separate, sever, stop, suspend.

Ant. resume.

interruption break, cessation, disconnection, discontinuance, dissolution, disuniting, division, hindrance, impediment, obstacle, obstruction, pause, separation, severance, stop, stoppage, suspension.

Ant. resumption.

intersect cross, cut, divide.

intersperse diversify, interlard, mix, scatter.

interstice chink, crack, crevice, fissure, gap, interval, opening, space.

intertwine cross, interlace, interweave, inweave, reticulate.

Ant. disentangle.

interval (1) gap, intermission, interstice, opening, space; (2) interlude, pause, period, season, space, term, time.

Ant. of (1) continuance.

intervene (1) intercede, interfere, intrude; (2) befall, happen, occur.

intervention agency, intercession, interference, interposition, intrusion, meditation.

Ant. neglect.

interview conference, consultation, meeting, parley, talk.

interweave cross, interlace, intertwine, inweave, reticulate.

Ant. disentangle.

intestines bowels, entrails, guts, insides, innards, viscera.

intimate (1) a. close, confidential, dear, friendly, near, private, secret; (2) n. acquaintance, associate, companion, comrade, confidant(e), crony, familiar, friend, helpmate, pal; (3) v. allude, announce, communicate, declare, hint, impart, insinuate, remind, suggest, warn.

Ant. of (1) distant; of (2) enemy.

intimation allusion, announcement, communication, declaration, hint, insinuation, reminder, suggestion, warning.

intimidate affright, alarm, appal, cow, daunt, dishearten, dismay, dispirit, frighten, scare, subdue, threaten, terrify.

Ant. reassure.

intimidation fear, terror, threat.

intolerable insufferable, insupportable, unbearable, unendurable.

Ant. endurable.

intolerant arrogant, bigoted, dictatorial, imperious, lordly, narrow-minded, overbearing.

Ant. condescending, forbearing.

intonation accentuation, cadence, modulation, tone.

intoxicated (1) drunk, drunken, fuddled, inebriated, muddled, tipsy; (2) (*Fig.*) excited, exhilarated, infatuated.

Ant. sober.

intoxication (1) drunkenness, inebriation, inebriety, insobriety; (2) (*Fig.*) excitement, exhilaration, infatuation.

Ant. sobriety.

intractability cantankerousness, indiscipline, indocility, obduracy, obstinacy, perverseness, pigheadedness, stubbornness.

Ant. docility.

intractable cantankerous, fractious, headstrong, obdurate, perverse, pigheaded, refractory, stubborn, unbending, undisciplined, ungovernable, unmanageable, unruly, unyielding, wilful.

Ant. amenable, docile.

intrenchment (1) defence, ditch, dyke, fortification, moat, protection, rampart, shelter, trench; (2) breach, encroachment, infringement, inroad, violation.

intrepid bold, brave, courageous, daring, dauntless, doughty, gallant, heroic, undaunted, valiant, valorous.

Ant. timid.

intrepidity boldness, bravery, courage, daring, fearlessness, fortitude, gallantry, heroism, prowess, spirit, valour.
Ant. timidity.

intricacy complexity, complication, entanglement, intricateness, involution, obscurity.
Ant. simplicity.

intricate complex, complicated, difficult, involved, obscure, perplexed, tortuous.
Ant. simple.

intrigue (1) *n.* artifice, cabal, conspiracy, machination, manoeuvre, plot, ruse, scheme, stratagem, wile; (2) *v.* conspire, plot, scheme.
Ant. of (1) frankness.

intriguing artful, crafty, cunning, deceitful, diplomatic, insidious, politic, scheming, sly, subtle, wily.
Ant. candid, frank.

intrinsic (1) essential, genuine, real, true; (2) inborn, inbred, inherent, native, natural.
Ant. of (1) artificial; of (2) acquired, extrinsic.

introduce (1) begin, commence, inaugurate, start; (2) acquaint, bring, conduct, lead, present.
Ant. of (1) withdraw.

introduction (1) inauguration, induction, presentation; (2) commencement, preamble, preface, prelude, prologue.
Ant. of (1) withdrawal; of (2) conclusion.

introductory initiatory, precursory, prefatory, preliminary, preparatory.
Ant. conclusive.

intrude encroach, infringe, interfere, obtrude, trespass, violate.

intrust commit, confide, consign, deliver.

intuition discernment, insight, instinct, perception, presentiment.
Ant. calculation.

intuitive instinctive, involuntary, spontaneous, unreflecting.
Ant. calculated.

intwine cross, interlace, intertwine, interweave, inweave, reticulate.
Ant. disentangle.

inundate deluge, drown, flood, overflow, overwhelm, submerge, swamp.
Ant. drain.

inundation deluge, flood, overflow.

inure accustom, familiarise, habituate, harden, train, use.

invade assail, assault, attack, encroach, infringe, occupy, raid, violate.

invalid (A) feeble, frail, ill, infirm, sick, weak.
Ant. strong.

invalid (B) baseless, fallacious, false, null, unfounded, unsound, untrue, void, worthless.
Ant. valid.

invalidate abrogate, annul, cancel, nullify, overrule, overthrow, quash, rescind, weaken.
Ant. ratify.

invaluable costly, inestimable, precious, priceless, valuable.
Ant. worthless.

invariable constant, immutable, unalterable, unchangeable, unchanging, uniform, unvarying.
Ant. variable.

invasion (1) aggression, assault, attack, foray, incursion, inroad, irruption, raid; (2) encroachment, infringement, violation.

invective abuse, censure, contumely, denunciation, diatribe, obloquy, raillery, reproach, sarcasm, vituperation.
Ant. commendation.

inveigh blame, censure, condemn, denounce, reproach, vituperate.
Ant. compliment.

inveigle allure, beguile, coax, decoy, ensnare, entice, entrap, lure, seduce, wheedle.
Ant. repel.

invent (1) conceive, contrive, create, design, devise, discover, imagine, originate; (2) fabricate, feign, forge.
Ant. of (1) copy, imitate.

invention (1) contrivance, creation, design, device, discovery; (2) deceit, fabrication, fiction, forgery.
Ant. of (1) copy, imitation.

inventive creative, fertile, ingenious, skilful.
Ant. uncreative.

inventory account, catalogue, list, record, register, roll, roster, schedule.

invert overset, overturn, upset.

invest (1) array, bedeck, clothe, deck, drape, dress, robe; (2) endow, endue; (3) (*Mil.*) beset, besiege, enclose, surround.
Ant. of (1) undress; of (3) relieve.

investigate consider, enquire, examine, explore, inquire, inspect, probe, scrutinise, search, sift, study.
Ant. ignore.

investigation enquiry, examination, exploration, inquiry, inspection, research, scrutiny, study.
Ant. neglect

investiture induction, installation, ordination.

investment (1) (*Arch.*) clothes, clothing, dress, garments, robes, vestment; (2) (*Mil.*) besieging, blockading, surrounding.

inveterate chronic, confirmed, deep-seated, established, habitual, hardened, ingrained, obstinate.
Ant. acquired.

invidious envious, hateful, odious, offensive.
Ant. charitable.

invigorate animate, brace, fortify, harden, nerve, quicken, stimulate, strengthen.
Ant. unnerve, weaken.

invincible impregnable, indomitable, inseparable, unconquerable, unsurmountable, unyielding.
Ant. conquerable.

inviolable (1) holy, sacred, sacrosanct; (2) obligatory, unalterable.

inviolate intact, sacred, stainless, unbroken, undefiled, unhurt, unpolluted, unstained, virgin.
Ant. corrupt.

invisible hidden, imperceptible, indiscernible, unperceivable, unseen.
Ant. visible.

invitation asking, begging, call, request, solicitation, supplication.

invite (1) ask, beg, bid, call, request, solicit, summon; (2) allure, attract, draw, entice, lead, tempt.
Ant. of (2) repel.

inviting alluring, attractive, captivating, engaging, enticing, fascinating, pleasing, winning.
Ant. forbidding.

invocation entreaty, petition, prayer, supplication.

invoke adjure, appeal, beg, beseech, conjure, entreat, implore, petition, pray, solicit, supplicate.
Ant. insist.

involuntary (1) compulsory, forced, obligatory, unwilling; (2) automatic, instinctive, spontaneous, unconscious, uncontrolled, unintentional.
Ant. of (1) voluntary; of (2) conscious.

involve (1) cover, envelop, enwrap; (2) comprehend, comprise, embrace, entail, imply, include; (3) bind, blend, complicate, connect, entangle, implicate, interlace, intertwine, tie, twine, unite.
Ant. of (1) uncover.

invulnerable insuperable, invincible, safe, unassailable.
Ant. vulnerable.

inwards n. pl. bowels, entrails, guts, intestines, insides, viscera.

inwrap cover, encase, enfold, envelop, infold, wrap.

iota atom, bit, grain, jot, mite, particle, scrap, tittle, trace, whit.

irascible cross, hasty, hot-tempered, irritable, petulant, quick-tempered, short-tempered, testy, touchy.
Ant. calm.

irate angry, annoyed, enraged, exasperated, incensed, irritated, piqued, provoked, wrathful.
Ant. pleased.

ire anger, annoyance, choler, exasperation, fury, indignation, passion, rage.

irksome annoying, boring, burdensome, disagreeable, tedious, tiresome, troublesome,

uninteresting, wearisome.
Ant. agreeable, easy.

ironical mocking, sarcastic, satirical, scoffing, sneering.
Ant. commendatory.

irons bonds, chains, fetters, gyves, manacles.

irradiate brighten, enlighten, illume, illuminate, illumine, shine.
Ant. darken.

irrational (1) absurd, foolish, injudicious, preposterous, silly, unreasonable, unwise; (2) aberrant, crazy, demented, insane; (3) brute, brutish.
Ant. rational.

irreconcilable implacable, incompatible, incongruous, inconsistent, inexorable, unappeasable.
Ant. appeasable, compatible.

irrefutable incontestable, indisputable, indubitable, invincible, irresistible, unanswerable, unassailable, undeniable, unquestionable.
Ant. doubtful, questionable.

irregular abnormal, anomalous, capricious, desultory, disorderly, eccentric, exceptional, immoderate, inordinate, uncertain, uneven, unmethodical, unpunctual, unsystematic, unusual, variable.
Ant. regular.

irrelevant impertinent, inapplicable, inapposite, inappropriate, inapt, unrelated.
Ant. apt, related.

irreligious impious, profane, sinful, undevout, ungodly, unholy, unrighteous, wicked.
Ant. godly, pious.

irremediable hopeless, incurable, irrecoverable, irreparable, remediless.
Ant. curable.

irreparable incurable, irrecoverable, irremediable, irretrievable.

irrepressible insuppressible, uncontrollable.
Ant. controllable.

irreproachable blameless, faultless, guiltless, inculpable, innocent, irreprehensible.
Ant. blameworthy.

irreprovable irreproachable, blameless, irreprehensible.

irresolute fickle, hesitant, hesitating, undecided, undetermined, unsettled, unstable, unsteady, vacillating, wavering.
Ant. decided.

irresponsible unaccountable, untrustworthy.

irreverent disrespectful, flippant.
Ant. reverent.

irreversible irrevocable, irreparable.

irrevocable changeless, immutable, invariable, irreversible, unalterable, unchangeable.
Ant. alterable.

irrigate flood, inundate, moisten, water, wet.

irrision derision, mockery, scorn.

irritable cantankerous, choleric, excitable, fiery, fretful, hasty, hot, irascible, passionate, peevish, petulant, testy, touchy.
Ant. good-tempered.

irritate anger, annoy, enrage, exasperate, fret, incense, inflame, infuriate, offend, provoke, vex.
Ant. delight, soothe.

irritation anger, annoyance, exasperation, excitement, indignation, provocation, resentment, wrath.
Ant. good-temper, pleasure.

irruption foray, incursion, inroad, invasion, raid.
Ant. evacuation.

isolate detach, disconnect, insulate, segregate, separate.
Ant. unite.

isolation disconnection, loneliness, seclusion, segregation, separation, solitude.
Ant. company, society.

issue (1) v. arise, emanate, emerge, originate, spring, proceed, rise; (2) conclude, end, result, terminate; (3) circulate, deliver, distribute, publish; (4) n. egress, exit, outlet, vent; (5) conclusion, consequence, effect, end, outcome, result, termination, upshot; (6) circulation, delivery, distribution, publication.

iterate reiterate, repeat.

itinerant journeying, nomadic, roaming, roving, travelling, unsettled, vagrant, wandering.
Ant. settled.

itinerary (1) circuit, journey, line, route, tour; (2) guide, guide-book.

J

jabber, babble, chatter, gabble, prate.

jade (1) v. exhaust, fag, fatigue, wear; (2) n. hussy, quean, slattern, slut, wench.
Ant of (1) revive.

jagged cleft, denticulated, indented, notched, rough, serrated, uneven.
Ant. even.

jam (1) v. crowd, crush, press, ram, squeeze, throng; (2) n. crowd, crush, mass, pack, throng

jar (1) *v.* bicker, clash, contend, disagree, interfere, oppose, quarrel, wrangle; (2) agitate, disturb, grate, irritate, jolt, offend, rasp, shake; (3) *n.* agitation, altercation, bickering, disagreement, discord, grating, irritation, jolt, quarrel, rasping, variance, wrangling.

Ant. of (3) harmony.

jargon (1) (*Pop.*) balderdash, gabble, gibberish, nonsense, palaver, rigmarole, twaddle; (2) argot, cant, dialect, patois, slang.

Ant. of (1) sense.

jaundiced (1) (*Med.*) bilious; (2) (*Fig.*) biased, bigoted, partial, prejudiced.

Ant. of (2) impartial.

jaunt excursion, outing, ramble, stroll, tour, trip.

jaunty airy, finical, garish, gay, showy, sprightly.

Ant. serious, staid.

jealous (1) covetous, emulous, envious, invidious, resentful, rival; (2) anxious, apprehensive, solicitous, suspicious, vigilant, watchful.

Ant. of (1) satisfied; of (2) carefree.

jeer (1) *v.* banter, deride, flout, gibe, mock, ridicule, scoff, sneer, taunt; (2) *n.* derision, gibe, ridicule, sneer, taunt.

Ant. praise.

jeopardise endanger, hazard, imperil, risk, venture.

Ant. preserve.

jeopardy danger, hazard, peril, risk.

Ant. safety.

jerk jolt, pull, throw, thrust, twitch.

jest (1) *n.* banter, fun, joke, play, pleasantry, quip, sport,

witticism; (2) *v.* gibe, jeer, joke, scoff, sneer.

Ant. of (1) solemnity.

jester (1) humorist, joker, wag; (2) buffoon, clown, fool, harlequin.

jilt (1) *v.* break, coquette, deceive, disappoint, discard, flirt; (2) *n.* coquette, flirt.

jingle clink, rattle, ring, tinkle, tintinnabulate.

jocose blithe, comical, droll, facetious, funny, humorous, jesting, jocular, jocund, jovial, joyous, merry, pleasant, sportive, waggish, witty.

Ant. sad, serious.

jog (1) nudge, prod, push, remind, shake; (2) lumber, trot, trudge.

join accompany, add, adhere, annex, append, attack, cement, combine, connect, couple, fasten, link, unite.

Ant. unfasten.

joint (1) *n.* articulation, connection, hinge, junction, juncture, seam, union; (2) *a.* combined, concerted, joined, united; (3) *v.* fit, join, unite.

joke *n.* fun, jest, play, quip, quirk, sally, sport, witticism.

jolly (1) cheerful, convivial, festive, frolicsome, funny, gay, gladsome, hilarious, jocund, jovial, joyous, jubilant, merry, mirthful, sportive; (2) chubby, lusty, plump, stout.

Ant. of (1) miserable; of (2) gaunt.

jostle crowd, jog, joggle, jolt, hustle, press, push, shake, squeeze, throng, thrust.

jot ace, atom, bit, fraction, grain, iota, mite, morsel, particle, scrap, tittle, trifle, whit.

journal diary, gazette, magazine, newspaper, paper, periodical, record, register.

journey (1) *n.* excursion, expedition, jaunt, outing, pilgrimage, ramble, tour, travel, trip, voyage; (2) *v.* fare, go, proceed, roam, rove, tour, travel.

jovial airy, blithe, cheery, convivial, gay, glad, happy, hilarious, jocose, jocund, jolly, jubilant, merry, mirthful.
Ant. cheerless, unhappy.

joviality fun, gaiety, hilarity, jollity, merriment, mirth.
Ant. sadness.

joy bliss, delight, ecstasy, exaltation, felicity, festivity, glee, hilarity, pleasure, rapture, ravishment, satisfaction, transport.
Ant. sorrow.

joyful blithesome, delighted, elated, glad, happy, jocund, jolly, jovial, jubilant, merry, pleased, satisfied.
Ant. gloomy, sorrowful.

jubilant elated, exultant, glad, rejoicing, triumphant.
Ant. despondent, downcast.

judge (1) *n.* adjudicator, arbiter, referee, umpire; (2) *v.* adjudicate, arbitrate, decide, determine; (3) *n.* critic, connoisseur, expert; (4) *v.* appreciate, criticise, esteem, estimate, rate; (5) *n.* justice, magistrate; (6) *v.* condemn, doom, sentence, try.

judgment (1) commonsense, discernment, discrimination, intelligence, penetration, perspicacity, prudence, sagacity, sense, shrewdness, taste, wisdom; (2) arbitration, award, conclusion decision, decree, determination, estimate, opinion, sentence, verdict.
Ant. of (1) stupidity.

judgment-seat bar, bench, court, tribunal.

judicious cautious, con-

sidered, discerning, discreet, discriminating, expedient, prudent, rational, reasonable, sagacious, sensible, skilful, sound, well-advised, well-judged, wise.
Ant. indiscreet.

juicy lush moist, sappy, succulent, watery.
Ant. sapless.

jumble (1) *v.* confound, confuse, disarrange, disorder, mix, muddle; (2) *n.* confusion, disarrangement, disorder, medley, mess, mixture, muddle.
Ant. of (1) arrange; of (2) order.

jump *v.* bound, caper, clear, hop, leap, skip, spring, vault.

junction alliance, combination, connection, coupling, joint, juncture, linking, seam, union.
Ant. separation.

juncture conjuncture, contingency, crisis, emergency, exigency, moment, occasion, point.

junta cabal, clique, combination, confederacy, coterie, faction, gang, league, party, set.

just (1) blameless, conscientious, equitable, fair, fair-minded, good, honest, honourable, impartial, lawful, pure, right, unbiased, upright, virtuous; (2) accurate, correct, exact, normal, proper, regular, true; (3) appropriate, apt, deserved, due, legitimate, merited, rightful, suitable; (4) *adv.* exactly, precisely.

justice (1) equity, fairness, honesty, impartiality, integrity, justness, law, reasonableness, rectitude, right; (2) judge, magistrate.
Ant. of (1) partiality.

justifiable defensible, excusable, fit, proper, right, vindicable, warrantable.

Ant. indefensible.

justification absolution, approval, defence, exculpation, excuse, exoneration, plea, vindication.

Ant. condemnation.

justify absolve, acquit, approve, defend, exculpate, excuse, exonerate, warrant.

Ant. accuse.

juvenile (1) *n.* boy, child, girl, youth; (2) *a.* boyish, childish, girlish, immature, puerile, young, youthful.

Ant. of (1) adult; of (2) mature.

juxtaposition adjacency, contact, contiguity, proximity.

Ant. remoteness.

K

keen (1) ardent, eager, earnest, fervid, zealous; (2) acute, biting, cutting, piercing, sharp; (3) astute, discerning, quick, sagacious, shrewd; (4) acrimonious, bitter, caustic, poignant.

Ant. of (1) apathetic; of (2) blunt; of (3) stupid; of (4) kind.

keenness (1) ardour, eagerness, earnestness, fervour, zeal, zest; (2) rigour, severity, sharpness, sternness; (3) astuteness, discernment, sagacity, shrewdness; (4) acrimony, asperity, bitterness, poignancy.

keep (A) *v.* (1) detain, guard, hold, maintain, preserve, protect, restrain, retain, support, withhold; (2) adhere, fulfil, obey, observe; (3) celebrate, commemorate, honour, observe, solemnise; (4) abide, dwell, endure, last, stay.

Ant. of (1) lose.

keep (B) *n.* (1) board, food, maintenance, subsistence, support; (2) castle, donjon, dungeon, stronghold, tower.

keeper curator, custodian, defender, gaoler, governor, guardian, jailer, preserver, superintendent, warden, warder.

keeping (1) care, charge, custody, guardianship, protection, trust; (2) agreement, conformity, congruity, consistency, harmony.

Ant. of (2) inconsistency.

ken (1) cognisance, knowledge, scope, sight, view; (2) *v.* (*Scot*) know.

key (1) clamp, lock-opener, opener, wedge; (2) (*Fig.*) clue, explanation, guide, solution, translation.

kick *v.* (*Fig.*) oppose, rebel, resist, spurn.

Ant. obey.

kidnap abduct, capture, remove, seize, steal.

Ant. restore.

kill (1) assassinate, butcher, despatch, destroy, murder, slaughter, slay; (2) (*Fig.*) calm, quell, scotch, still, suppress.

Ant. of (1) create.

kin (1) affinity, consanguinity, relationship; (2) connections, family, kindred, kinsfolk, kinsmen, relations, relatives; (3) *a.* akin, allied, cognate, kindred.

kind (A) (1) breed, class, family, genus, race, set, species; (2) character, description, manner, nature, sort, style, type.

kind (B) *a.* affectionate, amiable, amicable, beneficent, benevolent, benign, bland, bounteous, charitable, clement, compassionate, congenial, friendly, generous, gentle, good, gracious, humane, indulgent, kind-hearted, kindly, lenient, loving, mild, obliging, propitious, sympathetic, tender-hearted.

Ant. unkind.

kindle (1) fire, ignite, inflame, light; (2) (*Fig.*) animate, awaken, bestir, exasperate, excite, foment, incite, provoke, rouse, stimulate, stir, thrill.

Ant. of (1) extinguish.

kindliness amiability, beneficence, benevolence, benignity, charity, compassion, friendliness, gentleness, humanity, kind-heartedness, kindness, sympathy.

Ant. animosity.

kindly benevolent, benign, compassionate, cordial, genial, gentle, good-natured, hearty, kind, mild, pleasant, polite, sympathetic, warm.

Ant. unkindly, unsympathetic.

kindness affection, amiability, beneficence, benevolence, charity, clemency, compassion, fellow-feeling, generosity, gentleness, goodness, goodwill, grace, hospitality, humanity, indulgence, kindliness, tenderness.

Ant. malevolence.

kindred (1) affinity, consanguinity, relationship; (2) connections, family, kin, kinsfolk, kinsmen, relations, relatives; (3) *a.* akin, allied, cognate, kin, related, similar.

Ant. of (2) strangers; of (3) unrelated.

king monarch, sovereign.

Ant. commoner, subject.

kingdom (1) dominion,

dynasty, empire, monarchy, realm, reign, sovereignty; (2) commonwealth, county, division, nation, province, state, territory, tract.

Ant. republic.

kingly (1) imperial, monarchical, regal, royal, sovereign; (2) august, glorious, grand, grandiose, imposing, majestic, noble, splendid, stately.

Ant. of (1) low-born.

kink (1) bend, entanglement, knot, twist, wrinkle; (2) (*Fig.*) crotchet, whim.

kinsfolk connections, family, kin, kindred, kinsmen, relations, relatives.

Ant. strangers.

kit apparatus, effects, equipment, implements, outfit, tools.

knack adroitness, aptitude, dexterity, expertness, facility, handiness, quickness, skilfulness, skill.

Ant. awkwardness.

knave blackguard, cheat, rascal, rogue, scallywag, scamp, scapegrace, scoundrel, swindler, villain.

Ant. gentleman.

knavery deceit, deception, dishonesty, duplicity, fraud, imposture, rascality, roguery, trickery, villainy.

Ant. honesty.

knavish deceitful, deceptive, dishonest, fraudulent, rascally, roguish, scoundrelly, tricky, villainous.

Ant. honest.

knell ring, toll.

knit bind, connect, contract, fasten, join, loop, tie.

Ant. unravel, untie.

knob boss, bunch, door-handle, hunch, protuberance, stud.

knock (1) *v.* clap, cuff, hit, rap, slap, smite, strike, thump; (2)

n. blow, box, cuff, rap, slap.
Ant. caress.

knoll hill, hillock, mound.

knot (1) *v.* bind, complicate, entangle, knit, tie, weave; (2) *n.* bond, connection, joint, tie; (3) bunch, cluster, collection, tuft; (4) band, clique, company, crew, crowd, gang, group, squad.
Ant. of (1) untie.

knotty (1) gnarled, knotted; (2) complicated, difficult, hard, intricate, perplexing, puzzling.
Ant. of (2) simple.

know apprehend, ascertain, comprehend, discern, distinguish, learn, recognise, understand.

knowing acute, astute, clever, competent, cunning, discerning, experienced, expert, intelligent, qualified, sagacious, shrewd, skilful, well-informed.
Ant. unintelligent.

knowledge (1) education, enlightenment, erudition, instruction, learning, scholarship, science, wisdom; (2) apprehension, comprehension, discernment, judgment, recognition, understanding; (3) acquaintance, cognisance, information, notice.
Ant. of (1) ignorance.

knuckle *v.* cringe, crouch, stoop, submit, succumb, surrender, yield.
Ant. attack, resist.

L

laborious (1) arduous, difficult, fatiguing, hard, onerous, tiresome, toilsome, wearisome; (2) assiduous, diligent, hardworking, indefatigable, industrious, painstaking.

Ant. of (1) easy; of (2) lazy.

labour (1) *n.* drudgery, effort, exertion, industry, pains, painstaking, task, undertaking, work; (2) *v.* drudge, endeavour, slave, strive, suffer, toil, work; (3) *n.* childbirth, delivery, parturition, travail.
Ant. of (1) idleness, rest.

labyrinth entanglement, intricacy, maze, perplexity, windings.

labyrinthian confused, intricate, involved, labyrinthine, mazy, perplexing, winding.
Ant. simple.

lace *v.* attach, bind, fasten, intertwine, interweave, tie, twine.
Ant. untie.

lacerate (1) claw, cut, gash, maim, mangle, rend, rip, slash, tear, wound; (2) (*Fig.*) afflict, harrow, rend, torture, wound.
Ant. of (2) soothe.

lack (1) *n.* dearth, deficiency, destitution, insufficiency, need, scantiness, scarcity, shortage, shortcoming, shortness, want; (2) *v.* need, want.
Ant. of (1) plenty.

lackey attendant, flunkey, footman, lacquey, man-servant, valet.

laconic brief, concise, curt, pithy, sententious, short, succinct, terse.
Ant. loquacious.

lade burden, freight, load.

lading burden, cargo, freight, load.

lag dawdle, idle, linger, loiter, saunter, tarry.
Ant. hurry, speed.

laggard idler, lingerer, loafer, loiterer, lounger, saunterer, sluggard.
Ant. worker.

laic lay, secular.

lair (1) burrow, den, form, resting-place; (2) (*Scot.*) burial-plot, grave.

lambent flickering, gleaming, licking, touching, twinkling.

lame (1) crippled, defective, disabled, halt, hobbling, limping; (2) (*Fig.*) feeble, insufficient, poor, unsatisfactory, weak.
Ant. of (1) able-bodied; of (2) satisfactory.

lament (1) *v.* bemoan, bewail, complain, deplore, grieve, mourn, regret, wail, weep; (2) *n.* complaint, lamentation, moan, moaning, plaint, wail, wailing; (3) coronach, dirge, elegy, monody, requiem, threnody.
Ant. of (1) rejoice.

lamentable (1) deplorable, grievous, mournful, regrettable, sorrowful; (2) low, mean, miserable, pitiful, poor, wretched.
Ant. of (2) laudable.

lamentation dirge, grief, lament, moan, mourning, plaint, sorrow, wailing.
Ant. joy.

lampoon (1) *n.* calumny, libel, parody, satire; (2) *v.* calumniate, defame, libel, parody, satirise, slander.
Ant. of (1) eulogy.

land (A) (1) earth, ground, soil; (2) country, district, fatherland, motherland, nation, province, region, territory, tract.

land (B) *v.* debark, disembark.

landlord (1) host, hotel-keeper, hotelier, inn-keeper; (2) owner, proprietor.
Ant. of (1) guest; of (2) tenant.

language (1) conversation, dialect, idiom, jargon, speech, talk, terminology, tongue; (2) diction, expression, phraseology, style.

languid dull, faint, feeble, heavy, inactive, inert, listless, pining, sickly, sluggish, spiritless, torpid, weak.
Ant. energetic.

languish decline, droop, fade, fail, faint, pine, waste, weaken, wither.
Ant. revive.

languor apathy, debility, ennui, faintness, heaviness, lassitude, lethargy, listlessness, torpor, weakness, weariness.
Ant. energy, vigour.

lank attenuated, emaciated, gaunt, lean, scraggy, skinny, slender, slim, thin.
Ant. stout.

lap (1) cover, fold, turn, twist, wrap; (2) lick.

lapse (1) course, flow, flowing, gliding; (2) decline, descent, error, failing, fall, fault, indiscretion; (3) *v.* err, fail, fall, flow, glide, sink, slide, slip.

larceny pilfering, robbery, stealing, theft.

large abundant, ample, big, broad, bulky, capacious, colossal, comprehensive, copious, enormous, extensive, full, great, huge, immense, liberal, massive, plentiful, vast.
Ant. small, scarce.

largess bequest, bounty, donation, endowment, gift, grant.

lascivious lewd, libidinous, licentious, lustful, prurient, salacious, sensual, unchaste, voluptuous, wanton.
Ant. chaste.

lash (1) beat, castigate, chastise, flagellate, flog, (*Sl.*) lam, scourge, whip; (2) (*Fig.*) censure, lampoon, satirise; (3) bind, join, tie; (4) *n.* jambok, knout, scourge, sjambok,

thong, whip; (5) stripe, stroke.
Ant. of (1) caress.

lass damsel, girl, (*Scot.*) lassie, maid, maiden, miss.
Ant. lad.

lassitude dullness, ennui, exhaustion, fatigue, heaviness, languor, prostration, tiredness, weariness.
Ant. vigour.

last (1) *a.* closing, concluding, conclusive, extreme, final, hindmost, latest, terminal, ultimate, utmost; (2) *v.* abide, continue, endure, persist, remain.
Ant. of (1) first; of (2) fail.

lasting abiding, durable, enduring, perennial, permanent, perpetual, undying, unending.
Ant. ephemeral.

late (1) behind, behindhand, belated, delayed, slow, tardy; (2) recent; (3) deceased, former.
Ant. of (1) early.

latent concealed, hidden, invisible, occult, potential, secret, unseen, veiled.
Ant. open.

latitude (1) breadth, compass, extent, range, room, scope, space, width; (2) freedom, indulgence, laxity, liberty.
Ant. limit.

latter last, latest, modern, recent.

laud approve, celebrate, extol, glorify, honour, magnify, praise.
Ant. disparage.

laudable commendable, meritorious, praiseworthy.
Ant. blameworthy.

laughable amusing, comical, diverting, droll, farcical, funny, ludicrous, mirthful, ridiculous.
Ant. serious.

laughter cachinnation, chortle, chuckle, glee, laugh, laughing.
Ant. gloom.

launch (1) cast, dart, despatch, project, throw; (2) begin, commence, inaugurate, open, start; (3) descant, enlarge, expatiate.

lave bathe, cleanse, purge, wash.
Ant. soil.

lavish (1) *a.* excessive, extravagant, generous, immoderate, improvident, liberal, prodigal, profuse, thriftless, unreasonable, unrestrained, unstinted, wasteful; (2) *v.* dissipate, expend, spend, squander, waste.
Ant. of (1) stingy; of (2) economise.

law (1) act, code, command, commandment, covenant, decree, edict, enactment, formula, jurisdiction, order, ordinance, precept, principle, statute; (2) litigation, process, suit.

lawful allowable, authorised, constitutional, just, legal, legalised, legitimate, permissible, proper, rightful, valid.
Ant. illegal.

lawless disorderly, insubordinate, rebellious, reckless, riotous, seditious, wild.
Ant. orderly.

lawyer advocate, attorney, barrister, counsel, counsellor, solicitor.

lax (1) flabby, loose, slack, soft; (2) neglectful, negligent, remiss; (3) dissolute, lascivious, immoral, libertine, licentious, loose.
Ant. of (1) firm; of (2) heedful; of (3) moral.

lay (A) (1) deposit, establish, place, plant, produce, put, set, spread; (2) ascribe, attribute, charge, impute; (3) bet, hazard, risk, wager; (4) assess, impose, tax; (5) allay, appease, calm, quiet, still, suppress; (6) concoct, contrive, devise, prepare.

lay (B) ballad, carol, ditty, lyric, ode, poem, song.

lay (C) (1) laic, laical, unclerical; (2) amateur, inexpert, nonprofessional.

layer bed, row, seam, stratum.

laziness idleness, inactivity, indolence, slackness, sloth, slowness, sluggishness, tardiness.
Ant. industry.

lazy idle, inactive, indolent, inert, slack, slothful, slow, sluggish, supine, torpid.
Ant. active, industrious.

lead (1) v. command, conduct, direct, escort, govern, head; (2) draw, induce, influence, persuade, prevail; (3) conduce, contribute, serve, tend; (4) pass, spend; (5) n. advance, control, direction, guidance, precedence, priority.
Ant. of (1) follow.

leader captain, chief, commander, conductor, counsellor, director, guide, head, principal, ruler, superior.
Ant. follower.

leading chief, first, foremost, governing, highest, principal, ruling, superior.
Ant. subordinate.

league (1) n. alliance, association, coalition, combination, combine, compact, confederacy, confederation, consortium, union; (2) v. ally, associate, band, combine, confederate, unite.
Ant. of (2) divide.

leak (1) v. drip, exude, ooze, pass, percolate; (2) n. aperture, chink, crack, crevice, drip,

fissure, hole, oozing, opening, percolation.

leal attached, faithful, loyal, true-hearted.
Ant. disloyal.

lean (A) v. (1) abut, bear, bend, incline, recline, repose, rest, swerve, tend; (2) confide, depend, rely, trust.

lean (B) a. (1) bony, emaciated, gaunt, lank, pitiful, poor, scanty, skinny, slender, slim, spare, thin, unfatty; (2) bare, barren, inadequate, infertile, unfruitful, unproductive.
Ant. of (1) fat, obese; of (2) fertile.

leaning aptitude, bent, bias, disposition, inclination, liking, partiality, proneness, tendency.
Ant. disinclination.

leap v. (1) bound, caper, gambol, hop, jump, skip; (2) clear, vault.

learn acquire, ascertain, attain, collect, gain, gather, hear, memorise.
Ant. forget.

learned erudite, experienced, expert, knowing, lettered, literate, scholarly, skilled, versed, well-informed, well-read.
Ant. ignorant.

learner beginner, novice, pupil, student, tyro.
Ant. master, teacher.

learning acquirements, attainments, culture, education, erudition, information, knowledge, letters, literature, lore, scholarship, tuition.
Ant. ignorance.

least feeblest, last, lowest, meanest, minutest, smallest.
Ant. greatest.

leave (1) v. abandon, decamp, depart, desert, forsake, go, quit, relinquish, retire, with-

draw; (2) cease, desist, forbear, refrain, stop; (3) allow, let, permit; (4) commit, consign, refer; (5) bequeath, demise, transmit, will; (6) *n.* adieu, departure, farewell, good-bye, retirement, withdrawal; (7) allowance, concession, freedom, liberty, permission.
Ant. of (1) arrive.

leaven (1) *n.* barm, ferment, yeast; (2) (*Fig.*) influence, inspiration; (3) *v.* ferment, lighten, raise; (4) (*Fig.*) elevate, imbue, inspire, permeate, pervade; (5) infect, taint, vitiate.

leavings bits, dregs, fragments, left-overs, pieces, refuse, remains, scraps.

lecherous carnal, lascivious, lewd, libidinous, licentious, lustful, salacious, unchaste, wanton.
Ant. pure, chaste.

lecture (1) *v.* censure, chide, rate, reprimand, reprove, scold; (2) *n.* censure, reprimand, reproof, scolding; (3) *v.* address, harangue, teach; (4) *n.* address, harangue, lesson, teachings.

ledge projection, ridge, shelf.

lees dregs, precipitate, refuse, sediment, settlings.

legacy bequest, (*Law*) devise, gift.

legal allowable, authorised, constitutional, lawful, legalised, legitimate, proper, sanctioned.
Ant. illegal.

legalise authorise, legitimise, permit, sanction.
Ant. interdict.

legate ambassador, delegate, depute, deputy, envoy, nuncio.

legend fable, fiction, myth, narrative, story, tale.
Ant. fact, history.

legendary fabulous, fictitious, mythical, romantic.
Ant. factual, historical.

legible apparent, clear, decipherable, distinct, plain, readable.
Ant. illegible.

legion army, force, horde, host, multitude, number.

legislator law-giver, lawmaker.

legitimate (1) acknowledged, authorised, genuine, lawful, legal, proper, real, sanctioned; (2) correct, justifiable, logical, reasonable, sensible, valid, warranted.
Ant. of (1) illegitimate; of (2) unreasonable.

leisure convenience, ease, freedom, liberty, opportunity, quiet, recreation, retirement, vacation.
Ant. work.

lend advance, afford, bestow, confer, furnish, give, grant, impart, loan, present, supply.
Ant. borrow.

lengthen continue, draw, elongate, extend, increase, produce, prolong, protract, stretch.
Ant. shorten.

lengthy diffuse, lengthened, long-drawn, long-winded, prolix, prolonged, protracted, tedious, verbose.
Ant. concise.

leniency clemency, compassion, forbearance, gentleness, mercy, mildness, tenderness.
Ant. mercilessness.

lenient clement, compassionate, forbearing, gentle, merciful, mild, tender.
Ant. merciless.

lessen abate, abridge, contract, curtail, decrease, degrade, diminish, dwindle, impair,

lower, narrow, reduce, shrink, weaken.
Ant. increase.

lesson (1) exercise, instruction, lecture, precept, reading, task; (2) censure, chiding, rebuke, reproof, scolding, warning.

let (1) allow, permit, suffer; (2) hinder, impede, obstruct, prevent; (3) hire, lease; (4) n. hindrance, impediment, obstacle, obstruction, prohibition.

lethal baleful, deadly, destructive, fatal, mortal, murderous.
Ant. harmless.

lethargic apathetic, comatose, drowsy, dull, inactive, sleepy, sluggish, stupefied, torpid.
Ant. vigorous.

lethargy apathy, coma, drowsiness, dullness, inaction, inertia, sleepiness, sluggishness, stupor, torpor.
Ant. vigour.

lettered educated, erudite, learned, literate, versed, well-read.
Ant. ignorant.

levee ceremony, entertainment, gathering, party, reception.

level (1) a. even, flat, horizontal, plain, plane, smooth; (2) v. demolish, destroy, equalise, flatten, raze, smooth; (3) aim, direct, point.
Ant. of (1) uneven; of (2) restore.

levity buoyancy, facetiousness, fickleness, flightiness, flippancy, frivolity, inconstancy.
Ant. seriousness.

levy (1) collect, exact, gather, tax; (2) call, muster, raise, summon.

lewd impure, lascivious, libidinous, licentious, loose, lustful, profligate, unchaste, vile, wanton, wicked.
Ant. chaste.

lewdness debauchery, impurity, lasciviousness, lechery, licentiousness, profligacy, unchastity.
Ant. chastity.

lexicon dictionary, glossary, vocabulary, word-book.

liability accountability, duty, obligation, responsibility, tendency.
Ant. immunity.

liabilities (*Comm.*) debts, obligations.
Ant. assets.

liable (1) accountable, amenable, answerable, bound, responsible; (2) exposed, likely, subject.
Ant. of (1) unanswerable.

libel (1) v. calumniate, defame, lampoon, satirise, slander, vilify; (2) n. calumny, defamation, lampoon, obloquy, satire, slander, vituperation.
Ant. praise.

liberal (1) abundant, ample, bounteous, bountiful, charitable, generous, kind, lavish, open-handed, open-hearted, plentiful; (2) broad-minded, catholic, high-minded, magnanimous, tolerant, unbiased, unbigoted, unprejudiced.
Ant. of (1) stingy; of (2) bigoted.

liberality (1) beneficence, benevolence, bounty, charity, generosity, kindness, munificence; (2) benefaction, donation, gift, gratuity, present; (3) broad-mindedness, candour, catholicity, impartiality, magnanimity, toleration.
Ant. of (1) parsimony; of (3) bigotry.

liberate deliver, discharge,

disenthral, emancipate, free, release.

Ant. enslave.

libertine (1) *n.* debauchee, profligate, rake, roué, voluptuary; (2) *a.* corrupt, debauched, depraved, dissolute, licentious, profligate, rakish, voluptuous.

Ant. ascetic.

liberty (1) emancipation, freedom, immunity, independence, liberation, release; (2) leave, licence, license, permission, privilege.

Ant. restriction.

libidinous carnal, debauched, impure, lascivious, lecherous, loose, lustful, salacious, sensual, unchaste, wanton, wicked.

Ant. virtuous.

licence, license (1) *n.* authority, certificate, charter, immunity, leave, liberty, permission, permit, privilege, right, warrant; (2) anarchy, disorder, lawlessness, laxity; (3) *v.* allow, authorise, permit, suffer, tolerate.

Ant. of (1) restriction; of (3) forbid.

licentious disorderly, dissolute, immoral, impure, lascivious, lax, lewd, libidinous, lustful, profligate, rebellious, riotous, sensual, uncontrollable, uncontrolled, uncurbed, ungovernable, unruly, wanton, wicked.

Ant. virtuous.

lick (1) (*Sl.*) beat, flog, slap, spank, strike, thrash; (2) lap, taste.

Ant. of (1) caress.

lie (A) (1) *n.* falsehood, fabrication, prevarication, untruth; (2) *v.* fabricate, falsify, fib, prevaricate.

Ant. of (1) truth.

lie (B) *v.* (1) be, couch, recline, remain, repose, rest; (2) consist, pertain.

Ant. of (1) rise, stand.

lief freely, gladly, willingly.

liege master, overlord, sovereign, superior.

Ant. vassal.

lieu place, room, stead.

life (1) activity, animation, energy, sparkle, spirit, verve, vigour, vitality, vivacity; (2) being, duration, existence; (3) autobiography, biography, career, history, memoirs, story; (4) behaviour, conduct.

Ant. of (1) inactivity.

lifeless (1) dead, deceased, defunct, extinct, inanimate; (2) cold, dull, flat, frigid, lethargic, passive, pointless, slow, sluggish, spiritless, tasteless, torpid.

Ant. of (1) alive; of (2) lively.

lift elevate, hoist, raise, upheave, uplift, upraise.

Ant. lower.

ligament band, bandage, bond, ligature, tie.

light (A) (1) *n.* blaze, brightness, dawn, daybreak, daylight, flash, gleam, phosphorescence, radiance, ray, scintillation, sunrise; (2) candle, lamp, lantern, lighthouse, taper, torch, window-pane; (3) (*Fig.*) aspect, comprehension, elucidation, explanation, illustration, information, insight, instruction, interpretation, knowledge; (4) *v.* fire, ignite, inflame, kindle; (5) brighten, illuminate, illumine, irradiate, lighten; (6) alight, descend, land.

Ant. of (1) darkness; of (4) extinguish, quench; of (5) darken; of (6) board, mount.

light (B) *a.* (1) buoyant, easy,

imponderous, lightsome, portable; (2) easy, flimsy, inconsiderable, slight, small, trifling, trivial, unsubstantial; (3) airy, carefree, fickle, frivolous, gay, light-headed, unsteady, volatile; (4) (*Soil*) loose, porous, sandy, spongy; (5) bright, clear, whitish.

Ant. of (1) heavy; of (2) substantial; of (3) serious; of (4) clayey, heavy.

lighten (1) brighten, flash, gleam, illuminate, irradiate, shine; (2) enlighten, illumine, inform; (3) alleviate, ease, mitigate.

Ant. of (1) darken; of (3) aggravate.

light-hearted blithe, blithesome, carefree, cheerful, frolicsome, gay, glad, gleeful, jocund, jolly, jovial, joyful, merry.

Ant. morose, sad.

like (1) *v.* approve, cherish, choose, desire, enjoy, esteem, fancy, love, prefer, relish, select, wish; (2) *a.* alike, allied, analogous, cognate, corresponding, parallel, resembling, similar; (3) *n.* liking, partiality, preference; (4) equal, match.

Ant. of (1) dislike; of (2) different.

likely (1) liable, possible, probable; (2) agreeable, appropriate, pleasing, suitable.

Ant. of (1) unlikely.

likeness (1) appearance, form, parallel, resemblance, semblance, similitude; (2) copy, counterpart, effigy, facsimile, image, picture, portrait.

likewise also, besides, further, furthermore, moreover, too.

liking bent, bias, desire, fondness, love, partiality, predilection, preference, proneness, propensity, tendency.

Ant. dislike.

limb (1) arm, leg, member; (2) bough, branch, offshoot.

limber flexible, lithe, pliable, pliant, supple.

Ant. rigid.

limit (1) *n.* border, bound, boundary, check, confine, end, extent, frontier, limitation, obstruction, precinct, restraint, restriction, termination; (2) *v.* bound, check, circumscribe, confine, hinder, restrain, restrict.

limitation check, constraint, restraint, restriction.

limitless boundless, endless, illimitable, immeasurable, infinite, unbounded, undefined, unending, unlimited.

Ant. limited.

limp (1) *v.* halt, hobble; (2) *a.* flabby, flaccid, flexible, limber, pliable, relaxed, soft.

Ant. of (2) rigid.

limpid bright, clear, crystalclear, lucid, pellucid, pure, translucent, transparent.

Ant. cloudy, opaque.

line (1) cable, cord, rank, rope, row, streak, string, stripe, thread; (2) ancestry, family, lineage, race, succession; (3) business, calling, employment, job, occupation, post; (4) course, method.

lineage ancestry, birth, breed, descendants, extraction, family, forebears, forefathers, genealogy, house, line, offspring, progeny, succession.

lineament feature, line, outline, trait.

linger dally, dawdle, idle, lag, loiter, remain, stay, stop, tarry.

Ant. hurry.

link (1) *n.* bond, connection, joint, tie, vinculum; (2) *v.* bind, connect, fasten, join, tie,

unite; (3) *n.* division, member, part, piece.
 Ant. of (2) separate.
lion-hearted bold, brave, courageous, daring, dauntless, intrepid, valiant, valorous.
 Ant. chicken-hearted.
liquefaction dissolution, dissolving, fusion, melting, thawing.
liquefy dissolve, fuse, melt, thaw.
 Ant. solidify.
liquid (1) *n.* fluid, liquor; (2) *a.* clear, dulcet, flowing, fluid, mellifluous, melting, soft.
 Ant. of (1) solid.
list (1) catalogue, inventory, invoice, register, roll, schedule, series; (2) border, bound, edge, limit, selvage, selvedge, stripe; (3) *v.* heel, incline, lean; (4) (*Poet.*) choose, desire, like, please, prefer.
listen attend, hear, hearken, heed, obey, observe.
 Ant. disregard.
listless apathetic, careless, heedless, impassive, inattentive, indifferent, indolent, inert, languid, supine, vacant.
 Ant. active, attentive.
listlessness apathy, carelessness, heedlessness, inattention, indifference, indolence, languidness, languor, supineness, torpidity.
 Ant. activity, zeal.
literally actually, exactly, precisely, really, strictly.
literary bookish, erudite, learned, literate, scholarly, well-read.
 Ant. illiterate.
literature erudition, learning, letters, lore, writings.
lithe flexible, limber, pliable, pliant, supple.
 Ant. rigid.

litigation contending, disputing, lawsuit.
litigious contentious, disputatious, quarrelsome.
 Ant. conciliatory.
litter (1) *n.* confusion, disarray, disorder, fragments, rubbish, shreds, untidiness; (2) bedding, couch, straw-bed, stretcher; (3) brood, family; (4) *v.* derange, disarrange, disorder, scatter, strew.
 Ant. of (1) tidiness.
little (1) diminutive, feeble, infinitesimal, minute, pygmy, short, slender, small, tiny, wee; (2) brief, inconsiderable, insignificant, paltry, trivial, unimportant; (3) illiberal, mean, selfish, stingy.
 Ant. large.
live (1) *v.* be, breathe, exist, fare, feed, lead, pass, subsist; (2) abide, continue, dwell, endure, remain, reside, survive; (3) *a.* alive, animate, breathing, living, quick; (4) burning, glowing, hot, ignited; (5) active, earnest, vivid, wideawake.
 Ant. of (1) die; of (3) dead; of (5) inactive.
livelihood living, maintenance, subsistence, support, sustenance.
liveliness activity, animation, briskness, gaiety, smartness, spirit, sprightliness, vivacity.
 Ant. dulness, lifelessness.
lively active, agile, alert, animated, blithe, blithesome, forceful, gay, keen, moving, nimble, quick, sparkling, spirited, sprightly, spry, stirring, vigorous, vivacious.
 Ant. dull, torpid.
living (1) *a.* active, alive, animated, breathing, existing, extant, lively, quickening,

strong, vigorous; (2) *n.* livelihood, maintenance, subsistence, sustenance, support; (3) (*Eccl.*) benefice.

Ant. of (1) dead.

load (1) *n.* burden, encumbrance, incubus, onus, oppression, pressure, weight; (2) cargo, freight; (3) *v.* burden, cumber, encumber, freight, lade, oppress.

Ant. of (3) lighten.

loath averse, backward, disinclined, indisposed, reluctant, unwilling.

Ant. keen.

loathe abhor, abominate, detest, dislike.

Ant. love.

loathing abhorrence, abomination, antipathy, aversion, detestation, disgust, hatred, horror, repugnance, revulsion.

Ant. love.

loathsome abhorrent, abominable, disgusting, execrable, hateful, nauseating, obnoxious, odious, offensive, repugnant, repulsive, revolting.

Ant. delightful.

local district, limited, provincial, regional, restricted.

Ant. widespread.

locale locality, location, place, position, site, spot.

locality district, location, place, position, site, spot.

locate determine, establish, fix, place, settle.

Ant. remove.

lock (1) *v.* close, confine, fasten, join, restrain, seal, shut, stop, unite; (2) clasp, embrace, encircle, enclose, grapple, hug, press; (3) *n.* enclosure, fastening, hug; (4) handful, ringlet, tress, tuft.

Ant. of (1) open.

lodge (1) *v.* abide, dwell, inhabit, live, remain, rest, sojourn, stay, stop; (2) accommodate, cover, entertain, harbour, quarter, shelter; (3) deposit, fix, lay, place, plant, put, set; (4) *n.* cabin, cot, cottage, den, gate-house, haunt, house, hovel, lair; (5) assemblage, association, club, group, society.

lodging abode, apartments, cover, dwelling, habitation, harbour, protection, quarters, refuge, residence, shelter.

lofty (1) dignified, elevated, exalted, high, imposing, majestic, stately, sublime, tall, towering; (2) arrogant, haughty, proud.

Ant. of (1) low; of (2) humble.

logomachy altercation, argument, controversy, debate, dispute, wrangle.

Ant. agreement.

loiter dally, dawdle, delay, dilly-dally, idle, lag, linger, saunter, stroll.

Ant. hurry.

loneliness (1) desolation, isolation, seclusion, solitude; (2) dreariness, retirement.

lonely (1) alone, apart, forlorn, forsaken, friendless, lone; (2) deserted, desolate, dreary, isolated, remote, sequestered, solitary, unfrequented, uninhabited.

Ant. of (1) accompanied; of (2) crowded.

lonesome cheerless, deserted, desolate, dreary, gloomy, lone, lonely.

Ant. cheerful.

long (A) *a.* (1) extended, extensive, far-reaching, produced, prolonged, protracted, stretched; (2) backward, behindhand, dilatory, late, lingering, slow, tardy; (3) (*Fig.*) boring, diffuse, lengthy, long-winded, spun-out, tedious, wearisome, wordy.

Ant. of (1) short; of (2) quick; of (3) contracted.

long (B) v. covet, crave, desire, lust, pine, wish, yearn.

Ant. loathe.

longing aspiration, coveting, craving, desire, hankering, yearning.

Ant. loathing.

look (1) v. behold, consider, contemplate, examine, gaze, glance, observe, search, seek, watch; (2) anticipate, await, expect; (3) face, front; (4) appear, seem; (5) n. air, appearance, aspect, manner, mien, sight; (6) examination, gaze, glance, search.

loophole (1) aperture, opening; (2) (Fig.) excuse, plea, pretence, pretext, subterfuge.

loose (1) v. detach, disconnect, disengage, ease, free, liberate, loosen, release, slacken, unbind, undo, unfasten, unloose, untie; (2) a. free, movable, released, slack, unattached, unbound, unconfined, unfastened, unfettered, unrestricted, untied; (3) debauched, dissolute, immoral, licentious, unchaste, wanton; (4) diffuse, indefinite, indistinct, rambling, vague.

Ant. of (1) bind; of (2) bound; of (3) chaste; of (4) concise.

loosen liberate, relax, release, separate, slacken, unbind, unloose, untie.

Ant. tighten.

loot (1) v. pillage, plunder, ransack, rifle, rob, sack; (2) n. booty, plunder, spoil.

lop crop, curtail, cut, detach, dock, prune, sever, shorten, truncate.

loquacious babbling, chatty,

garrulous, talkative, voluble, wordy.

Ant. reserved.

loquacity babbling, chattering, gabbling, garrulity, volubility.

Ant. taciturnity.

lord (1) earl, noble, nobleman, peer, viscount; (2) governor, king, master, monarch, prince, ruler, sovereign, superior; (3) Christ, God, Jehovah.

Ant. of (1) commoner; of (2) subject.

lordly (1) aristocratic, dignified, exalted, grand, lofty, majestic, noble; (2) arrogant, despotic, domineering, haughty, imperious, overbearing, proud, tyrannical.

Ant. of (1) low; of (2) humble.

lordship authority, command, control, direction, domination, dominion, government, rule, sovereignty, sway.

Ant. subjection.

lore (1) erudition, knowledge, learning, letters, scholarship; (2) advice, doctrine, instruction, lesson, teaching, wisdom.

Ant. of (1) ignorance.

lose deprive, displace, drop, fail, forfeit, mislay, miss, misspend, squander, waste.

Ant. gain.

loss (1) bereavement, deprivation, failure, forfeiture, privation, squandering, waste; (2) damage, defeat, destruction, detriment, disadvantage, injury, ruin.

Ant. of (2) advantage.

lost (1) dissipated, forfeited, mislaid, missed, missing, misspent, squandered, wasted; (2) abstracted, bewildered, confused, distracted, dreamy, perplexed, preoccupied, puzzled; (3) conquered, defeated, vanquished; (4) abandoned, corrupt, depraved, dissolute, irreclaimable, licentious, profligate, unchaste, wanton.

Ant. of (1) found; of (4) chaste.

lot (1) accident, chance, destiny, doom, fate, fortune, hazard; (2) parcel, part, portion, share.

loth averse, disinclined, disliking, indisposed, reluctant, unwilling.

Ant. willing.

loud (1) boisterous, clamorous, deafening, high-sounding, noisy, obstreperous, sonorous, stentorian, strong, turbulent, vehement, vociferous; (2) (*Fig.*) flashy, gaudy, glaring, ostentatious, showy, vulgar.

Ant. of (1) low; of (2) elegant, tasteful.

lounge dawdle, idle, loaf, loiter, loll, recline, saunter, sprawl.

love (1) *n.* adoration, affection, amity, attachment, benevolence, courtship, delight, devotion, fondness, friendship, kindness, liking, passion, regard, tenderness, warmth; (2) lover, sweetheart; (3) *v.* adore, like, worship.

Ant. of (1) hatred; of (3) dislike, hate.

lovely admirable, adorable, amiable, beautiful, charming, delightful, enchanting, exquisite, graceful, handsome, sweet, winning.

Ant. ugly.

loving affectionate, dear, fond, kind, tender.

low (A) (1) deep, depressed, shallow, subsided, sunken; (2) short, small, stunted; (3) abject, base, degraded, dejected, ignoble, menial, servile, sordid, unworthy, vile, vulgar; (4) disgraceful, dishonourable,

disreputable, unbecoming, undignified, unrefined; (5) humble, lowly, meek, plain, poor, simple; (6) gentle, quiet, soft; (7) dying, feeble, exhausted, ill, reduced, weak; (8) cheap, moderate, reasonable.

Ant. high.

low (B) (1) *v.* bellow, moo; (2) *n.* bellowing, lowing, mooing.

lower (1) abate, decrease, diminish, lessen, reduce; (2) abase, debase, degrade, humble, humiliate; (3) depress, drop, fall, sink; (4) blacken, darken, frown, glower, scowl, threaten.

Ant. of (1) and (2) raise.

lowering clouded, cloudy, dark, darkening, gloomy, sullen, threatening.

Ant. bright, cheerful.

lowly (1) gentle, humble, meek, mild, modest, plain, poor, simple, unassuming, unpretentious; (2) low-born, mean, servile.

Ant. of (1) high, proud; of (2) high-born.

loyal attached, constant, devoted, faithful, patriotic, true.

Ant. disloyal.

loyalty allegiance, constancy, devotion, faithfulness, fealty, fidelity, patriotism.

Ant. disloyalty.

lucid (1) beaming, bright, brilliant, effulgent, luminous, radiant, resplendent, shining; (2) clear, crystalline, diaphanous, limpid, pellucid, pure, transparent; (3) clear, distinct, evident, intelligible, obvious, plain; (4) reasonable, sane, sober, sound.

Ant. of (1) dull; of (2) unclear; of (4) unreasonable.

luck accident, chance, fate, fortune, hap, hazard, success.

luckless ill-fated, ill-starred, unfortunate, unhappy, unlucky, unpropitious, unsuccessful.
Ant. lucky.

lucky auspicious, blessed, favoured, fortunate, prosperous, successful.
Ant. unlucky.

lucrative advantageous, gainful, paying, profitable, remunerative.
Ant. unprofitable.

lucre gain, money, profit, riches, wealth.
Ant. loss.

lucubration (1) cogitation, meditation, speculation, study; (2) composition, essay, writing.

ludicrous absurd, burlesque, comic, droll, farcical, funny, laughable, odd, ridiculous.
Ant. serious.

lugubrious doleful, gloomy, melancholy, morose, mournful, sad, serious, sombre, sorrowful.
Ant. gay.

lukewarm (1) blood-warm, tepid; (2) (*Fig.*) apathetic, cold, cool, indifferent, unconcerned.
Ant. of (2) wholehearted.

lull (1) *n.* calm, calmness, quiet, stillness; (2) *v.* abate, cease, decrease, diminish, subside; (3) calm, compose, hush, quiet, soothe, still, tranquillise.
Ant. of (2) increase; of (3) disturb.

lumber refuse, rubbish, trash, trumpery.

luminous (1) bright, brilliant, radiant, resplendent, shining, vivid; (2) clear, lucid, obvious, plain.
Ant. of (1) dark; of (2) obscure.

lunacy (1) aberration, craziness, derangement, insanity, madness, mania; (2) (*Med.*) dementia.
Ant. sanity.

lunatic (1) *n.* madman, maniac; (2) *a.* crazy, deranged, insane, mad.
Ant. of (2) sane.

lure (1) *v.* allure, attract, decoy, entice, inveigle, seduce, tempt; (2) *n.* allurement, bait, decoy, enticement, temptation.
Ant. of (1) repel.

lurid (1) dismal, ghastly, gloomy, lowering, murky, pale, wan; (2) (*Fig.*) fiery, glaring, sensational, startling, unrestrained.
Ant. of (1) bright; of (2) controlled, factual.

lurk hide, prowl, skulk, slink, sneak, snoop.
Ant. appear.

luscious cloying, delicious, honeyed, juicy, palatable, rich, savoury, sweet.
Ant. sour, unpalatable.

lust (1) *v.* covet, crave, desire, need, want, yearn; (2) *n.* appetite, carnality, craving, cupidity, desire, lasciviousness, lechery, lewdness, licentiousness, pruriency, salaciousness, sensuality, wantonness.
Ant. of (1) demand.

lustful carnal, concupiscent, craving, hankering, lascivious, lecherous, lewd, libidinous, licentious, prurient, sensual, unchaste.
Ant. virtuous.

lustily strongly, vigorously.

lustiness hardihood, power, robustness, stoutness, strength, sturdiness, vigour.
Ant. weakness.

lusty healthy, hearty, robust, stout, strong, vigorous.
Ant. weak.

luxuriance abundance, excess, profusion.

luxuriant abundant, excessive, exuberant, plenteous, plentiful, profuse, superabundant.
Ant. barren.

luxuriate abound, delight, enjoy, flourish, indulge, revel, wanton.
Ant. decay.

luxurious (1) opulent, rich, splendid, sumptuous; (2) effeminate, epicurean, pampered, pleasure-loving, sensual, voluptuous.
Ant. of (1) plain.

luxury (1) opulence, richness, sumptuousness, voluptuousness, wantonness; (2) comfort, delight, enjoyment, gratification, indulgence, pleasure.
Ant. of (1) austerity; of (2) discomfort.

M

macabre deathlike, ghastly, grim, gruesome, horrid, morbid.
Ant. charming, pleasant.

macerate (1) digest, soak, soften, steep; (2) harass, mortify, torture.

machiavellian arch, artful, astute, crafty, cunning, deceitful, designing, intriguing, perfidious, shrewd, sly, unscrupulous, wily.
Ant. straightforward.

machination artifice, cabal, conspiracy, design, intrigue, plot, ruse, scheme, stratagem, trick.

machine (1) engine, instrument, tool; (2) machinery, organisation, system; (3) (*Fig.*) agent, puppet.

maculate (1) *v.* blotch, blur, spot, stain; (2) *a.* blotched, blurred, spotted, stained; (3) (*Fig.*) corrupt, defiled, impure.
Ant. pure, spotless.

mad (1) aberrant, crazy, delirious, demented, deranged, frantic, frenzied, lunatic, rabid, raving; (2) (*Fig.*) angry, enraged, exasperated, furious, irate, raging, wild, wrathful; (3) foolish, imprudent, senseless, unsafe, unsound.
Ant. of (1) sane; of (2) calm; of (3) sensible.

madden annoy, craze, enrage, exasperate, incense, inflame, infuriate, irritate, provoke.
Ant. calm, soothe.

madness (1) aberration, craziness, derangement, distraction, insanity, lunacy, mania; (2) frenzy, fury, provocation, rage, raving, wildness; (3) (*Med.*) alienation, dementia, monomania.
Ant. sanity.

magazine (1) pamphlet, paper, periodical; (2) depot, store, storehouse, warehouse.

magic charm, conjuring, enchantment, juggling, legerdemain, necromancy, sorcery, witchcraft.

magician conjurer, conjuror, enchanter, juggler, necromancer, sorcerer, wizard.

magnificence brilliance, gorgeousness, grandeur, luxuriousness, luxury, majesty, pomp, splendour.
Ant. meanness.

magnificent brilliant, elegant, excellent, exquisite, imposing, lavish, luxurious, noble, outstanding, rich, splendid, stately, sublime, superb, superior.
Ant. mean, poor.

magnify (1) amplify, augment,

enlarge, exaggerate, increase; (2) celebrate, exalt, extol, glorify, praise.

Ant. of (1) decrease; of (2) disparage.

magnitude (1) bigness, bulk, extent, largeness, mass, size, volume; (2) grandeur, greatness, importance.

Ant. smallness.

maid damsel, girl, lass, (*Scot.*) lassie, maiden; (2) maidservant, servant.

maiden (1) *n.* girl, maid, virgin; (2) *a.* chaste, fresh, new, pure, undefiled, unmarried, unused, virgin.

maidenly demure, gentle, modest, reserved.

Ant. bold.

maim cripple, disable, injure, mangle, mar, mutilate, wound.

main (1) *a.* capital, cardinal, chief, foremost, leading, necessary, paramount, principal, vital; (2) absolute, direct, entire, pure; (3) *n.* effort, force, might, power, strength; (4) channel, conduit, duct, pipe; (5) continent, mainland, ocean, sea.

maintain (1) keep, preserve, provide, supply, support, sustain, uphold; (2) affirm, allege, assert, aver, contend, declare, hold, state; (3) claim, defend, justify, vindicate.

maintenance (1) aliment, allowance, food, keep, livelihood, subsistence, support, sustenance; (2) defence, justification, support, vindication.

majestic august, dignified, elevated, exalted, grand, imperial, imposing, kingly, lofty, magnificent, noble, pompous, princely, regal, royal, splendid, stately, sublime.

Ant. lowly.

majesty augustness, dignity, grandeur, loftiness, stateliness.

Ant. lowliness.

majority (1) greater, more, most, plurality, preponderance, superiority; (2) manhood, seniority.

Ant. minority.

make (1) create, compose, constitute, construct, fabricate, fashion, form, frame, manufacture, mould, originate, produce, shape; (2) acquire, gain, get, obtain, reach, secure, win; (3) cause, compel, constrain, force, require; (4) act, appoint, do, enact, establish, execute, ordain, perform, practise; (5) estimate, judge, reckon, suppose, think; (6) *n.* brand, build, constitution, construction, form, shape, style.

Ant. of (1) destroy.

maker (A) Creator, God.

maker (B) (1) builder, constructor, fabricator, framer, manufacturer; (2) author, composer, poet, writer.

maladroit (1) awkward, clumsy, inept, inexpert, unhandy, unskilful, unskilled; (2) tactless.

Ant. of (1) adroit; of (2) tactful.

malady affliction, ailment, complaint, disease, disorder, ill, illness, indisposition, sickness.

Ant. health.

malcontent (1) *a.* discontented, dissatisfied, rebellious, resentful, unsatisfied; (2) *n.* complainer, fault-finder, grumbler.

Ant. of (1) contented.

malediction anathema, curse, damnation, damning, denunciation, execration, imprecation, malison.

Ant. benediction, blessing.

malefactor convict, criminal, culprit, delinquent, evil-doer, felon, offender, outlaw.

Ant. benefactor.

malevolence hate, hatred, ill-will, malice, maliciousness, malignity, rancour, spite, spitefulness, vindictiveness.

Ant. benevolence.

malevolent evil-minded, hateful, hostile, ill-natured, malicious, malignant, mischievous, rancorous, spiteful, vindictive.

Ant. benevolent.

malice animosity, animus, enmity, hatred, ill-will, malevolence, maliciousness, malignity, rancour, spite, spitefulness, vindictiveness.

Ant. good-will.

malicious bitter, evil-minded, ill-disposed, injurious, malevolent, malignant, mischievous, rancorous, resentful, spiteful, vicious.

Ant. benevolent.

malign (1) v. abuse, calumniate, defame, disparage, harm, injure, libel, revile, slander, traduce, vilify; (2) a. baleful, baneful, evil, injurious.

Ant. of (1) praise; of (2) favourable.

malignant (1) bitter, hostile, malevolent, malicious, malign, mischievous, spiteful; (2) (*Med.*) dangerous, deadly, evil, fatal, virulent.

Ant. benign.

malignity (1) animosity, animus, bitterness, hate, hatred, hostility, ill-will, malice, maliciousness, rancour, spite; (2) deadliness, destructiveness, harmfulness, perniciousness, virulence.

Ant. benevolence.

malpractice evil, misbehaviour, misconduct, misdeed, sin, transgression.

Ant. goodness, well-doing.

maltreat abuse, harm, hurt, ill-treat, injure.

Ant. help.

mammoth colossal, enormous, gigantic, huge, immense, vast.

Ant. tiny.

man (A) (1) adult, being, body, humanity, individual, male, mankind, person, personage, somebody, soul; (2) attendant, employee, hand, servant, valet, workman.

Ant. of (1) beast; of (2) master.

man (B) v. furnish, strengthen, supply, re-enforce, reinforce.

manacle (1) v. bind, chain, fetter, handcuff, restrain, shackle; (2) n. bond, chain, handcuff, fetter, gyve, shackle, tie.

Ant. of (1) release.

manage (1) accomplish, administer, conduct, minister, concert, contrive, direct, effect, govern, manipulate, rule, superintend, supervise, transact; (2) control, dominate, handle, influence, train; (3) economise, husband, save.

Ant. mismanage.

manageable controllable, docile, easy, governable, tamable, tractable.

Ant. intractable.

management administration, care, charge, conduct, control, guidance, negotiation, operation, oversight, superintendence, supervision.

Ant. mismanagement.

manager comptroller, conductor, director, executive,

governor, overseer, superintendent, supervisor.

Ant. employee, underling.

mandate charge, command, commission, edict, injunction, order, precept.

Ant. request.

manful bold, brave, courageous, daring, heroic, intrepid, noble, stout, strong, vigorous.

Ant. weak.

mangle (1) cripple, crush, hack, lacerate, maim, mutilate, rend, tear; (2) (*Laundry*) calender, polish, press, smooth.

manhood (1) maturity, virility; (2) bravery, courage, firmness, fortitude, hardihood, manliness, resolution.

Ant. of (1) childhood; of (2) cowardice.

mania (1) aberration, craziness, delirium, dementia, derangement, frenzy, insanity, lunacy, madness; (2) (*Fig.*) craze, desire, enthusiasm.

Ant. (1) sanity.

manifest (1) *a.* apparent, clear, conspicuous, distinct, evident, glaring, obvious, open, patent, plain, unmistakable; (2) *v.* declare, demonstrate, display, evince, exhibit, expose, express, reveal, show.

Ant. of (1) obscure; of (2) conceal.

manifestation disclosure, display, exhibition, exposure, expression, revelation.

Ant. concealment.

manifold diverse, many, multiplied, multitudinous, numerous, varied, various.

Ant. few.

manipulate handle, operate, work.

manliness boldness, bravery, courage, fearlessness, firmness,

independence, intrepidity, resolution, valour.

Ant. cowardice.

manly (1) bold, brave, courageous, daring, dauntless, fearless, heroic, manful, noble, strong, valiant, valorous; (2) male, masculine, virile.

Ant. of (1) cowardly; of (2) feminine.

manner (1) air, appearance, aspect, bearing, behaviour, demeanour, deportment, look, mien; (2) custom, fashion, form, habit, method, mode, style, way; (3) kind, kinds, sort, sorts.

mannerly civil, courteous, polite, refined, well-behaved, well-bred.

Ant. rude.

manners bearing, behaviour, breeding, carriage, deportment.

manoeuvre (1) *n.* artifice, intrigue, plan, plot, ruse, scheme, stratagem, trick; (2) evolution, exercise, movement, operation; (3) *v.* contrive, intrigue, manage, plan, plot, scheme.

mansion abode, dwelling, habitation, hall, manor, residence, seat.

mantle (1) *n.* cloak, cover, covering, hood; (2) *v.* cloak, cover, disguise, hide, overspread; (3) (*Arch.*) cream, effervesce, foam, froth.

manufacture (1) *v.* build, compose, construct, create, fabricate, forge, form, make, mould, produce, shape; (2) *n.* construction, fabrication, making, produce, production.

Ant. of (1) destroy.

manumission deliverance, emancipation, enfranchisement, liberation, release.

Ant. slavery.

manumit deliver, enfranchise, free, liberate, release.
Ant. enslave.

many (1) a. abundant, divers, frequent, innumerable, manifold, multifarious, numerous, sundry, varied, various; (2) n. crowd, multitude, people.
Ant. few.

mar blot, damage, deface, disfigure, harm, hurt, impair, injure, maim, mutilate, ruin, spoil, stain.
Ant. improve.

marauder bandit, brigand, filibuster, freebooter, mosstrooper, outlaw, pillager, pirate, plunderer, raider, ravager, robber.

marches borders, boundaries, confines, frontiers, limits.

margin (1) border, bound, boundary, brim, brink, confine, edge, limit, rim, verge; (2) latitude, room, space, surplus.
Ant. of (1) centre, surface.

marine maritime, nautical, naval, oceanic, pelagic, sea.
Ant. land.

mariner navigator, sailor, salt, seafarer, seaman, tar.
Ant. landsman.

marital conjugal, connubial, matrimonial.
Ant. celibate.

maritime marine, nautical, naval, oceanic, sea.

mark (1) n. badge, brand, impression, incision, print, stamp; (2) index, indication, label, note, sign, symbol, token; (3) evidence, indication, symptom; (4) aim, end, object, purpose, target; (5) consequence, distinction, eminence, fame, importance, note, notice, regard; (6) foot-print, trace, track, vestige; (7) v. brand, characterise, denote, identify, impress,

imprint, indicate, label, stamp; (8) evince, heed, note, notice, observe, regard, remark, show, spot.

marked conspicuous, distinguished, eminent, notable, noted, outstanding, remarkable.
Ant. insignificant.

marriage (1) espousals, matrimony, nuptials, wedding, wedlock; (2) (*Fig.*) alliance, association, confederation, union.
Ant. of (1) celibacy; of (2) separation.

marrow (*Fig.*) cream, essence, gist, pith, quintessence, substance.

marsh bog, fen, morass, quagmire, slough, swamp.

marshal arrange, array, dispose, gather, guide, lead, muster, order, rank.
Ant. scatter.

marshy boggy, fenny, swampy, wet.
Ant. dry.

martial brave, heroic, military, warlike.
Ant. peaceful.

marvel (1) n. miracle, phenomenon, portent, prodigy, wonder; (2) (*Fig.*) admiration, amazement, astonishment, surprise, wonder.

marvellous (1) amazing, astonishing, astounding, extraordinary, miraculous, stupendous; (2) improbable, incredible, surprising, unbelievable.
Ant. of (1) ordinary; of (2) believable, credible.

masculine (1) male, manlike, manly, mannish, virile; (2) bold, brave, hardy, powerful, robust, strong.
Ant. of (1) feminine; of (2) weak.

mask (1) *v.* cloak, conceal, cover, disguise, hide, screen, veil; (2) *n.* blind, cloak, disguise, screen, veil, visor; (3) (*Fig.*) evasion, pretence, pretext, ruse, shift, subterfuge, trick.

Ant. of (1) uncover.

masquerade (1) *v.* cover, disguise, hide, mask, revel, veil; (2) *n.* mask, mummery, revel.

mass (1) accumulation, assemblage, bunch, collection, combination, heap, lump, quantity; (2) bulk, dimension, magnitude, size; (3) aggregate, body, sum, totality, whole.

massacre (1) *v.* annihilate, butcher, exterminate, kill, murder, slaughter, slay; (2) *n.* annihilation, butchery, carnage, extermination, killing, murder, slaughter.

massive big, bulky, colossal, enormous, heavy, huge, immense, ponderous, solid, substantial, vast, weighty.

Ant. light, thin.

master (1) *n.* captain, chief, commander, director, employer, governor, head, manager, overseer, owner, principal, superintendent; (2) instructor, pedagogue, preceptor, schoolmaster, teacher, tutor; (3) *a.* adept, expert, proficient; (4) chief, grand, great, main, leading; (5) *v.* conquer, defeat, direct, govern, overcome, overpower, rule, subdue, vanquish; (6) acquire, learn.

Ant. of (1) servant; of (2) student.

masterly (1) adroit, clever, dexterous, excellent, expert, skilful, skilled; (2) artistic, consummate, finished; (3) arbitrary, domineering, imperious.

Ant. of (1) clumsy.

mastery (1) ascendancy, command, conquest, dominion, preeminence, rule, superiority, supremacy, sway, upper-hand, victory; (2) ability, acquirement, attainment, cleverness, dexterity, proficiency, skill.

Ant. of (1) subjection; of (2) clumsiness.

masticate chew, eat, munch.

Ant. bolt, gulp.

match (1) *n.* companion, equal, mate, tally; (2) marriage, union; (3) competition, contest, game, test, trial; (4) *v.* equal, rival; (5) combine, couple, join, marry, mate, unite; (6) adapt, correspond, fit, harmonise, suit, tally; (7) oppose.

matchless consummate, excellent, exquisite, incomparable, inimitable, peerless, perfect, unequalled, unmatched, unparalleled, unrivalled.

Ant. commonplace, ordinary.

mate (1) *n.* assistant, associate, companion, compeer, comrade, crony, fellow-worker, friend, husband, subordinate, wife; (2) (*Naut.*) officer; (3) *v.* marry, match, wed.

material (1) *n.* body, element, stuff, substance; (2) *a.* bodily, corporeal, non-spiritual, physical, substantial; (3) essential, important, momentous, relevant, vital, weighty.

Ant. of (2) spiritual; of (3) unimportant.

maternal motherly.

matrimonial conjugal, connubial, espousal, hymeneal, nuptial, spousal.

matrimony marriage, wedlock.

matter (1) *n.* body, material, stuff, substance; (2) affair, business, concern, event, incident, question, subject, thing, topic; (3) consequence, importance, moment, significance; (4) difficulty, distress, trouble; (5) (*Med.*) purulence, pus; (6) *v.* import, signify, (*Med.*) suppurate.

mature (1) *a.* complete, fit, full-grown, mellow, perfect, prepared, ready, ripe; (2) *v.* develop, perfect, ripen.

Ant. of (1) immature, unripe.

maturity completion, matureness, perfection, ripeness.

Ant. immaturity.

mawkish (1) disgusting, flat, insipid, loathsome, nauseous, stale, vapid; (2) emotional, feeble, maudlin, sentimental.

Ant. of (1) well-flavoured; of (2) sensible.

maxim adage, aphorism, apothegm, axiom, proverb, saw, saying.

maze (1) intricacy, labyrinth, meander; (2) (*Fig.*) bewilderment, confusion, embarrassment, perplexity, puzzle, uncertainty.

mazy confused, confusing, embarrassing, intricate, labyrinthine, perplexing, puzzling, winding.

Ant. direct.

meagre (1) emaciated, gaunt, hungry, lank, lean, poor, skinny, starved, thin; (2) barren, deficient, poor, scanty, small, unfertile, unproductive.

Ant. of (1) plump; of (2) plentiful.

mean (1) *v.* contemplate, denote, design, express, imply, indicate, intend, purpose, signify; (2) *a.* common, humble, ignoble, inferior, low, ordinary, plebeian, vulgar; (3) abject,

base, beggarly, contemptible, degenerate, degraded, despicable, disgraceful, dishonourable, low-minded, menial, servile, shameful, sordid, vile, wretched; (4) contemptible, insignificant, paltry, petty, poor, shabby, squalid, wretched; (5) mercenary, miserly, niggardly, parsimonious, penurious, selfish, sordid, stingy, ungenerous; (6) average, intermediate, medium, middle, moderate; (7) *n.* average; (8) agency, measure, method, mode, way.

Ant. of (2) aristocratic; of (3) noble; of (4) superior; of (5) generous.

meander stroll, turn, wander, wind.

meaning (1) aim, design, end, idea, intention, object, purpose, trend; (2) connotation, explanation, force, gist, implication, import, interpretation, purport, sense, significance, signification.

means (1) expedient, instrument, measure, method, mode, way; (2) estate, income, money, property, resources, substance, wealth.

Ant. of (1) end; of (2) poverty.

measure (1) gauge, rule, standard; (2) allotment, amount, degree, extent, proposition, quantity, share; (3) means, step; (4) foot, metre, rhythm, tune, verse; (5) *v.* adjust, appraise, estimate, evaluate, judge, mete, value; (6) allot, distribute, proportion.

measureless boundless, endless, immeasurable, immense, infinite, limitless, unbounded, vast.

Ant. limited.

meat aliment, cheer, fare, flesh,

food, nourishment, nutriment, provender, provisions, rations, subsistence, sustenance, viands, victuals.

Ant. hunger.

mechanic artificer, artisan, craftsman, hand, machinist, operative, workman.

meddle interfere, intermeddle, interpose, intrude.

meddlesome interfering, intermeddling, intruding, intrusive, mischievous, officious, prying.

Ant. non-interfering.

mediate arbitrate, intercede, interpose, intervene, settle.

mediation arbitration, intercession, interposition, intervention.

mediator advocate, arbiter, arbitrator, interceder, judge, referee, umpire.

medicinal curative, healing, medical, sanatory, therapeutic.

medicine cure, drug, medicament, physic, remedy.

mediocre average, commonplace, indifferent, inferior, mean, medium, middling, ordinary.

Ant. superior.

meditate (1) cogitate, consider, muse, ponder, reflect, ruminate, study, think; (2) contemplate, devise, intend, plan, purpose, scheme.

meditation cogitation, contemplation, musing, pondering, reflection, ruminating, study, thought.

meditative contemplative, pensive, reflective, studious, thoughtful.

Ant. thoughtless.

medium (1) n. agency, instrument, instrumentality, means; (2) conditions, environment, influences; (3) average, mean

(4) a. average, mean, mediocre, middle.

medley confusion, farrago, hodge-podge, hotch-potch, jumble, miscellany, mixture.

Ant. order.

meed award, due, gift, premium, present, prize, recompense, remuneration, reward.

Ant. punishment.

meek calm, docile, forbearing, gentle, humble, mild, modest, patient, peaceful, soft, submissive, unassuming, yielding.

Ant. arrogant, immodest.

meekness docility, gentleness, humility, lowliness, modesty, patience, resignation, submission, submissiveness.

Ant. haughtiness.

meet (1) confront, contact, encounter, engage, find; (2) connect, converge, join, unite; (3) answer, comply, discharge, fulfil, gratify; (4) assemble, collect, congregate, gather, muster; (5) a. appropriate, apt, befitting, convenient, fit, fitting, proper, right, suitable, suited.

Ant. of (5) inappropriate.

meeting (1) assembly, audience, company, conference, congregation, convention, gathering, reunion; (2) confluence, junction, union.

melancholy (1) n. dejection, depression, despondency, gloom, gloominess, sadness, sorrow; (2) a. dejected, depressed, despondent, disconsolate, dismal, dispirited, doleful, downcast, downhearted, gloomy, glum, low-spirited, lugubrious, miserable, moody, sad, sorrowful, unhappy.

Ant. of (1) joy; of (2) joyous.

mêlée affray, brawl, broil, contest, fight, fray, scuffle.

mellifluous dulcet, euphonious, mellow, silvery, smooth, soft.
Ant. harsh.

mellow (1) delicate, full-flavoured, mature, perfect, rich, ripe, soft, well-matured; (2) dulcet, mellifluous, melodious, smooth, sweet, tuneful, well-tuned; (3) (*Sl.*) half-tipsy, jolly, jovial; (4) *v.* develop; improve, mature, perfect, ripen, soften.
Ant. of (1) immature.

melodious concordant, dulcet, harmonious, musical, silvery, tuneful.
Ant. tuneless.

melody air, descant, music, song, tune.

melt (1) colliquate, diffuse, dissolve, fuse, liquefy, soften, thaw; (2) (*Fig.*) mollify, relax, soften.
Ant. of (1) solidify; of (2) harden.

member (1) arm, component, constituent, element, leg, limb, organ, part, portion; (2) branch, clause, division, head; (3) associate, fellow, M.P., representative.

memento memorial, remembrance, reminder, souvenir.

memoir account, autobiography, biography, journal, life, narrative, record, register.

memorable celebrated, distinguished, extraordinary, famous, illustrious, noteworthy, remarkable, signal.
Ant. insignificant.

memorial (1) cairn, memento, monument, plaque, record, souvenir; (2) address, petition.

memory (1) recollection, remembrance, reminiscence; (2) celebrity, fame, renown, reputation.

Ant. of (1) forgetfulness.

menace (1) *v.* alarm, frighten, intimidate, threaten; (2) *n.* threat.
Ant. of (1) encourage.

mend (1) darn, patch, rectify, refit, reform, renew, repair, restore, retouch; (2) ameliorate, amend, correct, emend, improve.
Ant. of (1) break; of (2) mar.

mendacious deceitful, deceptive, fallacious, false, lying, untrue, untruthful.
Ant. truthful.

mendacity deceit, deceitfulness, duplicity, falsehood, lie, lying, untruthfulness.
Ant. truth.

mendicant beggar, pauper.

menial (1) *a.* abject, base, low, mean, servile, sorry, vile; (2) *n.* attendant, butler, domestic, flunkey, footman, lackey, serf, servant, slave, underling, valet, waiter.
Ant. of (1) noble; of (2) master.

mensuration measurement, measuring, survey, surveying.

mention (1) *v.* allude, cite, communicate, declare, disclose, divulge, impart, name, refer, report, reveal, state, tell; (2) *n.* allusion, reference.
Ant. of (1) conceal.

mentor adviser, counsellor, guide, instructor, monitor.

mephitic baleful, baneful, fetid, foul, noisome, noxious, pestilential.
Ant. pure.

mercantile commercial, marketable, trading.

mercenary (1) avaricious, covetous, grasping, mean, miserly, niggardly, parsimonious, penurious, sordid, stingy;

(2) hired, paid, venal; **(3)** *n.* hireling.

merchandise commodities, goods, wares.

merchant dealer, shopkeeper, trader, tradesman.

merciful beneficent, benignant, clement, compassionate, forbearing, forgiving, generous, gracious, humane, kind, lenient, mild, sympathetic, tender-hearted.
Ant. merciless.

merciless barbarous, callous, cruel, hard, hard-hearted, inexorable, pitiless, relentless, ruthless, severe, unfeeling, unmerciful, unsympathetic.
Ant. merciful.

mercurial active, changeable, fickle, flighty, gay, inconstant, light-hearted, mobile, spirited, sprightly, volatile.
Ant. constant.

mercy benevolence, charity, clemency, compassion, favour, forbearance, forgiveness, grace, kindness, leniency, pity.
Ant. cruelty.

mere (A) *a.* absolute, bare, entire, pure, sheer, simple, unmixed.

mere (B) *n.* lake, pool, pond.

meretricious deceitful, false, flashy, gaudy, sham, showy, spurious, tawdry.
Ant. plain, real.

merge dip, immerge, immerse, plunge, sink, submerge.

meridian (1) mid-day, noon, noon-tide; **(2)** (*Fig.*) acme, apex, climax, culmination, summit, zenith.
Ant. of **(2)** nadir.

merit (1) *v.* deserve, earn, incur; **(2)** *n.* claim, credit, desert, excellence, goodness, reward, virtue, worth, worthiness.

Ant. of **(2)** worthlessness.

merriment amusement, frolic, fun, gaiety, glee, hilarity, jocularity, jollity, joviality, laughter, liveliness, mirth, sport.
Ant. sadness.

merry blithe, blithesome, frolicsome, funny, gleeful, jocular, jocund, joyful, joyous, light-hearted, mirthful, sportive, vivacious, wanton.
Ant. sad.

mess (1) confusion, dirtiness, disorder, jumble, litter, medley, miscellany, mixture, untidiness; **(2)** (*Fig.*) difficulty, muddle, perplexity, plight, predicament.
Ant. of **(1)** order, tidiness.

message communication, intimation, missive, note, notice, word.

messenger carrier, courier, emissary, envoy, forerunner, harbinger, herald, precursor.

metamorphose change, transfigure, transform, transmute.

metamorphosis change, mutation, transfiguration, transformation, transmutation.

metaphysical abstract, general, ideal, intellectual, mental, psychological, subjective, unreal.
Ant. material.

mete (A) *v.* allot, apportion, deal, distribute, divide, measure, share.

mete (B) *n.* bound, boundary, limit, measure, term.

method (1) arrangement, classification, disposition, order, plan, regularity, rule, system; **(2)** course, fashion, manner, mode, procedure, way.

Ant. of (1) disorder, guess-work.

methodical orderly, precise, regular, systematic.
Ant. disorderly, irregular.

metropolis capital, city.

mettle (1) ardour, courage, fire, life, nerve, pluck, spirit, valour, vigour; (2) character, disposition, temper.
Ant. of (1) cowardice.

mettlesome ardent, brisk, courageous, fiery, frisky, high-spirited, sprightly.
Ant. cowardly.

microscopic infinitesimal, minute, tiny.
Ant. great.

middle (1) a. half-way, intermediate, intervening, mean, medial, medium, mid; (2) n. centre, half-way, mean, midst.
Ant. of (2) edge.

middling average, fair, indifferent, mediocre, medium, ordinary, passable, tolerable.
Ant. good.

midst centre, heart, middle, thick.
Ant. outside.

mien air, appearance, aspect, bearing, carriage, countenance, demeanour, deportment, look, manner.

might ability, capacity, efficacy, efficiency, energy, force, main, power, prowess, strength, valour.
Ant. weakness.

mighty (1) able, bold, capable, potent, powerful, robust, stalwart, strong, sturdy, valiant, vigorous; (2) bulky, enormous, huge, immense, tremendous, vast.
Ant. of (1) weak; of (2) small.

migratory nomadic, roving, shifting, wandering, unsettled.

Ant. settled.

mild (1) amiable, calm, clement, compassionate, equable, forgiving, gentle, indulgent, kind, meek, merciful, moderate, placid, pleasant, soft, temperate, tender, tranquil, warm; (2) demulcent, emollient, lenitive, mollifying, soothing.
Ant. of (1) unkind; of (2) harsh.

mildness clemency, gentleness, indulgence, kindness, meekness, moderation, softness, tenderness, warmth.
Ant. harshness.

milieu background, environment, sphere, surroundings.

militant belligerent, combating, contending, fighting.
Ant. peaceful.

military martial, soldierlike, soldierly, warlike.
Ant. civil.

militate conflict, contend, oppose.

mill v. comminute, grind, powder, pulverise.

mince (1) chop, cut, hash; (2) (Fig.) attenuate, diminish, extenuate, palliate.
Ant. of (2) enlarge.

mind (1) n. brains, intellect, intelligence, reason, sense, spirit, understanding; (2) bent, desire, disposition, inclination, intention, leaning, purpose, tendency, will; (3) belief, judgment, opinion, sentiment, thoughts; (4) memory, recollection, remembrance; (5) v. attend, heed, mark, note, notice, obey, observe, regard, watch; (6) care, dislike, object.
Ant. of (1) body; of (5) overlook.

mindful attentive, careful,

heedful, regardful, thoughtful.

mindless careless, forgetful, heedless, inattentive, neglectful, negligent.

mingle alloy, blend, combine, compound, confuse, intermingle, intermix, join, mix, unite.
Ant. dissolve, separate.

minion (1) darling, favourite, flatterer, pet; (2) dependent, hanger-on, parasite, sycophant.
Ant. of (2) master.

minister (1) *n.* churchman, clergyman, divine, ecclesiastic, pastor, priest; (2) administrator, ambassador, delegate, envoy, official, plenipotentiary; (3) agent, assistant, servant, subordinate; (4) *v.* administer, attend, officiate, serve; (5) aid, assist, help, succour, supply.

ministry (1) administration, cabinet, council, government; (2) agency, aid, help, service, support.

minor inferior, junior, less, petty, secondary, smaller, subordinate, unimportant, younger.
Ant. important, major.

minstrel bard, harper, musician, singer.

mint *v.* coin, fabricate, fashion, forge, invent, make, produce, stamp.

minute (1) *a.* diminutive, fine, little, microscopic, slender, slight, small, tiny; (2) critical, detailed, exact, precise; (3) *n.* account, memorandum, notes, proceedings, record.
Ant. of (1) large; of (2) inexact, vague.

miracle marvel, prodigy, wonder.

miraculous amazing, extraordinary, incredible, marvellous, supernatural, unaccountable, unbelievable, wonderful, wondrous.
Ant. natural, ordinary.

mirror (1) looking-glass, reflector, speculum; (2) (*Fig.*) example, model, paragon, pattern, prototype.

mirth cheerfulness, festivity, frolic, fun, gaiety, gladness, glee, hilarity, jollity, joviality, joyousness, laughter, merriment, pleasure, rejoicing, sport.
Ant. gloom.

mirthful cheerful, cheery, festive, frolicsome, gay, glad, gladsome, hilarious, jocund, jolly, jovial, merry, playful, sportive, vivacious.
Ant. dismal, gloomy.

misadventure accident, calamity, catastrophe, disaster, failure, ill-luck, mischance, misfortune, mishap, reverse.
Ant. success.

misanthrope cynic, egoist, egotist, mankind-hater, misanthropist.
Ant. philanthropist.

misapply abuse, misemploy, misuse, pervert.
Ant. apply.

misapprehend misconceive, mistake, misunderstand.
Ant. understand.

misbehaviour incivility, misconduct, misdemeanour, naughtiness, rudeness.

miscarriage (1) calamity, defeat, disaster, failure, misadventure, mischance, mishap, non-success; (2) (*Med.*) abortion, birth (*premature*).
Ant. of (1) success.

miscellaneous confused, diverse, diversified, heterogeneous, indiscriminate, jumbled, many, mingled, mixed, promiscuous, varied, various.
Ant. selected, selective.

miscellany collection, diversity, jumble, medley, mixture, variety.

mischance accident, calamity, disaster, infelicity, misadventure, misfortune, mishap.
Ant. luck.

mischief damage, detriment, disadvantage, evil, harm, hurt, injury, malice, misfortune, trouble.
Ant. good.

mischievous bad, destructive, detrimental, harmful, hurtful, injurious, malicious, naughty, pernicious, sinful, spiteful, troublesome, vicious, wicked.
Ant. beneficent.

misconceive misapprehend, misjudge, mistake, misunderstand.
Ant. understand.

misconduct misbehaviour, misdemeanour, naughtiness, rudeness, transgression.

misconstrue misconceive, misinterpret, misjudge, misread, misrender, mistake, mistranslate, misunderstand.
Ant. understand.

miscreant caitiff, knave, ragamuffin, rascal, rogue, ruffian, scamp, scoundrel, vagabond, villain.

misdeed crime, fault, misconduct, misdemeanour, offence, sin, transgression, trespass, wrong.
Ant. right.

misdemeanour misbehaviour, misconduct, misdeed, fault, transgression, trespass.

miser churl, niggard, screw, skinflint.

miserable (1) afflicted, dejected, disconsolate, distressed, doleful, downcast, melancholy, sorrowful, unhappy; (2) destitute, needy, penniless, poor; (3) abject, bad, contemptible, despicable, low, mean, worthless, wretched.
Ant. of (1) happy; of (2) rich; of (3) good.

miserly avaricious, beggarly, close-fisted, covetous, grasping, mean, near, niggardly, parsimonious, penurious, sordid, stingy.
Ant. generous.

misery affliction, agony, anguish, calamity, distress, grief, misfortune, sorrow, torment, torture, trial, unhappiness, woe, wretchedness.
Ant. joy.

misfortune accident, adversity, affliction, blow, calamity, failure, hardship, harm, illluck, misadventure, mischance, mishap, reverse, trial.
Ant. fortune.

misgiving apprehension, distrust, doubt, hesitation, suspicion, uncertainty.
Ant. trust.

mishap accident, calamity, disaster, ill-luck, misadventure, mischance, misfortune.
Ant. luck.

misinterpret distort, falsify, misapprehend, misconceive, misconstrue, misjudge, misrepresent.
Ant. interpret.

mislead beguile, deceive, delude, misdirect, misguide.
Ant. lead.

misprize slight, underestimate, underrate, undervalue.
Ant. prize.

misrepresent distort, falsify, misinterpret, misstate, pervert.

misrule anarchy, confusion, disorder, maladministration, misgovernment, mismanagement, tumult.

Ant. order.

miss (1) blunder, err, fail, forego, lack, lose, miscarry, mistake, omit, slip, trip; (2) need, want, wish; (3) *n.* blunder, error, failure, fault, loss, omission, oversight, want; (4) damsel, girl, maid, maiden, spinster.

misshapen deformed, ill-proportioned, ugly, ungainly, unshapely.

Ant. shapely.

missile projectile, weapon.

mission (1) business, charge, commission, duty, errand, office, trust; (2) delegation, deputation, embassy, legation, ministry.

missive communication, epistle, letter, message, note.

mist (1) cloud, drizzle, fog, haze, smog; (2) (*Fig.*) bewilderment, obscurity, perplexity.

Ant. of (1) clearness; of (2) clarity.

mistake (1) *v.* blunder, err, misapprehend, miscalculate, misconceive, misjudge, misunderstand; (2) *n.* blunder, error, fault, inaccuracy, miscalculation, misconception, misunderstanding, oversight, slip.

Ant. of (2) accuracy, correctness.

mistaken erroneous, inaccurate, incorrect, misinformed, wrong.

Ant. correct.

mistrust (1) *v.* apprehend, distrust, doubt, fear, suspect; (2) *n.* apprehension, distrust, doubt, fear, misgiving, suspicion.

Ant. trust.

misty cloudy, dark, dim, foggy, obscure, overcast.

Ant. clear.

misunderstand misapprehend, misconceive, misinterpret, mistake.

Ant. understand.

misunderstanding (1) error, misapprehension, misconception, misinterpretation, mistake; (2) difference, difficulty, disagreement, discord, dissension, quarrel.

Ant. of (1) understanding; of (2) agreement.

misuse (1) *v.* abuse, desecrate, dissipate, ill-treat, ill-use, maltreat, misapply, misemploy, profane, squander, waste; (2) *n.* abuse, desecration, dissipation, ill-treatment, ill-usage, misapplication, misusage, profanation.

Ant. use.

mitigate (1) abate, allay, assuage, diminish, lessen, moderate, modify, soften, subdue; (2) appease, calm, mollify, pacify, palliate, quiet, soothe, tranquillise.

Ant. aggravate.

mitigation abatement, allaying, alleviation, assuagement, diminution, moderation, palliation, relief.

Ant. aggravation.

mix amalgamate, associate, blend, coalesce, combine, commingle, commix, compound, incorporate, join, jumble, merge, mingle, unite.

Ant. separate.

mixture admixture, amalgamation, association, blend, combine, compound, conglomeration, jumble, hotchpotch, medley, mélange, miscellany, union, variety.

Ant. element.

moan (1) *v.* bemoan, bewail, deplore, grieve, groan, lament,

mourn, sigh; (2) *n.* groan, lament, lamentation, sigh, wail.
Ant. of (1) rejoice.

mob assemblage, canaille, crowd, multitude, rabble, riff-raff, scum, throng.
Ant. individuals.

mock (1) ape, counterfeit, imitate, mimic, satirise; (2) chaff, deride, insult, jeer, ridicule, scoff, taunt, tease; (3) cheat, deceive, delude, dupe, elude, fool, mislead; (4) *n.* banter, derision, gibe, mockery, ridicule, sneer; (5) *a.* counterfeit, faked, false, feigned, imitation, pretended, sham, spurious.
Ant. of (1) and (2) applaud, honour; of (5) genuine.

mockery contumely, deception, derision, jeering, mimicry, ridicule, scoffing, scorn, sham, travesty.
Ant. approval.

mode custom, fashion, form, make, method, plan, quality, state, style, way.

model (1) *n.* design, example, gauge, mould, original, pattern, prototype, standard, type; (2) copy, facsimile, image, imitation, representation; (3) *v.* fashion, form, mould, plan, shape.

moderate (1) abstemious, frugal, limited, restrained, steady, temperate; (2) cool, deliberate, equable, gentle, judicious, mild, reasonable; (3) cheap, fair, indifferent, inexpensive, mediocre, middling, ordinary; (4) *v.* abate, allay, appease, assuage, calm, control, diminish, lessen, mitigate, pacify, quiet, regulate, repress, soften, subdue, temper.
Ant. of (1) immoderate; of (4) increase.

moderation (1) abstemiousness, forbearance, frugality, restraint, temperance; (2) calmness, composure, coolness, equanimity, mildness, sedateness.
Ant. of (1) excess.

modern fresh, late, latest, new, novel, present, recent, up-to-date.
Ant. obsolete, old.

modest (1) bashful, becoming, coy, diffident, humble, meek, reserved, retiring, shy, unassuming, unpretentious; (2) chaste, pure-minded, virtuous.
Ant. of (1) bold; of (2) corrupt.

modesty (1) bashfulness, coyness, diffidence, humility, meekness, propriety, prudishness, shyness, simplicity, unobtrusiveness; (2) chastity, purity, virtue. [indecency
Ant. of (1) boldness; of (2)

modification alteration, change, form, manner, qualification, reformation, restriction, state, variation.

modify alter, change, form, limit, moderate, qualify, reduce, reform, restrict, vary.

modish conventional, courtly, fashionable, genteel.
Ant. unfashionable.

modulate adjust, attune, harmonise, inflect, tone, tune, vary.

moiety half, part, portion, share.
Ant. whole.

moist damp, dank, humid, wet.
Ant. dry.

moisture dampness, dankness, humidity, wetness.

mole breakwater, dike, dyke, embankment, jetty, pier, quay.

molecule atom, monad, particle.

molest annoy, assail, attack, badger, bore, bother, disturb, harass, incommode, inconvenience, irritate, pester, plague, tease, torment, upset, vex, worry.
Ant. please.

mollify abate, allay, appease, assuage, calm, compose, ease, mitigate, moderate, modify, pacify, relieve, soften, soothe, temper, tranquillise.
Ant. provoke.

moment (1) (*Sl.*) flash, instant, (*Colloq.*) jiffy, second, trice, twinkling; (2) consequence, force, gravity, import, importance, significance, value, weight; (3) drive, impetus, momentum, power.
Ant. of (2) insignificance.

momentous grave, important, serious, significant, vital, weighty.
Ant. insignificant, trifling.

monarch autocrat, despot, emperor, king, potentate, prince, queen, ruler.
Ant. subject.

monastery abbey, cloister, convent, nunnery, priory.

monastic celibate, cenobitic, conventual, monkish, recluse, secluded.
Ant. secular.

money banknotes, cash, coin, currency, riches, wealth.

monitor adviser, counsellor, instructor, mentor, overseer, teacher.
Ant. pupil.

monomania delusion, hallucination, illusion, self-deception.

monotonous boring, dull, tedious, uniform, uninflected, unvaried, wearisome.
Ant. varied.

monotony boredom, dullness,

tiresomeness, uniformity, wearisomeness.
Ant. variety.

monster (1) brute, demon, fiend; (2) ruffian, villain; (3) enormity, marvel, prodigy, wonder.
Ant. of (1) human.

monstrous (1) dreadful, enormous, frightful, hideous, horrible, huge, immense, terrible, vast; (2) abnormal, extraordinary, marvellous, prodigious, strange, unnatural, wonderful.
Ant. of (1) agreeable; of (2) normal.

monument cairn, cenotaph, gravestone, mausoleum, memento, memorial, pillar, record, remembrance, tombstone.

mood disposition, humour, temper, vein.

moody angry, capricious, crabbed, crusty, gloomy, glum, ill-humoured, irascible, irritable, melancholy, morose, pensive, sad, short-tempered, sulky, sullen, testy.
Ant. gay.

moor (1) bog, common, heath, morass, wasteland; (2) *v.* (*Naut.*) berth, fasten, fix, secure, tie.

moot *a.* arguable, debatable, disputable, doubtful, unsettled
Ant. indubitable.

moral (1) blameless, ethical, good, honest, just, honourable, right, righteous, virtuous; (2) abstract, ideal, intellectual, mental.
Ant. of (1) amoral, immoral.

morals behaviour, conduct, habits, manners, morality.

morass bog, fen, quagmire, slough, swamp.

morbid (1) ailing, diseased,

sick, unhealthy, unsound; (2) depressed, downcast, gloomy, pessimistic, sensitive.

Ant. of (1) healthy; of (2) cheerful.

moreover also, besides, further, furthermore, likewise, too.

morning dawn, daybreak, forenoon, morn, sunrise.

Ant. evening.

morose churlish, crusty, gloomy, glum, gruff, ill-humoured, ill-natured, moody, perverse, sulky, sullen, surly.

Ant. cheerful.

morsel bit, bite, fragment, mouthful, part, piece, scrap.

Ant. whole.

mortal (1) a. deadly, destructive, fatal, lethal, human, perishable, vital; (2) n. being, man, person.

Ant. immortal.

mortality corruption, death, destruction, fatality.

mortification (1) (Med.) gangrene, necrosis; (2) (Fig.) abasement, annoyance, chagrin, dissatisfaction, humiliation, shame, vexation.

Ant. of (2) joy.

mortify (1) (Med.) corrupt, deaden, fester, gangrene, necrose, putrefy; (2) (Fig.) abase, abash, annoy, confound, disappoint, displease, harass, humble, humiliate, shame, subdue, trouble, vex, worry.

Ant. of (1) heal; of (2) gratify.

mostly chiefly, customarily, especially, generally, mainly, particularly, principally.

Ant. seldom.

mote atom, corpuscle, flaw, mite, speck, spot.

motherly affectionate, kind, loving, maternal, tender.

motion (1) change, move, movement, passing; (2) ges-ture, impulse, proposal, proposition, suggestion.

Ant. of (1) rest.

motionless fixed, quiescent, stable, standing, static, stationary, still, unmoved.

Ant. mobile, moving.

motive cause, ground, incentive, incitement, inducement, influence, purpose, reason, spur, stimulus.

motley dappled, diversified, heterogeneous, mingled, mixed, mottled, specked, speckled, variegated.

Ant. unmixed.

mottled dappled, piebald, speckled, variegated.

mould (1) v. carve, cast, create, fashion, make, model, shape; (2) n. cast, character, fashion, form, matrice, matrix, pattern, shape; (3) blight, mildew, mouldiness, mustiness, smut; (4) earth, loam, material, matter, soil.

Ant. of (1) deform.

moulder crumble, decay, perish, waste.

mouldy decaying, fusty, mildewed.

Ant. fresh.

mound bank, bulwark, heap, hill, hillock, knoll, pile, rampart.

mount (A) (1) arise, ascend, rise, soar, tower, uprise; (2) ascend, bestride, climb, escalade, scale; (3) embellish, ornament.

Ant. of (1) and (2) descend.

mount (B) (1) charger, horse, steed; (2) hill, mountain.

mountebank charlatan, cheat, impostor, pretender, quack.

mourn bemoan, bewail, deplore, grieve, lament, sorrow.

Ant. rejoice.

mournful afflicting, calamitous, deplorable, distressing, grievous, heavy, lamentable, lugubrious, melancholy, sorrowful, unhappy, woeful.
Ant. bright, happy.

mouth (1) chaps, jaws; (2) aperture, cavity, crevice, entrance, inlet, opening, orifice; (3) v. clamour, rant, roar, vociferate.

movables chattels, effects, furniture, goods, property.
Ant. fixtures.

move (1) advance, budge, go, march, proceed, progress, stir, walk; (2) change, drive, impel, operate, propel, push, shift, shove, start, turn; (3) actuate, affect, agitate, excite, impress, incite, induce, influence, instigate, persuade, prompt, rouse, touch, urge; (4) flit, remove; (5) propose, recommend, suggest; (6) n. action, motion, movement.
Ant. stay, stop.

movement activity, agitation, change, excitement, motion, move, moving, progress, progression.

moving affecting, impelling, impressive, pathetic, persuasive, touching.

mucous glutinous, gummy, mucilaginous, ropy, slimy, viscid.

mud clay, dirt, mire.

muddle (1) v. confuse, disarrange, disorder, mess, spoil; (2) n. confusion, disorder, mess, plight, predicament.
Ant. order.

muddy dirty, foul, impure, miry, soiled, turbid.
Ant. clear, pure.

muffle (1) conceal, cover, disguise, envelop, shroud; (2) deaden, soften, stifle, suppress.

mulish headstrong, intractable, obstinate, stubborn.
Ant. docile.

multifarious different, diverse, diversified, manifold, many, multiform, multitudinous.
Ant. few.

multiply augment, extend, increase, spread.
Ant. decrease.

multitude army, assemblage, assembly, collection, concourse, congregation, crowd, horde, host, legion, mob, populace, swarm, throng.

mundane earthly, secular, temporal, terrestrial, worldly.
Ant. spiritual, unearthly.

munificence beneficence, bounteousness, bounty, generosity, liberality.
Ant. stinginess.

munificent beneficent, bounteous, bountiful, generous, liberal, princely.

murder (1) v. assassinate, butcher, destroy, kill, massacre, slaughter, slay; (2) (Fig.) mar, ruin, spoil; (3) n. assassination, butchery, homicide, manslaughter, massacre.
Ant. of (1) defend.

murderer assassin, butcher, cut-throat, man-slayer, slaughterer.

murderous barbarous, bloodthirsty, bloody, cruel, fell, sanguinary, savage, truculent.
Ant. gentle, pacific.

murky cheerless, cloudy, dark, dim, dusky, gloomy, hazy, obscure, overcast.
Ant. bright.

murmur (1) v. mumble, mutter, whisper; (2) complain, (Sl.) grouse, grumble; (3) n. complaint, (Sl.) grouse, grumble, plaint.

muscular athletic, brawny, lusty, powerful, robust, sinewy, stalwart, strong, sturdy, vigorous.
Ant. flabby, weak.

muse brood, cogitate, contemplate, deliberate, dream, meditate, ponder, reflect, ruminate, speculate, think.
Ant. attend.

musical dulcet, harmonious, melodious, sweet-sounding, tuneful.
Ant. discordant.

musing n. absent-mindedness, abstraction, contemplation, day-dreaming, dreaming, reflection, reverie, rumination.
Ant. attention.

muster (1) v. assemble, collect, congregate, convene, convoke, enrol, gather, marshal, meet, rally, summon; (2) n. assemblage, assembly, collection, congregation, convention, convocation, gathering, meeting, rally.
Ant. (1) disperse, scatter.

musty fetid, fusty, mouldy, rank, sour, stale.
Ant. fresh.

mutable alterable, changeable, changing, inconstant, irresolute, uncertain, unsettled, unstable, unsteady, vacillating, variable, wavering.
Ant. settled.

mutation alteration, change, variation.

mute dumb, silent, speechless, taciturn, voiceless.
Ant. vocal.

mutilate cripple, damage, disable, disfigure, injure, maim, mangle, mar.
Ant. repair.

mutinous insubordinate, rebellious, refractory, revolutionary, riotous, seditious, turbulent, unruly.
Ant. obedient.

mutiny insubordination, insurrection, rebellion, revolt, revolution, riot, rising, uprising.

mutter mumble.

mutual alternate, common, correlative, interchangeable, interchanged, reciprocal.

myopic near-sighted, short-sighted.

mysterious abstruse, concealed, cryptic, dark, enigmatic, hidden, incomprehensible, inexplicable, obscure, puzzling, recondite, secret, unfathomable.
Ant. clear, intelligible, open.

mystery enigma, puzzle, riddle, secret.

mystical abstruse, allegorical, cabalistic, emblematical, enigmatical, esoteric, hidden, inscrutable, mysterious, occult, symbolical.

mystify befog, bewilder, confound, confuse, embarrass, perplex, puzzle.
Ant. enlighten.

myth (1) allegory, fable, fiction, legend, parable, story, tradition; (2) falsehood, fancy, figment, imagination, lie, untruth.
Ant. fact.

mythical allegorical, fabulous, fanciful, fictitious, imaginary, legendary.
Ant. actual, historical.

N

nag annoy, harass, irritate, pester, provoke, scold, torment, vex, worry.
Ant. appease, soothe.

naïve artless, candid, frank, guileless, ingenuous, open, simple, unaffected, unsophisticated.

Ant. sly, sophisticated.

naked (1) bare, denuded, nude, unclothed, uncovered, undraped, undressed; (2) evident, manifest, open, plain, simple, undisguised, unexaggerated, unvarnished.

Ant. of (1) clothed; of (2) exaggerated.

name (1) *n.* appellation, denomination, designation, epithet, title; (2) distinction, fame, honour, note, praise, renown; (3) character, credit, reputation; (4) *v.* call, christen, denominate, dub, style, term; (5) designate, identify, mention, nominate, specify.

narcotic (1) *n.* anaesthetic, anodyne, opiate, sedative, tranquilliser; (2) *a.* sedative, stupefacient, stupefying.

narrate describe, detail, recite, recount, rehearse, relate, repeat, tell.

narration, narrative account, chronicle, description, detail, explanation, history, recital, rehearsal, relation, statement, story, tale.

narrow (1) circumscribed, close, confined, contracted, limited, near, scanty, straitened; (2) avaricious, close, covetous, mean, mercenary, niggardly, ungenerous; (3) biassed, bigoted, illiberal, intolerant, narrow-minded, partial.

Ant. of (1) broad; of (2) generous; of (3) broadminded.

nastiness (1) defilement, dirtiness, filth, filthiness, foulness, impurity, squalor, uncleanness;

(2) indecency, licentiousness, obscenity, pollution, ribaldry, smuttiness.

nasty (1) dirty, disagreeable, disgusting, filthy, loathsome, objectionable, offensive, sickening, unpleasant; (2) foul, gross, impure, indecent, lascivious, lewd, licentious, obscene, ribald, smutty; (3) annoying, bad-tempered, disagreeable, unpleasant.

Ant. of (1) clean; of (2) decent; (3) pleasant.

nation community, commonwealth, people, race, realm, state, tribe.

native (1) *a.* congenital, inborn, inbred, indigenous, inherited, innate, natal, natural; (2) genuine, original, real; (3) domestic, home, mother, vernacular.

Ant. of (1) acquired; of (3) foreign.

natural (1) legitimate, normal, ordinary, regular, usual; (2) characteristic, congenital, essential, indigenous, natal, native; (3) artless, candid, frank, genuine, ingenuous, open, real, simple, unsophisticated.

Ant. unnatural.

nature (1) character, constitution, essence, quality; (2) kind, sort, species, type; (3) creation, earth, universe, world; (4) disposition, humour, mood, temper, temperament.

naughty bad, disobedient, mischievous, perverse, sinful, wicked, worthless.

Ant. good, obedient.

nausea aversion, disgust, loathing, qualm, repugnance, sickness, squeamishness.

nauseous abhorrent, detestable, disgusting, distasteful, loathsome, nauseating, offensive, repulsive, revolting, sickening.

Ant. agreeable.

naval marine, maritime, nautical.

navigate cruise, direct, guide, pilot, plan, sail, steer.

near (1) adjacent, adjoining, bordering, close, contiguous, nearby, neighbouring, nigh, touching; (2) approaching, forthcoming, imminent, impending, near-at-hand; (3) allied, attached, connected, dear, familiar, intimate; (4) (*Fig.*) close-fisted, mean, miserly, niggardly, parsimonious, stingy, ungenerous.

Ant. of (1) remote; of (4) generous.

nearly *adv.* almost, approximately, well-nigh.

neat (1) dainty, nice, orderly, smart, spruce, tidy, trim; (2) adroit, apt, clever, expert, handy; (3) (*Spirits*) pure, straight, undiluted, unmixed.

Ant. of (1) untidy; of (2) clumsy; of (3) diluted.

nebulous cloudy, confused, hazy, misty, obscure.

Ant. clear, unclouded.

necessary compulsory, essential, indispensable, inevitable, involuntary, needed, obligatory, unavoidable.

Ant. needless.

necessitate compel, demand, force, oblige.

necessitous destitute, distressed, indigent, needy, penniless, poor, poverty-stricken.

Ant. rich.

necessity (1) compulsion, destiny, fate, indispensability, inevitability, needfulness, requirement, requisite, unavoidability; (2) indigence, need, poverty.

Ant. of (1) choice; of (2) plenty.

necromancy divination, enchantment, magic, sorcery, witchcraft, wizardry.

necropolis burial-ground, cemetery, churchyard, crematorium, God's Acre, graveyard, mortuary.

need (1) *v.* lack, require, want; (2) *n.* destitution, distress, lack, neediness, penury, poverty, privation; (3) emergency, exigency, necessity, urgency, want.

needful (1) necessitous, needy, poor; (2) essential, indispensable, necessary, requisite.

Ant. of (1) rich; of (2) needless.

needless unnecessary, useless.

needy destitute, indigent, penniless, poor, poverty-stricken.

Ant. wealthy.

nefarious abominable, atrocious, base, detestable, dreadful, enormous, execrable, heinous, horrible, infamous, iniquitous, monstrous, shameful, vile, villainous, wicked.

Ant. decent, good.

negation denial, disavowal, disclaimer, rejection, renunciation.

Ant. affirmation.

neglect (1) *v.* disregard, fail, forget, ignore, omit, overlook, slight; (2) *n.* carelessness, default, disregard, disrespect, failure, forgetfulness, heedlessness, negligence, remissness.

Ant. of (1) observe, remember; of (2) attention.

negligence carelessness, default, disregard, failure, forgetfulness, heedlessness, inadvertence, inattention, indifference, oversight, remissness, shortcoming, slackness, thoughtlessness.

Ant. carefulness.

negligent careless, disregardful, forgetful, heedless, inattentive, indifferent, neglectful, regardless, remiss, thoughtless.

Ant. careful.

negotiate arrange, bargain, deal, debate, discuss, settle, transact.

neighbourhood closeness, district, environs, locality, nearness, precincts, proximity, vicinity.

Ant. distance.

neighbourly civil, companionable, friendly, genial, kind, obliging, sociable, social.

Ant. standoffish, unsociable.

neophyte beginner, catechumen, disciple, learner, novice, novitiate, proselyte, pupil, student, tyro.

Ant. expert, teacher.

nerve (1) *n.* courage, endurance, energy, firmness, force, fortitude, hardihood, might, pluck, resolution, vigour, will; (2) *v.* brace, fortify, invigorate, strengthen.

Ant. of (1) weakness; of (2) undermine, weaken.

nervous apprehensive, excitable, fearful, hesitant, hysterical, shaky, timid, timorous, weak, weakly.

Ant. confident.

nestle cuddle, nuzzle, snuggle.

nettle chafe, exasperate, fret, harass, incense, irritate, provoke, ruffle, sting, tease.

Ant. soothe.

neutral impartial, indifferent, indistinct, neuter, unbiassed, undecided.

Ant. partial.

neutralise cancel, counteract,

counterbalance, invalidate, offset, undo.

nevertheless however, nonetheless, notwithstanding, yet.

new (1) fresh, latest, modern, novel, unused, up-to-date; (2) additional, further.

Ant. of (1) old.

news account, advice, information, intelligence, tidings, word.

nice (1) agreeable, amiable, courteous, delightful, friendly, good, kind, polite, refined, well-mannered; (2) dainty, fine, neat, tidy, trim; (3) accurate, critical, delicate, exact, exacting, fastidious, precise, rigorous, scrupulous, strict, subtle.

Ant. of (1) unpleasant; of (2) shabby; of (3) vague.

nicety (1) accuracy, exactness, minuteness, precision; (2) daintiness, delicacy, distinction, subtlety.

Ant. of (1) carelessness.

niggard churl, miser, screw, scrimp, skinflint.

Ant. spendthrift.

niggardly avaricious, close, covetous, mean, mercenary, miserly, near, parsimonious, penurious, sordid, sparing, stingy, tight-fisted, ungenerous.

Ant. generous.

nigh adjacent, adjoining, approximate, bordering, contiguous, near, next.

Ant. distant.

nimble active, agile, alert, brisk, lively, prompt, quick, ready, smart, sprightly, spry, swift.

Ant. clumsy, slow.

nobility (1) aristocracy, nobles, peerage; (2) dignity, eminence, excellence, grandeur, greatness, loftiness, nobleness, superiority, worthiness.

Ant. of (1) commonalty; of (2) humility.

noble (1) *n.* aristocrat, lord, nobleman, peer; (2) *a.* aristocratic, high-born, lordly, patrician, titled; (3) dignified, distinguished, elevated, eminent, excellent, grand, great, honourable, impressive, lofty, splendid, stately, worthy.

Ant. of (1) commoner; of (3) ignoble, plebeian.

noctambulist sleep-walker, somnambulist.

nod beck, bow.

noise blare, clamour, clatter, cry, din, hubbub, racket, row, sound, tumult, uproar.

Ant. peace, silence.

noiseless inaudible, quiet, silent, soundless, still.

Ant. noisy.

noisome bad, baneful, deleterious, disgusting, fetid, foul, hurtful, injurious, mischievous, nocuous, noxious, offensive, pestiferous, pestilential, poisonous, unhealthy, unwholesome.

Ant. wholesome.

noisy boisterous, clamorous, loud, obstreperous, riotous, tumultuous, turbulent, uproarious, vociferous.

Ant. quiet, silent.

nomadic migratory, pastoral, roving, vagrant, wandering.

Ant. settled.

nominal formal, inconsiderable, ostensible, pretended, professed, so-called, titular.

Ant. actual, fixed.

nominate appoint, choose, designate, name, present, propose.

nonchalant apathetic, calm,

careless, casual, cool, indifferent, unconcerned.

Ant. excitable.

nondescript indescribable, odd, peculiar, strange, unclassifiable, unclassified.

Ant. ordinary.

nonentity cipher, nobody, non-existence.

Ant. celebrity.

nonplus astonish, bewilder, confound, confuse, discomfit, disconcert, embarrass, perplex, puzzle.

Ant. enlighten.

nonsense absurdity, balderdash, folly, foolishness, jest, (*Colloq.*) stuff, stupidity, trash.

Ant. sense.

norm model, pattern, rule, standard.

normal natural, ordinary, regular, standard, typical, usual.

Ant. abnormal, unusual.

notable conspicuous, distinguished, evident, extraordinary, famous, manifest, memorable, noteworthy, noticeable, notorious, plain, rare, remarkable, striking, uncommon, unusual.

Ant. ordinary.

note (1) annotation, comment, communication, epistle, letter, memorandum, minute, record, remark; (2) indication, mark, symbol, token; (3) heed, observation, notice, regard; (4) celebrity, character, distinction, eminence, fame, renown, reputation; (5) *v.* denote, designate, indicate, mention, notice, observe, perceive, record, register, see.

Ant. of (5) overlook.

noted celebrated, conspicuous, distinguished, eminent, famous, illustrious, notable, notorious, renowned, well-known.

Ant. undistinguished.

nothing bagatelle, cipher, naught, nonentity, non-existence, nothingness, nought, trifle, zero.

Ant. something.

notice (1) v. discern, distinguish, heed, mark, mind, note, observe, perceive, remark, see; (2) n. cognisance, consideration, heed, note, observation, regard; (3) advice, announcement, communication, instruction, intelligence, intimation, news, notification, order, warning; (4) advertisement, comment, criticism, poster, review, sign; (5) attention, civility, respect.

Ant. of (1) overlook.

notify acquaint, advise, announce, apprise, declare, inform, publish, warn.

notion apprehension, belief, concept, conception, impression, inclination, judgment, knowledge, sentiment, understanding, view.

Ant. fact.

notoriety celebrity, fame, name, note, publicity, repute, vogue.

notorious (1) celebrated, famous, noted, remarkable, renowned, well-known; (2) dishonourable, disreputable, infamous, opprobrious; (3) obvious, open, overt, patent, undisputed.

Ant. of (1) unknown; of (2) creditable; of (3) obscure.

notwithstanding although, however, nevertheless, though, yet.

nourish (1) attend, feed, furnish, nurse, nurture, supply, tend; (2) comfort, encourage, foster, maintain, promote, support.

Ant. of (1) starve; of (2) neglect.

nourishment aliment, diet, food, nutriment, nutrition, sustenance.

Ant. want.

novel (1) a. different, fresh, new, rare, strange, uncommon, unusual; (2) n. fiction, narrative, romance, story, tale.

novice apprentice, beginner, convert, learner, neophyte, novitiate, probationer, proselyte, pupil, tyro.

Ant. teacher.

noxious baneful, corrupting, deadly, deleterious, destructive, detrimental, harmful, hurtful, injurious, insalubrious, noisome, pernicious, pestilential, poisonous, unhealthy, unwholesome.

Ant. harmless, wholesome.

nude bare, exposed, naked, unclothed, undraped, undressed.

Ant. clothed.

nugatory bootless, futile, ineffectual, inoperative, insignificant, trifling, trivial, unavailing, useless, vain, worthless.

Ant. important.

nuisance annoyance, bore, bother, infliction, offence, pest, plague, trouble.

Ant. delight.

null ineffectual, invalid, useless, vain, void, worthless.

Ant. effectual.

nullify abolish, abrogate, annul, cancel, invalidate, neutralise, repeal, rescind.

Ant. accomplish.

numb (1) a. benumbed, dead, deadened, insensible, paralysed, torpid; (2) v. benumb, deaden, stupefy.

Ant. of (1) active.

number (1) *n.* count, digit, figure, numeral, sum, total; (2) aggregate, collection, company, crowd, horde, many, multitude, throng; (3) *v.* account, add, calculate, compute, count, enumerate, include, reckon, tell, total.

numerous abundant, many, numberless.

Ant. few.

nuncio ambassador, envoy, legate, messenger.

nunnery abbey, cloister, convent, monastery.

nuptial *a.* bridal, conjugal, connubial, hymeneal, matrimonial.

nuptials espousal, marriage, wedding.

nurse (1) feed, nourish, nurture, suckle; (2) (*Fig.*) cherish, encourage, foster, promote, succour.

Ant. neglect.

nurture (1) *n.* diet, food, nourishment; (2) discipline, education, instruction; (3) *v.* feed, nourish, nurse, tend; (4) discipline, educate, instruct, rear, school, train.

nutriment aliment, diet, food, nourishment, nutrition, subsistence, support, sustenance.

Ant. starvation.

nutritious alimental, invigorating, nourishing, strengthening, wholesome.

Ant. unwholesome.

nymph damsel, girl, lass, maid, maiden, naiad.

O

oaf blockhead, dolt, dunce, fool, idiot, imbecile, nincompoop, simpleton.

oath (1) affirmation, pledge, promise, vow; (2) blasphemy, curse, imprecation, malediction, profanity.

obdurate callous, dogged, firm, hard, harsh, inexorable, inflexible, obstinate, perverse, pig-headed, relentless, stubborn, unbending, unrelenting, unshakeable, unyielding.

Ant. soft-hearted.

obedience acquiescence, agreement, compliance, duty, respect, reverence, submission, submissiveness, subservience.

Ant. disobedience, refusal.

obedient compliant, deferential, dutiful, observant, regardful, respectful, submissive, yielding.

Ant. disobedient.

obeisance bow, curtsey, curtsy, homage, respect, reverence, salutation.

Ant. arrogance, irreverence.

obese corpulent, fat, plump, podgy, portly, stout.

Ant. slim, thin.

obesity corpulence, embonpoint, fatness, fleshiness, portliness, stoutness.

Ant. thinness.

obey comply, follow, keep, observe, submit.

Ant. disobey.

obfuscate bewilder, cloud, confuse, darken, obscure.

Ant. clarify, enlighten.

object (1) *n.* fact, phenomenon, reality, thing; (2) aim, butt, design, end, goal, intention, motive, objective, purpose, target; (3) *v.* contravene, demur, oppose, protest, refuse.

Ant. of (3) agree.

objection cavil, censure, doubt, exception, opposition, protest, scruple.

Ant. acceptance.

oblation gift, offering, sacrifice.

obligation (1) accountableness, duty, requirement, responsibility; (2) agreement, bond, contract, debt, engagement.

obligatory binding, coercive, compulsory, enforced, necessary, unavoidable.
Ant. voluntary.

oblige (1) bind, coerce, compel, constrain, force, necessitate, require; (2) accommodate, benefit, favour, gratify, please, serve.
Ant. of (1) coax; of (2) disoblige.

obliging accommodating, civil, complaisant, considerate, courteous, friendly, kind, polite.
Ant. disobliging.

oblique aslant, inclined, indirect, slanting, sloping.
Ant. straight, upright.

obliterate cancel, delete, destroy, efface, eradicate, erase, expunge.
Ant. create.

oblivious careless, disregardful, forgetful, heedless, inattentive, neglectful, negligent.
Ant. heedful.

obloquy aspersion, blame, calumny, censure, contumely, detraction, discredit, disgrace, infamy, odium, reproach, shame, slander.
Ant. credit, praise.

obnoxious blameworthy, disgusting, hateful, horrid, objectionable, odious, offensive, reprehensible, unpleasant.
Ant. pleasant.

obscene bawdy, coarse, dirty, disgusting, filthy, foul, gross, immodest, immoral, impure, indecent, lewd, licentious, loose, offensive, pornographic, ribald, shameless, smutty, unchaste.
Ant. decent.

obscure (1) a. blurred, clouded, cloudy, dim, dusk, gloomy, indistinct, shadowy, sombre, veiled; (2) abstruse, ambiguous, doubtful, incomprehensible, intricate, involved, mysterious, vague; (3) humble, inglorious, nameless, undistinguished, unhonoured, unknown, unnoted; (4) v. cloud, darken, dim, eclipse, shade; (5) conceal, cover, disguise, hide.
Ant. of (1) bright; of (2) obvious; of (3) distinguished; of (4) brighten; of (5) uncover.

obsequious cringing, deferential, fawning, flattering, servile, submissive, sycophantic.
Ant. independent, overbearing.

observance (1) attention, celebration, discharge, fulfilment, observation, performance; (2) ceremonial, ceremony, custom, fashion, form, practice, rite, service.
Ant. of (1) inattention.

observant attentive, heedful, mindful, obedient, perceptive, quick, submissive, vigilant, watchful.
Ant. careless, inattentive.

observation (1) attention, cognition, information, knowledge, notice, observance, study; (2) annotation, comment, note, remarks.
Ant. of (1) inattention, neglect.

observe (1) detect, discover, notice, perceive, regard, see, view, watch, witness; (2) comment, mention, remark, say; (3) comply, follow, fulfil, heed, obey, perform; (4) celebrate,

keep, remember, solemnise.
Ant. of (1) overlook; of (3)
disregard.

obsolete ancient, antiquated,
archaic, disused, old, old-
fashioned, out-of-date.
Ant. modern, up-to-date.

obstacle bar, barrier, check,
difficulty, hindrance, impediment, interference, interruption, obstruction.
Ant. aid.

obstinacy firmness, inflexibility, perseverance, persis-
tency, pertinacity, obduracy,
resoluteness, stubbornness,
tenacity, wilfulness.
Ant. docility.

obstinate contumacious,
dogged, firm, headstrong, intractable, mulish, persistent,
pertinacious, perverse, pig-
headed, refractory, self-willed,
stubborn, unyielding.
Ant. docile, submissive.

obstreperous boisterous, clamorous, loud, noisy, riotous,
tumultuous, turbulent, uncontrolled, unruly, uproarious,
vociferous.
Ant. peaceful.

obstruct arrest, bar, barricade,
check, choke, clog, hinder, impede, interfere, interrupt, prevent, retard, stop.
Ant. assist.

obstruction bar, barricade,
barrier, check, difficulty, hindrance, impediment, stop, stoppage.

obtain achieve, acquire, attain,
earn, gain, get, procure, secure.
Ant. lose.

obtrude encroach, infringe, interfere, intrude, trespass.
Ant. retire, withdraw.

obtrusive forward, interfering,
intrusive, meddling, officious.
Ant. retiring.

obtuse (1) blunt; (2) (*Fig.*)
dull, dull-witted, heavy, slow,
stolid, stupid, unintelligent.
Ant. of (1) sharp; of (2) quick.

obviate anticipate, avert,
counteract, preclude, prevent,
remove.
Ant. help, permit.

obvious apparent, clear, distinct, evident, manifest, palpable, patent, perceptible, plain,
self-evident, unmistakable,
visible.
Ant. dark, obscure.

occasion (1) *n.* cause, ground,
inducement, influence, motive,
reason; (2) chance, convenience, event, incident, occurrence, opening, opportunity,
time; (3) *v.* cause, create, induce, influence, move, originate, persuade, produce.

occasional accidental, casual,
incidental, infrequent, irregular, uncommon.
Ant. frequent.

occult cabalistic, concealed,
hidden, invisible, latent,
mysterious, mystic, recondite,
supernatural, unknown, unrevealed, veiled.
Ant. natural.

occupation (1) business, calling, craft, employment, job,
post, profession, trade, vocation, work; (2) holding, occupancy, possession, tenure, use.

occupy (1) employ, engage,
fill, use; (2) inhabit, own,
possess; (3) capture, hold, invade, keep, seize.
Ant. of (3) evacuate.

occur appear, arise, befall, betide, chance, happen, result.

occurrence adventure, affair,
circumstance, happening, incident, proceeding, transaction.

odd abnormal, different, eccentric, exceptional, extraordin-

ary, peculiar, quaint, queer, rare, single, singular, strange, uncommon, uneven, unmatched, unusual, whimsical.

Ant. common, even, normal.

odds (1) bits, oddments, remnants, scraps; (2) advantage, superiority; (3) probability.

odious abominable, detestable, disgusting, execrable, forbidding, hateful, loathsome, obnoxious, offensive, repulsive, revolting, unpleasant.

Ant. lovable, pleasant.

odium abhorrence, antipathy, censure, condemnation, detestation, disapprobation, discredit, disgrace, dislike, hatred, obloquy, opprobrium, shame.

Ant. love.

odorous aromatic, balmy, fragrant, perfumed, redolent, scented, sweet-smelling.

Ant. malodorous.

odour aroma, fragrance, perfume, redolence, scent, smell.

offal carrion, dregs, garbage, refuse, rubbish, waste.

offence (1) crime, delinquency, fault, felony, misdeed, misdemeanour, sin, transgression, trespass, wrong; (2) affront, displeasure, harm, hurt, indignity, injury, injustice, insult, outrage; (3) anger, indignation, ire, resentment, umbrage, wrath; (4) aggression, assault, attack, onset.

Ant. of (3) delight, pleasure.

offend (1) affront, annoy, displease, fret, gall, harm, hurt, insult, irritate, molest, pain, provoke, vex, wound; (2) err, sin, transgress.

Ant. of (1) please.

offender criminal, culprit, delinquent, malefactor, sinner, transgressor.

offensive (1) abusive, annoy-

ing, detestable, displeasing, impertinent, insolent, insulting, irritating, rude; (2) abominable, disagreeable, disgusting, loathsome, obnoxious, revolting, unpleasant; (3) aggressive, attacking, invading.

Ant. of (1) pleasant; of (2) agreeable; of (3) defensive.

offer (1) v. bid, furnish, give, move, present, proffer, propose, show, tender; (2) immolate, sacrifice; (3) attempt, dare, endeavour; (4) n. attempt, bid, endeavour, essay, overture, proposal, proposition, tender.

Ant. of (1) refuse.

offhand abrupt, brusque, casual, curt, informal, unpremeditated.

Ant. attentive.

office appointment, business, charge, commission, duty, employment, function, place, post, responsibility, service, situation, station, trust, work.

officiate act, perform, serve.

officious dictatorial, forward, impertinent, interfering, meddlesome, meddling, mischievous, obtrusive, opinionated, over-busy, pragmatical.

Ant. retiring.

offspring child, children, descendant, descendants, issue, progeny.

Ant. parent.

often frequently, generally, oft, oftentimes, ofttimes, repeatedly.

Ant. seldom.

ogre bugbear, demon, devil, monster, spectre.

old aged, ancient, antiquated, antique, decayed, done, elderly, obsolete, old-fashioned, original, out-of-date, primitive, pristine, senile, worn-out.

Ant. new, young.

oleaginous adipose, fat, fatty, greasy, oily, sebaceous.

omen augury, foreboding, premonition, presage, prognostic, sign, warning.

ominous foreboding, inauspicious, premonitory, portentous, threatening, unpropitious.

Ant. auspicious.

omission default, failure, forgetfulness, neglect, oversight.

Ant. commission, fulfilment.

omit disregard, drop, eliminate, exclude, miss, neglect, overlook.

Ant. include.

omnipotent all-powerful, almighty.

Ant. feeble, weak.

omniscient all-knowing, all-seeing, all-wise.

Ant. ignorant.

onerous burdensome, difficult, grave, hard, heavy, laborious, oppressive, responsible, weighty.

Ant. light.

one-sided biassed, partial, prejudiced, unfair.

Ant. impartial.

onset assault, attack, charge, onslaught.

Ant. retreat.

onus burden, liability, load, responsibility.

Ant. relief.

ooze (1) v. drip, drop, exude, filter, percolate, seep, strain; (2) n. mire, mud, slime.

Ant. of (1) pour.

open (1) a. accessible, available, clear, free, unclosed, unenclosed, unrestricted; (2) bare, exposed, undefended, unprotected; (3) apparent, evident, obvious, plain; (4) artless, candid, fair, frank, guileless,

honest, ingenuous, sincere; (5) bounteous, bountiful, generous, munificent; (6) debatable, unsettled; (7) v. begin, commence, start; (8) unbar, unclose, uncover, unlock, unseal, untie; (9) disclose, exhibit, explain, show; (10) expand, spread.

Ant. of (1) closed; of (4) artful.

opening (1) aperture, breach, chink, cleft, fissure, gap, hole, orifice, perforation, rent, slot, space; (2) chance, opportunity, vacancy; (3) beginning, commencement, inauguration, initiation, start; (4) a. commencing, first, inaugural, initiatory, introductory.

Ant. of (1) closure; of (3) ending.

openly candidly, frankly, plainly, publicly.

Ant. secretly.

operate act, effect, function, influence, manage, perform, run, use, work.

operation action, affair, agency, business, effort, force, influence, manipulation, manoeuvre, motion, movement, performance, procedure, process.

Ant. cessation.

operative (1) n. artisan, craftsman, employee, labourer, mechanic, worker; (2) a. active, effective, efficient, serviceable; (3) important, indicative, influential, significant.

Ant. of (1) master; of (2) inoperative; of (3) insignificant.

opiate anodyne, drug, narcotic, sedative, tranquilliser.

Ant. stimulant.

opine believe, conceive, judge, presume, suppose, surmise, think, (Poet.) ween.

Ant. know.

opinion belief, conception, estimation, idea, impression, judgment, notion, persuasion, sentiment, view.

opinionated biassed, bigoted, dictatorial, dogmatic, prejudiced, obstinate, self-assertive, stubborn.
Ant. modest.

opponent adversary, antagonist, competitor, contestant, enemy, foe, rival.
Ant. ally, friend.

opportune appropriate, auspicious, convenient, favourable, felicitous, fit, fitting, fortunate, proper, propitious, suitable, timely, well-timed.
Ant. inopportune, unsuitable.

opportunity chance, convenience, moment, occasion, opening, time.

oppose bar, check, combat, confront, contradict, counter, hinder, obstruct, prevent, resist, thwart, withstand.
Ant. support.

opposite (1) facing, fronting; (2) adverse, antagonistic, conflicting, contradictory, contrary, different, differing, diverse, hostile, inconsistent, inimical, irreconcilable, opposed, reverse, unlike.

opposition antagonism, antagonist, competition, contrariety, counteraction, difference, diversity, hindrance, inconsistency, obstacle, obstruction, prevention, resistance.
Ant. support.

oppress burden, crush, depress, harass, load, maltreat, overpower, overwhelm, persecute, subdue, suppress, tyrannise, wrong.
Ant. relieve.

oppression abuse, calamity, cruelty, hardship, injury, injustice, misery, persecution, severity, suffering, tyranny.
Ant. freedom, kindness.

oppressive (1) burdensome, cruel, despotic, heavy, inhuman, overwhelming, severe, tyrannical, unjust; (2) close, muggy, stifling, suffocating, sultry.
Ant. of (1) light.

opprobrious abusive, contemptuous, dishonourable, disreputable, hateful, ignominious, infamous, insolent, insulting, offensive, scandalous, scurrilous, shameful, vituperative.
Ant. courteous.

opprobrium calumny, contumely, disgrace, ignominy, infamy, obloquy, odium, reproach, scurrility.
Ant. credit, encomium.

oppugn argue, assail, attack, combat, dispute, oppose, resist, withstand.
Ant. help.

option choice, election, preference, selection.
Ant. compulsion.

opulent affluent, luxurious, moneyed, plentiful, rich, sumptuous, wealthy, well-off.
Ant. poor.

oracular (1) auspicious, foreboding, ominous, portentous, prophetic; (2) grave, sage, venerable, wise; (3) authoritative, dictatorial, dogmatic, positive.
Ant. of (1) clear; of (3) undogmatic.

oral spoken, verbal, vocal.
Ant. written.

oration address, declamation, discourse, harangue, speech.

orb ball, circle, globe, ring, sphere.

orbit course, path, revolution, track.

ordain (1) appoint, call, consecrate, destine, elect, nominate; (2) decree, determine, enact, enjoin, order, predestine, prescribe; (3) establish, institute, regulate.

ordeal assay, experiment, proof, test, trial.

order (1) v. bid, command, decree, direct, enact, enjoin, instruct, ordain, prescribe, require; (2) adjust, arrange, classify, conduct, control, dispose, manage, regulate; (3) n. command, commission, direction, injunction, instruction, law, mandate, precept, regulation, rule; (4) arrangement, method, plan, regularity, symmetry; (5) discipline, law, peace, quiet, tranquillity; (6) arrangement, classification, disposition, sequence, succession; (7) association, brotherhood, community, fraternity, society; (8) (*Biol.*) class, family, genus, kind, sort, sub-class, tribe.

orderly (1) methodical, neat, regular, systematic, well-organised, well-regulated; (2) disciplined, peaceable, quiet, well-behaved.
Ant. disorderly.

ordinance (1) decree, edict, enactment, law, order, regulation, rule, statute; (2) ceremony, rite, ritual, observance, sacrament.

ordinary (1) accustomed, common, customary, everyday, habitual, normal, settled, usual, wonted; (2) commonplace, indifferent, inferior, mean, mediocre, second-rate.
Ant. of (1) uncommon; of (2) superior.

organisation constitution, construction, forming, making, organising, organism, structure, system.

organise arrange, constitute, construct, co-ordinate, dispose, establish, form, frame, shape.
Ant. disorganise, ruin.

orgy carousal, debauch, revel.

orifice aperture, cleft, mouth, opening, perforation, pore, rent, vent.

origin (1) beginning, cause, commencement, derivation, foundation, fountain, occasion, root, source, spring; (2) birth, heritage, lineage, parentage.
Ant. of (1) end.

original (1) a. aboriginal, first, primary, primitive, primordial, pristine; (2) fresh, inventive, new, novel; (3) n. archetype, model, pattern, prototype, type; (4) (*Colloq.*) a. eccentric, odd, peculiar.
Ant. of (1) secondary; of (2) old.

originate (1) arise, begin, emanate, flow, proceed, rise, spring; (2) create, discover, form, invent, produce.
Ant. of (1) end.

originator author, creator, father, founder, inventor, maker.

ornament (1) n. adornment, decoration, design, embellishment; (2) v. adorn, beautify, deck, decorate, embellish, garnish, grace.
Ant. of (1) blemish; of (2) spoil.

ornate beautiful, bedecked, decorated, elaborate, elegant, florid, flowery, ornamented.
Ant. unadorned.

orthodox conventional, correct, sound, true.
Ant. heretical.

oscillate fluctuate, sway, swing, vacillate, vary, vibrate.

ostensible apparent, exhibited, manifest, plausible, pretended, professed, specious.

ostentation boasting, display, flourish, pageantry, parade, pomp, pretension, show, showiness, vaunting.
Ant. modesty.

ostentatious boastful, dashing, extravagant, gaudy, pompous, pretentious, showy, vain.
Ant. modest.

ostracise banish, boycott, exclude, excommunicate, expatriate, expel, reject.
Ant. accept, admit.

oust dislodge, displace, dispossess, eject, evict, expel.
Ant. admit.

outbreak (1) affray, brawl, conflict, fray, revolt, riot, rising, row, uprising; (2) eruption, explosion, outburst.
Ant. of (1) discipline.

outcast castaway, exile, pariah, reprobate, vagabond, wretch.

outcome conclusion, consequence, end, issue, result.

outcry clamour, cry, exclamation, noise, scream, screech, uproar, yell.
Ant. peace, silence.

outdo beat, exceed, excel, outvie, overcome, surpass.

outlandish alien, barbarous, bizarre, exotic, foreign, queer, strange.
Ant. native.

outlaw bandit, brigand, criminal, highwayman, marauder, robber, thief.

outlet egress, exit, opening, vent.
Ant. inlet.

outline contour, delineation, draft, drawing, figure, plan, silhouette, sketch.

outlook future, prospect, sight, view.

outrage (1) n. abuse, affront, indignity, injury, insult, offence, shock, violation, violence; (2) v. abuse, injure, insult, maltreat, offend, shock, violate.
Ant. compliment.

outrageous abominable, atrocious, excessive, exorbitant, extravagant, furious, immoderate, mad, nefarious, raging, scandalous, villainous, violent, wild.
Ant. moderate.

outré excessive, extravagant, fantastic, far-fetched, immoderate, indecorous, inordinate, unreasonable.
Ant. reasonable.

outrun beat, exceed, excel, outdo, outstrip, surpass.

outset beginning, commencement, opening, start, starting-point.
Ant. finish.

outshine eclipse, outdo, outstrip, overshadow, surpass.

outspoken abrupt, blunt, candid, frank, free, open, unceremonious, unreserved.
Ant. reserved.

outstanding (1) conspicuous, eminent, prominent, striking; (2) due, owing, unpaid, unsettled.
Ant. of (1) inconspicuous; of (2) paid.

outwit cheat, circumvent, deceive, defraud, dupe, gull, out-manoeuvre, swindle, victimise.

overawe alarm, browbeat, cow, daunt, frighten, scare, terrify.
Ant. encourage.

overbearing arrogant, despotic, dictatorial, domineering, haughty, imperious, lordly, oppressive, supercilious.
Ant. humble.

overcast cloudy, darkened, hazy, murky, obscure.
Ant. bright, clear.

overcharge (1) burden, oppress, overburden, overload, surcharge, surfeit; (2) exaggerate, overstate.
Ant. (1) undercharge.

overcome beat, conquer, crush, defeat, overpower, overthrow, overwhelm, prevail, subdue, subjugate, surmount, vanquish.
Ant. yield.

overhaul (1) v. overtake; (2) check, examine, inspect, reexamine, repair, survey; (3) n. check, examination, inspection.

overlook (1) condone, excuse, forgive, pardon; (2) disregard, ignore, miss, neglect, omit, pass, slight; (3) examine, inspect, review, superintend, supervise, survey.
Ant. of (1) punish; of (2) include.

overpower beat, conquer, crush, defeat, overcome, overthrow, overwhelm, rout, subdue, subjugate, vanquish.
Ant. yield.

overreach cheat, circumvent, deceive, defraud, dupe, gull, outwit, swindle, trick, victimise.

override annul, cancel, nullify, outweigh, quash, supersede, upset.
Ant. approve.

overrule (1) control, direct, govern, influence, sway; (2) alter, annul, cancel, disallow, recall, repeal, rescind, revoke.

Ant. of (2) allow.

oversight (1) blunder, error, fault, inattention, lapse, mistake, neglect, omission, slip; (2) care, charge, control, direction, inspection, management, superintendence, supervision.

overt apparent, deliberate, manifest, notorious, open, patent, plain, public.
Ant. concealed, secret.

overthrow (1) v. beat, conquer, crush, defeat, master, overcome, overpower, overwhelm, subdue, subjugate, vanquish; (2) demolish, destroy, level, ruin, subvert, upset; (3) n. defeat, discomfiture, prostration, rout, ruin, subjugation, subversion.
Ant. of (2) restore.

overture (1) invitation, offer, proposal, proposition, resolution; (2) (Mus.) introduction, opening, prelude.
Ant. of (1) withdrawal; of (2) finale.

overweening arrogant, conceited, egotistical, haughty, opinionated, pompous, proud, supercilious, vain, vainglorious.
Ant. humble, modest.

overwhelm (1) drown, flood, inundate, overflow, sink, submerge; (2) conquer, defeat, overcome, overpower, subdue, vanquish.

overwrought (1) agitated, excited, overworked, stirred; (2) overdone, over-elaborated.
Ant. of (1) calm.

own (1) v. have, hold, possess; (2) acknowledge, admit, allow, avow, concede, confess, recognise.
Ant. of (2) deny.

owner holder, landlord, possessor, proprietor.

P

pacific appeasing, calm, conciliatory, friendly, gentle, mild, peaceable, peaceful, quiet, smooth, tranquil, unruffled.
Ant. violent.

pacify allay, ameliorate, appease, assuage, calm, compose, conciliate, moderate, mollify, quell, quiet, soften, soothe, still, tranquillise.
Ant. provoke.

pack (1) *n.* bale, bundle, burden, knapsack, load, package, packet, parcel; (2) assemblage, band, collection, company, crew, flock, gang, herd, lot, set; (3) *v.* burden, compact, compress, cram, load, store, stow.

pact agreement, alliance, arrangement, bargain, bond, contract, convention, covenant, deal, league, treaty, union.

pagan (1) *n.* gentile, heathen, idolater; (2) *a.* gentile, heathenish, idolatrous, irreligious.
Ant. believer, Christian.

pageantry display, magnificence, parade, pomp, splendour, state.

pain (1) *n.* ache, affliction, agony, anguish, bitterness, discomfort, distress, grief, misery, pang, suffering, throe, torment, torture, trouble, twinge, vexation, woe, wretchedness; (2) *v.* afflict, aggrieve, agonise, annoy, disquiet, distress, grieve, harass, harm, hurt, incommode, inconvenience, injure, irritate, torment, torture, vex, worry, wound.
Ant. of (1) pleasure; of (2) please.

painful (1) afflictive, agonising, annoying, disagreeable, displeasing, distressing, excru-

ciating, grievous, provoking, unpleasant, vexatious; (2) arduous, difficult, hard, laborious, severe.
Ant. of (1) harmless, painless; of (2) easy.

pains (1) care, effort, labour, trouble; (2) childbirth, labour.

painstaking assiduous, careful, conscientious, diligent, hard-working, industrious, persevering, sedulous, strenuous.
Ant. careless.

paint (1) *v.* delineate, depict, describe, draw, figure, picture, portray, represent, sketch; (2) adorn, beautify, colour, deck, embellish, ornament.

pal chum, companion, comrade, crony, friend, (*Colloq.*) mate.

palatable agreeable, delectable, delicate, delicious, enjoyable, luscious, pleasant, savoury, tasteful.
Ant. distasteful, unsavoury.

pale (1) *a.* ashen, ashy, colourless, dim, faint, pallid, sallow, wan, white; (2) *n.* barrier, boundary, confines, district, enclosure, fence, limit, region, territory.
Ant. of (1) bright, florid.

palliate (1) abate, allay, alleviate, assuage, diminish, ease, mitigate, mollify, relieve, soften, soothe; (2) cloak, conceal, cover, excuse, extenuate, hide, lessen.
Ant. of (1) increase; of (2) reveal.

pallid ashen, ashy, cadaverous, colourless, pale, sallow, wan, whitish.
Ant. florid.

palm (*Fig.*) bays, crown, laurel, prize, trophy.

palmy flourishing, fortunate, glorious, golden, happy, joyous, prosperous, thriving.

Ant. unfortunate.

palpable (1) material, real, tactile, tangible; (2) evident, manifest, obvious, plain, unmistakable.

Ant. of (2) doubtful.

palpitate beat, flutter, pulsate, quiver, shiver, throb, tremble.

paltry base, beggarly, contemptible, despicable, inconsiderable, insignificant, low, mean, minor, petty, pitiful, slight, small, trifling, trivial, unimportant, worthless, wretched.

Ant. important.

pamper coddle, fondle, gratify, humour, indulge, spoil.

Ant. neglect.

panacea cure-all, medicine, remedy.

panegyric commendation, encomium, eulogy, praise, tribute.

Ant. censure, condemnation.

pang agony, anguish, distress, gripe, throe, twinge.

panic alarm, consternation, fear, fright, terror.

Ant. calmness.

pant (1) blow, breathe, gasp, heave, palpitate, puff, throb; (2) (*Fig.*) desire, long, hunger, sigh, thirst, yearn.

paraclete advocate, comforter, consoler, intercessor.

parade (1) *n.* display, ostentation, pomp, show; (2) array, ceremony, pageant, procession, spectacle, review; (3) *v.* display, flaunt, show, vaunt.

Ant. of (1) restraint; of (3) conceal.

paradox absurdity, contradiction, mystery.

paragon ideal, masterpiece, model, pattern, standard.

paragraph clause, item,

notice, passage, section, sentence, sub-division.

parallel (1) *a.* analogous, correspondent, corresponding, like, resembling, similar; (2) *n.* analogy, comparison, counterpart, likeness, resemblance, similarity.

Ant. of (1) unlike; of (2) difference.

paramount chief, eminent, pre-eminent, principal, superior, supreme.

Ant. inferior.

paraphernalia accoutrements, baggage, belongings, effects, equipage, equipment, trappings.

parasite fawner, flatterer, hanger-on, sycophant, toady.

parched arid, dry, scorched, shrivelled, thirsty.

Ant. wet.

pardon (1) *n.* absolution, amnesty, condonation, discharge, excuse, forgiveness, grace, indulgence, mercy, release, remission; (2) *v.* acquit, absolve, condone, excuse, forgive, overlook, release.

Ant. blame.

parentage ancestry, birth, descent, family, line, lineage, origin, pedigree, race, stock.

parity analogy, correspondence, equality, equivalence, likeness, sameness, similarity.

Ant. inequality.

parody burlesque, caricature, imitation, travesty.

paroxysm attack, convulsion, fit, seizure, spasm.

parsimonious avaricious, close, close-fisted, covetous, frugal, grasping, mean, miserly, near, niggardly, penurious, saving, sparing, stingy, tight-fisted.

Ant. generous, open-handed.

parson clergyman, divine, ecclesiastic, incumbent, minister, pastor, priest, rector.

part (1) component, constituent, division, element, fraction, fragment, lot, piece, portion, section, share; (2) concern, faction, interest, party, side; (3) business, charge, duty, function, office, responsibility, work; (4) (*Theat.*) character, role; (5) *v.* break, detach, disconnect, disjoin, disunite, divide, separate, sever; (6) allot, apportion, deal, distribute, mete; (7) depart, go, leave, quit.

Ant. of (1) whole; of (5) unite; of (6) gather; of (7) remain.

partake participate, share.

partial (1) imperfect, incomplete, limited, unfinished; (2) biassed, influenced, interested, one-sided, predisposed, prejudiced, unfair, unjust.

Ant. of (1) perfect; of (2) unbiassed.

participate partake, share.

particle atom, bit, grain, iota, jot, molecule, mite, mote, piece, scrap, speck, tittle, whit.

Ant. whole.

parting (1) *n.* farewell, leave-taking; (2) breaking, detachment, division, rupture, separation; (3) *a.* breaking, dividing, last, separating, valedictory.

partisan (1) *n.* adherent, backer, champion, disciple, follower, supporter, votary; (2) *a.* biassed, interested, partial, prejudiced.

Ant. of (1) leader; of (2) impartial.

partition (1) barrier, screen, wall; (2) division, separation; (3) allotment, apportionment, distribution, portion, share; (4) *v.* apportion, divide, portion, separate, share.

partner (1) accomplice, ally, associate, coadjutor, collaborator, colleague, companion, confederate, helper, participant; (2) consort, husband, wife.

partnership association, company, connection, co-partnership, corporation, firm, house, interest, participation, society, union.

parts ability, accomplishments, capabilities, endowments, faculties, genius, gifts, intellect, intelligence.

party (1) alliance, cabal, clique, confederacy, coterie, faction, league, set, side; (2) assemblage, assembly, company, gathering, group; (3) individual, person, somebody, someone; (4) (*Law*) cause, defendant, litigant, plaintiff, pursuer, side, suit; (5) (*Mil.*) body, company, detachment, squad.

pass (A) *v.* (1) depart, elapse, go, lapse, leave, move, proceed; (2) cease, die, disappear, end, expire, fade, terminate, vanish; (3) experience, happen, occur, spend, suffer, undergo; (4) convey, deliver, send, transmit; (5) disregard, ignore, neglect; (6) exceed, excel, surpass; (7) approve, enact, ratify, sanction; (8) answer, do, succeed, suffice, suit; (9) deliver, express, pronounce, utter.

pass (B) *n.* (1) licence, passport, permission, permit, safe-conduct, ticket; (2) canyon, col, defile, gorge, ravine; (3) avenue, road, way; (4) condition, plight, situation, stage, state; (5) lunge, push, thrust.

passable (1) acceptable, admissible, allowable, fair, mediocre, middling, moderate, ordinary, tolerable; (2) navigable, traversable.

Ant. of (1) outstanding.

passage (1) avenue, course, lane, path, road, route, thoroughfare, way; (2) channel, crossing, journey, tour, trip, voyage; (3) corridor, doorway, entrance-hall, gallery, gate, vestibule; (4) clause, extract, paragraph, sentence, text, verse; (5) brush, combat, contest, encounter, exchange, incident, occurrence, skirmish; (6) fare.

Ant. of (1) barrier.

passion (1) animation, ardour, eagerness, emotion, excitement, feeling, fervour, joy, rapture, transport, zeal, warmth; (2) affection, attachment, desire, fondness, keenness, love, lust; (3) anger, fury, indignation, ire, rage, resentment, vehemence, wrath.

Ant. of (1) apathy; of (2) hate; of (3) calmness.

passionate animated, ardent, eager, enthusiastic, excited, fervent, fervid, impassioned, impetuous, impulsive, vehement, warm, zealous; (2) choleric, fiery, hot-headed, irascible, irritable, quick-tempered, violent.

Ant. of (1) apathetic; of (2) good-tempered.

passive enduring, inactive, inert, long-suffering, patient, quiescent, submissive, unresisting.

Ant. active, impassive.

past accomplished, elapsed, ended, finished, former, gone, spent.

pastime amusement, diver-

sion, entertainment, play, recreation, sport.

Ant. work.

pastor (1) churchman, clergyman, divine, ecclesiastic, minister, parson, rector; (2) shepherd.

patch v. fix, mend, repair, restore, settle, smooth.

patent (1) a. apparent, clear, conspicuous, evident, indisputable, manifest, obvious, open, palpable, unconcealed, unmistakable; (2) n. copyright, invention.

Ant. of (1) obscure.

path (1) avenue, course, passage, road, route, walk, way; (2) footpath, footway, pathway, track.

pathetic affecting, melting, moving, pitiable, plaintive, sad, tender, touching.

Ant. laughable.

patience calmness, composure, constancy, diligence, endurance, fortitude, long-suffering, perseverance, persistence, resignation, serenity, submission, sufferance.

Ant. excitement.

patient (1) a. calm, composed, constant, contented, enduring, indulgent, long-suffering, persevering, persistent, quiet, resigned, self-possessed, serene, submissive, uncomplaining, untiring; (2) n. invalid, sufferer.

Ant. of (1) excitable.

patron advocate, defender, guardian, helper, protector, supporter.

Ant. enemy.

patronise assist, befriend, countenance, defend, favour, help, maintain.

Ant. neglect.

pattern archetype, design, example, exemplar, guide,

model, norm, original, paragon, prototype, sample, specimen, style, type.

paucity deficiency, fewness, lack, poverty, rarity, shortage. Ant. plenty, sufficiency.

pauperism beggary, destitution, indigence, mendicancy, need, poverty, penury, want. Ant. wealth.

pause (1) n. break, cessation, delay, discontinuance, halt, hesitation, intermission, interruption, interval, respite, rest, stay, stoppage, suspense, wait; (2) v. cease, delay, deliberate, desist, halt, hesitate, interrupt, rest, wait, waver. Ant. of (1) continuance.

pawn v. gage, hazard, pledge, stake, wager. Ant. redeem.

pay (1) v. compensate, discharge, give, liquidate, offer, punish, recompense, reimburse remunerate, render, repay, requite, revenge, reward, settle; (2) n. allowance, compensation, emoluments, fee, hire, income, payment, remuneration, reward, salary, stipend, wages.

peace accord, agreement, amity, armistice, calm, calmness, concord, harmony, peacefulness, repose, rest, silence, stillness, tranquillity, truce. Ant. discord, war.

peaceable amiable, amicable, friendly, gentle, inoffensive, mild, pacific, peaceful, placid, quiet, serene, still, tranquil, undisturbed. Ant. noisy, quarrelsome.

peaceful calm, friendly, gentle, kind, pacific, placid, serene, tranquil, undisturbed, unexcited. Ant. disturbed.

peak acme, apex, crest, pinnacle, point, summit, top, zenith. Ant. bottom.

peasant countryman, hind, rustic, swain. Ant. towndweller.

peculate appropriate, defraud, embezzle, misappropriate, pilfer, purloin, rob, steal. Ant. refund.

peculiar (1) appropriate, characteristic, individual, particular, personal, private, special, specific; (2) eccentric, exceptional, extraordinary, odd, queer, singular, strange, uncommon, unusual. Ant. of (2) ordinary.

peculiarity characteristic, distinctiveness, eccentricity, idiosyncrasy, oddity, rarity, singularity, speciality.

pedantic conceited, fussy, officious, ostentatious, overlearned, particular, pedagogic, pompous, pragmatical, precise, pretentious, priggish, schoolmasterly, stilted. Ant. liberal, modest.

pedigree ancestry, breed, descent, family, genealogy, heritage, line, lineage, race, stock.

peer (1) associate, companion, compeer, equal, fellow, match, mate; (2) aristocrat, baron, count, duke, earl, lord, marquis, noble, nobleman, viscount. Ant. of (2) commoner.

peerless excellent, incomparable, matchless, outstanding, superlative, unequalled, unique, unmatched, unsurpassed. Ant. ordinary.

peevish acrimonious, captious, childish, churlish, crabbed, cross, crusty, fretful, ill-natured, ill-tempered, irritable, petulant, querulous, short-tempered, splenetic, testy, vexatious, waspish.

Ant. amiable.

pellucid bright, clear, crystalline, diaphanous, limpid, translucent, transparent.

Ant. opaque, turbid.

pelt (A) *v.* assail, batter, beat, belabour, cast, hurl, strike, throw.

pelt (B) *n.* coat, hide, skin.

penal corrective, disciplinary, punitive.

penalty amercement, fine, forfeiture, mulct, punishment, retribution.

Ant. reward.

penance humiliation, mortification, penalty, punishment.

penchant bias, disposition, fondness, inclination, leaning, liking, predilection, proclivity, propensity, taste, tendency, turn.

penetrate (1) bore, enter, perforate, permeate, pierce, probe; (2) (*Fig.*) affect, impress, touch; (3) (*Fig.*) comprehend, discern, understand.

penetrating (1) acute, keen, piercing, sharp; (2) (*Fig.*) astute, critical, discerning, discriminating, intelligent, quick, sagacious, sharp-witted, shrewd, subtle, wise.

Ant. of (1) blunt; of (2) stupid.

penitence compunction, contrition, regret, remorse, repentance, sorrow.

Ant. hard-heartedness, impenitence.

penitent (1) *a.* atoning, contrite, remorseful, repentant, sorrowful, sorry; (2) *n.* penance-doer, repentant.

penniless destitute, impecunious, indigent, moneyless, necessitous, needy, penuri-

ous, poor, poverty-stricken.

Ant. wealthy.

pensive (1) contemplative, dreamy, meditative, reflecting, serious, sober, thoughtful; (2) grave, melancholy, mournful, sad, solemn, sorrowful.

Ant. of (1) active; of (2) gay.

penurious avaricious, close, close-fisted, covetous, indigent, mean, mercenary, miserly, near, niggardly, parsimonious, sordid, stingy, ungenerous.

Ant. liberal.

penury beggary, destitution, indigence, need, poverty, privation, want.

Ant. plenty.

people (1) clan, family, nation, race, tribe; (2) community, men, persons, population, public; (3) crowd, herd, masses, mob, populace, rabble.

perceive (1) behold, descry, discern, discover, distinguish, espy, note, notice, observe, remark, see; (2) comprehend, feel, know, understand.

Ant. of (2) misunderstand.

perceptible apparent, appreciable, discernible, noticeable, perceiving, understandable, visible.

Ant. imperceptible, invisible.

perception apprehension, conception, discernment, feeling, idea, observation, recognition, sensation, sense, taste, understanding.

Ant. misunderstanding.

perchance haply, maybe, mayhap, peradventure, perhaps, possibly, probably.

percolate drain, drip, exude, filter, filtrate, ooze, strain.

Ant. block, penetrate, stagnate.

perdition damnation, demolition, destruction, downfall, hell, loss, overthrow, ruin.
Ant. blessedness, salvation.

peremptory absolute, arbitrary, authoritative, categorical, decisive, dictatorial, imperative, imperious, intolerant, irrefutable, positive, undeniable.

perennial ceaseless, constant, continual, deathless, enduring, eternal, everlasting, immortal, imperishable, permanent, perpetual, unceasing, undying, unfailing, uninterrupted.
Ant. temporary.

perfect (1) a. complete, completed, consummate, entire, finished, full, whole; (2) blameless, excellent, faultless, immaculate, pure, splendid, spotless, unblemished, untarnished; (3) accomplished, adept, expert, skilled; (4) v. accomplish, achieve, complete, consummate, elaborate, finish.
Ant. of (1) incomplete; of (2) impure; of (3) unskilled; of (4) mar.

perfection completeness, completion, consummation, excellence, exquisiteness, faultlessness, maturity, perfectness.
Ant. fault, imperfection.

perfidious deceitful, dishonest, disloyal, double-faced, faithless, false, traitorous, treacherous, unfaithful, untrustworthy.
Ant. loyal.

perfidy deceit, disloyalty, faithlessness, infidelity, perfidiousness, treachery, treason.
Ant. loyalty.

perforate bore, drill, penetrate, pierce, puncture.

perform (1) accomplish, achieve, act, complete, discharge, do, effect, execute, fulfil, observe, satisfy, transact; (2) (*Theat.*) act, play, represent.
Ant. of (1) fail.

performance (1) accomplishment, achievement, act, completion, consummation, execution, exploit, feat, work; (2) (*Theat.*) acting, exhibition, play, production, representation.

perfume aroma, attar, balminess, fragrance, incense, odour, redolence, scent, smell, sweetness.
Ant. stench.

perfunctory careless, heedless, indifferent, negligent, slovenly, superficial, thoughtless, unmindful.
Ant. careful.

peril danger, hazard, insecurity, jeopardy, risk, uncertainty, venture.
Ant. security.

perilous dangerous, hazardous, risky, unsafe.
Ant. safe.

period (1) age, course, cycle, date, epoch, era, stage, term, time; (2) bound, conclusion, duration, end, stop, termination.
Ant. of (1) eternity.

periodical (1) a. incidental, intermittent, recurrent, recurring, regular, stated, systematic; (2) n. magazine, paper, review, serial.
Ant. of (1) irregular.

perish decay, decease, die, expire, shrivel, vanish, waste, wither.
Ant. endure.

perishable decaying, destructible, dying, frail, fugitive, mortal, temporary.
Ant. durable.

perjured false, forsworn, perfidious, traitorous, treacherous, untrue.
Ant. true.

permanent abiding, constant, durable, enduring, everlasting, fixed, immutable, imperishable, indestructible, invariable, lasting, perennial, perpetual, persistent, stable, steadfast, unchanging.
Ant. temporary.

permissible admissible, allowable, lawful, legal, legitimate, proper, sufferable.
Ant. illegal, prohibited.

permission allowance, authorisation, consent, freedom, leave, liberty, licence, license, permit, sufferance, tolerance.
Ant. refusal.

permit (1) v. admit, agree, allow, authorise, consent, empower, endure, let, license, suffer, tolerate; (2) n. liberty, licence, pass, passport, permission, sanction, warrant.
Ant. of (1) refuse.

pernicious bad, baleful, baneful, deadly, deleterious, destructive, detrimental, evil, fatal, harmful, hurtful, injurious, malevolent, malicious, malign, malignant, noisome, noxious, offensive, poisonous, ruinous, wicked.
Ant. beneficial, harmless.

perpetrate do, commit, execute, perform.

perpetual ceaseless, constant, continual, continuous, endless, eternal, everlasting, incessant, infinite, interminable, never-ending, perennial, permanent, sempiternal, unceasing, unfailing, uninterrupted.
Ant. temporary.

perplex (1) beset, bewilder,

confuse, mystify, puzzle; (2) bother, disturb, harass, pester, plague, tease, vex, worry; (3) complicate, encumber, entangle, involve, tangle.
Ant. of (1) enlighten.

persecute afflict, annoy, distress, harass, hunt, injure, molest, oppress, pester, pursue, worry.
Ant. befriend.

perseverance constancy, determination, doggedness, indefatigability, persistence, pertinacity, resolution, steadfastness, tenacity.
Ant. inconstancy.

persevere continue, determine, endure, maintain, persist, remain, resolve, stick.
Ant. desist.

persist (1) continue, endure, last, remain; (2) insist persevere.
Ant. of (1) pass.

persistent constant, continuous, dogged, enduring, fixed, immovable, indefatigable, obdurate, obstinate, persevering, perverse, repeated, steadfast, steady, stubborn, tenacious.
Ant. inconstant.

personal (1) bodily, corporal, corporeal, exterior, material, physical; (2) individual, peculiar, private, special.
Ant. of (1) impersonal; of (2) general.

personate act, feign, imitate, impersonate, represent.

perspective (1) panorama, prospect, view, vista; (2) (Fig.) proportion, relation.

perspicacious acute, astute, clear-sighted, clever, discerning, keen, penetrating, sagacious, sharp-witted, shrewd.
Ant. slow-witted.

perspicacity acumen, acute-

ness, discernment, insight, sharpness, shrewdness.
Ant. dullness.

perspicuity clearness, distinctness, explicitness, intelligibility, lucidity, plainness, transparency.
Ant. obscurity.

perspicuous clear, distinct, explicit, intelligible, lucid, obvious, plain, transparent.
Ant. obscure.

persuade actuate, advise, allure, convince, counsel, entice, impel, incite, induce, influence, prevail, satisfy, urge.
Ant. dissuade.

persuasive cogent, convincing, inducing, logical, valid, sound, weighty.

pert bold, flippant, forward, impertinent, impudent, lively, nimble, presumptuous, saucy, smart, sprightly.
Ant. retiring.

pertain appertain, befit, behoove, belong, concern, regard.

pertinacious determined, dogged, headstrong, inflexible, intractable, obdurate, persevering, persistent, perverse, pig-headed, resolute, stubborn, tenacious, unyielding, wilful.
Ant. tractable.

pertinent applicable, apposite, appropriate, apt, fit, proper, relevant, suitable.
Ant. irrelevant.

perturb agitate, confuse, disorder, disquiet, disturb, trouble, unsettle, upset, vex.
Ant. calm.

pervade affect, diffuse, extend, fill, overspread, permeate, penetrate.

perverse (1) contrary, contumacious, dogged, headstrong, intractable, obdurate, pig-headed, stubborn, troublesome,

unmanageable, unyielding, wayward, wilful; (2) cantankerous, churlish, crabbed, cross, fractious, ill-natured, ill-tempered, peevish, petulant, spiteful, surly.
Ant. of (1) malleable, obedient; of (2) amiable.

perverted corrupt, debased, distorted, evil, impaired, misguided, vitiated, wicked.
Ant. good.

pessimistic cynical, dark, dejected, depressed, despondent, downhearted, foreboding, gloomy, melancholy, sad.
Ant. optimistic.

pest (1) bane, curse, epidemic, infection, pestilence, plague, scourge; (2) (*Fig.*) annoyance, nuisance.

pestilential catching, contagious, deadly, destructive, evil, foul, infectious, injurious, malignant, noxious, pernicious, pestiferous, poisonous, ruinous, venomous.
Ant. harmless, innocuous.

petition (1) address, appeal, application, entreaty, memorial, prayer, request, solicitation, supplication, suit; (2) *v.* ask, beg, crave, entreat, pray, solicit, sue, supplicate.
Ant. of (2) order.

petrify (*Fig.*) amaze, appal, astonish, astound, confound, dumbfound, stun, stupefy.

petty diminutive, inconsiderable, inferior, insignificant, little, mean, minor, negligible, paltry, slight, small, trifling, trivial, unimportant.
Ant. important.

petulant acrimonious, captious, cavilling, crabbed, cross, crusty, fault-finding, fretful, ill-humoured, irritable, peevish, perverse, querulous.

Ant. indulgent.

phantom apparition, ghost, spectre, (*Colloq.*) spook, vision, wraith.

pharisaical formal, hypocritical, sanctimonious.
Ant. sincere.

phenomenal marvellous, miraculous, prodigious, wondrous.
Ant. commonplace.

philanthropic benevolent, benignant, charitable, gracious, humane, kind.
Ant. selfish.

philosophic calm, collected, composed, cool, imperturbable, serene, stoical, tranquil, unruffled.
Ant. restless.

phlegmatic apathetic, cold, dull, frigid, heavy, impassive, indifferent, sluggish, stoical, stolid, unfeeling.
Ant. passionate.

phobia aversion, detestation, dislike, distaste, dread, fear, hatred.
Ant. love.

phraseology diction, expression, language, phrase, speech.

physical bodily, corporeal, material, mortal, natural, real, sensible, substantial, tangible.
Ant. spiritual.

physiognomy countenance, face, look, visage.

picture (1) *n.* account, description, drawing, effigy, engraving, image, likeness, painting, photograph, portrait, print, representation, resemblance, similitude, sketch; (2) *v.* delineate, depict, describe, draw, paint, represent, sketch.

picturesque beautiful, colourful, graphic, picture-like, scenic, striking, vivid.
Ant. dull.

piece (1) *n.* bit, fragment, morsel, mouthful, part, portion, scrap, shred; (2) *v.* cement, enlarge, extend, increase, join, mend, patch, unite.
Ant. of (1) all; of (2) decrease.

pied irregular, motley, mottled, parti-coloured, piebald, spotted, variegated.
Ant. regular, uniform.

pierce (1) bore, drill, enter, penetrate, perforate, puncture, transfix; (2) (*Fig.*) affect, excite, move, rouse, thrill, touch.

piety devotion, devoutness, godliness, grace, holiness, religion, reverence, sanctity, veneration.
Ant. impiety, irreverence.

pile (1) *n.* accumulation, collection, heap, mass; (2) building, edifice, structure; (3) fibre, filament, fur, hair, nap, thread, wool; (4) *v.* accumulate, amass, collect, gather, heap.

pilfer filch, purloin, rob, steal, thieve.
Ant. replace.

pilgrim crusader, palmer, traveller, wanderer, wayfarer.

pilgrimage crusade, excursion, expedition, journey, tour, trip.

pillage (1) *v.* despoil, loot, plunder, rifle, rob, sack, strip; (2) *n.* booty, depredation, devastation, loot, plunder, rapine, robbery, spoils, spoliation.
Ant. of (2) reparation.

pillar column, pier, post, prop, shaft, support.

pilot (1) *n.* aviator, conductor, director, guide, helmsman, navigator, steersman; (2) *v.* conduct, control, direct, guide, navigate, steer.

pinch (1) *v.* compress, gripe,

nip, press, squeeze; (2) (*Fig.*) afflict, distress, economise, oppress, press, spare, stint; (3) *n.* crisis, difficulty, emergency, exigency, oppression, pressure, stress.

pine (1) decay, decline, droop, fade, flag, languish, waste, wilt, wither; (2) desire, long, yearn.

Ant. of (1) revive.

pinion (A) *v.* bind, chain, confine, fasten, fetter, shackle.

Ant. release.

pinion (B) *n.* feather, pen, pennon, plume, quill, wing.

pinnacle acme, apex, crown, eminence, height, peak, summit, top, zenith.

Ant. bottom.

pious devout, godly, holy, religious, reverent, righteous, saintly.

Ant. irreligious.

piquant (1) biting, cutting, highly-seasoned, pointed, pungent, sharp, spicy, stinging, tart; (2) interesting, lively, racy, sparkling, stimulating.

Ant. of (1) mild; of (2) dull.

pique (1) *v.* affront, annoy, displease, irritate, offend, vex, wound; (2) *n.* annoyance, displeasure, grudge, irritation, offence, spite, umbrage, vexation.

Ant. of (2) pleasure.

pirate buccaneer, corsair, filibuster, freebooter, sea-robber, sea-rover.

pit abyss, cavity, chasm, coalmine, dent, depression, dimple, excavation, gulf, hollow, mine, trench.

pitch (1) *v.* cast, fling, heave, hurl, launch, throw, toss; (2) fix, locate, place, plant, settle, station; (3) fall, plunge.

piteous affecting, deplorable, distressing, doleful, grievous, lamentable, miserable, mournful, moving, pitiable, sad, sorrowful, woeful, wretched.

Ant. cheerful.

pith (1) core, essence, gist, heart, kernel, marrow, quintessence, substance; (2) energy, force, power, strength, vigour.

Ant. of (2) weakness.

pithy (1) energetic, forcible, powerful, strong, vigorous; (2) brief, compact, concise, expressive, laconic, pointed, short, terse.

Ant. of (1) weak; of (2) pointless.

pitiable deplorable, distressing, grievous, lamentable, miserable, mournful, piteous, woeful, wretched.

pitiful (1) compassionate, humane, kind, lenient, merciful, soft-hearted, sympathetic, tender, tender-hearted; (2) deplorable, lamentable, miserable, wretched; (3) abject, contemptible, despicable, insignificant, worthless.

pitiless callous, cruel, hardhearted, implacable, inexorable, merciless, relentless, ruthless, unfeeling, unmerciful, unsympathetic.

Ant. merciful.

pittance allowance, charity, drop, gift, modicum, portion, trifle.

Ant. abundance.

pity commiseration, compassion, condolence, fellow-feeling, kindness, mercy, sympathy.

Ant. cruelty.

place (1) *n.* area, district, locality, location, quarter, region, site, situation, spot; (2) city, hamlet, town, village; (3) employment, grade, job, position, post, rank, station; (4) abode, dwelling, home, house, manor, mansion, residence, seat; (5) room, space, stead; (6) cause, opportunity, reason; (7) v. allocate, appoint, arrange, assign, deposit, dispose, establish, fix, lay, locate, order, put, set, station.

placid calm, collected, cool, equable, gentle, imperturbable, mild, peaceful, quiet, serene, tranquil, undisturbed, unmoved, unruffled.

Ant. temperamental.

plague (1) n. contagion, disease, epidemic, infection, pest, pestilence; (2) (Fig.) affliction, annoyance, calamity, curse, evil, nuisance, scourge, torment, trial, vexation; (3) v. annoy, badger, bother, disturb, fret, harass, harry, molest, pester, tease, torment, torture, trouble.

Ant. of (2) boon; of (3) please.

plain (1) a. apparent, clear, distinct, evident, manifest, obvious, unambiguous, understandable, unmistakable; (2) artless, blunt, candid, direct, downright, frank, guileless, honest, ingenuous, open, outspoken, sincere; (3) common, commonplace, frugal, homely, ordinary, simple, unadorned, unpretentious; (4) even, flat, level, plane, smooth; (5) n. lowland, plateau, prairie, tableland.

Ant. of (1) ambiguous; of (2) deceptive; of (3) grand, ornate, of (4) uneven.

plaint complaint, cry, lament, lamentation, moan, wail.

Ant. cheerfulness, rejoicing.

plaintive doleful, grievous, melancholy, mournful, piteous, sad, sorrowful, woeful.

Ant. cheerful.

plan (1) n. blue-print, chart,

delineation, diagram, drawing, illustration, map, representation, sketch; (2) contrivance, device, method, plot, procedure, project, proposal, proposition, scheme, system; (3) v. arrange, concoct, contrive, design, devise, invent, plot, prepare, represent, scheme.

plane even, flat, level, plain, smooth.

Ant. uneven.

plant (1) v. establish, found, insert, institute, set, settle; (2) implant, scatter, sow.

plastic ductile, flexible, formative, pliable, pliant, soft, supple.

Ant. rigid, stiff.

platitude banality, bromide, cliché, commonplace, dullness, insipidity, triteness, triviality, truism, verbiage.

Ant. epigram, originality.

plaudit acclamation, applause, approbation, approval, clapping, commendation, praise.

Ant. abuse, booing, hissing.

plausible colourable, deceptive, fair-spoken, glib, hypocritical, ostensible, specious, superficial.

Ant. genuine, real.

play (1) v. caper, gambol, frisk, frolic, revel, romp, sport, trifle; (2) (Theat.) act, impersonate, perform, personate, represent; (3) bet, gamble, stake, wager; (4) n. amusement, caper, diversion, frolic, fun, gambol, game, jest, pastime, prank, recreation, romp; (5) comedy, drama, farce, performance, piece, show, tragedy; (6) gambling, gaming; (7) action, activity, exercise, motion, movement, operation, range, room, scope, sweep, swing.

Ant. of (1) work.

playful cheerful, frisky, frolicsome, gay, joyous, lively, merry, mischievous, sportive, sprightly, vivacious.
Ant. serious.

plea (1) apology, argument, claim, controversy, debate, defence, entreaty, excuse, justification, prayer, vindication; (2) (*Law*) action, allegation, cause, suit.

plead adduce, allege, argue, assert, defend, discuss, maintain.
Ant. deny, refuse.

pleasant acceptable, agreeable, amusing, charming, cheerful, delectable, delightful, gay, good-humoured, gratifying, humorous, jocular, merry, pleasing, sportive, welcome, witty.
Ant. disagreeable.

please (1) content, delight, gladden, gratify, humour, indulge, rejoice, satisfy; (2) choose, like, prefer.
Ant. of (1) displease.

pleasure (1) comfort, delight, enjoyment, gladness, gratification, happiness, joy, satisfaction, solace, voluptuousness; (2) choice, command, inclination, mind, preference, purpose, will, wish.
Ant. of (1) pain; of (2) disinclination.

plebeian base, common, ignoble, low-born, mean, vulgar.
Ant. aristocratic, patrician.

pledge (1) *n.* bond, deposit, earnest, gage, guarantee, security, surety; (2) (*Drinking*) health, toast; (3) *v.* bind, engage, gage, guarantee, plight; (4) toast.
Ant. of (3) redeem.

plenipotentiary ambassador, envoy, legate, minister.

plenitude abundance, completeness, fullness, plenteousness, plenty, plethora, profusion, repletion.
Ant. dearth.

plentiful abundant, ample, complete, copious, fruitful, plenteous, productive, profuse.
Ant. scarce.

plenty abundance, affluence, copiousness, fertility, fruitfulness, plenteousness, plentifulness, plethora, profusion, sufficiency.
Ant. scarcity.

pleonastic redundant, superfluous, verbose, wordy.
Ant. terse.

plethora excess, superabundance, superfluity, surfeit.
Ant. lack.

pliable adaptable, compliant, docile, ductile, flexible, limber, lithe, manageable, pliant, supple, tractable, yielding.
Ant. rigid, unyielding.

plight (1) *n.* case, condition, difficulty, dilemma, perplexity, predicament, situation, state; (2) *v.* engage, pledge, promise, propose.

plod drudge, labour, persevere, toil, trudge.

plot (1) *n.* cabal, conspiracy, intrigue, machination, plan, scheme, stratagem; (2) story, subject, theme, thread; (3) allotment, ground, lot, patch; (4) *v.* conspire, contrive, intrigue, plan, scheme; (5) concoct, contrive, devise, frame, project.
Ant. of (1) counterplot.

pluck (A) *n.* backbone, boldness, bravery, courage, determination, grit, hardihood, intrepidity, mettle, nerve, resolution, spirit.

pluck (B) *v.* (1) collect, gather, pick, pull; (2) pull, snatch, tear, tug.

plump (1) burly, buxom, chubby, corpulent, fat, fleshy, full, obese, portly, round, stout; (2) direct, downright, unqualified, unreserved.
Ant. of (1) thin.

plunder (1) *v.* despoil, devastate, loot, pillage, ravage, rifle, rob, sack, spoil, strip; (2) *n.* booty, loot, pillage, prey, rapine, spoils.

plunge descend, dip, dive, douse, drop, immerse, pitch, sink, submerge.

ply (1) assail, beset, employ, exercise, force, practise, press, strain; (2) beg, beseech, importune, solicit, urge.

poignant (1) bitter, distressing, heart-breaking, intense, irritating, keen, pointed, sarcastic, severe; (2) acrid, biting, caustic, penetrating, piercing, pungent, sharp, stinging.
Ant. (2) mild.

point (1) *v.* designate, direct, indicate, show; (2) aim, direct, level; (3) sharpen; (4) *n.* aim, design, end, object, purpose; (5) place, site, spot, stage, station; (6) apex, end, summit, tip, top; (7) matter, proposition, question, subject, text, theme; (8) aspect, peculiarity, respect, trait; (9) dot, mark, period, speck, stop; (10) cape, headland, naze, ness, promontory; (11) poignancy, sting.

point-blank categorical, direct, downright, explicit, express, plain, unreserved.

pointless (*Fig.*) aimless, dull, fruitless, futile, meaningless, stupid, vague.

poison (1) *n.* bane, pest, taint, toxin, venom, virus; (2) *v.* contaminate, corrupt, envenom, infect, pollute, vitiate.
Ant. of (1) antidote.

poisonous baleful, baneful, corruptive, noxious, pestiferous, pestilential, venomous.
Ant. healthful.

pole post, rod, shaft, stick.

policy action, approach, course, discretion, government, line, plan, procedure, rule, stratagem, wisdom.
Ant. rashness, simplicity.

polish (1) *v.* brighten, burnish, furbish, rub, shine, smooth; (2) finish, refine; (3) *n.* brightness, brilliance, gloss, lustre, sheen, smoothness; (4) (*Fig.*) elegance, finish, grace, refinement.
Ant. of (1) sully.

polished (1) bright, burnished, furbished, glossy, shining, smooth; (2) (*Fig.*) accomplished, cultivated, elegant, finished, polite, refined.
Ant. of (1) dull; of (2) uncouth.

polite accomplished, affable, civil, complaisant, courteous, courtly, elegant, finished, genteel, gracious, obliging, polished, refined, urbane, wellbred.
Ant. impolite.

politic artful, astute, crafty, cunning, diplomatic, discreet, intriguing, judicious, sagacious, scheming, shrewd, subtle, tactful, unscrupulous, wise.
Ant. honest, open, simple.

pollute (1) befoul, contaminate, corrupt, debase, deprave, dirty, soil, stain, taint; (2) debauch, defile, desecrate, dishonour, violate.
Ant. purify.

pollution contamination,

corruption, defilement, foulness, impurity, taint, uncleanness, vitiation.

Ant. purification.

poltroon coward, craven, dastard, recreant, (*Colloq.*) skunk.

Ant. hero.

pomp display, flourish, grandeur, magnificence, ostentation, pageant, pageantry, parade, show, splendour, state.

Ant. simplicity.

pompous august, boastful, bombastic, dignified, gorgeous, grand, inflated, ostentatious, pretentious, showy, splendid, sumptuous, superb.

Ant. simple.

ponder cogitate, consider, contemplate, deliberate, examine, meditate, reflect, study, think, weigh.

ponderous bulky, heavy, massive, weighty.

Ant. light.

poniard dagger, dirk, stiletto.

poor (1) destitute, hard-up, impecunious, impoverished, indigent, necessitous, needy, penniless, poverty-stricken; (2) deficient, inadequate, incomplete, insufficient, lacking, reduced, straitened; (3) faulty, feeble, inferior, mediocre, substandard, unsatisfactory, valueless, weak, worthless; (4) barren, fruitless, infertile, sterile, unproductive; (5) ill-fated, miserable, pitiable, unfortunate, unhappy, unlucky, wretched; (6) humble, lowly, mean, paltry, trivial.

populace crowd, mass, mob, multitude, people, rabble, throng.

popular (1) accepted, approved, favoured, liked; (2) common, current, general, prevailing.

Ant. of (1) disliked; of (2) unusual.

pore *v.* brood, dwell, examine, gaze, read, study.

port (1) (*Naut.*) anchorage, harbour, haven, roadstead; (2) door, embrasure, entrance, gateway, passage-way, portal; (3) air, appearance, bearing, behaviour, carriage, demeanour, deportment, mien, presence.

portable convenient, handy, light, manageable, movable.

Ant. bulky, heavy.

portend augur, betoken, bode, foreshadow, indicate, presage, prognosticate, threaten.

portent augury, foreboding, indication, omen, premonition, presage, presentiment, sign, warning.

portion (1) *n.* bit, fragment, morsel, part, piece, scrap, section; (2) allotment, division, lot, parcel, quantity, quota, share; (3) *v.* allot, apportion, deal, distribute, divide.

Ant. of (1) all, whole.

portly (1) dignified, grand, imposing, majestic, stately; (2) bulky, burly, corpulent, obese, plump, stout.

Ant. of (1) insignificant; of (2) thin.

portray delineate, depict, describe, draw, figure, paint, picture, represent, sketch.

pose (1) *v.* bewilder, confound, dumbfound, embarrass, mystify, perplex; (2) affect, attitudinise, pretend; (3) model, sit; (4) attitude, position, posture.

position (1) locality, place, post, site, situation, spot, station; (2) employment, job, office, place, post, situation; (3) place, rank, standing, status; (4) circumstances, condition, state; (5) attitude, posture.

positive (1) absolute, actual, certain, clear, definite, direct, explicit, express, incontrovertible, indisputable, unmistakable; (2) assertive, assured, confident, convinced, dogmatic, emphatic, peremptory, stubborn.

Ant. of (1) indefinite; of (2) undogmatic.

possess control, have, hold, keep, obtain, occupy, own, seize.

Ant. lose.

possession (1) control, custody, occupancy, occupation, ownership, proprietorship, tenure; (2) *pl.* assets, effects, estate, property, wealth.

Ant. of (1) loss.

possible feasible, likely, potential, practicable.

Ant. impracticable.

possibly maybe, mayhap, haply, peradventure, perchance, perhaps.

post (1) *n.* column, pillar, pole, shaft, support, upright; (2) appointment, assignment, berth, employment, job, office, place, position, situation; (3) place, station; (4) courier, letter-carrier, mail.

posterity (1) children, descendants, family, heirs, issue, offspring; (2) future.

Ant. of (1) ancestors; of (2) past.

postpone adjourn, defer, delay, prorogue.

Ant. expedite.

postscript addition, appendix, supplement.

posture (1) attitude, disposition, pose, position; (2) condition, phase, situation, state.

potency authority, control, efficacy, energy, force, influence, might, power, strength, sway.

Ant. weakness.

potent able, active, effective, efficacious, efficient, influential, mighty, powerful, strong.

Ant. impotent, weak.

potentate emperor, king, monarch, prince, ruler, sovereign.

Ant. subject.

potential (1) *a.* able, capable, inherent, latent, possible; (2) *n.* possibility, power.

Ant. of (1) impossible.

pound (1) beat, belabour, pommel, strike, thump; (2) bray, bruise, comminute, crush, powder, pulverise, triturate.

pouting cross, ill-humoured, moody, morose, sulky, sullen.

Ant. agreeable.

poverty (1) beggary, destitution, distress, indigence, lack, necessitousness, necessity, pauperism, penury, privation; (2) barrenness, deficiency, meagreness, poorness, sterility, unfruitfulness.

Ant. of (1) wealth; of (2) fertility.

power (1) ability, capability, capacity, competence, competency, energy, faculty, force, might, potency, strength; (2) authority, command, control, dominion, influence, rule, sovereignty, sway.

Ant. of (1) inability; of (2) subjection.

powerful active, convincing, effective, effectual, energetic, forceful, forcible, mighty, potent, robust, strong, vigorous.

Ant. powerless, weak.

practicable achievable, attainable, bearable, performable, possible, workable.

Ant. impracticable.

practical (1) accomplished, efficient, experienced, proficient, qualified, skilled, sound, trained; (2) serviceable, useful.
Ant. of (1) unskilled.

practice (1) custom, habit, usage, use, wont; (2) action, application, exercise, experience, operation, study.

practise apply, do, exercise, follow, observe, perform, pursue.

practised able, accomplished, experienced, proficient, qualified, skilled, trained.
Ant. unqualified.

pragmatical (1) matter-of-fact, practical; (2) impertinent, interfering, intrusive, meddling, meddlesome, officious.
Ant. of (1) theoretical; of (2) disinterested.

praise (1) *n.* acclamation, applause, approbation, approval, commendation, encomium, eulogy, laudation, panegyric, plaudit; (2) *v.* acclaim, admire, applaud, approve, compliment, eulogise, extol, laud; (3) adore, bless, exalt, glorify, magnify, worship.
Ant. of (2) blame, condemn, denigrate.

praiseworthy commendable, creditable, laudable, meritorious.
Ant. blameworthy.

prank antic, caper, frolic, gambol, trick.

pray adjure, ask, beg, beseech, crave, entreat, implore, importune, invoke, petition, request, solicit, supplicate.

prayer (1) entreaty, petition, request, suit, supplication; (2) (*Eccl.*) communion, devotion, invocation, litany, supplication.
Ant. of (1) command.

preamble exordium, foreword, introduction, preface, prelude.
Ant. conclusion.

precarious dangerous, doubtful, dubious, hazardous, insecure, perilous, uncertain, unreliable, unsettled, unstable, unsteady, unsure.
Ant. safe, secure.

precaution care, caution, foresight, forethought, providence, prudence, wariness.
Ant. carelessness.

precede head, introduce, lead, usher.
Ant. follow.

precedence antecedence, lead, pre-eminence, preference, priority, superiority, supremacy.
Ant. inferiority.

precedent *n.* antecedent, authority, example, instance, pattern, procedure, standard.

precept behest, command, commandment, decree, direction, edict, injunction, instruction, law, mandate, order, ordinance, principle, regulation.

preceptor (1) (*Scot.*) dominie; (2) instructor, lecturer, master, pedagogue, professor, schoolmaster, teacher, tutor.
Ant. student.

precincts borders, boundary, bounds, confines, district, enclosure, environs, frontier, limits, marches, neighbourhood, purlieus, region.

precious (1) cherished, costly, dear, inestimable, invaluable, priceless, prized, valuable; (2) adored, beloved, darling, dear, idolised.
Ant. of (1) cheap; of (2) hated.

precipitate (1) *v.* accelerate, advance, despatch, expedite, further, hasten, hurry, plunge, press, quicken; (2) *a.* abrupt, hasty, headlong, hurried, indiscreet, reckless, sudden, violent.

Ant. of (1) delay, retard.

precipitous abrupt, perpendicular, sheer, steep.

Ant. gradual, sloping.

precise (1) accurate, correct, definite, exact, explicit, fixed; (2) careful, ceremonious, exact, formal, prim, punctilious, puritanical, rigid, scrupulous, stiff.

Ant. of (1) incorrect; of (2) informal.

precision accuracy, correctness, definiteness, exactitude, exactness, nicety.

Ant. inaccuracy.

preclude check, debar, hinder, inhibit, obviate, prevent, prohibit, restrain, stop.

Ant. help.

precocious advanced, forward, over-forward, premature.

preconcerted concocted, prearranged, predetermined, premeditated, prepared.

precursory antecedent, introductory, preceding, preliminary, preparatory, previous, prior.

predatory greedy, pillaging, plundering, predacious, rapacious, ravaging, voracious.

predestination doom, fate, fore-ordainment, fore-ordination, necessity, predetermination.

predicament (1) attitude, condition, dilemma, emergency, plight, situation, state; (2) (*Sl.*) fix, mess.

predict augur, divine, forbode, forecast, foretell, portend, presage, prognosticate, prophesy.

predisposition bent, bias, disposition, inclination, proclivity, proneness, propensity, willingness.

Ant. dislike.

predominant ascendant, controlling, dominant, paramount, prevailing, prevalent, ruling, sovereign, supreme.

Ant. subordinate.

pre-eminent chief, consummate, excellent, outstanding, paramount, peerless, predominant, superior, supreme, unequalled, unrivalled, unsurpassed.

Ant. inferior.

preface foreword, introduction, preamble, preliminary, prelude, proem, prologue.

Ant. appendix, epilogue.

prefatory antecedent, introductory, precursory, preliminary, preparatory.

Ant. final.

prefer (1) choose, desire, elect, fancy, pick, select, wish; (2) advance, elevate, promote, raise.

Ant. of (1) reject; of (2) demote.

preference choice, desire, election, pick, precedence, predilection, priority, selection.

preferment (1) advancement, dignity, elevation, exaltation, promotion; (2) (*Eccl.*) benefice.

pregnant (1) fecund, fertile, fraught, fruitful, full, productive, prolific, replete, teeming; (2) (*Med.*) enceinte, gravid.

prejudice (1) bias, partiality, prejudgment, unfairness; (2) damage, detriment, harm, hurt, loss, mischief; (3) *v.* bias, influence, warp; (4) damage, harm, hurt, impair, injure.

Ant. of (1) impartiality.

prejudiced biassed, bigoted, influenced, one-sided, partial, partisan, unfair.

Ant. impartial.

preliminary (1) antecedent, initiatory, introductory, precedent, precursory, prefatory, preparatory, previous, prior; (2) *n.* beginning, initiation, introduction, opening, preamble, preface, prelude, start.

Ant. of (2) conclusion.

prelude beginning, exordium, foreword, introduction, preamble, preface, preliminary, proem, prologue, start.

Ant. conclusion.

premature (1) early, forward, pre-developed, unripe, unseasonable, untimely; (2) (*Fig.*) hasty, ill-considered, ill-timed, precipitate, rash, untimely.

Ant. of (1) mature; of (2) considered.

premeditation deliberation, design, forethought, intention, pre-arrangement, predetermination, purpose.

premium (1) bonus, boon, bounty, bribe, fee, prize, recompense, remuneration, reward; (2) appreciation, enhancement.

Ant. of (1) loss; (2) depreciation.

premonition forewarning, omen, portent, presage, sign, warning.

prepare adapt, adjust, arrange, equip, fit, form, make, plan, provide.

prepossessing alluring, amiable, attractive, bewitching, captivating, charming, fascinating, taking, winning.

Ant. ugly.

preposterous absurd, excessive, exorbitant, extravagant, foolish, irrational, monstrous, ridiculous, senseless, unreasonable, wrong.

Ant. reasonable, sensible.

prerogative advantage, claim, immunity, liberty, privilege, right.

presage (1) *v.* betoken, forebode, forecast, foreshadow, foretell, forewarn, portend, predict, prophesy, warn; (2) *n.* augury, foreboding, forecast, forewarning, omen, portent, prediction, premonition, presentiment, prognostic, prophecy, sign, warning.

prescribe appoint, command, decree, dictate, direct, enjoin, impose, order.

Ant. obey.

presence (1) attendance, company, nearness, neighbourhood, vicinity; (2) air, appearance, aspect, bearing, carriage, demeanour, mien, personality.

Ant. of (1) absence.

present (A) (1) *n.* now, to-day; (2) *a.* here, near, nearby, ready; (3) *a.* current, existing, immediate, instant.

present (B) (1) *n.* benefaction, boon, bounty, donation, favour, gift, grant, gratuity, offering; (2) *v.* bestow, confer, deliver, donate, furnish, give, grant, hand, offer, proffer.

present (C) *v.* exhibit, introduce, nominate, show.

presentiment anticipation, apprehension, fear, foreboding, forecast, forethought.

presently (1) anon, shortly, soon; (2) (*Obs.*) directly, forthwith, immediately.

Ant. of (1) eventually.

preservation conservation, maintenance, protection, safety, salvation, security, support.

Ant. destruction.

preserve (A) *v.* conserve, continue, defend, guard, keep, maintain, protect, retain, shield, sustain, uphold.
Ant. destroy.

preserve (B) *n.* confection, conserve, jam, jelly, marmalade, sweetmeat.

preside control, direct, govern, officiate.

press *v.* (1) clasp, compress, crush, embrace, gripe, hug, squeeze; (2) compel, constrain, enforce, enjoin, force, impress, urge; (3) crowd, hasten, hurry, push, rush, throng.
Ant. of (1) ease.

pressing constraining, imperative, important, importunate, serious, urgent, vital.
Ant. unimportant.

pressure (1) compressing, crushing, force, influence, squeezing, weight; (2) exigency, hurry, press, urgency.

prestige credit, distinction, importance, influence, reputation, weight.

presume (1) assume, believe, conjecture, infer, presuppose, suppose, surmise, think; (2) dare, undertake, venture.

presumption (1) anticipation, assumption, belief, conjecture, guess, opinion, probability, supposition, surmise; (2) assurance, audacity, boldness, effrontery, forwardness, presumptuousness.
Ant. of (2) modesty.

presumptuous arrogant, audacious, bold, foolhardy, forward, insolent, over-confident, presuming, rash, venturesome.
Ant. backward, modest.

pretence affectation, claim, cloak, colour, cover, excuse, feigning, garb, guise, mask,

pretext, semblance, show, simulation, subterfuge, veil.
Ant. sincerity.

pretend (1) affect, allege, counterfeit, deem, fake, falsify, feign, profess, sham, simulate; (2) aspire, claim.
Ant. of (2) renounce.

pretension (1) assertion, assumption, claim, demand, pretence, profession; (2) affectation, conceit, pertness, pretentiousness, priggery, priggishness, vanity.
Ant. of (2) modesty.

pretentious affected, assuming, conceited, priggish.
Ant. modest, natural.

preternatural abnormal, anomalous, extraordinary, inexplicable, irregular, marvellous, miraculous, mysterious, odd, peculiar, strange, supernatural, unnatural.
Ant. natural.

pretext affectation, appearance, cloak, excuse, guise, mask, pretence, semblance, show, simulation, veil.
Ant. truth.

pretty attractive, beautiful, bonny, comely, elegant, fair, fine, handsome, neat, nice, pleasing, tasteful, trim.
Ant. ugly.

prevail overcome, predominate, preponderate, succeed, triumph, win.

prevailing (1) controlling, dominant, effective, efficacious, operative, predominating, preponderating, ruling, successful; (2) common, current, established, general, ordinary, usual.
Ant. of (2) unusual.

prevalent (1) ascendant, compelling, governing, powerful, predominant, prevailing, successful, superior; (2) extensive, rife, widespread.

Ant. of (1) inferior; of (2) rare.

prevaricate cavil, dodge, equivocate, evade, quibble, shift, shuffle.

Ant. assert.

prevent anticipate, avert, bar, check, frustrate, hamper, hinder, impede, intercept, obstruct, obviate, preclude, restrain, stop, thwart.

Ant. help, support.

prevention anticipation, bar, check, frustration, hindrance, interruption, obstruction, stoppage.

Ant. help.

previous antecedent, earlier, foregoing, former, preceding, prior.

Ant. later.

prey (1) *n.* booty, loot, pillage, plunder, rapine, spoil; (2) captive, game, quarry, victim.

Ant. of (2) hunter.

price (1) amount, appraisement, charge, cost, estimate, expense, figure, outlay, valuation, value, worth; (2) compensation, recompense, reward.

priceless inestimable, invaluable.

Ant. cheap.

prick *v.* (1) bore, perforate, pierce, puncture, sting, wound; (2) (*Fig.*) drive, goad, incite, spur, stimulate, urge.

Ant. of (2) retard.

pride arrogance, conceit, haughtiness, hauteur, insolence, loftiness, presumption, self-esteem, self-importance, superciliousness, vainglory, vanity.

Ant. humility.

prim demure, formal, precise,

priggish, proper, starched, stiff, strait-laced.

Ant. hearty, informal.

primary (1) aboriginal, earliest, original, primeval, primordial, pristine, radical; (2) best, chief, first, highest, leading, main, principal; (3) basic, beginning, elementary, fundamental.

Ant. of (2) lowest; of (3) secondary.

prime (1) best, capital, chief, excellent, first-rate, highest, principal; (2) early, original, primary, primitive, pristine; (3) beginning, opening; (4) (*Fig.*) cream, flower, perfection.

Ant. of (1) inferior; of (2) later.

prince lord, monarch, potentate, ruler, sovereign.

princely august, dignified, grand, imperial, lofty, magnificent, majestic, noble, regal, royal, stately.

Ant. humble, lowly.

principal (1) *a.* capital, cardinal, chief, essential, first, foremost, highest, leading, main, paramount, pre-eminent, prime; (2) *n.* chief, head, headmaster, leader, master, ruler.

Ant. of (1) subordinate.

principally chiefly, especially, mainly, particularly, primarily.

Ant. least.

principle (1) axiom, canon, doctrine, dogma, law, maxim, opinion, rule, tenet; (2) goodness, honesty, honour, integrity, probity, rectitude, righteousness, trustworthiness, uprightness, virtue.

Ant. of (2) dishonesty.

print engrave, impress, imprint, issue, mark, publish, stamp.

prior antecedent, anterior, earlier, foregoing, former, preceding, previous.
Ant. later, posterior.

priority precedence, preference, superiority.
Ant. inferiority.

priory abbey, cloister, convent, monastery, nunnery.

prison confinement, dungeon, gaol, jail, lock-up, penitentiary.

pristine earliest, first, former, original, primary, primeval, primitive, primordial.
Ant. later.

privacy concealment, retreat, seclusion, secrecy, solitude.
Ant. publicity.

private (1) confidential, individual, particular, personal, reserved, special; (2) concealed, retired, secret, separate, solitary.
Ant. common, public.

privation destitution, distress, hardship, indigence, loss, necessity, need, poverty, want.
Ant. plenty.

privilege advantage, claim, immunity, leave, liberty, permission, prerogative, right.
Ant. disadvantage.

prize (1) n. booty, capture, loot, plunder, premium, reward, spoil, trophy; (2) v. appraise, rate; (3) appreciate, esteem, treasure, value.
Ant. of (3) disdain.

probability credibleness, likelihood, likeliness, presumption.
Ant. improbability.

probable credible, likely, presumable, reasonable.

probably likely, maybe, perchance, perhaps, possibly.
Ant. certainly.

probation examination, proof, test, trial.

probe examine, explore, investigate, prove, search, sift, sound, test, verify.

probity equity, fairness, goodness, honesty, integrity, rectitude, righteousness, sincerity, trustworthiness, truthfulness, uprightness, virtue, worth.
Ant. dishonesty.

problem dilemma, dispute, doubt, enigma, puzzle, question, riddle.
Ant. certainty.

problematical debatable, doubtful, dubious, enigmatical, puzzling, uncertain, unsettled.
Ant. certain.

procedure act, action, conduct, course, deed, measure, operation, performance, practice, proceedings, process, step, transaction.

proceed (1) advance, continue, progress; (2) arise, come, emanate, ensue, follow, issue, originate, result, spring.
Ant. of (1) recede, retreat.

proceeds gain, income, produce, products, profits, receipts, returns, yield.
Ant. outlay.

process (1) action, advance, course, measure, operation, performance, practice, procedure, proceeding, step, transaction; (2) (Law) action, case, suit, trial.

procession cavalcade, cortège, file, march, parade, retinue, train.

proclaim advertise, announce, circulate, declare, enunciate, publish, promulgate.
Ant. conceal.

proclamation announcement, ban, decree, edict, manifesto, notice, order, ordinance, promulgation, publication.

proclivity aptitude, bent, bias,

disposition, facility, inclination, leaning, proneness, propensity, tendency.

Ant. dislike, inaptitude.

procrastinate adjourn, dally, defer, delay, postpone, prolong, protract, retard.

Ant. expedite, hasten.

procreate beget, breed, engender, generate, produce, propagate.

procure (1) achieve, acquire, earn, effect, gain, get, obtain, manage, secure, win; (2) cause, compass, contrive.

Ant. of (1) lose.

prodigal (1) *a.* excessive, extravagant, immoderate, lavish, profligate, profuse, reckless, wasteful; (2) *n.* spendthrift, squanderer, wastrel.

Ant. of (1) thrifty.

prodigious (1) abnormal, amazing, astounding, extraordinary, marvellous, miraculous, portentous, strange, unusual, wonderful; (2) colossal, enormous, gigantic, huge, immense, monstrous, tremendous.

Ant. of (1) normal; of (2) tiny.

prodigy (1) marvel, miracle, portent, wonder; (2) monster, monstrosity.

produce (1) cause, create, effect, furnish, give, make, manufacture, originate; (2) afford, bear, beget, breed, engender, supply, yield; (3) demonstrate, exhibit, offer, show; (4) extend, lengthen, prolong, protract.

product consequence, effect, fruit, issue, outcome, performance, produce, production, result, returns, work, yield.

Ant. cause.

productive creative, fertile,

fruitful, generative, producing, prolific.

Ant. barren.

profane (1) *a.* godless, heathen, idolatrous, impure, pagan, secular, temporal, unconsecrated, unhallowed, unholy, unsanctified, worldly; (2) blasphemous, impious, irreligious, irreverent, sacrilegious, ungodly, wicked; (3) *v.* debase, defile, desecrate, pollute, violate.

Ant. of (1) sacred.

profanity blasphemy, impiety, irreverence, profaneness, sacrilege.

Ant. piety.

profess acknowledge, affirm, allege, avow, claim, confess, declare, own, pretend.

Ant. deny.

profession (1) acknowledgment, assertion, avowal, claim, confession, declaration, pretence; (2) business, calling, employment, office, trade, vocation.

Ant. of (1) denial.

proffer offer, propose, propound, suggest, tender, volunteer.

Ant. refuse.

proficiency accomplishment, aptitude, competency, dexterity, mastery, skill.

Ant. clumsiness.

proficient accomplished, adept, apt, capable, clever, competent, conversant, experienced, qualified, skilful, skilled, trained, versed.

Ant. unskilled.

profit (1) *n.* advantage, benefit, earnings, gain, emoluments, proceeds, produce, return, revenue, winnings; (2) *v.* benefit, better, gain, improve.

Ant. of (1) loss; of (2) lose.

profitable advantageous, beneficial, gainful, lucrative, productive, remunerative, serviceable.
Ant. disadvantageous.

profligate (1) *a.* abandoned, corrupt, debauched, depraved, dissolute, immoral, loose, shameless, vicious, vitiated, wicked; (2) *n.* debauchee, libertine, rake, reprobate.
Ant. of (1) moral, virtuous.

profound (1) abysmal, deep, fathomless; (2) abstruse, intense, learned, mysterious, mystic, obscure, occult, penetrating, recondite, sagacious, skilled, subtle.
Ant. of (1) shallow; of (2) superficial.

profuse abundant, bountiful, copious, diffuse, excessive, extravagant, exuberant, lavish, plentiful, prodigal.
Ant. scarce.

profusion abundance, bounty, copiousness, excess, extravagance, exuberance, lavishness, prodigality, superabundance, waste.
Ant. scarcity.

progeny breed, children, descendants, family, issue, lineage, offspring, posterity, race, stock.
Ant. ancestors.

prognosticate augur, betoken, forebode, foreshadow, foretell, portend, predict, presage.

progress (1) *n.* advance, advancement, betterment, development, growth, improvement, increase, progression; (2) *v.* advance, better, develop, gain, grow, improve, increase.
Ant. decrease.

prohibit ban, debar, disallow, forbid, hamper, hinder, interdict, obstruct, preclude, prevent.
Ant. allow, permit.

prohibition bar, ban, disallowance, embargo, interdict, interdiction, obstruction, prevention.
Ant. permission.

prohibitive forbidding, prohibiting, restraining, restrictive.

project (1) *v.* cast, fling, hurl, propel, throw; (2) contemplate, contrive, devise, plan, propose, purpose, scheme; (3) bulge, extend, jut, protrude; (4) *n.* contrivance, design, device, plan, proposal, scheme.

proletariat commonalty, masses, plebs, working-class.
Ant. aristocracy, middle-class.

prolific abundant, fertile, fruitful, productive, teeming.
Ant. barren.

prolix boring, diffuse, lengthy, long, long-winded, prolonged, protracted, rambling, tedious, tiresome, verbose, wordy.
Ant. concise, laconic.

prologue foreword, introduction, preamble, preface, preliminary, prelude, proem.
Ant. conclusion.

prolong continue, defer, extend, lengthen, postpone, protract.
Ant. curtail, shorten.

prominent (1) celebrated, chief, conspicuous, distinguished, eminent, famous, foremost, important, leading, main, noticeable, outstanding; (2) jutting, projecting, protruding, protuberant.
Ant. of (1) unimportant.

promiscuous confused, disordered, indiscriminate, intermingled, intermixed, mingled, miscellaneous, mixed.

Ant. selective.

promise (1) *n.* agreement, assurance, covenant, engagement, guarantee, pledge, undertaking, word; (2) *v.* agree, assure, engage, pledge, stipulate.

Ant. of (1) refusal; of (2) refuse.

promote (1) advance, aid, assist, encourage, forward, further, support; (2) dignify, elevate, exalt, honour, prefer, raise.

Ant. of (1) discourage; of (2) lower.

promotion (1) advancement, encouragement, furtherance; (2) elevation, exaltation, preferment.

prompt (1) *a.* agile, alert, apt, brisk, expeditious, hasty, quick, ready, smart; (2) early, punctual, timely; (3) *v.* impel, incite, induce, instigate, move, remind, stimulate, urge.

Ant. of (1) slow; of (2) tardy; of (3) discourage.

promulgate advertise, announce, broadcast, circulate, declare, disseminate, notify, proclaim, publish, spread.

Ant. suppress.

prone (1) apt, bent, disposed, inclined, tending; (2) flat, prostrate, recumbent.

Ant. of (1) disinclined; of (2) upright.

pronounce (1) articulate, enunciate, speak, utter; (2) affirm, announce, assert, declare, deliver, express.

Ant. of (2) suppress.

proof (1) experiment, ordeal, test, trial; (2) attestation, confirmation, demonstration, evidence, testimony.

prop (1) *v.* maintain, stay, support, sustain, uphold; (2) *n.* stay, support.

propagate (1) beget, breed, engender, increase, multiply, procreate, produce; (2) circulate, diffuse, disseminate, extend, promote, promulgate, spread.

Ant. of (1) destroy; of (2) conceal.

propel (1) cast, fling, hurl, project, throw; (2) drive, impel, push, urge.

Ant. of (2) dissuade.

propensity bent, bias, disposition, inclination, leaning, penchant, proclivity, proneness, tendency.

Ant. disinclination.

proper (1) appropriate, becoming, befitting, decent, decorous, fit, legitimate, meet, polite, respectable, right, seemly, suitable; (2) accurate, correct, exact, formal, precise; (3) individual, own, particular, peculiar, personal, special.

Ant. of (1) improper, indecent; of (2) incorrect.

property (1) assets, belongings, building(s), chattels, effects, estate, goods, house(s), ownership, possessions, riches, wealth; (2) attribute, characteristic, feature, quality.

Ant. of (1) poverty.

prophecy augury, divination, forecast, foretelling, prediction, prognostication, vaticination.

prophesy augur, divine, forecast, foretell, predict, presage, prognosticate, vaticinate.

propinquity (1) adjacency, nearness, neighbourhood, proximity, vicinity; (2) affinity, connection, consanguinity, kindred, relationship.

Ant. of (1) remoteness.

propitiate (1) appease, conciliate, pacify, reconcile; (2) atone, satisfy.

Ant. of (1) anger.

propitious (1) auspicious, favourable, fortunate, happy, lucky, opportune, promising, timely; (2) benevolent, benign, friendly, gracious, kind.

Ant. of (1) unlucky.

proposal design, offer, overture, plan, proposition, recommendation, scheme, suggestion, tender, terms.

Ant. rejection.

propose (1) design, intend, mean, plan, purpose, scheme; (2) nominate, offer, present, recommend, suggest, tender.

Ant. reject.

propriety accurateness, appropriateness, correctness, decency, decorum, fitness, justness, modesty, seemliness, suitableness.

proscribe banish, condemn, denounce, doom, exclude, exile, expel, interdict, ostracise, prohibit, reject.

prosecute (1) conduct, continue, follow, persist, pursue; (2) (*Law*) arraign, indict, sue, summon.

Ant. of (1) abandon.

prospect (1) display, field, landscape, outlook, perspective, scene, sight, spectacle, survey, view, vision; (2) anticipation, calculation, contemplation, expectation, hope, presumption, promise; (3) chance, likelihood, possibility; (4) *v.* explore, search.

prospectus announcement, conspectus, outline, plan, programme, scheme, syllabus.

prosper flourish, succeed, thrive.

Ant. decline.

prosperous flourishing, fortunate, lucky, rich, successful, thriving.

Ant. impoverished, unlucky.

prostrate (1) *a.* dejected, depressed, fallen, flat, prone, recumbent; (2) *v.* depress, exhaust, level, overcome, overthrow, overturn, reduce, ruin.

Ant. of (1) upright.

prostration (1) dejection, depression, exhaustion; (2) demolition, destruction, overthrow.

prosy boring, common-place, dull, flat, humdrum, prosaic, tedious, tiresome, unimaginative, uninteresting.

Ant. interesting.

protect cover, defend, foster, guard, harbour, preserve, save, screen, secure, shelter, support.

Ant. attack.

protest (1) *v.* affirm, assert, asseverate, attest, complain, declare, demur, disapprove, maintain, object, profess, testify; (2) *n.* complaint, declaration, disapproval, objection, protestation.

Ant. of (1) approve; of (2) approval.

prototype archetype, example, model, original, pattern, type.

protract continue, defer, delay, extend, lengthen, postpone, prolong.

Ant. shorten.

protrude bulge, extend, jut, project.

Ant. recede.

protuberance bulge, excrescence, knob, lump, process, projection, swelling, tumour.

proud (1) arrogant, boastful, haughty, imperious, lordly, overbearing, presumptuous, self-important, supercilious;

(2) grand, imposing, magnificent, majestic, noble, ostentatious, splendid; (3) conceited, egotistical, self-satisfied, vain.

Ant. of (1) humble; of (2) ignoble.

prove (1) ascertain, confirm, demonstrate, determine, establish, justify, show, substantiate, verify; (2) assay, examine, experiment, test, try.

Ant. of (1) disprove.

proverb adage, aphorism, apothegm, dictum, maxim, saw, saying.

proverbial acknowledged, current, notorious, unquestioned.

provide (1) afford, contribute, furnish, give, produce, supply, yield; (2) arrange, cater, collect, equip, fit, gather, prepare, procure.

Ant. of (1) deprive.

provident careful, cautious, considerate, discreet, economical, frugal, prudent, thrifty.

Ant. extravagant, improvident.

province (1) colony, county, department, dependency, district, domain, region, section, territory, tract; (2) (*Fig.*) business, calling, capacity, charge, duty, employment, function, part, post.

provision (1) arrangement, fund, hoard, preparation, reserve, stock, store, supplies; (2) (*Fig.*) agreement, clause, condition, proviso, stipulation.

Ant. of (1) want.

provisions eatables, fare, food, victuals, provender, supplies.

Ant. indigence, starvation.

provocation affront, annoyance, grievence, incitement, indignity, injury, insult, offence, vexation.

Ant. appeasement.

provoke affront, aggravate, anger, annoy, exasperate, fire, incense, incite, inflame, infuriate, injure, insult, irk, irritate, offend, rouse, vex.

Ant. appease, assuage.

provoking aggravating, annoying, exasperating, irksome, irritating, offensive, vexatious.

Ant. soothing.

prowess (1) bravery, courage, daring, fearlessness, gallantry, heroism, intrepidity, valour; (2) adroitness, aptitude, dexterity, expertness, facility, skill, talent.

Ant. of (1) cowardice; of (2) awkwardness.

proximity adjacency, contiguity, nearness, neighbourhood, vicinity.

Ant. distance, remoteness.

proxy agent, attorney, delegate, deputy, representative, substitute.

prudence care, caution, circumspection, commonsense, consideration, judgment, judiciousness, providence, wariness, wisdom.

Ant. recklessness.

prudent (1) careful, cautious, circumspect, discreet, judicious, wary, wise; (2) careful, economical, frugal, provident, sparing, thrifty.

Ant. of (1) rash; of (2) wasteful.

prune clip, cut, dock, lop, trim.

prurient covetous, desirous, hankering, itching, libidinous, longing, lustful.

pry examine, inspect, investigate, peep, peer, scrutinise, search.

Ant. disregard, ignore.

public common, general, notorious, open, popular, well-known.
Ant. private.

publication (1) advertisement, announcement, declaration, disclosure, notification, proclamation, promulgation; (2) book, booklet, brochure, handbill, issue, leaflet, magazine, newspaper, pamphlet, periodical.

publish advertise, announce, broadcast, declare, disclose, distribute, divulge, impart, issue, proclaim, promulgate, publicise, reveal.
Ant. conceal.

puerile boyish, childish, foolish, futile, immature, juvenile, petty, ridiculous, silly, trivial, weak, youthful.
Ant. manly, sensible.

pugnacious bellicose, contentious, disputatious, irascible, irritable, petulant, quarrelsome.
Ant. peaceable.

puissant forcible, mighty, potent, powerful, strong.
Ant. feeble.

pull (1) drag, draw, extract, haul, rend, tear, tug; (2) cull, gather, pick, pluck.
Ant. of (1) push.

pulsate beat, palpitate, quiver, throb, vibrate.

punctilious careful, ceremonious, conscientious, exact, formal, nice, particular, precise, scrupulous, strict.
Ant. careless, inexact.

punctual early, exact, precise, prompt, punctilious, seasonable, strict, timely.
Ant. late, tardy.

puncture v. bore, penetrate, perforate, pierce, prick.

pungent acrid, acrimonious, acute, biting, caustic, distressing, hot, keen, painful, penetrating, piquant, poignant, sharp, smart, stinging, trenchant.
Ant. mild.

punish beat, castigate, chasten, chastise, correct, discipline, flog, lash, scourge, whip.
Ant. praise.

puny diminutive, dwarfish, feeble, frail, inferior, insignificant, little, petty, pygmy, tiny, undersized, undeveloped, weak.
Ant. strong.

pupil beginner, catechumen, disciple, learner, neophyte, novice, scholar, student, tyro.
Ant. teacher.

puppet (1) doll, marionette; (2) (*Fig.*) cat's-paw, dupe, gull, pawn, tool.

purchase v. acquire, buy, gain, get, obtain, procure.
Ant. sell.

pure (1) clean, clear, genuine, perfect, simple, unadulterated, unmixed; (2) blameless, chaste, guileless, honest, immaculate, innocent, modest, true, undefiled, unspotted, unstained, upright, virtuous.
Ant. of (1) unclean; of (2) corrupt, wicked.

purge clarify, cleanse, clear, deterge, purify.
Ant. pollute.

puritanical ascetic, narrow-minded, prim, prudish, rigid, strait-laced, strict.
Ant. broad-minded.

purity (1) clarity, cleanness, clearness, fineness, genuineness; (2) chastity, guilelessness, honesty, innocence, integrity, piety, sincerity, virtue.
Ant. of (1) impurity; of (2) wickedness.

purlieus borders, confines, environs, limits, neighbourhood, outskirts, precincts, suburbs, vicinity.

purloin filch, pilfer, rob, steal, thieve.

Ant. restore.

purport (1) *n.* bearing, claim, drift, gist, import, intent, meaning, significance, spirit, tendency, tenor; (2) *v.* claim, express, imply, import, intend, mean, profess.

purpose (1) *v.* contemplate, design, intend, mean, plan, propose; (2) *n.* aim, design, end, intuition, plan, view.

pursue (1) chase, dog, follow, hunt, track; (2) conduct, continue, persist, prosecute, seek.

Ant. abandon.

pursy corpulent, fat, fleshy, obese, plump, podgy, short-winded.

Ant. thin.

purview compass, extent, field, limit, range, reach, scope, sphere.

push (1) drive, elbow, move, shoulder, shove, strive, thrust; (2) expedite, hurry, impel, persuade, press, urge; (3) *n.* assault, attack, charge, effort, onset.

Ant. of (1) pull; of (2) drag; of (3) retreat.

pusillanimous chicken-hearted, cowardly, dastardly, faint-hearted, feeble, recreant, timid, weak.

Ant. brave.

pustule abscess, boil, fester, gathering, pimple, ulcer.

put (1) bring, deposit, lay, place, set; (2) enjoin, impose, inflict, levy; (3) express, offer, propose, state, utter; (4) incite, induce, force, oblige, urge.

Ant. of (1) remove.

putative deemed, reckoned, reported, reputed, supposed.

putrefy corrupt, decay, decompose, rot, stink.

Ant. preserve.

putrid corrupt, decayed, decomposed, foul, rotten, stinking.

Ant. sweet-smelling.

puzzle (1) *n.* conundrum, enigma, poser, problem, riddle; (2) bewilderment, confusion, difficulty, dilemma, embarrassment, quandary; (3) *v.* bewilder, confound, confuse, embarrass, mystify, perplex.

Ant. of (3) enlighten.

pygmy (1) *n.* dwarf, midget, Lilliputian; (2) *a.* diminutive, dwarf, dwarfish, pygmean, stunted, tiny.

Ant. of (1) giant; of (2) colossal, gigantic.

Q

quack charlatan, humbug, impostor, mountebank, pretender.

Ant. dupe.

quagmire bog, fen, marsh, morass, slough, swamp.

quail blench, cower, droop, faint, flinch, quake, shrink, tremble.

Ant. confront.

quaint (1) antiquated, antique, bizarre, curious, droll, fanciful, fantastic, odd, old-fashioned, queer, singular, strange, unusual; (2) abstruse, artful, far-fetched, ingenious, recondite, subtle.

Ant. of (1) normal; of (2) ordinary.

quake move, quail, quiver, shake, shiver, shudder, tremble, vibrate.

qualification (1) ability, accomplishment, capability, capacity, endowment, fitness, suitableness; **(2)** allowance, condition, limitation, modification, proviso, restriction, stipulation.

Ant. of **(1)** disqualification.

qualify (1) adapt, capacitate, empower, equip, fit, prepare; **(2)** abate, diminish, limit, moderate, modify, reduce, regulate, restrain, restrict, modulate, soften, vary.

Ant. of **(1)** unfit.

quality (1) attribute, characteristic, condition, feature, nature, peculiarity, property, trait; **(2)** character, description, excellence, kind, make, position, rank, sort, standing, status, superiority; **(3)** aristocracy, gentry, nobility.

qualm (1) agony, attack, nausea, pang, sickness, throe; **(2)** compunction, misgiving, regret, remorse, scruple, twinge, uneasiness.

Ant. of **(1)** relief.

quandary bewilderment, difficulty, dilemma, doubt, embarrassment, perplexity, predicament, puzzle.

Ant. conviction.

quantity (1) aggregate, amount, number, part, portion, sum; **(2)** bulk, extent, greatness, length, measure, size, volume.

quarrel (1) *n.* affray, altercation, breach, broil, contention, controversy, difference, disagreement, dispute, dissension, feud, fight, fray, squabble, strife, tumult, wrangle; **(2)** *v.* bicker, brawl, clash, differ, disagree, dispute, fight, squabble.

Ant. of **(1)** peace; of **(2)** agree.

quarrelsome choleric, contentious, cross, ill-tempered, irascible, irritable, peevish, petulant, pugnacious, querulous.

Ant. affable.

quarter (1) district, locality, place, position, region, spot, station, territory; **(2)** mercy, pity.

quarters abode, barracks, cantonment, dwelling, habitation, lodging, post, residence, station.

quash (1) beat, crush, extinguish, quell, repress, subdue, suppress; **(2)** (*Law*) annul, cancel, nullify, overthrow.

queer abnormal, curious, droll, eccentric, extraordinary, odd, peculiar, quaint, singular, strange, unconventional, unique, unusual, weird.

Ant. normal.

quell (1) conquer, crush, defeat, extinguish, overcome, quash, stifle, subdue, suppress; **(2)** allay, alleviate, calm, compose, deaden, dull, mitigate, pacify.

Ant. of **(2)** arouse, excite.

quench (1) check, destroy, end, extinguish, stifle, suppress; **(2)** allay, cool, slake.

Ant. of **(1)** ignite; of **(2)** excite.

querulous carping, complaining, cross, discontented, dissatisfied, fault-finding, murmuring, peevish, petulant, testy, whining.

Ant. contented.

query (1) *v.* ask, inquire, question; **(2)** challenge, dispute, doubt; **(3)** *n.* inquiry, quesion.

question (1) *v.* ask, catechise, examine, inquire, interrogate, investigate; **(2)** challenge, controvert, dispute, doubt, query; **(3)** *n.* examination, inquiry,

interrogation, investigation;
(4) controversy, dispute,
doubt, query; (5) motion,
point, subject, theme, topic.
Ant. of (1) answer; of (2)
agree.

questionable controvertible,
debatable, disputable, doubtful, problematical, suspicious,
uncertain.
Ant certain.

quibble (1) n. cavil, equivocation, evasion, pretence, prevarication, quirk, shift, subterfuge,
subtlety; (2) v. cavil, equivocate, evade, pretend, prevaricate, shift.
Ant. of (1) truth.

quick (1) active, agile, alert,
animated, brisk, fast, fleet,
lively, nimble, rapid, speedy,
sprightly; (2) adroit, clever,
discerning, intelligent, sharp,
shrewd, skilful, smart; (3)
abrupt, curt, excitable, hasty,
impatient, irascible, irritable,
passionate, petulant, testy,
touchy; (4) alive, animate,
living.
Ant. of (1) slow; of (2) stupid;
of (3) patient; of (4) dead.

quicken (1) accelerate, expedite, hasten, hurry, speed; (2)
animate, excite, refresh, reinvigorate, resuscitate, revive,
rouse, stimulate, vivify.
Ant. of (1) delay, retard; of
(2) deaden.

quickly fast, immediately,
posthaste, promptly, quick,
rapidly, speedily, swiftly.
Ant. slowly.

quiescent calm, dormant,
motionless, peaceful, placid,
quiet, serene, silent, smooth,
still, tranquil, unagitated, undisturbed.
Ant. agitated.

quiet (1) calm, contented,

gentle, mild, motionless
pacific, peaceful, placid, serene,
silent, smooth, tranquil; (2)
isolated, retired, secluded,
sequestered, unfrequented; (3)
n. calmness, ease, peace, quietness, repose, rest, serenity,
silence, stillness, tranquillity;
(4) v. allay, alleviate, appease,
assuage, calm, compose, hush,
lull, mitigate, soothe, still,
stop, tranquillise.
Ant. of (1) noisy; of (2)
crowded; of (3) disturbance;
of (4) disturb.

quit (1) abandon, depart, desert, forsake, go, leave, renounce, resign, retire, surrender, withdraw; (2) absolve, acquit, clear, deliver, free, liberate, release, relieve; (3) act,
believe, discharge, perform; (4)
a. absolved, acquitted, clear,
discharged, free, released.
Ant. of (1) remain; of (2)
confine.

quite completely, considerably,
entirely, largely, perfectly,
totally, wholly.

quiver (1) v. agitate, quake,
shake, shiver, shudder, tremble, vibrate; (2) n. shake,
shiver, shudder, tremble, tremor, vibration.

quixotic fanciful, fantastical,
imaginary, impracticable, mad,
romantic, unrealistic, visionary, wild.
Ant. realistic.

quiz n. conundrum, enigma,
hoax, jest, joke, puzzle,
riddle.

quota allocation, assignment,
part, portion, proportion,
share.

quotation (1) (Comm.) estimate, figure, price, rate; (2)
(Lit.) citation, extract, selection.

R

rabble canaille, crowd, herd, horde, mob, populace, riff-raff, scum.

Ant. aristocracy.

rabid (1) frantic, furious, infuriated, mad, raging, wild; (2) bigoted, intolerant, narrow-minded, irrational.

race (A) (1) *n.* chase, competition, contest, course, pursuit, test, trial; (2) *v.* career, compete, contest, course, hasten, hurry, run, speed.

race (B) breed, clan, family, house, issue, kin, kindred, line, lineage, nation, offspring, people, progeny, stock, tribe.

rack (1) *v.* force, strain, stretch, wrench; (2) agonise, distress, excruciate, harass, torment, torture; (3) *n.* agony, anguish, pain, pang, torment, torture.

Ant. of (2) soothe.

racket clamour, din, disturbance, hubbub, noise, row, uproar, outcry.

Ant. peace.

racy (1) animated, lively, piquant, pungent; (2) (*Fig.*) rich, smart, spicy, spirited, stimulating, vigorous.

Ant. flat, uninteresting.

radiance brightness, brilliance, effulgence, glare, glitter, lustre, resplendence, shine.

radiant beaming, bright, brilliant, effulgent, glittering, glorious, luminous, lustrous, resplendent, shining, sparkling.

Ant. dull.

radiate emanate, emit, gleam, glitter, shine, spread.

radical (1) *a.* basic, constitutional, deep-seated, essential, fundamental, innate, native, natural, organic, original, primitive; (2) complete, entire, excessive, extreme, fanatical, thorough, violent; (3) *n.* Liberal, reformer.

Ant. of (1) superficial.

rage (1) *n.* anger, excitement, frenzy, fury, madness, mania, passion, raving, vehemence, wrath; (2) craze, enthusiasm, fashion, mode, rapture, vogue; (3) *v.* chafe, fret, fume, rave, storm.

Ant. of (1) calmness.

ragged (1) contemptible, mean, poor, shabby; (2) jagged, rent, rough, rugged, shaggy, tattered, torn, uneven.

Ant. of (1) well-dressed; of (2) neat.

raid *n.* attack, foray, incursion, inroad, invasion, irruption, onset, seizure.

rail *v.* abuse, censure, inveigh, scoff, scold, sneer, upbraid.

Ant. praise.

raillery banter, irony, joke, pleasantry, ridicule, satire.

Ant. geniality.

raiment apparel, array, attire, costume, dress, garb, garments.

raise (1) advance, elevate, erect, exalt, heave, hoist, lift, rear, uplift; (2) aggravate, augment, enhance, enlarge, heighten, increase, intensify; (3) arouse, awaken, evoke, stir; (4) assemble, collect, gather, get, levy, obtain; (5) cause, cultivate, engender, grow, originate.

Ant. of (1) lower.

rake (A) *v.* collect, gather, grope, ransack, scour, scrape, search.

Ant. disperse.

rake (B) *n*. debauchee, libertine, profligate, roué.

ramble (1) *v*. amble, range, roam, rove, saunter, straggle, stray, stroll, walk, wander; (2) *n*. excursion, roaming, roving, stroll, tour, trip, walk.

rambling desultory, discursive, incoherent, irregular.
Ant. coherent, direct.

ramification branch, divarication, division, forking, offshoot, sub-division.

ramify branch, divaricate, divide, separate.
Ant. unite.

rampant (1) excessive, exuberant, wanton; (2) aggressive, dominant, headstrong, impetuous, unbridled, uncontrollable, unrestrained, vehement, violent; (3) (*Her.*) erect, standing, upright.
Ant. of (1) and (2) restrained.

rampart barricade, breastwork, bulwark, defence, embankment, fence, fort, fortification, guard, security, stronghold.

rancid fetid, foul, fusty, musty, rank, sour, strong-smelling, tainted.
Ant. fresh.

rancorous bitter, implacable, malevolent, malicious, malign, malignant, resentful, spiteful, vindictive, virulent.
Ant. charitable.

rancour animosity, animus, antipathy, bitterness, enmity, hate, hatred, ill-will, malevolence, malice, malignity, resentment, spite, venom.
Ant. benevolence.

random aimless, casual, chance, fortuitous, guess, haphazard, stray.
Ant. definite, specific.

range (1) *n*. file, line, rank, row,

tier; (2) amplitude, compass, extent, latitude, reach, scope; (3) class, kind, order, sort; (4) excursion, expedition, ramble; (5) *v*. arrange, class, dispose, rank; (6) ramble, roam, rove, straggle, stray, stroll, wander.

rank (A) (1) *n*. line, range, row, tier; (2) class, degree, dignity, division, grade, nobility, order, quality, standing, station; (3) *v*. arrange, class, classify, sort.

rank (B) (1) *a*. disgusting, fetid, foul, fusty, musty, noxious, offensive, pungent, putrid, strong-smelling; (2) excessive, extravagant, gross, rampant, sheer, utter; (3) abundant, exuberant, luxuriant, productive, strong-growing, vigorous.

ransack (1) explore, rummage, search; (2) loot, pillage, plunder, ravage, rifle.

ransom (1) *n*. deliverance, liberation, redemption, release; (2) *v*. deliver, liberate, redeem, release.

rapacious avaricious, extortionate, grasping, greedy, plundering, predatory, preying, ravenous, voracious.
Ant. generous.

rapid expeditious, fast, fleet, hasty, hurried, quick, speedy, swift.
Ant. slow, tardy.

rapine depredation, loot, pillage, plunder, robbery, spoliation.
Ant. restoration.

rapt charmed, delighted, enraptured, entranced, fascinated, spell-bound.

rapture beatification, beatitude, bliss, delight, ecstasy, enthusiasm, exaltation, felicity, happiness, joy, ravishment, spell, transport.

Ant. misery.

rare (1) exceptional, infrequent, singular, strange, uncommon, unusual; (2) admirable, choice, excellent, fine, incomparable; (3) half-cooked, underdone.

Ant. of (1) common.

rarity infrequency, scarcity, uncommonness.

Ant. frequency.

rascal blackguard, caitiff, knave, miscreant, rapscallion, rogue, scamp, scoundrel, villain, wretch.

rash adventurous, audacious, careless, foolhardy, headlong, headstrong, heedless, impetuous, impulsive, incautious, precipitate, quick, rapid, reckless, thoughtless, unguarded, unwary, venturesome.

Ant. cautious, prudent.

rashness carelessness, foolhardiness, hastiness, heedlessness, inconsideration, indiscretion, precipitation, recklessness, temerity, thoughtlessness.

Ant. caution, prudence.

rate (A) (1) n. assessment, charge, cost, duty, estimate, price, tax, value, worth; (2) degree, proportion, ratio, speed, standard; (3) v. appraise, assess, estimate, reckon, tax, value.

rate (B) berate, blame, censure, chide, rebuke, reprimand, reprove, scold.

ratify approve, bind, confirm, corroborate, endorse, establish, sanction, settle, validate.

Ant. invalidate.

ration (1) n. allowance, food, portion, share; (2) v. apportion, deal, distribute, dole, restrict.

rational (1) enlightened, intelligent, lucid, sane, sensible,

sound, wise; (2) discreet, equitable, fair, judicious, moderate, reasonable.

Ant. of (1) insane, irrational; of (2) unreasonable.

raucous harsh, hoarse, husky, rough.

Ant. smooth.

ravage (1) v. despoil, destroy, devastate, loot, pillage, plunder, ransack, ruin, sack, spoil; (2) n. destruction, devastation, havoc, pillage, plunder, rapine, ruin, spoliation, waste.

Ant. of (1) restore.

ravenous devouring, ferocious, gluttonous, greedy, insatiable, predatory, rapacious, voracious.

Ant. satisfied.

ravine defile, gorge, gully, pass.

raving delirious, frantic, frenzied, furious, mad, raging.

Ant. sane.

ravish (1) captivate, charm, delight, enchant, enrapture, entrance, transport; (2) abuse, debauch, deflower, outrage, rape, violate.

Ant. of (1) displease.

raw (1) uncooked, undressed, unprepared; (2) ignorant, inexperienced, undisciplined, unpractised, unskilled, untried; (3) crude, green, immature, unrefined, unripe; (4) bleak, chilly, cold, damp, piercing, wet; (5) bare, naked, sensitive, sore, tender.

raze (1) demolish, destroy, extirpate, level, overthrow, prostrate, ruin, subvert; (2) efface, erase, obliterate.

Ant. of (1) rebuild; of (2) restore.

reach (1) v. arrive, attain, get, hit, obtain; (2) extend, stretch, touch; (3) n. capacity, compass, distance, extent, extension, grasp, power, range, spread.

Ant. of (1) miss.

readily cheerfully, easily, promptly, quickly, willingly.

Ant. unwillingly.

ready (1) adroit, apt, clever, dexterous, expert, handy, prompt, quick, sharp, skilful, smart; (2) disposed, inclined, keen, willing; (3) convenient, handy, near; (4) arranged, completed, prepared.

Ant. of (1) inexpert; of (2) unwilling; of (3) distant; of (4) unprepared.

real absolute, actual, authentic, certain, essential, genuine, intrinsic, positive, sincere, veritable.

Ant. false.

realise (1) comprehend, conceive, grasp, imagine, understand; (2) accomplish, acquire, complete, effect, gain, get, perform.

Ant. of (1) misunderstand; of (2) commence.

reality actuality, certainty, fact, truth, verity.

Ant. falsehood, imagination.

really absolutely, actually, certainly, indeed, positively, truly, undoubtedly, verily.

reap acquire, gather, get, harvest, obtain.

Ant. sow.

rear (A) (1) v. breed, educate, foster, nurse, nurture, raise, train; (2) elevate, hoist, lift, raise, rise, rouse; (3) build, construct, erect.

Ant. of (2) lower; of (3) demolish.

rear (B) n. back, end, rearguard, tail.

Ant. front, vanguard.

reason (1) n. aim, cause, design, end, motive, object,

purpose; (2) argument, excuse, explanation, exposition, ground, justification, proof; (3) judgment, intellect, mind, sense, understanding; (4) moderation, propriety, reasonableness, wisdom; (5) v. argue, conclude, debate, deduce, infer, think.

reasonable (1) equitable, fair, fit, honest, just, logical, proper, right; (2) intelligent, judicious, rational, sane, sensible, sober, sound, wise; (3) moderate, tolerable.

Ant. of (2) irrational; of (3) unreasonable.

rebate (*Comm.*) allowance, bonus, deduction, discount, reduction.

Ant. surcharge.

rebel (1) n. insurgent, mutineer, revolutionary; (2) a. insubordinate, insurgent, mutinous, rebellious; (3) v. revolt.

Ant. of (1) loyalist; of (2) law-abiding, loyal.

rebellious defiant, disloyal, disobedient, insubordinate, intractable, mutinous, rebel, refractory, seditious.

Ant. loyal, obedient.

rebuff (1) v. check, chide, discourage, reject, reprimand, resist, snub; (2) n. check, discouragement, opposition, refusal, rejection, repulse, resistance, snub.

Ant. of (1) encourage; of (2) approval.

rebuke (1) v. admonish, blame, censure, chide, remonstrate, reprehend, reprimand, reprove, scold, upbraid; 2) n. admonition, blame, censure, remonstrance, reprimand, reproach, reproof, reproval.

Ant. praise.

recall (1) recollect, remember;

(2) abjure, annul, cancel, countermand, nullify, rescind, retract, revoke.

Ant. of (1) forget; of (2) re-affirm.

recant abjure, disavow, disclaim, disown, recall, repudiate, retract, revoke.

Ant. affirm.

recapitulate epitomise, reiterate, repeat, restate, review, summarise.

recede desist, ebb, retire, retreat, return, withdraw.

Ant. advance.

receive (1) accept, acquire, derive, get, obtain; (2) admit, entertain, greet, welcome.

Ant. of (1) give; of (2) exclude.

recent fresh, late, latter, modern, new, novel.

Ant. old.

reception (1) acceptance, admission, receipt, receiving; (2) entertainment, levee, party, welcome.

Ant. (1) rejection.

recess (1) cavity, corner, niche, nook, privacy, retreat, seclusion; (2) holiday, intermission, interval, respite, vacation.

Ant. of (1) protrusion; of (2) work-time.

reciprocal alternate, correlative, interchangeable, mutual.

Ant. individual.

recital account, description, detail, narrative, recitation, rehearsal, relation, repetition, statement, story, tale.

recite describe, detail, enumerate, narrate, recapitulate, recount, rehearse, relate, repeat, tell.

reckless careless, foolhardy, hare-brained, headlong, heedless, imprudent, inattentive, incautious, indiscreet, mind-less, negligent, over-venture-some, rash, regardless, thoughtless, wild.

Ant. careful, heedful.

reckon (1) calculate, compute, count, enumerate, number; (2) consider, esteem, estimate, evaluate, infer, judge, regard; (3) imagine, suppose, think.

Ant. of (1) miscalculate.

reckoning (1) calculation, computation, counting, estimate; (2) account, bill, charge, score, settlement.

reclaim (1) recapture, recover, regain, reinstate, restore; (2) amend, correct, improve, reform.

Ant. of (1) renounce; of (2) impair.

recline lean, lie, repose, rest.

Ant. sit, stand.

recluse anchoret, anchorite, ascetic, eremite, hermit, monk, solitary.

recognise (1) acknowledge, admit, allow, avow, concede, confess, own; (2) identify, know, notice, recollect, remember; (3) greet, salute.

Ant. of (1) disavow; of (2) forget; of (3) ignore.

recoil (1) react, rebound, resile, retire, retreat, withdraw; (2) falter, flinch, quail, shrink.

Ant. advance.

recollect recall, remember.

Ant. forget.

recollection memory, remembrance, reminiscence.

Ant. forgetfulness.

recommend advise, approve, commend, counsel, praise.

Ant. disparage.

recommendation approbation, approval, commendation, praise.

Ant. disapproval.

recompense (1) v. compensate, indemnify, redeem, redress, reimburse, remunerate, repay, requite, reward, satisfy; (2) *n.* amends, compensation, indemnification, indemnity, remuneration, repayment, requital, reward, satisfaction.

reconcilable (1) appeasable, forgiving, placable; (2) compatible, congruous, consistent.
   Ant. of (2) inconsistent.

reconcile (1) appease, conciliate, pacify, propitiate, reunite; (2) adjust, compose, harmonise, settle.
   Ant. of (1) anger.

recondite abstruse, concealed, dark, deep, hidden, mystical, obscure, occult, profound, secret.
   Ant. open, simple, superficial.

record (1) *v.* chronicle, enrol, enter, note, register; (2) *n.* account, chronicle, entry, memoir, memorandum, memorial, minute, register; (3) annals, archives; (4) testimony, trace, witness.
   Ant. of (1) disregard.

recount describe, entail, enumerate, narrate, recite, relate, repeat, tell.

recover reclaim, regain, repair, restore, retrieve; (2) (*Med.*) cure, heal, mend, recuperate, revive.
   Ant. of (2) worsen.

recreant (1) *a.* apostate, backsliding, cowardly, craven, dastardly, faint-hearted, false, perfidious, treacherous, unfaithful, untrue; (2) *n.* apostate, coward, craven, dastard, renegade, traitor.
   Ant. of (1) bold, loyal; of (2) loyalist.

recreation amusement, diversion, entertainment, exercise, pastime, play, relief, sport.

   Ant. work.

recreative amusing, diverting, entertaining, relieving.

recruit (1) *v.* recover, refresh, regain, reinforce, renew, replenish, restore, revive, supply; (2) *n.* beginner, helper, learner, novice, tyro.

rectify (1) adjust, amend, correct, emend, improve, mend, redress, reform; (2) (*Chem.*) purify, refine.
   Ant. of (1) falsify.

rectitude equity, goodness, justice, honesty, integrity, righteousness, uprightness, virtue.
   Ant. turpitude.

recumbent lying, prone, prostrate, reclining.
   Ant. erect.

recur reappear, return, revert.

redeem (1) recompense, recover, regain, re-purchase; (2) deliver, free, liberate, ransom, rescue, save; (3) atone, compensate, discharge, fulfil, perform, satisfy.
   Ant. of (2) abandon.

redemption (1) recovery, repurchase; (2) deliverance, liberation, ransom, rescue, release, salvation; (3) discharge, fulfilment, performance.

redolent aromatic, fragrant, odorous, scented, sweet-smelling.
   Ant. malodorous.

redoubtable awful, dreadful, fearful, terrible, valiant.

redound conduce, contribute, result, tend.

redress (1) *v.* adjust, amend, rectify, reform, remedy, repair; (2) compensate, ease, relieve; (3) *n.* amends, atonement, remedy, reparation, satisfaction; (4) compensation, ease, relief.

Ant. of (1) destroy; of (3) damage.

reduce (1) abate, abridge, contract, curtail, decrease, diminish, lessen, shorten; (2) debase, degrade, depress, impair, lower, weaken; (3) conquer, master, overpower, subdue, vanquish; (4) impoverish, ruin.

Ant. of (1) augment; of (2) exalt; of (3) defend.

redundant (1) copious, excessive, overflowing, superabundant, su₊erfluous, unnecessaɪy; (2) diffuse, prolix, verbose.

Ant. of (1) deficient; of (2) laconic.

re-establish reinstate, renew, replace, restore.

reel falter, spin, stagger, waver, whirl.

refer (1) commit, consign, deliver, direct; (2) advert, allude, ascribe, attribute, hint; (3) apply, belong, pertain, point, relate.

referee (1) n. arbiter, arbitrator, judge, umpire; (2) v. arbitrate, judge, umpire.

Ant. of (1) player.

reference (1) allusion, citation, intimation, quotation, remark; (2) appeal, concern, regard, relation, respect; (3) testimonial.

refine (1) clarify, cleanse, purify; (2) cultivate, improve, polish.

refinement (1) clarification, purification; (2) civilisation, civility, courtesy, courtliness, culture, elegance, gentility, good-breeding, polish, politeness, style.

Ant. of (2) discourtesy, rudeness.

reflect (1) image, imitate, mirror; (2) cogitate, consider, contemplate, deliberate, meditate, muse, ponder, think, wonder.

reflection (1) cogitation, consideration, contemplation, deliberation, meditation, musing, opinion, rumination, thinking, thought;(2) aspersion, censure, imputation, reproach, slur; (3) counterpart, image.

Ant. of (2) praise.

reflective cogitating, contemplative, meditative, pensive, pondering, reasoning, thoughtful.

Ant. thoughtless.

reform (1) v. ameliorate, amend, better, correct, emend, improve, reclaim, reconstitute, reconstruct, rectify, regenerate, remodel, reorganise, repair, restore; (2) n. amelioration, amendment, betterment, correction, improvement.

Ant. of (1) worsen; of (2) deterioration.

refractory cantankerous, contentious, contumacious, disobedient, disputatious, headstrong, intractable, obstinate, perverse, stubborn, uncontrollable, unmanageable, unruly.

Ant. obedient.

refrain (A) v. abstain, cease desist, forbear, withhold.

Ant. persist.

refrain (B) (*Mus.*) burden, chorus, song.

refresh (1) renew, renovate, repair, restore; (2) cheer, cool, enliven, freshen, reanimate, reinvigorate, revive, stimulate.

Ant. of (2) oppress, fatigue.

refuge asylum, harbour, haven, protection, retreat, sanctuary, shelter.

refulgent bright, brilliant,

lustrous, radiant, resplendent, shining.

Ant. dark.

refund (1) v. reimburse, repay, restore, return; (2) n. reimbursement, repayment.

refuse (A) v. decline, deny, exclude, reject, repel, repudiate, withhold.

Ant. accept.

refuse (B) n. dregs, dross, garbage, lees, rubbish, scum, sediment, trash, waste.

refute confute, disprove, overthrow, repel, silence.

Ant. prove, substantiate.

regain recover, re-obtain, repossess, retrieve.

Ant. lose.

regale delight, entertain, feast, gratify, refresh.

regard (1) v. behold, eye, mark, notice, observe, remark, watch; (2) attend, heed, mind; (3) admire, esteem, honour, respect, reverence, value; (4) account, believe, consider, deem, estimate, hold, imagine, suppose, treat; (5) n. affection, attachment, attention, care, concern, deference, esteem, honour, love, respect, sympathy; (6) account, esteem, note, reputation, repute; (7) detail, matter, particular, point, reference.

regardful attentive, careful, mindful, observant, thoughtful.

Ant. careless.

regardless disregarding, heedless, inattentive, inconsiderate, indifferent, neglectful, negligent, unconcerned, unmindful.

Ant. mindful.

regenerate (1) change, renew, renovate, reproduce, restore; (2) convert, sanctify.

region (1) country, district, division, locality, province, quarter, territory, tract; (2) neighbourhood, part, sphere, vicinity.

register (1) n. annals, archives, catalogue, chronicle, ledger, list, memorandum, record, roll, roster, schedule; (2) v. catalogue, chronicle, enrol, enter, list, record.

regret (1) v. bemoan, bewail, deplore, grieve, lament, mourn, repent, rue; (2) n. compunction, contrition, grief, lamentation, penitence, remorse, repentance.

Ant. of (1) rejoice; of (2) pleasure.

regular (1) constant, established, fixed, habitual, stated, steady, uniform; (2) customary, formal, methodical, normal, orderly, punctual, systematic, unvarying, usual.

Ant. irregular.

regulate adjust, arrange, conduct, control, direct, fit, govern, guide, manage, order, rule, settle, systematise.

Ant. disarrange, disorder.

regulation adjustment, arrangement, control, direction, law, management, order, precept.

rehabilitate reconstitute, reconstruct, re-establish, reinstate, reinvigorate, renew, renovate, restore.

rehearse (1) delineate, depict, describe, detail, enumerate, narrate, recount, relate, tell; (2) (*Theat.*) act, practise, recite, repeat, train.

Ant. of (2) extemporise.

reign (1) v. administer, command, govern, influence, predominate, prevail, rule; (2) n. control, dominion, empire, influence, power, rule, sovereignty, sway.

Ant. of (1) obey.

reimburse compensate, indemnify, refund, repay, restore, return.

rein *v.* bridle, check, control, curb, hold, restrain.

reinforce augment, fortify, strengthen.

Ant. weaken.

reject decline, deny, despise, discard, eliminate, exclude, refuse, renounce, repel, repudiate, spurn.

Ant. accept.

rejoice cheer, delight, enliven, exult, gladden, glory, please, revel, triumph.

Ant. lament.

relate (1) chronicle, describe, detail, narrate, recite, recount, report, tell; (2) concern, refer.

Ant. conceal.

relation (1) account, description, detail, narration, recital, report, story, tale; (2) bearing, connection, interdependence, reference, regard; (3) affinity, kindred, kinsman, relationship, relative.

relative (1) *n.* connection, kinsman, relation; (2) *a.* comparative, definite, particular, pertinent, relevant.

Ant. of (1) stranger.

relax (1) abate, loosen, mitigate, slacken; (2) debilitate, diminish, enfeeble, lessen, reduce, weaken; (3) ease, rest, soften, unbend.

release (1) *v.* deliver, discharge, disengage, emancipate, extricate, free, liberate, loose, unfasten, unloose; (2) absolve, acquit, dispense, exempt, exonerate; (3) *n.* delivery, discharge, emancipation, freedom, liberation; (4) absolution,

acquittance, dispensation, exemption, exoneration.

Ant. of (1) fasten; of (3) imprisonment.

relentless cruel, hard, harsh, implacable, inexorable, merciless, pitiless, remorseless, unforgiving, unrelenting.

Ant. merciful.

relevant applicable, apposite, appropriate, apt, fitting, germane, pertinent, proper, suited.

Ant. irrelevant.

reliable dependable, honest, true, trustworthy, trusty.

Ant. unreliable.

reliance assurance, confidence, dependence, trust.

Ant. distrust.

relief aid, alleviation, assistance, comfort, help, mitigation, remedy, succour, support, sustenance.

Ant. distress.

relieve (1) aid, alleviate, assist, assuage, comfort, diminish, ease, help, soothe, succour, support, sustain; (2) free, redress, remedy.

Ant. of (1) increase.

religious devotional, devout, divine, faithful, godly, holy, pious, pure, reverent, righteous, sacred.

Ant. irreligious.

relinquish abandon, abdicate, cede, desert, forsake, leave, quit, renounce, resign, surrender, yield.

Ant. maintain.

relish (1) *v.* appreciate, enjoy, like, prefer, savour, taste; (2) *n.* appetite, appreciation, enjoyment, fondness, gusto, liking, partiality, zest; (3) appetiser, flavour, savour, seasoning, taste.

reluctance aversion, backwardness, disinclination, dislike, loathing, repugnance, unwillingness.

Ant. willingness.

reluctant averse, backward, disinclined, hesitant, indisposed, loath, unwilling.

Ant. keen, willing.

rely confide, depend, lean, reckon, repose, trust.

Ant. distrust.

remain abide, continue, delay, dwell, endure, last, rest, stay, survive, tarry, wait.

Ant. leave.

remainder balance, excess, leavings, remains, remnant, residue, residuum, rest, surplus.

Ant. shortage.

remark (1) v. heed, note, notice, observe, perceive, regard; (2) comment, express, observe, say, state; (3) n. attention, heed, notice, observation, regard; (4) assertion, comment, declaration, statement, utterance.

Ant. of (1) ignore; of (3) disregard; of (4) silence.

remarkable conspicuous, distinguished, extraordinary, famous, notable, noteworthy, pre-eminent, prominent, rare, strange, uncommon, unusual, wonderful.

Ant. common, ordinary.

remedy (1) n. antidote, counteractive, cure, medicament, medicine, relief, restorative, specific, treatment; (2) aid, assistance, help, redress; (3) v. cure, heal, help, palliate, relieve, restore, soothe; (4) aid, assist, redress, repair.

Ant. of (1) sickness.

remembrance (1) memory, mind, recollection, regard, reminiscence, thought; (2) keepsake, memento, memorial,

monument, souvenir, token.

Ant. of (1) forgetfulness.

reminiscence memory, recollection, remembrance.

remiss careless, dilatory, heedless, inattentive, indifferent, lax, neglectful, negligent, regardless, slack, slothful, slow, tardy, thoughtless, unmindful.

Ant. careful.

remission (1) absolution, acquittal, excuse, exoneration, forgiveness, indulgence, pardon; (2) abatement, decrease, diminution, lessening, moderation, rest, stoppage, suspense.

Ant. of (1) condemnation; of (2) increase.

remit (1) forward, send, transmit; (2) absolve, excuse, forgive, overlook, pardon; (3) abate, decrease, diminish, moderate, slacken; (4) replace, restore, return.

Ant. of (1) keep; of (2) punish; of (3) increase.

remnant balance, bit, fragment, remainder, remains, piece, residue, rest, scrap, shred, trace.

remorse compunction, contrition, penitence, regret, repentance, self-reproach, sorrow.

Ant. impenitence.

remorseless cruel, hard, harsh, implacable, inexorable, merciless, pitiless, relentless, ruthless, savage, uncompassionate, unmerciful, unrelenting.

Ant. merciful.

remote (1) far, distant, lonely, isolated, out-of-the-way, secluded; (2) alien, foreign, unconnected, unrelated; (3) faint, slight, small, inconsiderable.

Ant. of (1) close; of (2) related; of (3) considerable.

removal abstraction, dislodgement, dismissal, displacement, ejection, elimination, expulsion, extraction, relegation, transfer, transport, withdrawal.

remove (1) abstract, carry, dislodge, dismiss, displace, eject, eliminate, expel, extract, move, relegate, transfer, transport, withdraw; (2) (*Fig.*) assassinate, kill, murder.

Ant. of (1) retain.

remunerate compensate, indemnify, pay, recompense, reimburse, repay, requite, reward.

Ant. injure.

remuneration compensation, indemnity, pay, payment, recompense, reimbursement, reparation, repayment, reward, salary, wages.

Ant. injury.

remunerative gainful, lucrative, paying, profitable, recompensing, rewarding.

Ant. unremunerative.

rend break, burst, cleave, crack, divide, fracture, lacerate, rip, rive, rupture, separate, sever, split, sunder, tear.

Ant. join.

render (1) assign, contribute, deliver, furnish, give, pay, present, restore, return, supply, yield; (2) cause, do, make, perform; (3) construe, interpret, translate.

Ant. of (1) retain.

renegade apostate, backslider, coward, deserter, recreant, traitor, vagabond, wretch.

Ant. loyalist.

renew mend, recommence, recreate, re-establish, refit, regenerate, renovate, repair, repeat, replenish, restock, restore, transform.

renounce abandon, abdicate, decline, deny, disclaim, disown, forego, forsake, forswear, leave, quit, reject, relinquish, repudiate, resign.

Ant. accept.

renovate reconstitute, recreate, reform, renew, repair, restore.

renown celebrity, distinction, eminence, fame, glory, honour, note, reputation, repute.

Ant. dishonour.

renowned celebrated, distinguished, eminent, famed, famous, illustrious, noted.

Ant. unknown.

repair (1) fix, mend, patch, recover, redress, renew, renovate, restore, retrieve; (2) go, resort.

Ant. of (1) destroy.

reparable recoverable, restorable, retrievable.

Ant. irreparable.

reparation amends, atonement, compensation, indemnity, recompense, renewal, repair, restitution, satisfaction.

Ant. destruction.

repay (1) compensate, recompense, refund, reimburse, remunerate, requite, restore, return, reward; (2) avenge, retaliate, revenge.

repeal (1) *v.* abolish, abrogate, annul, cancel, recall, rescind, reverse, revoke; (2) *n.* abolition, abrogation, annulment, cancellation, rescinding, revocation.

Ant. of (1) confirm.

repeat duplicate, echo, iterate, quote, recapitulate, recite, rehearse, reiterate, relate, renew, reproduce.

Ant. discontinue.

repel beat, check, confront,

decline, drive, oppose, parry, rebuff, refuse, reject, repulse, resist.

Ant. attract, submit.

repent atone, regret, relent, rue, sorrow.

Ant. rejoice.

repentance compunction, contrition, grief, penitence, regret, remorse, self-reproach, sorrow.

Ant. impenitence.

repercussion rebound, recoil, result, reverberation.

repetition (1) iteration, recital, rehearsal, reiteration, relation, renewal; (2) pleonasm, prolixity, redundancy, tautology, verbosity.

Ant. of (2) terseness.

repine complain, fret, grieve, grumble, murmur.

Ant. acquiesce, rejoice.

replace re-establish, refund, reinstate, repay, restore, substitute, supersede, supplant, supply.

Ant. remove.

replenish fill, furnish, provide, refill, restock, stock, supply.

Ant. empty.

replete abounding, charged, full, glutted, gorged, satiated, well-provided, well-stocked.

Ant. empty.

repletion glut, overfulness, satiety, superfluity, surfeit.

Ant. emptiness.

replica copy, duplicate, facsimile, reproduction.

Ant. original.

report (1) v. announce, broadcast, circulate, communicate, declare, describe, detail, mention, narrate, proclaim, publish, recite, record, relate, state, tell; (2) n. account, announcement, communication, declaration description detail, hear-

say, narrative, news, recital, rumour, story, tale, tidings; (3) detonation, discharge, explosion, noise, sound; (4) fame, reputation; repute, (5) minute, note, record, statement.

Ant. of (2) and (3) silence.

repose (1) v. lie, recline, relax, rest, sleep, slumber; (2) lodge, place, put, store; (3) n. ease, peace, quiet, quietness, relaxation, respite, rest, sleep, slumber, tranquillity.

Ant. of (1) rise; of (3) unrest, weariness.

repository depository, depot, emporium, magazine, storehouse, treasury.

reprehend admonish, blame, censure, chide, rebuke, reprimand, reproach, reprove, upbraid.

Ant. praise.

reprehension admonition, blame, censure, condemnation, rebuke, reprimand, reproach, reproof.

Ant. approval.

represent (1) delineate, denote, depict, describe, designate, exemplify, express, portray, reproduce; (2) exhibit, perform, show, stage.

representation (1) account, delineation, description, narration, narrative, relation, statement; (2) image, likeness, model, picture, portrait, resemblance; (3) exhibition, performance, play, show, sight, spectacle.

representative (1) n. agent, commissioner, delegate, depute, deputy, proxy; (2) a. symbolic, typical; (3) chosen, delegated, elected.

Ant. of (1) principal.

repress chasten, check, control, crush, curb, overcome, overpower, quell, restrain, stifle, subdue, suppress.

Ant. encourage, support.

reprimand (1) *v.* admonish, blame, censure, chide, rebuke, reprehend, reproach, reprove, upbraid; (2) *n.* admonition, blame, censure, rebuke, reprehension, reproach, reproof.

Ant. praise.

reproach (1) *v.* abuse, blame, censure, condemn, defame, discredit, disparage, rebuke, reprehend, reprimand, reprove, upbraid; (2) *n.* abuse, blame, censure, condemnation, contempt, disapproval, disgrace, dishonour, disrepute, ignominy, indignity, obloquy, odium, opprobrium, scorn, shame.

Ant. of (1) approve; of (2) approval.

reproachful abusive, censorious, condemnatory, contemptuous, discreditable, disgraceful, dishonourable, infamous, offensive, opprobrious, shameful, upbraiding, vile.

reprobate (1) *a.* abandoned, base, corrupt, depraved, dissolute, hardened, profligate, shameless, vile, wicked; (2) *n.* caitiff, knave, miscreant, outcast, villain, wretch.

Ant. of (1) moral.

reproof admonition, blame, censure, chiding, condemnation, rebuke, reprehension, reprimand, reproach, reproval, upbraiding.

Ant. approval.

reprove abuse, admonish, blame, censure, condemn, rebuke, reprehend, reprimand, upbraid.

Ant. approve.

repudiate abjure, deny, disavow, discard, disclaim, disown, reject, renounce.

Ant. avow, recognise.

repugnance abhorrence, antipathy, aversion, dislike, distaste, hatred, loathing, reluctance, revulsion.

Ant. liking, sympathy.

repugnant adverse, antagonistic, averse, distasteful, hostile, inimical, objectionable, offensive, opposed.

Ant. agreeable.

repulse (1) *v.* check, defeat, rebuff, refuse, reject, repel; (2) *n.* check, defeat, disappointment, failure, rebuff, refusal, rejection, repulsion.

Ant. of (1) advance.

repulsive disagreeable, disgusting, forbidding, hateful, loathsome, nauseating, odious, repellent, revolting, sickening, unpleasant.

Ant. agreeable, pleasant.

reputable creditable, estimable, excellent, good, honourable, respectable, worthy.

Ant. disreputable.

reputation character, credit, distinction, esteem, fame, honour, name, renown, repute, standing.

reputed accounted, considered, deemed, estimated, held, reckoned, regarded.

request (1) *v.* ask, beg, beseech, desire, entreat, petition, pray, solicit, supplicate; (2) *n.* asking, begging, desire, entreaty, petition, prayer, solicitation, suit, supplication.

Ant. of (1) deny.

require (1) desire, lack, need, want, wish; (2) ask, beg, beseech, direct, enjoin, order, request.

Ant. of (2) refuse.

requisite (1) *a.* essential, indispensable, necessary, needed, needful, required; (2) *n.* necessity, need, requirement.
  Ant. of (1) unnecessary.

requite (1) compensate, pay, recompense, reimburse, remunerate, repay, reward, satisfy; (2) punish, retaliate.
  Ant. of (1) dissatisfy; of (2) pardon.

rescind abrogate, annul, cancel, countermand, quash, recall, repeal, reverse, revoke.
  Ant. ratify.

rescue (1) *v.* deliver, extricate, free, liberate, recover, redeem, release, save; (2) *n.* deliverance, liberation, recovery, release, salvation.
  Ant. of (1) imperil.

research examination, exploration, inquiry, investigation, scrutiny, study.

resemblance analogy, counterpart, facsimile, image, likeness, portrait, representation, semblance, similarity.
  Ant. dissimilarity.

resentful angry, exasperated, incensed, indignant, irascible, irate, irritable, malicious, malignant, revengeful.
  Ant. kind.

resentment anger, fury, indignation, ire, irritation, rage, vexation, wrath.
  Ant. pleasure.

reserve (1) *v.* hold, husband, keep, retain, store, withhold; (2) *n.* backwardness, bashfulness, constraint, coyness, modesty, reservation, restraint, reticence, shyness; (3) stock, store, supply.
  Ant. of (1) waste; of (2) forwardness.

reserved (1) backward, bashful, cautious, cold, coy, demure,

modest, restrained, shy, taciturn, unsociable; (2) held, kept, retained.
  Ant. of (1) ardent, forward; of (2) unreserved.

reside abide, dwell, inhabit, live, lodge, settle, sojourn, stay.

residence abode, domicile, dwelling, habitation, home, house, lodging.

residue balance, excess, remainder, remnant, residuum, rest, surplus.

resign abandon, abdicate, cede, for(e)go, leave, quit, relinquish, renounce, submit, surrender, yield.
  Ant. hold, keep.

resignation (1) abandonment, abdication, relinquishment, renunciation, submission, surrender; (2) acquiescence, endurance, forbearance, fortitude, patience, sufferance.
  Ant. of (2) impatience.

resist assail, attack, check, confront, counteract, curb, hinder, oppose, repel, thwart, withstand.
  Ant. submit.

resolute bold, constant, determined, dogged, firm, fixed, inflexible, persevering, purposeful, set, steadfast, undaunted, unflinching, unshaken, unwavering.
  Ant. undecided, weak.

resolution (1) boldness, constancy, courage, determination, doggedness, earnestness, energy, firmness, fortitude, perseverance, purpose, resoluteness, sincerity, steadfastness; (2) declaration, determination, intention, motion, purpose, resolve.
  Ant. of (1) hesitation.

resolve (1) v. conclude, decide, determine, fix, intend, purpose, settle; **(2)** clear, disentangle, dispel, explain, solve, unravel; **(3)** dissolve, liquefy, melt; **(4)** n. decision, determination, intention, purpose, resolution.

Ant. of **(1)** hesitate.

resonant echoing, resounding, reverberating, ringing, sonorous.

resort (1) v. go, repair, retreat; **(2)** n. haunt, holiday-place, refuge, retreat; **(3)** recourse, reference.

Ant. of **(1)** leave.

resound (1) echo, re-echo, reverberate, ring; **(2)** celebrate, extol, praise.

resource appliance, contrivance, device, expedient, means, resort.

resources funds, means, money, riches, supplies, wealth.

respect (1) v. admire, adore, esteem, honour, love, regard, revere, reverence, value, venerate; **(2)** attend, heed, notice, refer, regard, relate; **(3)** n. admiration, approbation, esteem, estimation, honour, reverence, veneration.

Ant. of **(3)** disrespect.

respectable decent, estimable, good, honest, honourable, reputable, respected, worthy.

Ant. unworthy.

respectful civil, courteous, courtly, deferential, dutiful, obedient, polite, reverential, submissive, well-mannered.

Ant. impolite.

respite break, cessation, delay, interval, pause, postponement, recess, reprieve, rest, stay.

Ant. continuance.

resplendent beaming, bright, brilliant, effulgent, gleaming,

glittering, glorious, lustrous, radiant, shining.

Ant. dull.

respond (1) answer, rejoin, reply; **(2)** accord, agree, correspond, suit.

Ant. of **(1)** question; of **(2)** differ.

response answer, rejoinder, reply.

responsible accountable, amenable, answerable, liable.

Ant. irresponsible.

rest (A) (1) v. cease, desist, halt, pause, stand, stay, stop; **(2)** n. break, cessation, halt, intermission, interval, pause, stop.

Ant. of **(1)** continue.

rest (B) (1) v. lean, lie, recline, relax, repose, sleep, slumber; **(2)** n. peace, peacefulness, repose, sleep, slumber, tranquillity.

rest (C) balance, excess, remainder, residue, surplus.

restitution amends, compensation, indemnity, recompense, remuneration, reparation, repayment, return, satisfaction.

restive impatient, obstinate, recalcitrant, refractory, restless, stubborn, uneasy.

Ant. patient.

restless (1) agitated, anxious, disturbed, restive, sleepless; **(2)** changeable, inconstant, irresolute, unsettled, unstable, unsteady.

Ant. of **(1)** composed; of **(2)** steady.

restoration (1) reconstruction, recovery, renewal, renovation, revival; **(2)** re-establishment, reinstatement, replacement, return.

Ant. destruction.

restore (1) reconstruct, recover, renew, renovate, revive;

(2) re-establish, reinstate, replace, return.

restrain bridle, check, confine, constrain, curb, debar, hamper, hinder, hold, keep, prevent, repress, restrict, subdue.

Ant. free.

restraint bridle, check, coercion, compulsion, constraint, curb, hindrance, limitation, prevention, restriction, suppression.

Ant. freedom.

restrict bound, circumscribe, confine, limit.

restriction confinement, constraint, limitation, restraint.

Ant. freedom.

result (1) n. conclusion, consequence, decision, effect, event, issue, outcome, sequel, termination; (2) v. arise, end, ensue, eventuate, follow, terminate.

Ant. of (1) cause.

resume recommence, restart.

Ant. stop.

resuscitate quicken, reanimate, renew, resurrect, restore, revive, revivify.

Ant. annihilate.

retain (1) detain, hold, keep, preserve, reserve, withhold; (2) employ, engage, hire.

Ant. of (1) lose; of (2) dismiss.

retaliate avenge, repay, requite, retort, revenge.

Ant. ignore, pardon.

retaliation repayment, reprisal, requital, retribution, revenge.

Ant. forgiveness.

retard check, clog, defer, delay, detain, hinder, impede, obstruct, postpone.

Ant. advance.

reticent reserved, silent, still, taciturn, uncommunicative.

Ant. communicative.

retinue attendants, cortège,

escort, followers, suite, train.

retire (1) depart, leave, withdraw; (2) recede, remove, retreat, retrograde.

Ant. of (1) arrive; of (2) advance.

retirement loneliness, privacy, retreat, seclusion, solitude, withdrawal.

retiring bashful, coy, demure, diffident, modest, reserved, shy.

Ant. forward.

retort (1) v. answer, rejoin, reply, respond, retaliate, return; (2) n. answer, rejoinder, reply, response.

Ant. question.

retract abjure, cancel, disavow, recall, recant, renounce, repudiate, rescind, revoke, unsay, withdraw.

Ant. affirm.

retreat (1) n. departure, retirement, withdrawal; (2) asylum, den, haunt, privacy, resort, retirement, seclusion, shelter; (3) v. depart, leave, recede, retire, withdraw.

Ant. of (3) advance.

retrench (1) curtail, cut, decrease, diminish, lessen, reduce; (2) economise, husband, limit, save.

Ant. of (1) increase; of (2) waste.

retribution compensation, recompense, repayment, requital, retaliation, revenge, reward, vengeance.

Ant. pardon.

retrieve recall, recover, regain, repair, rescue, restore, save.

Ant. lose.

retrospect re-examination, review, survey.

return (1) v. recoil, recur, revert; (2) recompense, refund, remit, render, repay, requite.

restore; (3) convey, remit, send, transmit; (4) answer, communicate, reply, respond, retort, tell; (5) *n.* advantage, benefit, profit; (6) recompense, reimbursement, repayment, requital, reward; (7) account, list, report, summary.

reveal announce, communicate, disclose, divulge, impart, open, proclaim, publish, show, tell, uncover, unveil.
Ant. conceal.

revelry carousal, debauch, festivity, jollification, jollity, merry-making, orgy.

revenge (1) *v.* avenge, repay, requite, retaliate, vindicate; (2) *n.* reprisal, requital, retaliation, retribution, vengeance, vindictiveness.
Ant. of (2) forgiveness.

revengeful implacable, malevolent, malicious, malignant, merciless, resentful, spiteful, unforgiving, vindictive.
Ant. forgiving.

revenue income, proceeds, profits, receipts, rewards.
Ant. expenditure.

reverberate echo, re-echo, resound.

reverence (1) *n.* adoration, awe, homage, honour, respect, veneration, worship; (2) *v.* adore, honour, respect, venerate, worship.
Ant. disrespect.

reverent deferential, humble, meek, respectful, submissive.
Ant. disdainful.

reverie abstraction, daydreaming, inattention, musing, preoccupation, rhapsody.
Ant. attention.

reverse (1) *v.* invert, overset, overthrow, overturn, transpose, upset; (2) alter, annul, change, countermand, quash,

repeal, rescind, revoke; (3) *n.* back, contrary, opposite, rear; (4) affliction, check, defeat, hardship, misadventure, misfortune, mishap, trial; (5) *a.* contrary, converse, opposite.
Ant. of (1) restore; of (2) confirm; of (3) front.

revert recur, return, reverse.

review (1) *v.* reconsider, re-examine, revise; (2) criticise, discuss, inspect, judge, overlook, scrutinise, study; (3) (*Mil.*) inspect; (4) *n.* reconsideration, re-examination, retrospect, revision; (5) commentary, criticism, critique, judgment, revision, scrutiny, study, survey; (6) (*Mil.*) inspection, parade.

revile abuse, calumniate, defame, malign, reproach, slander, traduce, vilify.
Ant. praise.

revise alter, amend, change, correct, reconsider, re-examine, review.

revival awakening, quickening, reanimation, restoration, resuscitation, revivification.

revive animate, awaken, cheer, comfort, invigorate, quicken, recover, refresh, renew, renovate, restore, resuscitate, rouse.
Ant. depress, repress.

revoke abolish, abrogate, annul, cancel, countermand, invalidate, quash, recall, recant, repeal, repudiate, rescind, retract.
Ant. ratify.

revolt (1) *n.* defection, insurrection, mutiny, rebellion, sedition, uprising; (2) *v.* mutiny, rebel, resist, rise; (3) disgust, nauseate, offend, repel, shock.
Ant. of (1) loyalty; of (2) submit; of (3) please.

revolting abhorrent, abominable, disgusting, nauseating, nauseous, noisome, obnoxious, offensive, repulsive, shocking.
Ant. attractive.

revolve (1) circle, gyrate, rotate, turn, twist, wheel, whirl; (2) consider, meditate, ponder, ruminate, study.

revulsion (1) abhorrence, disgust, loathing, repugnance; (2) change, reaction, reversal, withdrawal.
Ant. of (1) liking.

reward (1) v. compensate, honour, pay, recompense, remunerate, requite; (2) n. bounty, compensation, honour, merit, premium, prize, remuneration, repayment, requital; (3) desert, punishment, requital, retribution.
Ant. of (1) injure.

ribald base, bawdy, coarse, filthy, gross, indecent, mean, obscene, smutty, vile, vulgar.
Ant. pure.

rich (1) affluent, moneyed, opulent, wealthy; (2) costly, gorgeous, precious, sumptuous, superb, valuable; (3) abounding, abundant, ample, copious, fertile, fruitful, full, luxurious, plenteous, plentiful, productive; (4) delicious, luscious, savoury, sweet, tasty; (5) bright, gay, vivid.
Ant. of (1) poor; of (2) cheap; of (3) barren; of (4) insipid; of (5) dull.

riches abundance, affluence, fortune, opulence, plenty, richness, wealth.
Ant. poverty.

rickety broken, imperfect, insecure, shaky, tottering, unsteady, weak.
Ant. steady, strong.

riddance deliverance, freedom, release, relief.

riddle (A) conundrum, enigma, problem, puzzle, rebus.

riddle (B) (1) n. sieve, strainer; (2) v. perforate, pierce.

ridicule (1) n. banter, chaff, derision, gibe, irony, jeer, mockery, raillery, sarcasm, satire, sneer; (2) v. banter, chaff, deride, jeer, mock, satirise, scoff, sneer, taunt.
Ant. of (2) humour.

ridiculous absurd, comical, farcical, funny, laughable, ludicrous, nonsensical, stupid.
Ant. sensible.

rife common, frequent, general, prevailing, prevalent, widespread.
Ant. uncommon.

rifle v. despoil, pillage, plunder, ransack, rob, strip.

rift breach, chink, cleft, crack, cranny, crevice, fissure, fracture, gap, opening.

right (1) a. equitable, good, honest, just, lawful, true, upright; (2) becoming, fit, convenient, proper, seemly, suitable; (3) accurate, correct, genuine, sound; (4) direct, straight; (5) n. equity, goodness, integrity, justice, lawfulness, rectitude, truth, uprightness, virtue; (6) claim, prerogative, privilege, title; (7) v. correct, rectify, settle, straighten, vindicate.
Ant. of (1), (2), (3) and (4) wrong.

righteous devout, equitable, fair, godly, good, holy, honest, just, pious, pure, saintly, upright, virtuous.
Ant. dishonest, immoral.

righteousness devoutness, equity, faithfulness, godliness, goodness, honesty, integrity,

justice, uprightness, piety, purity, rectitude, virtue.
Ant. wickedness.

rightful just, lawful, legitimate, proper, suitable, true.
Ant. illegitimate.

rigid austere, exact, inflexible, rigorous, severe, stern, stiff, unbending, unpliant, unyielding.
Ant. pliable, pliant.

rigmarole balderdash, gibberish, jargon, nonsense, trash, twaddle.
Ant. sense.

rigour (1) asperity, austerity, hardness, harshness, inflexibility, rigidity, sternness, strictness; (2) (*Weather*) inclemency, severity.
Ant. mildness.

rile anger, annoy, irritate, upset, vex.
Ant. placate.

rim border, brim, brink, edge, margin.

riot (1) commotion, confusion, disorder, disturbance, fray, lawlessness, quarrel, row, strife, tumult, uprising, uproar; (2) carousal, excess, festivity, revelry.
Ant. of (1) peace; of (2) quiet.

riotous (1) disorderly, insubordinate, mutinous, rebellious, refractory, tumultuous, unruly, uproarious; (2) luxurious, unrestrained, wanton.
Ant. of (1) loyal; of (2) austere.

ripe (1) mature, mellow, ready; (2) accomplished, complete, finished, perfect, prepared.
Ant. immature, unripe.

rise (1) arise, ascend, enlarge, grow, increase, mount, swell; (2) appear, emerge, happen, occur, originate; (3) mutiny, rebel, revolt; (4) *n.* acclivity,

ascent, elevation, hillock; (5) advance, increase; (6) beginning, origin, source, spring.
Ant. of (1) descend; of (4) declivity, descent; of (5) decrease.

risible absurd, amusing, comical, droll, farcical, funny, laughable, ludicrous, ridiculous.
Ant. serious.

risk (1) *n.* chance, danger, hazard, jeopardy, peril, venture; (2) *v.* chance, dare, endanger, hazard, imperil, jeopardise, venture.
Ant. of (1) safety.

rite ceremony, custom, form, observance, ordinance, sacrament, usage.

rival (1) *n.* antagonist, competitor, contestant, emulator, opponent; (2) *v.* compete, contend, emulate, match, oppose; (3) *a.* competing, competitive, emulating, opposed, opposing.
Ant. of (1) friend.

road (1) course, highway, lane, path, pathway, route, street, thoroughfare, track, way; (2) (*Naut.*) anchorage, roadstead.

roam prowl, ramble, range, rove, stray, stroll, travel, walk, wander.

roar *v.* bawl, bellow, cry, shout vociferate, yell.
Ant. whisper.

rob cheat, defraud, deprive, despoil, filch, pilfer, pillage, pinch, plunder, rifle, sack, steal, strip.

robbery depredation, embezzlement, filching, fraud, larceny, pillage, plunder, spoliation, stealing, theft.

robust (1) athletic, brawny, hale, hearty, lusty, muscular, powerful, sinewy, sound, stout, vigorous; (2) boisterous, coarse, rough, rude.

Ant. of (1) feeble, weak; of (2) refined.

rogue caitiff, cheat, knave, rascal, scamp, scoundrel, sharper, swindler, villain.

Ant. gentleman.

roguish (1) dishonest, fraudulent, knavish, rascally, villainous; (2) frolicsome, mischievous, sportive, waggish.

Ant. of (1) honest; of (2) serious.

rôle (1) (*Theat.*) character, impersonation, part, representation; (2) duty, function, job, part, position, task.

roll (A) (1) gyrate, reel, revolve, rock, rotate, run, spin, trundle, turn, wheel, whirl; (2) bind, enfold, envelop, swathe, wind, wrap; (3) billow, rock, toss, tumble, sway, swing, wallow, welter; (4) (*Naut.*) n. billowing, pitching, rolling, tossing, wallowing.

roll (B) annals, catalogue, chronicle, document, inventory, list, record, register, schedule, scroll, volume.

rollicking frisky, frolicsome, jovial, lively, playful, sportive.

Ant. serious, solemn.

romance (1) fiction, legend, novel, story, tale; (2) exaggeration, falsehood, fiction, lie; (3) idyll.

romantic (1) chimerical, extravagant, fabulous, fanciful, fantastic, idyllic, imaginative, legendary, picturesque, quixotic, sentimental, unpractical; (2) exaggerated, fictitious, improbable, unrealistic, wild.

Ant. of (1) practical; of (2) realistic.

romp caper, frisk, frolic, gambol, skip, sport.

room (1) compass, expanse, extent, field, latitude, range, scope; (2) apartment, chamber, saloon; (3) place, stead; (4) chance, occasion, opportunity.

roomy ample, broad, capacious, extensive, large, wide.

Ant. cramped, narrow.

root (1) radicle, radix, rhizome, stem; (2) (*Fig.*) base, bottom, cause, foundation, occasion, origin, source; (3) v. establish, fasten, fix, set; (4) destroy, eradicate, exterminate, extirpate, remove, uproot.

Ant. of (1) top; of (4) plant.

rooted confirmed, deep, deep-seated, established, fixed.

Ant. shallow.

roseate blooming, blushing, red, rose-coloured, rubicund, ruddy.

rosy (1) blooming, healthy-looking, reddish, roseate, rubicund, ruddy; (2) (*Fig.*) bright, optimistic, promising.

Ant. of (2) black.

rot (1) v. corrupt, decay, decompose, degenerate, putrefy, spoil, taint; (2) n. corruption, decay, decomposition, putrefaction.

Ant. of (1) purify.

rotten (1) corrupt, decayed, decomposed, fetid, foul, putrescent, putrid, rank, stinking, tainted, unsound; (2) (*Fig.*) deceitful, faithless, treacherous, untrustworthy.

Ant. of (1) pure, sweet; (2) trustworthy.

rough (1) jagged, rugged, shapeless, uncut, uneven, unhewn, unpolished, unwrought; (2) bluff, blunt, brusque, churlish, coarse, impolite, indelicate, uncivil, ungracious; (3)

hard, harsh, severe, unfeeling, violent; (4) bristly, disordered, hairy, shaggy; (5) boisterous, inclement, squally, stormy, tempestuous; (6) discordant, inharmonious, unmusical.

Ant. of (1) even; of (2) polite; of (3) kind; of (4) smooth; (5) calm; (6) harmonious.

round (1) *a.* circular, cylindrical, globular, rotund; (2) complete, entire, full; (3) considerable, great, large, plump; (4) *n.* cycle, period, revolution, rotation, succession; (5) circuit, compass, tour, turn.

roundabout *a.* circuitous, devious, indirect, tortuous.

Ant. direct.

rouse (1) arouse, awaken, rise, wake; (2) agitate, anger, animate, disturb, excite, inflame, provoke, startle, stimulate, stir.

Ant. of (2) calm.

rout (1) *v.* beat, chase, conquer, defeat, dispel, overpower, overthrow, scatter; (2) *n.* defeat, overthrow, ruin.

Ant. of (2) victory.

route course, itinerary, passage, path, road, way.

routine custom, order, practice, way, wont.

rove ramble, range, roam, stray, stroll, wander.

row (A) file, line, range, rank, series.

row (B) brawl, commotion, disturbance, fray, quarrel, squabble, tumult, uproar.

Ant. peace.

royal (1) imperial, kinglike, kingly, monarchical, princely, regal; (2) august, magnificent, majestic, splendid, superb.

Ant. of (1) common; of (2) ordinary.

rub (1) abrade, chafe, clean,

grate, polish, scour, scrape, wipe; (2) apply, put, smear.

rubbish (1) débris, dregs, garbage, litter, lumber, refuse, trash; (2) (*Sl.*) balderdash, gibberish, nonsense, twaddle.

rubicund blushing, florid, flushed, reddish, rosy, ruddy.

Ant. pale.

rude (1) barbarous, boorish, coarse, ignorant, illiterate, loutish, low, rough, savage, uncivilised, undisciplined, uneducated, vulgar; (2) blunt, brusque, churlish, curt, discourteous, ill-mannered, impertinent, impolite, impudent, insolent, insulting, uncouth, unpolished, unrefined; (3) artless, crude, inartistic, inelegant, primitive, simple.

Ant. of (1) civilised; of (2) polite; of (3) elegant.

rudimentary elementary, embryonic, fundamental, initial, primary, undeveloped.

Ant. advanced.

rue bewail, deplore, grieve, lament, regret, repent.

Ant. rejoice.

rueful dismal, doleful, grievous, lugubrious, melancholy, mournful, sad, sorrowful, woeful.

Ant. bright, cheerful.

ruffian caitiff, miscreant, monster, rascal, rogue, scoundrel, villain, wretch.

Ant. gentleman.

ruffle (1) derange, disarrange, disorder, discompose, pucker, rumple, wrinkle; (2) (*Fig.*) agitate, annoy, confuse, disquiet, disturb, harass, perturb, torment, trouble, upset, vex, worry.

Ant. of (1) straighten; of (2) calm.

rugged (1) broken, furrowed,

jagged, ragged, uneven, wrinkled; (2) bristly, coarse, rough, shaggy; (3) austere, churlish, crabbed, hard, harsh, rude, severe, sour, stern, surly; (4) crude, unrefined.

Ant. of (1) even; of (2) smooth; of (3) gentle; of (4) refined.

ruin (1) v. crush, defeat, demolish, destroy, overthrow, overturn, overwhelm, wreck; (2) damage, disfigure, mar, spoil; (3) n. collapse, damage, decay, defeat, destruction, devastation, downfall, fall, havoc, ruination, subversion, undoing.

Ant. of (1) restore; of (2) improve; of (3) restoration.

ruinous baleful, baneful, calamitous, deleterious, destructive, devastating, injurious, noxious, wasteful.

Ant. beneficial.

rule (1) n. authority, command, control, domination, dominion, government, mastery, reign, sway; (2) criterion, guide, law, order, precept, principle, regulation, ruling, standard; (3) v. administer, command, control, direct, govern, guide, lead, manage, reign; (4) decide, decree, establish, judge, settle.

Ant. of (1) subjection; of (3) obey.

ruminate brood, chew, cogitate, consider, contemplate, deliberate, meditate, muse, ponder, reflect, think.

rummage examine, explore, ransack, search.

rumour (1) n. bruit, gossip, hearsay, news, report, story, talk, tidings; (2) v. bruit, circulate, publish, report, tell.

Ant. of (1) fact.

rumple crease, crumple, crush, derange, disorder, pucker, ruffle, wrinkle.

Ant. smooth, straighten.

run (1) v. dart, depart, escape, flee, hasten, hie, hurry, race, rush, scamper, speed; (2) discharge, flow, go, move, pour, proceed, stream; (3) fuse, liquefy, melt; (4) challenge, compete, contend; (5) extend, lie, stretch; (6) n. course, current, flow, motion, progress; (7) excursion, journey, outing, trip; (8) application, demand, pressure, rush.

rupture (1) v. break, burst, fracture, separate, sever, split; (2) n. breach, break, burst, fracture, split; (3) (*Fig.*) altercation, contention, disagreement, disruption, dissolution, feud, hostility, quarrel; (4) (*Med.*) hernia.

Ant. of (1) unite.

rural country, pastoral, rustic, sylvan.

Ant. town, urban.

ruse artifice, deception, device, dodge, imposture, manoeuvre, sham, stratagem, trick, wile.

rush (1) v. career, dart, fly, hasten, hurry, press, push, run, speed; (2) attack, charge, overcome.

Ant. of (1) linger.

rust blight, corrosion, crust, dross, mildew, mould, must.

rustic (1) n. boor, bumpkin, clod, clodhopper, countryman, peasant, swain, yokel; (2) a. countrified, homely, plain, simple; (3) awkward, boorish, coarse, outlandish, rough.

Ant. of (1) courtier, townsman; of (2) grand; of (3) refined.

ruthless adamant, barbarous, cruel, fierce, ferocious, hard, hard-hearted, inexorable, inhuman, merciless, pitiless, relentless, savage, severe, truculent.

Ant. humane, merciful.

S

sable *a.* black, dark, dusky, sombre.

Ant. white.

sack (1) *v.* demolish, despoil, destroy, devastate, loot, pillage, plunder, ravage, rifle, rob, ruin, spoil; (2) *n.* depredation, looting, destruction, devastation, pillage, plunder, (*Fig.*) rape, ravage, ruin, waste.

sacred (1) consecrated, divine, hallowed, holy, revered, venerable; (2) inviolable, protected, sacrosanct, secure.

Ant. of (1) profane.

sacrifice (1) *v.* forego, immolate, lose, offer, surrender; (2) *n.* destruction, immolation, loss, oblation, surrender; (3) *n.* atonement.

Ant. of (1) accept, receive.

sacrilege blasphemy, desecration, impiety, profanation, profaneness, violation.

Ant. piety.

sacrilegious blasphemous, desecrating, impious, irreverent, profane.

Ant. pious.

sad (1) cheerless, dejected, depressed, disconsolate, doleful, downcast, gloomy, lugubrious, melancholy, mournful, serious, sombre, sorrowful, woebegone; (2) bad, calamitous, dark, deplorable, disastrous, dismal, grievous.

Ant. of (1) cheerful; of (2) good.

saddle *v.* burden, charge, encumber, load.

Ant. rid.

sadness dejection, depression, despondency, dolefulness, gloominess, grief, melancholy, misery, mournfulness, sorrow.

Ant. joy.

safe (1) guarded, protected, secure, sound, unharmed, unhurt, unscathed; (2) dependable, reliable, sure, trustworthy; (3) *n.* chest, coffer, strongbox.

Ant. of (1) insecure; of (2) untrustworthy.

safeguard (1) *v.* defend, guard, protect, shield; (2) *n.* convoy, defence, escort, protection, security, shield.

Ant. of (1) endanger.

sagacious able, acute, apt, astute, clear-sighted, discerning, intelligent, judicious, long-headed, perspicacious, sage, sharp, sharp-witted, shrewd, wise.

sagacity acuteness, astuteness, discernment, insight, judiciousness, penetration, perspicacity, prudence, sense, sharpness, shrewdness, wisdom.

sage (1) *a.* acute, discerning, intelligent, judicious, prudent, sagacious, sapient, sensible, wise; (2) *n.* philosopher, savant.

Ant. of (1) stupid.

sailor mariner, navigator, (*Colloq.*) salt, seafarer, seaman, tar.

Ant. landsman.

saintly devout, godly, holy, pious, religious.

Ant. irreligious, sinful.

sake (1) cause, end, purpose, reason; (2) account, consideration, interest, regard, respect.

salacious carnal, lascivious, lecherous, lewd, libidinous, lustful, obscene, pornographic, prurient, voluptuous, wanton.
Ant. chaste.

salary allowance, hire, income, pay, remuneration, stipend, wages.

salient conspicuous, important, jutting, projecting, prominent, protruding, remarkable, striking.
Ant. inconspicuous, receding.

sally (1) v. issue, rush; (2) n. (*Mil.*) incursion, raid, sortie; (3) escapade, excursion, frolic, trip; (4) (*Fig.*) jest, joke, quip, retort, witticism.

salt (1) flavour, relish, savour, seasoning, taste; (2) (*Fig.*) piquancy, sarcasm, wit; (3) (*Colloq.*) mariner, sailor, seaman, tar; (4) a. saline, salted; (5) bitter, pungent, sharp.
Ant. of (4) fresh.

salubrious beneficial, health-giving, healthy, salutary, wholesome.
Ant. unwholesome.

salutary (1) healthful, healthy, salubrious; (2) advantageous, beneficial, good, helpful, profitable, useful.
Ant. of (1) unwholesome; of (2) useless.

salute (1) v. accost, address, greet, hail, honour, kiss, welcome; (2) n. address, greeting, kiss, salutation.

salvation deliverance, escape, preservation, redemption, rescue, saving.
Ant. loss.

sameness identicalness, likeness, monotony, oneness, resemblance, similarity, uniformity.
Ant. difference.

sample example, illustration, instance, model, pattern, specimen.

sanatory curative, healing, hygienic, remedial, sanative, sanitary, therapeutic.

sanctify consecrate, hallow purify.
Ant. defile.

sanctimonious canting, hypocritical, pharisaical, self-satisfied, smug.

sanction (1) n. allowance, approbation, approval, authorisation, authority, confirmation, countenance, support; (2) v. allow, approve, authorise, confirm, countenance, ratify, support, warrant.
Ant. of (1) refusal; of (2) refuse.

sanctity (1) devotion, godliness, goodness, holiness, piety, purity, religiousness, righteousness; (2) inviolability, sacredness, solemnity.
Ant. of (1) evil.

sanctuary (1) altar, church, shrine, temple; (2) asylum, protection, refuge, retreat, shelter.

sane healthy, lucid, sensible, sober, sound.
Ant. insane, unsound.

sang-froid calmness, composure, coolness, imperturbability, indifference, nonchalance, phlegm, self-possession.
Ant. excitability, passion.

sanguinary blood-thirsty, bloody, cruel, merciless, murderous, pitiless, ruthless, savage, truculent.
Ant. mild, pacific.

sanguine (1) animated, ardent, buoyant, cheerful, confident, hopeful, lively, optimistic, spirited, warm; (2) florid, red.
Ant. of (1) despondent; of (2) anaemic, pale.

sapient acute, discerning, intelligent, knowing, sagacious, sage, shrewd, would-be-wise.
Ant. stupid.

sarcastic biting, cutting, cynical, ironical, sardonic, satirical, sharp, sneering, taunting.
Ant. commendatory.

sardonic bitter, derisive, ironical, malevolent, malicious, malignant, sarcastic.
Ant. benignant.

satiate cloy, glut, gorge, overfill, sate, satisfy, surfeit.
Ant. dissatisfy, starve.

satire abuse, censure, diatribe, invective, irony, lampoon, pasquinade, philippic, ridicule, sarcasm, wit.
Ant. encomium, eulogy.

satirical biting, bitter, censorious, cutting, cynical, incisive, ironical, mordant, pungent, sarcastic, sardonic, taunting.
Ant. encomiastic, eulogistic.

satirise abuse, censure, criticise, lampoon, lash, ridicule.
Ant. commend.

satisfaction (1) comfort, contentment, ease, enjoyment, gratification, pleasure; (2) amends, atonement, compensation, indemnification, recompense, redress, remuneration, reparation, requital, restitution, settlement.
Ant. of (1) dissatisfaction; of (2) injury.

satisfy (1) content, fill, gratify, please, suffice; (2) atone, compensate, indemnify, recompense, remunerate, requite, reward; (3) answer, discharge, fulfil, pay, settle; (4) assure, convince, persuade.
Ant. of (1) and (4) dissatisfy; of (2) injure.

saturate drench, imbue, impregnate, soak, steep, wet.
Ant. dry.

saturnine dull, gloomy, grave, heavy, morose, phlegmatic, sedate, sombre.
Ant. gay.

sauciness flippancy, impertinence, impudence, insolence, pertness, rudeness,
Ant. modesty, staidness.

saucy disrespectful, flippant, forward, impertinent, impudent, insolent, pert, presumptuous, rude.
Ant. modest, staid.

saunter amble, dally, linger, loiter, ramble, roam, stroll, tarry.
Ant. hurry.

savage (1) a. aboriginal, heathenish, native, rough. rugged, uncivilised, uncultivated; (2) barbarous, beastly, brutal, brutish, cruel, ferocious, fierce, inhuman, rude, untamed, wild; (3) blood-thirsty, merciless, murderous, pitiless, ruthless, truculent; (4) n. aboriginal, aborigine, barbarian, heathen, native.
Ant. of (1) civilised; of (2) tame; of (3) merciful.

save (1) deliver, keep, liberate, preserve, rescue; (2) economise, gather, hoard, hold, husband, reserve, store; (3) hinder, obviate, prevent, spare; (4) prep. but, except, excepting.
Ant. of (1) abandon; of (2) squander.

saviour (A) defender, deliverer, guardian, preserver, protector, rescuer.
Ant. destroyer.

(our) **Saviour** (B) Christ, Jesus, Messiah, Redeemer.

savour (1) n. flavour, relish, smack, taste; (2) fragrance odour, scent, smell, taste; (3) v. appreciate, enjoy, like, partake, relish; (4) flavour, season.

savoury agreeable, appetising, delicious, luscious, palatable, piquant, tasty.

Ant. unpalatable, unsavoury.

saw adage, aphorism, apothegm, axiom, dictum, maxim, proverb, saying.

say (1) affirm, allege, assert, declare, express, pronounce, report, speak, state, tell, utter; (2) answer, reply; (3) recite, rehearse, repeat; (4) assume, presume, suppose.

saying (1) adage, aphorism, apothegm, axiom, dictum, maxim, proverb, saw; (2) declaration, observation, remark, statement.

scale (A) (1) v. ascend, clamber, climb, escalade, mount; (2) n. balance, gradation, measure, mile.

Ant. of (1) descend.

scale (B) n. flake, lamina, layer, plate.

scamper fly, hasten, hie, hurry, run.

Ant. dawdle.

scan con, examine, investigate, scrutinise, search.

scandal calumny, defamation, detraction, discredit, disgrace, dishonour, ignominy, infamy, obloquy, offence, opprobrium, reproach, shame, slander.

Ant. praise.

scandalise backbite, calumniate, defame, discredit, disgrace, disgust, dishonour, horrify, libel, offend, outrage, shock, slander, traduce, vilify.

Ant. honour.

scandalous atrocious, disgraceful, disreputable, ignominious, odious, opprobrious, shameful, slanderous.

Ant. reputable.

scanty bare, deficient, inadequate, insufficient, meagre, poor, scant, short, slender, sparing, sparse.

Ant. abundant.

scar cicatrix, injury, mark, wound.

scarce few, deficient, infrequent, insufficient, rare, uncommon, unusual, wanting.

Ant. sufficient.

scarcely barely, hardly, scarce.

scarcity dearth, deficiency, infrequency, insufficiency, lack, rareness, shortage, want.

Ant. abundance.

scare (1) v. affright, alarm, daunt, dismay, frighten, intimidate, shock, startle, terrify; (2) n. alarm, fright, panic, shock, terror.

Ant. of (1) reassure.

scatheless sound, undamaged, unharmed, unhurt, uninjured, unscathed, whole.

Ant. injured.

scatter (1) broadcast, diffuse, disseminate, spread, sprinkle, strew; (2) dispel, disperse, disunite, separate.

Ant. of (1) collect, gather; of (2) assemble.

scene (1) display, exhibition, pageant, representation, show, sight, spectacle; (2) place, situation, spot; (3) arena, stage; (4) landscape, prospect, view.

scent aroma, fragrance, odour, perfume, redolence, smell.

sceptical doubtful, doubting, dubious, hesitating, incredulous, unbelieving.

Ant. credulous.

schedule catalogue, chronicle, form, inventory, list, record, register, scroll, table, time-table.

scheme (1) *n.* contrivance, design, device, plan, programme, project, system, theory; (2) arrangement, draft, outline, pattern; (3) conspiracy, intrigue, plot, stratagem; (4) *v.* contrive, design, devise, frame, imagine, plan, project; (5) conspire, intrigue, plot.

schism breach, discord, disunion, division, separation, split.
Ant. union.

schismatic (-al) discordant, dissentient, dissenting, heretical, heterodox, seceding.
Ant. orthodox.

scholar (1) disciple, learner, pupil, student; (2) (*Univ.*) don, fellow, pedant, savant.

scholarship (1) accomplishments, attainments, education, erudition, knowledge, learning, lore; (2) bursary, exhibition, fellowship.
Ant. of (1) ignorance.

scholastic academic, lettered, literary.

school (1) academy, institute, institution, seminary; (2) class, denomination, sect; (3) disciples, followers.

scintillate flash, gleam, glisten, sparkle, twinkle.

scion (1) branch, graft, offshoot, slip, sprout, twig; (2) (*Fig.*) child, descendant, heir.
Ant. of (1) stock.

scoff deride, despise, flout, gibe, jeer, ridicule, scorn, scout, sneer, taunt.
Ant. praise.

scold berate, blame, censure, chide, rate, rebuke, reprimand, reproach, reprove, upbraid, vituperate.
Ant. encourage.

scope (1) extent, latitude, liberty, opportunity, range, room, space, vent; (2) aim, design, intent, intention, object, purpose, tendency, view.

scorch blister, burn, char, parch, roast, shrivel, singe.

scorn (1) *n.* contempt, contumely, derision, disdain, mockery, slight, sneer; (2) *v.* contemn, deride, disdain, slight, spurn.
Ant. esteem.

scornful contemptuous, defiant, derisive, haughty, insolent, reproachful, scoffing, supercilious.
Ant. approving.

scot-free (1) exempt, tax-free, untaxed; (2) clear, safe, scatheless, undamaged, unharmed, unhurt, uninjured, unscathed.
Ant. of (2) injured.

scoundrel caitiff, knave, miscreant, rascal, rogue, scamp, vagabond, villain, wretch.
Ant. gentleman.

scour clean, cleanse, furbish, polish, purge, rub, scrub, wash, whiten.
Ant. dirty.

scourge (1) *v.* beat, castigate, chasten, chastise, correct, lash, punish, whip; (2) (*Fig.*) afflict, curse, harass, plague, torment; (3) *n.* jambok, knout, lash, strap, thong, whip; (4) (*Fig.*) affliction, bane, curse, infliction, pest, plague, punishment.
Ant. of (1) pamper.

scout (A) contemn, deride, despise, disdain, ridicule, scoff, scorn, sneer, spurn.

scout (B) observe, reconnoitre, spy, survey, watch.

scowl (1) *v.* frown, glower; (2) *n.* frown, glower.
Ant. smile.

scraggy (1) broken, jagged, rough, rugged, uneven; (2) bony, emaciated, gaunt, lank, lean, scrawny, skinny.

Ant. of (1) even; of (2) plump.

scrap (1) bit, bite, crumb, fragment, morsel, mouthful, part, portion; (2) *v.* break, demolish, discard.

Ant. of (1) whole; of (2) retain.

scrape (1) *v.* abrade, grate, rasp, rub, scratch; (2) acquire, collect, gather, hoard, save; (3) clean, erase, remove; (4) *n.* difficulty, dilemma, distress, (*Colloq.*) fix, predicament, trouble.

scream *v.* and *n.* cry, screech, shriek, yell.

screen (1) *v.* cloak, conceal, cover, hide, mask, shroud, veil; (2) defend, protect, shelter, shield; (3) *n.* cover, guard, partition, shelter, shield.

Ant. of (1) reveal.

screw *v.* force, press, rack, squeeze, twist, wrench.

scribe amanuensis, clerk, copyist, notary, penman, scrivener, secretary, writer.

scrimmage brawl, fray, riot, row, scuffle, skirmish, squabble.

scrimp curtail, limit, pinch, reduce, shorten, stint, straiten.

Ant. squander.

scroll inventory, list, parchment, roll, schedule.

scrub clean, cleanse, rub, scour.

Ant. dirty.

scruple (1) *v.* demur, doubt, hesitate, vacillate, waver; (2) *n.* caution, compunction, difficulty, doubt, hesitation, misgiving, perplexity, qualm, reluctance.

Ant. of (2) confidence.

scrupulous careful, conscientious, exact, minute, nice, precise, punctilious, rigorous, strict.

Ant. unscrupulous.

scrutinise examine, explore, inspect, investigate, probe, scan, search, sift, study.

Ant. ignore.

scrutiny examination, exploration, inquiry, inspection, investigation, search, sifting, study.

scud fly, haste, hasten, hie, scamper, speed, trip.

scuffle (1) *v.* contend, fight, strive, struggle; (2) *n.* affray, altercation, brawl, fight, fray, quarrel, squabble, wrangle.

Ant. of (2) peace.

scurrilous abusive, coarse, foul, gross, indecent, infamous, insulting, low, mean, obscene, offensive, ribald, vulgar.

Ant. decent, polite.

scurvy abject, bad, base, contemptible, despicable, low, mean, pitiful, sorry, vile, worthless.

Ant. dignified, worthy.

scuttle bustle, hasten, hurry, run, scamper.

Ant. dawdle.

seal (1) *v.* close, enclose, fasten, shut; (2) assure, attest, authenticate, confirm, establish, ratify; (3) *n.* assurance, attestation, confirmation, notification.

Ant. of (1) open.

seamy disreputable, nasty, sordid, unpleasant.

Ant. pleasant.

sear burn, cauterise, dry, scorch, wither.

search (1) *v.* examine, explore, inquire, inspect, investigate, look, probe, pry, scrutinise, seek, sift; (2) *n.* examination, exploration, inquiry, inspection, investigation, pursuit, quest, scrutiny.

searching (*Fig.*) close, keen, minute, penetrating, severe, thorough, trying.
Ant. perfunctory, superficial.
season (A) *n.* interval, juncture, occasion, opportunity, period, spell, term, time.
season (B) *v.* acclimatise, accustom, habituate, harden, inure, mature, moderate, prepare, qualify. temper.
seasonable appropriate, convenient, fit, opportune, suitable, timely.
Ant. unseasonable, untimely.
seasoning condiment, relish, sauce.
seat (1) bench, chair, pew, settle, stall, stool; (2) location, place, site, situation, station; (3) abode, house, mansion, residence; (4) base, bottom, cause, foundation, ground.
secede resign, retire, separate, withdraw.
Ant. stay.
secluded isolated, private, remote, retired, sequestered, solitary, unfrequented.
Ant. busy, public.
second (1) *v.* advance, aid, approve, assist, back, encourage, forward, further, help, promote; (2) *n.* assistant, backer, helper, supporter; (3) instant, (*Colloq.*) jiffy, moment, trice; (4) *a.* inferior, secondary.
Ant. of (1) oppose; of (2) opponent.
secondary inferior, lower, mean, minor, second-rate, subordinate, unimportant.
Ant. primary, superior.
secrecy (1) concealment, privacy, stealth; (2) retirement, seclusion, solitude.
Ant. of (1) publicity.
secret (1) close, concealed, covered, covert, hid, hidden,

reticent, shrouded, sly, stealthy, underhand, unknown, unrevealed, unseen; (2) abstruse, cabalistic, clandestine, cryptic, latent, mysterious, occult, recondite; (3) private, retired, secluded.
Ant. apparent, open.
secrete conceal, cover, disguise, hide, screen, shroud, veil.
Ant. open.
sect denomination, faction, party, school.
section division, fraction, fragment, part, piece, portion, segment.
Ant. whole.
secular civil, laic, laical, lay, profane, temporal, worldly.
Ant. religious, unworldly.
secure (1) *a.* assured, certain, confident, sure; (2) protected, safe, sheltered; (3) fast, fastened, firm, fixed, immovable, stable; (4) *v.* assure, ensure, guarantee, insure; (5) fasten, guard, protect, safeguard; (6) acquire, gain, get, obtain, procure.
sedate calm, collected, composed, cool, demure, grave, imperturbable, placid, quiet, serene, serious, sober, staid, still, thoughtful, tranquil, unruffled.
Ant. excited, nervous.
sedative (1) *a.* allaying, calming, lenitive, relaxing, soothing, tranquillising; (2) *n.* anodyne, opiate, narcotic, tranquilliser.
Ant. of (1) stimulating; of (2) stimulant.
sedentary inactive, motionless, torpid.
Ant. active.
sediment dregs, grounds, lees, precipitate, residuum, settlings.

sedition insurrection, mutiny, rebellion, revolt, riot, treason, tumult, uprising.
Ant. loyalty.

seditious insurgent, mutinous, rebellious, refractory, revolutionary, riotous, treasonable, turbulent.
Ant. loyal.

seduce allure, attract, betray, corrupt, deceive, decoy, deprave, entice, inveigle, lure, mislead, tempt.

seductive alluring, attractive, beguiling, captivating, enticing, specious, tempting.
Ant. repulsive.

sedulous assiduous, busy, constant, diligent, industrious, laborious, painstaking, persevering, unremitting.
Ant. idle.

see (A) v. (1) behold, discern, distinguish, espy, heed, look, mark, note, notice, observe, perceive, regard, view; (2) comprehend, feel, know, understand; (3) ascertain, determine, discover, learn; (4) consider, deliberate, reflect.

see (B) n. bishopric, diocese.

seed (1) embryo, germ, grain, kernel, original, semen, sperm; (2) (*Fig.*) children, descendants, offspring, progeny, race.

seedy (1) faded, old, shabby, worn; (2) exhausted, miserable-looking, out-of-sorts.
Ant. of (1) smart; of (2) thriving.

seek attempt, endeavour, follow, inquire, pursue, search, solicit, strive, try.

seem appear, assume, look, pretend.

seeming (1) a. apparent, appearing, ostensible, specious; (2) n. appearance, semblance, look.

seemly appropriate, becoming, befitting, convenient, decent, decorous, fit, fitting, meet, suitable, suited.
Ant. unbecoming, unseemly.

seer augur, predictor, prophet, soothsayer.

segment bit, part, piece, portion, section.
Ant. whole.

segregate dissociate, isolate, select, separate.
Ant. unite.

seize apprehend, arrest, capture, catch, clutch, fasten, grab, grasp, grip, snatch, take.
Ant. loose, release.

seldom infrequently, occasionally, rarely.
Ant. frequently, often.

select (1) v. choose, pick, prefer; (2) a. choice, excellent, picked, preferable, rare, selected, special, superior.
Ant. of (2) cheap, inferior.

selfish egotistical, greedy, mean, mercenary, narrow, self-seeking, ungenerous.
Ant. generous.

self-willed headstrong, intractable, obstinate, stubborn, wilful.
Ant. docile.

sell (1) barter, exchange, trade, vend; (2) (*Fig.*) betray.
Ant. of (1) buy.

semblance air, appearance, aspect, bearing, figure, form, image, likeness, mien, resemblance, show, similarity.
Ant. difference.

seminary academy, college, high-school, institute, institution, school.

sempiternal endless, eternal, everlasting, interminable, perpetual, unending.
Ant. fleeting, transient.

send (1) convey, despatch,

forward, transmit; (2) cast, emit, fling, hurl, propel.

Ant. of (1) receive; of (2) keep.

senile aged, doting, imbecile.

Ant. sprightly, youthful.

seniority eldership, precedence, priority, superiority.

sensation (1) feeling, impression, sense; (2) agitation, commotion, excitement, furore, surprise, thrill.

sensational exciting, melodramatic, startling, thrilling.

Ant. dull, humdrum.

sense (1) n. feeling, sensation, sensibility; (2) import, interpretation, meaning, purport, significance, signification; (3) judgment, mother-wit, nous, reason, sagacity, tact, understanding, wisdom; (4) consciousness, intellect, mind, notion, opinion, sentiment; (5) v. appraise, appreciate, estimate, notice, observe, perceive, suspect, understand.

senseless (1) cold, insensible, unconscious, unfeeling; (2) absurd, foolish, idiotic, inane, meaningless, nonsensical, silly, simple, stupid, unreasonable, unwise.

Ant. of (1) sensitive; of (2) sensible.

sensible (1) perceptible, tangible, visible; (2) aware, conscious, convinced, observant, sensitive, understanding; (3) judicious, rational, reasonable, sagacious, sage, sober, sound, wise.

Ant. of (1) insensible; of (2) unaware; of (3) stupid.

sensitive (1) affected, impressionable, perceptive, responsive, sentient, susceptible; (2) delicate, tender, touchy.

Ant. of (1) insensitive; of (2) hard.

sensual (1) animal, bodily, carnal, fleshly, luxurious, unspiritual, voluptuous; (2) gross, lascivious, lewd, licentious, unchaste.

Ant. of (1) spiritual; of (2) chaste.

sentence n. - condemnation, decision, decree, doom.

sententious axiomatic, brief, compact, concise, epigrammatic, laconic, pithy, pointed, short, succinct, terse.

Ant. diffuse.

sentiment (1) emotion, sensibility, tenderness; (2) attitude, feeling, idea, judgment, opinion, saying, thought.

sentimental emotional, fanciful, impressionable, romantic, tender.

Ant. unromantic.

sentinel guard, picket, sentry, watchman.

separate (1) v. cleave, detach, disconnect, disjoin, disunite, divide, divorce, part, remove, sever, split, sunder; (2) a. detached, disconnected, disjointed, divided, divorced; (3) alone, apart, distinct, independent, individual.

Ant. of (1) unite; of (2) united.

separation disconnection, disjunction, dissociation, disunion, division, divorce, severance.

Ant. union.

sepulchral deep, dismal, funereal, gloomy, grave, hollow, lugubrious, melancholy, mournful, sad, sombre, woeful.

Ant. bright, cheerful.

sepulchre burial-place, grave, tomb, vault.

sequel conclusion, consequence, continuation, end, issue, result, upshot.

Ant. beginning.

sequence arrangement, order, series, succession.

sequestered isolated, lonely, quiet, remote, secluded, unfrequented.

Ant. busy.

seraphic angelic, celestial, divine, heavenly, holy, pure, sublime.

Ant. devilish.

serene (1) calm, composed, imperturbable, peaceful, placid, sedate, staid, undisturbed, unruffled; (2) bright, clear, fair, unclouded.

Ant. of (1) disturbed; of (2) clouded.

serenity (1) calm, calmness, composure, peace, peacefulness, placidity, quietness, sedateness, tranquillity; (2) brightness, clearness, fairness.

Ant. of (1) disturbance.

serf bondman, servant, slave, villein.

Ant. master.

series arrangement, course, line, order, sequence, set, succession.

serious (1) devout, earnest, grave, pious, sedate, sober, solemn, thoughtful; (2) critical, dangerous, grave, important, momentous, weighty.

Ant. of (1) capricious, flighty, inconstant; of (2) frivolous, trivial.

seriousness (1) devoutness, earnestness, gravity, piety, sedateness, solemnity, staidness; (2) danger, gravity, importance, moment, weight.

Ant. of (1) levity.

serpentine crooked, meandering, tortuous, twisting, winding.

Ant. straight.

servant dependent, domestic, drudge, employee, help, helper, maid, menial, retainer, slave, vassal.

Ant. master.

serve (1) aid, assist, help, minister, succour; (2) act, attend, discharge, do, observe, officiate, supply; (3) content, satisfy, suffice; (4) arrange, deal, distribute, handle.

service (1) attendance, business, duty, employment, labour, office, work; (2) advantage, avail, benefit, supply, use, utility; (3) ceremony, function, observance, rite, worship.

serviceable advantageous, beneficial, convenient, efficient, helpful, operative, profitable, useable, useful.

Ant. unserviceable.

servile abject, base, cringing, fawning, grovelling, low, mean, menial, obsequious, slavish, sycophantic.

Ant. independent, masterly.

servility abjection, baseness, bondage, fawning, meanness, obsequiousness, slavishness, sycophancy.

Ant. independence, liberty.

servitude bondage, enslavement, obedience, serfdom, service, slavery, thraldom, vassalage.

Ant. freedom.

set (1) v. appoint, arrange, assign, determine, establish, fix, locate, place, plant, regulate, seat, settle, situate; (2) decline, sink, subside; (3) adjust, rectify, regulate; (4) n. assortment, band, circle, class, clique, collection, company, coterie, group, sect; (5) a. customary, established, fixed, regular, settled, usual.

settle (1) adjust, agree, appoint, arrange, confirm, decide, determine, establish; (2) calm, compose, pacify, tranquillise; (3) discharge, liquidate, pay; (4) colonise, found, people, plant; (5) dwell, inhabit, live, reside; (6) decline, fall, sink, subside.

settlement (1) adjustment, agreement, arrangement, confirmation, establishment; (2) discharge, liquidation, payment; (3) colonisation, colony; (4) pacification, reconciliation.

sever cleave, cut, detach, disconnect, disjoin, disunite, divide, separate, sunder.
Ant. join.

several different, distinct, divers, diverse, individual, many, particular, single, sundry, various.

severe (1) austere, cruel, grave, hard, inexorable, morose, relentless, rigid, rigorous, serious, stern, strict, unrelenting; (2) chaste, plain, simple, unadorned; (3) caustic, cutting, satirical; (4) acute, distressing, extreme, intense, violent.

severely extremely, harshly, rigorously, sharply, sternly, strictly.
Ant. leniently.

shabby (1) faded, mean, poor, ragged, seedy, threadbare, worn; (2) (*Fig.*) contemptible, despicable, dirty, dishonourable, low, mean, scurvy, ungentlemanly, unworthy.
Ant. of (1) new, smart; of (2) praiseworthy.

shackle (1) bond, chain, fetter, gyve, handcuff, leg-iron, manacle; (2) *v.* bind, chain, fetter, hobble, manacle, tie; (3) (*Fig.*) embarrass, encumber, hamper,

impede, obstruct, restrain, restrict.
Ant. of (2) liberate.

shade (1) *v.* cloud, conceal, cover, darken, dim, hide, obscure, protect, shadow, veil; (2) *n.* dusk, gloom, gloominess, obscurity, screen, shadow; (3) blind, curtain, screen, veil; (4) colour, hue, stain, tint; (5) apparition, ghost, phantom, spectre, spirit; (6) (*Fig.*) amount, degree, difference, hint, suggestion, trace, variety.
Ant. of (1) illuminate.

shadow (1) *n.* cover, darkness, gloom, obscurity, protection, shade, shelter; (2) ghost, image, phantom, representation, spectre.
Ant. of (1) brightness; of (2) substance.

shadowy (1) dark, dim, gloomy, obscure, shady; (2) ghostly, imaginary, impalpable, intangible, spectral, unreal, unsubstantial.
Ant. of (1) bright; of (2) real.

shake (1) *v.* agitate, convulse, jar, jolt, quake, quiver, shiver, shudder, totter, tremble, vibrate; (2) frighten, intimidate, move; (3) *n.* agitation, convulsion, disturbance, jar, jolt, shiver, shock, shudder, trembling, tremor.

shallow (1) *n.* bank, flat, sandbank, shelf, shoal; (2) *a.* empty, flimsy, foolish, frivolous, ignorant, puerile, simple, slight, superficial, trivial, unintelligent.
Ant. of (2) profound.

sham (1) *v.* deceive, defraud, feign, imitate, pretend; (2) *a.* counterfeit, false, imitation, mock, pretended, spurious; (3) *n.* delusion, feint, fraud, humbug, imitation, imposture, pretence.

Ant. of (2) genuine.

shame (1) *v.* abash, confound, debase, disconcert, discredit, disgrace, dishonour, humble, humiliate, reproach, ridicule; (2) *n.* abashment, contempt, degradation, derision, disgrace, dishonour, humiliation, ignominy, mortification, obloquy, odium, opprobrium, reproach.

Ant. of (1) credit; of (2) honour.

shameful atrocious, base, degrading, disgraceful, dishonourable, ignominious, indecent, infamous, low, mean, outrageous, scandalous, unbecoming, vile, wicked.

Ant. decent, honourable.

shameless abandoned, audacious, brazen, corrupt, depraved, dissolute, immodest, impudent, incorrigible, indecent, insolent, profligate, reprobate, unabashed, unprincipled, vicious.

Ant. decent, modest.

shanty cabin, hovel, hut, shack, shed.

shape (1) *v.* create, fashion, form, frame, make, model, mould, produce, regulate; (2) *n.* appearance, aspect, build, cut, figure, form, make, model, mould, pattern.

shapely comely, elegant, graceful, neat, well-formed.

Ant. inelegant.

share (1) *v.* apportion, assign, distribute, divide, partake, participate, receive; (2) *n.* allotment, allowance, contribution, division, lot, part, portion, proportion, quota, ration.

Ant. of (2) whole.

sharp (1) acute, cutting, keen,

penetrating; (2) alert, apt, astute, bright, clever, cunning, discerning, ingenious, knowing, long-headed, observant, quick, quick-witted, ready, shrewd, smart, subtle; (3) acid, acrid, biting, burning, hot, piquant, pungent, sour, stinging; (4) distressing, excruciating, intense, severe, sore, violent; (5) acrimonious, caustic, cutting, sarcastic, sardonic, trenchant.

Ant. of (1) blunt; of (2) dull, stupid; of (4) mild; of (5) amicable.

shatter break, burst, crack, crush, demolish, shiver, smash, split.

Ant. repair.

shed *v.* cast, diffuse, drop, emit, scatter, spill, throw.

Ant. keep.

sheen brightness, gloss, lustre, polish, shine.

sheer (1) abrupt, perpendicular, precipitous, steep; (2) absolute, downright, pure, unadulterated, utter; (3) (*Fabrics*) diaphanous, fine, thin, transparent.

Ant. of (1) gradual; of (3) opaque.

shelter (1) *v.* cover, defend, guard, harbour, hide, protect, safeguard, shield; (2) *n.* asylum, cover, defence, guard, haven, protection, refuge, retreat, sanctuary, screen, security.

Ant. of (1) open, reveal.

shibboleth criterion, password, test, watchword.

shield (1) buckler, (*Her.*) escutcheon, targe; (2) (*Fig.*) aegis, bulwark, cover, defence, guard, protection, rampart, safeguard, shelter; (3) *v.* cover, defend, guard, protect, safeguard, screen, shelter.

shift (1) *v.* alter, change, displace, move, remove, transfer, vary, veer; (2) contrive, devise, manage, plan, scheme; (3) *n.* alteration, change, move, removal, transfer; (4) artifice, contrivance, craft, deceit, device, evasion, expedient, fraud, stratagem, trick, wile.

shine (1) *v.* beam, glare, gleam, glimmer, glisten, glitter, glow, radiate, shimmer, sparkle; (2) *n.* brightness, gloss, lustre, polish, radiance, sheen, sparkle.
Ant. of (2) dullness.

shining (1) beaming, bright, brilliant, effulgent, glistening, glittering, luminous, radiant, resplendent, shimmering, sparkling; (2) (*Fig.*) brilliant, conspicuous, distinguished, eminent, illustrious, outstanding, splendid.
Ant. of (1) dull; of (2) undistinguished.

shirk avoid, dodge, evade, shun.

shiver (1) break, shatter, smash; (2) quake, quiver, shake, shudder, tremble.

shock (1) *v.* appal, disgust, horrify, nauseate, offend, revolt, scandalise, sicken; (2) *n.* blow, clash, collision, encounter, impact.
Ant. of (1) please.

shocking abominable, appalling, detestable, disgusting, dreadful, foul, frightful, hideous, horrible, horrifying, loathsome, nauseating, odious, outrageous, repulsive, revolting, sickening.
Ant. pleasant.

shoot (A) *v.* dart, discharge, emit, fire, hit, hurl, kill, project, propel.

shoot (B) (1) *v.* bud, germinate, sprout; (2) *n.* branch, bud, off-shoot, scion, sprout, twig.

short (1) brief, compendious, concise, curtailed, laconic, pithy, sententious, succinct, summary, terse; (2) deficient, inadequate, insufficient, lacking, limited, poor, scanty, wanting; (3) abrupt, blunt, curt, discourteous, impolite, sharp, uncivil; (4) direct, near, straight; (5) (*Pastry*) brittle crisp, crumbly, friable.
Ant. of (1) lengthy; of (2) adeqate; of (3) polite.

shorten abbreviate, abridge, curtail, cut, diminish, dock, lessen, reduce.
Ant. lengthen.

shove drive, elbow, impel, jostle, press, propel, push, thrust.
Ant. pull.

show (1) *v.* disclose, display, divulge, exhibit, indicate, reveal; (2) assert, clarify, demonstrate, elucidate, evince, explain, manifest, prove, teach; (3) accompany, conduct, guide, lead; (4) *n.* demonstration, display, exhibition, pageant, pageantry, parade, pomp, representation, sight, spectacle; (5) appearance, likeness, ostentation, pretence, pretext, profession, semblance.

showy flashy, garish, gaudy, loud, ostentatious, pompous, tawdry.
Ant. quiet, refined.

shred (1) bit, fragment, piece, rag, scrap, tatter; (2) (*Fig.*) iota, jot, particle.

shrew fury, nag, scold, termagant, virago, vixen.
Ant. (*Fig.*) angel, darling.

shrewd acute, artful, astute, crafty, cunning, discerning, discriminating, far-seeing, intelligent, keen, long-headed, perspicacious, sagacious, sharp, sly, wily.

Ant. stupid.

shrill acute, high-pitched, piercing, sharp.

shriek v. and n. cry, scream, screech, yell.

shrink (1) contract, decrease, dwindle, wither, wrinkle; (2) flinch, recoil, retire, wince, withdraw.

Ant. of (1) expand; of (2) attack.

shrivel (1) burn, dry, parch; (2) dwindle, shrink, wither.

shroud (1) v. cloak, conceal, cover, envelop, hide, screen, veil; (2) n. covering, winding-sheet.

Ant. of (1) expose.

shudder v. quake, quiver, shake, shiver, tremble.

shuffle (1) confuse, disarrange, disorder, intermix, jumble, mix, shift; (2) cavil, dodge, equivocate, evade, prevaricate, quibble.

Ant. of (1) arrange.

shun avoid, elude, escape, eschew, evade.

Ant. seek.

shut bar, close, confine, enclose, fasten.

Ant. open.

shy backward, bashful, cautious, coy, diffident, distrustful, modest, reserved, retiring, suspicious, timid, wary.

Ant. forward.

sick ailing, diseased, disordered, feeble, indisposed, poorly, unwell, weak.

Ant. hale, healthy.

sickening disgusting, distasteful, loathsome, nauseating, offensive, repulsive, revolting.

Ant. pleasant.

sickly ailing, delicate, faint,

feeble, indisposed, infirm, languid, pining, unhealthy.

sickness ailment, complaint, disease, disorder, illness, indisposition, malady.

Ant. health.

side (1) border, edge, margin, rim, verge; (2) cause, faction, party, sect, team.

Ant. of (1) inside, middle.

sift (1) part, separate; (2) analyse, examine, fathom, investigate, probe, scrutinise.

sigh complain, grieve, lament, long, mourn.

sight (1) eye, seeing, vision; (2) perception, view, visibility; (3) exhibition, pageant, scene, show, spectacle; (4) v. observe, perceive, see.

Ant. of (1) blindness.

sign (1) n. badge, emblem, evidence, hint, indication, manifestation, mark, note, proof, signal, suggestion, symptom, token; (2) augury, auspice, foreboding, forewarning, omen, portent, presage; (3) v. endorse, initial, subscribe; (4) beckon, gesture, indicate, signal, signify.

signal (1) n. beacon, indication, mark, sign; (2) a. conspicuous, eminent, extraordinary, famous, memorable, notable, remarkable.

Ant. of (2) ordinary.

significance (1) import, meaning, purport, sense, signification; (2) consequence, consideration, force, importance, impressiveness, weight.

Ant. of (2) triviality.

significant (1) critical, important, momentous, vital, weighty; (2) denoting, expressing, indicative.

Ant. of (1) insignificant.

signify announce, betoken,

communicate, denote, express, imply, indicate, intimate, matter, mean, proclaim, represent.

silence (1) calm, hush, noiselessness, peace, quiescence, quiet, stillness; (2) dumbness, muteness, reticence, speechlessness, taciturnity; (3) *v.* allay, calm, hush, quell, quiet, stifle, subdue.

Ant. of (1) noise; of (2) speech; of (3) incite, rouse.

silly absurd, childish, foolish, frivolous, idiotic, imprudent, inane, preposterous, ridiculous, senseless, stupid, unwise, witless.

Ant. sensible.

similar alike, congruous, corresponding, resembling, uniform.

Ant. dissimilar.

simple (1) clear, intelligible, lucid, plain, understandable; (2) artless, frank, guileless, ingenuous, innocent, naïve, sincere, unaffected, unsophisticated; (3) credulous, dense, foolish, shallow, silly, stupid; (4) elementary, single, unblended, uncombined, unmixed.

simulate act, affect, counterfeit, feign, pretend, sham.

sin (1) *n.* crime, error, evil, iniquity, offence, transgression, trespass, ungodliness, wickedness, wrong; (2) *v.* err, offend, transgress, trespass.

Ant. of (1) goodness.

sincere artless, candid, earnest, frank, genuine, guileless, honest, open, real, straightforward, true, unaffected, upright.

Ant. false, insincere.

sincerity artlessness, candour, frankness, honesty, genuine-

ness, guilelessness, probity truth, uprightness.

Ant. deceit, insincerity.

sinewy athletic, brawny, lusty, muscular, powerful, robust, strong, sturdy, vigorous.

Ant. weak.

sinful bad, corrupt, criminal, depraved, immoral, iniquitous, irreligious, ungodly, unholy, unrighteous.

Ant. good, upright.

single (1) distinct, individual, one, only, particular, separate, sole, solitary; (2) unmarried, unwed; (3) simple, unblended, uncompounded, unmixed.

Ant. of (1) several; of (2) married; of (3) blended.

singular (1) individual, separate, single; (2) curious, eminent, exceptional, extraordinary, noteworthy, queer, rare, remarkable, strange, uncommon, unique, unusual, unwonted.

Ant. of (2) commonplace.

sinister (1) ill-omened, inauspicious, injurious, ominous, unfortunate; (2) bad, base, corrupt, dishonest, evil, perverse, sinful, wicked.

Ant. of (1) auspicious; of (2) good.

sink (1) abate, decay, decline, descend, droop, drop, drown, ebb, engulf, fall, flag, lower, merge, plunge, submerge; (2) degrade, depress, destroy, ruin; (3) dig, excavate.

Ant. of (1) rise.

sinless faultless, guileless, immaculate, innocent, pure, unblemished, undefiled, unsullied, virtuous.

Ant. sinful.

sinuous crooked, curved, serpentine, tortuous, winding.

Ant. straight.

situation (1) locality, location, place, position, seat, site, spot; (2) employment, job, office, place, post; (3) (*Fig.*) case, circumstance, condition, plight, state.

size amount, bigness, bulk, dimensions, extent, greatness, largeness, magnitude, mass, volume.

skeleton (*Fig.*) draft, framework, outline, sketch.

sketch (1) *v.* delineate, depict, draw, paint, portray, represent; (2) *n.* delineation, design, drawing, outline, plan, plot, skeleton.

skilful able, accomplished, adept, adroit, apt, clever, competent, dexterous, experienced, expert, handy, intelligent, knowing, masterly, practised, proficient, quick, ready, skilled, trained.
Ant. clumsy, inexpert.

skill ability, accomplishment, adroitness, aptitude, art, cleverness, competence, dexterity, experience, expertness, facility, handiness, ingenuity, intelligence, knack, proficiency, quickness, readiness, skilfulness.
Ant. clumsiness.

skirmish affair, battle, brush, combat, conflict, contest, encounter, engagement.

skirt (1) *n.* border, edge, hem, margin, rim; (2) flap, (*Colloq.*) petticoat.

slack (1) easy, loose, relaxed; (2) backward, dull, easy-going, idle, inactive, inattentive, lazy, negligent, remiss, slow, sluggish, tardy; (3) *v.* dodge, flag, neglect, relax, shirk, slacken.
Ant. of (1) tight; of (2) hardworking; of (3) work.

slacken diminish, lessen, loosen, moderate, reduce, relax, retard, slack, tire.
Ant. increase.

slander (1) *n.* aspersion, backbiting, calumny, defamation, detraction, libel, obloquy, scandal; (2) *v.* backbite, calumniate, decry, defame, detract, disparage, libel, malign, traduce, vilify.
Ant. praise.

slanderous abusive, calumnious, defamatory, libellous, malicious.

slatternly dirty, slovenly, sluttish, unclean, untidy.
Ant. spotless.

slaughter (1) *n.* bloodshed, butchery, carnage, killing, massacre, murder, slaying; (2) *v.* butcher, destroy, kill, massacre, murder, slay.

slave (1) *n.* bondman, drudge, vassal, villein, serf, servant; (2) *v.* drudge, toil.
Ant. of (1) freeman.

slavery bondage, captivity, enslavement, serfdom, servitude, thraldom, vassalage.
Ant. freedom.

slavish abject, base, cringing, despicable, drudging, grovelling, low, mean, menial, obsequious, servile, sycophantic.
Ant. masterly.

slay assassinate, butcher, destroy, kill, massacre, murder, slaughter.
Ant. spare.

sleepiness doziness, drowsiness, lethargy, somnolence.
Ant. wakefulness.

sleepless disturbed, restless, wakeful.

sleepy drowsy, dull, heavy, inactive, lethargic, slow, sluggish, slumbersome, somnolent, torpid.

Ant. lively.

sleight adroitness, artifice, dexterity, skill.

slender (1) feeble, flimsy, fragile, lean, slight, slim, thin, weak; (2) inadequate, inconsiderable, insufficient, little, meagre, scanty, small, spare.

Ant. of (1) stout; of (2) adequate.

slight (1) *a.* delicate, feeble, fragile, inconsiderable, insignificant, meagre, scanty, small, superficial, trifling, trivial, unimportant, unsubstantial, weak; (2) *v.* affront, despise, disdain, disparage, disrespect, ignore, insult, neglect, scorn; (3) *n.* affront, contempt, disdain, disregard, disrespect, inattention, indifference, insult.

Ant. of (1) significant; of (2) and (3) compliment.

slim gaunt, lank, lean, poor, slender, slight, small, thin.

Ant. fat.

slimy (1) miry, muddy, oozy; (2) clammy, glutinous, mucous, viscous.

sling (1) cast, fling, hurl, throw; (2) hang, suspend.

slink skulk, slip, sneak.

slip (1) *v.* fall, glide, slide, trip; (2) blunder, err, mistake; (3) *n.* blunder, error, fault, mistake, oversight.

slippery (1) glassy, perilous, smooth, unsafe, unstable, unsteady; (2) (*Fig.*) cunning, dishonest, evasive, false, shifty, treacherous, tricky.

Ant. of (1) firm; of (2) honest.

slipshod careless, slovenly, untidy.

Ant. careful.

sloping inclining, oblique, slanting.

Ant. horizontal, straight.

sloth idleness, inaction, inactivity, indolence, inertia, inertness, laziness, sluggishness, torpor.

Ant. activity, industry.

slothful idle, inactive, indolent, inert, lazy, sluggish, torpid.

Ant. hard-working.

slouching awkward, loutish, uncouth, ungainly.

Ant. smart.

slovenly careless, disorderly, dowdy, heedless, loose, negligent, perfunctory, slack, untidy.

Ant. careful.

slow behind, behindhand, deliberate, dilatory, dull, inactive, late, lingering, slack, sluggish, stupid, tardy, tedious, wearisome.

Ant. quick.

sluggish dull, inactive, indolent, inert, phlegmatic, slothful, slow, torpid.

Ant. brisk.

slumber doze, nap, repose, sleep, snooze.

Ant. wake.

slur *n.* affront, aspersion, brand, calumny, disgrace, innuendo, insinuation, insult, reproach, stain, stigma.

Ant. respect.

sly arch, artful, astute, clever, crafty, cunning, furtive, insidious, secret, stealthy, subtle, underhand, wily.

Ant. above-board, guileless.

small diminutive, inadequate, insufficient, miniature, minute, paltry, petty, puny, slender, slight, thin, trifling, trivial, unimportant.

Ant. large.

smart (A) (1) adept, agile, apt, bright, brisk, clever, intelligent, nimble, quick, ready, sharp; (2) chic, elegant, fashionable, fine, neat, spruce, trim.

Ant. of (1) dull; of (2) dowdy.

smart (B) (1) *v.* hurt, pain, sting; (2) *a.* keen, painful, piercing, pungent, sharp, stinging.

smash (1) *v.* break, crash, crush, shatter; (2) (*Fig.*) defeat, destroy, disrupt, overthrow, ruin; (3) *n.* collision, crash; (4) (*Fig.*) collapse, defeat, destruction, ruin.

Ant. of (1) repair.

smear blot, blotch, daub, patch, plaster, spot, stain.

Ant. clean.

smell (1) *n.* aroma, fragrance, odour, perfume, scent; (2) stench, stink; (3) *v.* scent, sniff.

smite (1) beat, buffet, destroy, kill, slay, strike; (2) (*Fig.*) afflict, chasten, punish.

smooth (1) *a.* even, flat, glossy, level, plain, polished, sleek, soft; (2) agreeable, bland, mild, oily, pleasant, soothing; (3) calm, equable, peaceful, tranquil, undisturbed; (4) *v.* flatten, level, plane, polish; (5) (*Fig.*) allay, alleviate, appease, assuage, calm, ease, extenuate, mitigate, mollify, palliate, soften.

Ant. of (1) uneven; of (5) aggravate.

smother (1) choke, extinguish, stifle, strangle, suffocate; (2) conceal, hide, repress, suppress.

Ant. of (2) reveal.

smug (1) complacent, conceited, self-opinionated, self-satisfied; (2) neat, nice, spruce, trim.

Ant. of (1) dissatisfied.

snap (1) break, crack; (2) bite, catch, grip, seize.

snare (1) *v.* catch, entrap, net,

seize, trap; (2) *n.* catch, gin net, noose, trap.

Ant. of (1) release.

snarl complain, growl, grumble, mumble, murmur.

snatch (1) *v.* clutch, grab, grasp, grip, pluck, pull, wrench, wrest; (2) *n.* bit, fragment, part, piece.

Ant. of (1) free.

sneak cower, lurk, skulk, slink, snoop, steal.

sneer (1) *v.* deride, disdain, jeer, gibe, laugh, mock, ridicule, scoff, scorn; (2) *n.* derision, disdain, jeer, gibe, mockery, ridicule, scorn.

Ant. respect.

sniff breathe, inhale, smell snuff.

snowy (*Poet.*) immaculate pure, spotless, unblemished, unsullied, white.

Ant. dirty.

snub (1) chide, humble, humiliate, mortify, rebuke, reprimand, reprove, shame, slight; (2) *n.* affront, check, insult, rebuke, reprimand, reproof.

Ant. compliment.

snug close, comfortable, compact, cosy.

soak damp, drench, moisten, saturate, steep, wet.

Ant. dry.

soar ascend, fly, mount, rise, tower.

Ant. descend.

sober (1) abstemious, abstinent, moderate, temperate; (2) calm, composed, cool, dispassionate, grave, peaceful, quiet, rational, reasonable, sedate, serene, serious, solemn, sound, staid, steady, subdued, unexcited, unruffled.

Ant. of (1) drunk; of (2) immoderate.

sobriety (1) abstemiousness

abstinence, moderation, soberness, temperance; **(2)** calmness, composure, coolness, gravity, reasonableness, sedateness, seriousness, solemnity, staidness, steadiness.

Ant. of **(1)** immoderation; of **(2)** excitability.

sociable accessible, affable, approachable, companionable, familiar, friendly, genial, neighbourly, social.

Ant. boorish.

society (1) association, community, companionship, company, fellowship, fraternity, partnership; **(2)** brotherhood, circle, club, corporation, fellowship, group, union.

soft (1) flexible, impressible, malleable, plastic, pliable, smooth, yielding; **(2)** bland, compliant, effeminate, gentle, lenient, sensitive, submissive; **(3)** kind, mild, sympathetic, tender, weak; **(4)** dulcet, melodious, pleasing, quiet, soothing, sweet; **(5)** foolish, silly, simple.

soften (1) melt; **(2)** abate, allay, alleviate, appease, assuage, calm, diminish, lessen, moderate, modify, mitigate, quell, soothe, still.

Ant. of **(2)** aggravate.

soil (1) *v.* begrime, besmirch, defile, dirty, foul, pollute, spot, stain; **(2)** *n.* dirt, earth, ground, loam; **(3)** country, land.

sojourn abide, dwell, lodge, reside, rest, stay, stop, tarry.

Ant. travel.

solace (1) *n.* alleviation, comfort, consolation, relief; **(2)** *v.* allay, alleviate, comfort, console, mitigate, soften, soothe.

Ant. of **(1)** grief.

sole alone, individual, one, only, singular, solitary.

Ant. several.

solemn (1) august, grand, grave, imposing, impressive, majestic, sedate, serious, sober, staid; **(2)** ceremonial, ceremonious, devotional, dignified, formal, religious, reverential, ritual, sacred, venerable.

Ant. of **(1)** jovial; of **(2)** informal.

solemnise celebrate, commemorate, honour, keep, reserve.

Ant. profane.

solemnity (1) celebration, ceremonial, ceremony, observance, rite, sacredness, sanctity; **(2)** gravity, impressiveness, seriousness.

solicit ask, beg, beseech, crave, entreat, implore, importune, petition, pray, seek, supplicate,

solicitous anxious, apprehensive, careful, concerned, disturbed, eager, earnest, troubled, uneasy, worried.

Ant. unconcerned.

solid (1) compact, dense, firm, genuine, good, hard, real, reliable, sound, stable, strong, sturdy, substantial, vigorous; **(2)** complete, unanimous, united.

Ant. of **(1)** unreliable.

solitary alone, desolate, isolated, lone, lonely, lonesome, remote, retired, secluded, sequestered, unfrequented.

Ant. busy.

solitude (1) isolation, loneliness, privacy, retirement, seclusion; **(2)** desert, waste, wilderness.

Ant. of **(1)** society.

solution (1) answer, elucidation, explanation, explication, key, resolution, result; **(2)**

disconnection, dissolution, liquefaction, melting.

Ant. of (2) union.

solve answer, clarify, disentangle, elucidate, explain, expound, interpret, unfold.

sombre dark, dim, dismal, doleful, dull, dusky, funereal, gloomy, lugubrious, melancholy, obscure, shady.

Ant. bright.

somnolent dozy, drowsy, sleepy.

Ant. wakeful.

song anthem, ballad, canticle, canzonet, carol, ditty, hymn, lay, ode, poem, poetry, psalm, sonnet, strain, verse.

sonorous high-sounding, loud, resonant, resounding, ringing, sounding.

Ant. soft.

soothe allay, alleviate, appease, assuage, calm, compose, ease, mitigate, mollify, pacify, quiet, relieve, soften, tranquillise.

Ant. excite.

soothsayer augur, diviner, foreteller, prophet, seer.

sophistry fallacy, quibble, stratagem, trick.

soporific *n.* anaesthetic, hypnotic, narcotic, opiate, sedative, tranquilliser.

sorcery charm, divination, enchantment, incantation, magic, necromancy, spell, witchcraft, wizardry.

sordid (1) base, degraded, dirty, foul, low, mean, vile; (2) avaricious, close-fisted, covetous, greedy, miserly, niggardly, stingy, ungenerous.

Ant. of (1) clean; of (2) generous.

sore (1) *n.* abscess, boil, gathering, ulcer; (2) (*Fig.*) affliction, grief, pain, sorrow, trouble; (3)

a. acute, distressing, grievous, irritated, painful, raw, severe, sharp, tender; (4) afflicted, aggrieved, grieved, pained, vexed.

sorrow (1) *n.* affliction, distress, grief, mourning, sadness, trouble, woe; (2) *v.* bemoan, bewail, grieve, lament, moan, mourn, weep.

Ant. of (1) joy; of (2) rejoice.

sorrowful afflicted, dejected, depressed, disconsolate, distressing, doleful, grievous, lamentable, lugubrious, melancholy, mournful, painful, piteous, sad, sorry.

Ant. happy.

sorry (1) afflicted, disconsolate, dismal, grieved, hurt, lugubrious, melancholy, mournful, sad, sorrowful; (2) abject, base, mean, miserable, paltry, pitiful, poor, shabby, vile, wretched.

Ant. of (1) pleased; of (2) splendid.

sort (1) *n.* character, class, denomination, description, family, genus, group, kind, nature, order, quality, race, species, type; (2) manner, means, method, style, way; (3) *v.* arrange, assort, choose, class, classify, distribute, divide, rank, select, separate.

Ant. of (3) disarrange.

soul (1) essence, intellect, life, mind, reason, spirit; (2) (*Fig.*) animation, ardour, courage, energy, fervour, vivacity; (3) individual, man, person.

Ant. of (1) body.

soulless (1) callous, cold, cruel, unfeeling, unkind, unsympathetic; (2) dead, lifeless, spiritless.

Ant. of (1) sympathetic.

sound (A) (1) *a.* complete, entire, firm, forcible, hale, healthy, hearty, lusty, perfect, robust, undamaged, unhurt, unimpaired, uninjured, vigorous, whole; (2) correct, fair, fixed, just, orthodox, proper, reasonable, reliable, right, true, trustworthy, valid, well-grounded.

Ant. unsound.

sound (B) (1) *n.* din, noise, report, resonance, tone, voice; (2) *v.* announce, echo, express, pronounce, resound, utter.

Ant. of (1) silence.

sound (C) (1) *v.* fathom, plumb, probe; (2) (*Fig.*) examine, inspect, investigate, test; (3) *n.* (*Geog.*) channel, passage, strait.

sour (1) acid, bitter, pungent, sharp, tart, unpleasant; (2) (*Fig.*) acrimonious, bad-tempered, churlish, crabbed, cross, cynical, harsh, ill-natured, ill-tempered, petulant, rude, testy, touchy, uncivil; (3) *v.* embitter, exacerbate, exasperate.

Ant. of (1) sweet; of (2) sweet-tempered.

source beginning, cause, commencement, fountain-head, origin, originator, rise, spring.

souvenir keepsake, memento, reminder.

sovereign (1) *n.* chief, emperor, empress, king, monarch, potentate, prince, queen, ruler, shah, tsar; (2) *a.* chief, dominant, imperial, kingly, monarchial, paramount, predominant, principal, regal, royal, supreme; (3) effectual, efficacious, efficient, excellent.

Ant. of (1) subject; of (2) subordinate; of (3) ineffectual.

space (1) amplitude, capacity, extension, extent, room; (2) distance, interval; (3) duration, period, time, while.

spaceman astronaut, cosmonaut.

spacious ample, broad, capacious, commodious, expansive, extensive, huge, large, roomy, vast.

Ant. confined.

span (1) amount, distance, extent, length (*Obs.* 9 inches), reach, stretch; (2) period, spell; (3) (*Animals*) couple, pair, team, yoke.

spare (1) *v.* afford, allow, bestow, give, grant; (2) hoard, husband, preserve, reserve, save, store; (3) *a.* economical, frugal, scanty, sparing; (4) gaunt, lank, lean, meagre, slender, slight, slim.

Ant. of (2) squander; of (3) wasteful; of (4) plump.

sparkle (1) *v.* beam, coruscate, flash, glare, gleam, glisten, glitter, glow, scintillate, shine, spark, twinkle; (2) bubble, effervesce.

spartan brave, bold, courageous, daring, dauntless, doughty, fearless, hardy, heroic, intrepid, valorous.

Ant. timorous, unmanly.

spasm fit, paroxysm, throe, twitch.

spasmodic convulsive, fitful, irregular.

Ant. regular.

speak (1) articulate, converse, discourse, enunciate, pronounce, say, talk, utter, voice; (2) address, argue, declaim, harangue, plead, speechify.

special (1) appropriate, certain, distinctive, especial, individual, particular, peculiar, specific; (2) exceptional, extraordinary, uncommon, unusual.

Ant. ordinary.

species class, collection,

description, group, kind, sort, variety.

specific characteristic, definite, especial, limited, particular, peculiar, precise.

Ant. vague.

specify define, designate, indicate, individualise, mention, name, particularise.

specimen copy, example, model, pattern, proof, sample, type.

specious deceptive, feasible, misleading, ostensible, plausible.

Ant. genuine.

speck (1) blemish, blot, defect, fault, flaw, spot, stain; (2) atom, bit, dot, mite, mote, particle.

spectacle (1) display, exhibition, pageant, parade, representation, review, show, sight; (2) curiosity, marvel, wonder.

spectator beholder, bystander, observer, onlooker, witness.

Ant. performer.

spectre apparition, ghost, phantom, shade, shadow, wraith.

speculate (1) cogitate, consider, contemplate, meditate, scheme, surmise, theorise; (2) gamble, hazard, risk.

speculation (1) conjecture, consideration, contemplation, guess, hypothesis, supposition, surmise, theory; (2) gamble, gambling, hazard, risk.

Ant. of (2) certainty.

speech (1) conversation, dialect, idiom, language, talk, tongue; (2) address, discourse, harangue, oration.

speechless (1) dumb, inarticulate, mute, silent; (2) (*Fig.*) aghast, amazed, astounded, dum(b)founded, shocked.

speed (1) *v.* despatch, expedite, hasten, hurry, press, quicken, urge; (2) advance, aid, assist, further, help; (3) *n.* celerity, fleetness, haste, hurry, quickness, rapidity, swiftness, velocity; (4) luck, prosperity, success.

Ant. of (3) slowness.

speedy fast, fleet, hasty, hurried, nimble, prompt, quick, rapid, swift.

Ant. slow.

spell (A) charm, exorcism, fascination, magic, witchery.

spell (B) interval, period, season, term, turn.

spell (C) decipher, interpret, read.

spend (1) consume, disburse, dispense, dissipate, exhaust, expend, lavish, squander, waste; (2) [bestow, employ, pass, use.

Ant. of (1) save.

spendthrift *n.* prodigal, spender, squanderer, waster.

spent *a.* exhausted, weakened, wearied.

spew disgorge, puke, throw, vomit.

sphere (1) ball, circle, circuit, compass, globe, orb, orbit; (2) capacity, department, employment, function, province, range, scope; (3) country, domain, field, realm, region.

spherical globular, orbicular, rotund, round.

Ant. square.

spicy aromatic, balmy, fragrant, piquant, pungent, racy.

Ant. tasteless.

spirit (1) air, breath, life, soul; (2) apparition, ghost, phantom, shade, shadow, spectre, sprite; (3) demon, elf, fairy; (4) character, complexion, disposition, essence, humour, quality, temper; **(5)** ardour, courage, earnestness, energy, enthusiasm, fire, force, liveliness, mettle, resolution, vigour, **warmth**; **(6)** alcohol, liquor.

Ant. of **(1)** body; of **(5)** apathy.

spirited active, animated, ardent, bold, courageous, energetic, lively, sprightly, vivacious.

Ant. calm.

spiritless (1) dead, inert, lifeless, soulless; **(2)** apathetic, dejected, depressed, despondent, dispirited, dull, languid, melancholy, torpid.

Ant. of **(2)** uplifted.

spiritual divine, ethereal, ghostly, holy, incorporeal, nonmaterial, pure, religious, sacred.

Ant. material, secular.

spite (1) n. animosity, gall, hate, hatred, ill-will, malevolence, malice, malignity, pique, rancour, spleen, venom; **(2)** v. annoy, harm, hurt, injure, offend, pique, vex.

Ant. of **(1)** benevolence.

spiteful ill-disposed, ill-natured, malevolent, malicious, malignant, rancorous, venomous, vindictive.

Ant. benevolent.

spleen (1) anger, animosity, hatred, ill-humour, malevolence, malice, malignity, pique, wrath; **(2)** dejection, depression, despondency, hypochondria, melancholy.

Ant. of **(1)** kindness; of **(2)** happiness.

splendid (1) beaming, bright, brilliant, glowing, lustrous, radiant, refulgent; **(2)** dazzling, gorgeous, imposing, magnificent, superb; **(3)** celebrated,

distinguished, eminent, famous, glorious, grand, heroic, illustrious, magnificent, remarkable, renowned, sublime.

Ant. of **(1)** dull; of **(3)** ordinary.

splendour brilliance, brightness, display, eminence, glory, grandeur, lustre, magnificence, pomp, refulgence, renown, show, stateliness.

Ant. dullness.

splenetic choleric, churlish, crabbed, cross, fretful, irascible, irritable, morose, peevish, petulant, sullen, testy, touchy.

Ant. genial.

split (1) v. break, burst, cleave, crack, divide, part, rend, separate, splinter; **(2)** n. breach, crack, division, fissure, rent, separation; **(3)** (*Fig.*) difference, discord, disruption, disunion, partition, schism.

Ant. of **(1)** join; of **(3)** unity.

spoil (1) pillage, plunder, ravage, rob, waste; **(2)** damage, destroy, disfigure, harm, impair, injure, mar, ruin, wreck.

Ant. of **(2)** restore.

spoils booty, gain, loot, pillage, plunder, prey, rapine.

spontaneous free, gratuitous, instinctive, natural, unbidden, uncompelled, unconstrained, voluntary, willing.

Ant. deliberate.

sporadic infrequent, irregular, occasional, scattered, separate.

Ant. continuous.

sport (1) amusement, diversion, entertainment, frolic, fun, game, mirth, play, recreation; **(2)** (*Fig.*) derision, laughing-stock, mockery, ridicule; **(3)** v. caper, frolic, gambol, play, romp.

Ant. of **(1)** work.

spot (A) (1) n. blemish, blot

flaw, mark, speck, stain, taint;
(2) v. blot, mark, soil, speckle,
stain, sully, taint, tarnish.
    Ant. of (2) clean.
spot (B) n. locality, place, position, site, situation.
spotless blameless, chaste,
immaculate, innocent, irreproachable, pure, unblemished,
unstained, unsullied, untarnished.
    Ant. impure.
spouse companion, consort,
husband, mate, partner, wife.
spread (1) dilate, expand,
extend, open, stretch, unfurl,
unroll; (2) advertise, broadcast, circulate, disseminate,
proclaim, promulgate, propagate, publicise; (3) arrange,
cover, furnish, prepare, set.
    Ant. of (1) contract; of (2)
conceal.
sprightly agile, airy, animated, blithe, brisk, cheerful,
frolicsome, gay, joyous, lively,
nimble, vivacious.
    Ant. spiritless.
spring (1) v. bound, hop, jump,
leap, rebound, recoil, vault; (2)
arise, emanate, emerge, grow,
issue, originate, proceed, start;
(3) n. bound, hop, jump, leap,
vault; (4) cause, fountain-
head, origin, source, well.
sprite apparition, elf, fairy,
goblin, imp, pixy, spirit.
sprout v. bud, germinate,
grow, push, spring, vegetate.
    Ant. die.
spruce dainty, elegant,
(*Colloq.*) natty, neat, smart,
trim.
    Ant. dowdy.
spry active, agile, alert, brisk,
nimble, quick, ready, sprightly,
supple.
    Ant. awkward, inactive.
spur (1) v. animate, drive, goad,

impel, incite, press, prick,
stimulate, urge; (2) n. goad,
prick, rowel; (3) (*Fig.*) impulse,
incentive, inducement, motive,
stimulus.
    Ant. of (3) discouragement.
spurious artificial, bogus,
counterfeit, deceitful, false,
feigned, mock, pretended,
sham, unauthentic.
    Ant. genuine.
spurn contemn, despise, disdain, disregard, reject, scorn.
    Ant. approve.
squabble v. bicker, brawl,
dispute, fight, quarrel, row,
wrangle.
    Ant. agree.
squalid dirty, disgusting,
filthy, foul, low, nasty, repulsive, sordid, unclean.
    Ant. clean.
squander dissipate, expend,
lavish, misuse, scatter, spend,
waste.
    Ant. save.
square v. (*Fig.*) accommodate,
accord, adapt, adjust, balance,
fit, harmonise, mould, regulate,
settle, suit.
squeamish (1) critical, delicate, fastidious, hard-to-please,
nice, particular, punctilious,
scrupulous; (2) qualmish,
sickish.
    Ant. of (1) indifferent.
squeeze (1) compress, crowd,
crush, grip, jostle, nip, press,
punch, squash; (2) hug,
embrace.
stab v. cut, gore, injure, spear,
thrust, transfix, wound.
stability constancy, dura-
bility, firmness, permanence,
steadiness, strength.
    Ant. instability.
stable abiding, constant, durable, established, fast, firm,
fixed, immutable, invariable,

lasting, permanent, secure, steadfast, steady, sure, unalterable, unchangeable.

Ant. inconstant, unstable.

stagger (1) falter, hesitate, lurch, reel, totter, vacillate, waver; (2) (*Fig.*) amaze, astonish, astound, dum(b)found, nonplus, shock, surprise.

stagnant inactive, inert, motionless, quiet, sluggish, standing, still, torpid.

Ant. running.

staid calm, composed, demure, grave, sedate, serious, sober, solemn, steady.

Ant. giddy.

stain (1) *v.* blemish, blot, discolour, dye, soil, tarnish, tinge; (2) contaminate, corrupt, defile, deprave, disgrace; (3) *n.* blemish, blot, discolouration, spot; (4) (*Fig.*) disgrace, dishonour, infamy, reproach, shame.

Ant. of (1) clean; of (4) honour.

stainless blameless, clean, faultless, guileless, innocent, pure, spotless, undefiled, untarnished.

Ant. dirty, unclean.

stake (A) picket, pole, stick.

stake (B) (1) *n.* bet, chance, hazard, peril, pledge, risk, venture, wager; (2) *v.* bet, hazard, imperil, jeopardise, pledge, risk, venture, wager.

stale (1) decayed, faded, flat, fusty, insipid, musty, old, sour, tasteless; (2) common, commonplace, effete, hackneyed, stereotyped, threadbare, trite.

Ant. of (1) fresh; of (2) original.

stalk *v.* follow, hunt, pace, pursue, stride, strut, walk.

stalwart athletic, brawny, daring, indomitable, intrepid,

lusty, manly, muscular, redoubtable, robust, stout, strapping, sturdy, valiant, vigorous.

Ant. weak.

stamina force, lustiness, power, resistance, strength, vigour.

Ant. weakness.

stammer falter, hesitate, pause, stutter.

stamp (1) *v.* beat, brand, impress, imprint, mark, mould; (2) *n.* brand, cast, imprint, mark, mould; (3) character, cut, description, fashion, form, kind, sort, type.

stand (1) *v.* continue, halt, pause, remain, rest, stay, stop; (2) abide, allow, bear, endure, suffer, support, sustain, tolerate; (3) *n.* halt, rest, stop; (4) determination, effort, resistance; (5) dais, grandstand, place, platform, stall, table, terrace, terracing.

Ant. of (1) move; of (2) resist.

standard (A) criterion, gauge, grade, guide, example, measure, model, norm, pattern, rule, sample, type.

standard (B) banner, colours, ensign, flag, pennant, pennon, streamer.

standing condition, credit, estimation, position, rank, status.

starchy (*Colloq.*) ceremonious, formal, precise, prim, punctilious, stiff.

Ant. informal.

stark (1) *a.* absolute, bare, arrant, downright, entire, pure, sheer, utter; (2) desolate, depressing, drear, dreary, grim, solitary; (3) rigid, stiff; (4) *adv.* completely, entirely, quite, wholly.

start (1) *v.* arise, begin, commence, depart, initiate, issue, originate; (2) alarm, disturb, frighten, jump, rouse, scare, startle, twitch; (3) begin, establish, found; (4) *n.* beginning, commencement, foundation, initiation, outset; (5) fit, jump, motion, spasm, twitch.

Ant. of (1) end.

startle agitate, alarm, amaze, astonish, astound, frighten, scare, shock, surprise.

Ant. calm.

startling alarming, astonishing, astounding, shocking, sudden, surprising, unexpected, unforeseen.

Ant. expected.

state (A) (1) *v.* affirm, assert, aver, declare, enumerate, explain, express, narrate, propound, represent, say, specify; (2) *n.* case, category, condition, plight, position, predicament, situation; (3) dignity, display, glory, grandeur, majesty, pomp, splendour.

state (B) commonwealth, federation, government, nation, republic, territory.

stately august, ceremonious, dignified, elegant, grand, imperial, imposing, lofty, majestic, noble, pompous, regal, royal, solemn.

Ant. lowly.

statement account, announcement, communication, declaration, description, explanation, narration, proclamation, relation, report, utterance.

station (1) *n.* depot, location, place, position, post, seat, situation; (2) appointment, business, calling, employment, grade, position, post, rank, standing, status; (3) *v.* assign, establish, fix, locate, post, set.

Ant. of (3) move.

status condition, degree, grade, position, rank, standing.

statute act, decree, edict, enactment, ordinance, regulation.

staunch constant, faithful, firm, loyal, reliable, resolute, sound, stout, steadfast, strong, true, trustworthy, trusty.

Ant. unfaithful.

stay (1) *v.* abide, continue, delay, halt, linger, lodge, pause, remain, reside, sojourn, stand, stop, tarry, wait; (2) arrest, check, curb, detain, hinder, hold, impede, obstruct, prevent; (3) bolster, brace, buttress, prop, strengthen, support, sustain, uphold; (4) *n.* delay, halt, pause, stop; (5) brace, buttress, prop, support.

Ant. of (1) leave.

steadfast constant, established, faithful, fast, firm, persevering, reliable, resolute, stable, staunch, unwavering.

Ant. fickle.

steady (1) balanced, constant, continuous, even, firm, fixed, regular, steadfast, unchangeable, uniform, uninterrupted; (2) sedate, sober, staid.

Ant. of (1) changeable.

steal embezzle, filch, peculate, pilfer, purloin, rob, swindle, take, thieve.

stealthy clandestine, covert, furtive, secret, skulking, sly, sneaking, surreptitious, underhand.

Ant. open.

steep (A) *v.* damp, drench, imbrue, immerse, macerate, moisten, soak, submerge.

steep (B) *a.* abrupt, headlong, precipitous, sheer.

Ant. sloping.

steer conduct, control, direct, govern, guide, pilot.

stem (A) *n.* branch, shoot, stalk, stock, trunk.

stem (B) *v.* check, dam, oppose, resist, stay, stop, withstand.
Ant. yield.

step (1) gait, footprint, pace, stride, trace, track, walk; (2) act, action, deed, expedient, means, measure, procedure, proceeding; (3) advance, advancement, degree, grade, progression; (4) round, rung, stair, tread.

sterile bare, barren, dry, empty, unfruitful, unproductive, unprolific.
Ant. fertile.

sterling genuine, pure, real, sound, standard, substantial.
Ant. counterfeit.

stern austere, bitter, cruel, forbidding, hard, harsh, inflexible, relentless, rigid, rigorous, severe, strict, unrelenting, unyielding.
Ant. lenient.

stick (A) *v.* adhere, attach, cement, cleave, cling, fix, glue, hold, paste, persist, remain, stop.
Ant. detach.

stick (B) *v.* gore, insert, penetrate, pierce, puncture, spear, stab, thrust, transfix.

stick (C) *n.* bat, baton, birch, bludgeon, cane, club, cudgel, pole, rod, staff, stake, switch, truncheon, wand.

sticky adhesive, gluey, glutinous, gummy, tacky, viscid, viscous.

stiff (1) austere, firm, inflexible, rigid, solid, unbending, unyielding; (2) obstinate, pertinacious, resolute, tenacious, unrelenting; (3) ceremonious, formal, pompous, priggish, prim, punctilious, (*Colloq.*) starchy; (4) awkward, clumsy,

crude, graceless, inelegant, ungainly; (5) austere, hard, harsh, inexorable, rigorous, severe, strict.
Ant. of (1) yielding; of (2) complaisant; of (3) unceremonious; of (4) graceful; of (5) kind, lax.

stifle (1) choke, garrotte, smother, strangle, suffocate; (2) check, conceal, deaden, extinguish, hush, prevent, repress, silence, still, stop, suppress.
Ant. of (2) encourage.

stigma (1) blot, blur, brand, mark, spot, stain; (2) (*Fig.*) disgrace, dishonour, reproach, shame, spot.

still (1) *a.* calm, hushed, inert, motionless, noiseless, peaceful, placid, quiet, serene, silent, stationary, tranquil; (2) *v.* allay, alleviate, appease, calm, hush, pacify silence, smooth, tranquillise; (3) *conj.* but, however, nevertheless, notwithstanding, yet.
Ant. of (1) disturbed.

stilted bombastic, grandiloquent, high-flown, high-sounding, inflated, pompous, pretentious.
Ant. simple.

stimulate animate, arouse, encourage, fire, goad, impel, incite, inflame, instigate, prompt, provoke, rouse, spur, urge.
Ant. depress.

stimulus encouragement, goad, incentive, spur.

sting afflict, hurt, pain, wound.

stingy avaricious, close-fisted, covetous, mean, miserly, niggardly, parsimonious, penurious.
Ant. lavish.

stipend allowance, compensation, emoluments, fees, living, honorarium, pay, remuneration, salary, wages.

stipulate agree, bargain, contract, covenant, engage, settle.

stipulation agreement, bargain, condition, contract, engagement, settlement.

stir (1) v. agitate, animate, disturb, excite, incite, instigate, move, prompt, raise, shake, spur, stimulate, urge; (2) n. ado, agitation, bustle, commotion, disorder, emotion, excitement, ferment, movement, tumult.

Ant. of (1) allay; of (2) quietness.

stock (1) v. accumulate, fill, furnish, gather, hoard, reserve, save, store, supply; (2) n. goods, hoard, reserve, store, supplies; (3) (*Animals*) cattle, horses, sheep; (4) (*Money*) capital, funds, property; (5) (*Gun*) butt, haft, handle; (6) ancestry, descent, family, house, lineage, parentage, pedigree, race; (7) body, stalk, stem, trunk; (8) a. commonplace, hackneyed, trite, usual.

stoical apathetic, calm, cool, impassive, imperturbable, indifferent, phlegmatic.

Ant. excitable.

stolid doltish, dull, heavy, obtuse, slow, stupid.

Ant. intelligent.

stony (*Fig.*) adamant, hard, inexorable, merciless, obdurate, pitiless, unfeeling.

Ant. compassionate.

stoop (1) bend, bow, crouch, descend, kneel, lean; (2) (*Fig.*) condescend, deign, descend, vouchsafe.

stop (1) v. cease, conclude, desist, discontinue, end, finish,

halt, terminate; (2) arrest, bar, block, break, check, close, hinder, impede, intercept, interrupt, obstruct, plug, prevent, repress, restrain, suspend; (3) lodge, rest, sojourn, stay, tarry; (4) n. cessation, conclusion, end, finish, halt, station, termination, terminus; (5) bar, block, break, check, control, hindrance, impediment, plug.

Ant. of (1) start; of (2) continue.

store (1) v. deposit, hoard, husband, reserve, save, stock; (2) n. abundance, accumulation, fund, hoard, plenty, provision, reserve, stock, supply; (3) emporium, market, shop, storehouse, storeroom, supermarket.

Ant. of (1) spend; of (2) scarcity.

storm (1) n. blast, blizzard, cyclone, gale, gust, hurricane, squall, tempest, tornado, whirlwind; (2) (*Fig.*) agitation, clamour, commotion, disturbance, outbreak, outburst, strife, tumult, turmoil; (3) v. assail, assault; (4) n. assault, attack, onset, onslaught, rush; (5) v. complain, fume, rage, rant, scold.

Ant. of (1) calm.

stormy blustering, blustery, boisterous, gusty, squally, tempestuous, turbulent, wild, windy.

Ant. calm.

story account, anecdote, chronicle, history, legend, narration, narrative, novel, recital, record, relation, romance, statement, tale.

stout (1) burly, corpulent, fat, obese, plump, portly; (2) athletic, brawny, hardy, lusty, robust, stalwart, sturdy, vigorous; (3) bold, brave, courageous, dauntless, doughty, gallant, intrepid, manly, resolute, valiant, valorous.

Ant. of (1) lean; of (2) weak; of (3) cowardly.

straight (1) erect, perpendicular, right, upright, vertical; (2) direct, near, short, undeviating, unswerving; (3) (*Fig.*) candid, equitable, fair, frank, honest, honourable, just, reliable, straightforward, upright.

Ant. of (1) sloping; of (2) winding; of (3) dishonest.

strain (1) *v.* exert, injure, overexert, sprain, stretch, tear, tighten, tire, twist, weaken, wrench; (2) filter, seep, sieve, sift, percolate, purify; (3) *n.* effort, exertion, force, injury, pressure, sprain, wrench; (4) ancestry, descent, family, lineage, pedigree, race, stock; (5) streak, tendency, trait; (6) lay, melody, music, song, tune.

Ant. of (1) relax.

strait (1) *a.* close, confined, constricted, contracted, limited, narrow, rigorous, severe, strict; (2) *n.* difficulty, dilemma, embarrassment, emergency, hardship, pass, perplexity, plight, predicament; (3) (*Naut.*) channel, narrows, sound.

Ant. of (1) broad; of (2) relief.

straitened difficult, distressed, embarrassed, limited, reduced.

Ant. relieved.

stranded (1) aground, ashore, beached, wrecked; (2) (*Fig.*) homeless, penniless.

strange abnormal, alien, astonishing, curious, eccentric, exceptional, extraordinary, foreign, irregular, marvellous, new, novel, odd, peculiar, queer, rare, singular, unaccountable, uncommon, unfamiliar, unknown, wonderful.

Ant. familiar, ordinary.

stranger alien, foreigner, guest, visitor.

Ant. acquaintance, native.

strangle choke, garrotte, smother, suffocate, throttle.

stratagem artifice, device, dodge, intrigue, manoeuvre, plan, plot, ruse, scheme, trick, wile.

stray (1) deviate, digress, ramble; (2) range, roam, rove, wander; (3) straggle, swerve.

Ant. of (2) stay.

stream (1) *n.* brook, burn, course, current, drift, flow, freshet, river, rivulet, run, rush, tide, tributary; (2) *v.* emit, flow, glide, gush, issue, pour, run, shed, spout.

streamer banner, colours, ensign, flag, pennant, pennon, standard.

strength (1) courage, energy, firmness, force, fortitude, might, potency, power, resolution, spirit, vehemence, vigour; (2) brawniness, lustiness, robustness, stoutness.

Ant. weakness.

strengthen (1) animate, encourage, fortify, harden, invigorate; (2) confirm, corroborate, establish, justify, substantiate, support.

Ant. of (1) weaken.

strenuous active, ardent, bold, eager, earnest, determined, energetic, intrepid, resolute, spirited, strong, vigorous, zealous.

Ant. ineffective.

stress (1) force, importance, pressure, strain, urgency, weight; (2) accent, emphasis.

Ant. of (1) relief.

stretch draw, elongate, expand, extend, lengthen, pull, reach, spread, strain, tighten, unfold.

strict (1) austere, harsh, rigorous, severe, stern, stringent; (2) accurate, close, exact, particular, precise, scrupulous.

Ant. of (1) lenient; of (2) loose.

stricture animadversion, blame, censure, criticism.

Ant. praise.

strife animosity, battle, clash, conflict, contention, contest, discord, quarrel, row, struggle.

Ant. peace.

strike (1) beat, buffet, chastise, hit, knock, pound, punish, slap, smite; (2) clash, collide, dash, touch; (3) drive, force, impel, thrust; (4) mutiny, revolt.

striking astonishing, extraordinary, forcible, impressive, wonderful.

stringent binding, exacting, rigid, rigorous, severe, strict.

Ant. lenient.

strip (1) v. disrobe, uncover, undress; (2) bare, denude, deprive, despoil, dismantle, divest, loot, peel, pillage, plunder, ransack, rob, sack, skin, spoil; (3) n. band, bit, piece, shred.

Ant. of (1) cover.

strive attempt, compete, contend, endeavour, exert, fight, struggle, toil, try.

stroke (1) n. blow, hit, knock, pat, rap, thump; (2) affliction, calamity, hardship, misfortune, reverse; (3) apoplexy, attack, fit, shock; (4) v. caress, rub.

stroll (1) v. ramble, range,

roam, rove, stray, wander; (2) n. excursion, promenade, ramble, tour, trip, walk.

Ant. of (1) run.

strong (1) athletic, brawny, capable, efficient, hale, hardy, healthy, lusty, muscular, powerful, robust, sinewy, sound, stalwart, stout, sturdy, tough; (2) ardent, eager, firm, staunch, tenacious, zealous; (3) biting, highly-flavoured, hot, intoxicating, piquant, pungent, sharp, spicy; (4) bright, brilliant, dazzling.

Ant. weak.

structure (1) arrangement, configuration, construction, form, formation, make; (2) building, edifice, erection, pile.

struggle (1) v. aim, contend, contest, endeavour, fight, labour, strive, toil, try, wrestle; (2) n. battle, conflict, contest, fight, strife; (3) aim, endeavour, exertion, labour, pains, toil.

stubborn contumacious, dogged, dour, headstrong, inflexible, intractable, obdurate, obstinate, persistent, refractory, unbending, unmanageable, unyielding, wilful.

Ant. docile.

studied deliberate, planned, premeditated, well-considered, wilful.

Ant. spontaneous.

studious assiduous, attentive, careful, diligent, eager, hardworking, meditative, reflective, scholarly, thoughtful.

Ant. inattentive.

study (1) v. cogitate, con, consider, contemplate, estimate, examine, learn, meditate, ponder, read, scrutinise, think, (2) n. application, attention, cogitation, consideration, contemplation, inquiry, learning, research, scrutiny, thought.

stumble fall, slip, stagger, trip.

stun amaze, astonish, astound, bewilder, confound, confuse, daze, dum(b)found, overcome, overpower, shock, stupefy.

stunted diminutive, dwarfish, little, small, tiny, undersized.
Ant. big.

stupendous amazing, astounding, huge, overwhelming, prodigious, surprising, tremendous, vast, wonderful.
Ant. ordinary.

stupid doltish, dull, foolish, inane, obtuse, senseless, simple, slow, sluggish, stolid, witless.
Ant. intelligent.

stupor coma, daze, lethargy, numbness, stupefaction, torpor.
Ant. liveliness.

sturdy athletic, brawny, firm, hardy, hearty, lusty, muscular, powerful, resolute, robust, vigorous, well-built.
Ant. weak.

style (1) v. address, call, christen, denominate, designate, dub, entitle, name, term; (2) n. chic, elegance, fashion, smartness; (3) approach, manner, method, mode; (4) appearance, characteristic, kind, sort, type; (5) diction, expression, phraseology, turn.

stylish courtly, fashionable, genteel, modish, polished.
Ant. slovenly.

suave affable, agreeable, bland, complaisant, gracious, obliging, pleasing, polite, smooth-tongued, sophisticated, svelte, urbane, worldly.
Ant. boorish.

subdue break, control, conquer, crush, defeat, discipline, master, overcome, overpower, quell, repress, soften, subject, suppress, vanquish.
Ant. yield.

subject (1) v. break, conquer, dominate, enslave, subdue, subjugate, quell, tame, vanquish; (2) abandon, expose, refer, submit; (3) a. dependent, inferior, obedient, submissive, subordinate, subservient; (4) exposed, liable, open, prone; (5) n. dependent, subordinate; (6) cause, ground, motive, reason; (7) matter, object, point, subject-matter, theme, topic.
Ant. of (4) immune; of (5) superior.

subjugate conquer, crush, defeat, master, overcome, overpower, overthrow, quell, reduce, subdue, subject, suppress, tame.
Ant. yield.

sublimate elevate, exalt, heighten, refine.

sublime elevated, eminent, exalted, glorious, grand, great, high, magnificent, majestic, noble.
Ant. lowly.

sublunary earthly, mundane, terrestrial.

submerge deluge, dip, drown, flood, immerse, inundate, overflow, (Fig.) overwhelm, plunge, sink.

submissive acquiescent, amenable, compliant, docile, humble, lowly, meek, obedient, passive, patient, resigned, subdued, tractable, uncomplaining, yielding.
Ant. intractable, obdurate.

submit (1) acquiesce, bend, bow, capitulate, comply,

endure, resign, stoop, surrender, tolerate, yield; (2) commit, propose, refer.

Ant. of (1) resist.

subordinate (1) *a.* ancillary, dependent, inferior, junior, minor, secondary, subject, subservient; (2) *n.* assistant, dependent, inferior, junior, subject.

subscribe (1) contribute, donate, give, offer, promise; (2) agree, assert, consent.

subscription aid, assistance, contribution, donation, gift, offering.

subsequent after, ensuing, following, later, succeeding.

Ant. former, prior.

subservient (1) inferior, obsequious, servile, subject, subordinate; (2) ancillary, conducive, helpful, instrumental, serviceable, subsidiary, useful.

Ant. of (1) superior.

subside (1) decline, descend, drop, ebb, lower, settle, sink; (2) abate, decrease, diminish, lessen, wane.

Ant. of (1) rise; of (2) increase.

subsidence (1) decline, descent, ebb, settling, sinking; (2) abatement, decrease, diminution, lessening.

subsidiary aiding, ancillary, auxiliary, co-operative, helpful, secondary, serviceable, subordinate, subservient, supplementary, useful.

Ant. primary, principal.

subsidy aid, assistance, grant, help, subvention, support.

subsist be, continue, endure, exist, last, live, remain.

Ant. starve.

subsistence aliment, existence, food, keep, living, livelihood, maintenance, provision,

support, sustenance, rations, victuals.

Ant. starvation.

substance (1) body, material, stuff, texture; (2) essence, gist, import, matter, meaning, pith, significance, subject, theme; (3) estate, means, property, wealth.

Ant. of (3) poverty.

substantial (1) actual, existent, material, positive, real, true; (2) efficient, firm, massive, solid, stout, strong, valid, weighty.

Ant. of (1) unreal; of (2) weak.

substantially adequately, essentially, firmly, materially, positively, really, truly.

substantiate confirm, corroborate, establish, prove, verify.

Ant. disprove.

substitute (1) *v.* change, commute, exchange, interchange, replace; (2) *n.* agent, depute, deputy, locum, makeshift, equivalent, expedient, proxy, representative.

Ant. of (2) chief, head.

subterfuge artifice, dodge, evasion, excuse, pretence, pretext, quibble, shift, trick.

Ant. confession.

subtle (1) arch, artful, astute, crafty, cunning, designing, intriguing, keen, shrewd, sly; (2) deep, delicate, ingenious, nice, penetrating, profound.

Ant. simple.

subtlety (1) artfulness, astuteness, craftiness, cunning, guile; (2) acumen, acuteness, cleverness, discernment, sagacity.

Ant. simplicity.

subtract deduct, detract, diminish, remove, take, withdraw.

Ant. add.

suburbs environs, neighbourhood, outskirts, precincts, purlieus.

subversive destructive, overthrowing, perversive, ruining, upsetting.

subvert (1) demolish, destroy, overturn, raze, ruin, upset; (2) confound, corrupt, pervert.

succeed (1) flourish, prosper, thrive; (2) ensue, follow, inherit, replace.

Ant. of (1) fail; of (2) precede.

success fortune, happiness, (*Colloq.*) hit, luck, prosperity.

Ant. failure.

successful auspicious, favourable, felicitous, fortunate, happy, lucky, prosperous, victorious.

Ant. unsuccessful.

succession (1) chain, course, order, sequence, series, suite; (2) descendants, descent, line, lineage, race.

succinct brief, compact, compendious, concise, condensed, laconic, pithy, summary, terse.

Ant. diffuse.

succour (1) aid, assist, comfort, encourage, foster, help, nurse, relieve; (2) *n*. aid, assistance, comfort, help, relief, support.

Ant. of (1) hinder; of (2) hindrance.

succulent juicy, luscious, lush, sappy.

Ant. dry.

succumb capitulate, die, submit, surrender, yield.

Ant. resist.

sudden abrupt, hasty, hurried, quick, rapid, rash, unexpected, unforeseen, unusual.

Ant. deliberate, foreseen.

sue (1) petition, plead, supplicate; (2) (*Law*) charge, indict, prosecute, summon.

suffer admit, allow, bear, experience, feel, permit, support, sustain, tolerate, undergo.

Ant. resist.

sufferable allowable, bearable, endurable, permissible, tolerable.

Ant. intolerable.

sufferance allowance, endurance, forbearance, misery, pain, patience, submission, suffering, toleration.

suffering affliction, agony, distress, endurance, hardship, misery, pain.

Ant. relief.

suffice content, satisfy.

Ant. dissatisfy.

sufficient adequate, ample, enough, full, plenteous, plentiful, qualified, satisfactory.

Ant. insufficient.

suffocate asphyxiate, choke, smother, stifle, strangle.

suffrage ballot, consent, franchise, (*Fig.*) voice, vote.

suggest advise, allude, hint, indicate, insinuate, intimate, propose, recommend.

Ant. withdraw.

suggestion allusion, hint, indication, insinuation, intimation, proposal, recommendation.

suit (1) *v*. accommodate, adapt, become, befit, fashion, fit, gratify, match, please; (2) agree, answer, correspond, harmonise, tally; (3) *n*. appeal, entreaty, invocation, petition, prayer, request; (4) (*Law*) action, case, cause, prosecution, trial; (5) clothing, costume, dress, habit.

Ant. of (2) differ; of (3) response.

suitable agreeable, applicable, appropriate, apt, becoming,

befitting, convenient, due, fitting, pertinent, relevant.
Ant. unsuitable.

suite (1) attendants, escort, followers, retainers, retinue, train; (2) collection, furniture, rooms, set.

sulky aloof, churlish, cross, ill-humoured, moody, morose, perverse, splenetic, sullen, testy, vexatious.
Ant. jovial.

sullen cheerless, cross, dismal, dull, gloomy, heavy, ill-natured, moody, mournful, obstinate, perverse, sour, stubborn, surly.
Ant. cheerful.

sully blemish, contaminate, darken, dirty, disgrace, dishonour, pollute, spoil, spot, stain, tarnish.
Ant. clean.

sultry close, damp, hot, humid, oppressive, stifling, stuffy,
Ant. cool, fresh.

sum aggregate, amount, entirety, quantity, total, whole.
Ant. part.

summary (1) abridgment, abstract, compendium, digest, epitome, essence, extract, outline, résumé; (2) *a.* brief, compact, compendious, concise, condensed, laconic, pithy, succinct.
Ant. of (2) lengthy.

summit acme, apex, crown, culmination, head, height, peak, pinnacle, top, zenith,
Ant. base, foot.

summon (1) arouse, bid, call, cite, convene, convoke, invite, rouse; (2) (*Law*) charge, indict, prosecute, sue.
Ant. dismiss.

sumptuous costly, dear, expensive, gorgeous, grand, lavish, luxurious, magnificent,

pompous, rich, splendid, superb.
Ant. austere, cheap, inexpensive.

sunburnt browned, bronzed, ruddy, tanned.
Ant. pale.

sunder break, disconnect, disjoin, disunite, divide, part, separate, sever.
Ant. attach, join.

sundry different, divers, several, some, various.
Ant. few.

sunny (1) bright, brilliant, clear, fine, luminous, radiant, unclouded; (2) (*Fig.*) cheerful, genial, happy, joyful, pleasant.
Ant. of (1) dark; of (2) morose.

superannuated aged, antiquated, decrepit, obsolete, old, pensioned, retired, senile, unfit.
Ant. youthful.

superb admirable, excellent, exquisite, fine, gorgeous, grand, magnificent, splendid, superior.
Ant. inferior.

supercilious arrogant, contemptuous, disdainful, haughty, high, imperious, lordly, overbearing, proud, scornful, vainglorious.
Ant. humble.

superfluity excess, exuberance, redundancy, surfeit.
Ant. deficiency.

superfluous excessive, needless, redundant, superabundant, unnecessary, useless.
Ant. deficient.

superintend control, direct, inspect, manage, overlook, oversee, supervise.

superintendence care, charge, control, direction, government, guidance, inspection, management, supervision.

superintendent conductor, controller, curator, custodian, director, governor, inspector, manager, overseer, supervisor, warden.

superior (1) a. better, excellent, good, high, higher, paramount, predominant, prevailing, surpassing, unrivalled, upper; **(2)** n. chief, principal.
Ant. inferior.

superiority advantage, ascendency, excellence, predominance, prevalence, supremacy.
Ant. inferiority.

superlative consummate, excellent, greatest, highest, peerless, surpassing, supreme, transcendent.
Ant. lowest.

supernatural abnormal, miraculous, unnatural, preternatural.

supernumerary excessive, odd, redundant, superfluous.

supersede annul, displace, oust, overrule, remove, replace, supplement, suspend.

supervise administer, conduct, control, direct, inspect, oversee, superintend.

supine (1) (Fig.) apathetic, careless, drowsy, heedless, idle, indifferent, indolent, inert, languid, lazy, lethargic, listless, negligent, sluggish, slothful, torpid; **(2)** lying, prone, prostrate, recumbent.
Ant. of **(1)** active; of **(2)** erect.

supplant displace, overthrow, remove, replace, supersede, undermine.
Ant. retain.

supple (1) bending, elastic, flexible, limber, lithe, pliable, pliant; **(2)** (Fig.) compliant, fawning, humble, obsequious, servile, submissive, yielding.
Ant. of **(1)** stiff, inflexible; of **(2)** stubborn, unyielding.

supplement (1) n. addition, appendix, codicil, postscript, sequel; **(2)** v. add, supply.
Ant. of **(2)** subtract.

suppliant (1) a. begging, beseeching, craving, entreating, imploring; **(2)** n. petitioner, solicitor, suitor, supplicant.

supplicate beg, beseech, crave, entreat, implore, importune, petition, plead, solicit.
Ant. demand.

supplication entreaty, invocation, petition, pleading, prayer, request, solicitation.
Ant. order.

supply (1) v. afford, contribute, fill, furnish, give, grant, minister, provide, replenish, satisfy, stock, store, yield; **(2)** n. hoard, provision, reserve, stock, store.
Ant. of **(1)** withhold.

support (1) v. bear, brace, cherish, maintain, nourish, prop, sustain, uphold; **(2)** advocate, aid, assist, back, confirm, defend, forward, help, promote, second, substantiate, uphold; **(3)** bear, endure, stand, submit, suffer, tolerate, undergo; **(4)** n. brace, pillar, prop, shore, stay; **(5)** aid, assistance, keep, help, livelihood, maintenance, relief, succour, sustenance.
Ant. of **(1)** hinder; of **(2)** oppose.

suppose (1) believe, conceive, conclude, conjecture, consider, imagine, judge, regard, view; **(2)** assume, imply, infer, presuppose.

supposition conjecture, doubt, guess, hypothesis, postulate, presumption, surmise.

suppress check, conquer, crush, overpower, overthrow, quash, quell, repress, restrain, smother, stifle, stop, subdue.

Ant. free, liberate.

supremacy domination, dominion, lordship, mastery, predominance, pre-eminence, sovereignty.

supreme chief, foremost, greatest, head, highest, leading, paramount, predominant, pre-eminent, prevailing, principal, sovereign, superlative.

Ant. least, lowest.

sure (1) accurate, assured, certain, confident, convinced, honest, indisputable, positive, precise, reliable, trustworthy, trusty, undoubted, unfailing; (2) firm, safe, secure, solid, stable, steady.

Ant. uncertain.

surety bail, bond, bondsman, certainty, guarantee, pledge, safety, security.

surfeit (1) n. excess, glut, satiety, superabundance, superfluity; (2) v. cram, fill, glut, gorge, overfeed, satiate, stuff.

Ant. of (1) paucity, scarcity.

surge (1) heave, rise, rush, swell; (2) n. billow, breaker, roller, swell, wave.

surly churlish, crabbed, cross, gruff, ill-natured, morose, perverse, pettish, petulant, sulky, sullen, testy, uncivil, ungracious.

Ant. genial.

surmise (1) v. conclude, conjecture, consider, fancy, guess, imagine, presume, suppose, suspect; (2) n. conclusion, con-

jecture, guess, idea, notion, possibility, suspicion, thought.

surmount conquer, exceed, master, overcome, overpower, overtop, pass, surpass, vanquish.

Ant. yield.

surpass beat, eclipse, exceed, excel, outdo, outstrip, override, transcend.

Ant. fail.

surplus balance, excess, remainder, residue, superabundance, surfeit.

Ant. deficit.

surprise (1) v. amaze, astonish, astound, bewilder, confuse, disconcert, startle; (2) n. amazement, astonishment, bewilderment, wonder.

surprising amazing, astonishing, extraordinary, marvellous, remarkable, startling, unexpected, unusual, wonderful.

Ant. ordinary.

surrender (1) v. abandon, capitulate, cede, forego, relinquish, renounce, resign, submit, succumb, waive; (2) n. capitulation, relinquishment, resignation, submission.

Ant. of (1) resist.

surreptitious clandestine, fraudulent, furtive, secret, sly, stealthy, unauthorised, underhand.

Ant. above-board, open.

surround (1) encircle, enclose, encompass, environ; (2) (Mil.) besiege, invest.

surveillance care, control, direction, inspection, oversight, superintendence, supervision, vigilance, watch.

Ant. neglect.

survey (1) v. examine, inspect, observe, review, scan, scrutinise, supervise, view, watch; (2)

estimate, measure, plan, plot, prospect; (**3**) *n.* examination, inspection, review, scrutiny; (**4**) estimating, measuring, planning, plotting, prospecting, work-study.

survive endure, last, outlive.
Ant. die, predecease.

susceptible impressionable, sensitive, tender, touchy.
Ant. unimpressionable.

suspect (**1**) distrust, doubt, mistrust; (**2**) believe, conclude, conjecture, consider, fancy, guess, suppose, surmise.
Ant. of (**2**) accept.

suspend (**1**) append, attach, hang; (**2**) arrest, cease, debar, defer, delay, discontinue, dismiss, interrupt, postpone, stay, withhold.
Ant. of (**2**) continue.

suspense (**1**) anxiety, apprehension, doubt, indecision, irresolution, wavering; (**2**) cessation, hesitation, interruption, pause, respite, rest, stop.
Ant. of (**1**) certainty.

suspicion (**1**) distrust, doubt, jealousy, misgiving, mistrust; (**2**) conjecture, guess, idea, notion, surmise.
Ant. of (**1**) trust.

suspicious distrustful, doubtful, jealous, mistrustful, questionable, suspecting.
Ant. trustful.

sustain (**1**) bear, carry, support, uphold; (**2**) aid, assist, comfort, help, maintain, nourish, relieve; (**3**) bear, endure, feel, suffer, undergo; (**4**) approve, confirm, ratify.
Ant. of (**1**) hinder; of (**2**) neglect; of (**4**) disapprove.

sustenance aliment, food, maintenance, nourishment, provisions, subsistence, support, victuals.

swagger bluster, boast, brag, bully, hector, strut.

swain (**1**) countryman, peasant, rustic; (**2**) (*Poet.*) lover.
Ant. of (**1**) townsman.

swallow absorb, consume, devour, drink, eat.
Ant. disgorge.

swamp (**A**) *v.* capsize, engulf, flood, overwhelm, sink, upset, wreck.

swamp (**B**) bog, fen, marsh, morass, quagmire.

swap, swop barter, exchange, trade, traffic.

sward grass, lawn, turf.

swarm (**1**) *n.* army, bevy, concourse, crowd, drove, flock, herd, horde, host, mass, multitude, shoal; (**2**) *v.* abound, crowd, teem, throng.

swarthy black, brown, dark, dark-skinned, dusky, tawny.
Ant. fair.

sway (**1**) *v.* bend, incline, lean, lurch, roll, swing, wave; (**2**) (*Fig.*) control, direct, dominate, govern, guide, influence, reign, rule; (**3**) *n.* (*Fig.*) ascendency, authority, command, control, dominion, government, influence, power, predominance, rule, sovereignty.
Ant. of (**2**) obey; of (**3**) subjection.

swear (**1**) affirm, assert, attest, avow, declare, promise, testify, vow; (**2**) blaspheme, curse.
Ant. of (**1**) deny.

sweep (**1**) *v.* brush, clean, clear, remove; (**2**) *n.* bend, curve; (**3**) range, scope.

sweeping (**1**) broad, comprehensive, extensive, wholesale, wide; (**2**) (*Fig.*) exaggerated, overdrawn, overstated, unqualified.
Ant. of (**1**) narrow; of (**2**) qualified.

sweet (1) honeyed, luscious, sugary, syrupy; (2) aromatic, balmy, fragrant, perfumed, redolent; (3) clean, fresh, new, pure; (4) dulcet, euphonious, harmonious, melodious, musical, silvery, soft, tuneful; (5) affectionate, agreeable, amiable, attractive, beautiful, charming, delightful, engaging, fair, gentle, loveable, tender, winning, winsome.
Ant. of (1) bitter, sour; of (4) cacophonous, discordant.

swell (1) *v.* bulge, dilate, enlarge, expand, extend, grow, heave, increase, protrude; (2) aggravate, augment, enhance, heighten; (3) *n.* (*Naut.*) billow, surge, wave; (4) (*Sl.*) beau, blade, dandy, fop.
Ant. of (1) diminish.

swerve bend, deflect, depart, deviate, diverge, incline, stray, turn, wander, wind.

swift expeditious, fast, fleet, nimble, prompt, quick, rapid, ready, speedy, sudden.
Ant. slow.

swiftness celerity, expedition, fleetness, quickness, rapidity, speed, velocity.
Ant. slowness.

swindle (1) *v.* cheat, deceive, defraud, dupe, hoax, trick; (2) *n.* deceit, deception, fraud, hoax, imposition, knavery, roguery, trickery.

swindler charlatan, cheat, impostor, knave, rascal, rogue, (*Sl.*) sharper, trickster.

swing dangle, hang, oscillate, rock, suspend, sway, vibrate, wave.

swoop (1) *v.* descend, pounce, rush, stoop, sweep; (2) *n.* descent, pounce, rush, stoop, sweep.

sword blade, brand, claymore,

cutlass, falchion, foil, rapier, sabre, scimitar.

sybarite epicure, epicurean, sensualist, voluptuary.
Ant. ascetic.

sycophancy adulation, cringing, fawning, flattery, grovelling, obsequiousness, servility, toadyism.
Ant. independence, self-respect.

sycophant cringer, fawner, flatterer, (*Colloq.*) hanger-on, lickspittle, parasite, toady, (*Colloq.*) yes-man.

syllabus abridgment, abstract, compendium, digest, epitome, outline, summary, synopsis.

symbol badge, emblem, figure, mark, representation, sign, token, type.

symbolical emblematic, figurative, representative, significant, typical.
Ant. actual.

symmetry balance, form, harmony, order, proportion, regularity, shapeliness.
Ant. disproportion.

sympathetic affectionate, commiserating, compassionate, condoling, kind, tender.
Ant. unsympathetic.

sympathy (1) commiseration, compassion, condolence, tenderness, thoughtfulness; (2) affinity, agreement, correspondence, harmony, union.

symptom indication, mark, note, sign, token.

synonymous equivalent, identical, interchangeable, similar.
Ant. dissimilar.

synopsis abridgment, abstract, compendium, conspectus, digest, epitome, outline, précis, résumé, summary, syllabus.

tab 347 **tar**

T

tabernacle cathedral, chapel, church, synagogue, temple.

table (1) board, counter, slab, stand, tablet; (2) catalogue, index, list, record, schedule, synopsis; (3) (*Fig.*) diet, fare, food, victuals.

tacit implicit, implied, inferred, silent, understood, unexpressed, unspoken.
Ant. explicit.

taciturn dumb, mute, reserved, reticent, silent, uncommunicative.
Ant. communicative.

tack affix, append, attach, fasten, nail, stitch.

tackle (A) *v.* capture, clutch, grasp, hook, seize.

tackle (B) *n.* apparatus, equipment, gear, implements, rigging.

tact ability, address, adroitness, cleverness, dexterity, diplomacy, discretion, judgment, perception, understanding.

tail conclusion, end, extremity.
Ant. head.

taint (1) *v.* blot, contaminate, corrupt, defile, imbue, impregnate, infect, pollute, soil, sully, tarnish, vitiate; (2) *n.* blemish, blot, defect, fault, flaw, spot, stain.
Ant. of (1) cleanse.

take (1) capture, catch, clutch, ensnare, entrap, grasp, grip, obtain, seize, win; (2) drink, eat, imbibe, inhale, swallow; (3) accept, adopt, assume, consider, hold, presume, regard.

tale (1) account, fable, fiction, legend, narration, narrative, novel, relation, report,

romance, story; (2) catalogue, reckoning, tally.
Ant. of (1) fact.

talent ability, aptitude, bent, capacity, faculty, forte, genius, gift, knack, parts, power.
Ant. stupidity.

tally (1) *v.* accord, agree, coincide, conform, correspond, harmonise, match, square, suit; (2) *n.* counterpart, match, mate; (3) reckoning, score.
Ant. of (1) conflict.

tame (1) amenable, disciplined, docile, domesticated, gentle, meek, mild, submissive, tractable; (2) (*Fig.*) boring, dull, tedious, vapid, wearisome; (3) *v.* conquer, curb, discipline, domesticate, enslave, repress, subdue, subjugate.
Ant. of (1) wild; of (2) interesting.

tamper alter, damage, interfere, meddle.

tang flavour, savour, taste.

tangible definite, discernible, evident, material, palpable, perceptible, positive, real, substantial tactile, touchable.
Ant. abstract, unreal.

tangle (1) interlace, interlock, intertwist, interweave, mat, twist; (2) (*Fig.*) complicate, embarrass, embroil, entangle, involve.

tantalise balk, disappoint, frustrate, irritate, provoke, tease, thwart, torment, torture, vex.
Ant. appease.

tantamount equal, equivalent, synonymous.
Ant. unequal.

tantrum fit, ill-humour, outburst, temper, whim.

tap (1) knock, rap, strike, touch; (2) broach, extract, pierce.

tardiness dilatoriness, lateness, procrastination, slowness.

tardy backward, behindhand, dilatory, late, loitering, procrastinating, slack, slow, sluggish.
Ant. early, quick.

tarnish blemish, blot, darken, dim, discolour, dull, soil, spot, stain, sully taint.
Ant. brighten.

tarry abide, delay, dwell, linger, lodge, loiter, put off, remain rest, sojourn, stay, wait.
Ant. depart.

tart (1) acid, acidulous bitter, piquant, pungent, sharp, sour; (2) acrimonious, biting, cutting, harsh, petulant, snappish, testy.
Ant. of (1) sweet; of (2) mild, placid.

task (1) n. business, duty, employment enterprise, exercise job, labour lesson, occupation, toil, undertaking, work; (2) v. strain, test.
Ant. leisure.

taste (1) v. experience, feel, relish, savour, sip. try, undergo; (2) n. flavour, relish, savour, sip; (3) (Fig.) desire, fondness, liking, predilection; (4) (Fig.) discernment, discrimination, elegance, judgment, style; (5) (Fig.) character.
Ant. of (2) insipidity; of (4) inelegance.

tasteful (1) palatable, savoury, toothsome; (2) (Fig.) elegant, refined, smart, stylish.

tasteless dull, insipid, uninteresting.

tattle v. babble, chatter, gossip, prate, prattle.

taunt (1) v. censure, deride, flout, insult, jeer, mock, reproach, revile, ridicule, sneer,

upbraid; (2) n. censure, derision, gibe, insult, jeer, reproach, ridicule.
Ant. respect.

taut strained, stretched, tense, tight.
Ant. loose.

tautology iteration, pleonasm, prolixity, redundancy, verbosity.
Ant. brevity.

tawdry flashy, gaudy, glittering, ostentatious, showy, tinselly.
Ant. refined.

tax (1) n. assessment, charge, custom, duty, excise, imposition, tariff, toll, tribute; (2) v. assess, demand, requisition; (3) burden load, strain; (4) accuse, charge.

teach advise, direct, discipline, drill, educate, impart, inculcate inform instruct, school, tutor, train.
Ant. learn.

teacher adviser, counsellor, director, (Scot.) dominie, educator, guide, instructor, master, mentor, pedagogue, professor, schoolmaster, tutor.
Ant. learner, pupil.

tear claw, divide, lacerate, mangle, rend, rip, sever, split, sunder.
Ant. mend.

tease bother disturb, harass, irritate, plague, provoke, tantalise, torment, vex, worry.
Ant. mollify.

tedious annoying, boring, dull, irksome, monotonous, prosy, tiring, uninteresting, wearisome.
Ant. interesting.

teem (1) abound, bear, produce, swarm; (2) discharge, empty, overflow.

teeming abundant, fruitful,

full, numerous, overflowing, replete, swarming.

Ant. scanty.

tell (1) acquaint, announce, communicate, disclose, divulge, express, impart, inform, mention, narrate, proclaim, relate, reveal, speak, state, utter; (2) discern, distinguish, identify; (3) bid, command, order; (4) calculate, count, enumerate, number, reckon.

temper (1) *n.* anger, annoyance, heat, ill-humour, irritability, irritation, passion, resentment; (2) disposition, frame, humour, mood, nature, temperament; (3) calmness, composure, coolness, equanimity, tranquillity; (4) *v.* abate, allay, assuage, calm, mitigate, moderate, mollify, restrain, soften, soothe.

Ant. of (4) aggravate.

temperament constitution, disposition, mood, nature, temper.

temperamental irritable, hypersensitive, moody, sensitive, touchy.

temperate abstemious, calm, continent, cool, dispassionate, mild, moderate, self-restrained.

Ant. immoderate.

tempest cyclone, gale, hurricane, squall, storm, tornado.

Ant. calm.

tempestuous blustery, boisterous, breezy, gusty, squally, stormy, windy.

Ant. calm.

temporal (1) earthly, mundane, secular, worldly; (2) fleeting, temporary, transient, transitory.

Ant. of (1) spiritual; of (2) eternal.

temporary brief, ephemeral, evanescent, fleeting, impermanent, momentary, short-lived, transient, transitory.

Ant. permanent.

tempt (1) attempt, prove, provoke, test, try; (2) allure, attract, decoy, entice, incite, instigate, inveigle, lure, seduce.

tempting alluring, attractive, enticing, inviting, seductive.

tenable defensible, maintainable, rational, reasonable, sound.

Ant. indefensible.

tenacious determined, firm, obstinate, persistent, pertinacious, resolute, retentive, stubborn, sure.

Ant. feeble, vacillatory.

tenacity determination, doggedness, firmness, obstinacy, perseverance, persistance, resoluteness, stubbornness.

Ant. slackness, vacillation.

tend (1) attend, feed, guard, keep, manage, nurse, protect, serve, wait, watch; (2) incline, lean; (3) conduce, contribute, lead.

tendency bent, bias, course, disposition, drift, inclination, liability, leaning, proclivity, proneness, propensity, susceptibility, trend.

tender (A) *a.* affectionate, compassionate, gentle, humane, kind, loving, merciful, pitiful, sentimental, soft-hearted, sympathetic; (2) delicate, feeble, fragile, soft; (3) acute, painful, raw, sensitive, sore.

Ant. of (1) unkind; of (2) strong.

tender (B) *v.* offer, present, proffer, propose, suggest.

tenebrous dark, dusky, gloomy, obscure, shady, sombre.

Ant. bright.

tenet belief, creed, doctrine, dogma, opinion, principle.

tenor aim, course, direction, drift, intent, meaning, purport, tendency, way.

tense (1) rigid, strained, stretched, taut; (2) (*Fig.*) exciting, moving.

tentative essaying, experimental, provisional, testing, toying.
Ant. certain.

tenure (*Law*) holding, occupancy, occupation, possession.

term (1) *v.* call, denominate, designate, entitle, name, style; (2) *n.* appellation, denomination, designation, expression, name, phrase, title; (3) bound, boundary, confine, limit, terminus; (4) period, season, space, spell, time.

termagant scold, shrew, spitfire, virago, vixen.
Ant. (*Fig.*) angel.

terminal (1) *a.* bounding, final, limiting, ultimate; (2) *n.* end, extremity, limit, termination.

terminate cease, close, complete, conclude, end, eventuate, finish, issue, result.
Ant. begin.

termination close, completion, conclusion, consequence, effect, issue, result.
Ant. beginning.

terrestrial earthly, mundane, worldly.
Ant. heavenly.

terrible appalling, awful, dire, dreadful, fearful, frightful, gruesome, horrible, horrid, horrifying, monstrous, shocking, terrifying.
Ant. pleasant.

terrify alarm, appal, awe, dismay, frighten, horrify, intimidate, scare, shock.

territory country, district, domain, province, region, state.

terror alarm, anxiety, awe, consternation, dismay, dread, fear, horror, intimidation.
Ant. unconcern.

terse brief, compact, concise, condensed, curt, laconic, pithy, sententious, short, succinct, summary.
Ant. diffuse, long-winded.

test (1) *v.* assay, examine, experiment, prove, try; (2) *n.* attempt, examination, ordeal, proof, trial.

testify affirm, assert, attest, certify, corroborate, declare, depone, depose, vouch, witness.
Ant. deny.

testimonial certificate, credential, recommendation, reference.

testimony affirmation, attestation, confirmation, corroboration, declaration, deposition, evidence, proof, witness.

testy acrimonious, captious, crabbed, cross, fretful, impatient, irascible, irritable, peevish, petulant, short-tempered, splenetic, touchy.
Ant. good-tempered.

tetchy crabbed, cross, fretful, irritable, peevish, sullen, touchy.
Ant. good-natured.

tether chain, fasten, fetter, manacle, rope, tie.

text (1) copy, subject, theme, topic, treatise; (2) (*Bib.*) paragraph, passage, sentence, verse.

texture constitution, fabric, grain, make, structure, tissue.

thankful beholden, grateful, indebted, obliged.

thaw dissolve, liquefy, melt, soften.

theatre (1) opera-house, playhouse; (2) (*Fig.*) arena, field, seat, stage.

theatrical (1) dramatic, histrionic, melodramatic, scenic; (2) (*Fig.*) affected, artificial, ceremonious, ostentatious, pompous, showy, unreal.
Ant. of (2) natural.

theft embezzlement, fraud, larceny, pilfering, purloining, stealing, swindling, thievery, thieving.

theme (1) subject, text, thesis; (2) idea, topic, trend; (3) composition, dissertation, essay, paper.

theoretical conjectural, hypothetical, impractical, speculative.
Ant. practical.

theory (1) assumption, conjecture, guess, hypothesis; (2) plan, proposal, scheme, system.
Ant. practice.

therefore accordingly, consequently, hence, so, then, thence, whence.

thesaurus dictionary, encyclopædia, repository, storehouse, treasury.

thick (1) close, compact, condensed, crowded, dense; (2) bulky, fat, plump, solid, squat; (3) abundant, frequent, numerous; (4) confused, inarticulate, indistinct; (5) (*Weather*) cloudy, foggy, hazy, misty; (6) (*Colloq.*) confidential, familiar, friendly, intimate.
Ant. of (1) sparse; of (2) thin; of (5) clear.

thicket clump, coppice, copse, grove, wood, woodland.

thief burglar, cheat, cracksman, embezzler, housebreaker, pickpocket, pilferer, plunderer, purloiner, robber, swindler.

thieve cheat, embezzle, peculate, pilfer, plunder, purloin, rob, steal, swindle.

thin attenuated, delicate, fine,

flimsy, gaunt, (*Poet.*) gossamer, lean, light, meagre, scanty, scraggy, scrawny, skinny, slender, slight, slim, spare, sparse, transparent, unsubstantial.
Ant. fat, thick.

thing being, body, matter, object, substance, part, portion, something.

think (1) cogitate, consider, contemplate, deliberate, meditate, muse, ponder, reason, reflect; (2) believe, conceive, conclude, determine, imagine, judge, surmise; (3) esteem, hold, reckon, regard, suppose.

thirst (1) drought, dryness; (2) (*Fig.*) appetite, craving, desire, eagerness, longing, yearning.

thirsty (1) arid, dry, parched; (2) (*Fig.*) eager, greedy, hungry, longing, yearning.
Ant. of (2) satisfied.

thorn (1) prickle, spike, spine; (2) (*Fig.*) annoyance, bother, curse, nuisance, pest, plague, torment, torture, trouble.
Ant. of (2) pleasure.

thorny (1) pointed, prickly, sharp, spiky, spinous, spiny; (2) (*Fig.*) difficult, harassing, hard, troublesome, trying, upsetting, vexatious, worrying.
Ant. of (2) easy.

thorough (1) complete, entire, finished, total; (2) absolute, downright, perfect.
Ant. of (1) incomplete.

though admitting, allowing, although, granted, granting, however, if, nevertheless, notwithstanding, still, yet.

thought (1) anxiety, attention, care, cogitation, conception, concern, consideration, contemplation, meditation, reflection, regard; (2) belief, concept, conviction, idea, judgment, notion, opinion; (3) design, intention, purpose.

thoughtful (1) contemplative, deliberative, meditative, pensive, reflective, serious, speculative, studious; (2) attentive, careful, cautious, circumspect, considerate, deliberate, discreet, heedful, mindful, prudent, wary.
Ant. thoughtless.

thoughtless careless, heedless, inattentive, inconsiderate, indiscreet, neglectful, negligent, rash, reckless, regardless, remiss, trifling, unmindful, unobservant.
Ant. thoughtful.

thraldom bondage, enslavement, serfdom, servitude, slavery, subjection, vassalage.
Ant. liberty.

thrash beat, castigate, chastise, drub, flog, maul, punish, whip.
Ant. caress.

thread (1) cord, fibre, filament, line, string; (2) (*Fig.*) course, direction, drift, tenor.

threadbare (1) old, used, worn; (2) (*Fig.*) common, commonplace, hackneyed, stale, trite.
Ant. new.

threaten denounce, endanger, forebode, foreshadow, impend, intimidate, menace, portend, presage, warn.

threshold (1) door, door-sill, entrance; (2) (*Fig.*) beginning, opening, outset, start.
Ant. of (2) end.

thrift economy, frugality, parsimony, saving.
Ant. waste.

thriftless extravagant, improvident, lavish, prodigal, unthrifty, wasteful.
Ant. thrifty.

thrifty careful, economical, frugal, prosperous, provident, saving, sparing.
Ant. wasteful.

thrilling affecting, exciting, gripping, moving, sensational, touching.
Ant. tame, unexciting.

thrive advance, flourish, grow, increase, prosper, succeed.
Ant. fail.

throe agony, anguish, fit, pain, pang, paroxysm, spasm.

throng (1) *n.* assemblage, concourse, congregation, crowd, horde, host, multitude, swarm; (2) *v.* crowd, fill, flock, press.

throw cast, fling, hurl, launch, overturn, pitch, project, propel, put, send, toss.
Ant. hold.

thrust (1) drive, force, impel, push, shove, urge; (2) lunge, pierce, stab, tilt.

thump bang, beat, belabour, hit, knock, strike, thrash.

thwart baffle, balk, defeat, frustrate, hinder, impede, obstruct, oppose.
Ant. encourage, help.

tickle (*Fig.*) amuse, delight, gratify, please, titillate.

ticklish (*Fig.*) critical, delicate, difficult, nice, uncertain, unstable, unsteady.
Ant. easy.

tide course, current, ebb, flow, stream.

tidings advice, greetings, information, intelligence, news, report, word.

tidy clean, cleanly, neat, orderly, spruce, trim.
Ant. untidy.

tie *v.* attach, bind, chain, connect, fasten, fetter, interlace, join, knot, link, lock, manacle, secure, shackle, unite.
Ant. loose, untie.

tier line, rank, row, series.

tight close, compact, fast, stretched, taut, tense.
Ant. loose.

till v. cultivate, plough.

tillage agriculture, cultivation, culture, farming, husbandry.

tilt n. cant, inclination, slant, slope, tip.

time (1) age, date, duration, epoch, era, generation, interval, period, season, space, span, spell, term; (2) (*Mus.*) measure, rhythm.

timely early, judicious, opportune, prompt, punctual, seasonable.
Ant. untimely.

timid afraid, bashful, cowardly, coy, diffident, faint-hearted, fearful, modest, pusillanimous, retiring, shrinking, timorous.
Ant. fearless.

tincture n. dash, flavour, hue, infusion, seasoning, shade, smack, spice, stain, tinge, tint, touch.

tinge v. and n. colour, dye, shade, stain, tincture, tint.

tint (1) n. colour, dye, hue, shade, stain, tinge; (2) v. colour, dye, stain, tinge.

tiny diminutive, dwarfish, little, microscopic, miniature, minute, puny, pygmy, small, wee.
Ant. big.

tip (A) v. cant, incline, lean, overturn, slant, tilt.

tip (B) cap, end, extremity, point, top.
Ant. bottom.

tip (C) donation, gift, gratuity, perquisite.

tirade abuse, denunciation, diatribe, harangue, outburst.
Ant. praise.

tire bore, exhaust, fatigue, harass, jade, weary.
Ant. rest.

tiresome annoying, arduous, boring, dull, exhausting, fatiguing, irksome, laborious, tedious, uninteresting, vexatious, wearisome.
Ant. interesting.

tissue (1) fabric, structure, texture, web; (2) accumulation, chain, combination, fabrication, mass, series.

titanic colossal, enormous, gigantic, herculean, huge, immense, mighty, stupendous.
Ant. small.

title (1) appellation, denomination, designation, epithet, name; (2) claim, privilege, right.

tittle atom, bit, iota, jot, particle, scrap, speck.

tittle-tattle babble, cackle, chatter, chit-chat, gossip, prattle.

toil (1) v. drudge, labour, moil, strive, work; (2) n. drudgery, effort, exertion, labour, pains, travail.
Ant. of (2) respite, rest.

toilsome difficult, fatiguing, hard, laborious, painful, severe, tedious, tiresome, wearisome.
Ant. easy, light.

token badge, evidence, indication, manifestation, mark, memento, memorial, note, sign, souvenir, symbol, type.

tolerable (1) bearable, endurable, sufferable, supportable; (2) indifferent, mediocre, middling, ordinary, passable, so-so.
Ant. of (1) unbearable; of (2) excellent.

tolerate abide, admit, allow, bear, brook, endure, permit, receive, suffer.
Ant. discourage.

toll assessment, charge, custom, demand, duty, impost, levy, rate, tax, tribute.

tomb catacomb, crypt, grave, sepulchre, vault.

tone (1) accent, emphasis, force, inflection, intonation, modulation, strength; (2) colour, effect, manner, shade, style; (3) character, drift, frame, mood, spirit, temper, tenor.

tongue dialect, discourse, idiom, language, parlance, speech, talk.

too also, besides, further, likewise, moreover.

toothsome agreeable, dainty, delicious, nice, palatable, savoury.
　Ant. unsavoury.

top acme, apex, cap, crown, culmination, head, height, meridian, pinnacle, summit, vertex, zenith.
　Ant. base, bottom.

topic matter, point, question, subject, theme.

torment (1) v. afflict, agonise, annoy, distress, harass, harry, irritate, pain, pester, plague, provoke; (2) n. agony, anguish, annoyance, distress, irritation, persecution, provocation.
　Ant. of (1) soothe.

tornado cyclone, gale, hurricane, storm, tempest, typhoon.
　Ant. calm.

torpid apathetic, benumbed, dull, inactive, indolent, inert, lazy, lethargic, motionless, numb, slothful, slow, sluggish.
　Ant. active.

torpor apathy, dullness, inactivity, inertia, inertness, lethargy, numbness, sloth, sluggishness.
　Ant. activity, vigour.

torrid arid, burning, dried,

fiery, hot, parched, scorched, tropical.
　Ant. frigid.

tortuous bent, circuitous, crooked, curved, indirect, serpentine, sinuous, twisting, winding.
　Ant. direct, straight.

torture (1) v. agonise, distress, excruciate, pain, rack, torment; (2) n. agony, anguish, distress, pain, pang, rack, torment.
　Ant. (1) ease; of (2) comfort.

toss (1) cast, fling, hurl, pitch, project, propel; (2) agitate, rock, roll, shake, tumble, writhe.
　Ant. of (2) rest.

total (1) n. aggregate, all, amount, mass, sum, whole; (2) a. complete, entire, full, integral, undivided, whole.
　Ant. of (1) part.

totally completely, entirely, fully, quite, wholly.
　Ant. partly.

totter oscillate, quiver, reel, rock, stagger, sway, tremble.

touch (1) v. feel, graze, handle, hit, pat, strike, tap; (2) affect, impress, move, stir; (3) concern, interest, regard; (4) grasp, reach, stretch; (5) n. blow, contact, hit, pat, tap; (6) hint, smack, soupçon, suggestion, suspicion, taste, trace.

touchiness fretfulness, irascibility, irritability, peevishness, pettishness, petulance.
　Ant. affability.

touching a. affecting, melting, moving, pathetic, piteous, pitiable, tender.

touchy cross, irascible, irritable, peevish, pettish, petulant, quick-tempered, splenetic, testy.
　Ant. affable.

tough (1) adhesive, cohesive, durable, firm, inflexible, rigid, stiff, strong, tenacious; (2) callous, difficult, obdurate, refractory, stubborn, troublesome.

Ant. of (1) weak; of (2) tractable.

tour (1) n. excursion, expedition, jaunt, journey, outing, travel, trip; (2) circuit, course, round; (3) v. journey, travel, visit.

tow v. drag, draw, haul, pull, tug.

Ant. push.

towering (1) elevated, great, lofty, surpassing, tall; (2) excessive, extreme, violent.

Ant. of (1) low.

toy (1) n. bauble, gewgaw, knick-knack, plaything, trinket; (1) v. dally, play, sport, trifle, wanton.

trace (1) v. delineate, draw, outline, sketch; (2) follow, pursue, track, trail; (3) n. evidence, hint, indication, mark, record, remains, sign, suggestion, token, vestige; (4) footmark, footprint, footstep, track, trail.

track (1) footmark, footprint, footstep, trace, trail, wake; (2) course, path, pathway, road, way; (3) v. chase, follow, pursue, trace, trail.

trackless pathless, solitary, unfrequented, untrodden, unused.

tract (A) district, extent, quarter, region, stretch, territory.

tract (B) booklet, brochure, dissertation, essay, homily, pamphlet, sermon.

tractable amenable, docile, governable, manageable, willing.

Ant. intractable, refractory.

trade (1) n. barter, business, commerce, dealing, exchange, traffic; (2) avocation, business, calling, craft, employment, occupation, profession; (3) v. bargain, barter, buy, deal, exchange, sell, traffic.

traditional customary, transmitted.

traduce abuse, calumniate, decry, defame, depreciate, detract, disparage, malign, misrepresent, revile, slander.

Ant. praise.

traducer calumniator, defamer, detractor, slanderer, vilifier.

traffic (1) n. barter, business, commerce, dealing, exchange, intercourse, trade; (2) (Road) transport; (3) v. bargain, barter, deal, exchange.

tragedy (1) n. adversity, calamity, catastrophe, disaster, misfortune; (2) (Theat.) drama, play.

Ant. of (2) comedy.

tragic calamitous, catastrophic, disastrous, dreadful, fatal, mournful, sad, shocking, sorrowful.

Ant. cheerful.

trail (1) v. drag, draw, haul, pull; (2) follow, hunt, pursue, trace, track; (3) n. footprint, footstep, path, scent, track.

train (A) (1) v. discipline, drill, educate, instruct, rear; (2) drag, draw, haul, tug.

train (B) (1) attendants, followers, retinue, staff, suite; (2) chain, series, succession.

trait (1) characteristic, feature, lineament, peculiarity; (2) line, mark, stroke, touch.

traitor apostate, betrayer,

deceiver, deserter, miscreant, quisling, rebel, renegade.
Ant. loyalist.

traitorous faithless, false, insidious, perfidious, treacherous, treasonable.
Ant. loyal.

trammel (1) v. curb, fetter, hamper, hinder, impede, restrain, restrict, tie; (2) n. bond, chain, clog, fetter, hindrance, impediment, shackle.
Ant. (1) free.

trample (1) crush, tread; (2) (Fig.) scorn, spurn.

tranquil calm, composed, peaceful, placid, quiet, serene, still, undisturbed, unruffled, untroubled.
Ant. disturbed.

tranquillise allay, alleviate, appease, assuage, calm, compose, lull, moderate, pacify, quell, soothe.
Ant. excite.

tranquillity calm, peace, peacefulness placidity, quiet, quietness, repose, serenity, stillness.
Ant. excitement.

transact conclude, conduct, do, enact, execute, manage, negotiate, perform, settle, treat.

transaction action, affair, business, deed, event, matter, negotiation, occurrence, proceeding.

transcend eclipse, exceed, outdo, outrival, outstrip, outvie, overstep, surpass.

transcendent consummate, exceeding, matchless, peerless, pre-eminent, superior, unequalled, unrivalled.
Ant. inferior.

transfer (1) v. carry, change, convey, move, translate, trans-

mit, transplant, transport. (2) n. change, removal.

transfigure change, metamorphose, transform, transmute.

transform alter, change, convert, metamorphose, transfigure, transmute.
Ant. retain.

transgress break, contravene, disobey, err, exceed, infringe, offend, sin, trespass, violate.
Ant. obey.

transgression breach, crime, error, fault, infringement, misdeed, misdemeanour, offence, sin, trespass, violation.
Ant. observance.

transgressor culprit, delinquent, evil-doer, malefactor, offender, sinner.

transient brief, ephemeral, fleeting, fugitive, momentary, passing, short, temporary, transitory.
Ant. permanent.

transitory brief, ephemeral, evanescent, fleeting, flying, momentary, passing, short, short-lived, temporary.
Ant. lasting.

translate (1) construe, interpret, paraphrase, render; (2) remove, transfer, transport.

translation (1) construction, interpretation, paraphrase, rendering, version; (2) removal, transference.

translucent diaphanous, pellucid, semi-transparent.
Ant. opaque.

transmit (1) bear, carry, convey, dispatch, forward, remit, send, transfer, transport; (2) (Radio) broadcast, relay.

transparent (1) bright, clear, crystalline, diaphanous, limpid, lucid, translucent; (2) (Fig.)

evident, manifest, obvious, patent.

transpire (1) befall, chance, happen, occur; (2) evaporate, exhale.

transport (1) v. bear, carry, fetch, move, remove, transfer; (2) (*Fig.*) delight, enrapture, entrance, ravish; (3) n. carriage, conveyance, transportation; (4) (*Fig.*) bliss, delight, ecstasy, felicity, happiness, ravishment.

Ant. of (4) indifference.

trap (1) v. catch, ensnare, entrap; (2) n. ambush, gin, net, pitfall, snare; (3) (*Fig.*) artifice, stratagem, wile.

trappings accoutrements, decorations, dress, equipment, furnishings, livery, ornaments, paraphernalia.

trash dregs, dross, refuse, rubbish, trumpery, waste.

travel (1) v. journey, ramble, roam, rove, tour, walk, wander; (2) n. excursion, expedition, journey, ramble, tour, trip, walk.

traveller (1) hiker, passenger, tourist, wanderer, wayfarer, voyager; (2) agent, salesman.

traverse contravene, frustrate, impede, obstruct, oppose, thwart.

Ant. support.

travesty burlesque, caricature, lampoon, parody.

treacherous deceitful, disloyal, faithless, false, insidious, perfidious, recreant, traitorous, treasonable, unfaithful, unreliable, untrustworthy.

Ant. faithful, loyal.

treachery betrayal, disloyalty, faithlessness, perfidiousness, perfidy, treason.

Ant. loyalty.

treason disaffection, disloyalty, perfidy, sedition, traitorousness, treachery.

Ant. faith, loyalty.

treasonable disloyal, false, traitorous, treacherous.

treasure (1) accumulate, collect, garner, hoard, husband; (2) (*Fig.*) cherish, idolise, prize, value, worship; (3) n. cash, funds, jewels, money, riches, valuables, wealth; (4) abundance, reserve, stock, store.

treat (1) v. attend, behave, deal, handle, manage, use; (2) entertain, feast; (3) bargain, negotiate; (4) n. banquet, delight, enjoyment, entertainment, feast, pleasure, refreshment.

Ant. of (1) mismanage.

treatise dissertation, essay, pamphlet, paper, thesis, tract.

treatment handling, management, manipulation, usage.

treaty agreement, alliance, bargain, compact, concordat, convention, covenant, entente, pact.

tremble oscillate, quake, quiver, rock, shake, shiver, shudder, totter, vibrate.

tremendous alarming, appalling, awful, dreadful, fearful, frightful, horrible, horrid, terrible, terrific.

Ant. ordinary.

tremor (1) agitation, quaking, quivering, shaking, trembling, trepidation, vibration; (2) earthquake.

tremulous afraid, fearful, quivering, shaking, shivering, timid, trembling.

Ant. steady.

trench channel, ditch, drain, gutter, pit, trough, waterway.

trenchant acute, biting, caustic, cutting, incisive, keen, piquant, pointed, sarcastic, severe, sharp, vigorous.

Ant. gentle.

trend (1) *v.* incline, lean, run, stretch, tend, turn; (2) *n.* course, direction, drift, inclination, leaning, tendency.

trepidation agitation, consternation, dismay, disturbance, emotion, excitement, fear, fright, perturbation, quivering, shaking, tremor.

Ant. tranquillity.

trespass (1) *v.* encroach, infringe, intrude; (2) offend, sin, transgress; (3) *n.* encroachment, infringement, intrusion; (4) crime, delinquency, error, fault, misdeed, misdemeanour, offence, sin, transgression, wrongdoing.

Ant. of (2) obey; of (4) observance.

trespasser (1) infringer, intruder; (2) offender, sinner, transgressor.

trial (1) examination, experience, experiment, proof, test, testing; (2) aim, attempt, effort, endeavour, exertion, struggle; (3) affliction, distress, grief, hardship, misery, pain, suffering, tribulation, trouble, woe, wretchedness; (4) (*Law*) action, case, cause, suit.

Ant. of (1) attainment.

tribe clan, class, division, family, race, sept, stock.

tribulation adversity, affliction, distress, grief, misery, pain, sorrow, suffering, trial, trouble, unhappiness, vexation, wretchedness.

Ant. happiness.

tribunal (*Law*) bar, bench, court, judgment-seat.

tribute charge, contribution, custom, duty, excise, grant,

impost, offering, subsidy, tax, toll.

trice flash, instant, (*Colloq.*) jiffy, moment, second, (*Colloq.*) tick, (*Colloq.*) twinkling.

trick (1) *v.* cheat, deceive, defraud, delude, dupe, gull; (2) *n.* artifice, deceit, dodge, hoax, imposture, ruse, stratagem, swindle, wile; (3) antic, caper, gambol, juggle, legerdemain; (4) habit, peculiarity, practice.

Ant. of (1) disillusion.

trickle *v.* dribble, drip, drop, ooze, percolate.

Ant. flow, rush.

tricky artful, cunning, deceitful, deceptive, subtle, trickish.

trifle (1) *v.* dally, dawdle, fritter, idle, play, toy, wanton; (2) *n.* bagatelle, bauble, gewgaw, plaything, toy, triviality.

trifling empty, frivolous, inconsiderable, insignificant, petty, shallow, slight, small, trivial, valueless, unimportant, worthless.

Ant. important.

trim (1) *v.* clip, curtail, cut, dock, lop, pare, prune, shave, shear; (2) adjust, adorn, arrange, array, bedeck, decorate, dress, embellish, order, prepare; (3) *a.* compact, neat, nice, prepared, smart, spruce, tidy, well-ordered; (4) *n.* condition, fettle, order, situation, state.

Ant. of (1) increase; of (2) untidy.

trinket bagatelle, bauble, gewgaw, knick-knack, trifle.

trinkets jewellery, jewels, ornaments.

trip (A) *n.* excursion, expedition, jaunt, journey, outing, ramble, tour, travel, voyage.

trip (B) (**1**) *v.* blunder, err, fall, miss, slip, stumble; (**2**) dance, frisk, hop, skip.

trite banal, common, commonplace, hackneyed, ordinary, stale, stereotyped, threadbare, worn.

Ant. original, uncommon.

triturate beat, bray, bruise, crush, grind, pound, pulverise.

triumph (**1**) *n.* achievement, conquest, exaltation, jubilation, ovation, success, victory; (**2**) *v.* exalt, flourish, prevail, prosper, rejoice, succeed, thrive, win.

Ant. of (**1**) failure; of (**2**) fail.

triumphant boastful, conquering, elated, exultant, jubilant, rejoicing, successful, victorious.

Ant. depressed.

trivial inconsiderable, insignificant, paltry, petty, slight, small, trifling, unimportant, valueless, worthless.

Ant. important.

trollop slattern, slut.

troop assemblage, band, body, company, contingent, crew, crowd, gang, gathering, group, multitude, squad.

troth allegiance, faith, fealty, fidelity, honesty, sincerity, word.

trouble (**1**) *v.* afflict, annoy, distress, disturb, fret, grieve, harass, inconvenience, perplex, perturb, pester, plague, torment; (**2**) *n.* adversity, affliction, annoyance, difficulty, disturbance, grief, inconvenience, irritation, misfortune, pain, sorrow, suffering, torment, tribulation, vexation, woe.

Ant. of (**1**) appease; of (**2**) happiness.

troublesome annoying, ar-

duous, difficult, harassing, hard, importunate, irksome, laborious, tiresome, trying, wearisome.

Ant. easy, simple.

troublous afflictive, agitated, disturbed, troublesome, trying, tumultuous, turbulent.

truant *n.* idler, laggard, loiterer, lounger, run-away, vagabond.

Ant. worker.

truce armistice, cessation, intermission, interval, peace, respite, rest.

truck *v.* barter, deal, exchange, trade, traffic.

truckle cringe, crouch, fawn, knuckle, stoop, submit, yield.

Ant. defy.

truculent barbarous, bloodthirsty, brutish, cruel, fierce, malevolent, overbearing, relentless, ruthless, savage, violent.

Ant. gentle.

true (**1**) accurate, actual, authentic, correct, exact, genuine, real, truthful, veracious, veritable; (**2**) constant, faithful, honest, honourable, loyal, pure, sincere, steady, trustworthy, upright.

Ant. of (**1**) untrue; of (**2**) false.

truism axiom, commonplace, platitude.

trumpery (**1**) *n.* nonsense, rubbish, stuff, trash, trifles; (**2**) *a.* meretricious, rubbishy, trashy, trifling, worthless.

Ant. of (**2**) valuable.

truncheon baton, club, cudgel, staff, wand.

trunk (**1**) stalk, stem, stock; (**2**) body, torso; (**3**) proboscis, snout; (**4**) box, chest, coffer, portmanteau.

truss (**1**) *v.* bind, bundle, cram,

hang, pack; (2) bundle, package, packet; (3) (*Med.*) bandage, support.

trust (1) *n.* assurance, belief, confidence, credit, expectation, faith, hope, reliance; (2) *v.* believe, commit, confide, defend, entrust, expect, hope, rely.

Ant. of (2) distrust.

trusty faithful, firm, honest, reliable, staunch, straightforward, strong, true, trustworthy, uncorrupt, upright.

Ant. unreliable.

truth (1) accuracy, exactness, fact, precision, reality, truthfulness, veracity, verity; (2) candour, faith, faithfulness, fidelity, frankness, honesty, integrity, uprightness.

Ant. of (1) lie.

truthful (1) accurate, correct, reliable, true, trustworthy;(2) artless, candid, frank, guileless, honest, ingenuous, straightforward.

Ant. of (1) inaccurate; of (2) lying.

truthless dishonest, faithless, false, insincere, lying, treacherous, untrustworthy.

Ant. truthful.

try (1) aim, attempt, endeavour, seek, strive, struggle; (2) examine, experiment, investigate, prove, test; (3) (*Law*) adjudge, adjudicate, examine, hear.

trying (1) arduous, difficult, fatiguing, hard, irksome, tiresome, wearisome; (2) afflicting, calamitous, dire, distressing, grievous, sad.

tryst (1) appointment, meeting, rendez-vous; (2) (*Scot.*) fair, market.

tuft bunch, clump, cluster, collection, knot.

tug drag, haul, heave, pull, tow.

Ant. push.

tuition discipline, education, instruction, schooling, training, tutoring.

tumble fall, roll, stumble, topple, toss.

tumid (1) distended, enlarged, inflated, protuberant, swollen; (2) (*Fig.*) bombastic, grandiloquent, grandiose, high-flown, pompous, turgid.

Ant. of (1) deflated; of (2) modest.

tumult ado, affray, altercation, brawl, commotion, disorder, fracas, hubbub, outbreak, quarrel, riot, row, stir, strife, turmoil, uproar.

Ant. peacefulness.

tumultuous agitated, boisterous, disorderly, irregular, lawless, noisy, obstreperous, restless, riotous, rowdy, seditious, uproarious.

Ant. peaceful.

tune air, concord, harmony, melody, strain.

Ant. discord.

tuneful harmonious, melodious, musical.

Ant. discordant.

turbid cloudy, dreggy, foul, impure, muddy, unsettled.

Ant. clear.

turbulent agitated, blustering, boisterous, disorderly, mutinous, obstreperous, rebellious, refractory, riotous, rowdy, seditious, tumultuous, undisciplined, unruly, uproarious, violent, wild.

Ant. orderly.

turf (1) clod, grass, sod, sward; (2) flat, horse-racing, racecourse.

turgid (1) bloated, distended, inflated, protuberant, swollen;

(2) (*Fig.*) bombastic, grandiloquent, grandiose, high-flown, ostentatious, pompous, stilted, tumid.

Ant of (1) deflated; of (2) modest.

turmoil agitation, bustle, commotion, confusion, disorder, disturbance, flurry, hubbub, noise, trouble, turbulence, uproar.

Ant. peacefulness.

turn (1) *v.* reverse, revolve, rotate, spin, twirl, twist, whirl; (2) adapt, alter, change, convert, divert, fashion, fit, form, mould, shape, transform; (3) bend, coil, curve, incline, mill, wind; (4) *n.* bend, change, curve, deviation, reversal, revolution, rotation, spin, turning, twist; (5) aptitude, bent, bias, drift, propensity, talent, tendency; (6) cast, fashion, form, manner, shape, style.

turncoat apostate, backslider, deserter, recreant, renegade, traitor, wretch.

turpitude baseness, depravity, vileness, wickedness.

Ant. goodness.

tussle (1) *v.* contend, fight, scuffle, struggle, wrestle; (2) *n.* conflict, fight, scuffle, struggle.

tutelage care, charge, dependence, guardianship, protection, wardship.

Ant. freedom.

tutor (1) *n.* coach, governor, guardian, instructor, preceptor, schoolmaster, teacher; (2) *v.* coach, discipline, educate, instruct, teach, train.

Ant. of (1) pupil.

twaddle *n.* balderdash, chatter, gabble, gossip, nonsense, rigmarole, tattle.

tweak pinch, pull, twist, twitch.

twig branch, shoot, spray, sprig.

twine (1) encircle, entwine, wind, wreathe; (2) bend, meander, twist, wind; (3) *n.* cord, string.

twinge gripe, pain, pang, pinch, spasm, tweak, twist, twitch.

twinkle (1) coruscate, glisten, scintillate, shine, sparkle; (2) blink, wink.

twinkling (1) flashing, glistening, scintillation, sparkle, twinkle; (2) flash, instant, (*Colloq.*) jiffy, moment, second, (*Colloq.*) tick, trice.

twirl revolve, rotate, spin, turn, twist, whirl.

twist contort, distort, encircle, entwine, screw, weave, wind, wreathe, writhe.

Ant. untwist.

twit *v.* banter, blame, censure, deride, taunt, tease, upbraid.

twitch (1) *v.* jerk, pull, snatch; (2) *n.* jerk, pull, spasm.

type (1) emblem, mark, representation, sign, stamp, symbol, token; (2) archetype, example, exemplar, model, original, pattern, prototype, specimen; (3) class, form, group, kind, order, sort.

typical emblematic, figurative, illustrative, indicative, representative, symbolical.

Ant. actual.

typify betoken, denote, figure, illustrate, indicate, represent, symbolise.

tyrannical arbitrary, autocratic, cruel, despotic, dictatorial, domineering, imperious, inhuman, oppressive, overbearing, severe, unjust.

Ant. human, just.

tyranny autocracy, despotism, dictatorship, oppression.

tyrant autocrat, despot, dictator, oppressor.

Ant. slave.

tyro beginner, learner, neophyte, novice.

Ant. expert.

U

ubiquitous omnipresent, present.

ugly disagreeable, frightful, hideous, horrid, ill-favoured, monstrous, offensive, plain, repulsive, revolting, shocking, terrible, unlovely, unpleasant, unsightly, vile.

Ant. attractive.

ulcer boil, fester, gathering, pustule, sore.

ulterior (1) final, further, remote, succeeding; (2) (*Fig.*) hidden, personal, secret, selfish, undisclosed.

ultimate conclusive, decisive, eventual, extreme, final, furthest, last.

Ant. first.

umbrage anger, displeasure, grudge, offence, pique, resentment.

Ant. pleasure.

umpire arbiter, arbitrator, judge, referee.

Ant. litigant, player.

unabashed bold, confident, undaunted, undismayed.

Ant. uncertain.

unable impotent, incapable, incompetent, powerless.

unacceptable disagreeable, displeasing, unpleasant, unsatisfactory, unwelcome.

Ant. satisfactory.

unaccomplished incomplete, unachieved, undone, unfinished, unperformed.

unaccountable incomprehensible inexplicable, inscrutable, mysterious, strange, unexplainable, unintelligible.

Ant. accountable.

unaffected (1) artless, genuine, honest, ingenuous, naïve, natural, plain, simple, sincere, unsophisticated; (2) unaltered, unimpressed, unmoved, unstirred, untouched.

Ant. of (1) artful, wily.

unanimity agreement, concert, concord, harmony, likemindedness, unity.

Ant. disagreement.

unanimous agreeing, concordant, harmonious, like-minded, united.

Ant. disagreeing.

unassuming humble, modest, reserved, retiring, unobtrusive, unostentatious, unpretentious.

Ant. forward, immodest.

unavailing abortive, fruitless, futile, ineffectual, unsuccessful, useless, vain.

Ant. successful.

unbearable insufferable, insupportable, intolerable, unendurable.

Ant. bearable.

unbecoming (1) inappropriate, unbefitting, unfit, unsuitable, unsuited; (2) improper, unseemly.

Ant. of (1) becoming; of (2) proper.

unbelief distrust, doubt, incredulity, scepticism.

unbeliever agnostic, disbeliever, free-thinker, infidel, sceptic.

unbiased disinterested, equitable, fair, impartial, indifferent, neutral, unprejudiced.

Ant. biased.

unbind free, release, unchain, undo, unfasten, unfetter, unloose, unshackle, untie.

Ant. bind.

unbounded boundless, endless, enormous, huge, immense, infinite, interminable, limitless, uncontrolled, vast, wide.
Ant. limited.

unbridled lax, licentious, uncontrolled, ungovernable, unrestrained, violent, wanton.
Ant. restrained.

unbroken complete, continuous, deep, entire, fast, intact, profound, sound, undisturbed.

uncanny eerie, mysterious, preternatural, strange, weird.
Ant. ordinary.

uncertain ambiguous, doubtful, dubious, indefinite, indistinct, insecure, irregular, precarious, questionable, unpredictable, unreliable, unsafe, unsure, vague, variable.
Ant. certain.

uncivil bearish, blunt, boorish, churlish, disrespectful, gruff, ill-bred, ill-mannered, impolite, impudent, rude, uncouth, unmannerly.
Ant. civil, polite.

unclean corrupt, dirty, evil, filthy, foul, impure, nasty, polluted.

uncommon exceptional, extraordinary, odd, queer, rare, remarkable, singular, strange, unusual.

uncompromising decided, firm, inflexible, obstinate, rigid, strict, unyielding.

unconditional absolute, categorical, complete, explicit, full, positive, unqualified, unreserved.

uncongenial antagonistic, discordant, displeasing, distasteful, unharmonious, unpleasant, unsuited, unsympathetic.

uncouth awkward, boorish, clownish, clumsy, gawky, loutish, lubberly, rough, rustic, ungainly, unrefined, unseemly.

uncover bare, disclose, discover, expose, reveal, show, strip.
Ant. cover.

unctuous (1) (*Arch.*) fat, (*Arch.*) fatty, greasy, oily, oleaginous; (2) (*Fig.*) bland, fawning, glib, gushing, insincere, obsequious, oily, plausible, smooth, suave, sycophantic. [genuine.
Ant. of (1) lean; of (2)

undaunted bold, brave, courageous, dauntless, fearless, gallant, intrepid, resolute, undismayed.
Ant. cowardly.

undeniable certain, clear, evident, incontestable, indisputable, indubitable, obvious, unassailable, unquestionable.
Ant. doubtful.

undergo bear, endure, experience, stand, suffer, sustain.

underhand clandestine, crafty, fraudulent, furtive, secret, sly, stealthy, surreptitious.
Ant. open.

understand (1) apprehend, comprehend, conceive, discern, know, perceive, recognise, see; (2) gather, learn.

undertake (1) attempt, try; (2) agree, bargain, engage, guarantee, promise, stipulate.

undesigned accidental, unintended, unintentional, unpremeditated.

undo (1) disengage, disentangle, loose, open, unfasten, untie; (2) annul, invalidate, neutralise, reverse; (3) destroy, impoverish, ruin.

undoubted certain, evident, incontrovertible, indisputable, indubitable, obvious, sure,

unquestionable, unquestioned.
Ant. questionable.

undue excessive, extreme, immoderate, improper, inordinate, unwarranted.
Ant. proper.

unearthly eerie, preternatural, supernatural, uncanny, weird.

uneasy (1) discomposed, disturbed, impatient, restive, restless, stiff, uncomfortable, unpleasing, unquiet; (2) awkward, constrained.

unending ceaseless, endless, eternal, everlasting, interminable, never-ending, perpetual.
Ant. brief.

unequal disproportionate, ill-matched, inferior, irregular, uneven.

unequalled exceeding, incomparable, inimitable, matchless, paramount, peerless, pre-eminent, surpassing, transcendent, unparalleled.
Ant. comparable.

unequivocal absolute, certain, clear, direct, evident, explicit, indubitable, manifest, plain, positive, unambiguous, unmistakable.
Ant. ambiguous.

uneventful commonplace, dull, humdrum, monotonous, unexciting, uninteresting.
Ant. exciting, momentous.

unexampled unequalled, unparalleled, unprecedented.

unexpected abrupt, sudden, unanticipated, unforeseen.
Ant. anticipated.

unfair biased, dishonest, dishonourable, faithless, false, hypercritical, one-sided, prejudiced, unjust.
Ant. just.

unfaithful (1) careless, deceitful, disloyal, faithless, false,

recreant, treacherous, treasonable, unreliable, untrustworthy; (2) changed, fickle, inconstant, untrue.
Ant. of (1) loyal; of (2) faithful.

unfeeling (1) insensible; (2) (*Fig.*) apathetic, callous, cold, cruel, hard-hearted, unsympathetic.
Ant. of (2) sympathetic.

unflinching bold, firm, resolute, steadfast, steady.
Ant. timid.

unfold (1) disentangle, expand, open, unravel, unroll; (2) (*Fig.*) clarify, disclose, evolve, explain, illustrate, reveal.
Ant. of (1) fold; of (2) withhold.

unfortunate calamitous, deplorable, disastrous, ill-fated, ill-starred, inopportune, unhappy, unlucky, unsuccessful.
Ant. fortunate.

unfrequented deserted, lone, lonely, sequestered, solitary, uninhabited.
Ant. busy.

unfruitful barren, fruitless, infecund, sterile, unproductive, unprolific.
Ant. fruitful.

ungainly awkward, clumsy, gawky, inelegant, lubberly, slouching, uncouth, ungraceful.
Ant. graceful.

uniform alike, consistent, constant, equable, regular, unchanging, undeviating, unvarying.
Ant. varying.

unintentional accidental, casual, fortuitous, involuntary, undesigned, unpremeditated.
Ant. deliberate.

union (1) combination, conjunction, junction; (2) alliance, association, coalition, confederacy, confederation; (3) agreement, concord, harmony, unanimity, unison, unity.

Ant. of (1) and (2) separation; of (3) disunity.

unique alone, exceptional, peerless, rare, single, sole, uncommon, unexampled, unmatched, unusual.

Ant. usual.

unison accord, agreement, concord, harmony.

Ant. discord.

unite add, amalgamate, associate, attach, blend, coalesce, combine, confederate, connect, consolidate, couple, incorporate, merge.

Ant. separate.

universal all, all-embracing, catholic, ecumenical, entire, general, total, unlimited, whole.

Ant. local, particular.

unjust (1) biased, partial, prejudiced, unfair, unjustified; (2) bad, fraudulent, heinous, iniquitous, wicked, wrong, wrongful.

Ant. just.

unjustifiable indefensible, inexcusable, unjust, unpardonable, unwarrantable, wrong.

Ant. justifiable.

unladylike ill-bred, impolite, rude, uncivil, ungentle, ungracious, unmannerly.

Ant. gracious.

unlamented undeplored, unmourned, unregretted, unwept.

Ant. lamented.

unlimited absolute, boundless, extensive, great, infinite, limitless, unbounded, unconstrained, unfettered, vast.

Ant. limited.

unlucky ill-fated, ill-omened, inauspicious, miserable, unfor-

tunate, unhappy, unsuccessful.

Ant. lucky.

unmanageable (1) awkward, cumbersome, unhandy, unwieldy; (2) difficult, intractable, refractory, unruly.

Ant. of (2) obedient.

unmatched consummate, incomparable, matchless, paramount, peerless, unequalled, unrivalled, unsurpassed.

Ant. equalled.

unmitigated absolute, complete, consummate, perfect, thorough.

Ant. mitigated.

unpremeditated extempore, impromptu, offhand, spontaneous, unprepared.

Ant. deliberate.

unreasonable (1) absurd, foolish, irrational, mad, nonsensical, preposterous, senseless, stupid; (2) excessive, exorbitant, extortionate, immoderate, unfair, unjust.

Ant. reasonable.

unremitting assiduous, constant, continual, diligent, incessant, indefatigable, sedulous, unabated, unceasing.

Ant. inconstant.

unrepentant abandoned, callous, hardened, incorrigible, merciless, obdurate, relentless, remorseless, rigorous, ruthless, shameless.

Ant. repentant.

unruly disobedient, disorderly, headstrong, insubordinate, intractable, mutinous, rebellious, refractory, riotous, turbulent, ungovernable, unmanageable, wild.

Ant. obedient.

unsafe dangerous, hazardous insecure, perilous, risky, uncertain.

Ant. safe.

unsatisfactory disappointing, inadequate, insufficient, mediocre, poor.
Ant. satisfactory.

unscrupulous dishonest, knavish, roguish, unconscientious, unethical, unprincipled.
Ant. honest.

unseemly improper, inappropriate, indecorous, unbecoming, unbefitting.
Ant. becoming.

unsettle confuse, derange, disorder, disturb, upset.
Ant. steady.

unsightly disagreeable, hideous, repulsive, ugly, unattractive, unpleasant.
Ant. attractive.

unsteady changeable, inconstant, irregular, reeling, tottering, unreliable, unsettled, unstable, variable, wavering.
Ant. steady.

unstinted abundant, ample, full, generous, large, lavish.
Ant. scanty.

unsullied clean, immaculate, pure, spotless, unblemished, uncorrupted, undefiled, unsoiled, untarnished.
Ant. dirty.

unsympathetic callous, cruel, hard, harsh, heartless, unfeeling, unkind.
Ant. sympathetic.

untimely early, ill-timed, inappropriate, inopportune, premature, unsuitable.
Ant. timely.

untiring incessant, indefatigable, patient, tireless, unremitting, unwearied.

unusual curious, exceptional, extraordinary, odd, queer, rare, remarkable, singular, strange, unwonted.
Ant. usual.

unwary careless, hasty, heedless, imprudent, indiscreet, rash, reckless, unguarded.
Ant. wary.

unwonted extraordinary, infrequent, peculiar, rare, singular, unaccustomed, uncommon, unusual.
Ant. customary, usual.

upbraid blame, censure, chide, condemn, reprimand, reproach, reprove.
Ant. praise.

uphold defend, elevate, justify, maintain, raise, support, sustain, vindicate.
Ant. attack.

upright (1) erect, perpendicular, vertical; (2) (*Fig.*) conscientious, faithful, good, honest, honourable, incorruptible, just, righteous, true, trustworthy, virtuous.
Ant. of (1) horizontal; of (2) dishonest.

uprightness fairness, faithfulness, goodness, honesty, incorruptibility, integrity, justice, probity, rectitude, righteousness, trustworthiness, virtue.
Ant. dishonesty.

uproar brawl, clamour, commotion, confusion, din, hubbub, noise, racket, riot, turbulence, turmoil.
Ant. peacefulness.

uproarious boisterous, clamorous, loud, noisy, tumultuous, turbulent.
Ant. peaceful.

upshot conclusion, consequence, end, event, issue, outcome, result.
Ant. beginning.

urbane civil, courteous, elegant, polished, refined, well-bred, well-mannered.

urge (1) constrain, drive, force, impel, incite, induce, instigate, press, push, solicit, stimulate; (2) beg, beseech, entreat, implore, recommend.

Ant. deter.

urgent cogent, compelling, immediate, imperative, important, insistent, instant, pressing.

Ant. unimportant.

usage custom, habit, practice, use, wont.

use (1) v. apply, employ, exercise, practise, utilise; (2) consume, exhaust, expend, waste; (3) accustom, familiarise, habituate, train; (4) n. application, employment, exercise, practice; (5) advantage, benefit, profit, service, treatment, utility; (6) custom, habit, usage, wont; (7) necessity, need, occasion.

Ant. of (1) and (4) disuse.

useful advantageous, beneficial, effective, helpful, profitable, salutary, serviceable.

Ant. useless.

useless bootless, disadvantageous, fruitless, futile, hopeless, ineffective, ineffectual, vain, valueless, worthless.

Ant. useful.

usual accustomed, common, constant, customary, familiar, fixed, general, habitual, ordinary, regular.

Ant. rare, unusual.

usurp appropriate, arrogate, assume, presume, seize.

Ant. renounce.

utility advantageousness, avail, benefit, profit, service, use, usefulness.

utmost extreme, farthest, greatest, remotest, uttermost.

Ant. least, nearest.

Utopian chimerical, fanciful, ideal, imaginary, visionary.

Ant. practical, real.

utter (1) v. articulate, enunciate, express, issue, promulgate, pronounce, say, speak, voice; (2) a. absolute, complete, entire, perfect, unqualified.

V

vacant (1) disengaged, empty, free, unemployed, unfilled, unoccupied, untenanted, void; (2) blank, dreaming, idle, inane, thoughtless, unthinking.

Ant. of (1) occupied; of (2) thoughtful.

vacillate fluctuate, hesitate, oscillate, reel, rock, sway, waver.

Ant. decide.

vacillation fluctuation, hesitation, inconstancy, reeling, staggering, swaying, unsteadiness, wavering.

Ant. firmness.

vacuity emptiness, inanity, vacuum, void.

vacuous (1) empty, unfilled, vacant, void; (2) inane, stupid, unintelligent, vacant.

vacuum emptiness, vacuity, void.

vagabond n. beggar, good-for-nothing, loafer, nomad, outcast, rascal, rogue, scamp, tramp, vagrant, wanderer.

vagary antic, caprice, fancy, freakishness, humour, prank, whim.

vagrant (1) n. beggar, itinerant, loafer, tramp, wanderer; (2) a. nomadic, roaming, roving, strolling, unsettled.

Ant. of (2) settled.

vague dim, doubtful, imprecise, indefinite, indeterminate, indistinct, lax, obscure, unclear, unknown.

Ant. definite.

vain (1) empty, fruitless, hollow, idle, trifling, trivial, unimportant, useless, worthless; (2) arrogant, conceited, egotistical, inflated, ostentatious, proud, vainglorious.

Ant. of (1) fruitful; of (2) modest.

valediction adieu, farewell, goodbye, leave-taking.

Ant. welcome.

valetudinarian delicate, feeble, frail, infirm, sickly, weakly.

Ant. healthy.

valiant bold, brave, courageous, dauntless, doughty, fearless, gallant, heroic, intrepid, redoubtable, stout-hearted, valorous.

Ant. cowardly.

valid binding, cogent, conclusive, efficacious, efficient, good, just, logical, powerful, sound, substantial, weighty, well-founded.

Ant. invalid, weak.

valley dale, dell, dingle, glen, hollow, vale.

Ant. hill.

valorous bold, brave, courageous, dauntless, doughty, fearless, gallant, heroic, intrepid.

Ant. cowardly.

valour boldness, bravery, courage, doughtiness, fearlessness, gallantry, heroism, intrepidity, spirit.

Ant. cowardice.

valuable costly, dear, estimable, expensive, precious, serviceable, useful, worthy.

Ant. worthless.

value (1) n. cost, desirability, importance, merit, rate, usefulness, utility, worth; (2) v. account, appraise, compute, estimate, rate; (3)

esteem, prize, regard, treasure.

Ant. of (1) worthlessness; of (3) disregard.

valueless miserable, useless, worthless.

vanish disappear, dissolve, fade, melt.

Ant. appear.

vanity (1) arrogance, conceit, egotism, pride, self-admiration; (2) emptiness, futility, inanity, triviality, unreality, unsubstantiality, worthlessness.

Ant. of (1) modesty.

vanquish conquer, crush, defeat, discomfit, master, overcome, overpower, quell, rout, subdue, subjugate.

Ant. yield.

vapid (1) dead, flat, flavourless, insipid, lifeless, stale, tasteless; (2) dull, tedious, tiresome, uninteresting.

Ant. of (1) tasty.

vapour exhalation, fog, fume, mist, smoke, steam.

variable changeable, fickle, fitful, fluctuating, inconstant, mutable, shifting, unsteady, vacillating, wavering.

Ant. constant.

variance difference, disagreement, discord, dissension, inconsistency, strife.

Ant. agreement.

variation alteration, change, departure, deviation, difference, discrepancy, diversity, modification.

Ant. constancy.

variegated diversified, many-coloured, motley, mottled, pied, streaked.

variety (1) assortment, difference, discrepancy, diversity, intermixture, medley, multiplicity; (2) class, kind, order, sort, species, type.

Ant. of (**1**) uniformity.

various different, differing, distinct, diverse, many, several, sundry, varied, variegated.
Ant. same.

varnish adorn, decorate, embellish, gild, glaze, lacquer, polish.

vary alter, alternate, change, differ, disagree, diversify, modify, transform.
Ant. continue.

vassal bondman, retainer, serf, slave, subject.
Ant. overlord.

vassalage bondage, dependence, serfdom, servitude, slavery, subjection.
Ant. freedom.

vast boundless, colossal, enormous, extensive, gigantic, great, huge, immense, unbounded, unlimited, wide.
Ant. minute.

vaticination augury, divination, prediction, prophecy.

vault (A) v. bound, clear, hurdle, jump, leap, spring.

vault (B) n. (**1**) arch, ceiling, roof; (**2**) catacomb, cellar, crypt, mausoleum, tomb.

vaunt boast, brag, swagger.

veer change, shift, turn.
Ant. remain.

vegetate (**1**) germinate, grow, shoot, spring, sprout, swell; (**2**) (*Fig.*) bask, idle, loaf, lounge.
Ant. of (**2**) work.

vehemence ardour, eagerness, earnestness, enthusiasm, fervour, fire, heat, impetuosity, intensity, keenness, passion, verve, violence, warmth, zeal.
Ant. apathy.

vehement ardent, eager, earnest, enthusiastic, fervent, fervid, forcible, impetuous, intense, passionate, power-

ful, strong, violent, zealous.
Ant. apathetic, cool.

veil (**1**) v. cloak, conceal, cover, disguise, hide, mask, screen; (**2**) n. blind, cloak, cover, curtain, disguise, mask, screen, shade.
Ant. of (**1**) uncover.

vein (**1**) course, current, lode, seam, streak, stripe; (**2**) (*Fig.*) bent, character, faculty, humour, mood, talent, turn.

velocity celerity, fleetness, quickness, rapidity, speed, swiftness.
Ant. slowness.

velvety (*Fig.*) delicate, smooth, soft.
Ant. coarse.

venal corrupt, mercenary, prostituted, purchasable, sordid.
Ant. upright.

vend dispose, hawk, retail, sell.
Ant. buy.

venerable grave, honoured, respected, reverenced, sage, sedate, wise, worshipped.
Ant. disdained.

venerate adore, esteem, honour, revere, reverence, worship.
Ant. dishonour.

veneration adoration, esteem, respect, reverence, worship.
Ant. disrespect.

vengeance retaliation, retribution, revenge.
Ant. forgiveness.

venial excusable, forgiveable, pardonable, trivial.
Ant. inexcusable.

venom (**1**) poison, virus; (**2**) (*Fig.*) bitterness, gall, grudge, hate, ill-will, malignity, rancour, spite, spitefulness, virulence.
Ant. of (**1**) antidote; (**2**) praise.

venomous (1) noxious, poisonous; **(2)** (*Fig.*) malicious, malignant, rancorous, spiteful, virulent.
Ant. of **(1)** harmless; of **(2)** benevolent.

vent (1) *n.* hole, opening, orifice, split; **(2)** *v.* emit, express, utter.

ventilate (1) air, fan, winnow; **(2)** (*Fig.*) discuss, examine, scrutinise, sift.

venture (1) *v.* endanger, hazard, imperil, jeopardise, presume, risk, tempt; **(2)** *n.* adventure, chance, hazard, jeopardy, risk.

venturesome adventurous, bold, courageous, daring, doughty, enterprising, fearless, intrepid.
Ant. cowardly.

veracious creditable, honest, reliable, straightforward, true, trustworthy, truthful.
Ant. false.

veracity candour, frankness, honesty, truth, truthfulness.
Ant. dishonesty.

verbal literal, oral, spoken, unwritten.
Ant. written.

verbose diffuse, prolix, wordy.
Ant. terse.

verdant flourishing, fresh, green.
Ant. withered.

verdict decision, finding, judgment, opinion, sentence.

verge (1) *n.* border, brim, brink, edge, limit, lip, margin; **(2)** *v.* approach, border, incline, lean, slope.
Ant. of **(1)** interior.

verification authentication, confirmation, corroboration.
Ant. falsification.

verify attest, authenticate, confirm, corroborate, prove.

Ant. disprove.

verily (*Arch.*) absolutely, certainly, positively, really, truly, veritably.
Ant. doubtfully.

verity certainty, reality, truth, truthfulness.
Ant. falsehood.

vernacular *a.* indigenous, mother, native, vulgar.
Ant. foreign.

versatile adaptable, changeable, fickle, flexible, inconstant, unsteady, variable.
Ant. constant.

versed accomplished, acquainted, conversant, experienced, practised, proficient, qualified, skilled.
Ant. inexperienced.

version account, exercise, interpretation, reading, rendering.

vertex apex, crown, culmination, height, summit, top, zenith.
Ant. bottom.

vertical erect, perpendicular, plumb, upright.
Ant. horizontal.

vertiginous (1) dizzy, giddy; **(2)** rotary, rotatory, whirling.

vertigo dizziness, giddiness.

verve animation, ardour, energy, enthusiasm, force, rapture, spirit.

very (1) *a.* actual, real, same, true; **(2)** *adv.* absolutely, exceedingly, excessively, extremely, highly, remarkably, surpassingly.

vesicle bladder, cell, cyst.

vest (1) *v.* clothe, cover, dress, envelop; **(2)** (*Fig.*) endow, furnish; **(3)** *n.* dress, garment, robe, vestment, (*U.S.A.*) waistcoat.

vestal chaste, immaculate, pure, unsullied.
Ant. impure.

vestibule hall, lobby, porch, portico.

vestige evidence, footprint, footstep, indication, remainder, remnant, residue, sign, token, trace, track.

vestment apparel, attire, clothing, costume, habit, raiment, robe, vesture.
Ant. nakedness.

veteran adept, expert, old, proficient, seasoned.
Ant. novice.

veto (1) *v.* ban, forbid, interdict, negative, prohibit; (2) *n.* ban, embargo, interdict, prohibition.
Ant. of (1) permit.

vex afflict, agitate, annoy, bother, displease, distress, disturb, harass, irritate, molest, offend, perplex, pester, plague, provoke, tease, torment, worry.
Ant. please.

vexatious afflicting, annoying, burdensome, disagreeable, distressing, harassing, irksome, irritating, provoking, teasing, tormenting, troublesome, unpleasant, worrying.
Ant. satisfying.

vexed (1) afflicted, agitated, annoyed, bothered, distressed, disturbed, harassed, irritated, perplexed, provoked, tormented, troubled, worried; (2) contested, disputed.
Ant. satisfied.

vibrate fluctuate, oscillate, quiver, shake, shiver, sway, swing, tremble, undulate.

vicarious commissioned, delegated, deputed, substituted.

vice blemish, corruption, defect, depravity, evil, failing, fault, immorality, imperfection, iniquity, sin, wickedness.
Ant. virtue.

vicinity district, locality, nearness, neighbourhood, propinquity, proximity.
Ant. distance.

vicious (1) abandoned, bad, corrupt, debased, degraded, depraved, faulty, foul, immoral, imperfect, malicious, profligate, sinful, unprincipled, worthless, wrong; (2) contrary, malevolent, refractory, unruly.
Ant. of (1) virtuous.

viciousness badness, corruption, depravity, immorality, profligacy.
Ant. virtuousness.

vicissitude alteration, alternation, change, mutation, revolution, variation.
Ant. permanence.

victim (1) sacrifice, sufferer; (2) dupe, gull.

victimise beguile, cheat, deceive, defraud, dupe, fool, gull, hoodwink, sacrifice, swindle.

victor conqueror, vanquisher, winner.
Ant. loser.

victorious conquering, successful, triumphant, vanquishing.
Ant. defeated.

victory conquest, mastery, success, superiority, triumph.
Ant. defeat.

victuals bread, eatables, food, meat, provisions, rations, viands.

vie compete, contend, contest, strive, struggle.
Ant. yield.

view (1) *v.* behold, contemplate, examine, explore, eye, inspect, scan, survey, watch; (2) consider, ponder, regard; (3) *n.* perspective, picture, prospect, scene, vista; (4) examination, inspection, sight, survey; (5) aim, belief, design, end, impression, intention, judgment, notion, opinion, sentiment.

vigilance alertness, attentiveness, carefulness, caution, circumspection, observance, watchfulness.
Ant. inattentiveness.

vigilant alert, attentive, careful, cautious, circumspect, wakeful, watchful.
Ant. inattentive.

vigorous active, effective, efficient, energetic, enterprising, forcible, hale, hardy, healthy, impetuous, intense, powerful, robust, sound, spirited, strong, virile.
Ant. weak.

vigour activity, animation, efficacy, energy, force, health, liveliness, might, power, robustness, soundness, strength, virility, vitality.
Ant. weakness.

vile abandoned, abject, bad, base, debased, depraved, despicable, ignoble, impure, loathsome, low, mean, miserable, sinful, vicious, wicked, worthless, wretched.
Ant. worthy.

vilify abuse, asperse, berate, calumniate, debase, decry, disparage, malign, revile, slander, traduce, vituperate.
Ant. praise.

villain caitiff, knave, miscreant, profligate, rascal, reprobate, rogue, scamp, scoundrel, vagabond, wretch.
Ant. hero.

villainous atrocious, bad, base, debased, degenerate, depraved, heinous, ignoble, infamous, mean, nefarious, outrageous, vile.
Ant. heroic.

vindicate advocate, assert,

claim, defend, establish, justify, support, uphold.
Ant. denounce.

vindication apology, assertion, defence, excuse, maintenance, plea, support.
Ant. denunciation.

vindictive implacable, malicious, malignant, rancorous, relentless, revengeful, spiteful, unforgiving, unrelenting.
Ant. forgiving.

violate (1) break, disobey, infringe, transgress; (2) abuse, debauch, defile, desecrate, outrage, pollute, profane, rape, ravish.

violent acute, boisterous, fiery, furious, impetuous, intense, outrageous, passionate, raging, severe, sharp, tumultuous, turbulent, ungovernable, vehement, wild.
Ant. calm.

virago scold, shrew, termagant, vixen.

virgin (1) n. damsel, girl, maid, maiden, spinster; (2) a. chaste, fresh, maidenly, modest, new, pure, undefiled, untouched, unused.

virile male, manly, masculine, robust, vigorous.
Ant. unmanly.

virtual essential, implicit, implied, indirect, potential.

virtue (1) chastity, goodness, morality, purity; (2) efficacy, excellence, integrity, justice, probity, quality, rectitude, uprightness, worth.
Ant. of (1) vice.

virtuous blameless, chaste, excellent, good, honest, moral, pure, righteous, upright, worthy.
Ant. vicious.

virulent (1) baneful, deadly, malignant, poisonous, toxic,

venomous; (2) (*Fig.*) acrimonious, bitter, malevolent, rancorous, spiteful, vicious.
Ant. of (1) harmless.

visage appearance, aspect, countenance, face, physiognomy.

viscera bowels, entrails, intestines.

viscous adhesive, clammy, gelatinous, gluey, glutinous, sticky, tenacious.

visible apparent, clear, conspicuous, discernible, distinguishable, evident, manifest, noticeable, observable, obvious, patent, perceptible.
Ant. invisible.

vision (1) discernment, image, perception, sight, view; (2) apparition, chimera, dream, ghost, illusion, phantom, spectre, wraith.

visionary (1) *a.* chimerical, dreaming, fanciful, fantastic, ideal, illusory, imaginary, romantic, speculative, unreal; (2) *n.* dreamer, enthusiast, idealist, theorist, zealot.
Ant. of (1) practical.

vital (1) alive, life-giving, living; (2) critical, essential, important, indispensable, necessary.
Ant. of (2) unessential, unimportant.

vitality animation, life, strength, vigour.
Ant. weakness.

vitiate contaminate, corrupt, defile, deprave, deteriorate, harm, impair, injure, pollute, taint.
Ant. purify.

vitiation contamination, corruption, debasement, degradation, deterioration, perversion, pollution.
Ant. purification.

vituperate abuse, blame, censure, denounce, rate, reproach, revile, upbraid, vilify.
Ant. praise.

vituperation abuse, blame, censure, invective, rebuke, reprimand, reproach, vilification.

vivacious animated, brisk, cheerful, frolicsome, gay, jocund, jolly, light-hearted, lively, merry, spirited, sportive, sprightly.
Ant. dull.

vivacity animation, briskness, energy, gaiety, liveliness, quickness, smartness, spirit, sprightliness.
Ant. lethargy.

vivid (1) bright, brilliant, clear, intense, lucid, striking; (2) active, animated, energetic, expressive, lively, quick, spirited, strong, vigorous.
Ant. dull.

vividness brightness, brilliancy, life, radiance, resplendence, sprightliness, strength.

vivify animate, arouse, awaken, enliven, quicken, vitalise.
Ant. stifle.

vixen (*Fig.*) scold, shrew, termagant, virago.

vocabulary dictionary, glossary, language, lexicon, wordbook, words.

vocation business, calling, employment, job, mission, office, post, profession, pursuit, trade.

vociferate bawl, bellow, clamour, rant, shout.
Ant. whisper.

vociferous clamorous, loud, noisy, obstreperous, ranting, uproarious.
Ant. peaceful, silent.

vogue custom, fashion, mode, practice, style, usage, use, way.

voice (1) *n.* articulation, expression, language, sound, tone, utterance, words; (2) *v.* declare, express, say, utter.

Ant. of (1) silence.

void (1) *a.* clear, destitute, empty, free, unfilled, unoccupied, vacant; (2) ineffective, ineffectual, invalid, useless, vain; (3) *n.* gap, opening, space.

volatile airy, changeable, fickle, flighty, gay, giddy, inconstant, lively, sprightly, unsteady, whimsical.

Ant. constant.

volition choice, determination, discretion, free-will, option, preference, purpose.

Ant. compulsion.

volley blast, burst, discharge, explosion, salvo.

voluble fluent, glib, loquacious, talkative.

Ant. dumb.

volume (1) book, tome; (2) body, bulk, compass, dimensions, mass.

voluminous ample, big, bulky, copious, full, large.

voluntary designed, discretional, free, gratuitous, intended, intentional, optional, spontaneous, uncompelled, unforced, willing.

Ant. obligatory.

volunteer *v.* offer, present, proffer, propose, tender.

Ant. refuse.

voluptuous epicurean, licentious, luxurious, sensual, sybaritic.

Ant. ascetic.

vomit disgorge, eject, emit.

Ant. swallow.

voracious gluttonous, greedy, hungry, rapacious, ravenous.

vortex eddy, maelstrom, whirlpool.   [ciple.

votary adherent, devotee, dis-

vouch affirm, assert, asseverate, back, confirm, guarantee, support, uphold.

Ant. deny.

vouchsafe accord, cede, deign, grant, yield.

Ant. refuse.

vow (1) *v.* affirm, consecrate, dedicate, devote, pledge, promise, swear; (2) *n.* oath, promise.

Ant. of (1) repudiate.

voyage cruise, journey, passage, trip.

vulgar (1) base, coarse, common, low-born, mean, plebeian, underbred; (2) general, native, ordinary, unrefined, vernacular.

Ant. of (1) polite, refined.

vulgarity baseness, coarseness, grossness, meanness, rudeness.

Ant. refinement.

vulnerable accessible, assailable, defenceless, exposed, susceptible, tender, weak.

Ant. invulnerable, protected.

W

waft bear, carry, convey, float, transmit, transport.

wag (A) *v.* shake, vibrate, waggle.

wag (B) *n.* humorist, jester, joker, wit.

Ant. dullard.

wage *v.* conduct, engage, undertake.

wager (1) *v.* bet, hazard, lay, pledge, risk, stake, venture; (2) *n.* bet, pledge, stake.

wages allowance, compensation, earnings, emolument, hire, pay, recompense, remuneration, reward, salary, stipend.

waggish comical, droll, funny, humorous, jocose, jocular, merry, sportive.

Ant. dull.

wail (1) v. bemoan, bewail, cry, deplore, grieve, lament, weep; (2) n. complaint, grief, lament, lamentation, moan, weeping.

Ant. of (1) rejoice; of (2) joy.

wait (1) abide, delay, expect, linger, pause, remain, rest, stay, tarry; (2) attend, serve.

Ant. of (1) depart.

waive abandon, defer, forego, relinquish, remit, renounce, resign, surrender.

Ant. demand, insist.

wake (1) arise, awake, awaken; (2) activate, animate, arouse, awaken, excite, kindle, provoke; (3) n. (*Naut.*) course, path, track, wash.

Ant. of (1) sleep; of (2) allay.

wakeful (1) restless, sleepless; (2) alert, observant, vigilant, wary, watchful.

Ant. of (1) sleepy; of (2) unobservant.

wale ridge, streak, stripe, weal.

walk (1) v. advance, go, march, move, pace, perambulate, step, stride; (2) n. promenade, ramble, stroll, tramp; (3) alley, avenue, footpath, path, pathway, pavement, sidewalk; (4) behaviour, carriage, conduct, gait, step; (5) action, beat, career, course, field, sphere.

wallet bag, pocket-book, pouch, purse.

wan ashen, bloodless, cadaverous, colourless, discoloured, pale, pallid, sickly.

Ant. florid, robust.

wander depart, deviate, range, roam, rove, straggle, stray, stroll, swerve.

Ant. settle.

wane (1) v. abate, decline, decrease, diminish, fail, sink; (2) n. abatement, decay, declension, decrease, diminution, failure.

Ant. of (1) wax.

want (1) v. crave, desire, need, require, wish; (2) n. craving, desire, longing, necessity, need, requirement; (3) dearth, deficiency, insufficiency, lack, scantiness, scarcity; (4) destitution, indigence, penury, poverty.

Ant. of (1) have, possess.

wanton (1) v. (*Poet.*) caper, disport, frisk, frolic, play, revel romp, sport; (2) a. frisky, frolicsome, gay, skittish; (3) dissolute, irregular, lewd, licentious, loose, lustful, unchaste; (4) careless, gratuitous, groundless, heedless, inconsiderate, reckless, unjustifiable, wilful.

Ant. of (2) demure, modest; of (3) chaste; of (4) heedful, justifiable..

war (1) n. contention, enmity, hostility, strife, warfare; (2) v. contend, fight, strive.

Ant. of (1) peace.

ward (1) v. defend, guard, protect, watch; (2) n. (*Arch.*) defender, keeper, guardian, warder; (3) (*Law*) minor, pupil; (4) (*City*) district, division, quarter; (5) (*Med.*) apartment, cubicle, room.

wares commodities, goods, merchandise.

warfare contest, discord, hostilities, strife, struggle, war.

Ant. peace.

warily carefully, charily, cautiously, circumspectly, guardedly, vigilantly, watchfully.

Ant. carelessly.

wariness care, caution, circumspection, foresight, vigilance, watchfulness.

Ant. carelessness.

warlike bellicose, belligerent, hostile, inimical, martial, military, unfriendly.

Ant. peaceful.

warm (1) heated, hot, lukewarm, sunny, tepid, thermal; (2) amiable, animated, ardent, cordial, enthusiastic, excited, fervent, friendly, genial, glowing, keen, lively, passionate, pleasant, vehement, violent.

Ant. of (1) cold; of (2) cool, phlegmatic.

warmth animation, ardour, cordiality, eagerness, earnestness, enthusiasm, excitement, fervency, heat, passion, transport.

warn admonish, advise, apprise, caution, forewarn, inform, notify, summon.

Ant. attend, encourage.

warning admonition, advice, augury, caution, notice, notification, omen, premonition, sign.   [ment.

Ant. attention, encourage-

warp bend, contort, deviate, distort, pervert, swerve, turn, twist.

Ant. straighten.

warrant (1) v. affirm, assure, attest, avouch, declare, secure; (2) approve, authorise, guarantee, justify, sanction; (3) n. assurance, authorisation, authority, guarantee, pledge, security, warranty.

Ant. of (1) disallow.

warrantable allowable, defensible, justifiable, lawful, permissible, proper.

Ant. unjustifiable.

warrior champion, fighter, hero, soldier.

wary careful, cautious, chary, circumspect, guarded, prudent, vigilant, watchful.

Ant. imprudent.

wash bath, bathe, clean, cleanse, lave, moisten, wet.

Ant. dry.

washy damp, diluted, moist, oozy, sloppy, thin, watery, weak.

waspish cantankerous, captious, fretful, irascible, irritable, peevish, pettish, petulant, snappish.

Ant. patient.

waste (1) v. consume, corrode, decay, decrease, destroy, devastate; (2) dissipate, dwindle, lavish, perish, pine, squander, wane, wither; (3) a. bare, barren, desolate, devastated, dismal, dreary, uncultivated, uninhabited, unproductive, worthless; (4) n. consumption, diminution, dissipation, expenditure, extravagance, loss, prodigality, squandering; (5) desolation, devastation, havoc, ravage; (6) débris, dregs, dross, refuse, rubbish; (7) desert, solitude, wild, wilderness.

wasteful extravagant, improvident, lavish, prodigal, unthrifty.

Ant. economical.

watch (A) v. (1) contemplate, look, mark, note, observe, see, view; (2) guard, keep, protect, tend; (3) n. alertness, attention, inspection, observation, vigil, watchfulness; (4) sentinel, sentry, watchman.

Ant. of (2) neglect.

watch (B) n. chronometer, clock, timepiece.

watchful alert, attentive, circumspect, guarded, heedful, observant, vigilant, wary.

Ant. unwary.

watchfulness attention, caution, cautiousness, circumspection, heedfulness, vigilance.

Ant. carelessness.

watchword countersign, password.

waterfall cascade, cataract, fall.

watery (1) aqueous, damp, humid, moist, wet; (2) diluted, insipid, tasteless, thin, waterish, weak.

Ant. of (2) concentrated, strong.

wave (1) v. beckon, brandish, flourish, flutter, oscillate, shake, sign, signal, stir, sway, undulate; (2) n. billow, breaker, ridge, ripple, sea-surf, swell, undulation, unevenness.

waver (1) flicker, fluctuate, quiver, shake, sway, tremble, undulate, wave; (2) fluctuate, hesitate, vacillate.

Ant. of (2) determine.

wax become, grow, increase, mount, rise.

Ant. wane.

way (1) course, highway, lane, path, pathway, road, route, street, track, trail; (2) advance, march, passage, progress; (3) fashion, manner, means, method, mode, plan, scheme, sort; (4) custom, habit, practice, usage.

wayfarer itinerant, nomad, passenger, traveller, walker, wanderer.

wayward capricious, contrary, cross-grained, headstrong, intractable, obdurate, obstinate, perverse, refractory, stubborn, ungovernable, unmanageable, unruly, wilful.

Ant. yielding.

weak (1) debilitated, delicate, feeble, fragile, frail, infirm,

languid, sickly, tender; (2) defenceless, exposed, unguarded, unprotected; (3) foolish, injudicious, irresolute, pliable, silly, simple, soft, unwise; (4) faint, flimsy, low, poor, slight, small; (5) diluted, insipid, thin, waterish, watery; (6) inconclusive, invalid, lame, unconvincing, unsatisfactory.

Ant. strong.

weaken debase, debilitate, depress, enervate, impair, invalidate, lower, reduce.

Ant. strengthen.

weakness (1) debility, feebleness, fragility, frailty, faintness, infirmity, languor, softness; (2) defect, failing, fault, flaw; (3) fondness, inclination, liking.

weal (A) good, happiness, profit, prosperity, utility, welfare.

Ant. ill-luck.

weal (B) ridge, streak, stripe, wale.

wealth (1) assets, cash, fortune, funds, goods, money, possessions, property, riches; (2) abundance, affluence, opulence, plenty, profusion.

Ant. of (1) poverty; of (2) dearth.

wean (Fig.) alienate, detach, disengage, withdraw.

Ant. attract.

wear (1) bear, carry, don; (2) endure, last; (3) consume, impair, rub, use, waste.

Ant. of (3) repair.

wearied exhausted, (Colloq.) fagged, jaded, tired, weary.

weariness exhaustion, fatigue, languor, lassitude, prostration, tiredness.

wearisome annoying, boring, dull, exhausting, fatiguing, humdrum, irksome, monotonous, prosaic, tedious, troublesome, trying, uninteresting.

Ant. interesting.

weary (1) exhausted, fatigued, jaded, spent, tired, worn; (2) irksome, tiresome, wearisome; (3) v. debilitate, dispirit, (*Colloq.*) fag, fatigue, harass, harry, jade, tire.

Ant. of (1) refreshed.

weave braid, contrive, interlace, intermingle, intertwine, mat, plait, unite.

Ant. disentangle, undo.

wed espouse, join, marry, unite.

Ant. divorce.

wedding espousals, marriage, nuptials, wedlock.

wedlock marriage, matrimony.

ween (*Poet.*) fancy, imagine, judge, suppose, think.

weep bemoan, bewail, complain, cry, lament, moan, sob.

Ant. laugh.

weigh (1) balance, counterbalance, lift, raise; (2) (*Fig.*) consider, deliberate, esteem, examine, ponder, study.

weight (1) burden, gravity, heaviness, load, pressure; (2) (*Fig.*) consequence, efficacy, importance, influence, moment, power, significance.

Ant. of (1) lightness.

weighty (1) burdensome, dense, heavy, ponderous; (2) (*Fig.*) forcible, grave, important, momentous, serious, significant.

Ant. of (1) light; of (2) unimportant.

weird eerie, ghostly, strange, supernatural, uncanny, unearthly.

Ant. natural.

welcome (1) a. acceptable, agreeable, gratifying, pleasant,

pleasing; (2) n. greeting, reception, salutation; (3) v. greet, hail, receive.

Ant. of (1) unwelcome.

welfare advantage, benefit, happiness, profit, prosperity, success, weal, well-being.

Ant. loss, misfortune.

well (A) fountain, origin, source, spring.

well (B) (1) a. hale, healthy, hearty, sound; (2) beneficent, fortunate, good, happy, profitable, satisfactory, useful; (3) adv. accurately, adequately, correctly, efficiently, properly, suitably; (4) abundantly, amply, considerably, fully, thoroughly.

Ant. of (1) ill.

welter roll, tumble, wallow.

wet (1) aqueous, damp, dank, drenched, humid, moist, moistened, soaked, watery; (2) drizzling, misty, raining, rainy, showery; (3) v. damp, drench, saturate, soak, spray, sprinkle.

Ant. dry.

whack bang, beat, belabour, rap, strike, thrash, thump, thwack.

Ant. fondle, stroke.

wharf dock, landing-stage, mole, pier, quay.

wheedle cajole, coax, court, entice, flatter, humour, inveigle.

Ant. force, repel.

wheel v. circle, gyrate, revolve, roll, rotate, spin, swing, turn, twirl, whirl.

whet (1) sharpen; (2) (*Fig.*) animate, arouse, excite, incite, increase, provoke, rouse, stimulate.

Ant. of (2) decrease, discourage.

whiff blast, gust, puff.

whim caprice, crotchet, fancy,

freak, frolic, humour, notion, sport, vagary, whimsy.
Ant. steadfastness.

whimsical capricious, crotchety, curious, eccentric, fanciful, fantastical, odd, peculiar, quaint, queer, singular.
Ant. serious.

whine complain, cry, grumble, moan, whimper.

whip (1) v. beat, castigate, flog, lash, punish, scourge, thrash; (2) jerk, seize, snatch, whisk.

whipping beating, castigation, flagellation, flogging, punishment, thrashing.

whirl gyrate, pirouette, roll, revolve, rotate, turn, twirl, twist, wheel.

whit atom, bit, grain, iota, jot, mite, piece, scrap, speck.
Ant. whole.

white (1) ashen, hoary, pale, pallid, snowy, wan; (2) clean, pure, spotless, unblemished.
Ant. of (1) black; of (2) dirty.

whole (1) all, complete, entire, integral, total, undivided; (2) good, faultless, perfect, unbroken, undamaged, unimpaired, uninjured.
Ant. of (1) partial; of (2) imperfect.

wholesome beneficial, good, helpful, invigorating, nourishing, nutritious, pure, salubrious, salutary, strengthening.
Ant. unwholesome.

wholly altogether, completely, entirely, fully, totally, utterly.
Ant. partially.

whoop halloo, hoot, shout, yell.

whore courtesan, harlot, prostitute, street-walker, strumpet.

wicked abandoned, amoral, bad, corrupt, debased, depraved, dissolute, evil, godless, guilty, heinous, immoral, impious, iniquitous, irreligious, nefarious, sinful, ungodly, unholy, unrighteous, vicious, vile, villainous, worthless.
Ant. virtuous.

wide (1) ample, broad, capacious, comprehensive, distended, expanded, extensive, large, spacious, vast; (2) distant, remote.
Ant. of (1) narrow.

wield brandish, control, employ, handle, manage, sway, swing, use.

wild (1) ferocious, fierce, savage, unbroken, undomesticated, untamed; (2) boisterous, furious, impetuous, lawless, rough, self-willed, turbulent, uncontrolled, undisciplined, ungovernable, unmanageable, unrestrained, unruly, violent, wayward; (3) extravagant, fantastic, foolish, impracticable, mad, rash, reckless; (4) anxious, enthusiastic, excited, over-eager; (5) deserted, uncivilised, uncultivated, uninhabited.
Ant. of (1) tame.

wilderness desert, waste, wild.

wile artifice, cheating, craft, cunning, device, dodge, fraud, guile, imposition, imposture, lure, manoeuvre, ruse, stratagem, trick.
Ant. ingenuousness.

wilful adamant, dogged, headstrong, intractable, intransigent, obdurate, obstinate, persistent, perverse, pig-headed, refractory, stubborn.
Ant. complaisant.

will (1) v. bid, command, decree, direct, ordain; (2) choose, desire, elect, wish; (3) (Law) bequeath, demise, devise, leave; (**4**) *n.* choice, decision, determination, volition; (**5**) desire, inclination, pleasure, wish; (**6**) (*Law*) testament.

willing desirous, disposed, eager, inclined, so-minded, prepared, ready.

willingly eagerly, gladly, readily, voluntarily.

Ant. reluctantly.

wily arch, artful, crafty, crooked, cunning, deceitful, designing, foxy, intriguing, scheming, sly, tricky, underhand.

Ant. straightforward.

win (**1**) accomplish, achieve, acquire, attain, catch, conquer, earn, gain, get, obtain, procure, secure, succeed; (**2**) allure, attract, convince, influence, persuade.

Ant. of (**1**) lose.

wind (A) (**1**) coil, encircle, twine, twist; (**2**) bend, curve, deviate, meander, turn.

wind (B) (**1**) *n.* air, blast, breath, breeze, draught, gust, respiration, zephyr; (**2**) (*Fig.*) hint, rumour, suggestion.

winding bending, curving, flexuous, meandering, serpentine, sinuous, turning, twisting.

Ant. straight.

windy (**1**) blustering, boisterous, breezy, squally, stormy, tempestuous; (**2**) (*Fig.*) airy, diffuse, empty, long-winded, verbose; (**3**) (*Sl.*) fearful, frightened, nervous.

Ant. of (**1**) calm; of (**2**) terse; of (**3**) fearless.

winning alluring, attractive, bewitching, captivating, charming, delightful, engaging, fascinating, lovely, prepossessing, winsome.

Ant. repulsive.

winnow divide, fan, part, select, separate, sift.

winsome agreeable, alluring, attractive, bewitching, captivating, charming, enchanting, engaging, fascinating, gay, light-hearted, lively, merry, winning.

Ant. repulsive.

wintry cold, frosty, icy, snowy.

wipe clean, dry, rub.

wisdom attainment, circumspection, discernment, enlightenment, erudition, foresight, insight, intelligence, judiciousness, judgment, knowledge, learning, prudence, reason, reasonableness, sagacity, sense.

Ant. folly.

wise (**1**) *a.* discerning, discreet, enlightened, erudite, intelligent, judicious, knowing, politic, prudent, rational, reasonable, sagacious, sage, sapient, sensible; (**2**) *n.* fashion, manner, mode, respect, way.

Ant. of (**1**) foolish.

wish (**1**) *v.* covet, crave, desire, hanker, lack, long, need, want, yearn; (**2**) bid, command, order; (**3**) *n.* desire, hankering, inclination, intention, liking, longing, want, will.

wistful (**1**) contemplative, meditative, musing, pensive, reflective, thoughtful; (**2**) eager, earnest, engrossed, longing.

wit (**1**) discernment, insight, intellect, mind, perception, reason, sense, understanding; (**2**) drollery, facetiousness, fun, humour, jocularity, pleasantry, repartee; (**3**) (*of a person*) humorist, wag.

Ant. of (**1**) ignorance.

witchcraft enchantment, incantation, magic, necromancy, sorcery, spell.

withdraw (1) depart, disengage, recede, retire, retreat, secede; (2) abjure, disavow, recall, recant, remove, rescind, retract, revoke.

Ant. of (1) stand; of (2) maintain.

wither decay, decline, droop, dry, fade, languish, perish, shrink, shrivel, waste.

Ant. bloom.

withhold check, forbear, keep, refuse, repress, reserve, resist, restrain, retain.

Ant. afford, grant.

withstand confront, face, oppose, resist, thwart.

Ant. yield.

witless dull, foolish, half-witted, senseless, silly, stupid.

Ant. intelligent.

witness (1) v. attest, confirm, corroborate, testify; (2) mark, note, notice, observe, perceive, see, watch; (3) n. attestation, confirmation, corroboration, evidence, proof, testimony; (4) beholder, corroborator, deponent, eye-witness, spectator, testifier.

Ant. of (1) disprove.

witty droll, facetious, fanciful, funny, humorous, jocular.

wizard conjurer, enchanter, juggler, magician, necromancer, soothsayer, sorcerer.

woe affliction, agony, anguish, curse, depression, disaster, distress, grief, melancholy, misery, pain, sadness, sorrow, trouble, unhappiness, wretchedness.

Ant. happiness.

woeful afflicted, agonised, anguished, calamitous, deplorable, disastrous, distressing, dreadful, grieved, grieving,

lamentable, miserable, mournful, piteous, pitiful, sorrowful, unhappy, wretched.

Ant. happy.

wonder (1) n. amazement, astonishment, awe, bewilderment, curiosity, surprise; (2) marvel, miracle, phenomenon, portent, prodigy, rarity; (3) v. marvel, meditate, ponder, question, speculate, think.

Ant. of (1) calmness.

wonderful amazing, astonishing, astounding, awesome, marvellous, miraculous, odd, peculiar, phenomenal, remarkable, startling, strange, surprising.

Ant. ordinary.

wont (1) n. custom, habit, practice, rule, use; (2) a. accustomed, customary, habitual, ordinary, usual.

Ant. of (2) unaccustomed.

wonted accustomed, common, customary, familiar, frequent, habitual, regular, usual.

Ant. unusual.

woo court.

wood (1) copse, grove, forest, thicket, woodland; (2) timber.

word (1) affirmation, assertion, declaration, expression, term, utterance; (2) account, advice, information, intelligence, news, report, tidings; (3) assurance, pledge, promise; (4) bidding, command, order; (5) countersign, password, signal.

wordy diffuse, garrulous, long-winded, prolix, verbose.

Ant. terse.

work (1) v. act, handle, manage, manipulate, move, operate, perform; (2) accomplish, achieve, effect, execute, fashion, make, produce; (3) drudge, labour, slave, toil; (4) n. production; (5) drudgery, exertion, labour, toil; (6) business, calling, employment, job, occupation, office, profession, trade.

Ant. rest.

workman artificer, artisan, craftsman, employee, hand, journeyman, labourer, mechanic, operative, worker.

Ant. employer.

world creation, earth, globe, universe.

worldly (1) earthly, mundane, secular, temporal, terrestrial; (2) covetous, greedy, selfish.

Ant. of (1) spiritual, unworldly; (2) selfless.

worry (1) v. annoy, bother, chafe, disturb, fret, harry, importune, irritate, pester, plague, tantalise, tease, torment, trouble, vex; (2) n. annoyance, anxiety, apprehension, care, concern, fear, misgiving, perplexity, solicitude, trouble, vexation.

Ant. of (1) comfort; of (2) joy.

worship (1) v. adore, deify, honour, idolise, love, respect, revere, reverence, venerate; (2) n. adoration, homage, honour, regard, respect, reverence.

Ant. of (1) detest.

worst beat, conquer, crush, defeat, master, overcome, overpower, overthrow, subdue, subjugate, vanquish.

Ant. yield.

worth (1) credit, desert, estimation, excellence, goodness, merit, usefulness, virtue, worthiness; (2) cost, price, rate, value.

Ant. of (1) worthlessness.

worthless (1) futile, miserable, paltry, poor, trivial, useless, valueless, wretched; (2) abandoned, abject, base, depraved, good-for-nothing, ignoble.

Ant. worthy.

worthy (1) commendable, deserving, estimable, excellent, laudable, meritorious; (2) good, honest, righteous, upright, virtuous.

Ant. unworthy.

wound (1) v. damage, harm, hurt, injure, irritate, lacerate, pierce; (2) (Fig.) annoy, offend, pain; (3) n. damage, harm, hurt, injury; (4) (Fig.) anguish, grief, pain, pang, torment, torture.

Ant. of (1) heal; of (2) salve.

wraith apparition, ghost, phantom, spectre.

wrangle (1) v. altercate, bicker, brawl, contend, disagree, dispute, quarrel, squabble; (2) n. altercation, bickering, brawl, contest, controversy, dispute, quarrel, squabble.

Ant. of (1) agree.

wrap cover, encase, enfold, envelop, muffle, wind.

wrath anger, choler, exasperation, fury, indignation, ire, passion, rage, resentment.

Ant. serenity.

wrathful angry, enraged, furious, incensed, indignant, irate, irritated.

Ant. serene.

wreak execute, exercise, inflict, work.

wreath chaplet, crown, festoon, garland.

wreathe encircle, enfold, intertwine, interweave, surround, twine, twist.

wreck (1) v. destroy, devastate, ruin, shatter, spoil; (2) founder, shipwreck, strand; (3) n. desolation, destruction, devastation, ruin; (4) shipwreck.

Ant. of (1) reconstruct.

wrench (1) twist, wring; (2) distort, sprain, strain.

wrest force, pull, strain, twist, wrench, wring.

wrestle contend, fight, strive, struggle.

wretch caitiff, knave, miscreant, outcast, profligate, rascal, rogue, ruffian, scoundrel, vagabond, villain.

wretched calamitous, comfortless, contemptible, dejected, deplorable, depressed, distressed, forlorn, melancholy, miserable, pitiable, poor, sorry, vile, woebegone, woeful, worthless.

Ant. fortunate, happy.

wring extort, force, twist, wrench, wrest.

wrinkle v. and n. crease, crumple, fold, furrow, gather, pucker, rumple.

Ant. v. smooth.

writ (*Law*) decree, order, summons.

write compose, copy, indite, inscribe, pen, scribble, transcribe.

writhe contort, distort, squirm, wrest, wriggle, wring.

wrong (1) *a.* erroneous, false, faulty, illegal, inaccurate, incorrect, injurious, mistaken, unjust; (2) *v.* abuse, injure, maltreat, oppress; (3) *n.* blame, error, grievance, guilt, immorality, iniquity, injustice, misdeed, sin, transgression, trespass, wickedness.

Ant. right.

wroth angry, enraged, exasperated, furious, incensed, indignant, irate, passionate, provoked, resentful.

Ant. unmoved.

wrought done, effected, performed, worked.

wry askew, awry, contorted, crooked, distorted, twisted.

Ant. straight.

X

X-rays Röntgen-rays.

xylograph wood-cut, wood-engraving.

Y

yarn anecdote, story, tale.

yearn covet, crave, desire, hanker, long.

yell (1) *v.* bawl, howl, scream, screech, shout, shriek, squeal; (2) *n.* cry, howl, scream, screech, shriek.

Ant. whisper.

yet besides, further, moreover, nevertheless, notwithstanding, now, still.

yield (1) afford, bear, furnish, produce, supply; (2) abandon, abdicate, capitulate, cede, relinquish, resign, submit, surrender; (3) allow, concede, grant, permit; (4) *n.* crop, harvest, produce.

Ant. of (2) resist; of (3) disallow.

yielding accommodating, affable, compliant, docile, easy, flexible, pliable, pliant, submissive, supple.

Ant. unsubmissive, unyielding.

yoke (1) *n.* bond, chain, link, tie; (2) bondage, service, servitude, slavery, thraldom, vassalage; (3) *v.* connect, couple, join, link, tie, unite.

Ant. of (2) freedom; of (3) disunite.

yokel boor, bumpkin, countryman, (*Obs.*) hind, peasant, rustic.

Ant. townsman.

youth (1) adolescent, boy, child, lad, stripling, teenager, youngster, (2) adolescence,

immaturity, juvenility.
Ant. of (1) adult; of (2) age, maturity.

youthful boyish, childish, immature, juvenile, puerile, young.
Ant. elderly, old.

Z

zeal ardour, eagerness, earnestness, enthusiasm, fervour, fire, keenness, passion, spirit, warmth.
Ant. coolness, disinterest.

zealot bigot, enthusiast, fanatic, maniac.

Ant. sceptic.

zealous ardent, eager, earnest, enthusiastic, fervent, fervid, keen, passionate, spirited, strenuous, warm.
Ant. cold, cool.

zenith apex, apogee, climax, height, pinnacle, summit, top, vertex.
Ant. base, nadir.

zero cipher, naught, nil, nothing, nought.

zest appetite, enjoyment, flavour, gusto, piquancy, relish, savour, smack, taste.
Ant. distaste.

zone area, belt, circumference, district, region, section, tract.

SYNONYMS OF FOREIGN
NOUNS AND PHRASES

A

abattu [Fr.] dejected, depressed, disheartened, dispirited, saddened.

Aberglaube [Ger.] credulity, superstition.

à bon chat, bon rat [Fr.] retaliation, tit-for-tat.

à bon droit [Fr.] justifiably, warrantably.

à bon marché [Fr.] cheap, inexpensive, low-priced.

ab ovo [Lat.=from the egg] initially, originally.

abrégé [Fr.] abridgment, abstract, epitome, précis, summary.

a capite ad calcem [Lat.= from head to heel] absolutely, completely, thoroughly, totally.

accablé [Fr.] despondent, discouraged, downcast, downhearted, overcome, overwhelmed.

Achtung [Ger.] attention! beware! care, caution, warning.

à cœur ouvert [Fr.] candidly, frankly, honestly, openly, straightforwardly, truthfully, unreservedly.

à contre cœur [Fr.] grudgingly, rancorously, reluctantly, ungracefully, unwillingly.

ad Calendas Graecas [Lat. =at the Greek Calends] never (*the Calends formed a division of the Roman month, but had no equivalent in Greek*).

addio [Ital.] adieu, farewell, goodbye.

à dessein [Fr.] intended, intentional, purposeful.

ad infinitum [Lat.] endlessly, illimitably, infinitely, interminably.

ad interim [Lat.] meantime, meanwhile.

ad invidiam [Lat.] enviously, invidiously, malevolently, maliciously, spitefully.

adscriptus glebae [Lat.= bound to the soil] bondsman, labourer, serf, slave, villein

adsum [Lat.] here, present.

ad unguem [Lat.=to the nail] accurate, admirable, choice, excellent, first-rate, perfect (*Roman sculptors tested the smoothness of a statue by drawing the finger-nail over it*).

aequo animo [Lat.] calmly, collectedly, composedly, equably, peacefully, serenely, tranquilly.

aere perennius [Lat.=more lasting than brass] eternal, everlasting, immutable, imperishable, infrangible, perennial, perpetual.

affiche [Fr.] bill, notice, placard, poster.

à fond [Fr.] completely, thoroughly, totally.

agaçant [Fr.] annoying, irritating, provoking.

à grands frais [Fr.] costly, expensively, sumptuously.

agréments [Fr.] blandishments, charms, courtesies, embellishments.

à haute voix [Fr.] aloud, loudly, openly.

aide-mémoire [Fr.] memory-aid, memorandum, reminder, summary.

aîné [Fr.] eldest, senior.

air distingué [Fr.] distinguished, gentlemanly, lady-like, refined (air).

aisé [Fr.] affluent, comfortable, easy, well-off.

à l'abri [Fr.] protected, sheltered.

à la dérobée [Fr.] secretly, slyly, stealthily.

à la mode [Fr.] current, fashionable, prevailing, smart, up-to-date.

alea jacta est [Lat.=the die is cast] irrevocable, irreversible (*said by Caesar when he crossed the Rubicon*).

allure [Fr.] bearing, gait, mien.

alma mater [Lat.] benign, gentle, mild (mother) (*used by graduates to designate their mother-university*).

alter ego [Lat.] counterpart, double, deputy, representative.

âme damnée [Fr.=lost soul] drudge, tool.

amor patriae [Lat.] patriotism.

amour propre [Fr.] conceit, self-admiration, self-esteem, self-love, vanity.

Anglia [Lat.] England.

animato [Ital.] animated, brisk, lively, vivacious.

Anschauung [Ger.] apprehension, instinct, intuition, perception, view.

Anschluss [Ger.] alliance, association, confederation, joining, union.

ante bellum [Lat.] pre-war.

aperçu [Fr.] outline, review, sketch, survey.

à peu près [Fr.] almost, nearly.

appartement [Fr.] flat, rooms, suite.

à propos [Fr.] about, concerning, opportunely, pertinently, timely.

à propos de rien [Fr.] irrelevantly.

arcanum [Lat.] enigma, mystery, secret.

Argadia [med. Lat.] Argyll.

arrière-garde [Fr.] rearguard.

arrière-pensée [Fr.] by-end, reservation.

à tâtons [Fr.] gropingly.

au courant, au fait [Fr.] acquainted, well-informed.

audax et cautus [Lat.] audacious, bold, venturesome, *and* careful, cautious, wary.

Aufklärung [Ger.] enlightenment, renaissance.

auf Wiedersehen [Ger.] adieu, farewell, good-bye.

au grand sérieux [Fr.] earnestly, seriously.

au secours! [Fr.] help!

Ausgleich [Ger.] adjustment, agreement, compromise, settlement.

aut Caesar, aut nullus [Lat. = Caesar or a nobody] *n.* ambition, haughtiness; *a.* haughty, imperious, lordly, over-bearing.

Autobahn [Ger.] highway, motor-way.

avant-coureur [Fr.] forerunner, harbinger, precursor.

avant-garde [Fr.] vanguard.

avant-propos [Fr.] foreword, introduction, preface.

ave! [Lat.] hail!

B

baccalauréat [Fr.] (School) leaving-certificate.

badinage [Fr.] jesting, joking, mockery, persiflage, pleasantry, ridicule.

badiner [Fr.] banter, chaff, deride, jest, joke, play, toy.

baignoire [Fr.] bath, tub; (*Theat.*) box.

ballon d'essai [Fr. = trial balloon] feeler, kite-flying, proposition, sounding.

banlieue [Fr.] outskirts, precincts, suburbs.

bas bleu [Fr.] bluestocking, highbrow, pedant.

bayer aux corneilles [Fr. = gape at the crows] day-dream, gape, stare, star-gaze, yawn.

beatae memoriae [Lat.] of blessed memory.

beau [Fr.] *a.* beautiful, handsome; *n.* Adonis, coxcomb, dandy, fop.

beau idéal [Fr.] perfection.

beau monde [Fr.] aristocracy, élite, society.

beau sabreur [Fr.] adventurer, cavalryman, swordsman.

beaux-arts [Fr.] arts, fine-arts.

bèche de mer [Fr. = spade of the sea] sea-slug, trepang (*when smoked and dried used as food in China*).

bec jaune [Fr. = yellow beak, *i.e., a fledging*] bejan, bejant (*a first year student at the Universities of Aberdeen and St. Andrews. In the Middle Ages applied to all young students*).

Bedeutung [Ger.] importance, meaning, signification.

benedicite [Lat.] blessing, a grace at table, prayer.

ben trovato [Ital. = well-found] apt, contrived, concocted, fabricated, feigned, invented.

berceuse [Fr.] lullaby.

bergère [Fr.] easy-chair; nymph, shepherdess.

bersaglio [Ital.] aim, butt, mark, target.

Besserung [Ger.] amelioration, betterment, improvement.

bête [Fr.] *a.* blockish, doltish, foolish, simple, stupid.

bête noire [Fr.] aversion, bogey, bugbear, detestation.

béton armé [Fr.] reinforced concrete.

bien–aimé [Fr.] darling, dear, sweetheart, well-beloved.

bien–être [Fr.] comfort, happiness, prosperity, welfare.

bienfaisance [Fr.] beneficence, benevolence, bounteousness, charity, liberality.

bienséant [Fr.] becoming, befitting, decorous, proper.

bigarré [Fr.] motley, particoloured, pied, variegated.

Bildung [Ger.] breeding, culture, education, formation, instruction.

billet-doux [Fr.] love-letter.

bis [Fr.] (*Mus.*) encore! repeat, twice.

Bitte! [Ger.] excuse (me)! pardon! please!

blafard [Fr.] lurid, pale, pallid, wan.

blague [Fr.] blarney, bounce, brag, bunkum, chaff, humbug, rubbish.

Blut und Eisen [Ger.=blood and iron] brutality, harshness, mercilessness, relentlessness, ruthlessness, truculence (*the essence of Bismarck's doctrine*).

bondad [Sp.], **bonté** [Fr.] clemency, courtesy, excellence, goodness, goodwill, graciousness, kindliness, suavity.

bon gré, mal gré [Fr.=goodwill, ill-will] willy-nilly.

bonhomie [Fr.] cordiality, frankness, geniality, good-nature, simplicity.

bonjour [Fr.] good day, good morning.

bonsoir [Fr.] good evening, good night.

bordereau [Fr.] abstract, list, memorandum, note, schedule, slip.

borné [Fr.] illiberal, limited, narrow-minded.

bouillabaisse [Fr.] fish-stew (*a speciality of the South of France*).

bouleversé [Fr.] distressed, overthrown, upset.

bourse [Fr.] bag, pouch, purse; (*Univ.*) exhibition, scholarship; (*Comm.*) Stock Exchange.

boutade [Fr.] caprice, crotchet, fancy, sally (*wit*).

boutique [Fr.] shop.

brasserie [Fr.] brewery, café-restaurant, public-house.

brava! [Ital.] splendid! well-done!

brevet [Fr.] certificate, diploma, licence.

breveté [Fr.] licensed, patented.

brindisi [Ital.] (*Drinking*) a toast, health.

brioche [Fr.] bun, roll.

Britannia [Lat.] Britain.

Brüderschaft [Ger.] brotherliness, fraternity, friendliness, good-fellowship.

bruit [Fr.] ado, clatter, din, noise, racket, row; gossip, news, report, rumour.

brut [Fr.] crude, raw; (*Gems*) uncut, unpolished; (*Wine*) unsweetened.

brutum fulmen [Lat.=insensible lightning] threat (loud but ineffectual).

Buch [Ger.] a book; *pl.* **Bücher.**

Buchhändler [Ger.] bookseller, publisher.

buon giorno [Ital.] good day, good morning.

buona notte [Ital.] good night.

buona sera [Ital.] good evening.

Bursche [Ger.] a student (at a German university).

Burschenschaft [Ger.] (student) society.

but [Fr.] aim, butt, end, intention, mark, point, purpose, target; (*Sport*) goal, winning-post.

C

Caaba [Arab.] mosque, temple (*Shrine at Mecca, enclosing a famous black stone, kissed by all Moslem pilgrims*).

caballero [Sp.] cavalier, gentleman, knight, nobleman.

cabinet [Fr.] lavatory, toilet, water-closet.

cachet [Fr.] seal, signet.

cachot [Fr.] cell, dungeon, gaol, jail, prison.

cachottier, *fem.* **cachottière** [Fr.] artful, astute, crafty, cunning, sly, underhand.

cacoëthes [Gk.] desire, itch, longing, mania, passion, urge (*never quoted alone; always followed by e.g. "loquendi", that is, a passion for speaking in public, or by "scribendi", that is an urge for writing*).

cadeau [Fr.] gift, present.

cadenzato [Ital.] measured, rhythmical.

cadet [Fr.] junior, minor, younger.

cadre [Fr.] compass, frame, framework, scheme, scope.

cagot [Fr.] deceiver, dissembler, hypocrite.

Caledonia [Lat.] Scotland.

câlin [Fr.] cajoling, caressing, coaxing, wheedling.

camarade [Fr.] chum, companion, fellow, mate.

camaraderie [Fr.] amity, attachment. fellowship, friendliness, friendship.

camarilla [Sp.] clique, coterie, junto, set.

Cambria [med. Lat.] Wales.

Camulodunum [Lat.] Colchester.

campeador [Sp. = surpassing in valour] champion, hero (*used of the Spanish hero* **el Cid**, *Rodrigo Diaz,* 1040-1099).

canaille [Fr.] blackguards, herd, mob, populace, proletariat, rabble, riff-raff, scum.

canción [Sp.] ballad, lay, lyric, song.

candidus [Lat.] beautiful, bright, radiant, white.

cantabile [Ital. = fit to be sung] (*Mus.*) flowing, graceful.

Cantabrigia [med. Lat.] Cambridge; *a.* **Cantabrigiensis.**

capa [Sp.] cape, cloak, mantle.

capuchon [Fr.] cowl, hood (*hence, a Capuchin or Franciscan monk from the hood he wears*).

caput mortuum [Lat.=dead head] ashes, remains, rubbish (*hence, useless details*).

carafe [Fr.] decanter, jug, water-bottle.

carême [Fr.] Lent.

cariñoso [Sp.] affable, affectionate, endearing, good, kind, loving.

carnet [Fr.] memorandum, note-book.

carpe diem [Lat.=enjoy the (present) day] opportunism.

carrefour [Fr.] cross-roads, round-about.

carte-blanche [Fr.=white or blank sheet of paper] a free-hand.

casus [Lat.] case, plea.

catalogue raisonné [Fr.] catalogue (*book with illustrations, literary notices, etc., arranged according to subjects*).

cauchemar [Fr.] bugbear, incubus, nightmare.

caudataire [Fr.] lick-spittle, toady, trainbearer.

cave [Fr.] cellar, vault.

cave! [Lat.] beware!

caveat [Lat.] a warning.

cela saute aux yeux [Fr.=that leaps to the eyes] (It's) apparent, clear, evident, obvious.

cela sert à faire bouillir la marmite [Fr.] a pot-boiler.

cela va sans dire [Fr.=that goes without saying] agreed, naturally.

célèbre [Fr.] celebrated, famous, noted.

cénacle [Fr.] a supper-room (*esp. the scene of the Last Supper*); (*Lit.*) coterie, gathering, group, meeting-place, salon, set (*referring to people with a common interest, esp. a literary one*).

censé [Fr.] deemed, reputed, supposed.

certificat [Fr.] certificate, character, scrip, testimonial.

certificat d'action(s) [Fr.] (*Stock Exchange*) scrip, (share) certificate.

c'est-à-dire [Fr.=that is to say] namely.

c'est égal [Fr.=it's equal] immaterial, unessential, unimportant.

cestus [Lat.] a girdle (*esp. of Venus which gave the wearer the power to awaken love*).

chaise-longue [Fr.=long chair] couch, sofa.

chamade [Fr.] drum-beat, trumpet-call (*esp. to announce challenge, parley or retreat*).

chambrer [Fr.] (*Wine*) unchill, warm (to room temperature).

champ de courses [Fr.] race-course.

chance [Fr.] bad-luck, chance, good-luck.

chanson [Fr.] song.

chantage [Fr.] blackmail.

chantier [Fr.] (*Shipbuilding*) shipyard, stocks.

chapeau claque [Fr.] opera-hat.

chapeau haut de forme [Fr.] silk-hat, top-hat.

chapeau melon [Fr.] bowler-hat.

château [Fr.] castle, country-seat, manor, mansion-house.

châteaux en Espagne [Fr.= castles in Spain] day-dreams.

chauvinisme [Fr.] jingoism, patriotism (*exaggerated*).

chef d'œuvre [Fr.] master-piece.

chevelure [Fr.] periwig.

che sarà sarà [Ital.] fatalism, inevitability.

chevalier d'industrie [Fr. = knight of industry] sharper, swindler, trickster.

chiaro [Ital.] bright, clear, illustrious.

chic [Fr.] natty, smart, stylish, swell.

chicanerie [Fr.] cavil, chic-anery, pettifoggery, shuffle.

cicerone [Ital.] attendant, courier, guide.

cicisbeo [Ital.] dangler, flirt, philanderer.

cid [Sp./Arab.] chief, leader (el **Cid, Campeador**, *titles given to the Spanish hero, Rod-rigo Diaz de Vivar*).

Cierra España! [Sp.] war-cry (of the ancient Spanish).

civiltà [Ital.] civilisation, civism, culture.

clairvoyance [Fr.] clear-sightedness, penetration, sharpness, shrewdness.

clameur publique [Fr.] scan-dal.

claqueur [Fr.] applauder, clapper, eulogiser, praiser (*per-son hired to applaud in a theatre*).

claviger [Lat.] club-bearer (*Hercules*), key-bearer (*Janus*).

clientèle [Fr.] connection, custom, customers, goodwill, public.

clin d'œil [Fr.] trice, twink-ling, wink.

clinquant [Fr.] foil, showiness, tinsel.

clique [Fr.] band, coterie, gang, set.

cloaca [Lat.] cesspool, drain, sewer.

Clota [Lat.] R. Clyde.

comitia [Lat.] assembly.

comitium [Lat.] meeting-place.

commedia [Ital.] comedy, play, theatricals.

comme il faut [Fr.] accurate, proper.

commis voyageur [Fr.] com-mercial-traveller.

compos mentis [Lat.] nor-mal, rational, sane.

compte rendu [Fr.] report, review.

con [Ital.] with.

con amore [Ital.] enthusiasti-cally, lovingly.

concetto [Ital.] a conceit.

concierge [Fr.] caretaker, door-keeper, porter, warden.

concordat [Fr.] agreement, compact, covenant, treaty (*esp. between the Pope and a temporal sovereign*).

concours [Fr.] competition, contest.

confer [Lat.] compare. Abbrev. **cf.**

confiteor [Lat.] (I) confess.

confrère [Fr.] brother, colleague, contemporary.

congé [Fr.] dismissal, holiday, leave (of absence).

congeries [Lat.] accumulation, heap, mass.

congrès [Fr.] assembly, conference, congress, convention, council, legislature.

conseil [Fr.] council.

consensus [Lat.] consent.

conservatoire [Fr.] (*Mus.*) academy, school of music (*esp. in Paris*).

con spirito [Ital.] animatedly, spiritedly.

conte [Fr.] (short) story, tale.

contra [Lat.] against, contrary (to).

contra bonos mores [Lat.= against good customs] ill-behaved, immoral, unmannerly.

contre–temps [Fr.] embarrassment, hitch, inopportunity, mischance, mishap.

convenances [Fr.] decencies, decorum, proprieties.

copita [Sp.] sherry-glass.

coram [Lat.] before.

coram publico [Lat.] publicly.

corps [Fr.] a body.

corpus [Lat.] the body.

corsage [Fr.] bodice, bust.

corsair [Fr.] pirate, privateer (*Moorish sea-marauder—person or vessel—of the Middle Ages*).

corsé [Fr.] (*Wine*) full-bodied; (*Language*) forcible, strong.

corsetière [Fr.] corset-maker.

cortège [Fr.] procession, retinue, train (*esp. used for a funeral procession*).

cortes [Sp.=courts] assembly, parliament (*legislative assembly of Spain and Portugal*).

cortese [Ital.] courteous, kind, polite.

corvée [Fr.] labour, task, toil (*medieval system of unpaid labour by a serf; hence any menial or unpleasant task*).

coterie [Fr.] circle, clique, set.

coulisses [Fr.] (*Theat.*) wings.

couloir [Fr.] corridor, passage; (*Geog.*) gorge, gulley.

coup [Fr.] blow, hit, stroke.

coup de grâce [Fr.=stroke of mercy] finishing-stroke, knock-out (*formerly, the stroke which finished the sufferings of those broken on the wheel*).

coup de hasard [Fr.] a fluke, luck.

coup de l'étrier [Fr.] stirrup-cup.

coup de sang [Fr.] (*Med.*) stroke.

coup d'état [Fr.=a stroke of state (policy)] rebellion, revolt (*sudden, and often unconstitutional, overthrow of a government*).

coup d'œil [Fr.] a glance, (quick) survey.

coup de théâtre [Fr.] a sensation (*dramatic and unforeseen happening*).

coupe [Fr.] bowl, chalice, cup, glass, goblet; (*Sport*) cup; (*Turf*) plate.

Cour de Cassation [Fr.= court of quashing] (Supreme) Appeal-Court.

coutume [Fr.] custom, habit, usage, wont.

couturière [Fr.] dressmaker, needlewoman, seamstress, tailoress.

craintif [Fr.] afraid, fearful, timid, timorous.

crèche [Fr.] crib, day-nursery; manger.

credat Judaeus Apella [Lat. = let the Jew Apella believe it! (I don't)] absurd (*applicable to anything too ridiculous to be believed except by a superstitious Jew, of Roman times*).

credenda [Lat.] creeds, tenets.

credo [Lat.= I believe] belief, credo, the Creed; (*Fig.*) gospel.

crimen [Lat.] accusation, charge, crime, guilt.

crimen laesae majestatis [Lat.] high-treason, lèse-majesté.

croûtons [Fr.] (*Cookery*) bread-cubes.

cru [Fr.] (*Wine*) vintage.

crux [Lat.= a cross, torture] issue, perplexity, problem.

cul [Fr.] bottom, end.

cul de sac [Fr.= bottom of the bag] blind-alley, dead-end.

Cumbria [Lat.] Cumberland.

curé [Fr.] padre, parson, priest, rector, vicar.

currente calamo [Lat.= with a running pen] extempore, improvised, off-hand.

custos [Lat.] guardian, keeper.

D

da capo [Ital.= from the beginning] (*Mus.*) repeat

d'accord [Fr.] agreed.

dame [Fr.] dame, lady; (*Cards, Chess*) queen.

dame d'honneur [Fr.] lady-in-waiting.

damnum [Lat.] damage, harm, loss.

Danke (schön)! [Ger.] thanks!

danse [Fr.] dance.

danseuse [Fr.] ballerina, ballet-dancer.

danse macabre [Fr.= gruesome dance] death-dance.

data [Lat.] facts, premises.

data et accepta [Lat.] debts *and* expenditures.

débâcle [Fr.] collapse, crash, landslide, reverse, rout.

déblai [Fr.] cut, cutting, excavation; (*Mil.*) parapet.

de bonne grâce [Fr.] cheerfully, gladly, gracefully, willingly.

débonnaire [Fr.] accommodating, affable, complaisant, debonair, easy, gracious, kind.

débris [Fr.] debris, litter, remains, scraps, wreck, wreckage.

débrouiller [Fr.] disentangle, extricate, unravel.

déchéance [Fr.] downfall, forfeiture, lapse, loss.

déclassé [Fr.] outcast.

décolleté [Fr.] low-necked (of a dress).

de facto [Lat.] actual, real.

défense [Fr.] forbiddal, interdiction, prohibition.

defensor [Lat.] averter, defender, guard, protector.

defensor (fidei) [Lat.] defender (of the faith). Abbrev. **F.D.** or **Fid. Def.**

de gaîeté de cœur [Fr.] lightheartedly, sportively, wantonly.

dégoût [Fr.] disgust, distaste.

de integro [Lat.] afresh, anew.

déjeuner [Fr.] breakfast or lunch.

de jure [Lat.] lawful, rightful.

dele [Lat.] (*Proof-reading*) delete.

delere [Lat.] annihilate, delete, destroy, efface.

délicatesse [Fr.] delicacy, fastidiousness, nicety.

délicatesses [Fr.], **Delikatessen** [Ger.] (*Cookery*) delicacies (*esp. cold cooked meats*).

delictum [Lat.] crime, offence, wrong.

delineavit [Lat.] (*Art*) (he) drew (this).

de luxe [Fr.] luxurious, sumptuous.

démarche [Fr.] bearing, gait; (*Diplomacy*) measure, proceeding, step.

démenti [Fr.] contradiction, denial, lie.

dementia [Lat.] (*Med.*) insanity, lunacy, madness.

demi–jour [Fr.] half-light, twilight.

démodé [Fr.] antiquated, old-fashioned, out-of-date.

Denkmal [Ger.] cenotaph, memorial, monument.

dénouement [Fr.=unknotting] conclusion, ending, finale, issue, upshot.

de nouveau [Fr.], **de novo** [Lat.] afresh, anew.

département [Fr.] (*Geog.*) county, shire.

dépêche [Fr.] despatch, message, telegram.

député [Fr.] delegate, deputy, M.P.

déraciné [Fr.] eradicated, uprooted.

Der Führer [Ger.] leader (*title accorded to Adolf Hitler by the German people during the Nazi régime*).

de rigueur [Fr.] compulsory, indispensable, obligatory (*demanded by etiquette*).

dernier cri [Fr.=the last cry] latest (thing out).

dernier ressort [Fr.=the last resort] expedient, resort, shift.

dernière heure [Fr.] (*Newspapers*) stop-press.

dérobé [Fr.] concealed, hidden, secret.

(à la) dérobée [Fr.] secretly, slyly, stealthily.

desideratum [Lat.=a thing desired] desire, essential, need, requisite; *pl.* **desiderata**.

désorienté [Fr.] confused, disorientated, lost, perplexed.

détente [Fr.] ease, relaxation.

détour [Fr.] circuit, detour, diversion, roundabout.

de trop [Fr.] out-of-place, superfluous, unwanted.

Deus [Lat.] God.

deus ex machina [Lat.= god out of the machine] intriguer, manipulator, plotter, schemer, wirepuller (*in the stage effects of the classical theatre this was an artificial device to resolve the difficulties of a dramatic plot*).

Deutsch [Ger.] German.

Deutschland [Ger.] Germany.

Deva [Lat.] Chester.

dévergondé [Fr.] licentious, profligate, shameless.

devinette [Fr.] conundrum, guess, puzzle, riddle.

devise [Fr.] device, motto; (*Finance*) bill, currency, exchange.

devoir [Fr.] duty, exercise, task.

dévouement [Fr.] devotion, self-sacrifice.

diable [Fr.] deuce, devil; (the) deuce! (the) devil!

diablerie [Fr.] devilment, devilry.

diabolique [Fr.] devilish, diabolic(al), fiendish.

dicenda bona [Lat.] (good) words.

Dichter [Ger.] poet.

dictum de dicto [Lat.] hearsay, report, rumour.

Dienst [Ger.] duty, function, service.

Dies irae [Lat.=day of wrath] Judgment-day (*opening words of a famous hymn*).

Dieu [Fr.] God; goodness!

difficile [Fr.] difficult, fastidious, hard-to-please, trying.

dilettante [Ital.] amateur, dabbler (in art).

diseur (*fem.* **diseuse**) **de bonne aventure**, fortuneteller.

distingué, *fem.* **distinguée**, aristocratic-looking, distinguished.

distrait [Fr.] absent-minded, absorbed, abstracted, engrossed, heedless, inattentive, musing, rapt.

divertissement [Fr.] amusement, entertainment, interlude.

divide et impera [Lat.] divide (your rivals) and rule.

dolce far niente [Ital.= sweet to do nothing] ease, idleness, relaxation, rest.

Dominus [Lat.] Lord.

dossier [Fr.] (*Law*) brief, documents, record.

dot [Fr.] bequest, dowry, endowment.

douane [Fr.] custom-house.

douanier [Fr.] custom-house officer.

douceur [Fr.=sweetness] bribe, present, "sweetener", tip.

douleur [Fr.] ache, pain, sorrow, throe.

drapeau [Fr.] colours, flag, standard.

dressage [Fr.] drilling, training (*esp. the training of a horse in deportment and response to control*).

dresseur de chevaux [Fr.] horse-breaker, horse-trainer.

droit [Fr.] due, duty, right.

droit d'auteur [Fr.] copyright, royalty.

droits de réproduction [Fr.] (serial) rights.

Duce [Ital.=leader] leader (*title accorded to Mussolini by the Italian people during the Fascist régime; see* **der Führer**).

dux [Lat.] chief, guide, head, leader; (*Mil.*) commander, general.

E

eau [Fr.] water.

eau de Cologne [Fr.= Cologne-water] a perfume.

eau de Nil [Fr.=Nile-water] a colour (pale-green).

eau de Seltz [Fr.=Seltz-water] soda-water.

eau de vie [Fr.=water of life] brandy.

ébauche [Fr.] draft, outline, sketch.

éblouir [Fr.] to dazzle.

éblouissement [Fr.] brightness, brilliance, splendour.

Eboracum [Lat.] (city of) York; *a.* **Eboracensis.**

écarté [Fr.] *a.* lonely, out-of-the-way, remote, secluded; *n.* (*Cards*) a game.

ecce! [Lat.] behold!

ecce Homo! [Lat.] behold the Man! (i.e. Christ).

eccidio [Ital.] carnage, massacre, slaughter.

échantillon [Fr.] (*Business*) pattern, sample.

échauffé [Fr.] a hot-head.

échéance [Fr.] (*Business*) date (payable), expiration. maturity.

échoir [Fr.] (*Business*) expire, mature.

échouer [Fr.] fail, miscarry; (*Shipping*) to beach, ground, strand, wreck.

éclair [Fr.] flash, gleam, glint; (*Pastry*) (chocolate) cake.

éclaircissement [Fr.] clarification, elucidation, enlightenment, explanation.

éclaireur [Fr.] Boy Scout, scout.

éclaireuse [Fr.] Girl Guide.

éclat [Fr.] brilliance, distinction, effect, lustre, notoriety, pageantry, pomp, show, showiness, splendour.

écossais, *fem.* **écossaise** [Fr.] Scottish.

écurie [Fr.] stable, stud, team.

Edinburgum [med. Lat.] Edinburgh; *a.* **Edinburgensis.**

éditeur [Fr.], **editore** [Ital.] publisher.

educazione [Ital.] good-breeding, manners, politeness, upbringing.

effluvium [Lat.=outlet] exhalation, (disagreeable) odour, vapour.

effréné [Fr.] frantic, unbridled, unrestrained.

effronté [Fr.] barefaced, brazen, impudent, shameless.

égalité [Fr.] equality.

égarement [Fr.] bewilderment, (mental) confusion.

ego [Lat.] I, self.

egregius [Lat.] distinguished, illustrious, outstanding, surpassing.

eh bien! [Fr.] well!

eheu! [Gk.] alas! (used in the quotation "eheu fugaces... labuntur anni!", alas! the fleeting years go swiftly by).

Eingang [Ger.] entrance.

Einsicht [Ger.] discernment, insight.

ejusdem generis [Lat.= of the same kind] alike, similar.

élan [Fr.] buoyancy, dash, enthusiasm, impetus.

élégant [Fr.] elegant, fashionable, stylish.

élevage [Fr.] (Agric.) breeding, rearing, stock-farming.

élite [Fr.] flower, (best) part, pick.

elixir [Arab.] quintessence.

elixir vitae [Lat.] life-prolonging liquor.

éloge [Fr.] encomium, eulogy, praise.

embarras [Fr.] embarrassment, encumbrance, inconvenience, superfluity (used in two well-known phrases, (a) **embarras de choix**, lit.= embarrassment of choice, i.e. so many as to make choice difficult, (b) **embarras de**

richesse(s), lit.= embarrassment of riches, i.e. a superfluity of good things, a perplexing abundance, an infinite variety).

embonpoint [Fr.] corpulence, fleshiness, plumpness, stoutness.

embusqué [Fr.= an ambushed person] dodger, evader, shirker (in World Wars I and II, one who took a civilian job in a reserved occupation in order to avoid military service).

emeritus [Lat.] superannuated (title given to a University professor who has retired from office).

émeute [Fr.] disturbance, riot, uprising.

émeutier [Fr.] rebel, rioter.

émigré [Fr.] emigrant, refugee (in French History, a French aristocrat, loyal to the royal house, who sought refuge and exile during the Revolution, in a foreign country).

Empfindung [Ger.] feeling, sensation, sentiment.

employé [Fr.] employee.

empressement [Fr.] alacrity, eagerness, readiness.

en [Fr.] in, into, while, within.

en attendant [Fr.] meantime, meanwhile.

en avant! [Fr.] forward! onward!

en clair [Fr.] clear, distinct, manifest, plain (describes a message or despatch sent in "plain" language, i.e. not in cipher or code).

en déshabillé [Fr.] (in) undress.

en fête [Fr.] merry-making.

en grande tenue [Fr.] (in) full-dress.

en grande toilette [Fr.] (*Ladies*) (in) full evening-dress.

en passant [Fr.] by-the-way, casually, incidentally.

en règle [Fr.] (in) order (*i.e. as it should be*).

en retraite [Fr.] retired, pensioned-off, superannuated.

en train [Fr.] agoing.

en vérité [Fr.] really, truthfully.

en ville [Fr.] (in) town.

enfant [Fr.] a child.

enfant gâté, *fem.* **gâtée** [Fr.] spoilt child.

enfant terrible [Fr.] precocious (child) (*esp. one who makes ill-timed or embarrassing remarks*).

enfant trouvé [Fr.] a foundling.

enfants perdus [Fr.=lost children] shock-troops, storm-troops (*originally troops stationed at advanced, dangerous, or isolated posts*).

engageant, *fem.* **engageante** [Fr.] attractive, inviting, winning.

engouement [Fr.] infatuation.

enjouement [Fr.] jocularity, playfulness, sprightliness, vivacity.

ennui [Fr.] boredom, listlessness, nuisance, tedium, worry.

ennuyeux [Fr.] irksome, prosy, tedious, tiresome.

entendu! [Fr.] agreed! right!

entente [Fr.] agreement, alliance, understanding (*the* **entente cordiale** *was the friendly understanding between France and Britain fostered by Edward VII in 1904*).

entêté [Fr.] headstrong, obstinate, stubborn.

entourage [Fr.] associates, attendants, retinue, suite.

entrain [Fr.] go, gusto, liveliness, spirit.

entraînement [Fr.] enthusiasm, heartiness, impulse; (*Sport*) training.

entre [Fr.] between.

entre deux âges [Fr.] middle-aged.

entrée [Fr.] admission, entrance.

entrefilet [Fr.] (*Newspaper*) (short) paragraph.

entremets [Fr.] (*Cookery*) side-dish, sweet.

entremetteur, *fem.* **entremetteuse** [Fr.] go-between, intermediary, intervener.

entre nous [Fr.] confidentially.

entrepôt [Fr.] emporium, mart, store, warehouse.

épanchement [Fr.] effusion, outpouring.

épée [Fr.] fencing-foil, sword.

éperdu [Fr.] desperate, distracted.

épergne [Fr.] (table) centre-piece.

ephialtes [Gk.] incubus, nightmare.

ephod [Heb.] a surplice.

épice [Fr.] spice (**pain d'épice** = gingerbread).

épicier [Fr.] grocer.

Epicuri de grege porcus [Lat. = hog from the sty of Epicurus] glutton, high-feeder, profligate.

epimuthion [Gk.] moral (of a fable).

epinikion [Gk.] triumphal ode, victory song.

epithalamion [Gk.] epithalamium, bridal ode, marriage hymn.

épouse [Fr.] spouse, wife.

époux [Fr.] consort, husband, spouse.

eppur(e) [Ital.] however, nevertheless, yet; (**eppur(e) si muove** = nevertheless it does move. *Words spoken by Galileo after being forced to deny his astronomical theory that the earth moves round the sun*).

épris [Fr.] enamoured, infatuated.

épuisé [Fr.] effete, exhausted, spent, worn-out.

équipe [Fr.] (*Sport*) crew, side, team.

Erbitterung [Ger.] exasperation, irritation.

Erde [Ger.] earth.

Erdgeist [Ger.] earth-spirit.

ergo [Lat.] therefore.

ergon [Gk.] work, business.

errare [Lat.] err (*used in the phrase* **errare est humanum** = to err is human).

erratum, *pl.* **errata** [Lat.] error(s), misprint(s).

Ersatz [Ger.] *n.* a substitute; *a.* synthetic.

eruditus [Lat.] accomplished, educated, learned.

eruditi [Lat.] scholars.

Erzählung [Ger.] narrative, story, tale.

escalier [Fr.] stair, staircase.

escamotage [Fr.] conjuring, juggling.

escroc [Fr.] cheat, crook, sharper, swindler.

Esel [Ger.] ass, donkey.

espada [Sp.] matador, rapier, sword; (*Cards*) spade.

espion [Fr.] spy.

espoir [Fr.] expectation, hope.

espresso [Ital.] express, hasty, hurried.

esprit [Fr.] animation, liveliness, mind, spirit, wit.

esprit de corps [Fr.] attachment, loyalty.

esprit follet [Fr.] hobgoblin, puck, sprite.

esprit fort [Fr.] free-thinker, independent (person).

esse [Lat.] (to) be.

essen [Ger.] (to) eat.

essence [Fr.] (*Motoring*) petrol.

est [Lat.] is.

estafette [Fr.] courier, messenger.

estaminet [Fr.] (cheap) café-restaurant, "pub".

estocade [Fr.] (*Fencing*) sword-thrust.

estrade [Fr.] dais, platform, stage.

étage [Fr.] flat, floor, storey.

étagère [Fr.] stand, whatnot (*with shelves arranged in tiers*).

étalage [Fr.] display, parade, show, window-dressing.

étape [Fr.] stage, stopping-place.

état [Fr.] condition, frame (of mind), state.

État [Fr.] Government, State.

État-major [Fr.] (*Mil.*) staff-headquarters.

et hoc genus omne [Lat. = and everything of this kind] suchlike.

etiam [Lat.] also, besides.

étoffe [Fr.] fabric, material, stuff.

étoile [Fr.] asterisk, star.

étourderie [Fr.] heedlessness, thoughtlessness.

étourdi [Fr.] flighty, heedless, thoughtless.

et sic de similibus [Lat. = and so of the like] similarly.

étude [Fr.] (*Law*) chambers, office, practice; (*Mus.*) exercise, preparation, study (*hence, a short musical composition intended mainly, to exercise, train or test the player's skill*).

étui [Fr.] box, case; (*Needlework*) reticule, work-box.

eu- [Gk. *pref.*] well.

euge! [Gk.] bravo! good! splendid!

Eulenspiegel [Ger. = owl's mirror] jester, wag (*a popular jester in medieval German folklore*).

eureka! [Gk. = I have found it] discovery, triumph, victory (*the exclamation of Archimedes when he discovered a method of measuring the purity of gold in King Hiero's crown; hence, an exclamation of triumph on making a discovery*).

événement [Fr.] event, happening, incident, occurrence, outcome.

evviva! [Ital.] hurrah!

ewig [Ger.] eternal, perpetual.

Ewigkeit [Ger.] eternity.

ex- [Lat. *pref.*] from, out.

ex aequo [Lat.] equally.

examen [Fr.] examination, scrutiny.

ex animo [Lat. = from the mind] conscientiously, earnestly, heartily, sincerely.

ex aprosdoketou [Gk.] unexpectedly.

exaucer [Fr.] grant, hear (prayer).

ex cathedra [Lat. = from the chair, pulpit, or throne] authoritatively, dogmatically, judicially.

excelsior [Lat.] higher.

exceptio [Lat.] exception (*N.B. the phrase* **exceptio probat regolam**, the exception proves the rule).

excerptum, *pl.* **excerpta** [Lat.] abstract(s), selection(s).

ex commodo [Lat.] leisurely.

ex confesso [Lat.] confessedly.

ex consequenti [Lat.] consequently.

ex continenti [Lat.] immediately.

ex curia [Lat.=out of court] (*Law*) privately.

excursus [Lat.] digression.

exeat [Lat.=let him go out], leave, permission (*formal leave of absence granted to a student in residence at certain universities; also to a priest*).

exeunt [Lat.=they go out] (they) leave (*a stage direction to actors; plural of* **exit**=he goes out).

exegi [Lat.] (I) erected, reared (*N.B. the phrase from Horace,* Ode III, **exegi monumentum aere perennius**=I have erected a monument more enduring than brass. *This was an allusion to his hope that his poems would endure to the end of time*).

ex facie [Lat.] evidently, manifestly.

ex facili [Lat.] easily.

ex fide [Lat.] faithfully.

ex gratia [Lat.=as an act of grace] free, gratuitous, voluntary.

ex hypothesi [Lat.] assuredly, hypothetically.

ex improviso [Lat.] unexpectedly.

exitus [Lat.] end, issue, outcome, result

ex officio [Lat.] officially (*i.e. by virtue of the office one holds*).

exordium [Lat.] beginning, introduction, preamble, preface, proem.

ex parte [Lat.] biased, one-sided.

experientia [Lat.] experience (*N.B. the phrase* **experientia docet**=experience teaches).

exposé [Fr.] account, explanation, statement, summary.

exposition [Fr.] exhibition, show.

ex posto facto [Lat.] retrospective.

exprès [Fr.] purposely.

expressis verbis [Lat.=in express terms] expressly.

ex professo [Lat.] avowedly.

exquis [Fr.] charming, choice, exquisite.

ex tacito [Lat.] silently.

extase [Fr.] delight, ecstasy, trance, transport.

externat [Fr.] day-school; (*Med.*) day-doctor (*i.e. a non-resident assistant in a hospital*).

extra [Lat.] beyond, outside.

extra modum [Lat.=beyond measure] extravagant, immoderate.

extra muros [Lat.] (beyond) the walls (of a city).

extravagance [Fr.] absurdity, exorbitance, extravagance.

F

Fabrik [Ger.] factory.

Fabrikant [Ger.] manufacturer.

façade [Fr.] (*Archit.*) front, frontage, frontispiece; (*Fig.*) pretence, showiness.

faccenda [Ital.] affair, business, matter, thing.

facetiae [Lat.] drollery, humour, wit, witticisms.

facéties [Fr.] facetiousness, jests, jokes, repartees.

fâcheux [Fr.] sad, tiresome, troublesome, unfortunate, worrying.

facile [Lat.] easily, indubitably, unquestionably (*N.B. the phrase* **facile princeps**= easily the first, the acknowledged leader).

facilis [Lat.] easy (*N.B. the well-known quotation from Virgil's "Aeneid"*—**facilis descensus Averni (Averno)**= easy is the descent from Avernus (to Hell); *Avernus is a lake near Cumae said to be an entrance to the lower world*).

façon [Fr.] fashion, make, manner, style, wise (**façon de parler**= way of speaking, form of speech).

facta [Lat.] deeds.

facultatif [Fr.] optional, voluntary.

fadaise [Fr.] a whim.

fade [Fr.] colourless, flat, insipid, tasteless.

faex populi [Lat.= dregs of the people] rabble, riff-raff, scum.

Fahne [Ger.] colours, ensign, flag.

faïence [Fr.] earthenware, pottery.

fainéant [Fr.] idler, good-for-nothing, loafer.

fainéantise [Fr.] idleness, laziness, loafing, sluggishness (cf. Ital. **dolce far niente**= sweet to do nothing).

faire [Fr.] do, make.

faire semblant [Fr.] pretend.

faire suivre [Fr.= cause to follow] (*Letters, etc.*) forward.

fait accompli [Fr.= an accomplished fact] completion, fulfilment, settlement.

falsi crimen [Lat.= crime of falsification] (*Law*) forgery.

fama [Lat.] report, rumour, talk, tradition.

fama clamosa [Lat.] a scandal (*esp. a current one*).

fanfaron [Fr.] blustering, bragging, bullying, swaggering.

fanfaronnade [Fr.] bluster, brag, swagger.

fantoccini [Ital.], **fantoches** [Fr.] marionettes, puppets.

farce [Fr.] antic, foolery, joke; (*Cookery*) force-meat, stuffing.

farceur [Fr.] humorist, joker, wag.

farci [Fr.] (*Cookery*) stuffed.

fard [Fr.] grease-paint, make-up.

fare [Ital.] do, make.

far niente [Ital.] idling, loafing.

farrago [Lat.] hodge-podge, hotch-potch, jumble, medley, mixture.

fas [Lat.] (divine) law, right.

fasces [Lat.] bundles (*esp. of rods and the executioner's axe carried in front of the high magistrates, in Ancient Rome, as the symbol of justice; in Italy, under Mussolini, the badge of Fascism*).

Fascio [Ital.] headquarters (of the Fascist party).

Fascismo [Ital.] Fascism (*the equivalent of German Nazism*).

Fascista [Ital.] a Fascist (*pl.* **Fascisti**).

fas est [Lat.] (it is) lawful.

Fastnacht [Ger.] carnival, Shrove-tide.

fastus [Lat.] lawful (**fasti**, *the days among the Romans when it was lawful to transact business before the praetor; also the books containing calendars of times, seasons and events*).

fata *pl.* [Lat.] the Fates.

Fata Morgana [Ital.=Morgan the Fairy], a mirage (*occasionally seen in the Strait of Messina; reference is to a lady of Arthurian legend who was the pupil of the wizard Merlin*).

fatum [Lat.] destiny, doom, fate, oracle.

faubourg [Fr.] a suburb.

faute [Fr.] error, mistake; lack, need, want (*N.B.* **faute de mieux** = for want of something better).

fauteuil [Fr.] arm-chair, easy-chair; (*Theat.*) stall.

fauve [Fr.] fawn-coloured, tawny.

Fauves [Fr. = wild beasts] term given in derision to a group of French impressionist painters (including Henri Matisse) who exhibited in Paris in 1906.

faux [Fr.] false.

faux pas [Fr.=false step] mistake, slip, tactlessness.

favete linguis [Lat.=favour by tongues, keep silence] silence! (*a solemn admonition repeatedly given while the superstitious rites of the Romans were being performed*).

favori [Fr.] favourite, pet.

favoris [Fr.] side-whiskers.

fecit [Lat.] (he or she) made it —used in artists' signatures; *pl.* **fecerunt**.

fécond [Fr.] fecund, fertile, fruitful, prolific.

fée [Fr.] fairy, pixy.

féerie [Fr.] fairyhood, fairy-land.

felicitas [Lat.] happiness, luck, prosperity (*N.B. the phrase,* **felicitas multos habet amicos** = prosperity has many friends).

feliciter [Lat.] successfully.

felix [Lat.] happy, successful.

felo de se [Lat.=a felon of himself] (*Law*) a suicide.

femme [Fr.] a woman.

femme auteur [Fr.] authoress.

femme de chambre [Fr.] chambermaid; (*Ship*) stewardess.

femme de journée [Fr.] daily-help.

femme de ménage [Fr.] charwoman, cleaner.

femme médecin [Fr.] lady-doctor.

femme savante [Fr.] blue-stocking.

fenêtre [Fr.] a window.

fenêtre à guillotine [Fr.] sash-window.

fer [Fr.] iron, sword.

feriae [Lat.] holidays.

fero, ferre [Lat.] bear, bring, carry.

ferrum [Lat.] iron.

ferrum et ignis [Lat.] devastation.

ferula [Lat.] rod, staff.

festa [Ital.] birthday, feast, festivity, holiday, merry-making.

festinare [Lat.] hasten, hurry (*N.B. the phrase* **festina lente** = hasten slowly, *i.e. the more hurry the less speed*).

fête [Fr.] birthday, feast, festivity, holiday, saint's-day; entertainment, treat.

fête champêtre [Fr.] garden-party.

Fête–Dieu [Fr.] Corpus Christi.

feu [Fr.] fire; (*Mil.*) fire!

feu [Fr.] *a.* deceased, late.

feu de joie [Fr.] bonfire, salute (*of guns*).

feu follet [Fr.] ignis fatuus, jack-o'-lantern, will-o'-the-wisp.

feu sacré [Fr.=sacred fire] inspiration.

feux d'artifice [Fr.] fireworks.

fiacre [Fr.] cab, four-wheeler.

fiasco [Ital.=a flask] failure.

fiat [Lat.=let it be done] decree, order (*N.B. two phrases,* (a) **fiat justitia ruat coelum**=let justice be done though the heavens should fall, (b) **fiat lux**=let there be light).

fidèle [Fr.], **fidelis** [Lat.] faithful, loyal, true.

fides et justitia [Lat.] faith and justice.

fides Punica [Lat.=Punic, *i.e. Carthaginian,* faith] treachery.

fi donc! [Fr.] shame!

fidus [Lat.] faithful, reliable, staunch, true (*N.B. the phrase* **fidus Achates**=faithful Achates, *i.e. a staunch friend In Virgil's "Aeneid", Achates was the friend and faithful companion of Aeneas*).

fidus et audax [Lat.] faithful and bold.

fier, *fem.* **fière** [Fr.] proud.

fierté [Fr.] haughtiness, pride.

fiesta [Sp.] entertainment, feast, festival, holiday, merriment.

figurine [Fr.] statuette (*usually in clay or metal*).

filius nullius [Lat.=son of nobody] a bastard.

filius terrae [Lat.=son of the soil] a nobody.

fille [Fr.] daughter, girl, lass, maid, maiden.

fille d'honneur [Fr.] maid-of-honour.

fille de joie [Fr.] prostitute.

filleul [Fr.] godson, protégé.

filleule [Fr.] god-daughter.

film d'actualités [Fr.] news-reel.

fils [Fr.] son; junior.

filtre [Fr.] filter, percolator.

fin, fine [Fr.] *a.* choice, delicate, fine, slender.

fin [Fr.], **finis** [Lat.] close, end, finish (*N.B. the phrase* **finis coronat opus**=the end crowns the work, *i.e. puts the finishing-stroke to it*).

finaud [Fr.] *a.* sly, wily; *n.* dodger, slyboots.

fin de siècle [Fr.=end of the (19th) century] decadent.

fine champagne [Fr.] liqueur-brandy.

finesse [Fr.] artifice, craftiness, cunning, slyness, stratagem, subtlety.

finis rerum [Lat.=the end of all things] the end.

Firenze [Ital.] Florence.

fisc [Fr.] (Inland) Revenue Treasury.

flacon [Fr.] bottle, flagon, flask.

flacon à odeur [Fr.] scent-bottle.

flagrante delicto [Lat.= while the crime is blazing] red-handed.

flair [Fr.] scent, smell; (*Fig.*) acumen, aptitude, keenness.

flamboyant [Fr.=flaming] elaborate, florid, over-ornate, showy.

Flammenwerfer [Ger.] (*Mil.*) flame-thrower.

flâner [Fr.] loaf, lounge, saunter, stroll.

flânerie [Fr.] idling, loafing.

flâneur [Fr.] idler, lounger, saunterer, stroller.

flatus [Lat.] blowing, breath, breeze; (*Fig.*) arrogance.

flèche [Fr.] arrow, shaft; (*Archit.*) spire.

Fledermaus [Ger.=a flying-mouse] a bat.

flétrir [Fr.] fade, wilt, wither.

fleur-de-lis [Fr.=flower of lilies] iris, lily-flower (*heraldic bearing borne by the Kings of France*).

fleuret [Fr.] fencing-foil.

fleurir [Fr.] bloom, blossom, flower, flourish.

fleuron [Fr.] floret, flower-work; (*Print.*) colophon.

floccus [Lat.] tuft (of hair or wool); *pl.* **flocci** (*N.B. the phrase,* **flocci non facio**= I don't care a straw for).

floreat! [Lat.] (let it) flourish!

Florentia [Lat.] Florence: *a.* **Fiorentinus**.

florilegium [Lat.]=a collection of flowers; (*Lit.*) an anthology; *pl.* **florilegia**.

floruit [Lat.] (he) flourished (*indicating the period of a person's eminence*; Abbrev. **fl.**

Flug [Ger.] flight, flying.

foi [Fr.] belief, faith, reliance, troth, trust.

foie [Fr.] liver (**foie gras**=fat liver (of goose) made into **pâté de foie gras**).

foire [Fr.] fair, market.

foison [Fr.] abundance, plenty (à **foison**=abundantly, galore).

folâtre [Fr.] playful, skittish, sportive, wanton.

foncé [Fr.] (*Colour*) dark, deep (**bleu foncé**=dark blue).

fonctionnaire [Fr.] functionary, official (**fonctionnaire public**=civil servant).

fond [Fr.] background, basis, fund.

fonda [Sp.] hotel, tavern.

fondant [Fr.] juicy, luscious, melting; *n.* sweetmeat.

fonds [Fr.] capital, cash, funds, money, stock.

fons et origo [Lat.=fountain and origin] cause, fount, source, spring, well.

foramen [Lat.] aperture, hole, opening.

forçat [Fr.] convict, prisoner.

force majeure [Fr.=superior force] coercion, compulsion, constraint.

foris [Lat.] abroad, out-of-doors, outside.

fors [Lat.] chance, luck.

forte [Fr.] ability, aptitude, capacity, talent.

forte [Ital.] (*Mus.*) loud, loudly.

fortiter [Lat.] firmly, strongly, vigorously.

fortune du pot [Fr.] potluck.

forum [Lat.] market, market-place, market-town; business, law-courts.

fossa [Lat.] ditch, moat, trench.

foyer [Fr.=fireside, hearth] (*Theat.*) ante-room, crush-room.

foyer des artistes [Fr.] (*Theat.*) greenroom.

foyer d'étudiants [Fr.] hostel.

fra [Ital.] (*Eccl.*) brother. friar.

fraîcheur [Fr.] coolness, freshness.

frais, *fem.* **fraîche** [Fr.] cool, fresh.

franco [Ital.] franked, free, post-paid.

franc–maçon [Fr.] freemason.

franc–tireur [Fr.] free-lance, guerilla-fighter, sharpshooter, sniper.

frappant [Fr.] affecting, striking.

frappé [Fr.] (*Cookery*) cooled, iced.

frate [Ital.] a friar.

fratello [Ital.] brother.

frater [Lat.] brother.

Frau [Ger.] a woman (married), Mrs.

Fräulein [Ger.] a woman (unmarried), Miss.

fraus [Lat.] deceit, fraud, offence, wrong.

fredaine [Fr.] caper, escapade, prank.

freddo [Ital.] chilly, cold, cool; (*Fig.*) indifferent.

frei [Ger.] free.

Freiheit [Ger.] freedom, liberty.

Freistaat [Ger.] commonwealth, republic.

frêle [Fr.] delicate, fragile, frail, weak.

Fremder [Ger.] foreigner, stranger.

frère [Fr.] brother.

fret [Fr.] (*Shipping*) freight.

fretta [Ital.] haste, hurry, speed.

Freude [Ger.] happiness, joy, mirth.

Freund [Ger.] friend.

friand [Fr.] dainty, delicate.

friandise [Fr.] dainty, delicacy, sweetmeat.

friction [Fr.] massage, shampoo.

Friede [Ger.] peace.

frigidarium [Lat.] cooling-room (*in Roman baths*).

fripon [Fr.] cheat, knave, rascal, rogue, swindler.

friponnerie [Fr.] dishonesty, knavery, rascality, roguery, trickery.

friser [Fr.] crimp, curl, frizzle.

friseur [Fr.] hairdresser.

frivole [Fr.] flighty, flimsy, frivolous, trivial, trumpery.

fröhlich [Ger.] cheerful, gay, glad, prosperous.

froid [Fr.] cold, cool, frigid.

froideur [Fr.] chilliness, coldness, coolness, frigidity.

Frondeur [Fr.] a malcontent, rebel (*a supporter of the* **Fronde,** *a political revolt in France* (1648-1653) *during the minority of Louis XIV*).

frou-frou [Fr.] rustling, swish (*esp. of silk*).

Führer [Ger.] guide, leader (*see* **Der Führer**).

funèbre [Fr.] *a.* funeral, funereal; (*Fig.*) dismal, ill-omened.

funérailles, funèbres [Fr.] burial, funeral, interment.

funeste [Fr.] baleful, baneful, fatal.

funiculaire [Fr.] cable-railway, funicular.

fuori [Ital.] beyond, outside.

fureur [Fr.] craze, excitement, enthusiasm, furore, rage.

furor [Lat.] frenzy, madness, passion (*N.B. the two phrases* (a) **furor loquendi,** *a passion for speaking, esp. in public, and* (b) **furor scribendi,** *a mania for writing. See also* **cacoëthes**).

fuselé [Fr.] spindle-shaped, stream-lined, tapering.

fusil [Fr.] gun, rifle.

fusiller [Fr.] shoot (*deserter, spy, etc.*).

fusil-mitrailleur [Fr.] machine-gun.

fuyant [Fr.] fleeing, receding, retreating; (*Perspective*) vanishing.

fuyard [Fr.] fugitive, runaway.

G

gaffe [Fr.] (*Colloq.*) blunder, howler, indiscretion.

gage [Fr.] pawn, pledge, security, token; *pl.* pay, wages.

gage d'amour [Fr.] keepsake, love-token.

gaieté [Fr.] cheerfulness, gaiety, glee, merriment, mirth.

gaillard [Fr.] hearty, jolly, merry.

gala [Ital.] festivity, finery, show.

galant [Fr.] *a.* amatory, elegant, gallant (*to ladies*), gay, stylish; *n.* beau, flirt, philanderer, spark.

galanterie [Fr.] politeness (*esp. to ladies*).

Gallia [Lat.] France.

gamin [Fr.] nipper, street-urchin, youngster.

gamine [Fr.] hoyden, romp, tomboy.

ganz [Ger.] entire, whole.

garçon [Fr.] bachelor, boy; waiter.

garde [Fr.] a guard.

garde-boue [Fr.] mudguard.

Garde du Corps [Fr.] bodyguard, Life-guards.

garde-malades [Fr.] sicknurse.

gardien [Fr.] attendant, caretaker, custodian, keeper.

gare [Fr.] railway-station; *interj.* beware! mind!

garni [Fr.] (*Room*) furnished; (*Cookery*) garnished.

gasconnade [Fr.] boasting, bragging.

Gasse [Ger.] alley, lane.

Gasthaus [Ger.] hotel, inn.

gâteau [Fr.] cake.

gauche [Fr.] left; awkward, clumsy, tactless.

gaucherie [Fr.] awkwardness, clumsiness, ungainliness.

gaudere [Lat.] (to) rejoice (*the name of a well-known students' song* is **Gaudeamus igitur** =Let us rejoice therefore).

gaufrette [Fr.] wafer-biscuit.

Geist [Ger.] ghost, intellect, spirit.

gemütlich [Ger.] comfortable, cosy, easy, homely.

Gemütlichkeit [Ger.] comfort, cosiness, ease, geniality, homeliness.

gendarme [Fr.] constable, policeman; [*Fig.*] martinet.

gêne [Fr.] constraint, discomfort, embarrassment, inconvenience (**sans gêne**=free-and-easy, unconventional).

genius [Lat.] (guardian) spirit; inclination, talent.

genre [Fr.] description, kind, sort, style.

genre humain [Fr.] mankind.

gens [Lat.] clan, family, nation, race, tribe.

gens [Fr.] folks, men, people.

gens d'armes [Fr.] men-at-arms.

gens de lettres [Fr.] authors, writers, etc.

gens de mer [Fr.] seamen.

gens de qualité [Fr.] gentlefolk(s).

gens de robe [Fr.] lawyers.

gens togata [Lat.]=race wearing a "toga" [i.e. a gown] Romans.

gentilhomme [Fr.], **gentiluomo** [Ital.], gentleman, nobleman.

genus [Lat.] kind, race, species, stock.

genus homo [Lat.] mankind.

gérant [Fr.] caretaker, manager.

gerbe [Fr.] sheaf, spray (of flowers).

Gesellschaft [Ger.] (*Business*) company, society. Abbrev. **Ges.**

gesund [Ger.] sound, healthy, wholesome.

Gesundheit [Ger.] health, healthiness.

gibier [Fr.] game (animals, birds).

gibier de potence [Fr.= game for the gallows] gallows-bird, jail-bird.

gitano, *fem.* **gitana** [Sp.] gipsy.

gîte [Fr.] home, lodging, shelter.

glace [Fr.] ice, ice-cream; mirror.

glacé [Fr.] iced (of a cake)

glacière [Fr.] freezer, ice-box, refrigerator.

gladius [Lat.] sword.

Gleichschaltung [Ger.] fusion, merging.

gloria [Lat.] ambition, fame, glory (*N.B.* **Gloria in Excelsis**= Glory (to God) in the Highest; **Gloria Patri**= Glory (be) to the Father).

Glück [Ger.] fortune, happiness, luck.

glücklich [Ger.] fortunate, happy, lucky. (*N.B.* **Glückliches Neujahr!** Happy New Year; **Glückliche Reise!** Bon voyage! Good journey!).

Gott [Ger.] God, a god (*N.B.* **Gott mit uns** (*the motto of Germany under the Kaisers*); **Gotterdämmerung**, the twilight of the gods).

gourmand [Fr.] gastronomist, glutton, gobbler.

gourmet [Fr.] connoisseur, epicure, judge.

goût [Fr.] flavour, fondness, inclination, liking, relish, style, taste.

grâce [Fr.] grace, gracefulness, favour, mercy, thanks (**grâce à Dieu**=thanks be to God).

gradatim [Lat.] gradually.

gradus [Lat.] a step.

Graf [Ger.] a Count.

Gräfin [Ger.] Countess.

grand [Fr.] big, great, high, large, tall.

grande passion [Fr.] infatuation.

grande route [Fr.] highway, main-road.

grande tenue [Fr.] (*Men*) full-dress.

grande toilette [Fr.] (*Women*) full-dress.

grandeur [Fr.] greatness.

gratia [Lat.] gratitude, thanks.

gratis [Lat.] free, gratuitous.

grazie! [Ital.] thanks!

Grenze [Ger.] boundary, frontier, limit.

gros [Fr.] big, great, large, stout.

grossier, *fem.* **grossière** [Fr.] coarse, uncouth, vulgar.

grossièreté [Fr.] coarseness, vulgarity.

guerre [Fr.] war (**guerre à outrance**= war to the death).

gusto [Ital.] taste.

gut [Ger.] good.

Guten Abend [Ger.] good evening.

Guten Morgen [Ger.] good morning.

Gute Nacht [Ger.] good night.

Guten Tag [Ger.] good day.

Gymnasium [Ger.] grammar-school.

H

habere [Lat.] have, hold, keep.

habitat [Lat.=he dwells] abode, dwelling-place, habitation.

habitué [Fr.] frequenter.

hablar [Sp.] to speak.

hachis [Fr.] hash, minced meat.

hacienda [Sp.] estate, farm, property, ranch.

Hafen [Ger.] harbour, haven, port.

halle [Fr.] a (covered) market (**Les Halles**, *the central market in Paris*).

Händler [Ger.] retailer, trader.

hardi [Fr.] bold, daring.

hardiesse [Fr.] boldness, daring.

haricot [Fr.] a bean (**haricots verts**=green beans, i.e. French beans).

Harpagon [Fr.] miser, skin-flint (*the name of the miser in Molière's "L'Avare"*).

hasta [Sp.] until (**hasta luego**=until presently, i.e. goodbye).

Hauptmann [Ger.] (*Mil.*) Captain.

Hausfrau [Ger.] housewife.

Hausmädchen [Ger.] maid, servant.

haut [Fr.] high, lofty, tall (**haut les mains!**=hands up!).

hautain [Fr.] arrogant, haughty, proud.

hautbois [Fr.] (*Mus.*) hautboy, oboe.

haute [Fr.] *fem.* of **haut** (**haute école**=advanced horsemanship, in circus-riding or equestrian displays).

hebdomadaire [Fr.] weekly.

Heil! [Ger.] hail! (*a reverential salutation but used during the Nazi régime, esp. in the phrase,* **Heil Hitler!** *as a common form of greeting*).

Heimweh [Ger.] home-sickness, nostalgia.

hermano [Sp.] brother.

hermandad [Sp.] brotherhood, fraternity.

Herr [Ger.] a gentleman, master, Mr., lord; *pl.* **Herren** (**Der Herr**, the Lord).

heure [Fr.] hour, o'clock, time.

heure d'allumer [Fr.] lighting-up (time).

heure de la jeunesse [Fr.] (*Radio*) children's-hour.

heures supplémentaires [Fr.] overtime.

heureux, *fem.* **heureuse** [Fr.] happy, fortunate, pleased, prosperous.

hiatus [Lat.] abyss, gap, opening.

Hibernia [Lat.] Ireland.

hic [Lat.] here (**hic jacet,** *on tombstones* = here lies).

hinc [Lat.] hence (*N.B. the phrase,* **hinc illae lacrimae** = hence these tears, *i.e.,* this is the source of discontent).

hoc [Lat.] this.

Hoch! [Ger.] (good) health! (*in drinking a toast*).

hodie [Lat.] today (*N.B. the phrase,* **hodie mihi, cras tibi** = today it is my turn, to-morrow will be yours).

Hof [Ger.] court, court-yard, yard.

hoi polloi [Gk. = the many] (common) herd, (the) masses, proletariat, riff-raff.

hombre [Sp.] a man.

homme [Fr.] a man (*N.B. the phrase,* **homme propose, mais Dieu dispose** = man proposes, but God disposes).

homme d'état [Fr.] politician, statesman.

homme de lettres [Fr.] author, writer, etc.

homme de paille [Fr. = man of straw] a nobody.

homo [Lat.] man (**homo sapiens** = lit. "a wise man"; man as a reasoning being).

honneur [Fr.] honour.

honnir [O. Fr.] to disgrace (*the pa. p. is used in the phrase* **hon(n)i soit qui mal y pense** = evil be to him who evil thinks — *the motto of the Order of the Garter.* **Honi** *is used in it, but erroneously for* **honni**).

honor [Lat.] award, esteem, honour, respect.

honoris causa [Lat. = out of respect] honorary (*esp. of a degree granted by a University*).

hora [Lat.] hour, season, time (*N.B. the phrase,* **in horam vivere** = to live from hand to mouth).

hors [Fr.] beyond, outside.

hors de combat [Fr.] disabled, unfit; (*Boxing*) knocked out.

hors de jeu [Fr.] (*Football*) offside.

hors de loi [Fr.] outlawed.

hors de saison [Fr.] unseasonable.

hospice [Fr.] asylum, home, hostel.

hostis [Lat.] enemy.

hôte, *fem.* **hôtesse** [Fr.] guest, host, hostess, visitor.

hôtel [Fr.] hotel, mansion, town-house.

Hôtel de Ville [Fr.] guild-hall, town-hall.

Hôtel-Dieu [Fr.] hospital (*usually the principal one in a town*).

hôtelier, *fem.* **hôtelière** [Fr.] hotel-keeper.

houri [Pers.] a nymph.

hübsch [Ger.] good-looking, pretty.

huissier [Fr.] bailiff, door-keeper, usher.

humus [Lat.] earth, ground, mould, soil.

hundertgradig [Ger.] centigrade.

Hütte [Ger.] cabin, hut.

I

ibi [Lat.] there.

ich dien [Ger.] I serve (*orig. the motto of Edward, the Black Prince; thereafter was the motto of the Prince of Wales till it was changed to the English version during World War I*).

ici [Fr.] here.

id [Lat.] it, that (*phrase* **id est** = that is. Abbrev. **i.e.**).

idée fixe [Fr. = a fixed idea] monomania, obsession.

idem [Lat.] also, likewise, same. Abbrev. **id.**

ignis [Lat.] fire.

il penseroso [Ital.] the thinker.

impayable [Fr.] invaluable; (*Colloq.*) amusing, inimitable, priceless.

imperator [Lat.] chief, commander, emperor, master.

impératrice [Fr.] empress.

imperium [Lat.] command, empire, power, sovereignty (*the phrase* **imperium in imperio** *means a government existing within another government; a body existing under, but wholly independent of, a superior body*).

in absentia [Lat.] in absence.

in aeternum [Lat.] forever.

in articulo mortis [Lat. = at the point of death] dying.

in camera [Lat. = in a room] (*Law*) privately, secretly (*said of a case heard in the judge's room instead of in open court*).

in curia [Lat. = in court] (*Law*) openly, publicly (*said of a case heard in open court, i.e. not 'in camera' as above*).

in esse [Lat. = in being] actual.

in excelsis [Lat.] in the highest.

in extremis [Lat. = in a critical state] dying.

in flagrante (or flagranti) delicto [Lat. = in the act of committing the crime] red-handed.

in initio [Lat. = in the beginning] initially.

in loco parentis [Lat. = in the position of a parent] parentally.

in nubibus [Lat. = in the clouds] speculative.

in perpetuum [Lat. = in perpetuity] forever.

in posse [Lat.] possible, potential.

in propria persona [Lat. = in one's own person] personally.

in re [Lat.] concerning.

in saecula saeculorum [Lat. = to the ages of the ages] for ever and ever.

in statu quo ante [Lat. = in the position in which it was before] originally.

in toto [Lat.] totally, utterly, wholly.

in transitu [Lat. = on its passage] progressing.

incognito, *fem.* **incognita** [Ital.] undistinguishable, unknown. Abbrev. **incog.**

inconnu [Fr.] *n.* a stranger; *a.* unknown.

inflatus [Lat.] inspiration.

infra [Lat.] below, beneath.

infra dignitatem [Lat.= beneath one's dignity] undignified. Abbrev. **infra dig.**

ingenium [Lat.] ability, genius, talent.

ingénu, *fem.* **ingénue** [Fr.] artless, ingenuous, naïve, unsophisticated.

inoxydable [Fr.] rustless, stainless.

insouciant [Fr.] careless, jaunty, unconcerned.

instanter [Lat.] instantly.

inter [Lat.] among, between.

interdit [Fr.] banned, forbidden, prohibited (*N.B. the phrase* **entrée interdite**= no entry).

intra [Lat.] within.

intransigeant [Fr.] *a.* intransigent, uncompromising; *n.* die-hard, intransigent.

ipso facto [Lat.= by the very fact, act, or deed) automatically.

ipso jure [Lat.= by the law itself] legally.

irredento [Ital.] unredeemed (*N.B.* **Italia irredenta** = unredeemed Italy, *the parts of Italy, esp. the South Tyrol still under Austrian domination after the war of 1866.* **Italia redenta**=redeemed Italy, *the former Italian territory restored to her after World War I*).

iterum [Lat.] again.

ivre [Fr.] drunk, intoxicated, tipsy.

ivre à pleurer [Fr.] maudlin.

ivresse [Fr.] drunkenness, intoxication; (*Fig.*) frenzy, rapture.

J

jadis [Fr.] formerly.

Jäger [Ger.] hunter, rifleman.

jamais [Fr.] ever, never.

jardin [Fr.] garden.

jardin d'enfants [Fr.] kindergarten, nursery-school.

Jardin des Plantes [Fr.] Botanic Gardens.

jardinière [Fr.] flower-stand.

jargon [Fr.] argot, gibberish, lingo, slang.

je ne sais quoi [Fr.= I do not know what] inexplicability.

jet d'eau [Fr.= a jet of water] fountain.

jeton [Fr.] counter, tally, token.

jetzt [Ger.] now.

jeu [Fr.] game, play, sport.

jeu d'esprit [Fr.] witticism.

jeu de mots [Fr.= play on words] pun.

jeu de patience [Fr.] jig-saw (puzzle).

jeune [Fr.] juvenile, young, youthful.

jeûne [Fr.] abstinence, fasting.

jeunesse [Fr.] boyhood, girlhood, youth, youthfulness (*N.B. the phrase* **jeunesse dorée**=gilded youth, fops).

joie [Fr.] glee, joy, merriment, mirth.

joie de vivre [Fr.] joy of living.

jour de fête [Fr.] festival, holiday.

Jour de l'An [Fr.] New Year's Day.

jour férié [Fr.] (Bank) holiday, (public) holiday.

jour maigre [Fr.] fast-day.

journal [Fr.] newspaper.

journal de modes [Fr.] fashion-paper.

Jude [Ger.] a Jew.

judex [Lat.] a judge.

juge [Fr.] a judge.

Jugend [Ger.] youth.

Jugendherberge [Ger.] youth-hostel.

Juif, *fem.* **Juive** [Fr.] Jew, Jewess.

Jungfrau [Ger.] maid, spinster, virgin.

Junker [Ger.] (young) nobleman.

junta [Sp.] assembly, conference, congress, council, meeting.

junto [Sp.] political group conspiring to seize power; a cabal.

jus [Lat.] law, right. (*N.B. the phrases:* **jus civile**=civil law; **jus gentium**=the law of nations; **jus primogeniturae**=the right of the eldest-born; **jus relictae**=the right of the widow; **jus supra vim**=right over might; **jus togae**=the right to wear the toga (or gown), *i.e. the right of the Roman citizen*).

jura, *pl.* of **jus** [Lat.] laws, rights (*N.B. the phrase,* **jura** negat sibi nata**=he says laws were not made for him— *this applies to the arrogant tyrant or usurper*).

K

Kamerad [Ger.] a comrade (*in both World Wars used for "I surrender" by a German soldier*).

Kampf [Ger.] conquest, fight, strife, struggle (**Mein Kampf***, i.e. "My Struggle", the title of Adolf Hitler's autobiography*).

Kapellmeister [Ger.=orchestra master] bandmaster, choirmaster, orchestra-director.

Kapital [Ger.] capital, funds.

kaput(t) [Ger.] broken, ruined, smashed.

Kartoffel [Ger.] potato.

kein [Ger.] no, none.

Kellner [Ger.] waiter.

képi [Fr.] peaked-cap.

kermesse, kermis [Dut.] fair, festival, fête.

kheda, khedah [Hind.] enclosure (*for trapping wild elephants*).

ketubah [Heb.] marriage-contract.

kia-ora! [Maori] (your) health!

Kindergarten [Ger.=children's garden] nursery-school.

Kinder, Kirche, und Küche [Ger.] children, church, and kitchen (*woman's proper sphere*).

Kinderspiel [Ger.=children's play] operetta.

kiosque [Fr.] bookstall, stall.

kiosque de jardin [Fr.] summer-house.

Kirschwasser [Ger.=cherry-water] cherry-brandy.

Klavier [Ger.] a piano.

klein [Ger.] small.

kloof [Afrikaans] cleft, gorge, gully, ravine.

Kopf [Ger.] the head.

Kopfweh [Ger.] headache.

Kraft [Ger.] force, strength.

Krieg [Ger.] war.

kriegerisch [Ger.] martial, military, warlike.

Kriegsdienst [Ger.] military service.

Kuh-horn [Ger.=cow-horn] (curved) horn (*used by Swiss herdsmen to call the cattle*).

Kümmel [Ger.=caraway-seed] a liqueur.

Kunst [Ger.] art, artifice, skill.

künstlerisch [Ger.] artistic.

L

là [Fr.] there.

là-bas [Fr.] yonder.

labor [Lat.] effort, exertion, labour, work (*N.B. the phrase*, **labor omnia vincit**=work conquers everything).

laborare (est) orare [Lat.] to work (is) to pray.

labourer [Fr.] to plough, to till.

lâche [Fr.] *n.* a coward; *a.* base, cowardly, faint-hearted, unmanly.

lâcheté [Fr.] baseness, cowardice, meanness, treachery.

lacrima, *pl.* **lacrimae** [Lat.] tear(s), weeping.

lacrimoso [Ital.] lachrymose, tearful.

lacuna [Lat.=a pit] hiatus, omission.

laesa majestas [Lat.] lèse-majesté, (high) treason.

laisser-aller [Fr.] carelessness, unconstraint.

laisser-faire [Fr.] drift, non-interference.

laissez-passer [Fr.] *n.* pass, permit.

lampe [Fr.] lamp; (*Radio*) valve.

Landwehr [Ger.=country defence] Home-Guard, militia.

langue [Fr.] language, tongue.

langue vulgaire [Fr.] vernacular.

lapis [Lat.] a stone.

lapsus [Lat.] error, failure, slip (*N.B. the phrase*, **lapsus linguae**=a slip of the tongue).

laquais [Fr.] flunkey, lackey, menial.

lares et penates [Lat.] household gods.

largesse [Fr.] bounty, liberality.

lasciare [Ital.] abandon, leave (*N.B. the phrase*, **lasciate ogni speranza, voi ch'entrate**="abandon all hope, ye who enter", *from Dante's "Inferno", the words written over the gates of Hell*).

laus [Lat.] approval, fame, glory, praise.

lealtà [Ital.] loyalty.

leben [Ger.] to live (*N.B.* **Lebensraum,** i.e. living space, *additional territory to satisfy the needs of a country with an increasing population*).

lector [Lat.] reader.

legatus [Lat.] ambassador, delegate.

le roi (**la reine**) [Fr.] the king (queen) (*N.B. the phrase* **le roy** (**la reyne**) **le veult** = the king (queen) wills it; *this is, in Norman French, the form of royal assent in Great Britain to a Bill*).

lettre [Fr.] letter (*N.B. the phrase,* **lettre de cachet** = a sealed letter; *it was a warrant under the private seal of former Kings of France ordering the imprisonment of a person without trial*).

levée [Fr.] (Royal) reception (*orig. a reception given by a Royal person, esp. in France, in his bed-chamber, on getting out of bed*).

lex [Lat.] law, statute (*N.B. the phrase* **lex talionis** = the law of talion or retaliation in kind, *i.e. an eye for an eye, a tooth for a tooth*).

liaison [Fr.] bond, connection; (*Mus.*) a tie; (*Cookery*) thickening.

liberté, égalité, fraternité [Fr.] liberty, equality, fraternity (*declaration by the revolutionaries at the time of the French Revolution*).

libido [Lat.] desire, passion, urge.

libra [Lat.] balance, scales; pound.

libraire [Fr.] bookseller.

librairie [Fr.] book-shop.

licence [Fr.] (*Univ.*) a degree (ordinary).

licencié [Fr.] (*Univ.*) a graduate.

Lied, *pl.* **Lieder** [Ger.] song(s).

limbus [Lat.] borderland, fringe, hem, limbo.

lingua [Lat., Ital.] language' speech, tongue.

literati [Lat.] scholars (*i.e. learned men, men of letters*).

literatim [Lat.] literally.

locum tenens [Lat. = holding the place] deputy, substitute (*temporary*).

locus [Lat.] a place (*N.B. the phrases,* **locus sigilli** = the place for the seal, *denoted on all official documents by the letters* **L.S.**; **locus standi** = lit. a place for standing, i.e. legal standing, right to interfere).

loge [Fr.] (*Theat.*) box, dressing-room.

Londinium [Lat.] London; *a.* **Londiniensis.**

loquitur [Lat.] (*Theat.*) speaks (*a stage direction*). Abbrev. **loq.**

louche [Fr.] shady, suspicious.

Logurallium [Lat.] Carlisle.

lumen [Lat.] light, torch.

lune de miel [Fr.] honeymoon.

Lusitania [Lat.] Portugal.

Lutetia [Lat.] Paris.

lutte [Fr.] contest, fight, struggle.

lutte à la corde [Fr.] tug-of-war.

lutte à l'américaine [Fr.] all-in-wrestling.

lutte-libre [Fr.] catch-as-catch-can.

lux [Lat.] light (*phrase* **Lux Mundi**=light of the world, i.e. Christ).

luxe, de [Fr.] luxury.

lycée [Fr.] high-school.

lycéen [Fr.] high-school boy.

M

madre [Ital.], **mater** [Lat.] mother.

maduro [Sp.=ripe] full-flavoured (of cigars).

maestoso [Ital.] (*Mus.*) dignified, majestic.

maestro [Ital.] a master (*esp. in music, etc.*).

magister [Lat.] master, scholar, teacher (*N.B. the phrase* **Magister Artium**=Master of Arts. Abbrev. **M.A.**).

Magnificat [Lat.] (he or she) magnifies (*the song of the Virgin Mary (Luke Ch. I) beginning "My soul doth magnify the Lord"*).

magnum bonum [Lat.=a great good] a boon.

magnum opus [Lat.=a great work] a masterpiece.

maigre [Fr.] lean, meagre, skinny, thin (*N.B. phrase,* **jour maigre**=a Fast Day).

maire [Fr.] mayor.

mairie [Fr.] mayoralty, town-hall.

maison [Fr.] a house.

maison publique [Fr.] a brothel.

maison de santé [Fr.] nursing-home.

maisonnette [Fr.=a small house] a flat.

maître, *fem.* **maîtresse** [Fr.] master, mistress (*it is also the courtesy title given to a lawyer*).

maître d'hôtel [Fr.] head-waiter, house-steward.

malade [Fr.] *a.* ill, sick; *n.* invalid, patient.

malade imaginaire [Fr.] hypochondriac.

maladresse [Fr.] awkwardness, clumsiness, tactlessness.

mala fide [Lat.=in bad faith] falsely, fraudulently.

mala fides [Lat.] faithlessness.

mal à propos [Fr.] ill-timed, inopportunely.

mal de mer [Fr.] sea-sickness.

mal(maladie) du pays [Fr.] homesickness, nostalgia.

malentendu [Fr.] misapprehension, misunderstanding.

malum [Lat.] evil (*N.B. the phrase* **malum in se**=a thing evil in itself, i.e. inherently wrong).

mañana [Sp.] tomorrow.

Mancunium [med. Lat.] Manchester.

manège [Fr.] horsemanship, riding, training (*of horses*).

manes [Lat.] shades (of the dead), souls; deities (*name given by the Romans to the souls of the departed, who were worshipped as deities. On sepulchres we* *find* **D.M.S.** *i.e.* **Dis manibus sacrum**=sacred to the departed spirits, now regarded as gods).

manière d'être [Fr.] bearing, deportment.

maquillage [Fr.] make-up, making-up.

mare [Lat.] the sea (*N.B. the proverb,* **mare, ignis, et mulier sunt tria mala**= the sea, fire, and a woman are three evils).

marionnette [Fr.] puppet.

marque de fabrique [Fr.]= trade-mark.

mauvais pas [Fr.] dilemma, fix, scrape.

mauvais quart d'heure [Fr.=a bad quarter of an hour] a trying-time.

mauvais sujet [Fr.] ne'er-do-well, scapegrace.

mauvais ton [Fr.] vulgarity.

mauvaise gestion [Fr.] mal-administration, mismanagement.

mauvaise langue [Fr.=a bad tongue] scandalmonger, slanderer.

mea culpa [Lat.] (through my) fault.

médisance [Fr.] backbiting, scandal, slander.

me judice [Lat.] (in my) judgment.

mélange [Fr.] blending, medley, mixture.

ménage [Fr.] family, home, housekeeping, housework.

mens [Lat.] the mind (*N.B. the phrase,* **mens sana in cor-**

pore sano=a healthy mind in a healthy body).

merci [Fr.] mercy; thanks! (no) thanks!

mésalliance [Fr.] misalliance.

mesquin [Fr.] mean, niggardly, stingy.

mesquinerie [Fr.] meanness, niggardliness.

meum et tuum [Lat.] mine and thine.

midi [Fr.] midday, noon; (*Fig.*) heyday (of life).

Midi [Fr.] South (of France).

midinette [Fr.] (Parisian) shop-girl.

mignon, *fem.* **mignonne** [Fr.] dainty, dear, lovable.

milieu [Fr.] environment, surroundings.

minutiae [Lat] trifles.

mirabile dictu. [Lat.] wonderful (to relate).

mirabilia [Lat.] wonders.

mise en scène [Fr.] (*Theat.*) mounting, production, stage-setting.

misericordia [Lat.] mercy, pity, sympathy.

mi-temps [Fr.] (*Football*) half-time.

modus [Lat.] manner, mode, way.

modus vivendi [Lat.=way of living] agreement, arrangement, compromise (*settlement of differences between parties and agreement to work together harmoniously*).

mœurs [Fr.] customs, habits, manners, morals.

Mona [Lat.] Anglesey.

mon Dieu! [Fr.=my God] goodness!

mont–de–piété [Fr.] a pawn-shop (*State-supervised for the relief of the poor*).

monumentum [Lat.] a monument (*N.B. the phrase from Horace*, **monumentum aere perennius**=a monument more enduring than brass).

morceau [Fr.] bit, fragment; (*Mus.*) piece.

morgue [Fr.] a mortuary.

morgue anglaise [Fr.] aloofness, coolness, haughtiness, indifference, standoffishness.

mors [Lat.] death (*N.B. the phrase* **mors janua vitae**= death is the gate of (eternal) life).

mos, *pl.* **mores** [Lat.] custom, habit, law, practice (*N.B. the phrase* **mos majorum**=the custom of one's ancestors).

mot [Fr.] a word (*N.B. the phrase* **mot juste**=the right word, the most appropriate term).

mot d'ordre [Fr.] password.

mot du guet [Fr.] watchword.

mousseux [Fr.] sparkling (*of wines*).

multum [Lat.] much (*N.B. the phrase* **multum in parvo**= much in little; *a compendium of knowledge*).

N

Nachkommenschaft [Ger.] posterity.

naïf, *fem.* **naïve** [Fr.] artless, ingenuous, unaffected, unsophisticated.

Napoli [Ital.] Naples; *a.* **Napolitano**.

natus [Lat.] born.

néant [Fr.] nothing(ness), nought.

Neapolis [Lat.] Naples.

nec [Lat.] neither, nor (*N.B. the phrase*, **nec tamen consumebatur**=nor was it (the bush) consumed; *See Exodus Ch. 3; the motto of the Church of Scotland*).

née (*fem. of* **né**) [Fr.] born (*used to designate a woman's maiden name*).

nemo [Lat.] no one, nobody (*N.B. the phrase* **nemo me impune lacessit**=no one shall attack me with impunity. *Motto of Scotland and of the Order of the Thistle*).

ne plus ultra [Lat.=nothing more beyond] acme, extreme, limit, perfection, superiority.

niais [Fr.] *a.* silly; *n.* fool, simpleton.

niaiserie [Fr.] folly, silliness, stupidity.

nihil, nil [Lat.] nothing (*N.B. the phrases*, (a) **nihil sine labore**=nothing without work; (b) **nil desperandum** =never despair).

nisi [Lat.] unless (*N.B. the phrase* **nisi Dominus, frustra**=unless the Lord be with you, all your efforts are in vain. *Motto of the city of Edinburgh*).

nitouche (sainte) [Fr.] a prude.

noblesse [Fr.] nobility, nobleness (*N.B. the phrase*, **noblesse oblige**=noble birth compels, *i.e. nobly born must nobly do; rank carries with it certain obligations*).

Noël [Fr.] Christmas.

nolens volens [Lat. = unwilling, willing] willy-nilly.

nom [Fr.] name.

nom de baptême [Fr. = baptismal name] Christian-name.

nom de famille [Fr.] surname.

nom de guerre [Fr. = war-name] alias, pen-name.

nom de théâtre [Fr.] stage-name.

nomen [Lat.] fame, name, reputation, title.

non [Lat.] not (*N.B. phrase*, **non olet pecunia** = the money does not stink, *i.e. money from doubtful or unclean sources*).

non compos mentis [Lat. = not of sound mind] insane.

non possumus [Lat.] (we) cannot (*i.e. inability to assist or unwillingness to co-operate, etc.*).

non sequitur [Lat. = it does not follow, *i.e. logically*] illogical.

Nonae [Lat.] the Nones (*7th day of March, May, July, October, and 5th day of other months*).

nonchalance [Fr.] coolness, indifference.

nonchalant [Fr.] cool, inactive, sluggish.

Nordovicum [med. Lat.] Norwich.

nota bene [Lat. = note well] note. Abbrev. **N.B.**

notanda [Lat.] details, notes, points, remarks.

nouveau [Fr.] new.

nouveau marié, nouvelle mariée [Fr.] bridegroom, bride.

nouveau-né [Fr.] new-born (child).

nouveau riche [Fr.] an upstart.

nouveauté [Fr.] newness, novelty.

novissima verba [Lat. = the last words] (*Fig.*) death.

novus homo [Lat. = a new man] an upstart.

nox [Lat.] night.

nulli secundus [Lat. = second to none] outstanding.

nunc [Lat.] now (*N.B.* **Nunc dimittis** = Now lettest thou depart. *These are the opening words of the canticle of Simeon (Luke Ch. 2) used following the Second Lesson at the evening service in the Anglican Church, and in the R.C. service of Compline*).

nunc est bibendum [Lat. = now is the time for drinking] drinking-time, jollification, merrymaking.

nunquam [Lat.] never (*N.B. the phrase* **nunquam minus solus, quam cum solus** = never less alone than when alone).

Nützlichkeit [Ger.] utility.

O

obiit [Lat.] (he or she) died. Abbrev. **ob.**

obiter [Lat.=on the way] by the bye, casually, incidentally (*the full Latin expression is* **obiter dictum**=a passing or casual observation. *Sometimes used in the plural* **obiter dicta**).

obole [Fr.] (brass) farthing, mite, offering.

observanda [Lat.] notes, observations.

octroi [Fr.] duty (on goods entering a town).

odium [Lat.] hatred (*N.B. the phrases,* (a) **odium theologicum**=theological rancour, *i.e. such as is shown between religious sects;* (b) **odium vicinorum**=hatred of one's neighbours, or of neighbouring countries).

œillade [Fr.] glance, ogle.

œuvres [Fr.] works (literary or artistic).

omne [Lat.] everything (*N.B. the phrase,* **omne nimium vertitur in vitium**=every excess becomes a vice, i.e. *even virtues pushed to extremes can become vices*).

omnia [Lat.=all things] everything (*N.B. the phrases,* (a) **omnia mutantur, nos et mutamur in illis**=all things change and we change with them; (b) **omnia vincit amor**=love conquers all things).

on dit [Fr.=one says] hearsay, rumour.

opera [Lat.] works (*pl. of* **opus**).

opusculum [Lat.] a (little) work.

orare [Lat.] to pray (*N.B. the phrases* (a) **ora pro nobis**=pray for us; (b) **orate pro anima**=pray for the soul of).

Orcades [Lat.] the Orkneys.

ordre du jour [Fr.=order of the day] agenda; (*Mil.*) orders.

oriflamme [Fr.] banner of the kings of France.

origo malorum [Lat.=source of evils] misfortunes.

orné [Fr.] adorned, ornate.

otium [Lat.] ease (*N.B. the phrase,* **otium cum dignitate**=the pleasure of retirement from business).

ouailles [Fr.] (*Church*) congregation, flock.

ouï-dire [Fr.] hearsay, rumour.

outré [Fr.=beyond] excessive, far-fetched, outrageous, overdone, unreasonable.

Oxonia [med. Lat.] Oxford; *a.* **Oxoniensis**.

P

pabulum [Lat.] aliment, food.

pactum [Lat.] agreement, compact.

Padova [Ital.] Padua.

paix [Fr.] peace.

palais [Fr.] a palace (**Palais de Justice**=the Law Courts).

Palladium [Lat.] a statue of Pallas in Troy, on the preservation of which depended the safety of the city; hence, (*Fig.*) protection, safeguard.

palma [Lat.] palm, prize, victory (*N.B. the phrase,*

palmam qui meruit, ferat=let him who has won the palm (of victory) wear it).

panis [Lat.] bread, loaf (*N.B. the phrase* **panem et circenses**=bread and circuses, *i.e.* (*give us*) *food and entertainment* (*at the public expense*); *a demand of the populace of Ancient Rome*).

par [Fr.] by.

par excellence [Fr.] pre-eminently.

Parigi [Ital.] Paris.

pari passu [Lat.=with equal step] likewise.

parti [Fr.] a decision, marriage-match, (political) party.

parti pris [Fr.=decision (already) taken], bias, preconception, prejudice.

partie [Fr.] game, match, round.

partie double [Fr.] (*Golf*) foursome; (*Tennis*) doubles.

partim [Lat.] mostly, partly.

pas [Fr.] pace, step, stride; precedence.

Pas de Calais [Fr.] Straits of Dover.

pasquinade [Fr.] lampoon.

passager, *fem.* **passagère** [Fr.] fleeting, fugitive, passing, short-lived, transient.

passé, *fem.* **passée** [Fr.] faded, gone, out-of-date, past (the prime of life).

passe-partout [Fr.] latch-key, master-key, passport (*also used in English for a simple method of framing photographs with the use of cardboard and gummed tape*).

passim [Lat.] everywhere, indiscriminately.

pater [Lat.] father (**Pater noster**=our Father, *the opening words of the Latin version of the Lord's prayer*).

paterfamilias [Lat.] master of the house.

patres (*pl.* of **pater**) [Lat.] fathers (**patres conscripti** =lit. the conscript fathers, the Roman Senate).

patria [Lat.], **patrie** [Fr.] fatherland, homeland, motherland.

paucis verbis [Lat.=in a few words] briefly, shortly.

pax [Lat.] peace; *interj.* enough! (**pax vobiscum**= peace be with you).

pays [Fr.] country, district, land (**pays de Cocagne**, land of milk and honey, land of plenty, *N.B. Cocagne is an imaginary country*).

paysage [Fr.] landscape, scenery; (*Art*) a landscape-painting.

paysagiste [Fr.] (*Art*) landscape-painter.

peccavi [Lat.] I have sinned (to cry **peccavi** is to acknowledge oneself in the wrong).

pecunia [Lat.] money, property.

penates [Lat.] home, (household) gods.

penchant [Fr.] bent, fondness, inclination, propensity.

pension [Fr.] boarding-house, board (and lodging).

pensionnaire [Fr.] boarder, paying-guest.

pensionnat [Fr.] boarding-school.

pensum [Lat.] duty, task; (*in French schools*) an imposition.

Pentecôte [Fr.] Pentecost, Whitsun(tide).

per [Lat.] by, through (*N.B. the motto of the Royal Air Force*, **per ardua ad astra** =through difficulties to the stars).

per annum [Lat.] yearly.

per capita [Lat.=(counting) by heads] individually.

per diem [Lat.] daily.

per mensem [Lat.] monthly.

per procurationem [Lat.= by the agency of] by proxy (*Abbrev.* **per pro.** or **p.p.**, *used when signing for another person*).

per se [Lat.=by itself] essentially.

persona [Lat.] a person (**persona grata**, an acceptable person; **persona in-grata**, an objectionable, offensive, or unacceptable person).

personnage de carton [Fr. =a character of cardboard] a figurehead.

petitesse [Fr.] littleness, pettiness, smallness.

petitio [Lat.] appeal, claim, petition, request (**petitio ad misericordiam**=an appeal to mercy, compassion).

piazza [Ital.] (town) square.

pièce [Fr.] bit, piece; (*Theat.*) a play; (*Cookery*) (**pièce de résistance**=principal dish of a meal, esp. the meat course; (*Fig.*) the principal item on the programme).

pièces de rechange [Fr.] spare-parts.

pied-à-terre [Fr.] temporary lodging.

Pilsener [Ger.] lager-beer.

pinxit [Lat.] (he or she) painted (this); usually preceded by the artist's signature.

pioupiou [Fr.] (*Colloq.*) an infantryman.

piquant [Fr.] cutting, pungent, racy.

pis [Fr.] worse, worst.

pis aller [Fr.] a makeshift (the last resource).

più [Ital.] more.

pius, *fem.* **pia** [Lat.] good, holy, pious, upright (**pia fraus**=a pious fraud, *i.e. a fraud originating from charit-able motives*).

place [Fr.] place, room, seat, town-square (**place aux dames!**=(make) room for the ladies! ladies first!).

plat [Fr.] (*Restaurant*) course, dish (**plat du jour**=lit. dish of the day, *i.e. a special dish*).

plaza [Sp.] town-square (**Plaza del Sol**=lit. Square of the Sun, the principal square in Madrid).

plebs [Lat.] (common) people, masses, plebeian.

podestà [Ital.] (chief) magistrate.

poeta [Lat.] a poet (**poeta nascitur, non fit**=the poet is born, not made).

poilu [Fr.] (*Colloq.*) a (French) soldier.

poisson [Fr.] a fish (**poisson d'avril**=lit. an April fish) an April fool.

poli [Fr.] glossy, mannerly, polished, polite, refined.

politesse [Fr.] politeness (**toujours la politesse**, politeness at all times).

polichinelle [Fr.], **polichinello** [Ital.] buffoon, clown, Punch.

pollex [Lat.] the thumb (**pollice verso**=with thumb turned down—*the sign made by the spectators for the death of a gladiator; hence, a sign of disapproval*).

Poltergeist [Ger.=uproar ghost] (noisy) ghost, hobgoblin.

poltron [Fr.] a coward, poltroon.

poltronnerie [Fr.] cowardice.

pons [Lat.] a bridge (**pons asinorum**=the bridge of asses, *nickname for the 5th proposition of Euclid, Book I; hence, a difficult test for beginners*).

pontifex [Lat.] a bishop, pontiff, priest. (**Pontifex Maximus**=the highest pontiff or chief priest, one of the designations of the Pope).

pont-levis [Fr.] a drawbridge.

populus [Lat.] the people, the populace (**populus vult decipi et decipiatur**=the people like to be fooled so let them be fooled).

post [Lat.] after, behind (**post factum nullum consilium**=after the deed is done, consultation is useless).

post meridiem [Lat.] after noon.

post mortem [Lat.] after death.

post prandium [Lat.] after dinner.

postiche [Fr.] *a.* artificial, false, sham; *n.* a wig.

pot-au-feu [Fr.=pot at the fire] (*Cookery*) broth, stock-pot.

pot pourri [Fr.=a rotten pot] mixture (of dried rose petals in a jar); (*Mus.*) a medley.

pourboire [Fr.=in order to drink] gratuity, tip.

pour comble de bonheur [Fr.=the height of happiness] ecstasy.

pour comble de malheur [Fr.] a crowning misfortune.

praemium [Lat.] prize, reward (**praemia virtutis**=the rewards of virtue).

praemonitus, praemonitus [Lat.] forewarned, forearmed.

préfet [Fr.] a prefect (chief magistrate of a French *département*).

préfecture [Fr.] headquarters (of a *préfet*).

preux [Fr.] doughty, valiant (**preux chevalier** = a doughty champion, a valiant knight).

premier, *fem.* **première** [Fr.] first (**première**=first performance of a play; **première danseuse**, principal female dancer in a ballet).

primo [Lat.] firstly.

primus [Lat.] first (**primus inter pares**=the first among equals).

princeps [Lat.] chief, first.

principia [Lat.] elements, (first) principles.

prix [Fr.] price, prize.

pro [Lat.] for (**pro bono publico**=for the public good; **pro et con**=for and against; **pro patria**=for one's country; **pro re nata**=for special business; **pro tempore**=for the time being. Abbrev. **pro. tem.**).

procès [Fr.] (*Law*) action, case, proceedings.

procès-verbal [Fr.] minutes, report, summary (*pl.* **procès-verbaux**).

proxime [Lat.] nearest, next.

proxime accessit [Lat.] the runner-up (he or she came next to the prize-winner).

Punica fides [Lat.=Punic, *i.e. Carthaginian*, faith] treachery.

pur [Fr.] pure, unalloyed.

purée [Fr.] (*Cookery*) mash, (thick) soup.

purée de pommes de terre [Fr.] mashed-potatoes.

pur sang [Fr.=pure blood] thoroughbred.

puy [Fr.] cone, mountain, peak (*often the name of an extinct volcano in Auvergne*).

Q

qua [Lat.] as (in the capacity of), whereby.

quadriga(ae) [Lat.=a team of four] a chariot.

quaere [Lat.] ask, enquire, question, seek.

quaestor [Lat.] tax-collector, treasurer (*in ancient Rome, the finance magistrate*).

quai [Fr.] embankment, quay (**Quai d'Orsay**=the title given to the French Ministry of Foreign Affairs occupying buildings on the "quai" of that name along the Seine).

qualis [Lat.] as, like (**qualis rex, talis grex**=like king, like people).

quam celerrime, quam primum [Lat.=as quickly as possible] hastily, speedily.

quand même [Fr.] nevertheless, notwithstanding.

quantum [Lat.] amount, (as) much, proportion (**quantum libet**=as much as you please (*on prescriptions*). Abbrev. **q.l.**; **quantum sufficit**=as much as is needed. Abbrev. **quant. suff.** or **q.s.**).

quartier [Fr.] district, quarter (*of a town*).

quartier-général [Fr.] (*Mil.*) Headquarters.

quasi [Lat.] almost, apparently, seeming, seemingly.

Quattrocento [Ital.=one thousand four hundred]15th century.

quebrada [Sp.] a ravine.

quem [Lat.] whom (**quem deus perdere vult, primus dementat**=a god wishes to destroy, he first makes mad; **quem di diligunt adolescens moritur**

=whom the gods love dies young).

quenelles [Fr.] (*Cookery*) forcemeat-balls.

qui [Fr.] who (**qui s'excuse, s'accuse**=he who excuses himself, accuses himself; **qui va là?**=who goes there?—a sentry's challenge).

quid pro quo [Lat.=something for something] an exchange, an equivalent, (mutual) consideration.

quintus [Lat.] fifth.

quis? [Lat.] who? (**quis custodiet ipsos custodes?** who will guard the guards themselves?—*quotation from Juvenal, meaning what check have you on those whom you have set to guard you?*).

quo? [Lat.] whither? (**quo vadis?**=whither goest thou?).

quoad [Lat.] so far as (**quoad sacra**=as to, or with respect to sacred matters, *i.e. so far as the offices of the church are concerned, in contradistinction to matters of a parochial nature*).

quod [Lat.] that, what, which (**quod erat demonstrandum**=which was to be demonstrated or proved; Abbrev. **Q.E.D.—quod erat faciendum**=which was to be done; Abbrev. **Q.E.F.**).

quoque [Lat.] also, too.

quot [Lat.] so many (**quot homines, tot sententiae**=so many men, so many different opinions. *This quotation from Terence is an allusion to the continued diversity of taste and opinion*).

R

raison d'être [Fr.=reason for existence] justification.

raisonné [Fr.] reasoned, systematised.

rapprochement [Fr.] reconciliation, re-establishment (*esp. of friendly relations between countries*).

rara avis [Lat.=rare bird] prodigy, wonder.

rauchen [Ger.] to smoke (**rauchen verboten**=smoking forbidden; no smoking).

rébarbatif [Fr.] grim, surly.

recherché [Fr.=sought after] affected, choice, elaborate, far-fetched, rare, select.

récidiviste [Fr.] (confirmed) criminal, (old) offender.

reculer [Fr.] to recoil, to retreat (**reculer pour mieux sauter**=to draw back in order to leap better; *hence, to retreat temporarily before attack*).

rédacteur [Fr.] editor.

redivivus [Lat.] reborn, renovated.

reductio [Lat.] reduction, restoration (**reductio ad absurdum**=reducing to an absurdity).

régime [Fr.] government, order, system; (*Med.*) diet (**ancien régime**=the old order, *i.e. the old or former form of government in France before the Revolution*).

regina [Lat.] queen; Abbrev. **R.** or **Reg.**

régisseur [Fr.] (*Theat.*) stage-manager.

Reich [Ger.] kingdom, republic, state.

Reichstag [Ger.] parliament.

relâche [Fr.] relaxation, rest; (*Theat.*) closed (*i.e. no performance*).

renommée [Fr.] fame, renown.

rentes [Fr.] annuities, income, stock.

rentier [Fr.] annuitant, fundholder, stockholder (*i.e. one who lives on investments or is of independent means*).

répondre [Fr.] to answer (**répondez s'il vous plaît** = answer if you please, i.e. please reply to this invitation; Abbrev. **R.S.V.P.**

requiescere [Lat.] to rest (**requiescat in pace** = may he (or she) rest in peace; Abbrev. **R.I.P.**).

res [Lat.] thing, things.

res adversae [Lat.] adversity.

res augustae [Lat.] straits (*i.e. pecuniary difficulties*).

res gestae [Lat.] deeds, exploits.

res non verba [Lat.] deeds, not words.

résumé [Fr.] recapitulation.

resurgere [Lat.] revive, rise (again) (**resurgam** = I shall rise again).

revanche [Fr.] revenge.

revenir [Fr.] to return (**revenons à nos moutons** = let us return to our sheep, i.e. let us come back to the subject we were discussing. *The origin of the expression is to be found in the medieval farce* "*L'Avocat Pathelin*").

rêveur, *fem.* **rêveuse** [Fr.] a day-dreamer.

rex [Lat.] a king (**rex regnat sed non gubernat** = the king rules but does not govern).

Rex et Imperator [Lat.] King and Emperor; Abbrev. **R.I.**

reine [Fr.] queen.

rien [Fr.] nothing (**rien ne va plus** = no more goes, i.e. no more stakes accepted— *the call of the croupier at the gaming-table*).

ris de veau [Fr.] (*Cookery*) sweetbreads.

risorgimento [Ital.] renascence, revival.

rognons [Fr.] (*Cookery*) kidneys.

roi roy [Fr.] king (**le roy (roi) le veult (veut)** = the king wills it, *the phrase indicating the royal assent to an Act of Parliament*).

roman [Fr.] a novel (**roman policier** = a detective story).

rôti [Fr.] roast (**rôti d'agneau, de bœuf, de porc, de veau** = roast lamb, beef, pork, veal).

roué [Fr.] libertine, profligate, rake, scamp.

rus [Lat.] the country, countryside (**rus in urbe** = the country in the city, *i.e. a residence enjoying the advantages of both town and countryside*).

S

sabreur [Fr.] cavalryman (*armed with a sabre*) (**beau sabreur**=dashing cavalryman).

Sabrina [Lat.] the R. Severn.

sacré [Fr.] sacred (**Sacré Cœur**=the Sacred Heart, *name of a famous church in Paris*).

saignant [Fr.=bleeding] (*Cookery*) underdone (of meat).

sal [Lat.] salt; (*Fig.*) humour, wit, witticism (**sal Atticum** =Attic salt, *i.e. delicate, subtly sharp wit*).

salle [Fr.] a hall, a room.

salle à manger [Fr.] dining-room.

salle d'armes [Fr.] fencing-school.

salle d'attente [Fr.] waiting-room.

salve! [Lat.] hail!

sanctus [Lat.] holy, sacred (**sancta simplicitas** = child-like simplicity; **sanctum sanctorum**=the holy of holies).

sans cérémonie [Fr.] un-ceremoniously (*i.e. without fuss*).

sans gêne [Fr.] free-and-easy, off-handed.

sans peur [Fr.] fearless.

sans peur et sans reproche [Fr.] without fear and without reproach (*used to describe the medieval knight, Bayard*).

sans souci [Fr.] care-free, happy-go-lucky.

sartor [Lat.] a tailor (**Sartor Resartus**=the tailor re-tailored, *the title of a work by Thomas Carlyle*).

Sarum [Lat.] Salisbury.

sauver [Fr.] to save (**sauve qui peut**=let him save himself who can, *the phrase of panic, indicating headlong flight, rout, stampede*).

savate [Fr.] an old shoe (*also a kind of French boxing in which feet and head, as well as fists, are used*).

savoir-faire [Fr.=to know how to do] common-sense, gumption, nous, tact.

savoir-vivre [Fr.=to know how to live, to behave oneself] good-breeding.

Schnitzel [Ger.] (*Cookery*) a cutlet.

scripsit [Lat.] (he or she) wrote (this).

sculpsit [Lat.] (he or she) sculptured (this).

se [Ital.] if (**se non è vero, è ben trovato**=if it is not true, it is at least well invented).

sec [Fr.] (*Wines*) dry, un-sweetened.

secundo [Lat.] secondly.

secundum [Lat.] according to.

secundum artem [Lat.] artistically, professionally, skilfully.

secundum legem [Lat.] judicially, legally.

secundus [Lat.] second (to bear the name).

semper [Lat.] always, ever (**semper fidelis**=always faithful; **semper idem**= always the same man or character; **semper paratus**= ever ready).

sempre [Ital.] always (**sempre il mal non vien per nuocere**=misfortune does not always come to injure, i.e. it may be a blessing in disguise).

senatus [Lat.] the (Roman) senate (**senatus populusque Romanus**=the senate and the Roman people. Abbrev. **S.P.Q.R.**).

Sequana [Lat.] R. Seine.

sequens [Lat.] the following; Abbrev. **seq.** *pl.* **sequentes, sequentia**; Abbrev. **seqq.**

sequitur [Lat.] (he, she, it) follows, a consequence.

si [Lat.] if (*N.B. the two phrases;* (a) **si monumentum requiris, circumspice**=if you seek my monument look around (you), i.e. if you question my merit, behold my works—*part of the epitaph of Sir Christopher Wren in St. Paul's Cathedral;* (b) **si vis pacem, para bellum**=if you wish peace, be ready for war).

sic [Lat.] thus (**sic transit gloria mundi**=thus passes away the glory of the world; **sic vos non vobis**=thus you (labour) not for yourselves).

siècle [Fr.] a century (**siècle d'or**=the Golden Age, *i.e. the period of Louis XIV of France, the 17th Cent.*).

simpliciter [Lat.] absolutely, simply.

sine [Lat.] without (**sine die** =without a day (being named), i.e. indefinitely; **sine prole**= without issue, childless; **sine qua non**=an indispensable condition; an essential).

siste, viator! [Lat.] halt, traveller!

société [Fr.] association, company, society (**société anonyme**=a limited liability company; **Société des Nations**=the League of Nations. Abbrev. **S.D.N.**).

soigné, *fem.* **soignée** [Fr.] neat; trim, well-finished, well-groomed.

sperare [Lat.] to expect, to hope (**spero meliora**=I hope for better things).

splendide [Lat.] brilliantly, magnificently, nobly (**splendide mendax**=nobly lying, i.e. being false in a good cause).

statim [Lat.] immediately.

status [Lat.] position, situation, state (**status quo (ante bellum)**=the position as it was (before the war), *i.e. the pre-existing state of affairs*).

stimulus [Lat.] incentive, inducement, spur.

Sturm und Drang [Ger.] storm and stress.

suaviter [Lat.] gently, pleasantly, sweetly (**suaviter in modo, fortiter in re**= pleasantly in manner, vigorously in action, *i.e. a pleasant manner combined with firm discharge of duties*).

sub [Lat.] under (**sub judice** = under consideration; **sub rosa** = under the rose, i.e. secretly; **sub sigillo** = under the seal, i.e. confidentially).

succès [Fr.] success (**succès d'estime** = when speaking of books and plays, a success founded not on popular favour, but on the appreciation of the cultured; **succès fou** = a howling success, enthusiastic reception).

succursale [Fr.] (*Comm.*) branch (*of a firm, bank, etc.*)

sui generis [Lat. = of its own kind] peculiar, unique (i.e. the only one of its kind).

summus [Lat.] highest, supreme, top (**summum bonum** = the supreme good).

sursum [Lat.] up, upwards (**sursum corda** = lift up your hearts!; **sursum semper** = ever upwards).

sutor [Lat.] cobbler, shoemaker (**sutor ne supra crepidam** = let not the shoemaker venture beyond his sandal, i.e. let the cobbler stick to his last. *This is a reference to the rebuke made by Apelles (the most famous painter of antiquity) when a cobbler while criticising one of his pictures passed from the sandals to the legs*).

T

tabula [Lat.] writing-tablet (**tabula rasa** = a smoothed tablet, hence a blank page, a clean sheet).

tacere [Lat.] to be silent (**tacent, satis laudant** = their silence is sufficient praise).

taedium vitae [Lat. = tedium of life] boredom, ennui, weariness.

Tamesis [Lat.] R. Thames.

tant [Fr.] so, so much (**tant mieux** = so much the better; **tant pis** = so much the worse).

te [Lat.] thee (**Te Deum laudamus** = we praise, Thee, O God).

télégraphie [Fr.] telegraphy (**télégraphie sans fil** = wireless telegraphy; Abbrev. T.S.F.).

tempora [Lat.] times (**tempora mutantur, et nos (or nos et) mutamus in illis** = times are changed and we change with them).

tempus [Lat.] time (**tempus edax rerum** = time is the consumer, of all things; **tempus fugit** = time flies; **tempus omnia revelat** = time reveals all things).

terra [Lat.] earth, land, soil (**terra firma** = solid earth, *i.e. dry land*; **terra incognita** = unknown country; **terrae filius** = a son of the soil, *i.e. one of humble birth*).

tertio [Lat.] thirdly.

tertius [Lat.] the third (also the third to bear the name); **tertium quid** = a third something, *i.e. intermediary between two opposite principles*).

tête [Fr.] the head (**tête-à-tête** = head to head, a private conversation between two people; (**tête-de-pont**) (*Mil.*) a bridgehead; **tête de série** (*Tennis*) seeded player).

tiers [Fr.] third (**tiers état**= the third estate, *formerly in France, the common people as distinguished from the nobility and higher clergy*).

timere [Lat.] to fear (**timeo Danaos et dona ferentes** =I fear the Greeks, (even) when bearing gifts).

toga [Lat.] a robe (**toga virilis**=the manly robe, *i.e. the mantle of manhood, worn by Roman youths when they came of age*).

toison [Fr.] a fleece (**La Toison d'Or**=The Golden Fleece).

tombola [Ital.] lottery, raffle (*modern*=Bingo, Housey-Housey).

toujours [Fr.] always (**toujours la politesse**=politeness at all times).

tour [Fr.] an effort, feat, trick (**tour de force**=a feat of strength or skill, an outstanding effort).

tout [Fr.] all, everything (**tout à fait**=completely, entirely; **tout court**, briefly, in short; **tout de suite**=at once, immediately; **tout ensemble**=all together; (*Fig.*) the general effect; **tout le monde**=everybody.)

troika [Russ.] a sleigh, carriage (drawn by 3 horses abreast).

troppo [Ital.] (*Mus.*) too.

trouvaille [Fr.] godsend, windfall.

tu [Lat.] thou (**tu quoque**= lit. "thou also", *used as a retort in accusing an opponent of action, conduct, etc., similar to the charge made against oneself*).

tutte *fem. pl.* [Ital.] all (**tutte le strade conducono a Roma**=all roads lead to Rome).

U

ubique [Lat.] everywhere (*motto of the Royal Artillery*).

Uhlan [Pol. & Ger.] cavalryman, lancer.

ultima, *fem. of* **ultimus** [Lat.] last (**ultima ratio regum**=the last argument of kings, *i.e. war*; **ultima Thule** =the furthest Thule, i.e. the utmost boundary or limit. *Thule was the most remote northern land known to the Romans*).

ultimus [Lat.] last (**ultimus haeres**=the last heir. (*Law*) the crown, to which passes the property of those who die intestate without heirs).

ultra [Lat.] beyond (**ultra vires**=beyond the powers possessed).

Umlaut [Ger.] a diaeresis (*the change in the sound of a vowel indicated by two dots placed over it, as in Führer*).

und [Ger.] and (**und so weiter**=and so on. Abbrev. **u.s.w.**)

uno animo [Lat.] unanimously.

urbs [Lat.] a city (**Urbi et Orbi**=to the city, *i.e. Rome*, and to the world. *This phrase is applied to the Pope's blessing, given from the balcony of St. Peter's on special occasions*).

ut [Lat.] as (**ut infra**=as below, *e.g. in a book*; **ut supra**=as above, *e.g. in a book*).

V

vadere [Lat.] to go (**vade mecum**=go with me; a handy reference book, a pocket manual; **vade in pace!**=go in peace!).

vae! [Lat.] alas! woe! (**vae victis**=woe to the conquered!).

vale! [Lat.] farewell!

vallum [Lat.] a ditch, rampart.

vanitas [Lat.] vanity (**vanitas vanitatum**=vanity of vanities).

varius [Lat.] changeable, fickle (**varium et mutabile semper femina**=woman is ever fickle and inconstant).

vaurien [Fr.] a good-for-nothing, rascal, scamp.

vedere [Ital.] to see (**vedi Napoli e poi muori**=see Naples, and then die).

Venezia [Ital.] Venice.

veni, vidi, vici [Lat.] I came, I saw, I conquered (*the famous words of Julius Caesar announcing the great speed of his defeat of King Pharnaces II, son of Mithridates, at Zela in* 47 B.C.).

ventre à terre [Fr.=belly to the ground] flat-out, top-speed.

verbatim [Lat.] word for word.

verboten [Ger.] forbidden.

verbum [Lat.] a word (**verbum sapienti sat est**= a word to the wise is enough. Abbrev. **verb. sap.**).

Verein [Ger.] association, society, union.

vestigium [Lat.] foot-print, footstep, track (**vestigia . . . nulla retrorsum**=no footprints going back (*i.e. from the lion's den—hence, a danger from which there is no retreat*).

via [Lat.] a way (**via dolorosa**=the painful road, i.e. The Way of Calvary; **via media** =a middle course).

via, veritas, vita [Lat.] the way, the truth, the life (*motto of the University of Glasgow*).

vide [Lat.] see (**vide infra**= see below; **vide supra**=see above).

videlicet [Lat.] clearly, evidently, namely, to wit. Abbrev. **viz.**

vigilate et orate [Lat.] watch and pray.

vin [Fr.] wine (**vin blanc**= white wine; **vin mousseux** =sparkling wine; **vin rouge** =red wine; **vin de marque** =vintage wine; **vin du pays** =local wine).

virgo [Lat.] a maid, a virgin (**Virginibus Puerisque**= for maidens and youths—*title of a work by R. L. Stevenson*).

virtus [Lat.] valour, virtue (**virtus in arduis**=valour in difficulties; **virtus incendit vires**=virtue kindles strength).

vis [Lat.] force, power, strength (**vis inertia**=the power of inertia, passive resistance).

vita [Lat.] life (**vita brevis, ars longa**=life is short, art is long).

vivat! [Lat.] (long) live! (**vivat rex (regina)**=long live the king (queen).

vive! [Fr.] (long) live! (**vive le roi, la reine, la république**=long live the king, the queen, the republic).

voguer [Fr.] to row, to sail (**vogue la galère**=let the galley drift; row on, come what may!).

voilà [Fr.] there!

volage [Fr.] fickle, inconstant, changeable.

vox [Lat.] voice (**vox et praeterea nihil**=a voice and nothing more, i.e. a fine speech without matter, or a mere display of words; **vox populi, vox Dei**=the voice of the people, i.e. public opinion is the voice of God).

vulgus [Lat.] crowd, herd, populace, rabble.

W

wandern [Ger.] to travel, wander (**Wanderjahr**="a travelling year". *An old Teutonic custom by which an apprentice, having finished his time, "wandered" for a year through the country, plying his trade and gaining experience; cf. Eng. "journey-man";* **Wanderlust**="travel desire", an irrepressible urge to travel or wander).

Wandervögel [Ger.=wandering birds or songsters] hikers, hostellers. (*An association founded in Germany; the beginning of the Youth Hostel movement*).

Wechsel [Ger.] (*Comm.*) bill, change, exchange.

Wein, Weib, und Gesang [Ger.] wine, woman, and song.

Welt [Ger.] world (**Weltgeist** =the world-spirit; the spirit of the age; **Weltschmerz**= "World pain", *i.e. the affected pessimism about the sorrows of mankind*).

Wiener Schnitzel [Ger.= Vienna cutlet] (*Cookery*) vealcutlet.

Wirt [Ger.] host, innkeeper, landlord.

wunderbar [Ger.] wonderful.

X

Xantippe [Gk.] scold, shrew, termagant (*wife of Socrates*).

xoanon [Gk.] a wooden-statue.

xystus [Gk.] colonnade, portico.

Y

Yahveh, Yahweh [Heb.] Jehovah.

yaourt [Turk.] yoghourt (fermented milk).

Z

zambo [Sp.] a half-breed.

Zeit [Ger.] time.

Zeitung [Ger.] newspaper.

zenana [Hind.] harem.

Zigeuner, *fem.* **Zigeunerin** [Ger.] a gipsy.

zincalo [Sp.], **zingaro** [Ital.] gipsy.

Zweifel [Ger.] doubt.

Zollverein [Ger.] customs-union.

zuppa inglese [Ital.] (*Cookery*) trifle (*a sweet*).

CHRISTIAN NAMES

L=*Latin*, F=*French*, I=*Italian*, S=*Spanish*, G=*German*

A

Abraham; (L) Abrahamus; (F) Abraham; (I) Abrahamo; (S) Abrahán; (G) Abraham.

Adam; (L) Adamus; (F) Adam; (I) Adamo; (S) Adán; (G) Adam.

Adelaide; (F) Adélaïde; (I) Adelaida; (S) Adelaida; (G) Adelheid.

Adolph; (L) Adolphus; (F) Adolphe; (I) Adolfo; (S) Adolfo; (G) Adolf.

Adrian; (L) Hadrianus; (F) Adrien; (I) Adriano; (S) Adrián, Adriano; (G) Hadrian.

Agatha; (L) Agatha; (F) Agathe; (I) Agata; (S) Agata, Agueda; (G) Agathe.

Agnes; (L) Agneta; (F) Agnès; (I) Agnese; (S) Inés; (G) Agnes.

Albert; (L) Albertus; (F) Albert; (I) Alberto; (S) Alberto; (G) Albert, Albrecht.

Alexander; (L) Alexander; (F) Alexandre; (I) Alessandro; (S) Alejandro; (G) Alex.

Alfred; (L) Alfredus; (F) Alfred; (I) Alfredo; (S) Alfredo; (G) Alfred.

Alice; (L) Alicia; (F) Alice; (I) Alicia; (S) Alicia; (G) Alice.

Alphonsus; (L) Alphonsus; (F) Alphonse; (I) Alfonso; (S) Alfonso, Alonso; (G) Alfons, Alfonso.

Amadeus; (L) Amadeus; (F) Amédée; (I) Amedeo; (S) Amadeo.

Ambrose; (L) Ambrosius; (F) Ambroise; (I) Ambrogio; (S) Ambrosio; (G) Ambrosius.

Amelia; (F) Amélie; (I) Amelia, Amalia; (S) Amelia; (G) Amalie.

Andrew; (L) Andreas; (F) André; (I) Andrea; (S) Andrés; (G) Andreas.

Ann(e); (L) Anna; (F) Anne, Annette, Nannette, Ninon; (I) Anna; (S) Ana; (G) Anna, Ännchen.

Anthony; (L) Antonius; (F) Antoine; (I) Antonio; (S) **Antonio**; (G) Anton.

Arabella; (F) Arabelle; (I) Arabella; (S) Arabela; (G) Arabelle.

Archibald; (L) Archibaldus; (F) Archambault; (I) Arcibaldo; (S) Archibaldo; (G) Archimbald.

Arnold; (F) Arnaud, Arnaut; (I) Arnoldo; (S) Arnaldo; (G) Arnold.

Arthur; (L) Arturus; (F) Arthur; (I) Arturo; (S) Arturo; (G) Arthur.

Augustin(e); (L) Augustinus; (F) Augustin; (I) Agostino; (S) Augustino; (G) Augustin.

Augustus; (L) Augustus; (F) Auguste; (I) **Augusto**; **(S)** Augusto; (G) August.

B

Baldwin; (L) Balduinus; (F) Baudouin; (I) **Baldovino**; **(S)** Baldovino; (G) Balduin.

Balthazar, Balthasar; (L) Belshazzar; (F) Balthazar; (I) Baldassare; (S) Baltasar; (G) Balthasar.

Baptist; (L) Baptista; (F) Baptiste, Batiste; (I) Battista; (S) Bautista; (G) Baptist.

Barbara; (L) Barbara; (F) Barbe; (I) Barbara; (S) Barbara; (G) Barbara.

Bartholomew; (L) Bartholomaeus; (F) Bartholomé; (I) Bartolomeo; (S) Bartolomeo, Bártolo; (G) Bartholomäus, Barthel.

Basil; (L) Basilius; (F) Basile; (I) Basilic; (S) Basilio; (G) Basilius.

Beatrice; (L) Beatrix; (F) Béatrice, Béatrix; (I) Beatrice; (S) Beatriz; (G) Beatrix.

Benedict; (L) Benedictus; (F) Benoît; (I) Benedetto; (S) Benedicto, Benito; (G) Benedikt.

Benjamin; (F) Benjamin; (I) Beniamino; (S) Benjamin; (G) Benjamin.

Bernard; (L) Bernardus; (F) Bernard; (I) Bernardo; (S) Bernardo; (G) Bernhard.

Bertha; (L) Bertha; (F) Berthe; (I) Berta; (S) Berta; (G) Berta, Bertha.

Bertram; (F) Bertrand; (I) Bertrando; (S) Beltrán; (G) Bertram, Bertrand.

Blanche; (F) Blanche; (I) Bianca; (S) Blanca; (G) Blanka.

Bridget; (L) Brigitta; (F) Brigitte; (I) Brigida; (S) Brigida; (G) Brigitte.

C

Camilla; (L) Camilla; (F) Camille; (I) Camilla; (S) Camila.

Caroline; (F) Caroline; (I) Carolina; (S) Carolina; (G) Caroline, Karoline.

Cassandra; (L) Cassandra; (F) Cassandre; (I) Cassandra.

Catherine, Catharine; (L) Catharina; (F) Catherine; (I) Caterina; (S) Catalina; (G) Katharine, Katrina.

Cecilia, Cecily; (L) Caecilia; (F) Cécile; (I) Cecilia; (S) Cecilia; (G) Cäcilia.

Celia; (L) Caelia; (F) Célie; (I) Celia.

Charles; (L) Carolus; (F) Charles; (I) Carlo; (S) Carlos; (G) Carl, Karl.

Charlotte; (L) Carola; (F) Charlotte; (I) Carlotta; (S) Carlota; (G) Charlotte.

Christian; (L) Christianus; (F) Chrétien; (I) Cristiano; (S) Cristiano; (G) Christian.

Christopher; (L) Christophorus; (F) Christophe; (I) Cristoforo; (S) Cristóbal; (G) Christoph.

Clara; (L) Clara; (F) Claire; (I) Chiara; (S) Clara; (G) Klara.

Claud(e) ; (L) Claudius; (F) Claude; (I) Claudio; (S) Claudio; (G) Claudius.

Clement; (L) Clemens; (F) Clément; (I) Clemente; (S) Clemente; (G) Clemens.

Conrad; (L) Conradus; (F) Conrad(e); (I) Corrado; (S) Conrado; (G) Konrad.

Constance; (L) Constantia; (F) Constance; (I) Costanza; (S) Constenza, Costenza; (G) Constanze, Constantia.

Cordelia; (L) Cordeilla; (F) Cordélie; (G) Cordelia, Cordula.

Corinna; (L) Corinna; (F) Corinne; (I) Corinna; (S) Corina.

Cornelius; (L) Cornelius; (F) Cornélius; (I) Cornelio; (S) Cornelio; (G) Cornelius.

Cosmo; (L) Cosmus; (F) Cosme, Côme; (I) Cosmo, Cosimo; (S) Cosme.

Crispin; (L) Crispus, Crispinus, Crispianus; (F) Crispin, Crépin; (I) Crispino, Crispo; (S) Crispo; (G) Crispus.

Cyprian; (L) Cyprianus; (F) Cyprien; (I) Cipriano; (S) Cipriano.

Cyril; (L) Cyrillus; (F) Cyrille; (I) Cirillo; (S) Cirilo; (G) Cyrill.

D

Daniel; (F) Daniel; (I) Daniele; (S) Daniel; (G) Daniel.

Daphne; (F) Daphné; (I) Dafne; (S) Dafne.

David; (F) David; (I) Davide; (S) David; (G) David.

Deborah; (L) Debora; (F) Déborah; (I) Debora; (S) Débora; (G) Debora.

Demetrius; (L) Demetrius; (F) Démétrius; (I) Demetrio; (S) Demetrio; (G) Demetrius.

Denis; (L) Dionysius; (F) Denis; (I) Dionigi; (S) Dionisio; (G) Dionys.

Diana; (L) Diana; (F) Diane; (I) Diana; (S) Diana; (G) Diana.

Dorothy; (L) Dorothea; (F) Dorothée, Dorette; (I) Dorotea; (S) Dorotea; (G) Dorothea.

E

Edgar; (L) Edgarus; (I) Edgaro; (G) Edgar.

Edith; (L) Editha; (F) Édith; (I) Edita; (S) Edita; (G) Editha.

Edmund; (L) Edmundus; (F) Édmond; (I) Edmondo; (S) Edmundo; (G) Edmund.

Edward; (L) Eduardus; (F) Édouard; (I) Eduardo; (S) Eduardo; (G) Eduard.

Edwin; (L) Edvinus; (I) Edvino; (G) Edwin.

Eleanor, Elinor; (F) Éléonore, Aliénor; (I) Eleonora; (S) Leonor; (G) Eleonore.

Elijah; (L) Elija; (F) Élie; (I) Elia; (S) Elias; (G) Elias.

Elisha; (L) Elisebus; (F) Élisée; (I) Eliseo; (S) Eliseo; (G) Elisa.

Elizabeth; (L) Elisabeth; (F) Élisabeth; (I) Elisabetta; (S) Isabel; (G) Elisabeth.

Ellen. *See* **Helena.**

Emery, Emory; (L) Almericus, Amalricus; (F) Émery; (G) Emmerich.

Emilius; (L) Aemilius; (F) Émile; (I) Emilio; (S) Emilio; (G) Emilius.

Emily; (L) Aemilia; (F) Émilie; (I) Emilia; (S) Emilia; (G) Emilie.

Emmanuel; (F) Emmanuel; (I) Emmanuele; (S) Manuel; (G) Emanuel.

Ephraim; (L) Ephraim; (F) Éphraïm; (I) Efraimo; (S) Efrain; (G) Ephraim.

Erasmus; (L) Erasmus; (F) Érasme; (I) Erasmo; (S) Erasmo; (G) Erasmus.

Eric; (L) Ericus; (F) Erico; (I) Erico; (S) Erico; (G) Erich.

Ernest; (L) Ernestus; (F) Ernest; (I) Ernesto; (S) Ernesto; (G) Ernst.

Esther; (L) Esther; (F) Esther; (I) Ester; (S) Ester; (G) Esther.

Eugene; (L) Eugenius; (F) Eugène; (I) Eugenio; (S) Eugenio; (G) Eugen, Eugenius.

Eugenia; (L) Eugenia; (F) Eugénie; (I) Eugenia; (S) Eugenia; (G) Eugenie, Eugenia.

Euphemia; (L) Euphemia; (F) Euphémie; (I) Eufemia; (G) Euphemia.

Eustace; (L) Eustachius; (F) Eustache; (I) Eustachio, Eustasio, Eustazio; (S) Eustaquio; (G) Eustachius.

Eva; (L) Eva; (F) Ève; (I) Eva; (S) Eva; (G) Eva.

Ezekiel; (L) Ezechiel; (F) Ézéchiel; (I) Ezechiele, Ezechiello; (S) Ezequiel; (G) Ezechiel.

Ezra; (L) Ezra, Esdras; (F) Esdras; (G) Esra.

F

Felicity; (L) Felicitas; (F) Félicie, Félicité; (I) Felicia; (S) Felicia, Felisa.

Felix; (L) Felix; (F) Félix; (I) Felice; (S) Félix; (G) Felix.

Ferdinand; (F) Ferdinand, Ferrand; (I) Ferdinando, Ferrando; (S) Fernando; (G) Ferdinand.

Florence; (L) Florentia; (F) Florence; (I) Fiorenza; (S)
Florencia; (G) Florentia.

Frances; (L) Francisca; (F) Françoise; (I) Francesca; (S)
Francisca; (G) Franziska.

Francis; (L) Franciscus; (F) François; (I) Francesco; (S)
Francisco; (G) Franz.

Frederick; (L) Fredericus; (F) Frédéric; (I) Federico; (S)
Federico; (G) Friedrich, Fritz.

G

Gabriel; (L) Gabriel; (F) Gabriel; (I) Gabriello; (S) Gabriel;
(G) Gabriel.

Genevieve; (F) Geneviève; (I) Genoveffa; (S) Genoveva.

Geoffrey; (L) Gaufridus, Galfridus; (F) Geoffroi.

George; (L) Georgius; (F) George(s); (I) Giorgio; (S) Jorge;
(G) Georg.

Gerald; (L) Geraldus; (F) Gérald, Géraud, Girauld; (I)
Geraldo; (G) Gerold.

Gerard; (L) Gerardus; (F) Gérard; (I) Gerardo, Gherardo; (G)
Gerhard.

Gertrude; (F) Gertrude; (I) Gertrude, Gertruda; (S) Ger-
trudis; (G) Gertrud, Gertraude.

Gilbert; (L) Gilbertus; (F) Guilbert, Gilbert; (I) Gilberto; (S)
Gilberto; (G) Gilbert.

Giles; (L) Aegidius; (F) Gilles, Égide; (I) Egidio; (S) Egidio,
Gil; (G) Egidius.

Gillian; (L) Juliana; (F) Giuliana; (I) Giuliana; (S) Juliana;
(G) Julchen.

Godfrey; (L) Godefridus; (F) Godefroi; (I) Goffredo; (S)
Godofredo; (G) Gottfried.

Gregor(y); (L) Gregorius; (F) Grégoire; (I) Gregorio; (S)
Gregorio; (G) Gregor.

Griselda; (F) Griselda; (I) Griselda; (G) Griseldis, Griselde,
Grishilde.

Gustavus; (L) Gustavus; (F) Gustave; (I) Gustavo; (S)
Gustavo; (G) Gustav.

Guy; (L) Guido; (F) Guy; (I) Guido; (S) Guido; (G) Guido.

H

Hadrian. *See* **Adrian.**

Hannah. *See* **Ann.**

Harold; (F) Harold; (I) Araldo, Aroldo; (S) Haraldo; (G) Harald.

Hector; (F) Hector; (I) Ettore; (S) Hector; (G) Hektor.

Helen; (L) Helena; (F) Hélène; (I) Elena; (S) Elena; (G) Helene.

Henry; (L) Henricus; (F) Henri; (I) Enrico; (S) Enrique; (G) Heinrich.

Herbert; (L) Herbertus; (F) Herbert; (I) Erberto; (S) Heberto; (G) Herbert.

Hercules; (F) Hercule; (I) Ercole; (S) Hércules; (G) Herkules.

Herman; (L) Arminius; (I) Ermanno; (G) Hermann.

Hezekiah; (F) Ézéchias; (I) Ezechia; (S) Ezéquias; (G) Hiskia.

Hilary; (L) Hilarius; (F) Hilaire; (I) Ilario; (S) Hilario; (G) Hilarius.

Horace; (L) Horatius; (F) Horace; (I) Orazio; (S) Horacio; (G) Horaz.

Hortensia; (L) Hortensia; (F) Hortense; (I) Ortensia; (G) Hortensia.

Hubert; (L) Hubertus; (F) Hubert; (I) Uberto; (S) **Huberto**; (G) Hubert.

Hugh; (L) Hugo; (F) Hugues; (I) Ugo; (S) Hugo; (G) Hugo.

Humbert; (F) Humbert; (I) Umberto; (S) Humberto.

Humphrey; (F) Onfroi; (I) Onofrio; (S) Hunfredo; (G) Humfried.

I

Ida; (L) Ida; (F) Ide, Ida; (I) Ida; (S) Ida; (G) Ida.

Ignatius; (L) Ignatius; (F) Ignace; (I) Ignazio; (S) **Ignacio**; (G) Ignaz.

Ines, Inez; (F) Inès; (S) Inés [*Form of* **Agnes**].

Irene; (L) Irene; (F) Irène; (I) Irene; (S) Irene; (G) **Irene.**

Iris; (L) Iris, Iridis; (F) Iris; (I) Iride.

Isaac; (L) Isaacus; (F) Isaac; (I) Isacco; (S) Isacar; (G) **Isaak.**

Isabel, Isabella; (F) Isabeau, Isabelle; (I) Isabella; (S) Isabel; (G) Isabel [N.B. in Spain, **Isabel** has taken the place of **Elizabeth**].

Isaiah; (L) Isaias; (F) Isaïe; (I) Isaia; (S) Isaías; (G) **Iesaias.**

Isidore; (L) Isidorus; (F) Isidore; (I) Isidoro; (S) **Isidoro,** Isidro; (G) Isidor.

J

Jacob; (L) Jacobus; (F) Jacob; (I) Giacobbe; (S) Jacob; **(G)** Jakob.

Jacqueline; (F) Jacqueline; (I) Giacomina.

James; (L) Jacobus; (F) Jacques; (I) Giacomo; (S) **Jaime,** Diego; (G) Jakob.

Jane, Janet, Jean. *See* **Joan.**

Jasper; (F) Gaspar; (I) Gasparo; (S) Gaspar; (G) Kaspar.

Jeffrey; *See* **Geoffrey.**

Jeremiah, Jeremy; (L) Jeremias; (F) Jérémie; (I) Geremia; (S) Jeremias; (G) Jeremias.

Jerome; (L) Hieronymus; (F) Jérôme; (I) Geronimo; **(S)** Jerónimo; (G) Hieronymus.

Joan; (L) Joanna; (F) Jeanne; (I) Giovanna; (S) Juana, Juanita; (G) Johanna.

John; (L) Jo(h)annes; (F) Jean; (I) Giovanni; (S) Juan; **(G)** Johann.

Joseph; (L) Josephus; (F) Joseph; (I) Giuseppe; (S) José; **(G)** Joseph, Josef.

Joshua;(L) Josua; (F) Josué; (I) Giosué; (S) Josué; (G) **Josua.**

Judith; (L) Judith; (F) Judith; (I) Giuditta; (S) Judit; **(G)** Judith.

Julian; (L) Julianus; (F) Julien; (I) Giuliano; (S) Julián; **(G)** Julianus.

Juliana. *Fem. of* **Julian**; (F) Julienne; (I) Giuliana; **(S)** Juliana; (G) Juliane, Julie, Jule.

Julius; (L) Julius; (F) Jules; (I) Giulio; (S) Julio; (G) **Julius.**

K

Kate, Katharine, Katherine. *See* **Catherine.**

Kit *(masc.).* *See* **Christopher.**

Kit *(fem.),* **Kitty.** *See* **Catherine.**

L

La(u)ncelot; (F) Lancelot; (I) Lancelotto.

Laura; (L) Laura; (F) Laure; (I) Laura.

Lawrence; (L) Laurentius; (F) Laurent; (I) Lorenzo; (S) Lorenzo; (G) Lorenz.

Leander; (L) Leander; (F) Léandre; (I) Leandro; (S) Leandro.

Leo; (L) Leo; (F) Léon; (I) Leone; (S) León.

Leonard; (L) Leonardus; (F) Léonard; (I) Leonardo; (S) Leonardo; (G) Leonhard.

Leonora; (F) Éléonore, Aliénor; (I) Leonora, Eleonora; (S) Leonor; (G) Leonore, Lenore.

Leopold; (F) Léopold; (I) Leopoldo; (S) Leopoldo; (G) Leopold, Liutpold.

Lewis, Louis; (L) Ludovicus; (F) Louis; (I) Luigi; (S) Luis; (G) Ludwig.

Louise; (L) Ludovica; (F) Louise; (I) Luigia, Luisa; (S) Luisa; (G) Luise.

Lucy; (L) Lucia; (F) Lucie; (I) Lucia; (S) Lucía; (G) Lucie.

Luke; (L) Lucas; (F) Luc; (I) Luca; (S) Lucas; (G) Lukas.

M

Magdalen(e), Madeleine; (L) Magdalene; (F) Magdelaine, Madeleine, Madelon; (I) Maddalena; (S) Magdalena, Madelena; (G) Magdalene.

Manuel. *See* **Emmanuel.**

Marcel; (L) Marcellus; (F) Marcel; (I) Marcello; (S) Marcelo; (G) Marcellus.

Margaret; (L) Margarita; (F) Marguerite; (I) Margherita; (S) Margarita; (G) Margarete.

Marian, Marion; (L) Mariana; (F) Marianne; (I) Marianna; (S) Mariana; (G) Marianne.

Marjory. *See* **Margaret**; (G) Gretchen.

Mark; (L) Marcus; (F) Marc; (I) Marco; (S) Marcos; (G) Markus

Martha; (L) Martha; (F) Marthe; (I) Marta; (S) Marta; (G) Martha, Marthe.

Mary; (L) Maria; (F) Marie; (I) Maria; (S) Maria; (G) Marie.

Mat(h)ilda; (F) Mathilde; (I) Matilde; (S) Matilde; (G) Mathilde.

Matthew; (L) Matthaeus; (F) Mathias; (I) Matteo; (S) Mateo; (G) Matthias.

Maurice; (L) Mauritius; (F) Maurice; (I) Maurizio; (S) Mauricio; (G) Moritz.

Maud. *See* **Mathilda**.

Michael; (L) Michael; (F) Michel; (I) Michele; (S) Miguel; (G) Mich(a)el.

Millicent; (F) Mélisande.

Miriam. *See* **Mary**.

Moses; (L) Moses; (F) Moïse; (I) Moisè, Mosè; (S) Moisés; (G) Moses.

N

Nancy. *See* **Ann, Agnes**; (G) Ännchen.

Naomi; (F) Noémi; (S) Noemí.

Nathan; (F) Nathan; (I) Náthan; (S) Natán.

Nathaniel; (L) Nathanael; (F) Nathaniel; (I) Nathaniel; (S) Nataniel; (G) Nathanael.

Nehemiah; (F) Néhémie; (I) Neemia; (S) Nehemías.

Nell. *Dim.* of **Helen**.

Nic(h)olas; (L) Nicolaus; (F) Nicolas, Nicole; (I) Niccolò, Nicolo, Nicola; (S) Nicolás; (G) Nikola(u)s.

Nicola (*fem.*); (F) Nicole—*Dims.* Nicolette, Colette.

Nicodemus; (F) Nicodème, Nicomède; (I) Nicodemo; (S) Nicodemo.

Noah; (F) Noé; (I) Noè; (S) Noé.

Noel; (L) Natalis; (F) Noël; (I) Natale, Natalino; (S) Natal.

O

Oliver; (F) Olivier; (I) Oliviero; (S) Oliverio; (G) Olivier.

Ophelia; (L) Ophelia; (F) Ophélie; (I) Ofelia; (S) Ofelia.

Oscar; (L) Oscarus; (F) Oscar; (I) Oscar, Oscarre; (S) Oscar; (G) Oskar.

P

Patrick; (L) Patricius; (F) Patrice; (I) Patrizio; (S) Patricio; (G) Patricius.

Paul; (L) Paulus; (F) Paul; (I) Paolo; (S) Pablo; (G) Paul(us).

Peg, Peggy. *Dims.* of **Margaret.**

Penelope; (L) Penelope; (F) Pénélope; (I) Penelope; (S) Penelope.

Percival; (F) Perceval; (S) Perceval; (G) Parzival.

Peter; (L) Petrus; (F) Pierre; (I) Pietro; (S) Pedro; (G) Peter.

Philemon; (F) Philémon; (I) Filemon; (S) Filemón.

Philip; (L) Philippus; (F) Philippe; (I) Filippo; (S) Felipe; (G) Philipp.

Phoebe; (L) Phoebe; (F) Phébé; (I) Febe; (S) Febe; (G) Phöbe.

Q

Quentin; (F) Quentin; (I) Quintino; (S) Quintin; (G) Quintin.

R

Rachel; (L) Rachel; (F) Rachel; (I) Rachele; (S) Raquel, Rachel; (G) Rahel.

Ralph; (L) Radulfus; (F) Raoul; (I) Rodolfo; (S) Rodolfo; (G) Rudolf, Rudi.

Raymond; (F) Rémond; (I) Raimondo; (S) Ramón, Raimundo; (G) Raimund.

Rebecca; (L) Rebecca; (F) Rébecca; (S) Rebeca; (G) Rebekka.

Reginald; (L) Reginaldus; (F) Regnault, Regnauld, Renaud; (I) Rinaldo, Reinaldo; (S) Reinaldo; (G) Reinwald, Reinhold, Reinald.

Richard; (L) Ricardus; (F) Richard; (I) Riccardo; (S) Ricardo;
(G) Richard.

Robert; (L) Robertus; (F) Robert; (I) Roberto; (S) Roberto;
(G) Robert.

Roderick; (L) Rodericus; (F) Rodrigue; (I) Rodrigo, Roderico;
(S) Rodrigo, Ruy; (G) Roderich.

Roger; (L) Rugerus; (F) Roger; (I) Rugg(i)ero; (S) Rogerio;
(G) Rüdiger.

Roland; (L) Rolandus; (F) Roland; (I) Orlando; (S) Orlando,
Rolando; (G) Roland.

Ronald. *See* **Reginald.**

Rupert; (L) Rupertus; (G) Ruprecht.

S

Samuel; (L) Samuel; (F) Samuel; (I) Samuele; (S) Samuel;
(G) Samuel.

Sarah; (L) Sara; (F) Sara, Sarah; (I) Sara; (S) Sara; (G) Sara.

Simon; (L) Simon; (F) Simon; (I) Simone; (S) Simón; (G)
Simon.

Sophia; (F) Sophie; (I) Sofia; (S) Sofía; (G) Sophia.

Stephen; (L) Stephanus; (F) Étienne; (I) Stefano; (S) Esteban;
(G) Stephan.

Susan; (L) Susanna; (F) Suzanne; (I) Susanna; (S) Susana;
(G) Susanne.

T

T(h)eresa; (L) Therasia; (F) Thérèse; (I) Teresa; (S) Teresa;
(G) Therese.

Theodore; (L) Theodorus; (F) Théodore; (I) Teodoro; (S)
Teodoro; (G) Theodor, Theo.

Thomas; (L) Thomas; (F) Thomas; (I) Tomáso; (S) Tomás;
(G) Thomas.

Timothy; (L) Timotheus; [(F) Timothée; (I) Timoteo; (S)
Timoteo; (G) Timotheus.

Tobias, Toby; (L) Tobias; (F) Tobie; (I) Tobia; (S) Tobías;
(G) Tobias.

U

Uriah; (F) Urie; (I) Uria; (S) Urías; (G) Uria(s).

V

Valentine; (L) Valentinus; (F) Valentin; (I) Valentino; (S) Valentín; (G) Valentin.

Veronica; (L) Veronica; (F) Véronique; (I) Veronica; (S) Veronica.

Victor; (L) Victor; (F) Victor; (I) Vittore; (S) Victor; (G) Viktor.

Vincent; (L) Vincentius; (F) Vincent; (I) Vincenzo; (S) Vicente; (G) Vincenz.

W

Walter; (L) Gualterus; (F) Gaut(h)ier; (I) Gualtiero;' (S) Gualterio; (G) Walter.

William; (L) Gulielmus; (F) Guillaume; (I) Guglielmo; (S) Guillermo, Guillelmo; (G) Wilhelm.

X

Xavier; (S) Xavier; (G) Xaver.

Y

Yves; (F) Yves, Yvon.

Yvette, Yvonne; (F) *fems.* of **Yves** and **Yvon**.

Z

Zachariah, Zachary; (F) Zacharie; (I) Zaccaria; (S) Zacarías; (G) Zacharias.

Zenobia; (F) Zénobie; (I) Zenobia; (S) Zenobia.